Business Law in Canada

Sixth Edition

Richard A. Yates
SIMON FRASER UNIVERSITY

Prentice Hall

TORONTO

Canadian Cataloguing in Publication Data

Yates, Richard
    Business law in Canada

Triennial (irregular)
Description based on: 4th ed. (1995).
Supplements accompany some vols.; some supplements on computer disk.
ISSN 1190-9587
ISBN 0-13-088190-2 (6th ed.)

1. Commercial law – Canada.   I. Title.

KE919.Y37   346.71'07   C95-300897-5
KF889.3.Y37

0-13-088190-2

Vice President, Editorial Director: Michael Young
Director of Marketing: Michael Campbell
Developmental Editor: Suzanne Schaan
Production Editor: Marisa D'Andrea
Copy Editor: Rohini Herbert
Production Coordinator: Deborah Starks
Page Layout: Carol Magee
Photo Research: Susan Wallace-Cox
Art Director: Mary Opper
Interior Design: Lisa LaPointe
Cover Design: Lisa LaPointe
Cover Image: PhotoDisc

3 4 5   05 04 03

Printed and bound in Canada.

Brief Table of Contents

Table of Contents

Preface

Creating a new edition of a successful textbook presents a number of interesting challenges, not the least of which is balancing the need to keep what works well against the demand to address the needs of new learners in a changing business environment. The text must also be kept short enough to be useful in a 12–13 week term and yet long enough to cover the variety of topics that instructors in different disciplines might want to address. This requires some compromises, and in this edition I have carefully considered how to best respond to those conflicting needs.

Changes to the Sixth Edition

The text has retained the unit divisions implemented in the fifth edition, but has changed the order of some of the topics covered in them. Part 1, Introduction, now includes a new chapter that focuses on dispute resolution processes, including the courts and alternatives to litigation. Because the subject of administrative law seems to fit best in close proximity to the topic of dispute resolution, we have added that chapter to the Introduction, along with its discussion of environmental law. Chapters 4 to 8 (Part 2) cover the fundamentals of tort and contract law and should be studied together and in order. The other sections can be covered in whichever order the instructor feels is best for the class. There has always been a strong temptation to reduce the discussion of negotiable instruments, and some instructors feel that it could be eliminated altogether, but in this edition I have condensed it and added it to the discussion of credit relationships in Chapter 10, which along with sale of goods and consumer transactions, make up Part 3. (Note that a full-length discussion of negotiable instruments is available on the Companion Website.) Employment and agency are the topics covered in Part 4, and business organizations are the subject matter of Part 5. The final division, Part 6, is covered in two chapters and deals with personal, real, and intellectual property.

I have updated legal information and added new cases, business comments, and notes on new technology to every chapter. In order to do this and retain a manageable text, I have worked hard to condense the rest of the content. I think students will find the discussions more succinct, accessible, and closely connected to the business environment. Two areas where the discussion has been significantly expanded are professional liability, in the chapter on tort law, and electronic technology, in the chapter on intellectual property.

The business-oriented legal problems in the appendix of the fifth edition have been moved to the Instructor's Manual in a form that can be easily duplicated if you choose to use them in your classes. Students will also be able to access them on the Companion Website. More cases for discussion are also available in the *Business Law in Canada Casebook*, prepared by D'Anne Davis and Maria Koroneos, which has been updated to a third edition to correlate with this edition of *Business Law in Canada*.

I am gratified by the reception *Business Law in Canada* has received over the years; I have tried to limit changes to those that contribute to the usefulness of the text or are a needed response to a changing legal environment.

Finally, I would like to remind all those who use this text that it is designed as a tool for learning business law and not as an authoritative source for legal advice. When faced with a specific legal problem, the reader is advised to seek the assistance of a lawyer.

Features

The following are the main pedagogical elements of the sixth edition:

Chapter Highlights: Each chapter opens with a brief list of highlights, providing students with a map of what is to come.

Case Summaries: The number of cases discussed has been increased in this edition. They appear throughout each chapter and are used to introduce topics and provide concrete examples that help students understand the key legal issues.

Case Synopses: These brief, boxed summaries of cases support the legal rule, principle, or concept being discussed.

"What Should a Business Consider?": *New to this edition,* this feature highlights business considerations throughout the text, focusing students' attention on how the law applies in business situations.

"Untangling the Web": *New to this edition,* this feature offers comments relative to new technologies. Interspersed throughout the text, these boxes cover topics such as Internet privacy and issues related to e-commerce.

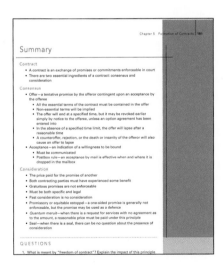

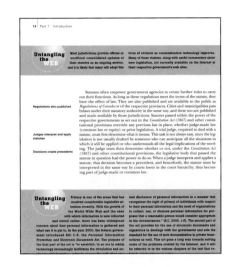

Marginal Notes: The marginal notes act as running summaries of the key points in the text.

Figures: A number of simple figures have been added to illustrate important points in the text.

Summaries: The end-of-chapter summaries have been set out in point form for quick review and reference.

Questions and Cases: Each chapter closes with a number of questions that cover the main points of the chapter, as well as several cases for discussion.

Weblinks: Addresses for helpful Internet sites can be found in Appendix C at the end of the text.

References: Additional business law resources are also listed at the end of the text.

Supplements

Business Law in Canada, Sixth Edition, is accompanied by a complete supplements package:

Instructor's Resource Manual: This manual contains summaries of each chapter, answers to the questions found at the end of each chapter in the text, as well as solutions to the cases and their full citations. New issues have been added to facilitate class and group discussion.

Test Item File: This test bank contains over 1600 multiple choice, true/false, and short essay questions with answers. Each question has been checked for accuracy and is available in both printed and electronic format.

Pearson Education Canada Test Manager: This powerful testing software incorporates all the questions from the Test Item File. This user-friendly package allows instructors to create and edit tests and exams, administer them traditionally or online, and evaluate and track students' results.

Electronic Transparencies: Over 250 PowerPoint slides highlight the key concepts featured in the text.

Student Study Guide and Workbook: This Study Guide provides an overview of each chapter, review questions with answers and text references, and a glossary providing definitions of all the terms highlighted in the text. It also contains guidelines for conducting legal research and briefing a law report.

Companion Website: The Companion Website for *Business Law in Canada,* Sixth Edition, offers student resources such as practice questions, key terms and concepts, Weblinks to related sites and legislation, and more. Visit the site at **www.pearsoned.ca/yates**.

Business Law in Canada Casebook: The third edition of this casebook by D'Anne Davis and Maria Koroneos is correlated with the sixth edition of *Business Law in Canada.* Following the changes in the text, the casebook covers a number of new topics, including such technology-related issues as spamming and the human genome project.

Online Learning Solutions: Pearson Education Canada supports instructors interested in using online course management systems. We provide text-related content in WebCT, Blackboard, and our own private-label version of Blackboard, called CourseCompass. To find out more about creating an online course using Pearson content in one of these platforms, contact your local Pearson Education Canada representative.

Acknowledgements

Reviewers have played an important role in reshaping and updating this edition of the text. I would like to thank the instructors who have patiently gone over the text and made suggestions for revision, including:

George Cummins, Memorial University
Maureen Donnelly, Brock University
Allan Elliott, Southern Alberta Institute of Technology
Ronald McDonald, Mohawk College

Peter McKeracher, Durham College
Patricia Margeson, New Brunswick Community College (Moncton)
Trevor Schindeler, Canadore College
Brian Shaughnessy, Humber College
Kenneth Thornicroft, University of Victoria
Fulvio Valentinis, St. Clair College

Special thanks are due to Teresa Bereznicki-Korol and Trevor Clarke from the Northern Alberta Institute of Technology, the co-authors of the Alberta version of *Business Law in Canada*, for their suggestions. Teresa's work on the copyright material in Chapter 16 was especially appreciated.

I am also indebted to the staff at Pearson Education Canada, particularly Suzanne Schaan and Mike Ryan, who worked hard to coordinate the suggestions of reviewers and overcome my inherent reluctance to go through this material yet another time. My wife Ruth continues to be my most avid supporter in the preparation of this work for publication. Were it not for her, it would not be.

Dedication

This edition marks my first year away from the British Columbia Institute of Technology, which has been the academic ground upon which all previous editions of this text have been nurtured. In recognition of the role that the Institute and my many colleagues and friends there have played, and particularly my longest-standing and most valiant cohorts, D'Anne Davis and Bill Hooker, I would like to dedicate this edition to them.

Richard A. Yates,
LLB, MBA

Your Internet companion to the most exciting, state-of-the-art educational tools on the Web

T he Pearson Education Canada Companion Website is easy to navigate and is organized to correspond to the chapters in this textbook. The Companion Website comprises these distinct, functional features:

Customized Online Resources

Online Interactive Study Guide

Interactivities

Communication

Explore these areas in this Companion Website. Students and distance learners will discover resources for indepth study, research, and communication, empowering them in their quest for greater knowledge and maximizing their potential for success in the course.

A NEW WAY TO DELIVER EDUCATIONAL CONTENT

Course Management

Our Companion Websites provide instructors and students with the ability to access, exchange, and interact with material specially created for our individual textbooks.

- **Syllabus Manager** provides instructors with the option of creating online classes and constructing an online syllabus linked to specific modules in the Companion Website.
- **Grader** allows the student to take a test that is automatically marked by the program. The results of the test can be e-mailed to the instructor and then added to the student's record.
- **Help** includes an evaluation of the user's system and a tune-up area that makes updating browsers and plug-ins easier. This new feature will facilitate the use of our Companion Websites.

Instructor Resources

This section features modules with additional teaching material organized by chapter for instructors. Downloadable PowerPoint Presentations, Electronic Transparencies, and an Instructor's Manual are just some of the materials that may be available in this section. Where appropriate, this section will be password protected. To get a password, simply contact your Pearson Education Canada representative or call Faculty Sales and Services at 1-800-850-5813.

General Resources

This section contains information that is related to the entire book and that will be of interest to all users of the site. A Table of Contents and a Glossary are just two examples of the kind of information you may find in this section.

The General Resources section may also feature *Communication facilities* that provide a key element for distributed learning environments:

- **Message Board** – This module takes advantage of browser technology to provide the users of each Companion Website with a national newsgroup to post and reply to relevant course topics.
- **Chat Room** – This module enables instructors to lead group activities in real time. Using our chat client, instructors can display website content while students participate in the discussion.

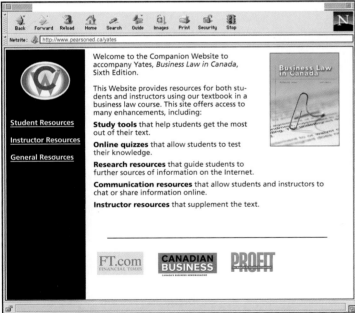

Introduction

The study of business law involves an examination of the obligations associated with specialized legal relationships as well as the rights and duties created by various types of commercial transactions. This section lays the foundation essential for understanding the laws related to business activities by setting the Canadian legal system in its historical context and describing the institutions that have been developed to resolve the legal problems that are too often associated with commercial transactions. Chapter 1 reviews the sources of our law, the Canadian constitutional structure, including the *Charter of Rights and Freedoms,* particularly the human rights provisions that have important implications for business people. In Chapter 2, we examine the civil court structure and litigation process, but because the majority of legal problems are resolved outside the courts, Chapter 2 also looks at alternatives to litigation and the reforms the courts have made to further encourage people to retain control of and resolve their own disputes. Chapter 3 is concerned with the important area of administrative law or the government regulation of business. When government administrators make decisions that affect individuals or businesses, they must meet procedural standards that are monitored and can be reviewed by the courts. This chapter concludes with an overview of environmental law particularly, as this area of law illustrates how the courts, administrative decision-making, and alternative methods have been used to apply, enforce, and mediate the impact of statutory law.

Introduction to the Legal System

CHAPTER HIGHLIGHTS

- A workable definition of the term "law"
- Sources of Canadian law
- Distinctions between common law and civil law
- Constitutional law
- The parliamentary system
- The *Charter of Rights and Freedoms*
- Fundamental human rights

We live in a complex world in which our success depends largely on how effectively we interact with one another. An understanding of the legal concepts and principles that govern personal and commercial relationships is essential for orderly progress in our society.

What Is Law?

No wholly satisfactory definition of law

Problems applying theory

Most of us recognize the rules and regulations that are considered law and understand that law plays an important role in ordering society, but knowing that does not make it easy to come up with a satisfactory, all-inclusive definition. Philosophers have been trying for centuries to determine just what "law" means, and their theories have profoundly affected the development of our legal system. Law has been defined in moral terms, where only good rules are considered law (natural law theorists). Others have defined law by looking at its source, stipulating that only the rules enacted by those with authority to do so qualify as law (legal positivists). And some have defined law in practical terms, suggesting that only those rules that the courts are willing to enforce qualify as law (legal realists). Legal positivism helped shape the concept of law in Canada, where parliamentary supremacy requires that we look to the enactments of the federal parliament or provincial legislatures as the primary source of law. In the United States, however, a more pragmatic approach to law based on legal realism has been adopted that allows judges to factor in current social and economic realities when they make their decisions.

Definition

For our purposes, the following simplified definition is helpful, if we remember that it is not universally applicable. **Law is the body of rules that can be enforced by the courts or by other government agencies.** We are exposed to many rules in our daily activities that do not qualify as law. Courtesy demands that we do not interrupt when someone is speaking. Social convention determines that it is inappropriate to enter a restaurant shirtless or shoeless. Universities and colleges often establish rules of conduct for their students and faculty. These rules do not fall into our definition of law because the courts do not enforce them. But when there is a disagreement over who is responsible for an accident, a question as to whether a crime has been committed, or a difference of opinion about the terms of a contract or a will, the participants may find themselves before a judge. Rules that can be enforced by the courts govern these situations; thus, they are laws within the definition presented here.

A person dealing with government agencies, such as labour relations boards, the Workers' Compensation Board, or city and municipal councils, must recognize that these bodies are also able to render decisions in matters that come before them. The rules enforced by these bodies are also laws within this definition. The unique problems associated with government agencies and regulatory bodies will be discussed in Chapter 3.

While the definition of law as enforceable rules has practical value, it does not suggest what is just or moral. We must not assume that so long as we obey the law we are acting morally. Legal compliance and ethical behaviour are two different things, and people must decide for themselves what standard they will adhere to. Many choose to live by a personal code of conduct demanding adherence to more stringent rules than those set out in the law, while others disregard even these basic requirements. Some think that moral values have no place in the business world, but in fact, the opposite is true. There is now an expectation of high ethical standards in business activities, and it is hoped that those who study the law as it relates to business will appreciate and adhere to those higher standards. We must at least understand that whether we are motivated by divine law, conscience, moral indifference, or avarice, serious consequences may follow from non-compliance to the body of rules we call law.

Do not confuse law and morality

Categories of Law

Law consists of rules with different but intersecting functions. The primary categories are substantive and procedural laws. **Substantive law** establishes both the rights an individual has in society and also the limits on their conduct. The right to travel, to vote, and to own property are examples of the many laws that guarantee our rights. Prohibitions against theft and murder as well as other actions that harm our neighbours are also examples of substantive law. **Procedural law** determines how the substantive laws will be enforced. The rules governing arrest and criminal investigation, pre-trial and court processes in both criminal and civil cases are examples. Law can also be distinguished by its public or private function. **Public law** includes constitutional law that determines how the country is governed and the laws that affect an individual's relationship with government, including criminal law and the regulations created by government agencies. **Private law** involves the rules that govern our personal, social and business relations, which are enforced by one person suing another in a private or civil action. Knowing the law and how it functions allows us to structure our lives as productive and accepted members of the community and to predict the consequences of our conduct. As business students, we study law because it defines the environment of rules within which business functions. In order to play the game, we must know the rules.

Kinds of law

Origins of Law

Nine of the 10 Canadian provinces and the three territories have adopted the common law system developed over the last millennium in England. For private matters, Québec has adopted a system based on the *French Civil Code*. Although this text focuses on common law, understanding it may be assisted by briefly examining the basic differences between the common law and civil law systems. It is important to note that the term civil law has two distinct meanings. The following discussion is about the legal system developed in Europe and now used in many jurisdictions, including Québec. The terms civil court, civil action, and civil law are also used within our common law system to describe private law matters and should not be confused with the *Civil Code* or civil law as used in Québec.

Québec civil law; all other provinces common law

Civil Law

Modern civil law traces its origins to the Emperor Justinian, who had Roman law codified for use throughout the Roman Empire. This codification became the foundation of the legal system in continental Europe. Its most significant modification occurred early in the 19th century when Napoleon revised it. The *Napoleonic Code* was adopted throughout Europe and most of the European colonies. Today, variations of the *Civil Code* are used in all of continental Europe, South America, most of Africa, and many other parts of the world, including Québec. The most important feature of French civil law is its central *Code*—a list of rules stated as broad principles of law that judges apply to the cases that come before them. Under this system, people wanting to know their legal rights or obligations refer to the *Civil Code*. For example, if a person were to suffer injury in Québec because of the careless acts of an employee delivering fuel oil, the victim would turn to the Québec *Civil Code* to determine his or her rights. Articles 1457 and 1463 of the most recent *Code* state the following:

Civil Code used throughout the world

> 1457. Every person has a duty to abide by the rules of conduct which lie upon him, according to the circumstances, usage or law, so as not to cause injury to another. Where he is endowed with reason and fails in this duty, he is responsible for any injury he causes to another person and is liable to reparation for the injury, whether it be bodily, moral, or material in nature.
>
> He is also liable, in certain cases, to reparation for injury caused to another by the act or fault of another person acting on his behalf.
>
> 1463. The principal is liable to reparation for injury caused by the fault of his agents and servants in the performance of their duties; nevertheless, he retains his recourses against them.

In the example above, the injured party would have a claim against the employee under article 1457 and a claim against the employer under article 1463.

Québec courts rely on the *Code* for guidance and solutions in private disputes. While civil law judges are influenced by decisions made in other cases, and lawyers will take great pains to point out what other judges have done in similar situations, the key to understanding the *Civil Code* system is to recognize that ultimately the *Code* determines the principle to be applied. Prior decisions do not constitute binding precedents in a civil law jurisdiction. The most recent Québec *Civil Code* came into

Civil Code provides predictability

effect on January 1, 1994. One-quarter of the 1994 *Code* is new law, making its introduction a very significant event in the evolution of the law of Québec.

One of the effects of the new *Code* was to make the doctrine of good faith (recently developed in common law and discussed in Chapter 6) part of Québec's contract law. Prior to this, the law was similar to common law, where the obligation to act in good faith towards the person you are dealing with applied only when special relationships existed. Article 1375 of the new code states that contracting parties "shall conduct themselves in good faith both at the time an obligation is created and at the time it is performed or extinguished." This means that the parties can no longer withhold important information or fail to correct erroneous assumptions that they know have been made by the other side without exposing themselves to an action for violating this obligation of good faith.

There are many important differences between civil law and the principles of common law. In this text, we have limited the discussion to common law, and while there are many similarities, care should be taken not to assume that the same principles apply to Québec or other civil law jurisdictions.

Common Law

As Roman civil law was taking hold in Europe, relations between the existing English and French kingdoms were frequently strained. It has been suggested that this strain is the reason England maintained its unique common law system of justice rather than adopting the more widely accepted Roman civil law. The early Norman Kings established a strong feudal system in England that centralized power in their hands. As long as they remained strong, they maintained their power, but when weak kings were on the throne, power was surrendered to the nobles. The growth of the common law system was much affected by this ongoing struggle for power between kings and nobles and later between kings and parliament.

Common law grew from struggle for power

During times when power was decentralized, the administration of justice fell to the local lords, barons, or sheriffs, who would hold court as part of their feudal responsibility. Their courts commonly resorted to such practices as trial by battle or ordeal. Trial by battle involved armed combat between the litigants or their champions, and trial by ordeal involved some physical test. The assumption was made that God would intervene on behalf of the righteous party. Strong kings, especially Henry II, enhanced their power by establishing travelling courts, which provided a more attractive method of resolving disputes. As more people used the king's courts, their power base broadened, and their strength increased. The fairer the royal judges, the more litigants they attracted. Eventually, the courts of the nobles fell into disuse. The function of the royal courts was not to impose any particular set of laws but to be as fair and impartial as possible. To this end, they did not make new rules but enforced the customs and traditions they found already in place in the towns and villages they visited. The judges also began to look to each other for rules to apply when faced with new situations.

Henry II established courts

Stare Decisis

Gradually, a system of justice developed in which the judges were required to follow each other's decisions. This process is called *stare decisis*, or following precedent. Another factor that affected the development of *stare decisis* was the creation of appeal courts. Although the process of appeal at this time was rudimentary, trial judges would try to avoid the embarrassment of having their decisions overturned

Judges follow each other's decisions

What should a business consider?

and declared in error. Eventually, the practice of following precedent became institutionalized. The most significant feature of our legal system today is that the decision of a judge at one level is binding on all judges in the court hierarchy who function in a court of lower rank, provided the facts in the two cases are similar.[1] Thus, today, a judge hearing a case in the Court of Queen's Bench for Alberta would be required to follow a similar decision laid down in the Court of Appeal for Alberta or the Supreme Court of Canada but would not have to follow a decision involving an identical case from the Court of Appeal for Manitoba. Such a decision would be merely persuasive, since it came from a different jurisdiction. Because the Supreme Court of Canada is the highest court in the land, its decisions are binding on all Canadian courts.

Re Transgas Ltd. and Mid-Plains Contractors Ltd. et al.[2]

In this case, which questioned the constitutionality of section 224(1.2) of the *Income Tax Act*, the Saskatchewan Court of Queen's Bench judge was presented with a Manitoba Court of Appeal decision that had dealt with the same provision. The Saskatchewan judge, referring to the Manitoba Court of Appeal decision that had found the provision to be valid, said, "While not binding on me, that decision is persuasive, but with the greatest respect, I must disagree with that conclusion." Thus, a trial judge in Saskatchewan was not bound by the decision of the highest court of a neighbouring province. For the businessperson, this case not only illustrates how precedents are applied in the different jurisdictions but also points out the fact that rules, even federal statutes, may not be interpreted and applied in the same way in each province.

Stare decisis provides predictability

Results in an inflexible system

A judge must choose between precedents

The role *stare decisis* plays in the English common law system is similar to the role the *Civil Code* plays in the French system. It allows the parties to predict the outcome of the litigation and thus avoid going to court. However, a significant disadvantage of following precedent is that a judge must follow another judge's decision even though social attitudes may have changed. The system is anchored to the past, with only limited capacity to make corrections or to adapt and change to meet modern needs. Opposing legal representatives present a judge with several precedents that support their side of the argument. The judge's job is to analyze the facts of the precedent cases and compare them with the case at hand. Since no two cases are ever exactly alike, the judge has some flexibility in deciding whether or not to apply a particular precedent. Judges try to avoid applying precedent decisions by finding essential differences between the facts of the two cases if they feel that the prior decision will create an injustice in the present case. This process is referred to as **distinguishing the facts** of opposing precedents. Still, judges cannot stray very far from the established line of precedents.

1. Strictly speaking, a judge is not bound to follow decisions made by other judges in a court at the same level in that province. However, the practical effect is the same, since these judges must follow their colleagues' decisions "in the absence of strong reason to the contrary." Rex Ex Rec. McWilliam v. Morris [1942] O.W.N. 449 High Court of Justice

2. 86 D.L.R. (4th) (Sask. Q.B.) 251

Sources of Law

Common Law

At an early stage, in the development of common law, three great courts—the court of common pleas, the court of king's bench, and the exchequer court, referred to collectively as the **common law courts**—were created. The rules developed in the courts were called "common law" because the judges, at least in theory, did not create law but merely discovered it in the customs and traditions of the people to whom it was to be applied. However, the foundation for a complete legal system could not be supplied by local custom and tradition alone, so common law judges borrowed legal principles from many different sources. **Roman civil law** gave us our concepts of property and possessions. **Canon or church law** contributed law in relation to families and estates. Another important European system that had an impact on common law was called the **law merchant**. Trading between nations was performed by merchants who were members of guilds (similar to modern trade unions or professional organizations), which developed their own rules to deal with disputes between members. As the strength of the guilds declined, common law judges found themselves dealing increasingly with disputes between merchants. The law merchant was then adopted as part of the English common law, and it included laws relating to negotiable instruments, such as cheques and promissory notes.

Customs and traditions major source of common law

Common law borrows from Roman law

Canon law

Law merchant

Equity

Common law courts had some serious limitations. Parties seeking justice before them found it difficult to obtain fair and proper redress for the grievances they had suffered. Because of the rigidity of the process, the inflexibility of the rules applied, and the limited scope of the remedies available, people often went directly to the king for satisfaction and relief. The burden of this process made it necessary for the king to delegate the responsibility to the chancellor, who, in turn, appointed several vice-chancellors. This body eventually became known as the **Court of Chancery**, sometimes referred to as the **Court of Equity**. It dealt with matters that, for various reasons, could not be handled adequately or fairly by the common law courts. The Court of Chancery did not hear appeals from the common law courts; rather, it provided an alternative forum. If people seeking relief knew that the common law courts could provide no remedy or that the remedy was inadequate, they would go to the Court of Chancery instead. Initially, the Court of Chancery was unhampered by the rules of precedence and the rigidity that permeated the common law courts and could decide a case on its merits. The system of law developed by the Court of Chancery became known as the **law of equity**. This flexibility, which was the most significant asset of equity, was also its greatest drawback. Each decision of the Court of Chancery appeared arbitrary; there was no uniformity within the system; and it was difficult to predict the outcome of a given case. This caused friction between the chancery and the common law judges, which was solved, to some extent, by the chancery adopting *stare decisis*. This caused the same problems found in the common law courts. The chancery courts eventually became as formal and rigid as the common law courts. Finally, the two separate

Common law rigid

Courts of chancery provide relief

Resulting in the law of equity

Conflict results in rigidity in chancery as well

court systems were amalgamated by the *Judicature Acts of 1873-1875*.[3] This merger happened in Canada as well, and today there is only one court system in each of the provinces.

Equity today does not simply mean fairness

Although the two court systems merged, the bodies of law they had created did not, and today, it is still best to think of common law and equity as two distinct bodies of rules. Originally, the rules of equity may have been based on fairness and justice, but today, when a person asks a judge to apply equity, they are not asking for fairness, they are asking that the rules developed by the courts of chancery be applied to the case. Equity should be viewed as a supplement to, rather than a replacement of, common law. Common law is complete, albeit somewhat unsatisfactory, without equity, but equity would be nothing without common law. The courts of chancery were instrumental in developing such new principles in law as the trust (in which one party holds property for another) and also provided several alternative remedies, such as injunction and specific performance, which we will examine later in the text.

Equity supplements the common law

The common law provinces in Canada administer both common law and equity, and judges treat matters differently when proceeding under equity as opposed to common law rules. Of course, judges must always be alert to the fact that any applicable parliamentary statute will override both.

Statutes

In many situations, justice was not available in either the common law or chancery courts, and another method was needed to correct these inadequacies. The English Civil War of the 17th century firmly established the principle that parliament, rather than the king, was supreme, and from that time, parliament handled any major modification to the law. Parliamentary enactments are referred to as statutes or legislation and take precedence over judge-made law based on either common law or equity.

Statutes and regulations override judge-made law

It is important to remember that government has several distinct functions: legislative, judicial, and administrative. Parliament legislates or creates the law, the judicial branch is the court system, and the executive branch and its agencies administer and implement that law. Such organizations as the RCMP, the Employment Insurance Commission, and the military are part of the executive branch of government. Many of these bodies have the power to create regulations by which they accomplish the goals of the statute and enforce its terms. Therefore, legislation includes regulations created by government agencies. In the same way, municipal bylaws have the authority of the statute under which they were passed.

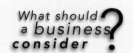

For the businessperson, these statutes and regulations have become all important, setting out the specific rules governing business activities in all jurisdictions. Although judge-made law still forms the foundation of our legal system, it is statutes and regulations that control and restrict what we can do and determine what we must do to carry on business in Canada today.

---

3. *Judicature Acts* (1873–1875) 31 Geo.III

The Law in Canada

Confederation

Canada came into existence in 1867, with the federation of Upper and Lower Canada, Nova Scotia, and New Brunswick. Other provinces followed, with Newfoundland being the most recent to join the Confederation. Every jurisdiction, except Québec, adopted the English common law system. Québec elected to retain the use of the French *Civil Code* system for private matters falling within provincial jurisdiction.

Confederation was accomplished when the British Parliament passed the *British North America Act (BNA Act)*, now renamed the *Constitution Act (1867)*. The *BNA Act*'s primary significance is that it created the Dominion of Canada and determined the functions and powers of the provincial and federal levels of government. The preamble to the *BNA Act* says that Canada has a constitution "similar in principle to that of the United Kingdom," that is, we claim as part of our constitution all the great constitutional institutions of the United Kingdom, such as the *Magna Carta* and the *English Bill of Rights*. Also included are such unwritten conventions as the **rule of law**, which recognizes that although parliament is supreme and can create any law considered appropriate, citizens are protected from the arbitrary actions of the government. In addition, our constitution includes those acts passed by both the British and Canadian Parliaments subsequent to the *Constitution Act (1867)* that have status beyond mere statutes, such as the *Statute of Westminster* (1931) and the *Constitution Act (1982)* which includes the *Charter of Rights and Freedoms*.

For the person in business, it must be remembered that the effect of Confederation was not simply to create one country, with one set of rules. Each province was given the power to establish rules in those areas over which it had jurisdiction. As a consequence, businesses operating within and between provinces must comply with federal, provincial, and municipal regulations. In spite of the opportunity for great divergence among the provinces, it is encouraging to see how similar the controls and restrictions are in the different jurisdictions.

BNA Act **created Canada and divided powers**

More to Canadian Constitution than *BNA Act*

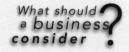
What should a business consider?

Constitution and Division of Powers

In Canada, as in Britain, parliament is supreme and traditionally has had the power to make laws that cannot be overruled by any other body and subject only to the realities of the political system in which they function. In addition, the *Constitution Act (1867)* and the *Charter of Rights and Freedoms* place some limitations on this supremacy. Unlike the United Kingdom, Canada has a federal form of government with 11 different legislative bodies, each claiming the supreme powers of parliament. The *Constitution Act (1867)* assigned different powers to the different levels of government. The powers of the federal government are set out primarily in Section 91 of the *Constitution Act (1867)*, and those of the provincial governments in Section 92 (see Appendix A). The federal government has power over such matters as banking, currency, the postal service, criminal law (although not its enforcement), and the appointment of judges in the federal and higher-level provincial courts. The federal government passes considerable legislation affecting such matters as the regulation of

Constitution Act **and** *Charter* **limit power of federal and provincial governments**

Constitution Act (1867) **divides powers between federal and provincial governments**

Federal powers set out in Sec 91

all import and export activities, taxation, environmental concerns, money and banking, interprovincial and international transportation, as well as important areas of intellectual property, such as copyrights, patents, and trademarks. The provinces have jurisdiction over such matters as hospitals, education, the administration of the courts, and commercial activities carried on at the provincial level. Thus, most business activities that are carried on within the province are governed by provincial

Provincial powers set out in Sec 92

legislation or municipal bylaw, including statutes dealing with the sale of goods, consumer protection, employment, workers' compensation, collective bargaining, secured transactions, incorporation, real estate, and licensing. For industries that fall within the federal jurisdiction, such as banking and the railways, there are corresponding federal statutes, such as collective bargaining and incorporation legislation. Under the "peace, order, and good government" clause (found in the introduction to Section 91) the federal government has residual power to make law with respect to things not listed in the *Constitution Act (1867)*, such as broadcasting and air transportation. Under Section 92(16), the provinces are given broad powers to make law with respect to all matters of a local or private nature. It is important to note

Sections 91 and 92 deal with types of legislations, not things

that these assigned areas of jurisdiction are concerned with the nature of the legislation being passed, rather than the individuals or things affected. Thus, the federal government's power to pass banking legislation allows them to control anything to do with banking, including interest rates, deposits, and how those deposits are invested. The division of powers accomplished by Sections 91 and 92 of the *Constitution Act (1867)* has been very important in the development of Canada as a nation and, until the recent entrenchment of the *Charter*, was the main consideration of courts when faced with constitutional questions.

U.T.U. v. Central Western Railway[4]

The railway in question was built in 1911, consisting of over 1930 kilometres of track, entirely within the province of Alberta. The Canadian National Railroad (CNR) operated the line as part of its overall operation until it made application to abandon it in the 1980s. Permission to do so was refused, and instead, the CNR sold the line to Central Western Railway Company in 1986. The rail line was then separated by a 10-centimetre gap from the CNR tracks. When the CNR delivered empty grain cars to that section, a gap-connecting device was installed, the cars were transferred to the Central Western lines, and the device was removed. The cars were then taken by Central Western locomotives to various grain elevators, filled, and returned to the CNR.

There was no doubt that the railway, while part of the CNR system, fell under federal jurisdiction and federal laws, including the *Canada Labour Code*. A number of unions were involved with the CNR employees and the *Canada Labour Code* provided that when a business was sold, the employees involved had "successor rights," meaning that a new owner would be bound by the same collective agreement that was in place with the old owner. In this case, the Supreme Court of Canada had to decide whether that federal legislation with its successor rights still applied or whether this was now subject to provincial law. While Section 92(10) of the *Constitution Act (1867)* declares that local works and undertakings are under the provincial power, it also sets out a number of exceptions, including interconnecting railways with other provinces.

The problem is that while this line once connected with the rest of the CNR, it no longer does; and for this reason, the Supreme Court found that the line was

4. 76 D.L.R. (4th) 1 (S.C.C.)

no longer under federal jurisdiction, that the successor provision of the *Canada Labour Code* did not apply to this sale, and that now provincial labour legislation would apply to those working for this railway.

Conflicting Powers

On occasion, one level of government passes legislation that may infringe on the powers of another.

For example, municipal governments have tried to control prostitution or pornography, using their zoning or licensing power, when, in fact, these matters are controlled by criminal law, a federal area. To keep prostitutes out of the west end of Vancouver, the city used its zoning power to prohibit that activity. The courts struck down this bylaw, stating that it was an attempt to pass criminal law, since it was designed to control moral conduct. Municipalities sometimes try to increase the licensing fee charged to a business to accomplish the same purpose, often with the same result.

Validity of statute determined by its true nature

One level of government cannot invade the area given to another by trying to make it look like the legislation is of a different kind. The court simply looks at the substance of what the governing body is trying to do as opposed to what it claims to be doing and asks whether or not it has that power.

The powers of the federal and provincial governments can overlap considerably.

For example, the Alberta government passed legislation prohibiting the production and sale of the hallucinogenic drug LSD shortly after it came on the market. This legislation was valid under the province's public health power. Subsequently, the federal government passed similar legislation under its criminal law power, which was also valid.

When overlap does take place, the principle of **paramountcy** requires that the federal legislation be operative and that the provincial legislation go into abeyance and no longer apply. If the overlap between provincial and federal legislations is merely incidental, both are valid, and both are operative. An individual must obey both by adhering to the higher standard, whether provincial or federal. It is only when the laws are such that only one can be obeyed that a true conflict exists, and then, the federal provision will prevail.

When provincial and federal laws conflict, follow federal

Finning Ltd. v. Federal Business Development Bank[5]

In this British Columbia case, Finning repaired the engine on a boat, which was then returned to service. Finning properly registered a lien against the boat under valid provincial legislation.[6] The Federal Business Development Bank also had a claim against the boat in the form of a mortgage and, upon default, seized the boat and sold it as they were entitled to do. Finning then sued the bank seeking repayment of the repair loan, and federal and provincial laws came into conflict. The *Federal Court Act* said that such a lien only persisted while the ship was in Finning's possession; they had allowed the boat to return to service, thus losing their lien. The provincial legislation provided for the continuation of the lien even after possession of the boat was returned to the owner. The court found that the two acts were in conflict and that by the doctrine of paramountcy, the federal legislation prevailed. Finning had no claim against the boat or the bank that had sold it.

5. 56 D.L.R. (4th) 379(B.C.S.C.), 56 D.L.R. (4th) 379 (B.C.S.C.)

6. *Repairers Lien Act*, R.S.B.C. (1979) c. 363.

Statutes May Not Conflict

Ripplinger operated an art gallery that did not provide wheelchair access. He acquired the building next door, made renovations, and still did not provide this access. Ryan, who used a wheelchair, made a complaint to the Saskatchewan Human Rights Tribunal. They found Ripplinger in violation of the *Human Rights Code*. This was appealed and reversed at trial on the basis that the *Uniform Building Accessibility and Standards Act* does not require such accessibility. When this decision was itself appealed, the Court of Appeal held that the duty to accommodate established in the *Human Rights Code* of Saskatchewan and this act were not in conflict. The *Human Rights Code* merely created a higher standard that had to be adhered to. There was a duty to accommodate.

Ripplinger v. Ryan, 131 D.L.R. (4th) 697 (Saskatchewan Court of Appeal)

Untangling the WEB

The use of the Internet raises some constitutional questions in Canada. Since telephone and cable services and broadcasting generally fall within federal jurisdiction under the "peace, order, and good government" clause of Section 91, Internet service will fall within the federal jurisdiction as well. This will become increasingly true as broadcast and Internet services become indistinguishable. However, straight textual material conveyed over the telephone lines, such as fax or e-mail, will likely not be considered as a broadcast, since it is directed to a specific individual and therefore will not be subject to the federal broadcasting rules. Also, provincial laws of general application, such as consumer protection legislation, will apply to provincial businesses even if they fall within this federal control. Thus, a provincial company providing services or products to consumers in any location will likely be covered by the provincial consumer protection legislation despite the fact that their services are offered over the Internet. Internet phone service is now being offered, and regular phone companies are concerned that while they are regulated, the Internet phone service is not. Federal legislation gives the Canadian Telecommunication Corporation (CRTC) the power to regulate this area, but the CRTC has decided not to do so, for the time being at least.

Delegation of Powers

Direct delegation prohibited

Since neither the federal nor the provincial levels of government are considered inferior legislative bodies, both are supreme parliaments in their assigned areas. Over the years, for various reasons, these bodies have sometimes found it necessary to transfer the powers given to them to other levels of government. However, direct delegation between the federal and provincial governments is prohibited. For example, during the depression of the 1930s, it became clear that a national system of unemployment insurance was needed. The provinces, which have jurisdiction in this area, attempted to delegate their power to the federal government. The court held that they could not do so, as it was an "abdication" of the "exclusive powers" given to the provinces under the *Constitution Act (1867)*. To make unemployment insurance an area of federal responsibility, the British Parliament needed to amend the constitution. This amendment is now incorporated in Section 91, Subsection (2A) of the *Constitution Act (1867)*.

Although direct delegation is prohibited, it is possible for the federal and provincial governments to delegate their powers to inferior bodies, such as boards and individual civil servants; in fact, this is usually the only way that governmental bodies can conduct their business. It is also possible for the federal government to delegate its power in a particular area to a provincial board or a provincial civil servant. Similarly, a province can give powers to federal boards, since these are also inferior bodies. In this way, governments overcome the prohibition against delegation.

But indirect delegation permitted

Legislation

Legislation is introduced to the parliamentary process in the form of a **bill,** which goes through a sequence of introduction, debate, modification, and approval, referred to as first, second, and third readings. When it is finally enacted, it has the status of a statute (although it may still be referred to as a bill or an act). Such a statute does not have the status of law until it receives the approval (signature) of the Governor General at the federal level or the Lieutenant Governor in a province, a process referred to as receiving **royal assent**. They are the Queen's representatives in Canada and can sign on behalf of the Crown. Because the Queen is essentially a figurehead in Canada, her representatives sign as the government in power directs them, and such approval is therefore usually a formality. The government may use this requirement to delay the coming into effect of legislation, and care should therefore be taken when examining an act to make sure that it has received royal assent. The statute itself may have provisions for different parts of it to come into force at different times. There are many examples of whole acts or portions of them that look like normal statutes but have no legal effect for these reasons.

Statutes must receive royal assent

Federal and provincial statutes summarized and published

The Government of Canada publishes a compilation of these statutes annually; they can be found in most libraries, under *Statutes of Canada.* The federal government summarized and published all current statutes in the *Revised Statutes of Canada* in 1985, cited as R.S.C. (1985). It is not necessary to go back any earlier than this compilation to find current legislation. Indexes and guides are provided to assist in the process of finding the federal statutes and subsequent amendments.

Similarly, each province annually publishes the statutes passed by its legislative assembly. Each province also provides a compilation of all current legislation to that date in the form of revised statutes. Unfortunately, there is no uniformity in the timing of the revisions, and each province has revised and summarized its statutes in a different year.

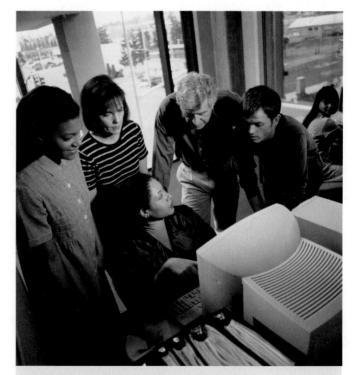

Human rights acts protect employees from discrimination in the workplace.

PhotoDisc

Regulations also published

Statutes often empower government agencies to create further rules to carry out their functions. As long as these regulations meet the terms of the statute, they have the effect of law. They are also published and are available to the public as *Regulations of Canada* or of the respective provinces. Cities and municipalities pass bylaws under their statutory authority in the same way, and these too are published and made available by those jurisdictions. Statutes passed within the power of the respective governments as set out in the *Constitution Act (1867)* and other constitutional provisions override any previous law in place, whether judge-made law (common law or equity) or prior legislation. A trial judge, required to deal with a statute, must first determine what it means. This task is not always easy, since the legislation is not usually drafted by someone who can anticipate all the situations in which it will be applied or who understands all the legal implications of the wording. The judge must then determine whether or not, under the *Constitution Act (1867)* and other constitutional provisions, the legislative body that passed the statute in question had the power to do so. When a judge interprets and applies a statute, that decision becomes a precedent, and henceforth, the statute must be interpreted in the same way by courts lower in the court hierarchy, thus becoming part of judge-made or common law.

Judges interpret and apply statutes

Decisions create precedents

Human Rights Legislation

Re Ontario Human Rights Commission et al. and Simpsons Sears Ltd.[7]

The clerks employed at a particular branch of Simpson Sears Limited were required to work some Friday nights and two out of every three Saturdays. Mrs. O'Malley who was a clerk at Sears for three years before joining the Seventh Day Adventist Church informed her manager that she could no longer work on their Sabbath day (Friday night to Saturday night). Her employment was terminated, and she was hired back part time to accommodate these restrictions. She wanted to continue working full time and laid a complaint with the Ontario Human Rights Commission on the basis of discrimination against her because of her creed. The matter went all the way to the Supreme Court of Canada, which held that discrimination had, in fact, taken place. It was not necessary to show that there was an intention to discriminate, only that there was discrimination in fact. Even where the rule or practice was initiated for sound economic and business reasons, it could still amount to discrimination. The employer was required to take reasonable steps to try to accommodate the religious practices of this employee, short of creating undue hardship on the business. The court decided that there was evidence of discrimination and that the business had failed to show any evidence of accommodation or that to accommodate would have created undue hardship, and so the complaint was upheld. Simpson Sears was required to pay her the difference in wages between what she had made as a part-time employee and what she would have made as a full-time employee.

Re Bhinder et al. and Canadian National Railway Co.[8]

Mr Bhinder was a Sikh, who was required by his religion to wear a turban and as a result would not wear a hard hat. He was terminated because of this refusal. The Supreme Court held that the requirement that Mr. Bhinder wear a hard hat was not discrimination but rather a *bona fide* requirement of the job. The court held that where such requirements were a *bona fide* occupational requirement to do the job, there was no discrimination and therefore no duty to accommodate.

Canada inherited the British tradition of protecting human rights and individual freedoms through an unwritten constitution, common law, and the culture and practices of its people. There were few statutes specifically designed to protect individuals against discrimination and intolerance until after World War II, when an awareness of the problems became more widespread and steps were taken to address the rights of individuals and minority groups. Initially, these statutes were designed to stop discrimination in such specific service areas as hotels and restaurants. In 1944, Ontario passed the *Racial Discrimination Act*, and other provinces followed with similar statutes shortly thereafter.

Common law did not provide adequate protection of personal freedoms

7. 23 D.L.R. (4th) 321 (S.C.C.)
8. 23 D.L.R. (4th) 481 (S.C.C.)

Provincial Statutes

During the 1960s and 1970s, these acts were expanded, and today, all provinces have specific statutes designed to protect individuals against human rights violations in all areas of public activities and, to some extent, in private relationships as well. Entertainment, accommodation, food services, membership in professional organizations, and employment are all areas controlled by human rights statutes. These acts prohibit discrimination relating to gender, religion, ethnic origin, race, age, disabilities, and sexual orientation. Where protection against discrimination on the basis of sexual orientation has been left out of provincial human rights legislation, the Supreme Court of Canada has written it into the offending act, making the statute conform to the requirements of the *Charter of Rights and Freedoms*.

Vriend v. Alberta[9]

In 1987, Delwin Vriend was employed by a private religious school in Alberta. His performance of his job was not in question, but he was dismissed after he "disclosed his homosexuality." He complained under the *Alberta Individual Rights Protection Act* to the Alberta Human Rights Commission, claiming that he had been discriminated against because of his sexual orientation. He was told that he could not make such a complaint because the act did not provide protection against discrimination due to sexual orientation.

This case went to the Supreme Court of Canada, which agreed with the trial court but decided to read sexual orientation into the act as one of the protected grounds. In effect, the Supreme Court rewrote the provincial statute so that it complied with Section 15 of the *Charter of Rights and Freedoms*. Although this was a private matter, the legislation protecting those rights involved an act of government and was, therefore, subject to the *Charter*.

Recently, harassment has become an area of particular focus. The offending conduct usually involves the misuse of a position of authority or power to obtain a sexual or some other advantage. Protection against such harassment has not yet been provided in many provincial statutes, but businesses often include this in their policy manuals and in collective agreements. The federal government has also enacted human rights legislation that governs abuses in areas controlled by federal legislation, such as the broadcast and telecommunication industries.

Another important development in this field is when there is discrimination in the workplace or where public services are provided. In such circumstances, there is not only a duty not to discriminate but also a duty to take reasonable steps to accommodate any person who may be discriminated against. This may require anything from creating wider space between desks to accommodate a wheelchair to the provision of a digital reader for a blind person. In the Sears case used to open this discussion, the discrimination took the form of failure to accommodate religious beliefs, and the employer and union were required to take what was determined to be the reasonable action of rearranging the work schedule so that Mrs. O'Malley did not have to work on her Sabbath day.

Perhaps the most significant area affected by human rights legislation is in the field of employment. This will be treated as a specific topic in Chapter 11. Both

9. (1998) 156 D.L.R. (4th) 385 (S.C.C.)

the federal and provincial governments have set up special human rights tribunals authorized to hear complaints about human rights violations, to investigate and, where appropriate, impose significant sanctions and remedies. These are not courts. They are administrative tribunals, and a person's rights when dealing with such tribunals are discussed in Chapter 3.

Human rights tribunals enforce act

Although the *Charter of Rights and Freedoms* (discussed below) has justifiably been given more attention in recent times to business people, it is the human rights codes in place in the various provinces that are much more important. These codes govern not only how employees must be treated but all those with whom we do business as well. In fact, a significant portion of the cases that come before the various human rights commissions deal with complaints arising from business interactions, usually because of questionable employment practices. A person in business is well advised to become familiar with the human rights legislation in place where they do business and to make sure that their activities comply with those regulations.

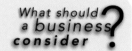

Federal Statutes

Federal legislation, such as the *Canadian Bill of Rights* and the *Canadian Human Rights Act,* protect citizens in their relations with the federal government, but like all statutes based before 1982, they could be repealed, amended, or overruled by the legislative bodies that had passed them, when that course of action became politically expedient. The *Canadian Human Rights Act* corresponds to the provincial human rights codes and simply controls these abuses when federally regulated industries and activities are involved. But the *Canadian Bill of Rights* was intended to be different. It was to set overriding principles against which other federal statutes would be measured. Unfortunately, the courts were reluctant to apply the *Bill of Rights* or, if they did, interpreted it in the same narrow and restrictive way that they did any other legislation, thus significantly limiting its scope and effect. It became clear that the only sure way to protect people from abuse by government was to have such protections entrenched in the Constitution.

***Bill of Rights* not effective in curbing government**

Charter of Rights and Freedoms

After a series of constitutional conferences, the *Constitution Act (1982)* was simultaneously enacted in Canada and England. An important aspect of this act was the inclusion of the *Canadian Charter of Rights and Freedoms.* The effect of including the *Charter* in our Constitution is twofold. First, neither the federal government nor the provincial government has the power to modify or otherwise interfere with the basic rights set out in the *Charter,* except through constitutional amendment. Thus, the provisions are said to be "entrenched" in the Constitution and became, as declared in Section 52 of the *Constitution Act (1982)*, "the supreme law of Canada." The section goes on to state that "any law that is inconsistent with the provisions of the Constitution is, to the extent of that inconsistency, of no force or effect." The burden of protecting those rights has shifted from the politicians to the judges. Now, an individual who feels that his or her rights have been interfered with by legislation or other forms of government action can seek redress in the courts, relying on the provisions of the *Charter.* Hence, the doctrine of parliamentary supremacy has been, to some extent, limited, the courts now being able to check the power of parliament and the legislatures in those areas covered by the *Charter.*

Freedom of expression

Constitution is supreme law in Canada

Burden of protecting the rights now on the courts

RJR MacDonald Inc. v. Canada (Attorney General)[10]

The *Tobacco Products Control Act*,[11] created a complete and total prohibition on the advertising and promotion of tobacco products in Canada. The act also required a health warning of a specific nature to be put on tobacco packaging and prohibited the manufacturers from putting any other information on those packages. The manufacturer challenged the legislation, claiming that it was an incursion into provincial powers under the *Constitution Act (1867)* and also that it interfered with the manufacturer's right to freedom of expression under the *Charter of Rights and Freedoms*. This matter went to the Supreme Court of Canada, which held that this was properly enacted federal legislation under the criminal law power. But the Supreme Court also found that the requirement of the health warning and the prohibition of information that could be included on the packaging as well as other advertising and promotion of tobacco products generally was clearly a violation of the manufacturer's freedom of expression which included the right not to express. The court then had to consider whether this was justifiable as a "reasonable limit" under Section 1 of the *Charter*. The case is interesting in that it illustrates the court's approach to the application of Section 1 of the *Charter*. For Section 1 to apply, the legislation must be sufficiently important to justify infringement; the provisions in question must be designed to achieve the objective (rational connection test); the provision must interfere no more than is necessary to accomplish the objective (minimal interference); and the results must not be worse than the original problem (proportionality test). In this case, the Supreme Court found that the objective of encouraging people to refrain from using tobacco products justified the interference and that the methods used accomplished that purpose. The problem was that the government did not meet the minimal impairment requirement. They could not demonstrate that their legislation went no further than was necessary to accomplish the objective. The court overturned the legislation because it was not satisfied that the government could not have imposed some less intrusive level of control. And the failure of this statute has had far reaching effects.

Limitations

Government cannot interfere with basic rights and freedoms, except:

There are three important limitations on the entrenchment of these basic rights. Section 1 of the *Charter of Rights and Freedoms* allows "reasonable limits" on those rights and freedoms when limiting them can be "demonstrably justified in a free and democratic society." This gives the courts the power to interpret the provisions of the *Charter* so as to avoid an unreasonable result. The rights and freedoms set out in the *Charter* are, therefore, not absolute. For example, the *Charter* guarantees freedom of expression, but there would be little dispute that libel, slander, or hardcore pornography must be controlled.

If reasonable to do so

The Supreme Court was asked in *Hill v. Church of Scientology of Toronto (1995)*[12] to give effect to the freedom of expression provision of the Charter by dismissing a defamation action against the Church and their representative, especially where the remarks were directed at a government official. The court found that the laws of defamation were, under Section 1, a reasonable limitation on the operation of the freedom of expression clause of the *Charter*, thus confirming the lower court's finding of defamation and the highest defamation award up to that time in Canada.

10. [1995] 3 S.C.R. 199
11. S.C. 1988, c. 20
12. (1995) 126 D.L.R. (4th) 129 (S.C.C.)

Section 1 of the *Charter* is also used to impose reasonable limits on the rights of prisoners and the requirement of invoking special powers in times of emergency, such as war (*Emergencies Act*). But the interests of the public must be weighed before applying Section 1. An exception, even though reasonably justified, might be rejected if it goes too far. This is why it was not applied in the *Re Bhinder et al. and Canadian National Railway Co.* case discussed above.

The second limitation is contained in Section 33, which allows each of the provinces and the federal government to override the basic rights contained in Section 2 and Sections 7-15 of the *Charter* simply by stating that the new legislation "operates notwithstanding" the specific provision of the *Charter* that would otherwise make the new legislation inoperative. The sections that can be overridden in this way include such provisions as freedom of conscience and religion, of thought and belief, of opinion and expression, and of assembly and association; the right of life, liberty, and security of person; security against unreasonable search and seizure, arbitrary imprisonment and detention; the right not to be discriminated against on the basis of gender, age, religion, race, or colour; and the guarantee of equality before the law.

If legislature so declares

Does not apply to all sections

It would appear that Section 33 weakens the *Charter of Rights and Freedoms* considerably. The supremacy of parliament appears to have been restored, at least in relation to the designated sections. It was originally hoped that most provinces would find the political cost too great to override the *Charter* in this way and, as a result, would refrain from doing so; and for the most part, this has been the case. Québec, however, used the "notwithstanding" clause to support language legislation restricting the use of English on business signs in that province. This legislation clearly violated the *Charter* and would have been invalid had it not been for the invocation of the "notwithstanding" clause. Since there are very few other examples of the clause being used, original expectations seem to be validated. This provision does not apply to the sections guaranteeing the right to vote, to elect members to the parliament and legislative assemblies, to enter and leave Canada, or to use both official languages. In addition, the rights of the aboriginal people and the rights guaranteed to both genders cannot be overridden by the federal or provincial governments by the application of the "notwithstanding" qualification in Section 33.

A "sunset clause" is applied to the operation of Section 33. If the "notwithstanding" clause is invoked, it must be re-enacted by that legislative body every five years. This forces a re-examination of the decision to override the *Charter,* which will likely involve different legislators who may not be as willing to pay the political cost of using the "notwithstanding" clause.

Sunset clause

The third limitation is the restriction of the operation of the *Charter* to government and government-related activities. Section 32(1) a declares that the *Charter* applies only to matters falling within the authority of "the Parliament and Government of Canada" and the Territories, and Section 32(1) b "to the legislature and government of each province." A serious problem facing the courts is determining just where government stops and government institutions acting in a private capacity start. Are government institutions, such as universities, schools, and hospitals, and Crown corporations, such as the CBC, affected? While there are still many questions, it does seem clear that when such institutions are acting as an arm of government, the *Charter* applies. Certainly the *Charter* applies to the legislation creating them and to the services provided directly by government departments, including the police and military. When government agencies act in their private capacity (for example, employee relations), the appropriate federal or provincial human rights legislation applies, and such legislation must, in turn, comply with the

Charter restricted to government-related activities

provisions of the *Charter*. If a section of a statute is in conflict with the provisions of the *Charter*, the offending section will be void, or an appropriate section will be added. In the *Vriend* case discussed above, the Supreme Court of Canada showed its willingness to interpret into the Alberta statute a provision prohibiting discrimination on the basis of sexual orientation rather than overturning the statute.

While the *Charter* directly affects an individual's relationship with government, it only indirectly affects the relationships between individuals and between individuals and private institutions because provincial human rights codes must comply with the *Charter*. It is also important to remember that the provisions of the *Charter* apply not only to the regulations and enactments of these government bodies and institutions but also to the conduct of government officials employed by them. These officials derive their authority from provincial or federal enactments. If they are acting in a way that violates the provisions of the *Charter*, either they are not acting within their authority, or their action itself is in violation of the *Charter*. In either case, such offending conduct can be challenged under the *Charter*.

Charter Provisions

A brief summary of the types of rights and freedoms Canadians now enjoy because of the *Charter of Rights and Freedoms* follows. (The complete *Charter* is set out in Appendix B.) The *Charter* sets out several rights that are available, in some cases, just to citizens of Canada and, in other cases, to everyone in the nation. The extent of the rights and freedoms set out in the *Charter*, their meaning and the limitations on those rights are still being defined by the litigation that is taking place in the courts.

Available remedies expanded

Recourse is available in the courts if the declared rights set out in the *Charter* are interfered with by legislation, regulations, laws, or the acts of public servants. The courts have been empowered under Section 24 of the *Charter* to "provide such remedies as the court considers appropriate and just in the circumstances." These powers are in addition to the inherent power of the court when faced with offending legislation or conduct by government officials, to declare that the offending legislation or conduct will be of no effect and will have no impact on the person complaining. This provision allows the courts to award damages, injunctions, and other remedies, when otherwise they would have had no power to do so. Section 24 also gives a judge the power in a criminal matter to exclude evidence that has been obtained in a way that violates the *Charter* rights of the accused, if its admission "would bring the administration of justice into disrepute."

The types of rights protected under the *Charter*

Personal Freedoms

Costco Wholesale Canada Ltd. v. British Columbia (Board of Examiners in Optometry)[13]

The rules of the optometrists' professional association enacted under the authority of the provincial *Optometrists Act*,[14] prohibited optometrists from carrying on their profession in association with any other non-optometrist business. Costco, a large retail outlet that often provides space in their stores for various professionals to practise, wanted to include optometrists but was prohibited from doing so by this rule. Costco and the two optometrists are challenging this rule as a violation of

13. 157 D.L.R. (4th) 725, British Columbia Supreme Court
14. 13 R.S.B.C. 1996, c. 342

their right to freedom of association under the *Charter of Rights and Freedoms*. Costco failed because it lacked standing in the matter, being unaffected by the application of these rules. But the two optometrists were successful in their challenge. Because these rules were authorized by provincial statute, they had to comply with the *Charter of Rights and Freedoms*, and the freedom of association provision applies even to economic associations. This rule clearly contravened the section and could not be overcome by Section 1. The association claimed that the rule was necessary to maintain high standards and protect the public by ensuring their members were free of any conflicts of interest. However, the court did not support this argument, especially considering that there was no prohibition against optometrists selling glasses directly to their patients.

Section 2 of the *Charter* declares certain underlying fundamental freedoms available to everyone in Canada. These are the freedoms of conscience and religion and of belief, opinion, and expression, as well as freedom of assembly and association, all of which relate to our right to believe in whatever we wish, to express that belief, and to carry on activities associated with it free from interference. Only where the expression of those freedoms or the activities associated with them interferes with the freedoms of others will those freedoms be restricted through the operation of Section 1 of the *Charter*.

Freedom of belief, expression, press

Regina v. Big M Drug Mart Ltd.[15]

In this case, the corporation was charged with violation of the *Lord's Day Act*, which required that all such businesses be closed on Sunday. This statute was enacted by the federal government under their criminal law power long before the enactment of the *Charter*. This matter went to the Supreme Court of Canada which held that the *Lord's Day Act* was invalid and of no effect because it interfered with the right of freedom of conscience and religion. It did not matter that the applicant was a corporation incapable of having a conscience or beliefs, the provision was invalid because it was in contravention of the *Charter* guarantee of freedom of conscience and religion. Since that time, many municipalities have passed bylaws requiring that businesses be closed on Sunday or some other day. Some of these have been overturned for the same reason, but others have been upheld.

Peel (Regional Municipality) v. Great Atlantic & Pacific Co. of Canada Ltd.[16]

In this case, the Ontario Court of Appeal held that the legislation requiring Sunday closing but allowing other days to be substituted had a secular purpose and did not substantially interfere with religious freedom and did not violate the provisions of the *Charter of Rights and Freedoms*. "The fact that a day selected for a common pause day coincides with a day which is a religious holiday for some does not render that choice unconstitutional." Any interference with religious freedom is trivial and insubstantial, and even if it were in conflict with the freedom of religion provision, it would be a reasonably justified limitation under Section 1.

15. (1985) 3 W.W.R. 481 (S.C.C.)

16. 78 D.L.R. (4th) 333, Ontario Court of Appeal

Freedom of the press and freedom of expression are extremely important provisions for preserving the democratic nature of Canada, and our courts are very careful to uphold these rights. Still, there are many limitations on them, such as the laws of defamation and obscenity. Similarly, the right to peaceful assembly and the freedom of association have been limited when riots may occur or in the field of employment when employer rights are interfered with by inappropriate trade union activity.

Gameday Publication(s) Ltd. v. Keystone Agricultural and Recreational Centre Inc.[17]

An arena was used by minor hockey league teams to play and practise. The minor hockey league produced a magazine that was distributed to the players, parents, and fans. On two occasions, a publishing company came to the arena and distributed their own rival magazine to people in the areas outside the arena. This was a free magazine all about minor hockey, with statistics and photos, supported by advertising. The owners of the arena had them evicted, prompting this action. The publishing company claimed that this interfered with their freedom of speech, but the Appeal Court found that their right to freedom of speech did not extend to carrying on what was essentially a commercial activity on the private property of the arena owners, even when that property was open to the public.

Rights to vote and to hold office

Democratic Rights

Sections 3, 4, and 5 protect our rights to vote and to qualify to be elected to the House of Commons or the provincial legislative assemblies. Reasonable limitation can be put on the right to vote, restricting those underaged and most likely the mentally incompetent, but the abuses of the past, where racial groups were denied the vote, are now prohibited. These rights were protected in the past by constitutional convention, but now they are enshrined in the *Charter*. Section 4 ensures that there will be an election at least every five years, except in times of war, and Section 5 requires that the elected body be called into session at least once every 12 months. The government in power still has the right to decide when to call an election within that five-year period and also whether to call the session into sitting more often than the "once every 12 months" minimum. The government also has the power to determine what that session will consist of, which also gives some potential for abuse. These sections cannot be overridden by the "notwithstanding" clause.

Mobility Rights

Basile v. Attorney General of Nova Scotia[18]

Under the *Direct Sellers' Licensing and Regulation Act*,[19] anyone involved in the activity of direct selling (door-to-door sales) in Nova Scotia had to be a resident of that province. Mr. Basile was a bookseller and a resident of Québec. He applied for a licence to sell in Nova Scotia and was refused because he was not a permanent resident as required by the statute. He challenged this decision as a violation of his mobility rights under the *Charter of Rights and Freedoms*. The Court of Appeal held that this was clearly an infringement of the mobility rights under the *Charter*, which

17. 170 D.L.R. (4th) 617, Manitoba Court of Appeal
18. 11 D.L.R. (4th) 219, Nova Scotia Supreme Court, Appeal Division
19. 1975 (N.S.), c. 9

gave any Canadian the right to travel to and earn a living in any part of the country. The main difficulty was to decide whether this fell into one of the exceptions set out in either Section 6(3a) (laws of general application) or the reasonable limitation clause in Section 1 of the *Charter*. The court held that this did not qualify as a law of general application, since it was directed at one specific group—non-residents—and also that no evidence had been presented that would support the argument that this was a reasonable limitation as required under Section 1 of the *Charter*. Mr. Basile was successful, and the offending section was declared by the court to be "of no force and effect."

This section ensures that Canadians can travel and live anywhere within the geographic limitations of Canada as well as enter and leave the country at will. It also ensures that all Canadians have the right to earn a livelihood in any part of Canada. But again these assurances are qualified. Programs that are of general application in a province or region can be valid even though they appear to interfere with these rights. In the field of employment, for instance, provincial licensing and educational requirements may prevent people trained and licensed in other parts of the country from carrying on their chosen profession without requalifying in that province. Section 6(4) specifically allows for programs that are designed to better the condition of those "who are socially or economically disadvantaged," even when those programs interfere with the mobility rights of other Canadians who might want to take advantage of the programs but are prohibited from doing so.

Right to enter and leave Canada, and work and live anywhere in Canada

Legal Rights

The rights listed under this heading are intended to protect individuals from unreasonable interference from the government or its agents, to ensure that when there is interference, it is done according to the rules of natural justice and that any punishment is neither excessive nor unreasonable. Section 7 states that we have the right to life, liberty, and the security of person and the right not to have these rights taken away, except in accordance with the "principles of fundamental justice." A 1972 judgment by Fateaux J. summarized what is meant by these basic rules of procedural fairness. He said, "The tribunal which adjudicates upon his [an individual's] rights must act fairly, in good faith, without bias, and in a judicial temper and must give him [her] the opportunity adequately to state his [her] case."[20] It is important to note that the protection provided in this section does not extend to interference with property rights. There is no specific reference to property rights in the *Charter*.

Rights to life, liberty, and security; fair trial and punishment

Subsequent sections under this heading prohibit such activities as unreasonable search and seizure and arbitrary imprisonment and provide for the right to be informed of the reason for an arrest, the right to retain counsel, the right to be tried within a reasonable time, the presumption of innocence, the right not to be tried twice for the same offence, and the right not to be subjected to any cruel or unusual punishment. The common theme here is to protect people from abusive, arbitrary, or unequal application of police and prosecutorial power. Not only is the individual protected in the event of such an abuse, but the provisions also serve to discourage the police and prosecutors from acting outside the law. The powers given to the courts, especially under Section 24(2) discussed above, further help to persuade the law enforcement community to act properly by allowing the court to exclude evidence obtained in violation of these provisions, where not to do so "would bring the administration of justice into disrepute." These basic legal rights can be overridden by the invocation of the "notwithstanding" clause.

Wrongfully obtained evidence may be excluded

20. Duke v. The Queen (1972) S.C.R. 917 at p. 923

Equality Rights

The equality rights set out in Section 15 of the *Charter* prohibit discrimination in the application of the law on the basis of gender, religion, race, age, or national origin and ensure that all people in Canada have the same claim to the protection and benefits of the law. This means that the various provisions of the federal and provincial laws must be applied equally to all and that anytime a distinction is made in any provincial or federal law or by a government official on the basis of one of these categories, it can be challenged as unconstitutional. Even where the discrimination relates to a category not listed, there is a general prohibition against such discrimination, and so victims will be protected. Thus, even though Section 15 makes no reference to sexual preference, the courts have had no difficulty in concluding that a denial of benefits to same-sex couples because of sexual preference is prohibited. It is important to note that Section 15(2) provides for affirmative action programs. When a provision is intentionally introduced that has the effect of discriminating against one group of people, it may still be allowed if its purpose is to correct an imbalance that has occurred through discrimination in the past.

Thus, the government may intentionally set out to hire women or specific ethnic minorities in order to get a better balance in the civil service. This is permissible even though it will have the effect of preventing people of other groups, such as Caucasian men, from having an equal opportunity to obtain those same jobs. Universities often have similar programs to encourage minorities to enter faculties or professions to correct historical imbalance. These basic equality rights can also be overridden by the operation of the "notwithstanding" clause.

In addition to the provisions set out in Section 15, there are other provisions in the *Charter* setting out equality rights. Section 28 guarantees that the provisions of the *Charter* apply equally to males and females. Section 35 states that the *Charter* in no way affects the aboriginal and treaty rights of the native people of Canada. Although this last provision may have the effect of preserving inequality rather than eliminating it, the object of this section was to ensure that during the process of treaty negotiations and land claims disputes between the provincial governments and the native groups of Canada, nothing in the *Charter* would interfere with the special status rights associated with that group. Section 33 cannot be used to affect the gender equality rights or the protection given to the position of the aboriginal people of Canada.

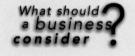

Although these *Charter* provisions only apply in our dealings with government, it is important for business people to remember that these equality provisions are the essence of most provincial and federal human rights legislations. Since those statutes must comply with the *Charter* provisions, the *Charter* indirectly controls business practices. In addition, there are many examples of provincial and federal legislations that require all those working on government-funded projects to comply with special federal and provincial programs aimed at correcting past injustices. These special requirements may range from fair-wage policies where non-union businesses must pay wages comparable with union-negotiated wages to programs requiring the hiring or promotion of disadvantaged minorities or the correction of gender imbalances in the workforce.

Language Rights

The part of the *Charter* headed "Official Languages of Canada" outlined in Sections 16 to 22 ensures that French and English have equal status and that the rights of minorities to use those languages are protected. Of the Canadian provinces, only New Brunswick is officially bilingual, and so Section 16 of the *Charter* declares that

English and French are the official languages of Canada (federally) and of New Brunswick. All federal government activities, including court proceedings, publications, and other services where numbers warrant, must be available in both official languages. Similar rights are established for New Brunswick. Note that some language rights are set out in the *Constitution Act (1867)*. For example, Section 3 requires that Québec provide court services in English as well as French. The *Constitution Act (1867)* also requires that Manitoba provide many government services in both English and French.

French and English language rights guaranteed

Minority language educational rights are outlined in Section 23 and guaranteed for the citizens of Canada, ensuring that those whose first language is English or French who received their primary education in English or French, or have had one of their children educated in English or French, have the right to have their other children educated in that language. People who are immigrants to Canada have no such rights, no matter what their native language may be. Note that the right to be educated in English or French only applies where community numbers warrant the expense of setting up such a program. Language rights and minority language educational rights cannot be overridden by Section 33 of the *Charter*.

Section 52

The *Constitution Act (1982)* makes other important changes to Canada's constitution. In addition to declaring that the Constitution is the "supreme law of Canada," Section 52 also sets out all the statutes that have constitutional status in an attached schedule. Important amendments are also made to the *Constitution Act (1867)*, creating Section 92(A), which expands the power of the provinces to make law with respect to non-renewable natural resources, including the generation of electric power and forestry resources.

Constitution supreme law

The Importance of the Changes

The significance of the 1982 additions to the Canadian Constitution cannot be overemphasized. The *Charter of Rights and Freedoms* will continue to affect the development of Canadian law over the next century. Traditionally, Canadian courts had adopted the position that their function was to apply the law as it existed. If the law needed to be changed, the judiciary left the job to parliament and the legislative assemblies. It is clear that the courts have been forced to play a more active role and create new law through their interpretation and application of the provisions of the *Charter*. The broad, generalized nature of the *Charter* provisions contributes to this more expansive role of the courts. Statutes have traditionally been interpreted in a very narrow way, and because of this, they are always very carefully and precisely worded. But the *Charter* provisions are generalizations, and the courts must therefore interpret these broad statements, filling in the gaps, thus making new law.

***Charter* leads to a more active court**

The *Constitution Act (1982)* also eliminated the requirement that any major change involving Canada's Constitution had to be made by an act of the Parliament of Great Britain. Because the original *BNA Act* was an act of the British Parliament, any changes to it had to be made by that body. When the provinces and the federal government agreed on a formula for amending the Constitution, the British Parliament passed the *Canada Act* making Canada completely independent of Britain. Québec, however, did not assent to this document. Since then, another important agreement, known as the *Meech Lake Accord*, which attempted to change this amending formula, was drawn up. The *Accord* did not receive the required

British power eliminated

Meech Lake Accord

unanimous approval by the provinces within the specified time limit. Its failure and the failure of the subsequent *Charlottetown Accord*, which went to a national referendum has created a constitutional crisis in Canada, with Québec seeking independence. The pro-separatist government in Québec took the question of sovereignty to a provincial referendum in 1996, which failed by only a 1 percent margin. Discussions regarding granting Québec special status in Canada have occasioned much debate and dissension within the federation.

It should be emphasized that although Canada's ties to the British Parliament have been severed, our relationship with the monarch remains. The Queen remains the Queen of Canada, just as she is the Queen of England, Australia, New Zealand, and other independent nations.

Summary

A workable definition
- Law is the body of rules that can be enforced by courts or government agencies

Categories of law
- Substantitive law governs behaviour
- Procedural law regulates enforcement process
- Public law comprises constitutional, criminal, and administrative laws
- Private law involves one person suing another

Origins of law
- Codes in civil law jurisdictions
- Judge-made laws and precedents in common law jurisdictions

Sources of law
- Common law
- Equity from chancery courts
- Statutes—legislations of federal and provincial governments

Constitution of Canada
- *Constitution Act (1867)* (*BNA Act*)
- Conventions and traditions of Britain
- *Constitution Act (1982)*
- The *Charter of Rights and Freedoms*

Constitution Act (1867)
- Divides power between federal and provincial governments
- Powers can be indirectly delegated to other levels of government

Legislative powers
- Set out in *Constitution Act (1867)* Sections 91 and 92
- Courts interpret and apply statutes

Charter

- All legislation must be compliant with *Charter*
- Applies to relationships with government
- Limited by Sections 1 and 33

Human rights

- Federal—provides protection against abuses by businesses within federal jurisdiction
- Provincial—protects individuals in private relationships

QUESTIONS

1. Why is it difficult to come up with a satisfactory definition of law?

2. Where do we look to predict the outcome of a legal dispute:

   a. in a common law system?

   b. in a civil law system?

3. Explain how the use of previous decisions differs in civil law and common law jurisdictions.

4. Describe what is meant by the following statement: "Common law judges did not make the law, they found it."

5. Explain the advantages and the disadvantages of the system of *stare decisis*.

6. Explain which disadvantages in the common law system led to the development of the law of equity.

7. Explain what was accomplished by the *Judicature Acts* of 1873-1875.

8. Explain what is meant by the phrase "the supremacy of parliament."

9. Explain what effect a properly passed statute will have on inconsistent judge-made law (cases).

10. Explain how a parliamentary bill becomes law.

11. Using the principles of *stare decisis*, explain how judges determine whether or not they are bound by another judge's decision in a similar case.

12. What is included in Canada's Constitution?

13. Explain the limitations of human rights legislation.

14. Explain how the *Constitution Act (1982)*, including the *Charter of Rights and Freedoms*, affects the doctrine of supremacy of parliament?

15. Explain how the provisions of the provincial human rights codes differ in their application from the *Charter of Rights and Freedoms*.

16. Give examples of democratic rights, mobility rights, legal rights, and equality rights as protected under the *Charter*. Give examples of three other types of rights protected under the *Charter*.

17. What is the effect of Sections 91 and 92 of the *British North America Act*, also known as the *Constitution Act (1867)*?

18. How did the *Constitution Act (1867)* limit the power of the federal and provincial governments? How is it possible, given the division of powers, to have identical provisions in both federal and provincial legislations and have both valid? Explain what is meant by the doctrine of paramountcy. When does the doctrine apply?

19. Describe the limitations on the federal or provincial governments' powers to delegate their authority to make laws.

CASES

1. Re The Queen in Right of British Columbia and Van Gool et al.

Mr. Van Gool owned property in Surrey, a municipality outside Vancouver, on which he operated an airfield for ultralight planes. His property was in an area designated as an agricultural zone in Surrey, which prevented the use of the property as an airfield except for his own personal use. Since Van Gool rented out space to others, he was in violation of that bylaw. He was also without a permit, license, or other accreditation or certificate from the federal government to operate an airfield. The problem here is whether or not the municipal bylaw applies and whether he can be found in violation of it, considering the constitutional division of powers and the jurisdiction of the federal government over aeronautics. Discuss. Would your answer be different if the bylaw in question simply listed what the property could be used for and did not include an airfield? (See Venchiarutti v. Longhurst.)

2. B. (R.) v. Children's Aid Society of Metropolitan Toronto

In this case, the parents were Jehovah's Witnesses, and when their child was born prematurely with several physical ailments, they resisted the recommendations of the doctors to use blood transfusions. An application was made to a provincial court judge to make the child a ward of the court. This was done, and the transfusion was administered. The parents objected to this as an interference with their *Charter* rights. Discuss what sections of the *Charter* they might use in these circumstances as well as the arguments that can be put forward to support the position of the authorities and the likely outcome. Discuss the operation of the *Charter* in these circumstances and whether the transfusion administered to the child violated these basic rights and freedoms.

3. Dartmouth/Halifax Country Regional Housing Authority v. Sparks

According to the *Residential Tenancy Act* in place in Nova Scotia, residents who have been renting premises for over five years have security of tenure, which means that they can only be given notice to leave if they are in violation of their obligations under the lease. The act, however, specifically excludes people who are living in public housing, and Mrs. Sparks, a single mother with two children, had been living in the public housing for 10 years when she was given one month's notice to leave. She claimed that the *Residential Tenancy Act* provision which makes an exception in the case of public housing discriminated against her. Mrs. Sparks was a black woman, and she argued that because many of the people in public housing were black women on social assistance, they were, as a group, being discriminated against by this provision. What do you think?

4. Roberts v. Ontario

The Ministry of Health in Ontario started a program to assist disabled children by providing them with various types of devices. That program was gradually expanded to provide services to other disabled people. Part of this service was to assist in providing vision aids for the blind. In 1986, Mr. Roberts, who was legally blind, applied for financial assistance to purchase such a vision aid and was turned down. The reasons given was that he was 71 years of age and too old. Mr. Roberts purchased the device himself and filed a complaint under the *Human Rights Code* of Ontario. Explain the likely outcome of that complaint.

The Resolution of Disputes—The Courts, Litigation, and Its Alternatives

CHAPTER HIGHLIGHTS

- The court system in Canada
- The process of litigation
- Problems in the courts
- The alternatives to litigation
- Alternative dispute resolution methods
- Their advantages and disadvantages

In addition to hearing criminal matters, the courts have been charged with the duty of adjudicating civil or private disputes, including assessing liability for injuries and awarding compensation when someone has been harmed by the actions of another. But having the court settle those claims can be an expensive and time-consuming process. While it is always a good idea for the parties to try to resolve their own disputes, when this is not possible, they can turn to the courts to adjudicate a resolution. In this chapter, we examine the structure of the courts in Canada and then look at the litigation process from the initial claim to the enforcement of a judgment. This process is not without its drawbacks and may result in a decision that neither party is happy with or a judgment that cannot be enforced. The second half of this chapter outlines a variety of alternatives to the litigation process along with a review of the reasons why business people might choose negotiation, mediation, or arbitration over courts in resolving their disputes.

The Courts

The process described below is an extrapolation of the various procedures used at the trial level of the superior courts, but students should note that the actual procedure may vary with the jurisdiction. Procedural laws ensure that the hearing will be fair, that all citizens have equal access to the courts, and that parties have notice of an action against them and an opportunity to reply.

As a general rule, Canadian courts are open to the public. The principle is that justice must not only be done but must be seen to be done; no matter how prominent the citizen and no matter how scandalous the action, the procedures are open and available to the public and the press. There are, however, important exceptions to this rule. When juveniles are involved or when the information coming out at a trial may be prejudicial to the security of the nation, the courts may hold **in camera hearings**, which are closed to the public. When children are involved, the more common practice is to hold an open hearing but prohibit the publication of the names of the parties.

Trials open to public

The courts in Canada preside over criminal prosecutions or adjudicate in civil disputes. While civil matters are the major concern of this text and criminal law is only incidentally discussed, it should be noted that there are some important differences between civil and criminal actions. In civil actions, two private persons use the court as a referee to adjudicate a dispute, and the judge, or in some cases the judge with a jury, chooses between the two positions presented. The decision will be made in favour of the side advocating the more probable position. The judge, in such circumstances, is said to be deciding the matter on the balance of probabilities.

Both criminal and civil functions

Criminal prosecutions are quite different. When a crime has been committed, the offence is against the state, and the victims of the crime are witnesses at the trial. The government pursues the matter and prosecutes the accused through a Crown prosecutor. Since the action is taken by the government (the Crown) against the accused, such cases are cited as, for example, "R v. Jones" (the R stands for either Rex or Regina, depending on whether a king or queen is enthroned at the time of the prosecution). While a civil dispute is decided on the balance of probabilities, in a criminal prosecution the judge (or judge and jury) must be convinced beyond a reasonable doubt of the guilt of the accused. This is a much more stringent test in that even when it is likely or probable that the accused committed the crime, the charge must be dismissed if there is any reasonable doubt about guilt.

Civil test—balance of probabilities

Criminal test—beyond reasonable doubt

Rizzo v. Hanover Insurance Co.[1]

Mr. Rizzo owned a restaurant that was seriously damaged by fire. When he made a claim under his insurance policy, the insurance company refused to pay on the basis that he had started the fire himself. It was clear that the fire was intentionally set and that it was done with careful preparation. Because the restaurant business had not been doing well and Mr. Rizzo was in financial difficulties, the finger of blame was pointed at him. Other evidence damaged his credibility. The Ontario High Court in this case had to decide what burden of proof the insurance company should meet. Because the conduct that Mr. Rizzo was being accused of was a crime, he argued that it should be proved beyond "a reasonable doubt." The court held that because this was a civil action, it was only necessary that the insurance company establish that Mr. Rizzo was responsible for setting the fire "on the balance of probabilities" and that they had satisfied that burden. "I have found on balance that it is more likely than not that the plaintiff did take part in the setting of the fire." As a result, Mr. Rizzo's action against the insurance company was dismissed. Note that the fact that Mr. Rizzo had been acquitted of arson in a criminal proceeding was inadmissible in a civil proceeding as proof that he had not committed the arson.

1. 103 D.L.R. (4th) 577, (Ont. C.A.)

May face both criminal and civil trial for same matter

As occurred in this case, a person who has been either acquitted or convicted of a criminal act may still be sued in a civil court for the same conduct. A person causing an automobile accident may be charged with criminal negligence. Whether convicted or not, the person will likely be sued by the injured party for the damages caused. A recent example of this is the case of a woman in British Columbia who won a $500 000 judgment against the man she accused of raping her even after he had been acquitted in a criminal prosecution of the assault.[2]

Criminal law is restricted to the matters found in the *Criminal Code* as well as certain drug control legislations and a few other areas under federal control that have been characterized as criminal matters by the courts. There is a much broader area of law that subjects people to fines and imprisonment but does not qualify as criminal law. These are regulatory offences, sometimes referred to as quasi-criminal matters, and include such areas as environmental, fishing, and employment offences, as well as offences created under provincial jurisdiction, such as motor vehicle regulations, securities regulations, and hunting violations. Only the federal government has the power to make criminal law, and although people may be punished with fines and sometimes even imprisonment for violations of these provincial offences, the violations do not qualify as criminal acts. People charged under these provisions usually go through a process similar to a summary conviction offence under the *Criminal Code*.

Regulatory offences

Court Hierarchy (Each province will vary to some extent)

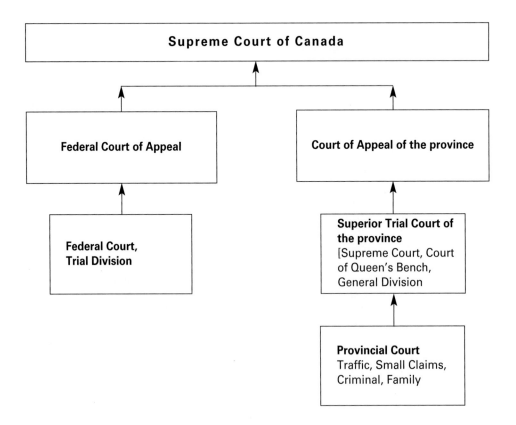

2. Lawson v. Ambrose B.C.S.C. (Reported in *Vancouver Sun,* Feb. 25, 2000)

Trial Courts of the Province

The nature and structure of the courts vary from province to province, but there are essentially three levels (see table). At the lowest level are the provincial courts (called the Court of Québec in that province, and the territorial courts in the Northwest Territories and the Yukon), with a criminal jurisdiction over the less serious criminal matters that are assigned to judges under the *Criminal Code of Canada.* Most jurisdictions also have small claims courts and family courts, sometimes as separate bodies, but usually as divisions of the provincial courts. Family courts deal with such matters as custody of children during a separation or after a divorce, maintenance, and in some cases youth offences. Some provinces maintain separate youth courts that deal with offences under the *Youth Criminal Justice Act.* In Canada, youth offenders, ages 12 to 18 years, are subject to the same *Criminal Code* provisions as adults but are subject to a different level of punishment, and so the role of youth courts is very important. Small claims courts deal with civil matters that involve, depending on the province, amounts up to $10 000.

Lower, intermediate, superior, and appellate courts

The highest trial level or superior court has an unlimited monetary jurisdiction in civil matters and deals with serious criminal matters. Some provinces also have specialized courts, referred to as surrogate or probate courts, dealing with the administration of wills and estates. But in most jurisdictions, this is just a specialized function of the superior court.

It is before the trial courts that the disputing parties in a civil case first appear and testify, witnesses give evidence, the lawyers make arguments, and a decision is reached. When both a judge and a jury are present, the judge makes findings of law, and the jury makes findings of fact. When the judge is acting alone, which is much more common, the judge decides both matters of fact and matters of law. Matters of fact are those regarding the details of an event. For example, was Erasmus at the corner of Portage and Main in the city of Winnipeg at 7:00 a.m. on March 5, 1997? Did a portion of the building owned by Washington fall on Erasmus? Was he paralyzed as a result of his injury? Was Washington aware of the danger? Had he taken steps to correct it? Questions of law, on the other hand, concern the rules or laws that are to be applied in the situation. For example, was Washington obliged to keep the outside of his building in good repair? Would this obligation be affected if Washington were unaware of the danger? The trial itself is discussed in more detail under "The Process of Civil Litigation" (see below).

Questions of law and fact

Courts of Appeal of the Province

These courts hear appeals from the other courts in their respective provinces. They must hear a matter before it can go to the Supreme Court of Canada. In most cases, this is the court of last resort. When one of the parties is dissatisfied with the decision of a provincial trial court and an error in law or procedure is identified, the decision may be appealed. As a general rule, an appeal court will only consider a case when questions of law are in dispute, not questions of fact. But many of the decisions of appeal courts are ones of mixed law and fact, where the rules that are applied are inseparably connected to the facts that are found. Whether a person lived up to the standards of a reasonable person in a given situation would be an example of such a question of mixed law and fact.

Only questions of law can be appealed

The court exercising an appellate jurisdiction does not hold a new trial. The assumption is made that the people best qualified to determine questions of fact are the judge (or judge and jury) who heard all the evidence presented by witnesses at the trial. The appeal court judges (usually three) read the trial court record and deal

Courts of the Provinces

	Alberta	**British Columbia**	**Manitoba**	**New Brunswick**	**Newfoundland**	**Yukon Territory**
Appellate Court (Superior Court)	Court of Appeal	Court of Appeal	Court of Appeal	Court of Appeal	Supreme Court • Appeal Division • Trial Division	Court of Appeal
Highest Trial Court (Superior Court)	Court of Queen's Bench	Supreme Court of B.C.	Court of Queen's Bench • Family Division • Special Small Claims Procedure • Special Probate Procedure	Court of Queen's Bench • Trial Division • Family Division	Unified Family Court	Supreme Court
Lower Trial Court	Provincial Court • Criminal Division • Youth Division • Family Division • Civil Division	Provincial Court • Small Claims • Family Court • Criminal Court	Provincial Court • Criminal Court • Family Division • Youth Court	Provincial Court • Criminal Court • Family Division • Small Claims Court	Provincial Court • Criminal Court • Unified Family Court • Small Claims Court	Supreme Court • Small Claims Court

	Nova Scotia	**Ontario**	**Prince Edward Island**	**Québec**	**Saskatchewan**	**Northwest Territories and Nunavut**
Appellate Court	Court of Appeal	Court of Appeal • Appeal Division	Supreme Court of P.E.I. • Appeal Division	Court of Appeal	Court of Appeal	Court of Appeal for the Northwest Territories
Highest Trial Court	Supreme Court of Nova Scotia	Ontario Court, General Division • Divisional Court • Small Claims Court • Family Court	Trial Division • Estates Section • Family Section • Small Claims • General Section	Superior Court • Family Law Division	Court of Queen's Bench	Supreme Court of the Northwest Territories
Lower Trial Court	Provincial Court • Small Claims Court • Family Court • Criminal Court	Ontario Court, Provincial Division • Criminal Court	Provincial Court • Criminal Court	Court of Québec • Civil Division • Criminal and Penal Division • Youth Division • Expropriation Division • Municipal Courts	Provincial Court	Territorial Court of the Northwest Territories • Youth Court • Criminal Jurisdiction • Civil Jurisdiction

with the specific objections to the trial judge's decision submitted by the appellant's lawyers and then hear the arguments of both the appellant and the respondent.

The judges who serve on provincial superior and appeal courts are appointed by the federal government from a list of candidates supplied by the provinces. Once appointed, the judges have tenure until they retire or are appointed to new positions. They can only be removed from the bench for serious misconduct but not as the result of a decision.

Federal Courts

The Federal Court of Canada serves a function similar to that of a provincial superior court. It has a trial division and an appellate division. The Federal Trial Court hears disputes that fall within the federal sphere of power, such as those concerning copyrights and patents, federal boards and commissions, federal lands or money, and federal government contracts. The Federal Court of Appeal hears appeals from the trial division. Both divisions of the Federal Court can hear appeals from decisions of federal regulatory bodies and administrative tribunals. The role of these quasi-judicial bodies will be discussed in Chapter 3. An appeal from the appellate division goes directly to the Supreme Court of Canada. The Tax Court of Canada is another very specialized court, which was established in 1983 to hear disputes concerning federal tax matters. This body hears appeals from assessment decisions made by various federal agencies enforcing taxation statutes.

The Supreme Court of Canada is the highest court in the land.
The Canadian Press/Tom Hanson

Federal Court, Trial, and Appellate divisions

The Supreme Court of Canada is the highest court in the land and has a strictly appellate function as far as private citizens are concerned. There are nine judges appointed by the Government of Canada, according to a pattern of regional representation. It has become customary, since the court now deals with matters relating to the *Charter*, that all nine judges hear the cases that come before the Supreme Court. There is no longer an automatic right of appeal to the Supreme Court of Canada; leave must be obtained from the Supreme Court, and this will usually only be granted if the case has some national significance. It hears criminal and civil cases and is sometimes asked to rule directly on constitutional disputes involving federal and provincial governments. Decisions of the Supreme Court set binding precedents for all other courts in Canada.

Supreme Court of Canada

The Process of Civil Litigation

Consumer Glass Co. Ltd. v. Foundation Company of Canada Ltd.[3]

In 1963, Foundation, a contracting and engineering company, designed and built a warehouse for Consumer Glass. There were no problems with the building and no indication of any difficulty until the roof collapsed suddenly in 1981. Consumer Glass sued Foundation for negligence in the design and construction of the building. The builder claimed that the action should have been brought in contract and within the six-year period set out in the *Limitation Act*. The questions the

3. 20 D.L.R. (4th) 126, (Ont.C.A.)

Ontario Court of Appeal had to resolve were (1) whether the action should be based on negligence—a tort action—or as a breach of contract, and (2) whether the limitation period started running in 1963, when the work was done, or in 1981, when the damage occurred.

The Court of Appeal, after examining several important precedents, decided that when a person was suing because of a failure to live up to a duty to be careful, that person was free to sue for the tort of negligence, even though the relationship that gave rise to that duty was based on a contract between the parties. After the court decided that Consumer Glass could sue in negligence, it looked at when the limitation period should start to run. The justices considered several important precedents, but in effect, they found that it would be inappropriate if the victim of such negligence was barred from suing before he knew of the damage. The court also found that this would be equally unjust in contract law or negligence.

Timely start to action necessary

This case is cited here to illustrate how important it is to start the process of suing properly. Not only do you have to sue for the right thing, in this case negligence or breach of contract, but you have to do so in a timely manner. Failure to sue within the time limits set out in a limitation statute can bar an action from proceeding.

Most of this text deals with matters of substantive law, that is, law that summarizes rights and obligations of the "you can" or "you can't" variety, rather than procedural law, which deals with the process by which we enforce those rights and obligations. But it is important to be familiar with the procedures involved in bringing a dispute to trial, if only to understand the function of lawyers and the reasons for the expense and delay involved. Before a decision is made to sue someone, all

Should try to settle dispute

avenues for settling the dispute outside of court ought to be exhausted. Alternative methods for resolving legal disputes, including negotiation, mediation, and arbitration, have been developed, and often the court requires the disputing parties to

Some variations from province to province

have tried these dispute resolution mechanisms before a trial procedure will be instigated. The litigation procedures may vary somewhat from province to province, but they are substantially the same in all common law jurisdictions, and they apply to most superior courts. (One of the distinguishing characteristics of small claims courts is that this involved procedure has been streamlined significantly, eliminating many of the steps described.) The procedure set out below is taken from the system used in British Columbia.

Jurisdiction

The first step in a legal suit is to determine which court should hear the action. The geographic jurisdiction of a court can be a very difficult question, but generally, the plaintiff, or person bringing the action, can choose a court in the area where the defendant resides or in the area where the matter complained about arose.

If a traffic accident happened in Alberta involving a driver from British Columbia and one from Ontario, the Ontario driver would have to sue in British Columbia or Alberta. The question of selecting the appropriate jurisdiction has become complicated by the prevalence of commercial and other kinds of transactions on the Internet. This communication system virtually eliminates distances between people as well as the ability to clearly determine which jurisdiction's law should prevail if the transaction leads to a dispute.[4] As a rule, however, the courts seem willing to take jurisdiction where there has been some interaction between the residents in that jurisdiction and the offending company.

Jurisdiction requires some interaction

Untangling the WEB

Jurisdiction is an important area of concern when dealing with commercial transactions on the Internet. There is already a considerable body of law covering the area referred to as **conflict of laws,** but these rules may not always be appropriate where the Internet is concerned. The problem is to determine whether an action can be brought in a particular court in one state or province against a person doing business through the Internet and residing in another state or province. The problem can arise when two companies do business with each other through e-mail but becomes acute when a retail business offers a product or service over the Internet. Do retailers face the risk of being sued or prosecuted in every area that the Internet message is received? This is especially a problem where activities that are prohibited in one area may be permissible in others, such as pornography and gambling. When people advertise or do business over the Internet, the message goes into every jurisdiction in the world, but there has to be something more than information delivery or advertising to give a particular court jurisdiction to hear a complaint. The transaction involved must create a special link or connection with the particular state or province that wants to take jurisdiction. A passive web site will usually not create a problem in any particular jurisdiction where it is read. For a court to have jurisdiction, there must be some degree of interactivity. A resident of that state or province, ordering or purchasing a product or paying a fee for some service over the Internet (such as the use of a game, music, pornography, etc.) would likely establish the appropriate amount of interconnectivity to give rise to jurisdiction. When doing business on the Internet, it is not always obvious where the service provider or the business originates, and so, it is often not good enough to simply follow the rules of your own jurisdiction. This is an area that will likely require international treaties to provide solutions.

Another problem with respect to jurisdiction is that once a state or province has taken jurisdiction, held a trial, and made a judgment, can that decision be enforced in the jurisdiction where the business resides or has assets? Cases in Canada and the United States have demonstrated that the judgment will only be enforced if there is a degree of connectivity or interactivity so that the business in question could clearly be said to be active and functional in the jurisdiction of the court that came up with the judgment. Courts have also refused to hear some cases where they felt that another jurisdiction would be more appropriate.

In order to avoid these problems, those doing business over the Internet should specify what law is to apply and, where business is solicited, include disclaimers that limit who they will do business with. Such disclaimers would be similar to those contained in product warranties: "Void where prohibited by law" or "Only available to residents of Canada." If a business creates a web site and uses it to do business in other jurisdictions, it will be subject to the law of those jurisdictions.

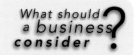

Once the appropriate jurisdiction has been chosen, the plaintiff must then choose the court. In a civil action, this is either the small claims court or the superior trial court of the province. The small claims court has a monetary limit of $10 000 (this varies with the province), but in several jurisdictions, cases involving more can be tried in the small claims court if the plaintiff waives any claim to a

4. For more information on this topic, see *Canadian Business Law Journal*, July 1999, Vol. 32, No. 1.

higher amount. Although it is simpler and less expensive to bring an action in the small claims court, a major disadvantage from a plaintiff's point of view is that the court is restricted in the costs it can award. Costs incurred for representation by a lawyer usually cannot be recovered, unless the action is brought at a superior court level.

Pre-trial

Writ of summons

Appearance

Statement of claim

Statement of defence

To commence an action in a superior court, the plaintiff must issue a **writ of summons**, have it authorized by a court clerk, pay the appropriate fees, and serve it on the defendant. The writ contains the names and addresses of the parties and a brief summary of the nature of the plaintiff's claim. If the defendant chooses to dispute the claim, he or she must promptly file an **appearance** with the court clerk. This is an important step, for without it, the plaintiff can short-circuit the rest of the procedure and ask for a summary judgment. Once the appearance has been filed and a copy sent to the plaintiff's lawyer, the plaintiff must draw up a **statement of claim**. The statement of claim sets out in more detail the plaintiff's allegations and must be filed with the court clerk and sent to the defendant, who then must file a **statement of defence,** in which he or she provides answers to the claims of the plaintiff. In some jurisdictions, notably Ontario, the writ of summons has been eliminated and an action begins with a statement of claim being served on the defendant.

Counterclaim

If the defendant feels that he or she is the real victim, he or she can also file a **counterclaim**. This is like a statement of claim and requires the submission of a statement of defence from the plaintiff in response. This exchange of documents is not to argue and justify positions; rather, the parties are merely stating the claims giving rise to the dispute and establishing the required elements of the legal action. If either of the parties feels that the documents do not make the position of the other completely clear, they may ask for clarification or further information. These documents constitute the **pleadings,** and once they have been closed, the parties have the right to apply to set a date for trial and begin the process of discovery. Throughout the pre-trial process, the parties have the right to, and often do, make applications to the court for direction regarding what details have to be disclosed, what questions have to be answered, and other matters that may arise. These are referred to as **chambers applications** because the judge deals with them in a less formal atmosphere than the regular trial process. The effect of the resulting court orders, however, can be extremely important to the outcome of the action.

Discovery may involve two distinct parts:

Discovery

1. **Discovery of documents.** The lawyers of the parties have the right to arrange for the inspection of any document in the possession of the other party that may be used as evidence in the trial.
2. **Examination for discovery.** The parties and their lawyers meet before a court reporter and, under oath, are asked detailed questions about the problem to be tried.

The parties are required to answer these questions fully and truthfully. Anything that is said is recorded and may be used later at the trial. This examination process generally applies only to the parties to the action, not to witnesses. When corporations are involved, a representative who has personal knowledge of the matter is examined. As part of a general reform of the litigation process in Ontario, and in an attempt to reduce the costs of an action to the parties, the discovery process has been eliminated in actions involving under $25 000. Other provinces have initiated similar reforms. In most jurisdictions, a pre-trial conference between the lawyers and a judge is held to determine whether there is an issue to try and if the parties can themselves resolve their dispute. All these procedures are designed to provide as much information as possible to the parties before the trial and encourage the parties to settle their dispute between themselves. In fact, most private disputes are settled between parties during this pre-trial process.

The discovery stage is an extremely important part of the litigation process, and cases are often won or lost at this point. When parties testify under oath at this stage, they often make admissions or incorrect statements that come back to haunt them at the trial. Admissions of fact that may not seem important at the time may be crucial by the time of the actual trial, and the party is bound by that admission. A false claim can be investigated before trial, and the party can be forced to recant at the trial, bringing his or her credibility into question. The result is that what is said at the discovery stage often determines the outcome of the case, compelling the parties to come to a settlement. For people in business, it is extremely important that the person who testifies at such a discovery process is not only familiar with the matter but is well prepared and appreciates the importance of his or her testimony and its potential impact on the legal action.

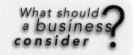

Another tool often available to parties before a trial is **payment into court**. A defendant being sued for damages may admit liability but think that the amount being demanded by the plaintiff is too high. The defendant makes a payment to the court acknowledging the amount he feels is owed. The judge is not aware of such a payment, and if the judgment is for less than the amount deposited by the defendant, the plaintiff will not be compensated for any of the costs incurred after the payment was made and will actually be responsible for the costs of the defendant. The plaintiff has had an opportunity to accept a fair settlement, and any costs incurred after failure to do so must therefore be borne by him or her. If the amount awarded is more than the payment into court, the defendant's payment obviously was not sufficient, and the plaintiff will be able to claim compensation for any costs that have been incurred. This encourages the defendant to make a fair offer of payment and the plaintiff to accept it and not risk unrecoverable expenses.

If Resnick fails to perform the terms of his contract with Wong, he may freely admit his liability and be willing to pay $15 000 but balk at Wong's claim for $25 000 damages. Resnick can deposit $15 000 with the court and notify Wong of the payment. Wong can either take the money, thus ending the action, or ignore the payment and proceed to trial in hopes of getting the additional $10 000. But in doing so, she risks losing not only the $10 000 but also being responsible for the plaintiff's legal costs incurred after that payment into court was made.

In some provinces, a related provision exists for the plaintiff to file an offer to settle which has a similar effect.

If Resnick sues for $25 000 but is willing to settle for $15 000, he can make the offer and file it with the court and notify the defendant. If Wong refuses to accept the offer and insists on a trial, she runs the risk of the judgment being for more than the offer to settle. If this happens, Wong will be required to pay double Resnick's costs incurred after the offer to settle was made. If the judgment is less than what was offered, of course, the defendant will only have to pay the costs of the plaintiff in the normal way.

Purpose of Pre-trial Proceedings

While it is obvious that the purpose of this long, involved, and expensive pre-trial process is to encourage the parties to reach a settlement, thus avoiding a trial, it is also clear that the process results in frustrating delays for the parties. For this reason,

Streamlining the process

Ontario and other provinces have initiated a reform process to streamline litigation, especially when lower amounts are involved. For example, in British Columbia, the option of a summary proceeding in a supreme court action is available, where instead of holding a trial with witnesses and testimony, the matter is decided on **affidavit evidence**. Also, jurisdictions, including Ontario, have introduced mediation as part of the pre-trial procedure to encourage parties to settle without a trial. The objective of reducing costs and delay and making the justice system more accessible has motivated all jurisdictions to create small claims courts where the procedures have been dramatically simplified.

What should a business consider?

The delay and costs associated with litigation as well as the lack of control over the process and outcome have contributed to its decreasing popularity. For business people, finding themselves in court should normally be viewed as a failure, and considerable care should be taken to avoid such disputes or settle them once they arise. When this cannot be done and the other party is willing, it is sometimes advantageous to explore some of the alternatives to litigation that are available (discussed below). However, in some situations, especially where it may be necessary to enforce the decision backed by the power of the court, litigation is the only option available.

The Trial

At the trial, the burden of proof rests with the plaintiff, and so, the plaintiff's case and witnesses are presented first. The plaintiff's lawyer will assist witnesses in their testimony by asking specific questions that get at the facts essential to their argument, but the types of questions that may be asked are restricted. Leading questions, in which the answer is suggested, are prohibited, e.g., "You were there on Saturday, weren't you?" The defendant's lawyer can cross-examine the witness and is permitted more latitude in the type of questions that can be asked, including leading questions. If something new arises from the cross-examination, the plaintiff's lawyer can then re-examine witnesses on those matters. Opposing lawyers may object to questions and have the judge rule whether to permit the question or order the lawyer to withdraw it. The complex rules governing what evidence is admissible and the kinds of testimony that can be obtained from witnesses are referred to as the **rules of evidence**, the details of which are beyond the scope of this text. After both sides have finished calling witnesses, the lawyers summarize the evidence and make arguments to the court.

Judgment and Its Enforcement

If there is a jury involved, the judge instructs them on matters of law. The jury then retires to consider the case and returns to announce its decision to the judge. The function of the jury in such cases is to decide on questions of fact; the judge decides on the questions of law. If a judge alone hears the case, a decision may be rendered immediately, but in a superior court trial, it is more common for the judge to hand down a judgment in writing some time later. The judge will include reasons for the decision as part of the judgment. These reasons can form the basis for an appeal. The successful claimant in a superior court action obtains judgment for both the amount owed and a portion of their legal costs from the defendant. A variety of factors can be considered in calculating the amount of costs to be awarded. Several tariffs or categories of costs exist. **Party and party costs** are the costs the

Obtaining judgments can be a costly process

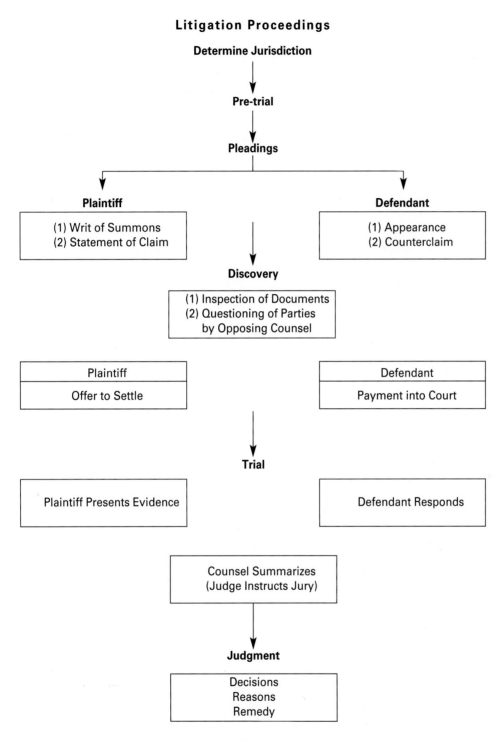

Litigation Proceedings

Determine Jurisdiction

Pre-trial

Pleadings

Plaintiff	**Defendant**
(1) Writ of Summons (2) Statement of Claim	(1) Appearance (2) Counterclaim

Discovery

(1) Inspection of Documents
(2) Questioning of Parties
by Opposing Counsel

Plaintiff	Defendant
Offer to Settle	Payment into Court

Trial

Plaintiff Presents Evidence	Defendant Responds

Counsel Summarizes
(Judge Instructs Jury)

Judgment

Decisions
Reasons
Remedy

losing party must pay to the winner; **solicitor-client costs** are the fees a lawyer is normally expected to charge his or her own client above and beyond the party and party costs, but there is nothing to stop a lawyer from charging more if the client is willing to pay. In addition to the fees of the lawyer, there may be other costs, such as the costs of photocopying documents, the costs of obtaining transcripts from the

**Costs not completely
recoverable**

examination process, and the fees associated with obtaining specialized reports from engineers and other such experts. Even when successful, the winning party will have to pay some of their own legal costs. In most provinces, the cost of court services is minimal. Parties have the right to represent themselves, but lawyers are generally the rule in higher-level courts, and the cost of hiring a lawyer is often prohibitive. This is one of the reasons that small claims courts have been introduced in most common law jurisdictions. In small claims courts, the presence of a lawyer is discouraged by not awarding legal costs for their services, and so, litigants often represent themselves.

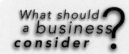

Concern about the delays and costs that plague the civil dispute resolution process has prompted reforms in the system. Bryan Williams, former Chief Justice of the Supreme Court of British Columbia, says that currently in British Columbia, "after the close of pleadings…litigants must wait two years for a trial date. Even then, if not enough judges are available, they may have their trial bumped for a further six months or more. To help remedy the problems, he recommended and implemented, on an experimental basis, the following reforms among others: (1) The judge appointed to hear a case that will last longer than 10 days will manage it from beginning to end; (2) parties in a less complicated trial can opt for a fast track, which will see the matter completed within six months; (3) a number of judges assigned to a settlement division within the court to conduct settlement/mediation conferences at the request of both sides; (4) telephone- and video-conferencing systems that allow judges in one area to hear applications made in another, allowing courts to balance the workload; and (5) a review of some of the more costly and time-consuming pre-trial procedures. Ontario and other jurisdictions have also introduced reforms to the same end.[5]

Remedies

Damages

The most common remedy requested by a plaintiff is monetary payment in the form of **damages**, which are designed to compensate the victim for any loss suffered. They may take the form of **general damages,** where the amount is estimated in terms of future wages or pain and suffering, or **special damages,** where the exact amount lost can be calculated. In serious cases involving clear wrongdoing, **punitive** or **exemplary damages** may be awarded to the victim to punish the wrongdoer.

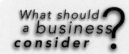

Some Canadian companies have discovered to their regret that juries in the United States are less reluctant to make huge damage awards. The Loewen Group of Funeral Homes faced a jury award of $500 million in a civil action in Mississippi when the company was found liable in a breach of contract action in the purchase of a family funeral home business. Although relatively uncommon, businesses must take the possibility of such an outcome into consideration when deciding how to meet this kind of challenge in another jurisdiction. It might well be better to settle or turn to alternative dispute resolution mechanisms, where the results can be controlled better, rather than face the risk-laden prospect of such a jury trial.

Other remedies

The court can order money incorrectly paid to the defendant to be restored to the rightful owner. In some circumstances, it is also possible to obtain an **accounting**, which results in any profits wrongfully obtained by the wrongdoer to be paid over to the victim. The court also has the power to order an **injunction** stopping wrongful conduct or correcting some existing wrong. The court may compel proper performance of a legal obligation by **specific performance**. In some situations, it may be appropriate for the courts to simply make a **declaration** as to the law and the legal rights of the parties.

5. *Vancouver Sun,* Jan. 2000

Semelhago v. Paramadevan et al.[6]

Although damages or monetary compensation is the common remedy in a civil action, sometimes the court will order the equitable remedy of specific performance. In land transactions, it was thought that because all land is unique, specific performance would always be available, at least until the following case was decided by the Supreme Court of Canada. Mr. Semelhago agreed to purchase a house, under construction, from Paramadevan for $205 000 at the time of the agreement. When it was the time to perform the contract, the vendor refused to go through with it, and this action was brought. Mr. Semelhago asked for the remedy of specific performance or, as permitted by statute, damages in lieu of specific performance. At the trial, he elected to receive damages, and the court awarded him $125 000 damages in lieu of specific performance. The reason for this high award was that the market value of the house had risen from the $205 000 agreed upon at the time of the contract to $325 000 at the time of trial. Paramadevan appealed the award, and the appeal court reduced the award by the interest that Semelhago would have had to pay to finance the purchase of the house over the period of time from the contract to the trial, saying that the damages should not only reflect the increase in the value of the house from the time of the contract but also reflect normal interest that would have been paid out had the deal gone through. This reduced the damages he was entitled to to just less than $82 000. The purpose of such damages is to put him in the position he would have been in had the contract been properly performed, and so, the interest he would have had to pay should have been taken into consideration. The Supreme Court of Canada refused to further reduce the award and refused to take into consideration the increased value of the house that Mr. Semelhago had intended to sell to acquire the one in question but which he had retained. In making their judgment, an important statement that came out of the case was that it should no longer be thought that all land is unique and that specific performance would always be appropriate in a land transaction.

Enforcement

Even when the process is complied with and judgment obtained, there is no guarantee that the amount awarded will be paid. There may be no dispute over liability, but if the judgment debtor refuses to pay, steps must be taken by the plaintiff to enforce that judgment. If the judgment debtor has no assets (this is a dry judgment), it was likely unwise to pursue the action in the first place. Not only will the successful plaintiff get nothing from the defendant but will also have to pay his own legal expenses. On the other hand, if the debtor has prospects of future assets, the judgment remains enforceable for a considerable period of time, up to 20 years in some cases.

A judgment does not ensure payment

Enforcing Judgment

Once judgment has been obtained, most provinces provide for a further hearing, sometimes called an **examination in aid of execution**, to determine which of the defendant's assets are available to satisfy the judgment. The plaintiff can question the defendant who is under oath about his or her assets, wages, bank accounts, safety deposit boxes, and so on. The plaintiff can also ask about any property transfers involving the defendant. At the conclusion of the process, the plaintiff can ask

Hearing to aid execution

6. [1996] 2 S.C.R. 415

for an order to execute against a particular property or garnishee wages, bank accounts, and rental or mortgage income.

Seizure of Property

Property seized

The execution process involves the seizure and eventual sale of the debtor's property to satisfy the judgment. The property is seized by an official, who, after deducting a fee, sells it, usually through public auction. The proceeds are distributed first to secured and preferred creditors, then on a *pro rata* or percentage-of-claim basis to the rest of the creditors. Secured creditors used the property in question to secure the loan, and so, they have first claim to the proceeds from its sale but only up to the amount secured. Preferred creditors are those who, by legislation, must be paid before general creditors. Landlords for unpaid rent and wage earners for unpaid wages, both for a limited number of months, are examples. Some properties are exempt from seizure, including food, clothing, bedding, furniture, tools needed to perform a trade, fuel, motor vehicles used in the course of employment, and goods under a certain value. It should be noted that real property (land and buildings) can be seized to satisfy a judgment, but the method employed varies with the jurisdiction. Often, registering the judgment against the property is enough to pressure the debtor to pay. But when this is not enough, the court can order the property sold to satisfy the debts.

Proceeds of sale shared by all creditors

Some properties are exempt from seizure

Garnishment

Funds owed to debtor can be seized pursuant to judgment

When wages are intercepted before being paid to the judgment debtor or bank accounts seized to satisfy a judgment, the process is referred to as garnishment or **attachment of debt**. The legislation covering this area may be found in one act dealing with the execution process generally or in some jurisdictions in separate attachments of debts statutes. These acts, while allowing the creditor to garnishee wages, typically limit the amount that can be intercepted. This amount may vary, depending on the debtor's earnings and number of dependants. In Ontario, for instance, only 20 percent of the wage earner's net income can be garnisheed. Once the garnishee order is served on the employer or person holding the funds, that person must pay those funds into the court, which then supervises their disbursement.

GRH Ventures Ltd v. DeNeve[7]

Mr. DeNeve owned property and contracted with GRH to build a house on that property. DeNeve failed to pay, and GRH registered a builders' lien against the property and sought an order to garnishee his bank account. The order was granted, and the bank paid the money to the court to hold, pending the outcome of the litigation. This decision was appealed by Mr. DeNeve. A garnishee order to intercept funds before trial is an extraordinary remedy, and the court will only grant it when authorized by statute and when the amount owing is a debt or a liquidated demand (a fixed and certain amount). The judge in this case relied on a statement from a Saskatchewan judge who said…. "I would not interpret the words 'debt or liquidated demand' so broadly. In my view, debt or liquidated demand means the amount must be agreed upon or ascertained either by the parties, by operation of law or otherwise. It must be a claim which can be determined with exactness by a

---

7. 37 D.L.R. (4th) 155, (Man. C.A.)

mathematical computation." In this case, because there was dispute over the specific amount owed, the appeal court overturned the pre-judgment garnishee order and returned the money seized to Mr. DeNeve. Once judgment is awarded to the plaintiff, a garnishing order would be completely appropriate because the amount owing would then be certain, having been determined by the court in its judgment.

Judicial Remedies before Judgment

Some judicial remedies may be available to the creditor even before judgment is obtained. These are extraordinary remedies that are normally only granted where there is risk that the property will be removed or otherwise made unavailable to the creditor. While bank accounts and other sources can sometimes be attached before judgment, intercepting wages before judgment is usually not permitted. New Brunswick and Nova Scotia do not permit any form of garnishment before the judgment. Where property other than money is involved and there is risk of it being removed or sold, the creditor usually must get a court order allowing seizure. This is not a judgment but an interim order by the court granted before the actual trial to ensure that the goods will be available to satisfy a judgment.

Pre-judgment remedies limited

Another remedy available in some situations is to make a request to the court for an **injunction** to prevent a third party from paying out money owed to the debtor. This does not direct those funds to the creditor, but it does prevent them from going to the debtor who may abscond with or dissipate them. The process of collection and enforcement of judgment as described here may appear cumbersome, but it is quite effective because of the diversity of options available. However, the process can be expensive and may not be justifiable economically, considering the amount of the debt and the likelihood of recovery. Note that when property has been used to secure a debt and the security has been properly registered, the creditor has a right to seize the property upon default, without recourse to the courts. Bankruptcy will also affect the debtor's obligation to pay. Secured transactions involving personal property as well as the bankruptcy process are dealt with in Chapter 10.

Limitation Periods

Whether to remove ongoing uncertainty or to ensure fairness when memories dim or witnesses become unavailable, court action must be brought within a relatively short period of time from the complained of event. These are referred to as limitation periods, and in Ontario, for example, a person who is owed money from a simple sale of goods transaction, must bring an action against the debtor within six years of the failure to pay the debt. It is not necessary to actually go to trial before the limitation period expires, only to initiate the action by filing the writ (or statement of claim in Ontario). Failing to fulfill that step within the limitation period will result in the plaintiff being barred from pursuing the action. This time limitation will vary, depending on the jurisdiction and the nature of the complaint involved, and may be embodied in several different statutes in a province. Whether this limitation period had expired was the problem facing the court in the *Consumer Glass* case cited at the beginning of this section. With the expiry of the limitation period, the plaintiff is left without recourse. This is one reason why a person involved in a potential lawsuit should put the matter in the hands of a lawyer as quickly as possible.

Expiration of limitation period prohibits suing

Alternatives to Court Action

Business people involved in private disputes are well advised to avoid litigation, whenever possible, because of the high cost, the long delays, and the general dissatisfaction with the results. In this section, we will discuss the various alternatives that are available and can be used instead of or in conjunction with the litigation process. It has been suggested that the capacity of the civil justice system has been severely tested in the effort to resolve disputes, and many jurisdictions in Canada are actively supporting the use of alternative mechanisms for avoiding court-adjudicated settlements. Some of the tools the courts have implemented, and in some cases made mandatory, are very similar to the mechanisms that have become increasingly popular. Alternative dispute resolution and litigation are neither inconsistent nor rival systems. In fact, each depends on the other. If the alternative processes fail, it may still be possible to initiate a lawsuit, and that threat may be enough to make the alternative processes more productive. And even if the matter does go to the courts, these mechanisms can be used at any stage in the litigation process, including post judgment, when the parties wish to avoid an appeal. Because of the essential privacy of the matters resolved by alternative means, it is difficult to cite actual case examples in this discussion. As a consequence of that, hypothetical examples of the processes described are used. They should not be relied on as actual case studies.

What is Alternative Dispute Resolution?

Any strategy that is used as a substitute for court action qualifies as a method of alternative dispute resolution (ADR), but they can be divided into three main approaches. The first is when the decision making is left in the hands of the disputing parties, the second is when a neutral third party assists the parties to come to a resolution, and the third is when a third party makes a binding decision in the matter under dispute. **Negotiation** is the process by which the disputants agree to discuss the matter between themselves in an attempt to resolve the problems. The goal of **mediation** is to bring in an outsider to facilitate discussions and assist disputing parties to resolve their problem and come to a settlement on their own. **Arbitration** involves a third party holding a hearing and actually making a decision that is binding on the parties. There are some variations on these methods and they will be discussed below in more detail.

Negotiation

Mediation

Arbitration

ADR versus Litigation

Advantages

Control. There are some significant advantages in choosing an alternative to litigation. The first is that control of the matter remains in the hands of the people most affected by it. When people turn to the courts to solve their problems, they abdicate their personal responsibility and right to control the decision-making process. Litigants may expend significant amounts of time, money, and personal and business resources pursuing or defending an action. They may feel some satisfaction and relief if the final decision is in their favour but powerless if the decision goes against them. Rarely does the judgment compensate the parties for all the costs incurred, and because they are not part of the decision-making process, they may find them-

ADR leaves control in the hands of the parties

selves unwilling to comply with the decision, making it more difficult to enforce. It is, therefore, vitally important that business people appreciate the advantages of maintaining control over the problem-solving process and the disadvantages of placing it in the hands of others.

Avoidance of Delay. Most of the delays in litigation are because of the lengthy pre-trial process and the problems of scheduling court personnel and facilities. When other resolution processes are used, there are fewer procedural delays because the structure of the process is determined by the parties themselves. Scheduling only has to involve a time and a place to meet that are convenient to the parties, their representatives, and a mediator, if one is involved.

Less delay with ADR

Avoidance of Lost Productivity. An ongoing court battle can be very distracting to the managers and employees of a company. Key people may find themselves involved in overseeing the process, providing information, or preparing to testify over a considerable period of time. This is non-productive time that may cost a company its competitive advantage. Other business opportunities may be lost because of this distraction, not to mention the negative publicity that may be given to the case. The much quicker resolution process offered by ADR reduces that problem.

Less distraction with ADR

Lower Cost. ADR is less costly because of the simplified procedure but also because fewer parties are involved. There is less need for lawyers, and the general expense caused by delay is not usually a factor. The costs of producing documentary evidence and preparing witnesses are largely avoided. Also the unpredictable risks associated with an adverse court decision are avoided. No matter how sure a person is of their legal position, it is impossible to be certain of the outcome of an action. There is no obligation to assume the other party's costs as would be the case if the decision was in their favour. Also, there is no danger that punitive damages will be awarded. This is true especially in the United States, where the risk of a jury awarding crippling punitive damages has become an important consideration in doing business.

Less expense

In an American case against McDonalds, the burger chain, a woman was injured when a cup of extremely hot coffee spilled on her as she removed the top to add sugar. She suffered serious burns and spent some time in hospital. She had asked for some small compensation from McDonalds and was rebuffed. When the matter when to trial, the jury awarded over $2.7 million in punitive damages.[8] Similarly, the Loewen Group was involved in an $8 million contract dispute, and the jury awarded $500 million in punitive damages against them, a judgment that contributed significantly to the financial difficulties of the company.[9] These cases illustrate the great risk that can be faced by litigants and why ADR can be much more attractive.

No risk of unexpected damage awards

Privacy. The fact that ADR is a private process gives it several advantages, not the least of which is that the media can be excluded and the general public will be unaware of the dispute, thus protecting the reputations of the people involved and the public image of the business. Confidential information, trade secrets, profitability, and

8. Liebeck v. McDonalds, cited in: Ponte LM, Thomas DC. *Alternative Dispute Resolution in Business*, (Cincinnati, Ohio: West Educational Publishing Company, 1999).
9. *Lawyers Weekly*, February 7, 1997, Vol. 16, No. 36.

Confidentiality retained with ADR

other sensitive information remain private. There may be no records kept of the process, and therefore, one agreement cannot set a precedent for subsequent, similar disputes. Other claimants will not be tempted to take a run at the company because they were attracted by the amount of a previous settlement, simply because they will not be aware of it.

Good Will. One of the costs of a protracted conflict is the breakdown in the relationship between the parties. Litigation is adversarial in nature, where questioning the opposition's credibility and honesty is routine. The emotional costs can be extreme, leaving bitterness and animosity between the parties. When the parties in conflict have a business relationship and an adjudicated decision favours one party at the expense of the other, often it becomes impossible for them to resume that business relationship. When they have worked together to resolve their differences and come to a relatively quick settlement that is mutually agreeable, their relationship may be strengthened. In addition, because they maintain control of the process, they are more likely to abide by the terms of the agreement.

Good relationship can be retained with ADR

International Disputes. Most other trading nations use the civil law system, which is much less adversarial in nature and much more compatible with ADR. North American companies accustomed to solving disputes through cooperation rather than confrontation will function more effectively in the global business environment. There are no international courts that deal with private matters, and it is difficult to determine the best jurisdiction to hear the dispute. Even where the parties agree ahead of time, by putting a clause in the contract specifying which country's law will apply, there will likely be a suspicion of bias towards their own nationals. In such circumstances, ADR culminating in international arbitration is the logical alternative, and organizations have been established in the major cities in Canada to manage such disputes.[10]

Avoids conflicts under international laws

Flexibility. One of the most attractive features of ADR is its flexibility. The process and method used to resolve conflicts remain in the control of the parties and can be tailored to the particular dispute. The needs of multiple parties or several competing interests can be accommodated. It can take into consideration not only the interests of the company but those of the shareholders, employees, suppliers, customers, and creditors as well. Even cultural differences can be taken into consideration. When there are internal conflicts within an organization, such as disputes between different divisions or between management and employees, ADR is the only satisfactory solution, since it can resolve the matter quickly and allow the parties to continue to work together in an improved environment. Litigation, on the other hand, takes place in a very formal atmosphere and must adhere to rigid rules of evidence and procedure.

ADR less formal than litigation

Disadvantages

ADR is not always the best option. The qualities of judicial fairness, impartiality, predictability, and certainty associated with the litigation process are not always present in ADR. The court has no prior interest in the parties or their problems, but it does have extraordinary powers to extract information from the parties, which is not the case outside the courts. In the courts, there are safeguards in place to en-

ADR cannot assure full disclosure

10. For example, the British Columbia International Commercial Arbitration Centre, www.bcicac.com

Summary Chart

	Adjudication	Arbitration	Mediation	Negotiation
Control	Low	Low	High	Highest
Delay	Lengthy	Moderate	Brief	Briefer
Cost	High	Moderate	Low	Low
Privacy	Low	Moderate	High	Complete
Flexibility	Low	Moderate	High	Highest
Good Will	Unlikely	Possible	Likely	Assured
Predictability	High	Reasonable	Low	Low
Appealability	Usually	Reviewable	None	None
Visibility	High	Moderate	None	None

sure that the rules are followed and that each side gets a fair hearing. Because there are few rules or required procedures, ADR may not be able to provide this assurance. The court strives to balance the process so that neither side can take unfair advantage of the other, although this advantage may be compromised when only one side can afford extensive legal help. When there is a power imbalance between the parties, there is the danger that the weaker party will be taken advantage of in an ADR setting. The court process preserves the basic rights of due process and, through the discovery process, does much to level the playing field where such inequality exists.

ADR cannot assure fair process

Another important advantage of the courts over ADR is the consistency of the decisions. A court case will establish a precedent that can govern future dealings and avoid disputes between other parties. Because judges are bound to refer to similar previous cases and base their decisions on the earlier judgment, the decisions are quite predictable and can be challenged if they are inconsistent. Where disputes are resolved independently and privately as is the case with ADR, not only is there no precedent, there is also no record and no knowledge of the outcome outside of the immediate parties to it. As a result, each dispute must be dealt with on its own merits, and the same kind of problems may be faced over and over again. But this is a two-edged sword in that other potential claimants will not learn of the settlement or the amount they might claim. The availability of effective tools of enforcing the judgment may also be an important consideration in choosing litigation over ADR. Litigation also retains the right of appeal if the loser feels an injustice has taken place.

ADR cannot assure consistent outcomes

Agreements may not be enforceable

The publicity given to high-profile cases makes court decisions an effective deterrent to similar offending conduct. For example, a software company, discovering that their product is being copied and used without permission, might select a particularly blatant offender and initiate an action to get across the idea to others that such conduct will not be tolerated.

Findings unavailable to public

It must also be emphasized that the public interest may not be served by the privacy of ADR. Where public policy matters, such as pollution or unfair competition, are involved, the information that would normally be available to the press and public in the court process is withheld. When there is public scrutiny and businesses are forced to do their business in the plain light of day, they are likely to be much better citizens. It must always be remembered that what is a disadvantage to one party may be the most appealing feature of the chosen process to another. As in all business decisions, sound, properly informed judgment is needed in deciding between ADR and litigation in any given situation.

ADR Mechanisms

Upon concluding that ADR is a viable option, the businessperson must then decide which of the various strategies would be most effective in resolving the dispute.

Negotiation

This should be the first recourse for people who find themselves in a disagreement—too often, it is the last. Negotiation involves the parties meeting to discuss the problem in order to come to an agreement as to how it should be resolved. Both sides must be willing to enter into negotiations, and the goal must be to find a solution, even if that means making concessions. Negotiation can be as simple as a phone conversation, an exchange of correspondence, or two people sitting down together in a private meeting, but any meeting with the goal of resolving a dispute qualifies as a negotiation. It may take place through agents and include legal representation, and the stakes may be very high as in the treaty negotiations that take place between governments and aboriginal groups. As the size and significance of the meetings increase, so must the formality of the process to ensure that the position of each side is fairly represented. Because the process is cooperative and non-binding, either side can withdraw if the other is being unreasonable or intransigent. The parties may then elect to move on to some other means of dealing with the matter. An understanding of the law surrounding the dispute will help the parties recognize the consequences of a failure to settle. This puts pressure on the parties to negotiate a settlement consistent with their legal rights, but they are free to reach a settlement independent of those legal rights and obligations if it better suits the needs of both parties. This flexibility is one of the great attractions of ADR.

People approach negotiation with a variety of attitudes, skills, and objectives, and it is helpful to be aware of them and recognize the role they play in the process. Some will come to the table with the idea of getting the best return for their side, even if it is at the expense of the other. They may take an aggressive position, with little regard for the needs of the other party. This competitive style may be successful in achieving certain goals, but it will do little to resolve underlying problems or prevent the development of others in the future. It destroys rather than enhances business relationships. Another style would be one where a person is too willing to accommodate the other's demands, sacrificing personal interests for the good of the relationship. This, too, can be a pitfall, as it may lead to unfair results, which, in turn, will jeopardize future relations.

The successful model for negotiation requires people who are acutely aware of their own position but are also capable of understanding the position of the other party. Cooperation and compromise are the central concepts to fruitful negotiation, and the objective is to come to a solution where both sides win. Bullying and coercion have no place in such negotiations. Because the parties put themselves in a vulnerable position, there is some risk of one of the parties indulging in unethical behaviour, such as withholding essential information, deceit, or coercion. Not everyone is a good negotiator, and if a businessperson recognizes this in himself of herself or a particular talent in the other party, they would be well advised to appoint or employ others to represent them at the table or invite a third party to facilitate the process.

Negotiating through representatives has both advantages and disadvantages. It creates more formality and less privacy. Relying on third parties, whether they are lawyers, experts in the subject matter, or trained negotiators, puts some distance between the parties and brings another point of view to the dispute. Experts may introduce other considerations or suggest solutions that were not apparent to the actual parties. This may be more a hindrance than help if those new points of view simply complicate the picture. And since these third parties are negotiating with each other, they must be satisfied before any solution will be taken to the principals, which will increase the time and money spent on the process. In this way, the actual parties lose some measure of control over the matter. Where lawyers are involved and the negotiations fail, they are already up to speed and will be better prepared for the litigation that follows. However, that can be a problem as well. If a lawyer is predisposed to the litigation process and approaches the negotiations expecting them to fail, he or she will not be an effective representative. The added costs must also be taken into consideration before hiring outsiders to do the negotiations.

Representatives may conduct negotiation

It is important to remember that while negotiation might involve significant compromise, if the negotiations fail, those concessions will not necessarily follow the parties to the next stage. Legal concessions, compromises, and admissions that take place in the negotiation process are generally made "without prejudice," which means that they cannot be used against the party making the admission or compromise in subsequent litigation. These compromises should not come back to haunt the parties later. Finally, it should be taken into consideration that well-handled negotiations will not harm an ongoing relationship and, in fact, may actually strengthen it, the parties having gone through a process of cooperation and compromise, resulting in increased trust and interdependence.

Relationship may be enhanced

It is more likely the case that a failure at negotiation leads to litigation, but it is also interesting to observe that sometimes a failure to achieve a settlement through litigation can lead to more effective negotiation. Native tribes in British Columbia have long contested their rights to lands and territories in the province. Their demands led to several protracted and unsatisfying legal battles culminating in several hearings before the Supreme Court of Canada. In the Delgamuukw decision rendered in 1997,[11] the Supreme Court ordered a new trial but also made it clear that the best route to follow was through the negotiation process. Armed with that counsel, both sides embarked on serious negotiations that accomplished in a little over a year what had not been accomplished in decades of legal wrangling. A treaty acceptable to both sides has resulted, reminding us that negotiation, the most basic of all dispute resolution processes, should hold a significant place in all business relationships.

Mediation

Mediation also has a long history in resolving disputes. Its use in labour relations has been mandated by statutes for most of the century, and its use in family disputes is commonplace. Mediation has always played a role in commercial relations but has

---

11. Delgamuukw v. British Columbia [1997] 3 S.C.R. 1010

Neutral third party facilitates communication

become much more visible in recent years. The main difference between negotiation and mediation is that mediation involves a neutral third party who is trained to assist the parties in coming to an agreement. Their role is to facilitate the discussion, making sure that each side has the opportunity to put their side forward, eliciting information, finding areas of possible compromise, and encouraging settlement. Mediators do not impose decisions but may make recommendations if they have some expertise in the matter under dispute.

Mediator finds common ground

The mediation process can be very informal or can be carefully structured with rules of procedure and a set timeframe that all parties must adhere to. Usually, only a few meetings are necessary, and the process begins by the mediator summarizing his facilitator's role and what will occur during the proceedings, and then both parties make an opening statement describing their positions. One of the main objectives of the mediator is to find some common ground that can be used as the basis of a settlement. The mediator will meet with both parties together and separately, actually forming a communication link between them. And then, by determining what compromises each party is willing to make, the parties are encouraged to move bit by bit towards a solution.

Many different techniques and variations are available to the mediator, and it is this flexibility that makes the process so effective in the hands of a skilled mediator. Because the mediator is so involved in the decision-making process, it is vitally important that the mediator be free of bias, ethical, and highly skilled. The key to understanding the success of mediation is to realize that the persuasiveness, fresh thinking, skills, and neutrality of a trained third party that both parties trust are brought into the equation, while control of the problem is retained by each party.

Mediator does not make decision

The mediator does not impose a solution on the parties but encourages them to come to one on their own. If the parties cannot come to an agreement, they are still free to seek other solutions. If the matter does end up in court before an agreement is concluded, any concessions made at the mediation will not be taken into consideration. Of course, if a settlement is reached and put into an agreement, it can be enforced just like any other contract. In addition to this, a settlement that has been reached by both parties is more likely to be adhered to than one that has been imposed on them. When the parties have cooperated and been part of the decision making process, it has been found that they are more willing to live up to the terms of that agreement. This saves the enforcement costs that often accompany a court order.

The skills involved require considerable specialized training, and organizations are now in place to provide this training. Membership and certification are provided by organizations that set recognized professional standards. The disputing parties will normally choose a mediator who is a member in good standing with such an organization or actually choose the mediator from a list provided by the organization.

Mediation may be required

Mediation has been mandated by statute in several situations in various jurisdictions. Perhaps the highest profile is in collective bargaining. In most jurisdictions, either party or the government can call for the services of a mediator. They are supplied from a trained pool of professional labour mediators, and as they try to help the disputing parties reach a settlement, other forms of labour action, including strikes and lockouts, are prohibited. Mediation in these circumstances is more structured and formal. Still, mediators have many different strategies they can bring to the process and are often successful in bringing the dispute to an end. Even in the litigation process itself, mediation, in the form of a pre-trial conference, is mandated in most jurisdictions before the trial can proceed.

Mediation in Health Care

Some hospitals in Canada have standing mediation committees that are prepared to deal with problems arising between patients and hospital staff. George had developed an acute illness and had been admitted to hospital for treatment. He had been a healthy and vigorous man, but because it was flu season, his symptoms were mistaken for the flu, and he was being treated like most of the other patients in the hospital at the time with something short of benign neglect. After several days, it became apparent that George was not recovering. It was at this stage that the doctors attending him suspected that he might have a rare case of what is commonly known as "flesh-eating disease," and they began immediate and dramatic efforts to save his life, including amputating his leg when an infection became untreatable. In spite of their efforts, George died within a week of being admitted to the hospital. His widow was distraught at his unexpected death, but she was even more horrified at the treatment he had received, both the seeming neglect at the beginning of his hospital stay and the almost violent method of treatment at the end. She could not be consoled and considered suing the attending doctors, nurses, and the hospital for medical malpractice. The director of the hospital suggested to her that she first might want to take her concerns to the hospital mediation committee that had been struck to help patients with such complaints. Members of the medical staff who had treated George were called to make statements to explain and justify their actions in the presence of George's relatives. They explained how the extreme flu season had caught them unawares and of the variety of symptoms the many new patients were exhibiting. They had been short staffed and had been working a lot of overtime because their own employees were also being struck by the flu. They explained the rareness of the disease that struck George and that no one at the hospital had ever seen it before. They also explained how quickly the disease progressed and what extreme measures were required to treat it and were able to report on other cases and the survival rate of patients. They were also able to express their feelings of sorrow to the family for its loss and their regret for the circumstances of the death. In this case, the family was primarily looking for answers as to how George died and some expression of sympathy from the people who were responsible for his care.[12]

In spite of the obvious advantages of mediation, such as being private, less costly, faster, and more flexible, there are some important disadvantages to consider before using mediation. In the case of the hospital mediation, it is clear that a patient and his family are in a vulnerable position, compared with the hospital and its staff. Where there has been actual malpractice, it is unlikely that the full truth of the situation would come out in mediation. Therefore, mediation is not a good forum where blame needs to be established or where some other legal right or precedent should be set. If it is necessary to obtain confidential or secret information, it is more likely to be forthcoming through the discovery part of litigation. Mediators have little power to compel parties to produce evidence and documentation when they are unwilling to do so. When compensation for loss and damages for injuries are being sought, there is no power to enforce such agreements. In other situations

Mediation may be inappropriate

---

12. Adapted from a report of a case in Alberta, from: Portlock PL. "Code Green dispute resolved through mediation." *Law Now*, May 1994, pp. 9–12.

**Successful mediation
requires balance of power**

where one of the parties is weaker, mediation may just exacerbate that weakness. This can be a serious problem in family disputes where the weakness of one of the parties, or their desire to accommodate, leads to an unbalanced result. It is important in such situations for the parties to have legal counsel throughout the process or, at the very least, have their lawyer review the terms of the agreement before they sign it. The job of the mediator is to help the parties reach an agreement, not to ensure that the agreement is fair and balanced. But where one of the parties is suspected of acting in bad faith, mediation is simply inappropriate, trust being such an important component of the mediation process.

**and willingness to disclose
relevant information**

There is no public record of a mediated settlement, and because of that, it cannot become a precedent and may not be consistent with past practice. And if the decision is later regretted, there is no appeal to a higher court. Many people find the very flexibility of the mediation process uncomfortable, preferring a more formal and rule-oriented process.

Mediation does work well where highly confidential or sensitive information which should not be disclosed to the public is involved, where a speedy resolution is vital, where good ongoing relations must be maintained, where there is some trust involved, and where both parties are desirous of reaching a settlement.

*What should
a business
consider* ?

There are a variety of circumstances in which mediation would bring more satisfying results than other means of resolution might. For example, in the construction industry, when the successful bidder on a building is unable to complete the project within the time or the budget originally agreed upon. Normally, the owner could sue for compensation and damages from the delinquent contractor. If the shortfalls in the project were obvious before the project's completion and if the owner were otherwise satisfied with the work that was being done and anxious that the public not become aware of troubles on the job site, it would make little sense to claim a breach of contract and pursue the matter in court. In such an instance, it is likely that work on the project would stop as the parties gather evidence to support their claims and the reasons for the delays, ill feeling would damage the working relationship, and it is possible that the two parties would not be able to continue working on the project together. If required changes or unforeseen circumstances contributed to the delay or the cost overrun and if there was a likelihood of the project failing altogether because of the disagreement as to who was responsible for the problems, it would be wise to call in a mediator who understands the construction industry. This mediator could help the two parties come to an understanding of the problems each has faced in the process of the development and establish the consequences of continuing under new arrangements or breaking off the relationship. When each party understands all the implications of the breach and what a court battle might involve, it is likely that compromises and new agreements at this stage would be the most reasonable way to solve the difficulties facing both parties to the contract. In fact, in the construction sector, it is reported that millions of dollars are saved annually in jurisdictions where the first recourse in the event of problems is to mediate rather than litigate.

Simulated court hearings

Variations. Mini-trials are much more formal models that still leave the actual decision to the people most concerned with the matters in dispute. **Mini-trials** are quite valuable as an alternative dispute mechanism, especially within the context of a company. Here, the senior managers hear the case presented by lawyers, much as it would be presented in a court. Usually, there has been some discovery process, and witnesses are called and cross-examined, or the lawyers can simply summarize what they would have said. It is quite a formal process involving some cost and time, but it is still a private process and still in the control of the parties. This is an effective way to get across the various positions of the parties as well as the legal ramifications for both the individuals and the company. The managers listen to the evidence and the arguments as if they were the judges and make a decision. Because all the pertinent information is out and both parties have had an opportunity to be heard, it is more likely that they will accept the managers' decision. Even if they are not in agreement with the decision, everyone is aware of their legal position and can determine whether it would be beneficial to pursue the matter in court. Because the process is private, confidentiality is maintained and adverse publicity avoided. Yet, many of the advantages of a trial, such as the formality and structure as well as adherence to due process, are present. This approach is particularly useful where the issues and information are quite technical and require considerable expertise. Expert witnesses are commonly called on to testify, and complicated documentation can be introduced. Of course, it is a much more formal, costly, and time-consuming process than simple negotiation or even mediation.

Mediating Gender Bias

Gillian had been working with a large and reputable architectural firm for a couple years as a junior architect. She was a talented designer and had demonstrated a unique ability in the assignments she had been given. Unfortunately, they were limited ones, and she often found herself drawing up blueprints for the projects of the more senior members of the firm. It eventually became clear to her that younger male architects, more recently hired than she, were getting their own interesting projects, while she was being kept in the background busy with the mundane tasks of the firm. She approached her supervisor for an explanation, and he brushed her off claiming that the clients were not interested in having women work for them and that she had better get used to that fact if she wanted a job at all in this industry. The head office for the firm was in Toronto, so she took her complaints to the senior partner. He had not seen her work, nor did he know much about her, but he was not anxious to have a gender discrimination complaint lodged against his firm, and so, after some deliberation, he suggested to her that they deal with the problem through a mini-trial and that the firm would cover the costs of legal representation for both sides of the issue. After explaining the process to Gillian and her supervisor and allowing them both the opportunity to prepare their cases, the three senior partners convened a mini-trial, in which both sides were able to put forward their evidence, concerns, and arguments as to their positions. Each side was treated with respect, and each was encouraged to make a full case for themselves. Gillian was able to demonstrate her capabilities, and her supervisor brought in the clients who had expressed their disinclination to work with women. After a full hearing, in which all the legal and human rights issues were raised, and during their private deliberations, the three-judge panel reconsidered the firm's traditional policies, recognizing that even though it had never been explicitly stated as such, the message had been understood by most of their employees that this was not an environment in which women were encouraged to progress or expected to succeed. Their decision to change that policy and demonstrate it by giving Gillian a broader range of responsibilities and assignments demonstrates the unique opportunities given to executives hearing and dealing with sensitive issues within the confines of their own workplace.

Arbitration

The third major category of alternative dispute resolution involves surrendering the decision making to a third party. In most cases, arbitration is voluntary, but in some situations, such as labour relations, the parties are required by statute to agree to some arbitration mechanism as part of the collective agreement process. In other instances, though, the requirement to arbitrate disputes and the method for choosing an arbitrator are contained in the original contract between the parties. In such a case, arbitration is agreed upon before any dispute has arisen. Or the parties may agree to use arbitration as the best method of resolution after the conflict has developed. Arbitration can be very effective when external disputes arise with creditors, suppliers, and customers and even internally with employees and shareholders and between departments.

Typically, the arbitrator is chosen from a pool of trained and certified professionals. Organizations of professional arbitrators have been established, and the members offer their services like any other professional. These organizations not only provide training and certification, they also set professional and ethical standards requiring that their members be properly trained, avoid conflict of interest, be free of bias, and keep all information they obtain in strict confidence. Arbitrators are sometimes lawyers, retired judges, or business people with expertise in the particular area in dispute. Sometimes a panel of three arbitrators is chosen, with each side selecting one of them and then those two choosing a third neutral member. Because this is a private undertaking, the process to be followed as well as the power given to the arbitrator can be established by the parties. The original agreement between the parties and the agreement of employment of the arbitrator will set out fees, any time limits, and restrictions on the decision that can reached. For example, in a hearing to determine whether an employee was improperly dismissed, a decision to reinstate the employee may be beyond the mandate of the decision maker. As well, the power to award punitive damages will likely be withheld.

The procedure to be followed may be set out in the agreement, but the arbitrators themselves often design it to meet the needs of the parties and the dispute. Prior to the hearing, some discovery of information usually takes place, which may take the form of a pre-arbitration hearing. At the hearing itself, the lawyers or other representatives begin by introducing their cases. They examine witnesses, present documents, make arguments, and then summarize. Formal rules of evidence need not be adhered to, although they should conform to standard practice, nor is the arbitrator required to follow precedent in reaching the decision. Where the process is mandated by statute, as in labour disputes, the requirements are much more stringent, and the decision may be reviewed by a court if the arbitrator has strayed too far from the normally accepted legal rules. Arbitration mandated by statute may, in fact, approach a court hearing in its formality and adherence to legal rules of process. The arbitrator(s) then make(s) a decision, usually rendering it in writing giving reasons. The decision is binding on the parties and is generally

not appealable. But because this is a quasi-judicial process, the courts will still exercise supervisory power over the arbitrator. If they have exceeded their powers, the process used has not provided for a fair hearing, or there is bias or some other disqualifying factor present, the courts may overturn the decision. If the arbitrator has not adhered to the agreed upon procedure or if there has been a clear error of law either in the decision or reasons, the decision may also be reviewed.

The unique feature of arbitration is that a third party makes the decision. To be effective, it is vital that the parties be required to honour that decision. Most jurisdictions provide that the decisions reached by arbitrators are binding and enforceable. As a result, arbitration is effective because the decisions are as enforceable.

Third party makes a decision that is binding

Arbitration is still essentially adversarial in nature. In this sense, it is like litigation, with the attendant danger that bitterness and hard feelings may be aggravated. Arbitration is more costly than other forms of ADR, being more formal and involving more people, but it is still much less expensive than the litigation process.

Ideally, arbitration should be voluntary, but clauses requiring arbitration are finding their way into standard form contracts at an alarming rate. These contracts often cover consumer transactions, with the consumer unaware that he has surrendered the right to a court hearing until the dispute arises. Because the decision is binding and non-appealable, the disgruntled party may challenge the validity of the arbitration clause in court, compounding an already complex resolution procedure.

Arbitration may look much like litigation, but it is still private and still within the control of the parties. Where expertise is important in complex matters, an arbitrator with that expertise can be chosen. Arbitration is faster, less costly, and more private than litigation, but it also has many disadvantages. There may be little certainty or predictability in such a process, and there is no appealing the decision, although in some cases, the process may be reviewed by the courts. Animosity between the parties may actually increase as a result of the process. And where disclosure of information is important, obtaining that information will not be as effective as with the discovery process in litigation.

Arbitration is private

CAMVAP's Successful Arbitration

Miguel bought a new vehicle from a dealer in town and was very pleased with the first car he had purchased straight off the showroom floor. That is, until the CD player stopped working, as did the clock and the interior lights. He took the car back to the dealer, and they agreed to have it repaired, the dealer even going to the trouble of replacing the stereo. In fact, the service department spent hours at no charge to the customer trying to find the problem in the electrical system. After each visit, things would work normally in the car for a short while, but inevitably some quirky new electrical problem would arise bringing Miguel back to the shop every week or so for months. The service people could not locate the source of the problem. Finally, Miguel was fed up with the inconvenience of all this and demanded a new car and was adamant that he would not pay another cent for it. By this time, the dealer was certain that Miguel was tampering with

the car and that he was, in effect, creating his own problems. Their good relationship had deteriorated to the extent that there was a shouting match every time Miguel came into the dealership. Fortunately, the manager of the dealership became involved and suggested that the customer apply to the CAMVAP (The Canadian Motor Vehicle Arbitration Plan) to have his case heard. He explained the role of CAMVAP, and Miguel, recognizing that he would be unlikely to get satisfaction any other way, booked an appointment with the arbitrator. In this instance, the manufacturer, the dealership, and the owner all had the opportunity to put forward their stories, and the arbitrator who was experienced in the issues and complaints surrounding the purchase of new cars was able to make a decision that was binding on all the parties.

For more information on CAMVAP, try http://camvap.ca, or Peter Portlock, "Fair fast free friendly and final" *Law Now*, April/May 1997, p. 19.

Mediator may become an arbitrator

Variations. Often, the tools of mediation and arbitration will be brought together in a mediation-arbitration process. This involves the third party starting out as a mediator, and when it is clear that the parties cannot reach a settlement, even with the mediator's help, the mediator then becomes an arbitrator making a decision binding on both parties. The advantage is that mediation is attempted in a non-adversarial atmosphere, preserving the good will and trust relationship between the parties. Still, the parties have the added pressure of knowing that if they fail to reach an agreement, one will be imposed on them. Where a fast decision is needed, this approach can be very effective.

Private judging is also a variation on arbitration but much more formal in its nature. The parties, in effect, hire a judge to hold a private trial, using formal rules of evidence, due process, precedent, and other legal requirements but where the process and the outcomes are still private and confidential. This is just a very formal form of arbitration. In some jurisdictions in the United States, parties can hire a retired magistrate or judge to hold a private trial. Where such a process is authorized by statute, it takes on the same characteristics as a trial with the hired judge having the same power and authority as a regular judge. In these situations, the decision has the status of a court decision and can be enforced using the power of the court. There is also a right of appeal.

Private judges may be hired

In general, as the courts have become more congested, with corresponding increases in delay and costs, they have resorted to their own methods of reducing the caseload by also adopting forms of mediation and arbitration. Private alternative dispute resolution is becoming much more commonplace, and as it becomes even more acceptable, we can expect it to play a greater role in the future.

Untangling the WEB

ADR services are now being offered online. Since there is little regulation in this field generally, it is likely that there will be even less in the electronic environment. People should ensure that the services are being offered by qualified professionals and be aware that they may have little recourse if things go wrong. Given that, online dispute resolution services can be very helpful in attempting to mediate between companies and their customers, when information, service, or products do not meet expectations or where customers have not fulfilled their obligations. Perhaps such intermediaries may serve to set standards, monitor compliance, and warn potential customers where problems exist.

The Internet has become a valuable source of information about alternative dispute resolution. Students should check the weblinks listed at the end of the book to find additional resources.

Summary

The courts

- Procedural rules govern structure and function, which may vary with jurisdiction
- Open to the public with some exceptions
- Both criminal and civil functions at trial and appellate levels

Provincial Courts
- Handle less serious criminal offences

- civil matters under $10 000; custody and maintenance in family divisions; young offenders

Superior Courts
- Handle serious criminal offence; civil matters in excess of $10 000; divorce

Appeal Level Courts
- Deal with appeals of law from trial level courts; usually has three judges; does not rehear the facts; usually holds final hearing for most criminal and civil matters

Federal Courts
- Trial division hears disputes within federal jurisdiction and administrative tribunals; appellate division hears appeals from trial division, tax court, and some administrative tribunals

Supreme Court of Canada
- Highest level appeal court; deals primarily with Constitutional and *Charter* matters and questions from federal government; all but lower level provincial court judges are appointed by federal government

Process of civil litigation

Pre-trial
- Plaintiff files writ of summons and statement of claim
- Defendant responds with appearance and statement of defence
- Discovery of documents and questioning of parties by opposing counsel
- Payment into court to encourage reasonable demands and offers
- Purpose—to bring information to light and encourage settlement

Trial
- Examination of witnesses and presentation of evidence

Judgment
- Jury decides questions of fact
- Judge decides questions of law
- Legal costs usually paid by loser

Remedies
- Damages—general, specific, punitive
- Accounting, injunction, specific performance, declaration

Enforcement
- Examination in aid of execution
- Seizure of property
- Garnishment

Limitation periods
- Set by statute

Alternative dispute resolution (ADR)

- Recent trend to avoid costs and delays associated with litigation

Advantages of ADR

- Control, timeliness, productivity, cost, privacy, good will, flexibility

Disadvantages

- Unpredictable, no precedents set, cannot deal with complex legal problems
- Must be voluntary, must have a balance of powers between the parties
- Parties must cooperate to ensure agreement and resolution

Methods

- Negotiation—direct discussion between parties
- Mediation—neutral third party facilitates discussion
- Arbitration—neutral expert makes a binding decision

QUESTIONS

1. Describe the court hierarchy in Canada, including provincial and federal courts.

2. Who appoints provincial superior court judges?

3. What kind of matters are heard before the Supreme Court of Canada?

4. Distinguish between questions of law and questions of fact and explain why this distinction is significant.

5. How does the discovery process take place, and what is its significance in civil litigation?

6. Explain how a payment into court can affect the judgment award made by the court to the plaintiff.

7. Why might a creditor be reluctant to sue a debtor even when he or she can be sure of successfully obtaining a judgment? What advantage might there be to obtaining a judgment even when the defendant can't pay?

8. Distinguish between the various remedies available to a successful plaintiff in a civil action.

9. Explain what an examination in aid of execution is and describe its value in the execution process.

10 How can a judgment be enforced against a debtor who is trying to avoid payment?

11. Explain the value of an injunction as a pre-judgment remedy. Discuss other pre-judgment remedies available to aid in the collection of debt.

12. What is a limitation period, and what effect can it have on the right of parties to litigate a matter in dispute?

13. List and describe the principal advantages of alternative dispute resolution.

14. Describe the process of negotiation and suggest circumstances where it would be beneficial.

15. Distinguish between negotiation and mediation.

16. While a mediated settlement is not binding on the parties, it brings with it certain benefits. What are they?

17. What are the essential differences between mediation and arbitration?

18. How are arbitration and adjudication similar?

19. What are the disadvantages of having matters resolved outside the courts?

20. When should litigation be the choice in a dispute?

CASES

1. A.B. v. Stubbs et al.

In this case, the plaintiff was suing for medical malpractice. He had undergone a plastic surgery procedure that had not had the desired results and claimed that Dr. Stubbs had been negligent and also failed to inform him of the risks and follow-up procedures that had to take place with respect to the surgery. Prior to the hearing of the action, the plaintiff brought a motion asking the court to prohibit the publication of any aspect of the case that would identify him. He said that because of the sensational nature of the procedure, identifying him would cause acute embarrassment and discourage others from seeking redress in similar cases. Is such serious embarrassment enough reason for the judge to hold the hearing in-camera or refuse to allow the identity of the plaintiff to be published?

2. Royal Trust Corp. of Canada v. Dunn et al.

The Royal Trust lent just over $200 000 to four defendants, taking security in the form of a mortgage for the loan. The loan was defaulted, and an action was commenced against these four defendants. The lawyers acting for Royal Trust served a copy of the statement of claim on the lawyer who had acted for the defendants when they had purchased the property, and that lawyer, in turn, forwarded the statement of claim to the one defendant he had dealt with. None of the defendants responded to the statement of claim, and so Royal Trust proceeded and obtained a default judgment against them. In this action, the defendants are applying to have the judgment set aside claiming improper service. Explain the nature of their complaint and the likely outcome.

3. Libman v. The Queen

Libman participated in a scheme whereby he solicited funds from residents of the United States by phone from Ontario. They were persuaded to purchase shares in a Central American mining operation and were instructed to send their money to that location. These shares were worthless. Libman collected his share of the proceeds by meeting his co-conspirators in another country where he was paid. He took some of the proceeds back to Canada with him. When charged with conspiracy and fraud in an Ontario court, he argued that the Canadian court had no jurisdiction, the events having taken place in other countries. Explain whether you think the Supreme Court of Canada should accept this position or not.

4. Sanwa Bank California et al. v. Quebec, North Shore & Labrador Railway Co. Inc.

A railway company operating in Québec and Labrador leased locomotives from the plaintiff, Sanwa Bank, and a term of the lease agreement provided that the railway company had the right to purchase the locomotives at the end of the lease period at a "fair market value." This value was to be established by a qualified independent appraiser, if they could agree on the choice, and if not, by a panel of three appraisers, one to be appointed by each side and those two then choosing a third. The railway company recommended an individual appraiser, but the Sanwa Bank did not agree. They then appointed their chosen appraiser to the panel, and the panel chose a third as set out in the agreement. The railroad chose as their representative on the panel the very appraiser that had been rejected as an individual appraiser by the supplier. The panel reached a unanimous decision on a price, but this was unacceptable to the plaintiff, Sanwa Bank, who sought to have that decision set aside and have the court determine what price should be paid. Set out the arguments for each side and the likelihood of their success.

Would the presence of a private clause in the lease making the decision of the panel of appraisers final and not reviewable make a difference to your answer?

5. Automatic Systems Inc. v. Bracknell Corp. et al.

An American company (Automatic Systems Inc.) entered into a contract with an Ontario company to do electrical work on an Ontario construction project involving the assembly line of an automotive manufacturing plant. The work was subcontracted to Bracknell Corp. This subcontract provided that the agreement was to be subject to Missouri law and that any disputes arising under the contract were to be settled by arbitration in Missouri. When disputes arose which were not resolved, Bracknell filed a construction lien against the property, as permitted under Ontario law. This application was brought by Automatic Systems Inc. to have that lien set aside and force the dispute to be resolved by arbitration. Explain any arguments that might be presented by the parties and the likely outcome.

CHAPTER 3

Government Regulation and the Environment

It should be evident to students that not all disputes can or should be heard by the courts. In fact, the most likely forum where business people will face disputes will be before administrative tribunals. One of the characteristics of our society is the ever-expanding role of government, especially where business activities are concerned. Government, through its statutory power, creates agencies to oversee the implementation and enforcement of the statutes that are passed. In the process, government agents are authorized to create regulations that have a wide-reaching impact on business people. When government officials overstep the authority granted to them under the statute or otherwise abuse their powers, individuals have some recourse against unfair treatment. Our rights before such tribunals and the role of the courts in resolving such disputes are the first concerns of this chapter. We conclude this chapter by demonstrating how judge-made, statutory, and regulatory laws work together to facilitate the functioning of business and, at the same time, to preserve societal interests and standards in the area of environmental law. In the process, we will see how the various dispute resolution processes discussed in this chapter and the previous one complement and balance each other in this area that has been so controversial and conflict ridden for politicians, business people, and private citizens alike.

Nasrala v. Association of Professional Engineers of Ontario (Discipline Committee)[1]

Mr. Bill Nasrala was a professional engineer and the subject of a complaint that went before a panel of the Discipline Committee of the Association of Professional Engineers of Ontario. He made several complaints about the process, but the one the court accepted was that Mr. Gill, the deputy registrar of the association, who played a significant role in the process, was biased. He had acted as investigator and prosecutor before the panel. He had also selected the five-person panel from a pre-approved committee of 50. It was clear in the evidence that Mr. Gill had convinced one of the expert witnesses to amend his report and remove parts that were in favour of Mr. Nasrala. It was also clear that he allowed himself to be manipulated by the actual complainant, Mr. Williams, who, as a result, played a much greater role in the process than he should have. The court held that because of Mr. Gill's role as investigator and prosecutor and because of his wrongful conduct, together with the fact that he had selected the panel, there was a reasonable apprehension that the panel itself was biased. The court was careful to point out that they were not finding bias in fact, only that a reasonable person would have assumed that such bias was likely given these factors. That was enough to overturn the decision of the panel. Still, the court did not give Mr. Nasrala what he wanted. He had asked that the matter be stayed (ended). Instead, the court decided that the appropriate course of action was to send the matter back and have a completely new panel struck to hear the complaint and make a decision.

Most business activities are scrutinized and controlled either by government regulators and administrators or by professional and business organizations that, while private, are created by statute. These bodies have considerable power, but it must be exercised fairly; otherwise, the decision can be challenged in court. This case also illustrates that while the right to challenge such abuse may be present, it is not always wise to do so. This portion of the chapter discusses the role of government, its regulatory agencies, and the rights of people who deal with them.

Regulatory Role of Government

The commercial and industrial progress of this past century has been matched by the growth of government agencies to regulate it. In the last few decades, the size of government has expanded at an astonishing rate, intruding into the lives of its citizens in an unprecedented way. This process reached a peak in the 1980s, and there has been some relief since through deregulation, but still, businesses face a daunting variety of stringent government restrictions and regulations. While in most cases the intrusions are beneficial and the decisions of administrators justifiable, government officials sometimes abuse their positions or go beyond their authority when they make decisions that affect individuals or businesses.

Government consists of legislative branch, judicial branch, and executive branch

Government is divided into three different functions: legislative, judicial, and executive. While parliament or the **legislative branch** is supreme in Canada, its powers have been limited in two significant ways. First, the *Constitution Act (1867)* divides power between the federal and provincial governments, thus limiting the power of each to their assigned areas. Second, the *Charter of Rights and Freedoms* places

---

1. 58 D.L.R. (4th) 379, (Ont. Div. Ct. Gen. Div.)

specific limits on what parliament, the provincial legislatures, and their representatives can do.

There is little difficulty in distinguishing the **judicial branch** of government
(the courts) from the rest of government activity. However, the legislative branch
and the executive branch have become somewhat blurred in Canada. Parliament
and the provincial legislatures are the principal law-making bodies. From those assemblies are drawn the prime minister, premiers, and cabinet ministers, who are,
in turn, responsible for the various ministries and departments that perform the
work of government. This is the **executive branch** of government. In Canada, the
theoretical head of the executive branch is the Queen, and so, this aspect of government is often referred to as the Crown.

When people have dealings with government, it is usually with the executive
branch of government in the persons of the civil servants who make up its bureaucracy. The executive branch is divided into categories on the basis of primary function: for example, service agencies, such as law enforcement, education, health and
welfare; administrative departments, which include revenue, taxation, and the internal
management of government systems; and regulatory bodies, concerned with such
matters as the environment, product safety, employment, and human rights. When
a legislative body creates a statute that needs to be enforced, the statute will normally provide for the establishment of a department and the regulations that will control the affairs of that department. Such regulations stipulate how the terms of the
statute will be implemented and enforced and how complaints will be dealt with.

Administrators of the statutes then have decision-making powers that can profoundly affect the people with whom they have dealings. They must act not only in
accordance with the statute but also according to standards of justice that have
been recognized in our democratic tradition. They may not be required to follow
all the rules found in the judicial system and may have been given considerable
discretionary powers, but they still must act within the terms of the act that empowers them, adhere to certain basic procedural fairness requirements, and not
abuse their powers, or their decisions may be reviewed by the courts.

The Government of Canada exercises its power and control over businesses
and individuals in many ways. The power may be exercised directly through the
government departments and their bureaucrats or indirectly through Crown corporations, such as the Canadian Broadcasting Corporation (CBC), and independent
agencies, such as the Telecommunications Corporation (CRTC) or the National
Energy Board. The method used to wield this power can take several forms. Often,
that control is exercised directly through rules enforced with various kinds of penalties. This means of achieving compliance is supplemented by other less direct methods, such as economic incentives and other forms of political persuasion, including
public education. One of the main functions of government and the most significant aspect of their power is the distribution of government funds through grants,
loans, investments, and various types of joint initiatives. It is also common for government to influence how businesses operate, through advertising, educational
programs, and public awareness campaigns.

The following discussion is primarily concerned with the rules and controls
created under the various statutes and imposed on businesses and individuals by administrative bodies and agencies. The administrator may be implementing government policy, choosing between applicants when distributing government funds,
granting licenses and permits, or determining when there has been an infringement of the regulations. There are as many different ways that government exerts
control over business as there are statutes and regulations, and it is not possible

**Executive branch also
known as the Crown**

**Executive branch creates
and enforces regulations**

**Must follow recognized
standards of justice**

**Compliance achieved
through rule enforcement,
by economic incentives and
education**

to examine them all. Rather, we will concentrate on what can be done when these government activities collide with our basic rights and interests and then look at the impact of the regulatory system on environmental law as an example.

Administrative Law

Regulators

The regulation of business is conducted through many government institutions, including ministries, departments, boards, commissions, agencies, tribunals, and individual bureaucrats at the federal, provincial, and municipal levels. Government departments, such as the Department of Transport or the Department of Health and Welfare, administer programs, while other departments, such as Consumer Affairs and Environment, are primarily regulators responsible to see that private individuals and organizations conform to statutory regulations. Often, the functions of government departments overlap, as in transportation and environment, when they are concerned with the transport of hazardous products. Crown agencies or Crown corporations have regulatory responsibilities assigned to them under the act that created them. They have been granted more political autonomy to provide some distance between the decisions they make and the government. The CRTC operating under the terms of the *Broadcasting Act* is an example of such a commission.

Comeau's Sea Foods Ltd. v. Canada (Minister of Fisheries and Oceans)[2]

In 1990, the federal minister, pursuant to powers given to him in the *Fisheries Act,* instituted a quota system for the fishing of halibut on the west coast of B.C. The quotas imposed were based on the best year of fishing of the holder of the license. Some newer license holders objected, claiming that they were treated unfairly by this system. In this case, the minister was accused of acting in bad faith because the policy hurt one group and benefited another. The trial judge found that such bad faith was present. The Court of Appeal decided that because this was an exercise of legislative or policy-making discretion, it was not subject to review in the court. Although it is true that discretionary power should not be exercised in bad faith or based on considerations irrelevant to the purpose of the statute, the Court of Appeal found that the process of policy creation and implementation often favoured one group over another. The question was whether the quota system was introduced for a valid purpose, not whether it affected one group over another.

Standards set for regulators

Whether the government administrators are merely implementing government policy (such as a clerk granting a building permit or business license) or acting as a referee or judge (such as a labour relations board), there are certain standards they must maintain. When acting as judges or referees, government decision makers are often referred to as administrative tribunals (whether the decisions are made by a committee, a commission, a tribunal, or an individual). The area of law that describes an individual's rights before such a tribunal is called administrative law. The administrator's authority is granted by statute.

2. (1997) 142 D.L.R. (4th) 193, (S.C.C.)

Advantages

Keeping in mind that one of the purposes of these administrative bodies is to keep matters out of the courts, it is important to note some functional advantages. Administrative decision makers are appointed to their positions because they have expertise in the area. They are often career public servants, who, through their continuity of service, acquire a detailed knowledge of the terms and goals of the statute as well as the programs and activities of their departments. They often have considerable discretionary power to allow for decisions that can serve the interests of both the department and the complainant. In most cases, they are not bound by precedent, and so, each case can be judged on its merits. Tribunals can hear a matter and make a decision promptly, overcoming the delay and expense often associated with court hearings. While their job is to enforce the regulations, the possibility that a court will review the process by which their decision was made hopefully constrains them to act within the jurisdiction of the statute and the limits prescribed by the court.

Administrative decision makers have special expertise

When powers are abused, judicial review available

To determine whether the decision of a civil servant or administrative tribunal can be challenged or reviewed by a court, reference should be made to two basic principles that govern the actions of decision makers. First, the decision must have been made within the authority of the official or board. Second, the process involved and the conduct of the decision maker must have been proper. As a general rule, the merits of the decision itself are not questioned, as would be the case in an appeal. It is not the function of the court to revisit the decision; rather, it is to supervise the process. For this reason, it is called **judicial review** rather than an appeal. It is only where the decision is completely unreasonable that the court will use this as a ground to overturn that decision.

The courts recognize that administrative tribunals have special expertise in the matters being considered and that their decisions should not be interfered with lightly. The Supreme Court of Canada has established a standard to determine when a decision of a tribunal can be challenged. "So long as the administrative decision maker has acted within the authority granted and any discretion has been exercised in a fair and honest way so that the decision can be said to be reasonable, the decision should stand."[3] The following discussion should be read, keeping in mind this clear policy of a general reluctance on the part of the courts to interfere with the decisions of properly functioning administrative bodies.

The Authority of the Decision Maker

A fundamental aspect of the constitutional tradition we inherited from Britain is the **rule of law**. The rule of law holds that even given the supremacy of parliament, neither parliament nor any government official representing parliament can act arbitrarily. They cannot rely on their status to justify their action but must be able to point to some authorizing statute or regulation. When a government official or board cannot point to some valid statute that authorized their conduct or decision, the decision can be challenged as *ultra vires* or beyond their power and set aside. Both the courts and the executive branch are bound by the rule of law, and even when they have been given discretionary power, that discretion cannot be exercised arbitrarily. Such discretionary power must be exercised within a framework of rules based on fairness, equality, and justice.

Government agents must act within existing law

3. Canada (Director of Investigation and Research) v. Southam Inc. [1997] 1 S.C.R. 748

Statutory Authority

The first step in challenging an administrative tribunal, then, is to examine the statutory authority and determine if the tribunal's conduct or actions were authorized under it. This statutory authority may be found not only in the statute itself but also in the regulations passed under that statute. While parliament and the provincial legislative assemblies create law primarily through legislation, the resulting statutes often give government institutions, such as workers' compensation boards, human rights commissions, and labour relations boards, the power to make further rules called **regulations** under that legislation. These regulations have the same force as the statute under which they were created. When an administrative tribunal makes a decision, it must be authorized by the statute or regulation in question. Even when the decision is within the authority granted by the regulation, the validity of the regulation itself can be questioned. If that regulation has not been properly passed or exceeds the scope of the statute authorizing it, the regulation is *ultra vires* (without authority) and cannot support the action of the decision maker. When the decision or conduct is unauthorized the courts will have no hesitation in overturning it.

Does administrative tribunal have authority?

Apotex Inc. v. Québec (Minister of Health and Social Services)[4]

Québec, like other provinces, subsidizes medicinal drugs used by the public. In furtherance of this program, they have established a list of approved drugs that qualify for such subsidy. To be put on the list, the drug has to be approved for marketing in Canada (a federal responsibility) and also recommended by the Conseil Consultatif de Pharmacologie (the "Council"). The basis for their recommendation is that it has therapeutic value and is fairly priced. In this case, Apotex developed a drug, Apo-Enalapril, which had the same properties as a similar drug developed by a rival company which was already on the approved list for the Québec subsidy. The rival company Merck instituted an action against Apotex, claiming that the new drug infringed their patent. Both drugs were federally approved for sale in Québec. When Apotex applied to have their new drug added to the Quebéc's list of subsidized drugs, the minister refused on the basis that it violated the Merck patent. In fact, "the Council" learning of the litigation between Apotex and Merck sought legal advice with respect to the Apotex application. That advice was to wait until the patent dispute was resolved before approval, and this was the advice they gave to the minister, which he followed. The problem was that the statute that set out the approval process for such a drug said nothing about litigation or patent disputes. The council had no authority to consider anything other than therapeutic value and fair pricing in making their recommendation. While the minister could consider other things and was not bound by the recommendation, those things could not be extraneous to the purpose of the act. The ongoing litigation was an irrelevant consideration. This case is important not only because it shows that even the minister must act within the authority of the statute authorizing the action but also for the remedy granted. Here, the court granted an order of *mandamus*, whereby they ordered that the new drug developed by Apotex be added to the list.

Statutory Interpretation

When determining whether a regulation has been properly imposed under the statute in question or whether any other aspect of the statute is being properly en-

4. (1994) 111 D.L.R. (4th) 622, (Qué.S.C.)

forced, the courts will apply accepted rules of statutory interpretation. These rules have been developed from three basic principles. First, if a provision of the statute is clear and unambiguous and conveys a certain meaning that is not inconsistent with other sections of the statute, the court is obligated to apply the plain or literal meaning. If the statute is ambiguous, either because the provisions are inconsistent with other sections of the legislation or because the wording is capable of more than one meaning, the courts may apply either the golden rule or the mischief rule. The **golden rule** means that a reasonable interpretation based on common sense will be used and that the literal meaning of the statute will be departed from only as far as necessary to overcome the ambiguity or inconsistency. The **mischief rule** means that the courts will try to give effect to the specific purpose for which the statute was enacted. For example, when a statute has been passed to cure some defect or injustice in common law or in some other statute, the court can identify the defect or injustice and, in face of the ambiguity, interpret the statute in such a way as to give the best effect to the original intent of the legislation. Thus, if there were a problem of interpretation with the federal *Youth Justice Act*, the application of the mischief rule would require that any ambiguity be interpreted to give effect to the intention of the act, that is, to give the youth involved the same kind of rights and protection given to adults. Today, these rules are rolled into one basic principle that the words of a statute should be read in their ordinary grammatical sense, unless it is clear from the overall statute that they were intended to have a different meaning, and then the words should be read in such a way as to be in harmony with the objective and other provisions of the statute.

Rules of statutory interpretation

• plain meaning

• golden rule

• mischief rule

Watters v. Glace Bay (Town)[5]

Mr. Watters purchased two properties in the town of Glace Bay that were in a deplorable condition. One judge even described them as an abomination. Mr. Watters received several notices ordering him to correct the condition of the buildings. On those occasions, he obtained building permits to make the appropriate repairs, but the repairs were never done. Finally, the municipal council, relying on Section 222 of the *Town Act* that authorized them to "enter onto the land and remedy the condition," had the buildings demolished. After the demolition, Mr. Waters stood in the middle of the debris refusing to let the bulldozers clean it up. A constable took him to the police station. In this action, Mr. Watters was seeking damages for wrongful demolition of the building and for trespass. The problem was the meaning of the word "remedy." Does that include the right to demolish the building? The judge, after careful examination of the rules of statutory interpretation, held that "remedy" does not include "demolition." If the legislature had meant that, they would have used the term demolition, as they did in other parts of the statute. The judge based his decision on what he referred to as the "golden rule" of statutory interpretation, summarizing the rule in these words: "Cases flowing from these authorities make it clear that the grammatical and ordinary sense of the words used in the statute are to be adhered to and may be modified where that meaning results in some objective repugnance, inconsistency, or absurdity. If the words of a statute are in themselves precise and unambiguous, then no more can be necessary than to expound those words in their natural and ordinary sense. Consideration must be given to both the spirit and the letter of the legislation." Applying these rules to this case, he said, "Demolishing a structure is drastic action. Undoubtedly, that is why the legislature gave the specific authority so to do in certain sections of the *Towns*

5. (1987) 34 D.L.R. (4th) 747, (N.S.C.A.)

Act, the *Municipal Act,* and the *Health Act,* and refrained from giving authority in other sections, such as that in issue before us, as Section 222 of the act." Mr. Watters was successful in his action, but the judge awarded only $500 damages on the basis that the buildings could not have been repaired.

Statutes strictly interpreted

Another rule of statutory interpretation available to the courts is that a judge is not obligated to follow a statute, unless it clearly and unambiguously overrules the common law provision. This is referred to as **strict interpretation** of the statute. Other specific rules have been developed to assist the courts to interpret statutes. These rules may range from principles of grammatical construction to rules favouring one interpretation over another in different situations. The courts may also turn to similar statutes, both within and outside the legislative jurisdiction involved, and to the official translations of statutes and other publications, such as dictionaries and academic articles.

Each jurisdiction in Canada has passed legislation setting out general principles and specific rules judges must follow when determining the meaning of statutes or regulations. These rules are called **interpretation statutes**. Most statutes begin with a definition section that sets out specific meanings that must be applied to words used throughout that particular statute.

It is beyond the scope of this chapter to discuss statutory interpretation in any greater detail. However, it should be apparent that when faced with disputes over the meaning of statutory provisions, the courts have a cohesive framework of rules and guidelines to help them determine the appropriate interpretation. The interpretation eventually settled on by the court may affect whether the particular regulation in question was valid, whether the conduct complained of has violated a particular statute, or whether the particular regulatory body or government agency had the power to make the decision or impose the control it did. Once this has been determined, the question remains whether or not the legislation itself was validly passed pursuant to the division of powers as set out in the *Constitution Act (1867).*

Jurisdiction of the Statute

Statutes must be passed by appropriate level of government

As mentioned in Chapter 1, the powers of government are divided between the federal and provincial levels of government as set out primarily in Sections 91 and 92, respectively, of the *Constitution Act (1867).* When the statute empowering the administrator to act has been passed by a level of government that does not have the power to do so under this division of powers the courts will find the statute to be *ultra vires* and void. The conduct of the decision maker acting under the void statute will also be *ultra vires.*

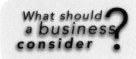

If a city council were to pass a bylaw prohibiting the sale of adult videos within the city boundaries and the council, on the strength of that bylaw, were to deny such a business a license to operate, the business could challenge that decision. Neither the province nor a city deriving its authority from the province can pass such a bylaw because it encroaches on the federal government's criminal law powers. Since the bylaw was invalid, any decision made under its authority is also invalid, and the courts would, upon application, declare the decision ultra vires and void.

In the same way, the statute or regulation must be consistent with the provisions of the *Charter of Rights and Freedoms,* also discussed in Chapter 1. A statute that had the effect of discriminating on the basis of gender, religion, or ethnic ori-

gin or one that denied a person the right to a hearing (where life, liberty, and security of person was involved) or restricted freedom of the press or religion could
be challenged, and a decision made under such a statute would be invalid.

Re United Nurses of Alberta, Local No. 17 et al. and High Prairie General Hospital & Nursing Home District No. 98[6]

Nurses working in a hospital in Alberta were required to retire at age 65 years. A
grievance was initiated on the basis that this was age discrimination prohibited by
a non-discrimination clause in the collective agreement. The arbitration board
had considered this prohibition against age discrimination but had decided that because the provincial *Individual's Rights Protection Act*, defined age as between 45 and
65 years, they could use the same definition of age, and so, this forced retirement
was not an example of age discrimination. This decision was challenged, and the
judge determined that for the challenge to be successful, the decision must be
shown to be patently unreasonable. The judge found that the definition of age
used in the act as 45 to 65 years was obviously an "emasculated" definition and that
there was no reason that the meaning used in the collective agreement should be
referable to that restricted definition. The effect of the arbitration decision would
be to allow age discrimination in face of the parties' obvious intention to prohibit
it in their collective agreement. This was patently unreasonable, and so the decision
of the arbitration board was overturned. This case is interesting in that it illustrates
the appropriate remedy of *certiorari* that was used to quash the decision. It also
shows that in the face of a privative clause stating that the decision is "final and
binding," the appropriate standard for a court to interfere with the decision of
such a tribunal is when the decision is "patently unreasonable."

Proper Process

Once it has been established that the decision maker has acted within the authority given under a valid statute or regulation, the question remains whether that authority was exercised in a proper way. Historically, the obligation of the administrator
to act in a procedurally fair manner varied to a great extent depending on the
function performed. The decision maker might be acting as a judge adjudicating
disputes or simply acting as an administrator implementing government policy.
The distinction is less important today. Even when the decision maker is acting as
an administrator, there is an obligation to maintain at least a minimum standard of
procedural fairness. The courts are much more likely to find an obligation on the
decision maker to act fairly when the issues being dealt with are important, when
the decision maker's function is to decide between competing parties or interests,
or when the remedies or penalties that can be imposed will have a significant impact on the parties. These minimum standards of fairness have been imposed on
the cabinet and the ministers of the Crown as well, although it should be noted
that such obligations may be modified by statute. What constitutes fairness in these
situations is determined by the rules of natural justice; the minimum requirements
of justice or procedural fairness are set out below.

6. (1985) 17 D.L.R. (4th) 532, (Alta. Q.B.)

Rules of Natural Justice

Sinkovich v. Police Board of Commissioners (Strathroy)[7]

After some serious problems, including an inquiry and a negative report from the Ontario Police Commissioner, a new police chief, Mr. Sinkovich, was hired for the police force in the town of Strathroy. Unfortunately, the new chief and the mayor of the town did not get along. There were also several negative reports about the management style of the new chief. Finally, the Ontario Police Commission was persuaded to hold an inquiry.

Chief Sinkovich was told that the inquiry was looking at the management and administration of the force, and he came to the hearing prepared to discuss the matter. It turned out, however, that it was the competence and personal conduct of the police chief himself that were being reviewed. His performance was found to be unsatisfactory, and the commission recommended that he be dismissed.

Upon his application, the court quashed the decision and report of the commission, finding that no proper hearing had been held before the chief's dismissal. Although Mr. Sinkovich had been told of when the hearing was to take place, he had not been told that his performance was in question or that his position was in jeopardy; thus, the notice was improper, resulting in an unfair hearing.

This case illustrates that in order for a proper hearing to take place, a person must be notified of that hearing, and a significant aspect of such notification requires that they be told the nature of the charges to be dealt with so that a proper response can be formulated. Notice and a fair hearing are central to the rules of natural justice.

Statutes may improve or modify duty

Often, the statute governing the area will set out procedural requirements that must be followed, and so, the first step in determining whether there has been procedural fairness is to see whether these statutory requirements have been complied with. Such statutory procedural requirements must also conform to the *Charter of Rights and Freedoms*, in particular, when the administrative action interferes with the "life, liberty, or security of person." Such action can only be taken in accordance with "the principles of fundamental justice." The **principles of fundamental justice** have been taken to mean the same thing as procedural fairness and natural justice.

Fair Hearing

The most fundamental requirement of the rules of natural justice is that the party being affected by the decision of an administrator has an opportunity to a fair hearing. What constitutes a fair hearing will vary from situation to situation, but essentially, the person being affected by the decision must have been notified that a decision is to be made and must have been given an opportunity to put his or her side forward. The courts have held that a fair hearing has not taken place when proper notice of the hearing was not given and when the person was not informed of the nature of the complaint or given the information needed to present their case. This was the basis of Chief Sinkovich's complaint in the case used to open this discussion. The failure to notify him that his security in his position was the subject of the hearing he was to attend denied him the opportunity to properly defend himself. There can be no fair hearing without notice and an opportunity to prepare a defence.

All information must be disclosed before hearing

7. (1988) 51 D.L.R. (4th) 750, (Ont. Div. Ct.)

Fair Hearing Requires Opportunity to Be Heard

Ladney and others wished to propose an amendment to the official plan for the Township of Moore. They appeared before a session of the Ontario Municipal Board to make this application. The board called one expert witness and then recessed for 20 minutes. When they returned, they proceeded to turn down the Ladney application without hearing evidence from the other side and without hearing submissions from the lawyers. The question for the court was whether the board had the power to make a decision without having given Ladney or his council an opportunity to make their arguments. The court held that the board had exceeded its jurisdiction; the decision was set aside and a new hearing scheduled. To be given a fair hearing on a decision, a person must have the opportunity to call evidence and submit his or her arguments before the decision is rendered.

Re Ladney et al. and Township of Moore, 10 D.L.R. (4th) 612, Ontario High Court of Justice, Divisional Court

Supermarches Jean LabrecqueInc. v. Labour Court et al.[8]

This is a Québec case, and although the process is somewhat different, the essential requirements of natural justice are the same. Here, Supermarches Jean Labrecque Inc. was charged with several violations of the labour code and was to be tried on those charges. The appellant appeared on May 12 and pleaded not guilty to the charge. A date was set for the hearing to be held in the Val d'Or courthouse on June 10 of the same year. On that date, counsel for the parties showed up as required, but the judge was not present. In fact, the hearing had been changed by order of the Chief Judge to Montreal, but the parties had not been notified. The Supreme Court of Canada decided that even though the chief judge had the authority under the statute to make such a change, it was a basic requirement of natural justice that proper notice of a hearing be provided, and by failing to do so, the labour court had lost jurisdiction (authority) to deal with the matter.

Part of the requirement of a fair hearing is that all the evidence that forms the basis of the decision be disclosed to the individual being affected by it. An individual must be given the opportunity to cross-examine witnesses who present material testimony or to refute any written declarations. Similarly, it is essential to a fair hearing that the individual be given an opportunity to present arguments and evidence to support them.

A fair hearing may extend to the right to demand an adjournment in certain circumstances. But there is no requirement that the decision maker follow the strict rules of evidence or even that the person affected have a right to counsel, although legal representation is a right if the proceedings might result in criminal charges. There is no general obligation on the decision maker to give reasons for the judgment, but many statutes do impose a duty on the decision maker to give reasons and often require that these reasons be put in writing. The test is reasonableness, and an unreasonable imposition on the time of an administrator will not be tolerated. In some situations, the opportunity to present a case by letter is enough to satisfy the fair hearing requirement. This illustrates that the applications of the rules of natural justice or procedural fairness involve a considerable degree of flexibility. No set rules can be stated, since what is required will be a reflection of what constitutes fairness in any given circumstance.

No obligation to allow counsel or follow rules of evidence

8. (1987) 43 D.L.R. (4th) 1 (S.C.C.)

McCaw v. United Church of Canada[9]

Mr. McCaw was an ordained minister in the United Church, and in 1982, there was a considerable controversy in his congregation as to his style of ministry. The procedural manual required his immediate superiors (the council) to make recommendations to a higher council (the presbytery), which then would act on that recommendation. On January 3, 1982, the council recommended that he take a special program and then on January 6, only three days later, recommended that his services be discontinued. There was much activity that followed, including negotiation and appeals, but the presbytery eventually followed the recommendation and discontinued his service. Mr. McCaw turned to the courts, claiming wrongful dismissal on the basis that he was not given a fair hearing. A series of meetings had taken place to decide his fate, and in the first three, he was not given notice of those meetings. In the fourth meeting, he was not even allowed to hear the testimony of the witness. In the end, the court only concerned itself with the recommendation by the council of January 6 to the presbytery that Mr. McCaw be dismissed. The court found, according to the manual that governed the situation, that this recommendation could only be made where there was a neglect or refusal to take a specified program. There was no evidence of such a neglect or refusal or even that such a program had been set out for him to take. The court of appeal did not find it necessary to deal with the fairness of the meetings, having determined that all subsequent proceedings were inappropriate because of the wrongful January 6 recommendations. Mr. McCaw succeeded in his wrongful dismissal action. This case is interesting because it treats the manual of the United Church much like a statute, determining the authority of the council and other bodies in the church. It also shows the need for a fair hearing and illustrates that the courts will review the decisions of even non-statutory quasi-judicial bodies.

Heard by Decision Maker

Decision must be made by person hearing evidence

Another requirement of the rules of natural justice is that the decision must be made by the person hearing the evidence. If a board of inquiry is convened requiring five people to participate in the decision and something happens to one of them after the commencement of the hearing, that person cannot be replaced by

Decision Maker Must Hear All Evidence

Pursuant to the *Canada Corporations Act*, the Restrictive Trades Practices Commission had an investigator examine the affairs of Javelin International Ltd. Once such an investigation takes place, the Commission holds a hearing in which the inspector presents evidence of what he or she has found, and the other party is given an opportunity to respond. During the Javelin hearing, three members of the commission sat and listened to the proceedings. At various stages, one of them stepped out, always leaving two members present, which was required for a quorum. The commission found evidence of fraud and made recommendations to the minister. Mr. Doyle, a principal of Javelin, brought this application to have the findings of the commission set aside. The court agreed. People who had not heard all the evidence had participated in the decision, resulting in an unfair hearing.

Doyle v. Canada (Restrictive Trade Practices Commission) (1985) 21 D.L.R. (4th) 366, (Fed. C.A.), leave to appeal to S.C.C. ref'd (1985) 7 C.P.R. (3rd) 235 n (S.C.C.).

9. (1991) 82 D.L.R. (4th) 289, (Ont. C.A.)

another because the new person would not have heard all the evidence presented. Similarly, the board of inquiry cannot proceed and make the decision with only four people because the statute requires five. It is permissible for the decision maker to use staff services to gather and summarize the evidence, but the decision must be made only by those who have heard all the evidence.

Decision maker must hear all evidence

Bailey v. Saskatchewan Registered Nurses' Assn.[10]

In this case, a resident at the Sherbrook Community Centre died, and an investigation of the three nurses working at the centre was commenced by the professional association.

The investigation and subsequent hearing, resulting in the termination of the nurses, gave rise to a number of procedural complaints. Not only did the investigation committee fail to interview a number of individuals whose statements might have been in favour of the nurses but also the lawyer for the nurses was not given proper access to the information gathered by that committee, even when demanded. The investigation file itself was not disclosed until they were four days into the hearing. Even the physical structure of the hearing was set up in a way that was not fair. The hearing room was set up in such a way that the lawyer for the nurses was unable to see the witnesses who were testifying and the disciplinary committee at the same time. No room was provided for the nurses to meet with their lawyers during the hearing, and there was a sense of urgency to get on with the matter whenever the nurses were presenting their defences. A complaint was made also that their supervisor at the Sherbrook Community Centre who had laid the complaint against them was on the council deciding the matter, creating possible bias. She was also the president elect of the Saskatchewan Nurses Association wielding considerable influence. There was no response to the complaints.

Even the lawyer acting for the Nurses Association was in a difficult position. He had been the general lawyer for the association, then the lawyer for the investigating body, and now was acting as prosecutor against the three nurses. He had also been involved in the orientation of the members of the disciplinary committee itself and had conducted education days for them. The firm for which he worked had made financial donations to the association's building fund, and there was a general air of familiarity between him and the members of the committee, giving the nurses the feeling that this was just a one-sided process out to get them.

All these factors created an atmosphere where there was a reasonable apprehension of bias. The court held that a proper hearing had not taken place, which was a breach of natural justice, and therefore the decision of the committee was quashed.

This case illustrates very well the problems that can arise when there is a conflict of interest or bias on the part of decision makers. The court said the investigation committee should have looked at the evidence of all the witnesses with more diligence and given proper hearing and interview facilities to the nurses. They should not have conducted the hearing in an atmosphere of haste. The nurses should have been given an opportunity to give full answers in defence of the charges that were laid against them. It was extremely important that full disclosure be made in a timely manner so that the nurses could have known what they were responding to. Disclosing information in the middle of a meeting was not sufficient. This was not a fair hearing as required under the rules of natural justice, the main problem being a lack of impartiality on the part of the decision makers.

10. 137 D.L.R. (4th) 224, (Sask. C.Q.B.)

Impartiality

A significant requirement of the rules of natural justice is that the decision be made in good faith and impartially. If it can be shown that the decision maker is biased, the decision can be overturned. Because it is so difficult to establish a condition of bias, the courts have developed the principle that a reasonable likelihood of bias is enough to invalidate the decision. Bias is assumed when the matter being decided involves a relative, friend, or business acquaintance of the decision maker. Similarly, if there has been an exhibition of bad feelings or hostility between the decision maker and the individual being affected by the decision, there is a real likelihood of bias, and the decision can be challenged. Where it can be shown that the decision maker has an interest in the matter being decided or has already decided the matter, that person will be disqualified from the decision-making process. A monetary interest in the subject matter affected by the decision will be grounds for challenge, and the size of such an interest should not be relevant.

Bennett v. British Columbia (Superintendent of Brokers)[11]

Mr. Bill Bennett, former Premier of British Columbia, was charged with insider trading, a violation of the *Securities Act* of the province. One of the people accused with him, Mr. Herb Doman, was the president of a large forestry company. Under the legislation, Mr. Bennett and Mr. Doman had the right to a hearing before a panel of commissioners. During the hearing, an objection was heard that Mr. David Divine, one of three decision makers, should not be sitting on the panel. He also was a director of a forestry company. In this case, the British Columbia Court of Appeal held that there was a reasonable apprehension of bias and overturned the decision of the panel. If Mr. Doman were convicted of the charge, he would be prohibited from managing his company. This would deprive his company of his expertise, giving an advantage to other competing forest companies, including Mr. Devine's company, and this created a reasonable apprehension of bias. Note that it was not necessary to actually show that Mr. Devine was influenced by this consideration, only that there was an appearance to a reasonable person that this was likely.

Decision-making bodies are sometimes structured to incorporate a bias. For example, those appointed to labour relation boards and arbitration panels are usually appointed as representatives from labour and management. Often, a panel of three arbitrators is struck, each side appointing one of the arbitrators who together then choose a third. The principle involved is that the bias represented by one side will be balanced by the bias of the other and the third arbitrator chosen by both will mediate between them. This emphasizes the point that the rules of natural justice are guidelines only. The courts retain a considerable amount of flexibility in the exercise of their supervisory jurisdiction as they ensure that the procedures involved are fair to all parties.

What should a business consider?

It is vital that business people remember that challenging government regulators and administrators should only be done as a last resort. As in all litigation, it can be a frustrating, costly, often fruitless exercise and should be avoided, if at all possible. Further, this is a specialized field where the costs are even higher then normal litigation and the complainant is dealing with government officials who have access to large funds and are generally more than willing to spend those funds to save themselves the embarrassment of being found in the wrong.

11. (1993) 109 D.L.R. (4th) 717, (B.C.C.A.)

Judicial Review

Many statutes establishing decision-making boards or commissions provide for an appeal to another level of decision maker. This may be another board, a commissioner, a director, or even the minister in charge, and in some instances, the appeal can go eventually to the courts. Judicial review must be distinguished from this appeal process. **Appeal** is the process whereby the decision of an inferior court or tribunal is reconsidered at a higher level. Judicial review involves the superior court's inherent right to supervise the judicial process. Whether or not an appeal is provided for and whether or not there are other courses of action open to the person affected by the decision, the courts retain the right to supervise and oversee the administration of justice. They have to correct the action of a decision maker who acts improperly, and so, it is the process itself that is of more concern in a judicial review.

Judicial review—inherent right of courts

As a rule, the courts require that all other remedies be exhausted before they exercise their supervisory capacity in the form of judicial review. If an appeal is available under the statute or regulations, that appeal process must be finished before turning to the courts. Generally, judicial review is available "where an administrative body has acted without authority, or has stepped outside the limits of its authority, or has failed to perform its duties."[12]

The following is a summary of the situations in which a person affected by the decision of an administrator or administrative tribunal can go to the courts for relief.

1. When the decision maker has no authority to make the decision or has stepped outside of his or her authority in some way, that decision can be challenged in the courts. In determining whether or not the decision maker has the required authority, the courts must look not only to the contents of the statute or regulations to determine if the decision or act was authorized but also to the validity of the statute itself under the *Charter of Rights and Freedoms* and the *Constitution Act (1867)*. If the statute is valid, the decision can still be challenged on the grounds that the administrator was not functioning within the **authority** granted under the statute. For example, if a school board is required by statute to review a dismissal application but appoints a committee of the board to hear the complaint because of the inconvenience of meeting over the summer, the decision of that committee can be challenged if the school board does not have the statutory power to delegate its authority to a committee.

   Authority of decision maker may be reviewed

   Another such error can be made if the decision maker makes an initial incorrect decision that brings the matter in dispute under his or her jurisdiction. For example, if a labour relations board is given the authority by statute to hear disputes between employees and employers and decides that a dispute between independent fishers and the fish-packing companies they do business with falls within its jurisdiction, this primary jurisdictional determination can be challenged in the courts. Another type of jurisdictional error occurs when a decision-making body takes it upon itself to rehear a matter after it has made a final decision. Usually, statutes will empower such a body to decide in the first place but not authorize them to rehear the matter. Therefore, the second hearing is outside the jurisdiction of the decision maker and void. Note that often, such a body will hold another hearing after the first has been

   Must function within prescribed jurisdiction

---

12. *Judicial Review Procedure Act*, R.S.O. (1990) c.J.1

found to be invalid because of some procedural defect. This is not a rehearing because in law, the first hearing being void never took place.

Process must be fair

2. The decision-making process itself is subject to the scrutiny of the court. There is a requirement of **procedural fairness**, as discussed above, that must be followed whenever a decision is made that has an adverse impact on an individual.

In some cases, the decision itself may be reviewed

3. If the decision maker is functioning within the proper jurisdiction and the process is procedurally fair, the courts are generally reluctant to interfere with the decision. But if the decision incorporates a remedy beyond the decision maker's power to grant, it will be reviewable on the grounds of jurisdiction. For example, under labour legislation, an arbitrator is given the authority to determine whether an employee was properly dismissed. If that arbitrator were to impose some other kind of consequence, such as a suspension from employment for a number of weeks, rather than simply deciding whether the dismissal was justified or not, the arbitrator would be assuming authority he or she does not have, and that decision would then be invalid.

    Under rare circumstances, the court may find that there was not sufficient legal evidence for the administrator to reach a particular decision. The legal standard requires that there be at least some evidence to justify the conclusion reached by the decision maker.

Abuse of discretionary power

    The courts have been willing to overturn a decision when the decision maker has committed an abuse of power. If a decision maker acts dishonestly, out of malice, or with fraudulent intent in the exercise of his or her power (including discretionary power), even though the decision may be within his or her power to reach, that decision is reviewable on the basis of abuse of power. The case of *Roncarelli v. Duplessis*[13] is a classic example of the abuse of power by a minister of the Crown, which was reviewable by the courts. In that case, a restaurant owner in Montreal supported some Jehovah's Witnesses facing charges by paying their legal expenses. The premier of the province exerted his influence to have the plaintiff's liquor license cancelled. This act was clearly outside the jurisdiction he had as premier and an abuse of his power. The court ordered the premier to pay compensation to the plaintiff.

    The decision maker must consider all relevant matters and must not make a decision for an improper purpose. The exercise of any discretion must be a genuine exercise. For example, if a decision maker with discretionary power merely follows the direction of a superior, that is an abuse of such power and reviewable in the courts.

Error of law on record

4. Finally, the courts are willing to interfere with any decision that involves an **error of law**, which is incorporated into the record of the hearing. The record consists of the decision, the reasons for it, and any documents involved in the process of reaching the decision. A transcript of the proceedings can also be included as part of the record. The supervising judicial body cannot tolerate such an error of law on the record, and the decision will be overturned whenever such an error is substantial enough to affect the decision. Of course, an error of law must be distinguished from an **error of fact**. The decision maker is generally empowered to decide questions of fact and those decisions will not be interfered with. But when there is an incorrect declaration as to the

13. [1959] S.C.R. 121, (S.C.C.)

law, this is of concern to the superior court and will not be tolerated. The error of law may be in misconstruing common law or statutes or a procedural error, such as the refusal to hear evidence or hearing evidence that ought to have been excluded. The court will not usually interfere with the decision merely because it does not like the decision or would have come to a different one itself.

Robinson Plymouth Chrysler Ltd. v. Nova Scotia (Minister of Finance)[14]

Robinson Plymouth Chrysler traded and sold vehicles. Often, they did not actually have these vehicles in their possession but acquired them from or traded them to other out-of-province dealers. In those cases, they would resell the trade-in directly to that out of province dealer and never actually have possession of the vehicle. Under the provincial *Revenue Act*, a tax was payable on the purchase price of the vehicle minus the value of the trade. But in this case, because the trade-in was never actually in their possession, they were required to pay tax on the full purchase price. In this action, that decision was challenged. The act required that the reduction take place where the car was "accepted in trade," and so, the meaning of that phrase had to be determined. In its reasons, the Nova Scotia Utility and Review Board stated that the term "accepted" requires actual delivery of the goods, and since this did not take place, tax had to be paid on the full purchase price. This interpretation was in error. The judge in this case said that acceptance or control can take place in many different ways, not just delivery. The proper question was whether the dealership had allowed a trade-in credit, not whether they had taken delivery. Because of this error of law, the decision of the board was overturned, and the matter sent back for a rehearing. This case is a good illustration of how the court will overturn a decision made by a tribunal when there has been a clear error of law. Note as well that the remedy was to send the matter back for rehearing, since the decision still had to be made applying the correct interpretation of the law.

Methods of Judicial Review

Prerogative Writs

The courts have traditionally used the method of prerogative writs in exercising their supervisory power over administrative tribunals. These are ancient remedies traceable to the prerogative power of the Crown. Four main prerogative writs are in use today, the best known of which is the writ of **habeas corpus**, a court order to the custodial authority to present a person being kept in custody before the court. *Habeas corpus* is used whenever there is concern over whether a person is being improperly detained. While this remedy is primarily used in criminal matters, it is also used in immigration and child custody cases and when people have been institutionalized for mental health reasons. Many jurisdictions have passed legislation modifying the application of this judicial remedy, such as Ontario's *Habeas Corpus Act*.[15]

An order to release a person improperly detained

The other three prerogative writs, *certiorari*, prohibition, and *mandamus*, play a significant role as the courts exercise their supervisory jurisdiction over administrative tribunals. A writ of **certiorari** renders the decision of the inferior body as having no legal effect and, thus, null and void. The granting of an application for *certiorari*

***Certiorari* overrules a decision**

14. (1998) 170 D.L.R. (4th) 498, (N.S.C.A.)

15. *Habeas Corpus Act*, R.S.O. (1990) c.H.1

Prohibition prevents a decision from being made

nullifies an administrator's decision and eliminates any impact that decision might have. Prohibition is similar to *certiorari*, but certiorari overturns and voids a particular decision, whereas prohibition prevents the decision from being made in the first place. For *certiorari* to apply, a decision must have been made that can be challenged. **Prohibition**, on the other hand, is used to prevent administrators or decision makers from using their power to make a decision in an unfair or otherwise inappropriate procedure. Prohibition is obtained before any decision and can be extremely effective in stopping an unfair or abusive process at an early stage.

Mandamus forces decision

Mandamus has quite a different application. When an individual is dealing with an administrator, delay in reaching a decision can be every bit as devastating as an improper decision or an abuse of procedure. *Mandamus* can force the administrator to perform his or her duty and make the decision. It should be noted that administrators sometimes have the discretion to act or not; in such circumstances, *mandamus* cannot be used. But where the administrator has a duty to decide, usually imposed by statute, *mandamus* can be used to force a decision, although this may not be the decision you would like. But at least a decision has been made, and then other means can be used to challenge it. In the rare case in which there is only one decision the decision maker can legally reach, *mandamus* can be used to compel that decision.

Re McDonald and Rural Municipality of North Norfolk[16]

Mr. McDonald owned property near a lake and obtained a license from the province to get water from that lake for his farm. In order to access the water, he had to lay a pipe beside and under a municipal road to get to the lake. He applied to the municipality for permission to lay the pipe, and the municipality refused. They made it clear that the reason for the refusal was that they had concerns about the water supply for municipal and residential use. That decision was challenged, and the judge found that only the province had the right to consider the availability of the water. For the municipality to base its decision on this factor was to base it on irrelevant matters, making the decision reversible. The court then considered the appropriate remedy. While it could not order the municipal council to make a particular decision, it could order them to do their duty, that is, to make a decision based only on relevant considerations related to the road itself, such as safety, cost, and indemnification. The court then, by *mandamus,* ordered the municipality to make a decision based on only these relevant matters.

Declaratory Judgment

Although the use of prerogative writs is the backbone of judicial review today, there are many situations in which this type of remedy is ineffective. They are available only when a duty to act fairly is not met; they do not provide remedies when the impact of the decision has already been felt. For example, if Yamada owns property and builds a home on it that Adolfo, the city engineer, feels does not comply with the zoning regulations, and Adolfo then orders and supervises the demolition of the house, it would be little comfort to Yamada to go to the court, obtain a writ of *certiorari* and have Adolfo's decision quashed. The damage has already been done, and a court order nullifying the decision will not undo it.

Court can make declaratory judgment

To deal with situations in which there is no other appropriate action, the court has developed the concept of the declaratory judgment. The court reserves the right to declare the law, assess damages, and grant compensation in almost all situations. Declaratory judgments are available in situations in which prerogative

16. (1992) 98 D.L.R. (4th) 436, (Man. C.A.)

writs are not and are often more effective in application. They have become an effective tool to assist the courts' exercise of their supervisory jurisdiction over administrators. The eminent English jurist Lord Denning went so far as to say, "I know of no limitations to the power of the courts to grant a declaration, except such limit as it may in its discretion impose upon itself."[17]

Injunction

Another remedy available to the courts to help them in their supervisory jurisdiction is the injunction. An injunction is simply an order by the court to an individual or body to stop breaking the law or otherwise interfering with another's rights. In the example above, an appropriate remedy for Yamada after the decision was made but before it was put in place would have been to obtain an injunction to prevent the implementation of the decision. If the decision involved is merely the application for a license, however, an injunction would not be available, since no private rights of Yamada are being interfered with.

Injunction stops illegal conduct

An injunction is somewhat limited in its application. In fact, there are many situations in which an injunction is completely inappropriate, such as when the damage has already taken place. In addition, there are limitations concerning whom an injunction can be obtained against. In many cases, the Crown and servants of the Crown are immune to the effect of an injunction.

Modification by Statute

While the declaratory judgment and the injunction are more straightforward than prerogative writs in their application, they are inappropriate in some circumstances and may not be available in some jurisdictions where *certiorari*, prohibition, or *mandamus* are available. And the procedure to obtain a declaratory judgment or an injunction is quite different from that to obtain one of the prerogative writs.

Judicial review is often not achieved in administrative law proceedings because of the failure to meet technical requirements. Because of this, many jurisdictions have passed statutes incorporating these methods of judicial review into a consolidated and simplified procedure (for example, the British Columbia and Ontario *Judicial Review Procedure Acts*[18]). The statutes go so far as to say that whenever an application for *certiorari*, prohibition, *mandamus*, declaratory judgment, or injunction is made, the application will be deemed to be one for judicial review under the statute. The court then has the power to grant any relief available under statute or common law.

Complex requirements modified by statute

It must be emphasized that one of the dominant elements present in the common law provisions has been carried over into statutory judicial review, that is, the discretionary power of the judges. The courts always reserve the right to refuse to grant a prerogative writ or declaratory judgment when it would be inappropriate to do so. This is an exercise of pure discretionary power, and under the *Judicial Review Procedures Acts* of Ontario and British Columbia, this power has been retained.

Ontario has also enacted specialized legislation with respect to the procedure to be used by administrative tribunals in that province. The *Statutory Powers Procedures Act*[19] sets out the standards that must be observed by all such statutory bodies in that province, except where they have been specifically exempted or where the enabling statute creating the body requires a different procedure to be followed or

17. Barnard v. National Dock Labour Board [1953] 2 Q.B. 18 at 41 (C.A.)

18. *Judicial Review Procedure Act,* R.S,B,C. (1996) c. 241. and R.S.O. (1980) c. J.1

19. *Statutory Powers Procedure Act,* R.S.O (1990) c. S.22

different standards to be observed. It should also be noted that in Ontario, a special court (Divisional Court) has been established to deal with these kinds of disputes.

Privative Clauses

Historically, the courts have been reluctant to give up their power, and so, with the creation of administrative tribunals, the legislators have also included in the statutes clauses that specifically prohibit review by the courts of the tribunal's decision. Because of the principle of supremacy of parliament, one would expect these privative clauses to effectively keep the courts from interfering with such administrative decisions. The courts, however, must interpret such statutes and determine what they mean, and in the process, the judges often find ways to avoid the operation of privative clauses. It is important not to take privative clauses at face value. They may appear to clearly prevent the court from interfering, but the actual effect may be quite different. A typical example of a privative clause, taken from the current *Ontario Labour Relations Act*, is:

Privative clauses attempt to prevent judicial review

> No decision, order, direction, declaration, or ruling of the board shall be questioned or reviewed in any court, and no order shall be made or process entered, or proceeding taken in any court, whether by way of injunction, declaratory judgment, *certiorari, mandamus*, prohibition, *quo warranto*, or otherwise, to question, review, prohibit, or restrain the board or any of its proceedings.[20]

The intent of this legislation is obvious, but the courts interpret this to apply only when the board is acting within its jurisdiction. Thus, the original question as to whether or not the administrator has jurisdiction is still open to review. In fact, the way the courts have interpreted this type of privative clause varies with circumstances. If the courts wish to review a decision, they will often find a way to do so despite the presence of a privative clause.

Syncrude Canada Ltd. v. Michetti[21]

An employee of Syncrude died, and after a joint investigation by the provincial Workers' Compensation Board and the Occupational Health and Safety Branch, it was determined that the person died of an electric shock received while on the job. This resulted in an increased assessment in workers' compensation premiums to be paid by Syncrude. Syncrude appealed the decision without success, eventually applying for judicial review and ending up at the Court of Appeal. Syncrude's complaint was that a staff physician of the Workers' Compensation Board, who was also an advisor to the appeals commission, made the report with respect to the cause of death. When they appealed, Syncrude was not permitted to cross-examine the physician or to introduce any further evidence. Their hands were effectively tied, even though under the statute, the appeal must provide an opportunity for the parties to be heard and to submit new or additional evidence. Further, the appeals commissions refused to let Syncrude keep any record of the process and eventually destroyed their own notes. In the judge's words, "The whole course of conduct recited above is unfair, in every sense of the word, and deeply unfair. It was not a real hearing, but a mere simulacrum. If carefully analyzed, it will be seen to violate most of the traditional rules of natural justice."

20. *Ontario Labour Relations Act (1995),* S.O (1995) c. 1
21. (1994) 120 D.L.R. (4th) 118, (Alta. C.A.)

A major argument against review by the court was the presence of a very strong privative clause that prohibited review of the appeal commission's decisions by a court. The judge had no difficulty overcoming this provision for several reasons. First, when the appeal commission did not permit Syncrude to submit further evidence as required by the statute, they had declined jurisdiction (failed to act as they were required). Second, by their failure to follow the rules of natural justice, including their refusal to allow Syncrude an opportunity to be heard and cross-examine the witnesses, the commission went beyond their jurisdiction. And, finally, the court held that the decision was, in the circumstances, patently unreasonable and unfair. In each of these circumstances, the presence of a privative clause would not protect the decision from judicial review. The decision of the appeal commission was quashed and a new hearing ordered. It must be stressed that the courts will not lightly intrude on a decision made by such an administrative tribunal, but in the face of such abuses, the presence of a privative clause will not deter such judicial review.

In addition to privative clauses that directly prohibit judicial review, the legislators have embodied in statutes other clauses that indirectly have the same effect. Legislative provisions that assign the right to review specific questions of law or other matters to a minister or other administrator can exclude the courts from this function. Other clauses try to define the nature of the power exercised as discretionary, by using subjective wording: "The director may," "Where the administrator is satisfied," "Where it appears to be," and "Where in the opinion of." It is difficult to tell when discretionary power is being abused when it is assigned in a subjective way. Subjective assignments of power are, therefore, quite effective in keeping the courts from reviewing a decision.

Although privative clauses take many different forms, it must be remembered that it is up to the courts to determine what they mean. As a result, it should not be assumed that judicial review has been excluded because a privative clause is present. The effect of such privative clauses must also be viewed as subject to the operation of the *Charter of Rights and Freedoms*, which guarantees and enshrines the right to fundamental justice when a person's life, liberty, or security is at stake. If these rights are interfered with by an administrative tribunal, the decision can be reviewed in the courts regardless of a privative clause.

Courts resist operation of privative clauses

Even when there is no privative clause present, the courts must be very cautious when intervening in the area given to an administrative tribunal. Usually, there is good reason to give this decision-making function to such a body rather than to a court. The tribunal is usually more efficient and quicker in dealing with a particular kind of problem. It is possible to tailor the procedures involved to the types of disputes and parties involved, and the decision maker usually has particular expertise not found in a court. For these and other reasons, shifting the decision-making power from the courts to such administrative bodies may be both prudent and efficient. When parliament or the legislature gives authority to administrators, the courts must be very cautious in interfering, even without a privative clause and only do so where the decision itself appears unreasonable.[22]

Other Remedies

The powers and rights discussed in this section are largely extraordinary rights present when administrators or bureaucrats abuse their power or act incorrectly when making a decision that affects the position of an individual. In addition to the

22. Pezim v. British Columbia (Superintendent of Brokers) [1994] 2 S.C.R. 557

Contract and tort remedies may be available

unique and special remedies discussed, the normal rights that arise when one individual has been injured by the act of another may be available. For example, if a contract is breached, all the rights relating to breach of contract are applicable, even when one of the parties is the government or a Crown corporation. Similarly, if the actions of the decision maker involve the commission of a tort, such as negligence, defamation, trespass, or even assault and false imprisonment, the injured individual has the right to pursue tort remedies against the administrator. We will examine these remedies in more detail in the following chapters.

Enforcement of judgment may be difficult

However, there are some limitations to the availability of remedies under these headings. Until recently, an individual had no power to sue the Crown, on the premise that since the government was the source of the law, it was not subject to it and therefore could not be sued in its own courts. All jurisdictions in Canada have passed legislation making it possible to take the government to court and pursue judgment for breach of contract, tort, and so on. However, most jurisdictions have retained some of the Crown's former immunity, so it is difficult, if not impossible, to execute a judgment against the Crown. For example, it is almost impossible to get an injunction against the Crown, although it may be possible against an individual bureaucrat abusing his or her power. Similarly, the property of the Crown will not generally be available to satisfy judgment. Once a judgment is obtained, the good faith of the government agency has to be relied on to satisfy that judgment. No force can be used to ensure payment. This restriction does not apply to Crown corporations.

It should also be noted, as a matter of common law, that when an administrator exercises a statutory power properly, it will not give rise to tort action, even if damage to an individual results from it. Some jurisdictions have extended this protection by statute. New Brunswick's *Protection of Persons Acting Under Statute Act*[23] is an example. The effect of such legislative protections may be to exclude a right of action in any given case, and the student should be aware of any such local legislation.

You Can't Fight City Hall

When a person is adversely affected by the decision of a government official or tribunal, they should consider some of the following factors before initiating any action. First, it should be carefully determined whether there is any benefit to the action. When an administrator has made a decision that is disliked, even where there is some ground to challenge that decision, it may be of no use to do so. For example, when the tribunal has made a decision and not provided proper notice or there was bias or an unfair hearing, it may be possible to have the decision overturned, but to what end? If the tribunal simply holds another hearing reaching the same decision, this time making sure everything is done correctly, it is just a waste of time and money. There has to be some realizable objective that can be accomplished by the challenge, and creating a delay is usually not good enough. When a person proceeds in such an action as a matter of principle, the question usually asked is, just how much principle can you afford?

Challenging administrative decisions may be
- **futile**

23. *Protection of Persons Acting Under Statute Act,* R.S.N.B. (1973) c. P-20

The second major concern, then, is the cost. These government agencies usually have considerable funds available to fight any challenge to their actions or authority, and they usually are very willing to use all the options at their disposal to resist such a challenge. Remember, to them, the matter might be much more important than this particular case, and the danger of setting a precedent may drive them to focus all their efforts on defeating the challenge. The costs of such an action as a result will usually be considerable. To make matters worse, this is a difficult area of law requiring specialization, which drives the cost of legal representation up so that it is only in the most serious of cases where large sums are at stake that legal action will be advisable. Even then, it is normal practice for the lawyer to require a large retainer to cover the costs of the action. Normally, a contingency fee arrangement is out of the question.

- **costly**

Other criticisms have been leveled against the tribunal process, particularly when dealing with human rights commissions. Often, lengthy delays are involved, or the decision maker is perceived as having a particular axe to grind because of the political nature of their appointment.

- **lengthy**

These factors should be taken into consideration whenever a person pursues litigation, and many a justified complaint is abandoned because of the costs or questionable outcomes that may result. This is one reason that the alternatives to court action discussed in Chapter 2 are becoming much more attractive. And even government agencies that have a specific mandate, such as protecting the environment or ensuring fair competition, are willing to look to alternatives to the mandated enforcement process and litigation. Many of these bodies are more than willing to turn to methods of alternative dispute resolution, such as mediation and negotiation, and people involved in such disputes, especially businesses, should explore this avenue before directly challenging the validity of their decisions in court.

ADR may provide better resolution

It should also be remembered that these principles only apply where a person's rights or interests have been directly affected by a government decision maker. But the government often wields its power and implements its policies in more indirect ways through financing projects, joint ventures, government grants and various government initiatives, and public relations mechanisms. In these situations, the only real method of responding is a political one rather than through litigation. Even when there may be an avenue through litigation, a political response where public pressure is brought to bear or even internal pressure, such as talking to a superior, may be much more effective than turning to the courts.

Political pressure may be most effective

Regulating the Environment

One of the characteristics of our modern society is the ever-expanding role of government within it. This involvement is even more extensive where business activities are concerned. The first part of this chapter was concerned with government regulation of business generally. The rest of the chapter overviews the impact of law and government regulation on the environment. The environmental statutes, government departments, and enforcement bodies that businesses have to deal with illustrate the expanding regulatory environment within which businesses must function. We will also look at what happens when interactions between regulatory bodies and business come into conflict.

R. v. Bata Industries Limited[24]

The Bata shoe organization is a large corporation operating several different factories and facilities in southern Ontario. At one of these locations, inspectors from the Ministry of the Environment discovered metal drums leaking industrial waste into the soil. Tests were performed, and it was discovered that the ground water had been contaminated. Despite the fact that Bata had shown a willingness to cooperate on environmental matters and that members of the family had made significant contributions to cleaning up the environment, charges were laid against the corporation and also against the individual directors who were in charge of the sites where the contamination was discovered. The ministry disposed of the offending material with the cooperation of the corporation and at corporation expense. Fines were imposed on the corporation as well as on the individual directors. These fines were reduced somewhat on appeal, but the fines remained significant and had to be individually paid by the directors in question. In fact, when the corporation tried to reimburse the directors for the cost of the fines and legal expenses, the courts prohibited it from doing so.[25] On appeal, the court held that the corporation did have the right to indemnify their directors for the fines they had to pay, and what was expected to be an effective deterrent became considerably less so.

Reducing pollution is a significant cost of doing business.

PhotoDisc

Environmental concerns have great impact on business

Laws to protect the environment are significant and an important consideration in calculating the cost of doing business. As can be seen from this example, directors and officers of a corporation must carefully consider the risks and the potential costs associated with their positions. Some directors are extremely reluctant to serve on boards of companies where they may experience such exposure.

The Protection of the Environment

Our society and the natural world are interdependent in a way that historically has not been recognized in either our economic system or our laws. The production of wealth is the underlying objective of the business world (which the economic system facilitates), and wealth is produced, to a large extent, through the consumption of natural resources. In the wake of economic progress, forests are cleared, fish stocks are depleted, mineral, oil, and gas reserves are exhausted, and great scars are left on the earth in the process. Species of animal life are decimated as they are either directly consumed or their environment is destroyed around them. The byproducts of all this in the form of waste materials are discharged into the atmosphere, into the seas, and onto the lands, further degrading the environment. Such industries as mining, fishing, forestry, farming, construction, transportation, and manufacturing have all greatly contributed to Canada's environmental problems.

24. (1992) 70 C.C.C. (3d) 394 (Ont. Prov. Div.); varied (1993) 11 C.E.L.R. (N.S.) 208 (Ont. Gen. Div.); varied (1995) 101 C.C.C. (3d) 86 (Ont. C.A.)

25. *Ibid*, p. 394

The economic structures that form the basis of business and industry have traditionally not factored in these environmental costs. The range of problems contributing to the environmental crises is vast. From nuclear disasters to automobile emissions, from the disposal of chemical wastes to domestic sewage, and from the depletion of the ozone layer to the depletion of the soil—all have serious consequences for the environment. We have been forced to consider the depletion of the environment as one of the important factors in the economic equation.

The law has been even slower to react to these modern realities; it has only been in the last few decades that our legislators have considered it necessary to create statutes to introduce some balance into the system. In the 1970s and 1980s, there was a rash of statutory enactments to try to remedy the problems, and with those statutes came government departments and agencies to administer and promote compliance with the regulations. A product of public pressure and general concern for the preservation of the environment, the statutes have sometimes failed to ensure the necessary balance between the production of wealth and the preservation of the environment. Most of the statutes were remedial in nature and became increasingly stringent as the extent of the damage that had already been done to the environment was realized. The goal of the original legislation was to bring polluters into compliance, and governments sought to achieve it by restricting certain practices and imposing harsh penalties. That process created new problems, as the economic cost of compliance began to discourage and even destroy industries, particularly those based on harvesting natural resources. Over the past decade, there has been a realization that the primary mandate of legislative action should be investigation, education, and negotiation so that government and industry work together to resolve common problems. The courts, administrative tribunals, and alternative dispute resolution methods all have important roles to play in achieving the essential balance.

> **Statutes designed to protect environment have had varying degrees of success**

Common Law

Common law has always had some provisions that relate to the preservation of the environment. These generally take the form of individual rights associated with a person's right to property. **Riparian rights** give people living near rivers and streams the right to have the water come to them in undiminished quantity and quality, subject to limited domestic usage, such as washing, drinking, and normal sewage disposal. These rights are fragile, however, and the government commonly overrides them by issuing permits allowing for the withdrawal of large quantities of water for irrigation or for other uses or the discharge of waste into those streams and rivers.

> **Common law protections**
> * **riparian rights**

The law of torts is the subject of the following chapter. Suffice it to say here that tort law has been used with some significant limitations to control environmental damage. When a person uses his property so as to interfere with his neighbour's use of his property through the escape of noise, fumes, or other substances, the tort of "private nuisance" gives that neighbour the right to sue to put a stop to the offending conduct and for compensation. The torts of negligence and trespass can also be used to enforce a person's right not to be interfered with in this way by others, including municipal, provincial, and federal government agencies, which are to some extent liable for their wrongful conduct in tort law. Although tort law and the other common law remedies are an important source of individual rights against those who pollute, the downside is that personal involvement is required. An individual must bear the costs and, in order to qualify, must show that they have personally suffered damage from the offending conduct. Although some modern statutes give individuals the right to sue in tort under the statute and receive private compensation for personal loss, it still requires the personal involvement and

> * **nuisance**
>
> * **negligence**
>
> * **trespass**

> **Plaintiff must suffer personal injury**

commitment of that individual to the litigation process. One of the main advantages of the modern approach of statutory control and regulation is that the government agency specifically charged to do so can use various methods, including education, cooperation, and negotiation, before applying sanction and penalties, to ensure that the appropriate standards of environmental protection are determined and complied with.

Common Law Rights to Water

Mr. Steadman had a spring on his property feeding a small reservoir from which he took water mainly for domestic use. The Erickson Gold Mining Corporation built a road on the adjacent property and, in the process, silted the water supply. Even after some corrective action was taken, the water remained unusable, and Steadman had to truck water in. He sued for nuisance. The court said that although the Crown owned the water, Mr. Steadman had a right to the use of it, that Erickson's conduct amounted to a nuisance, and that they were liable for their interference. This is an example of common law control of environmental interference. Mr. Steadman's right to use the water is said to be a riparian right, and his remedy in nuisance illustrates the effectiveness of this common law tort action.

Steadman v. Erickson Gold Mining Corp., (1987) 43 D.L.R. (4th) 712, (B.C.S.C); aff'd (1989) 56 D.L.R. (4th) 577 (B.C.C.A)

R. v. Consolidated Maybrun Mines Ltd.[26]

Consolidated Maybrun operated a copper-gold mine in northwestern Ontario. Employees of the Ministry of Environment inspected the site about 10 years after its shutdown and discovered the mine site had been completely abandoned. It had been vandalized, windows were broken, chemicals were strewn around, the mine shaft had filled with water, and oils contaminated with PCBs had leaked from several electrical transformers located in a generator building in a fenced-off area.

The ministry officials wrote to the owners of the mine asking them to correct the situation, but they did nothing. They then served notice on the mine owners that they would be issuing an order in 15 days requiring them to take specific steps to clean up the property. The owners were given 15 days to make written submissions to the ministry before the orders were made. The mine owners responded that the order was ridiculous and blamed the government for their problems. The ministry then made the order on June 2, 1987. They also informed Consolidated Maybrun that they had the right to appeal the order by making written submissions, again within 15 days.

No appeal was made, and the order was generally ignored. The ministry stepped in, took the necessary steps to clean up the site, and laid charges against Consolidated Maybrun for failing to comply with the order, which in the *Environmental Protection Act*[27] is identified as an offence.

The case was quite complex, but for our purposes, it is sufficient to note that the accused responded to the charges by saying that the order of the director was unreasonable and that was the reason the accused did not comply. At the trial level, they were allowed to argue on the merits of whether it was a reasonable order or not.

26. 133 D.L.R. (4th) 513, (Ont. C.A.); aff'd [1998] 1 S.C.R. 706
27. R.S.O. 1990 c. E 19

On appeal, the court held that whether the order was reasonable did not really matter and that Consolidated Maybrun was required to respond to the order given by the director under the act. The accused had had other methods to deal with the merits of the charge. It could have appealed and challenged the decision, in effect gaining a new hearing. It did not take advantage of this option but simply ignored the order. It was the failure of the accused to respond to the order that resulted in the charge, and Consolidated Mayburn was convicted.

This case is instructive because it illustrates not only the statutory liability of business people for long-forgotten operations, such as this old mine, but also the power given to the ministry officials by the *Environmental Protection Act*. Such orders should not be ignored or treated lightly, for the impact can be profound. From the point of view of dealing with these kinds of government agencies, it is important to understand that prompt action must be taken in response to such orders. It is important to take advantage of all remedies within the structure of the regulatory body involved—in this case, the original right to make written submissions in response and, once the order was given, the right to make an appeal. It was failure to take advantage of those options and the mine owners' lack of willingness to treat these matters seriously that got them into trouble.

Common law (and the civil law in Québec) was basically ineffectual in providing any kind of general environmental protection. Because of this, most effective environmental law is embodied in federal and provincial statutes that not only prohibit polluting activities but provide for government enforcement whether or not individuals have been harmed.

Common law ineffective against polluters

Jurisdiction

Both federal and provincial governments have powers to make law with respect to the environment as they exercise their assigned responsibilities primarily under Sections 91 and 92 of the *Constitution Act (1867)*.

Environment shared responsibility between federal and provincial governments

R. v. Hydro-Québec[28]

This dispute arose over allegations that Hydro-Québec dumped PCBs into a river at a higher rate than allowed under the appropriate regulations. They were charged with violating an order of the *Canadian Environmental Protection Act* and entered a plea of not guilty. They claimed that the provisions relied on were not within the authority of the federal government, since environmental protection did not fall under the responsibilities assigned to the federal government under Section 91 of the *Constitution Act (1867)*. The charges were dismissed at trial, and an appeal to the Québec Superior Court was also dismissed. The matter was further appealed in the Supreme Court of Canada.

The court agreed that the environment had not been specifically assigned to the federal government but went on to observe that it had not been given to either level—federal or provincial. "It is a diffuse subject that cuts across many different areas of constitutional responsibility. If a provision in pith and substance falls within the parameters of a power assigned to the body that enacted the legislation, then it is constitutionally valid."

28.[1997] 3 S.C.R. 213

The problem then was to decide whether the *Canadian Environmental Protection Act* fell under any other existing federal responsibility, such as criminal law. It was found that the protection of the environment through the regulation of toxic substances was a legitimate public interest that needed to be protected and therefore a proper use of criminal law power. The legislation was valid and proper, and so, the matter was sent back to the original court for trial.

The case is important because it establishes beyond question that the federal government has authority to make laws with respect to the environment and enforce them as a valid exercise of their criminal law power, even where it does not relate to subjects given specifically to them under the *Constitution Act (1867)*. It also illustrates that there can be overlapping jurisdictions in this area. Similar provincial legislation could also have been valid, but on different grounds.

Businesses may face federal and provincial regulations

Forests, minerals, air, and water are all local matters and under the jurisdiction of provincial governments. But when activities involving such resources become interprovincial or international in scope or when they take place on federal lands or in coastal waters, the federal government then has jurisdiction. The federal government can enact environmental protection legislation under its criminal law power as evidenced by the Hydro-Québec case discussed above. It can also exercise a considerable amount of indirect control by requiring that provincial environmental projects satisfy federal standards to qualify for federal funding.

Often, both federal and provincial regulatory authorities become involved when businesses initiate projects and activities that have significant environmental implications. These businesses must receive permits and licenses and submit to environmental regulations from various levels of government. Businesses engaged in smaller projects that are local in nature will likely deal only with provincial and municipal regulations. There is growing cooperation between the three levels of government, which should lead to the harmonization and consolidation of legislation that will require business people to deal with only one level of bureaucracy. In January 1998, the provincial, territorial, and federal environmental ministers (with the exception of Québec) reached an agreement that made a significant step towards this objective. But we are not there yet, and there is legislation at both the federal and provincial levels with respect to environmental regulation which businesses must comply with.

Provincial Legislation

All provinces have some form of environmental legislation intended to control pollution and environmental deterioration. These statutes regulate the transport and disposal of waste, the use and transportation of hazardous materials, the clean up of contaminated sites, the treatment of sewage, and the disposal of byproducts from manufacturing, mining, and other activities. Statutes also control specific locations by limiting industrial, commercial, and residential uses. They control contamination of the air, land, and water. Even noise and odour are controlled by statute. Essentially, the laws are designed to ensure that the natural state of the environment is retained as much as reasonably possible and that pollution in all its forms is kept to a minimum.

This is accomplished in several ways. The statutes provide for the creation of a ministry or government department charged with establishing standardized codes for the use of natural resources and the elimination of waste products or any other kind of activity that might degrade the environment. They then enforce those standards through inspection, investigation, the holding of hearings, and the levying of fines and other penalties.

Typically, government agencies concerned with the environment are divided into several departments. One section requires that permits be obtained before engaging in an activity that causes pollution and provides those permits setting appropriate limits and controls. Another section is responsible for research and development designed to establish standards and identify possible future threats to the environment. A third section is devoted to prevention education, achieving compliance, investigation of violations, and prosecutions.

Government departments set standards

The first major point of interaction between government and the business person is at the assessment stage, which is a mandated process imposed on businesses and other undertakings to determine what impact those activities may have on the environment before permits and approvals are issued. The main area of potential conflict, however, is at the enforcement stage, where the agency must determine whether the established standards are being adhered to. Inspectors have the power to enter and inspect premises, plants, and other sites to determine compliance. Typically, the agencies and their representatives have the power to investigate violations, search and inspect premises, seize documents, hold hearings, impose fines and other penalties, and even close down the business when the infractions are serious enough. This is where the matters discussed in the first part of this chapter will be of particular interest to the business person. This enforcement aspect of the legislation is often not taken as seriously as it should be. These agencies have considerable power and authority, as the owners of Consolidated Maybrun Mines discovered in the case used to open this discussion. In that case, the mine owners, in effect, ignored the orders to clean up the property under the Ontario *Environmental Protection Act*[29] and, as a result, were in much more serious trouble than they otherwise would have been.

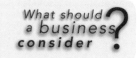

The criminal prosecution model has largely been incorporated into the environmental field, including the imposition of fines and even imprisonment for violations. It is much debated whether this approach is appropriate when the offenders in most cases have not acted intentionally or maliciously. Other models are now being explored, and Nova Scotia's *Environmental Act,*[30] for instance, puts more emphasis on settlement and provides for the mediation of environmental disputes and other ways of working with business to solve these problems.

New tort rights created by statutes

Another major point of potential contention occurs at the assessment stage, which is discussed in more detail below. When a new project or activity is proposed, before granting approval and issuing a license or permit, most jurisdictions require that an environmental impact assessment be carried out in order to determine whether the activity will be a danger to the environment. These processes can be long, involved, and costly to business and are applied both to new and established projects where there is renovation, modification, or expansion being done. Ontario has made significant changes in their legislation significantly reducing the red tape and streamlining the process in that province.

Nova Scotia has also taken steps to reform their environmental protection legislation. Their *Environmental Act,* consolidates 16 previous acts and puts more emphasis on settlement mediation and negotiation. Like recent amendments in other provinces, the act also broadens the range of people who can be held responsible

29. R.S.O. 1990 c. E 19
30. S.N.S. 1994-95, c. 1

for violations and significantly increases the penalties, the philosophy being that polluters should be the ones to pay for the damages.

The primary statutes in British Columbia are the *Environmental Management Act*[31] that deals primarily with the assessment process and the *Waste Management Act*[32] that, among other things, requires permits for the discharge of anything that would degrade the environment. It also deals with spills and their cleanup and the containment, haulage, and disposal of waste, including municipal waste, sewage, vehicle, and fuel emissions. It allows for contaminated site identification and cleanup with the associated liability for costs as well as significant enforcement and penalty provisions.

Individual rights include freedom from pollution

The most recent trend in legislation, found in such acts as the Yukon Territory's *Environment Act*[33] and the Northwest Territories' *Environmental Rights Act,*[34] is the declaration that the people have the right to have their environment free from pollution. These acts allow individuals to take action against the polluter to enforce those rights. The Northwest Territories' act, for example, allows an individual to bring a private action when someone polluting the environment has committed a statutory offence. This may seem attractive but is arguably a step backwards with all the disadvantages associated with the common law solutions, where an individual must assume the substantial burden of time, effort, and cost of pursuing an individual action. Québec's *Environmental Quality Act*[35] creates a right to a healthy environment, which is bestowed on every person in the province and to the protection of living species.

Devolution of Powers

It should also be noted that there is a movement to devolve more and more power and responsibilities in these areas to lower levels of government. Just as the federal government has moved to place more responsibility for environmental matters onto the provinces, there is a growing movement for the provinces to place more responsibility and cost onto the municipalities. Ontario, as part of its legislative reforms, has made major changes to the *Municipal Act,* giving cities and towns more capacity to regulate these matters. For example, the responsibility for sewage treatment facilities has been handed over to the municipal level, and these bodies have also been given the authority to regulate environmental concerns in a number of areas, including "nuisance, noise, odour, vibration, illumination, and dust." It should be noted in passing that this devolution of power and responsibility is not always greeted with enthusiasm. For example, Ontario ministry officials have been enforcing the federal *Fisheries Act*[36] with respect to the Great Lakes for some time, and when the federal government refused to pay for the service, Ontario decided to discontinue enforcement, leaving a significant vacuum which the small contingent of federal officials could not fill.[37]

Provinces and municipalities acquiring new responsibilities

31. R.S.B.C. (1996), c. 118
32. R.S.B.C. (1996) c. 482)
33. S.Y. (1991) c. 5
34. R.S.N.W.T. (1988) c. 83 (Supp.)
35. R.S.Q. (1977) c. E-24
36. *R.S.C. (1985) c. F-14*
37. "Environmental Perspectives," *The Lawyers Weekly*, Vol. 17 No. 25

Penalties

Another significant reform is the trend to generally increase the penalties that are imposed for violations and expand the number of people who are liable. Waste disposal, for instance, is a particularly difficult problem to control, and the Ontario reforms make it possible to prosecute the producer of waste, even when the violation has been committed by a subcontractor, or for using waste haulers, handlers, or disposal sites that do not have the appropriate licenses permits or authorization.

Penalties increasing

Company Commits Offence

The parties concerned were in the business of collecting, transporting, and re-refining waste oil. This business is closely regulated, including the requirement of a number of manifests which must be filled out by the generator of the waste, by the transporter of it, and by the receiver of it. Mr. Cochrane picked up oily waste from a Petro-Canada facility with the proper manifest. On the way, his truck broke down, and he contacted Mr. Howitt, a representative of Safety-Kleen, who brought his truck and transferred the oil from one truck to the other. This required verbal permission from the ministry as well as the completion of a new manifest. Although an attempt had been made, neither the appropriate documentation nor the necessary authorization was present, and false information was filled in on the original manifest. Mr. Howard's truck was pulled over by a ministry official as soon as it got out on the highway, and the violations that had taken place became apparent. There were two offences here: failing to comply with the regulations and providing false information. The question the court had to determine was whether the corporate personality of Safety-Kleen could be responsible in its own capacity for the offences committed by its employee. The court held that the failure to comply with the completion of the manifests was a strict liability offence. The only way the corporation could avoid liability would be to show due diligence, that is, show that they had taken reasonable steps to set up a system to avoid this sort of thing. The court looked at the complete independence allowed to employees and decided that no such system had been in place and that therefore the offence had been committed by the company. The second offence of providing false information was a *mens rea* offence: it required intent to do the wrongful deed. This intent was not possible in the "mind" of the corporation, and therefore, it was not liable for the second offence of making a false declaration.

R. v. Safety-Kleen Canada Inc., 145 D.L.R. (4th) 276, Ontario Court of Appeal

Federal Legislation

The federal government exercises its power over the environment both directly and indirectly. As mentioned above, it has the power to make law with respect to the environment under the *Constitution Act (1867)* in matters that have an international or interprovincial scope, in matters that take place on federal land or coastal waters, and in those areas that have been determined to have been assigned to the federal government, such as the fisheries, military areas, airports, and air transportation. The federal government exercises an indirect control over the environment when it provides funding to the provinces to help pay for their environmental programs. The federal government can stipulate how the funds will be used and, to some degree, control the extent of the environmental legislation in place in the provinces. When the federal government finances a project under provincial jurisdiction, it can require compliance with both federal as well as provincial regulations.

Federal regulations control provincial areas through funding

The *Canadian Environmental Protection Act* (CEPA, 1999)[38] is the principal federal statute dealing with the environment. It controls the manufacturing, import, and use of many toxic substances, such as PCBs and asbestos, sets standards for and regulates the use of these substances, and establishes a reporting process that must be followed. The act authorizes the assessment of domestic (existing) and new substances, to determine if they are toxic. The legislation then requires that plans for managing toxic substances are developed to prevent pollution that could harm the environment or human health. Individuals are obliged to report any release of toxic substances that contravene a regulation. Whistleblower protection is available to any employee who voluntarily reports a release. It governs international air pollution, allowing for cooperation with the provinces; it controls contamination of the oceans and dumping; it provides for research and data collection, including the publication of guidelines; it regulates crown corporations, undertakings, and lands. The act can impose personal liability on directors and officers of corporations who fail to comply or cooperate with officials. This is a comprehensive statute meant to prevent pollution, provide for research and development, investigate and measure pollution levels, and monitor industry. It has become a model for other levels of government to follow. An important aspect of this legislation is that where there are equivalent provincial regulations in place, the federal government may declare that specific regulations made under *CEPA 1999* do not apply in that province.

Federal statute
- **hazardous materials**
- **international concerns**
- **holds directors liable for company's damage to environment**

Hazardous Wastes

Another area of federal attention is the handling and disposal of hazardous wastes and material. The *Transportation of Dangerous Goods Act*[39] controls the transport of dangerous chemicals and goods. The act applies when goods are transferred between provinces or internationally, including between Canada and the United States. Again, at the federal level, the *Fisheries Act*[40] with its 1970 amendments is very important because of its provision prohibiting the discharge of any dangerous substances into waterways, lakes, and oceans. This act has been used effectively to control the discharge of sewage from municipalities as well as effluents from pulp mills. It stipulates that "no person shall carry on any work or undertaking that results in the harmful alteration, disruption, or destruction of fish habitat." The act prohibits any discharge into waters (referred to as a HADD) that may have a deleterious effect on fish. Since almost any alteration of a waterway or anything discharged into it, including silt or gravel from a construction site, road building, mining, or forestry operation, can have such an effect, even if short term, the act has been very effectively used to control pollution and deterioration of the waterways. To illustrate just how far this has been taken, a Newfoundland municipality was convicted of a violation of the act, even though they were dredging their local river in order to clean it up and restore the fish habitat.[41]

Transportation of dangerous goods

Pollution of waterways

The Queen v. Township of Richmond[42]

In this case, the township of Richmond in British Columbia was charged with a violation of the federal *Fisheries Act* by discharging a pollutant into a river. The act provided that "no person shall deposit or permit to be deposited any deleterious substance or cause any such deleterious substance to enter any such water." At the

38. S.C. (1999) c.33
39. S.C. (1992) c. 34
40. *R.S.C. (1985) c. F-14*
41. R. v. Mount Pearl Council (1986), 5 F.P.R. 298 (Nfld. Prov. Ct.)
42. (1983) 4 D.L.R. (4th) 189, (B.C.C.A.)

provincial trial level, the charge was dismissed on the basis that the judge did not have jurisdiction because the township did not qualify as a person under the act. The Court of Appeal examined the statute and found that the matter hinged on the definition of a person in the eyes of the law. The *Interpretation Act* holds that a person may be male or female or a corporation. The court found that even though Richmond was a unique kind of corporation, it was indeed a corporation and that the act applied to it. The chief justice stated, "I think it is only common sense that parliament, in providing for the protection of waters from pollution, intended that that should apply to all persons in Canada and could not, unless there was some specific language, exclude a municipal corporation."

This case illustrates just how extensive the provisions of the *Fisheries Act* are and that it applies even to cities and towns. It is also interesting in that it shows that a corporation is a person in the eyes of the law, a matter that will be discussed in some depth later in the text.

The *Arctic Waters Pollution Prevention Act*[43] is an attempt to preserve the relatively pristine conditions found in the north and avoid the kind of disasters that have happened in other areas, such as oil spills and other forms of contamination. Many other federal acts have some aspect of environmental protection to them, such as the *Canada Shipping Act*[44] that controls the handling of cargo and the use of fuel and ballast and provides inspectors with the power to enforce these regulations. The *Nuclear Energy Act*,[45] the *Hazardous Products Act*,[46] and the *Navigable Waters Protection Act*[47] are other examples of federal legislation that are related to the environment.

Special protections in the north

Enforcement

Federal and provincial environment statutes grant considerable enforcement powers to the government officials charged with their application, including the power to enter premises, to inspect, to seize documents, to take samples, and, in some circumstances, to order certain activities stopped. But in most cases, that power stops short of the right to use force. In fact, except in the most blatant cases of intentional dumping of waste, the enforcement branches find it much more productive to work with the offending business to help it live up to the standards rather than punish it for failing to do so. In fact, environmental protection alternative measures (EPAMs) are used as an alternative to court prosecution under *CEPA 1999.* An EPAM is a negotiated agreement entered for the purpose of restoring the violator to compliance with the legislation. The Crown may propose an EPAM to a party who previously had a good compliance history but who is now charged with a *CEPA 1999* offence. If that party is willing to take remedial steps (without first having the charges tried in court), then it may avoid the costs and delays inherent in judicial proceedings, as well as the stigma of a possible conviction.

Extensive enforcement power

Companies may be required not only to refrain from future activities that threaten the environment but may also face prosecution for past uncontrolled dumping and the costs of cleanup. It is not only the companies that face these responsibilities, since the statutes often lift the corporate veil, making the directors personally responsible for the offences committed by the corporations they direct.

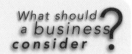

43. R.S.C. (1985) c. A-12
44. R.S.C. (1985) c. S-9
45. R.S.C. (1985) c. A-16
46. R.S.C. (1985) c. H-3
47. R.S.C. (1985) c. N-22

Even secured creditors, such as mortgagees, landlords, and receivers, can be held responsible for the cost of such cleanup. Note that amendments to the *Bankruptcy and Insolvency Act* provide additional protection to trustees and receivers in such circumstances. It is uncertain just how far this responsibility will or should go, but it is clear that if such secured creditors realize their security by taking possession of the property, the responsibility to clean it up goes with it. Because of this responsibility, many lenders choose not to exercise their security in the face of default. It is now incumbent on lenders, investors, and potential purchasers of property or business, to make a careful examination to determine any risks before they become involved.

Environmental audits make businesses account for their activities

Environmental audits are fast becoming an essential aspect of modern business practice and can take one of two forms: the **site audit**, used to determine contamination problems associated with a business or site before a transaction is made, and the **compliance audit**, used by an ongoing business to examine its own practices to determine whether they are in compliance with the legislation. The latter form is a necessary part of establishing **due diligence,** where the director or officer of a corporation must show that he or she has taken all reasonable steps to do everything necessary to live up to his or her personal responsibilities under the act and regulations.

Penalties have increased

Although the enforcement approach used in these statutes is primarily regulatory, controlling rather than prohibiting environmentally sensitive activities, the penalties involved in environmental offences have been greatly increased. Under *CEPA 1999,* fines range up to a million dollars a day and up to five years in prison. The court may also levy a fine equal to any profits earned as a result of the offence. The directors of the responsible government departments (or, in some cases, the ministers responsible) also have the power under these statutes to issue **stop orders** for any activity that violates the standards established in the regulation. In other circumstances, less drastic control orders can be issued that direct compliance with the standards. In some cases, orders can be issued that require an offender to repair any damage caused by the activity. These penalties involve criminal or quasi-criminal prosecution. One alternative being used in some jurisdictions is the use of the "administrative monetary penalty (AMP)," a non-criminal alternative to the criminal prosecution model and is intended to create a less adversarial and more cooperative administrative environment. One of the effects of using AMPs, however, may be to overcome the due diligence defence now available to those charged with responsibility for violations, reimposing strict liability.

De-regulation

Costs and complexities have led to deregulation

Although the federal government has considerable power to create and enforce regulations with respect environmental protection, it is important to realize that having the power is not the same as exercising it. As part of the general process of cost cutting at the federal level, there have been significant reductions in staff and funding of the federal agencies charged with implementing and enforcing these regulations, to the point where they have been criticized as becoming dangerously ineffective. In addition, wherever possible, the federal government has been devolving the enforcement side of the equation to the provinces. The recent *Accord on Environmental Harmonization* reached by the Canadian Council of Ministers of the Environment (excluding Québec) is an example of that process in operation. The idea is to develop a common and coordinated approach to dealing with the environment on the basis of the "polluter pays" principle. A framework is provided for bilateral agreements between each province and the federal government to deal with these matters. The end result will be the federal government surrendering more of its responsibility for enforcement to the provinces. If the consequences are less attention to preservation of the environment, we may all be worse off. But if this simply removes duplication and streamlines the process, eliminating inconsistent or conflicting regulations and making compliance clearer and easier, the public generally may benefit from the changes.

Public awareness enhances compliance

Re Mac's Convenience Stores Inc. and Minister of the Environment for Ontario[48]

This case involved a gas station with a leaking gasoline storage tank. When the leak was discovered, the Ontario Minister of the Environment under Section 16 of the *Environmental Protection Act*,[49] ordered that the operators of the gas station, the owners of the property, and the gasoline supplier to clean up the spill and remove the contaminated soil. It is important to realize that there was some urgency in the matter, since the city water supply was in danger of contamination. When they failed to clean up the soil within the specified time, the minister made an order under Section 143, which allowed the ministry to do the cleanup and charge the cost back to those who had failed to comply with the order. They were also charged with failure to comply with the order to clean up the contaminated soil. This application for judicial review of the minister's action was based on a claim that they had no jurisdiction and that there was a failure to follow procedural fairness.

As far as jurisdiction was concerned, it was clear that the minister had a duty to identify who caused or permitted the pollution before an order to clean it up was made. This had to be done reasonably. In this case, no hearing was held, but there was evidence to support the decision that was made. It was not up to the court to interfere with such a finding of fact on the part of the minister. Remember that this was an emergency and to require the minister to hold a hearing would have interfered with the very purpose of the legislation, which is to provide a quick response in the event of an emergency such as this. Once the minister had jurisdiction to make the order to clean up the property, it is clear that the jurisdiction was also present to have someone else do it and charge the costs back under Section 143 if they failed to comply. As far as the duty of procedural fairness is concerned, it is true there was no hearing before the action complained of, but that was necessary because of the emergency. In order to collect the money, that had to be done through a court process, and at that time, those charged had time enough to make their case, and so, the requirements of procedural fairness were satisfied.

This case illustrates the power of the minister to order the cleanup under the EPA of Ontario and, if it is not done, to have it done and collect the costs from those responsible. It also illustrates just how far the responsibility can be assessed. Here, not only the operators but also the suppliers of gasoline as well as the owners of the property were held responsible for the spill. It also shows how the process of judicial review is to take place, and it is interesting to note that the requirement of procedural fairness was not satisfied before the action but after. Often, regulators must exercise their power quickly to prevent some greater harm. In emergency situations, procedural fairness must still be satisfied, but it often takes place after the required emergency response, not before.

48. (1984) 12 D.L.R. (4th) 443, (Ont. Div. Ct.)
49. R.S.O. (1980) c. 141

The Environmental Assessment Process

Following the American example of the *National Environmental Policy Act (1969),* the trend in Canadian legislation at both the federal and provincial levels is to impose an environmental assessment review process on those wishing to undertake some new, potentially hazardous project. The objective is to require the parties proposing the project to file a report with a designated government agency that highlights its potential impact on the environment, including any health risks. The government authority studies this report, seeks public input, and holds a public hearing to air all the various points of view. The authority then decides whether to give its permission for the activity, to withhold it, or to grant the permit with conditions. Environmental assessment reviews were initially limited to public activities, but now environmental impact studies are generally required for private industrial and resource-based projects as well. Producing such reports has significantly increased the cost of doing business. Such reports are now required not only for large projects, such as steel plants, pulp mills, and hydroelectric dams, but also for smaller types of business activities that use specific types of chemicals or otherwise threaten the environment.

The *Canadian Environmental Assessment Act,* proclaimed in January 1995, replaces non-legislated cabinet guidelines and imposes significant reporting obligations on businesses dealing with the federal government. The proclaimed purposes of the act are the following:

1. To ensure that the environmental effects of projects receive careful consideration before any action is taken

2. To promote sustainable development and thus a healthy environment and a healthy economy

3. To ensure that projects on federal lands do not cause adverse environmental effects to other lands

4. To ensure an opportunity for public participation in the environmental assessment process

The act requires an environmental assessment for any project done on federal lands, any project the federal government finances, or any project for which it provides a permit or license. The environmental review process consists of a comprehensive study of the environmental impact of the project, evaluation by a review panel, and the implementation of a follow-up program, where necessary. The panel also considers the purpose of the project, any alternative means that could be used and their environmental effect, and how renewable resources might be affected. Once approval has been given by the review panel, it issues a certificate, and the project can proceed. To ensure public access and involvement, a registry is established to make available all information collected or submitted relative to the environmental review process for the various projects. The act also establishes the Canadian Environmental Assessment Agency, which advises and assists the minister by administering and promoting the environmental assessment process, encouraging research, promoting uniformity throughout Canada, and ensuring an opportunity for public input. In the process, the agency provides administrative support, training, and information. This act is an important step towards establishing a comprehensive process for protecting the environment. Other jurisdictions have followed the federal example and now require similar environmental review processes. Some jurisdictions, such as British Columbia (in their *Environmental Management Act*), only require such an assessment when ordered by the minister (or the designated official).

Modifying Regulations

There has been a great deal of criticism concerning the considerable burden complying with these environmental assessment regulations imposed on businesses. A zero-tolerance policy has required businesses that impact the environment even in only a minor way to embark on a lengthy and complicated process with little tangible benefit and great cost.

Ontario's *Environmental Assessment Act* required extensive reporting and public input, including hearings in some cases, to the point where businesses were overwhelmed.

In an effort to alleviate this burden on industry by reducing red tape and to make regulations that are "better, stronger, and clearer," the government brought in significant changes to the *Environmental Protection Act* and other statutes that generally streamline the process, reducing and, in some cases, eliminating altogether the procedural requirements. Where major projects are involved, instead of having to specifically comply with a complicated and cumbersome process that was often unclear and was subject to change as the application proceeded, under the new legislation, standards and guidelines are provided, and the business submits "terms of reference" setting out how they propose to satisfy the environmental assessment requirement. This is a plan setting out what the business proposes to do to appropriately assess the impact of the project on the environment and ensure compliance with the standards, including provision for public consultation. Once approved, all parties, including the ministry, are required to comply with that plan. The process is clear, and businesses need only follow those terms of reference to be in compliance. Where the activity impacts the environment only in a minor way, usually where small businesses are involved, the assessment and approval process may be eliminated altogether. The recent amendments have provided certain regulations (Standard Approval Regulations) that must be followed for a qualifying business or activity, and so long as they are complied with, the requirements for approvals for these minor discharges are removed altogether. If they follow the regulation, they are deemed to have obtained valid approval. Some businesses have simply been exempted from the regulations altogether. These are specific types of activities, such as the exhaust fans from restaurants and laundromats. It remains to be seen whether the changes to the Ontario legislation removes a stifling imposition on commercial and other activities or is a significant step backwards in the war against environmental contamination. In some jurisdictions, this environmental assessment process is only required where the minister (or a designated government official) specifically identifies the project as a potential problem and requires it.

Efforts are being made to simplify process

Economy versus Environment

The tendency of government towards increasing interference into business activities in relation to the environment may appear to be an unwarranted and unfair intrusion, but there is considerable justification for it. As our economy worsens and costs increase, businesses sometimes have difficulty surviving as profitable enterprises. Pressing bottomline concerns are bound to affect the attention given to environmental issues. This creates a dilemma in that as the environment is threatened, businesses become less economically viable and less able to take the steps necessary to preserve it. The increased attention that government is paying to the environment may be justified, but it is understandable that the imposition of more government regulation is not popular in business circles. It is usually in this regulatory arena that the clash between government bureaucrats, businesses, and private individuals takes place.

Environmental costs threaten businesses

Imposition of strict regulations often harms business

The ongoing dispute between the environmental movement and various industries is forcing a reassessment of how government should deal with these matters; business people must not only concern themselves with a costly and interfering regulatory environment but also must contend with uncertainty and flux. Government regulatory officials impose standards, establish environmental screening processes, and require reports when any new project is undertaken. An involved process of public hearings and submissions may be required before a license or permit is granted. Once the project is under way, inspectors may measure compliance, and for industries that are considered dangerous, such inspections become routine.

Industries must consider the costs of complying with environmental standards and the costs of prosecution when offences do take place. Even if a site was previously contaminated, modern statutes may require that it be cleaned by or at the expense of the polluter or current owner and that compensation be paid to those injured. These statutes may apply even when no regulations were in place at the time the pollution occurred or if the standards in place were lower than they should have been.

Even with the trend towards de-regulation, government departments are still involved in industrial and other forms of business activity in a powerful way. Almost any business decision taken today must consider the environmental factors and the procedures that are laid down by the government agencies established to protect it and must recognize the fact that all businesses are subject to inspection and prosecution when their day-to-day activities pose a risk to the environment. It is crucial that any business plan contain provisions for compliance to current and projected regulations. In order to protect directors, officers, and the company itself, strategies must be developed so that the reasonable conduct required to establish due diligence is built into the business operation.

Due diligence and self regulation necessary

The controversy extends to whether development ought to take place at all—whether the forests ought to be cut down; rivers ought to be dammed; plants ought to be built. The recurring examples of environmental activists risking jail terms to stop logging in sensitive areas or strapping themselves to oil drilling rigs or trees illustrate that the problem is more fundamental than waste disposal and pollution. The impact of these disputes can have a profound effect on businesses to the point of raising the question of whether they will be able to carry on business at all.

Protesters face stiff penalties

For example, when a company applied to develop a copper mine in the Tatshenshini Wilderness area, the outcry and pressure were so great that the British Columbia government stepped in, declared the area a provincial park, and put an end to the project. The Oldman River hydro-electric project in Alberta ran into many obstacles, most hinging on environmental concerns. The fixed-link bridge between Prince Edward Island and the mainland ran into similar difficulties. The Kemano completion project in British Columbia was stopped completely because of concerns about the fish habitat in the Fraser and Nechako river systems. Fast ferries ran into difficulty because the wake they created destroyed shorelines.

Even when a government has given approval for a project, protesters may continue their activities. On the west coast of Vancouver Island, the provincial government gave permission to MacMillan Bloedel to log in the Clayoquot Sound area, but the protests of environmentalists in the area (the arrests were in the hundreds) put great pressure on the government to backtrack from its decision. These protests continue there and elsewhere in the province, with several people jailed for their beliefs (one concerned senior citizen was given a one-year jail term for contempt). An important aspect of these protests is the involvement of private groups, such as Greenpeace, the Sierra Club of Canada, the World Wildlife Fund, and the Sierra Legal Defence Fund, positioning themselves against the government and businesses. These groups not only provide a vehicle for promoting the position of their members but also play an important role in intervening in litigation or providing the financial support for those involved. To further complicate matters, recent court decisions and treaty negotiations with respect to native rights bring one more group into the equation that must be satisfied before projects can be advanced.[50]

As our population continues to grow, and with it our consumption of resources and production of goods, the pressure on the environment will increase. Government is the only body that can mediate conflicting interests. It has managed to create a greater public awareness and interest in environmental issues and has legislated and otherwise encouraged solutions that address the major problems. A spirit of cooperation, consultation, and compromise will allow government and industry to develop and maintain workable programs and policies that satisfy the needs of both sides.

Negotiation and mediation may be preferred alternatives

This discussion with respect to environmental law is just one (albeit an important one) of the areas where business must deal with government, but it illustrates the extensive regulatory environment within which businesses must function today. Although a businessperson has some right to resist the improper use of government power, it should be clear that individuals and businesses are usually at a disadvantage not having access to unlimited resources. Confrontation should be avoided, if at all possible. Usually, the controls imposed are necessary, and government officials are just trying to do their jobs. In these circumstances, negotiation is more appropriate than resistance, and most government agents are encouraged to find collaborative mediated solutions rather than deal with them in the courts. Business people and environmental activists alike should explore this avenue first and exercise great caution before turning to the courts for relief.

Summary

Government agents

- Derive their power from statutes
- Powers consist of the right to create, apply, and enforce regulations that accomplish the goals of the legislation

Administrative tribunals

- Enforce policies and resolve disputes when private individuals challenge the regulations
- Act within the jurisdiction granted by the statute
- Comply with the terms of the *Charter of Rights and Freedoms*
- Have a duty to conduct a fair and unbiased hearing
- Follow the rules of Natural Justice
- Fair hearing with adequate notice

50. This seems to be the effect of the Supreme Court of Canada decision in *Delgamuukw v. British Columbia* [1997] 3 S.C.R. 1010

- Decision made by person who heard the evidence
- Process must be free of bias

Courts

- Review administrative decisions when there has been a failure to follow these rules
- Can apply sanctions by way of prerogative writs including *quo warranto* and prohibition
- Declaratory judgment and injunction

Privative clauses

- Statutory terms that attempt to prevent judicial review

Environmental protection

- Statutes designed to protect the environment are examples of government regulation and the administrative process
- Common laws, such as tort of nuisance, negligence, and riparian rights
- Both federal and provincial governments have jurisdiction
- Goals of statute law is to prohibit environmental offences; assess damage of proposed projects; levy fines and penalties for violations; and educate public and encourage good practices
- Resolving environmental conflicts by negotiation and incentives generally more effective than imposing administrative decisions and judicial remedies

---

QUESTIONS

1. Identify and describe the three different functions of government. Explain how the concept of supremacy of parliament affects how the three functions interrelate.

2. Describe the principle of the rule of law. Explain how it affects the exercise of government power.

3. What is meant by the term *ultra vires*, and how does it relate to federal and provincial legislation?

4. What is meant by the golden rule and the mischief rule? Under what circumstances can the courts apply these rules of statutory interpretation?

5. What is an administrative tribunal?

6. What obligations are placed on an adjudicative decision maker, even if not included in the legislation under which he or she is acting?

7. What three main elements constitute the rules of natural justice? Under what circumstances must a decision maker follow these rules of natural justice?

8. What requirements must be met for a person to receive a fair hearing?

9. Under what circumstances will judicial review be available?

10. Distinguish between *certiorari*, prohibition, *mandamus*, and declaratory judgment.

11. What is a privative clause? How do courts usually react to them?

12. Give examples of three different types of privative clauses.

13. What are some of the disadvantages of having a dispute resolved before an administrative tribunal?

14. What common law provisions protect the environment? Why was it necessary to pass new federal and provincial legislation?

15. What is the negative impact of these environmental statutes on business?

16. What is the extent of the power of the government officials who enforce environmental laws?

17. Explain the purpose of environmental assessment strategies.

18. What other processes are in place to encourage compliance?

19. How would you recommend that businesses deal with environmental issues and regulations?

CASES

1. Re Eastern Provincial Airways Ltd. and Canada Labour Relations Board et al.

During a labour dispute between the employer and the union, a series of events took place that led to charges by both sides of unfair labour practices. The Canada Labour Relations Board heard these complaints. The union's complaint was that the employer had failed to bargain in good faith, had interfered in the administration of a trade union, and had discriminated against, intimidated, and threatened striking employees. The employer's complaint was that the union had failed to bargain in good faith, and intimidation and coercion were used to get people to join or quit the union. After the union had put its case and after the employer had presented some of its evidence, the board declared that it had heard enough evidence and decided in favour of the union. The employer brought this action to have the decision of the board overturned.

Explain the nature of its complaint and the likely outcome. How would your answer be affected if the board gave the employer an opportunity to complete the presentation of evidence with the possibility that it might change its decision after the decision had been rendered?

2. Re Saskatchewan Oil and Gas Corporation and Leach et al.

Mr. and Mrs. Leach, the owners of a property on which Saskatchewan Oil and Gas Corporation operated an oil well had a dispute with the gas company over what Mr. and Mrs. Leach ought to be paid as compensation for a well site and access roadway on their property. In Saskatchewan, the owner of surface rights to property does not own the mineral and gas rights. Saskatchewan Oil and Gas Corporation had the right to develop the subsurface minerals and oil and was only required to pay suitable compensation for the disruption of the surface rights.

When such a disagreement takes place, the *Surface Rights Acquisition and Compensation Act* (R.S.S., 1978) provides for arbitration. This legislation gives broad powers to the arbitrator and great flexibility as far as what evidence can be heard. A hearing was held and evidence presented, but after the hearing was finished, the chairperson of the arbitration board wrote to a professional evaluator, Racine, for his opinion. Racine responded in the form of a letter. Neither the owners nor the operators were aware of the request to Racine nor of his use of the information in his response.

The owner challenged the arbitration award. What is the nature of the complaint? Explain the probable outcome.

3. Re Workers' Compensation Board of Nova Scotia and Cape Breton Development Corp.

Mr. Slade, an employee of Devco, allegedly fell down the stairs and suffered an incapacitating injury. When he made a claim to the Workers' Compensation Board, Devco objected, as permitted under the legislation. At the hearing, the tribunal said that it was going to follow its policy and common practice of not allowing the employer's lawyer to cross-examine Mr. Slade. They also refused to give the employer access to the medical examination reports that formed the basis of the decision. The employer refused to proceed and challenged the board in court.

Explain the arguments on both sides and the appropriate remedy. Would your answer relating to the disclosure of the confidential medical information be any different if you realized that the tribunal was relying on the following section?

> "No officer of the board and no person authorized to make an inquiry under this part shall divulge or allow to be divulged, except in the performance of his duties under the authority of the board, any information obtained by him or which has come to his knowledge in making or in connection with inspection or inquiry under this part."

4. Bailey v. Local Board of Health for Corporation of Township of Langley, McDonald, and Attorney General for British Columbia

Mr. McDonald owned property in the township of Langley on which he wanted to build. He brought an application before the medical health officer of the township (the petitioner in this action) for permission to build a conventional septic tank system. This request was turned down because of the disposal regulations passed under the *Health Act*. In October 1978, the council of the Township of Langley issued a building permit for the construction of a house on that property, provided McDonald obtained approval for the septic tank system from the medical health officer.

He proceeded to build, but instead of obtaining approval, McDonald sought an appeal of the medical health officer's refusal before the local board of health, which then held a hearing in several sessions. An election took place, and the makeup of the council changed after the first session. In subsequent sessions, some members were absent for part of the hearings, but all members of the council participated in the decision at the end. The decision was to permit the septic tank system over the medical health officer's objections.

The medical health officer appealed this decision in court. What is the nature of his complaint and the likely outcome of the action?

5. Regina v. Canadian Pacific Limited

The Canadian Pacific Railway Company is a transcontinental railway that falls under the legislative jurisdiction of parliament. Under the *Railway Act,* the railway is obligated to keep its right of way clear of dead grass and other unnecessary combustible matter.

To do so, on several occasions, the railway instituted what is called a full burn. This procedure produced a considerable amount of smoke, including obnoxious odours, which were offensive and caused discomfort to the people in the various towns along the tracks. The *Ontario Environmental Protection Act* prohibits such activities, and the railway was charged with violating the act.

Explain some of the arguments available to the railway in its defence and the likely outcome.

6. Bank of Montreal v. Lundrigans Ltd.

Lundrigans operated a series of businesses in Newfoundland, including interests in "road construction, civil engineering construction, building supply sales, mixed and pre-cast concrete production and sales, gypsum wallboard production, and sales and residential, commercial, and industrial real estate development." It was having financial difficulties and could not meet its obligations to the Bank of Montreal. The bank wished to appoint a receiver, but the receiver insisted that a clause be included in the court order stating that the receivers would not be personally liable for any environmental liability incurred.

Discuss whether the creditors and receivers appointed by them should be responsible for environmental damage and cleanup costs. Discuss the extent of this liability. In your answer, consider whether the receiver ought to be responsible for the continuing environmental problems that arise while they operate the business as a going concern in order to preserve its value.

The Fundamentals

Before dealing with the specialized legal relations and transactions that are the major focus of this text, it is necessary to understand the basic concepts and principles upon which they are built. These fundamentals are covered in Chapters 4 to 8. Chapter 4 is an examination of tort law, the basis of liability imposed on professional and business people for their wrongful conduct that causes injury to others. Chapters 5 to 8 examine the law of contract, including the requirements for a valid contract, problems that can arise between contracting parties, and how a contractual relationship ends. Most of the transactions and relationships discussed in the rest of the text are specialized forms of contracts with their own unique rules.

First Light/The Stock Market/Peter Beck

CHAPTER 4

Torts and Professional Liability

The law of torts involves private disputes decided in the civil courts. When one person harms another, either intentionally or carelessly, a tort has been committed, and an action can be brought seeking compensation for injuries suffered from the person who committed the wrong. In this chapter, we discuss the distinctions between intentional and negligent torts, the defences that the person being sued may raise, and the conditions that must be met for the plaintiff to be awarded compensation. Tort law is particularly important to business people who deal with the public, as they can erroneously give out advice to clients and others who may suffer losses when they rely on that advice. Professional and product liability, which are based primarily on the tort of negligence, and other types of business torts are a growing concern in our modern business environment.

Introduction

Vachon et al. v. Roy et al.[1]

While washing their truck at a service station, the parents of a four-year-old boy allowed him to play without supervision behind the station. There was an open cesspool there, which was unknown to the parents. It was unmarked, and its opening was flush with the ground. The boy fell in and, although rescued, became very ill, required hospitalization, and suffered significant physical problems as a result

1. (January 29, 1987) Doc. 4248/83 (Ont. Dist. Ct)

of the accident. The parents brought an action against both the oil company that owned the station and the operators who leased it. The judge found that the defendants were negligent and liable under the *Ontario Occupiers' Liability Act*, since they had known of the open cesspool. By doing nothing about it, they had failed to take reasonable steps to protect the little boy from its dangers.

When people engage in commercial activities, conflicting interests or simple interactions often lead to the commission of torts. It is difficult to find a wholly satisfactory definition for torts because of the different kinds of acts that may be considered tortious. Some general principles, however, do apply. A tort is committed when one person causes injury to another, harming their person, property, or reputation. The right to sue for compensation arises when the injurious conduct falls below a minimum social standard. A tort, then, is a social or civil wrong that must be distinguished from a crime or a breach of contract. The approach we use in this text is to look at different categories of torts, and though this is convenient, it can be somewhat misleading. It is convenient because different rules sometimes apply and different remedies are available. But it is misleading in that only some kinds of torts are dealt with here. The court may find a tort has been committed that does not conveniently fit into the identified categories. From a business perspective, it might be better to approach tort as one basic principle of law that provides remedies where wrongful conduct is involved. The discussion in the latter portion of the chapter related to professional liability does not deal with separate torts but is simply an application of the principles already discussed in the rest of the chapter, especially the law of negligence. Grouping the principles together under the topic of professional liability should be more helpful to business students.

> **A tort is a civil or social wrong**

Crimes must be distinguished from torts. Harmful conduct that is so serious that it poses a threat to society generally is said to be criminal in nature, and the prosecution for such acts is done by the state in a criminal court where the goal is to punish the wrongdoer, not to compensate the victim. A tort is considered a private matter where the victim of the injurious conduct sues the person responsible for the injury. With many crimes, the victim has the right to sue for tort, even if the prosecution results in an acquittal. Thus, wrongful conduct is often both a crime and a tort. Most of the torts discussed in this chapter have a *Criminal Code* counterpart. The O.J. Simpson trial is a good example. Although a jury acquitted him of murder, he was found liable in a subsequent civil action for the tort of causing wrongful death and had to compensate the relatives of the victims. It is much easier to successfully sue for tort because the standard of proof is based on a "balance of probabilities," while in a criminal action, the standard is "beyond a reasonable doubt," a much higher standard than required in a civil action.

> **Crimes are wrongs that affect society as a whole**

A tort must also be distinguished from a breach of contract. An act that breaches a contract may not be inherently wrong, but the contractual relationship makes the violation of its terms unacceptable. A tort, on the other hand, is inherently wrongful conduct that falls below a minimal social standard. When the victim sues, the court imposes the standard and determines who should bear the loss for the injuries suffered and also the amount that will adequately compensate the victim.

There are two major categories of tortious activity: intentional or deliberate acts and unintentional (careless) or negligent acts. Business people can find themselves in trouble over both intentional and unintentional torts, but the latter is, by far, the most important area of tort law for business people and professionals to understand. One important difference between deliberate torts and negligence is in the remedies that the courts are willing to grant to the injured party. When the interference has been

> **Torts may involve intentional or inadvertent conduct**

intentional, the courts may be persuaded to grant punitive damages in addition to the more common general and special damages. **Special damages** are awarded to cover actual expenses and calculable losses and **general damages** are the estimated costs of incalculable factors, such as pain and suffering. **Punitive** or **exemplary damages** are designed to punish the wrongdoer and do not relate to the injury suffered. To avoid excessive awards, the Supreme Court of Canada has put an upper limit of approximately $250 000 that can be awarded to compensate for pain and suffering and loss of enjoyment of life. Occasionally, the court will also order the return of property or an injunction to stop some offending activity.

What should a business consider?

Perhaps the most valuable thing to gain from the study of tort law, or any of the rules discussed in this text for that matter, is the habit of mind that anticipates and avoids legal problems. This is called risk avoidance or risk management. Business people have a responsibility to manage their legal affairs in the same way they manage the production, marketing, and distribution of their products. Too often, managers wait for something to go wrong, then put the matter into the hands of a lawyer, and wait for the results of a lawsuit. Managing responsibly means avoiding the problem in the first place. As you learn about torts and other aspects of the law, you might observe the conditions and practices that pose a danger to the public, customers, suppliers, or employees and decide how they should be corrected. This might be as simple as checking the credit-worthiness of customers, keeping a record of e-mails, putting a warning sticker on a plate glass window, or lighting a darkened stairwell. Business people should adopt an attitude of risk avoidance to reduce exposure to costly and time-consuming legal actions.

Employer may be vicariously liable for employees' torts

It is important for business people to keep the concept of **vicarious liability** in mind while studying tort law. An employer can be held liable for the tortious act an employee commits while at work. This liability is limited to torts committed while carrying out employment duties. The employer will not be vicariously liable when the employee is off doing his or her own thing during working hours. The importance of vicarious liability in the business world cannot be overemphasized. A detailed examination of the master/servant (employer/employee) relationship and vicarious liability can be found in Chapter 11. Several provinces have imposed vicarious liability by statute on the owners of motor vehicles, making them liable for damage and injury caused by the people they allow to drive their cars.

Intentional Torts

Assault and Battery

Bruce v. Coliseum Management Ltd. et al.[2]

Jeffery Bruce was a 22-year-old college student at the time that he went with a friend to a local nightclub. While there, after consuming a moderate amount of beer, he and his friend got into a friendly tussle. Unfortunately, the doorman in the club saw this as a fight and ordered the two off the premises. The friend left quietly, but Bruce put up a struggle. He verbally abused the bouncer, swore, and resisted eviction. Finally, he was forced out onto a second story balcony, and after continued resistance, the bouncer pushed him in the chest causing him to fall backwards down the stairs. Bruce broke his kneecap causing serious pain and suffering. The court found that even in the face of the provocation, the doorman had used excessive

2. 165 D.L.R. (4th) 472, (B.C.C.A.)

force. While the provocation did not justify the excessive use of force, it did mitigate the damages awarded, which were considerable. Bruce was awarded $50 000 special damages and, on appeal, a further $40 000 general damages. The award was reduced by 30 percent because of the provocation.

This case shows how careful commercial establishments must be in who they hire and how the staff are trained. In the face of this kind of provocation, only a saint could have kept his composure, and still, the employee and the business, because of the principle of vicarious liability, were responsible for the excessive force used.

Assault and battery (or **trespass to person**) is the intentional physical interference with another person. This tort is an important consideration for business people who serve the public. An action that makes a person think they are about to be struck is an assault. If someone fakes a punch, points a gun, or picks up a stone to threaten another person, an assault has been committed. A battery takes place when someone is in actual physical contact with another person. Since battery almost invariably involves an assault, the term "assault" is often used to refer to both assault and battery. Assault and battery are actionable, even where there is no injury; "the least touching of another in anger is battery."[3]

Intentional physical interference

Fear of contact—assault

Actual contact—battery

The test to determine whether an assault has taken place is to look to the victim and ask if they were fearful or anticipated unwanted physical contact. The contact might be anything from a physical blow, unwanted medical treatment, or a kiss. The motive or good will of the person attacking is not relevant. The words, as well as the gestures and actions, are taken into consideration. A person walking towards another can be an assault when accompanied by threatening words, whereas the words "How nice to see you again" remove the threat.

Intent to harm not required

Defences

There are several defences that can be raised to an assault claim. Normally, doctors escape liability for their actions, when operating on or otherwise treating patients, through the principle of **consent**. Essentially, a person who consents, either expressly or by implication, to conduct that which would otherwise constitute an assault or battery loses the right to sue. This is the reason injured boxers cannot sue their opponents.

Consent is a defence

It is important to remember, however, that the level of interference cannot exceed the consent. Excessive violence in a hockey game or other sporting activity will constitute a battery despite the consent. Also, the consent must be informed consent; people must know what they are consenting to. People may refuse or give only limited consent to medical treatment. Followers of a certain religion, for example, refuse blood transfusions. If this is made clear to a doctor and he administers the refused treatment anyway, even where the patient would die without it, he can be sued for the battery he has committed.[4]

Self-defence can also be raised to counteract an assault and battery accusation. The law entitles people who are being attacked to use as much force as is necessary to defend themselves. The test is reasonable force. An attack is not a license to respond with unrestrained violence. Of course, the experience of the person being attacked will be taken into account in determining what is reasonable. Thus, a boxer is held to a higher standard than an ordinary person not accustomed to such violence.

Reasonable force to defend permitted

3. Cole v. Turner (1705) 87 E.R. 907 (K.B.)

4. This right may not extend to others within their care. When parents refuse treatment needed to save the lives of their children for religious reasons, the courts are often willing to interfere by taking custody of the children away from the parents and ordering treatment.

Reasonable force permitted to eject trespasser

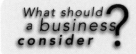

When ejecting an unruly patron, the same principle applies. If a patron refuses to leave when asked, he becomes a trespasser, and reasonable force can be used to eject him.

In one case, a bartender removed a drunken patron and then, in the alley, struck him in the face when he thought he was about to be hit, causing serious injury to the patron.[5] This was excessive force. The state of the patron was such that the blow was not necessary. He posed no threat and was out of the establishment. The importance of careful training of employees with respect to how to interact with customers and the public cannot be overemphasized. When faced with shoplifting, fraud, and other improper conduct, employees must know what they can and cannot do, in order to protect the business from the possibility of devastating lawsuits. The courts may be somewhat sympathetic to the plight of businesses when faced with the considerable losses caused by shoplifting, fraud, and other wrongs committed by customers, but they have to protect the rights of people who have done nothing wrong from assault, intimidation, or improper restraint. The damages awarded are based not only on what the employee has done but also the plaintiff's status in the community and any injury they might have suffered. This can be out of all proportion to any loss suffered by the business by the alleged wrongdoing.

Trespass to Land

On land without authority

Trespass can be indirect

Trespass to land involves going onto another person's property without having either the lawful right or the owner's permission to do so. Such a trespass is an actionable wrong, even when no damage or injury takes place and even if the intruder does not know they were trespassing. Ignorance of the location of the property line is no excuse. Only if the intruder had no control of where they were would there be a defence. Thus, if they were struck by a car and thrown on the property, there would be no trespass. But if they were running away and went on the property to escape a threat, it is still a trespass, and they would be responsible for any damage caused. Trespass can also take place indirectly. When a person throws some item on another's property, a trespass has taken place.

People acting in an official capacity, such as postal workers, meter readers, municipal inspectors, and the police, have the right to come on private property and are not trespassing. In shopping malls and other premises where the public is welcome, there is an implied right to be there, even where the visitor has not come to shop. Permission is also implied when visitors have been allowed on the property over time without steps being taken to remove them. If such visitors become unruly or dangerous to other patrons, they can be asked to leave. If they refuse, they become trespassers, and reasonable force can be used to eject them.

McLachlan v. Canadian Imperial Bank of Commerce et al.[6]

Mr. McLachlan operated Kay Motors Ltd., a business that had been in operation for some 30 years before suffering its first loss. The company had two demand loans with the CIBC, one an operating line of credit and the other chattel mortgages on their inventory of new cars. Mr. McLachlan was called into the bank by the manager and there presented with a demand that the loans be repaid. One hour later, Mr. Topley, an employee of a company hired by the bank, attended at the car lot and seized all the property, including the building, land, cars, tools, and equipment, as

5. Cottreau v. Rodgerson (1965) 53 D.L.R. (2d) 549 (N.S.S.C.)

6. 1989 57 D.L.R. (4th) 687, (B.C.C.A.)

authorized under the *Bank Act*. He even seized a fleet of cars belonging to Budget rental cars. A few days later, Mr. McLachlan was able to arrange funds to pay the operating line of credit, but Mr. Topley refused to take the money, demanding that all outstanding funds be paid. Because the premises and assets had been taken over, the business failed, and an action was brought for trespass to chattels and trespass to land. It was argued that the one-hour notice to pay was completely unreasonable and, therefore, there was no right to seize the business. While the court agreed, it did not base its decision on this ground. The chattel mortgage for the new cars was a separate deal between GM and the bank and should not have been included in this process. In effect, the bank already owned these cars, and so, they could not be used to justify the seizure of the other property. When Mr. McLachlan presented the funds to pay off the operating line of credit, that ended Mr. Topley's authority to be on the premises, and his continued control of the business became a trespass both to the chattels involved and to the land. The damages ordered, based on the value of the business as a going concern as of the date of the seizure, were substantial, and even punitive damages were awarded. This case shows how careful we have to be in exercising what we think are our rights in these kinds of transactions.

Trespassers who cause damage while on private property bear responsibility for any injury or loss caused, whether it was foreseeable or not. A trespasser who is injured while on the property generally has no claim against the occupier. Provincial occupier's liability acts only require the occupier of property not to willfully or recklessly cause harm to a trespasser or someone on the property for a criminal purpose. Children are often not considered trespassers in these circumstances, having been enticed to enter by some attractive feature on the property.

Occupier's Liability Act

Trespass can also involve a permanent incursion onto the property of another. This is referred to as a continuing trespass and can take the form a building or other structure that encroaches on the property of another. Where multi-storied buildings are involved, the costs of correcting the problem can be enormous.

Injunction available to remedy continuing trespass

In the case of *Gross v. Wright*,[7] the owners of two adjoining properties agreed to establish a common wall on the property line. The wall was to be 24 inches (0.6 metres) at its base and taper evenly on both properties as it went up several stories. The builder put the taper on only one side and so the wall at the top was entirely on the property of the neighbour in violation of the agreement. In the resulting action, the court decided that there was a continuing trespass and ordered that the problem be corrected. The court suspended the operation of the injunction to give the defendant time to make adjustments so that the wall would conform to the agreement.

False Imprisonment

False imprisonment including false arrest occurs when people are intentionally restrained against their will and the person doing the restraining has no lawful authority to do so. This may be in the form of complete imprisonment, where the person is held in a cell or room, or may take the form of an arrest. In either case, the person must be completely restrained without a ready means of escape. Even a person who submits to authority or threat can be considered imprisoned, since in

Restraint without lawful excuse—false imprisonment

Submission to authority can constitute imprisonment

7. [1923] 2 D.L.R. 171 (S.C.C.)

their minds, they have been restrained. The second requirement is that the restraint be unlawful. When a security guard arrests someone found shoplifting, there has been no false imprisonment. Generally, a private person has the power to make an arrest, but only when they find someone in the process of committing a crime, such as shoplifting.

Imprisonment false—where no authority

Bahner v. Marwest Hotel Company Ltd., Muir et al.[8]

This case is typical of the kind of problems faced by restaurants, hotels, and retail stores. The defendant, a patron in a Vancouver restaurant, was unfamiliar with the provincial liquor laws when he ordered and obtained a bottle of wine shortly before 11:30 p.m. When Mr. Bahner discovered just before midnight that he had to consume the wine in only the few minutes remaining, he left it and refused to pay for it. He paid for the meal but not the wine, and when he attempted to leave, he was detained by the manager and a security guard until the police arrived. Mr. Bahner was arrested and spent the night in jail. The court held that he had been falsely imprisoned twice, once at the restaurant and once by the police. Although there was a way to escape at the restaurant, he had submitted to the authority of the security guard. The judge said, "The plaintiff, commanded by the security officer to stay and prevented by the officer from leaving by the ordinary exit, behaved with admirable restraint in making no forcible attempt to pass the security officer. After what the officer had said and done, he could reasonably expect to be restrained by force if he tried to leave by any exit, and he was not required to make an attempt to run away."[9] The court also found that the imprisonment was without authority. There was no right to arrest here because no criminal act had taken place. There was a dispute as to whether the wine should be paid for, and if the proprietor wanted to, he could have sued for breach of contract. Only where it is clear that a patron is trying to sneak out without paying can he be restrained. Because these facts were known to the police when they arrested Mr. Bahner, their action constituted a second false arrest, which was also actionable. Although police have broader powers of arrest, because they knew the facts, they could not show that they had "reasonable and probable grounds" to suppose a crime had been committed.

Punitive damages may be available for false imprisonment

The court went further and awarded the victim punitive damages. Normally, in a tort action, the courts will only order one party to pay damages to compensate the other for his loss. This is one of the few situations where a court will award damages to punish the perpetrator to discourage them from doing it again.

This, like most such cases, was an instance where the legal costs and judgment overwhelmed the few dollars that would have been lost had the employees not detained the customer.

A charge of false imprisonment is a significant risk for any business involved in serving the public, including restaurants, hotels, retail stores, and bars. This risk is especially strong when, either because of store policy or inexperienced staff, customers are detained whenever they are suspected of wrongdoing. It may be well for managers to discourage their employees from apprehending shoplifters, since the potential loss from goods stolen is far outweighed by the danger of losing a false imprisonment action. This is one area in which training of staff to know when they can detain a person and when they cannot is a well-justified expense.

8. (1969) 6 D.L.R. (3d) 322 (B.C.S.C); aff'd (1970) 12 D.L.R. (3d) 646 (B.C.C.A.)
9. *Ibid.*, p. 325–326

Private Nuisance

This tort is committed when an individual or business uses property in such a way that it interferes with a neighbour's use or enjoyment of their property. Such interference is usually ongoing and continuous. When a commercial building, such as a mill, is built near a residential neighbourhood, and the resulting odour and noise interfere with the neighbours' enjoyment of their yards, it is appropriate for them to sue for nuisance. Such an action is only possible where the property is being used in an unusual or unreasonable way, and the problem caused must be a direct consequence of this unusual activity. A person living in an industrial section of a city cannot complain when a factory begins operating in the neighbourhood and emits noise, smoke, and dust. Nor could the residents of a rural area complain about the normal odours associated with farming.

Private nuisance—use of property interferes with neighbour

Normally, the properties would need to be in close proximity for private nuisance to apply and for a nuisance action to be brought. However, in an Alberta case, a telephone was used to harass a resident on the other side of the city, interfering with the enjoyment of their property. The court found this to be a private nuisance, even though they were miles apart.[10] It is quite likely that we will see similar nuisance cases in the future arising from abuses of fax transmissions and other forms of electronic communications.

Private nuisance at a distance

Untangling the WEB

Thus, electronic mail transmissions from advertisers or purveyors of indecent materials or computer viruses that become so prevalent that people are unwilling to open their e-mail boxes, let alone read their contents, will increasingly be the basis of actionable nuisances in the future.

It must also be noted that for a private nuisance to be actionable, the consequences must be reasonably foreseeable to the defendant. Reasonable foreseeability is discussed in the section on Negligence. And because nuisance often involves offending substances, it is one of the few common law tools that can be used to enforce environmental protection.

Noise and Fumes Are Nuisance

The plaintiff operated a motel adjacent to some lands that Ontario Hydro had leased to the defendants, who operated an amusement business that consisted of a racecourse for scaled-down versions of Grand Prix racing cars. The noise from the motors and screeching tires as the cars raced around the track was constant during the summer season from 11:00 a.m. until 11:00 p.m. The court found that this constituted a nuisance and awarded damages to the plaintiff and granted an injunction. The court deemed that this was an unusual use of the property. Both the noise and the air pollution generated from the activity were out of keeping with what was normally expected from the area.

Banfai v. Formula Fun Centre Inc. (1984) 19 D.L.R. (4th) 683 (Ont. H.C.)

10. Motherwell v. Motherwell (1976) 73 D.L.R. (3d) 62 (Alta C.A.)

Defamation

Hiltz and Seamone Co. v. Nova Scotia (Attorney General)[11]

Hiltz and Seamone is an engineering company that builds sewage treatment plants in Nova Scotia. It designed and built a particular installation to serve a small subdivision, and when came the time to expand the subdivision, permission to expand the treatment plant was also needed. Plans and approvals were required, and when a newly appointed government engineer inspected the present facilities, she was critical of the work done. A consultant was hired to do a report, and that report, along with a letter attached to it by the government engineer, and subsequent correspondence critical of the company, became the subject of this defamation action. The letter was critical of what had been done and contained a note suggesting that another specified firm could do a better job. The government engineer and her supervisor wrote another letter justifying the position taken and further criticizing the company. These letters were sent to the municipality, made available to the public, and caused the company the loss of a considerable amount of business. The court found both letters to be defamatory and refused the defences raised, including qualified privilege. Although this was an occasion of qualified privilege, that privilege was lost because of the malice present in the subsequent correspondence. The court found that the engineer and the supervisor knew that the statements included in the correspondence were false. They engaged in other conduct to justify their actions, including persuading the municipality to demolish the original treatment facility. All this was taken into consideration by the judge in awarding significant general and punitive damages. Great care must be taken in business communications, especially where the comments are critical of the competence or performance of other professionals.

Detrimental false statement

Defamation is a published false statement about a person to their detriment. It is a primary concern for businesses involved in media communications. But all commercial enterprises face some risk over defamation, even if it is only from a carelessly worded letter of reference. For the statement to be an actionable defamation, it must be derogatory, false, published, and refer to the plaintiff. If the false statement causes people to avoid or shun someone, it is derogatory. In the *Youssoupoff* case, Lord Justice Scrutton said that a statement was defamatory if it was "a false statement about a man to his discredit."[12] A complementary statement about a person, even if it is false, is not defamation. Thus, if a manager were to say of an employee that he was the best worker in the plant, it would not be actionable even if false. Once the plaintiff establishes that the derogatory statement was made, he need not prove it was false. This is assumed, and it is up to the defendant to prove the truth if he can. If the statement can be shown to be true, it is an absolute defence to a defamation action.[13]

For a statement to be actionable, it must be clear that it refers to the person suing. Thus, a general negative reference to a group, such as the faculty or student body of a university, will not qualify.

11. (1999) 172 D.L.R. (4th) 488 (N.S.C.A.).

12. Youssoupoff v. Metro-Goldwyn-Mayer Pictures Ltd. (1934) 50 T.L.R. 581 at 584 (C.A.).

13. Elliott v. Freison et al. (1982) 136 D.L.R. (3d) 281 (Ont. H.C.); aff'd (1984) 6 D.L.R. (4th) 388 (Ont. C.A.); leave to appeal refused (1984) 6 D.L.R. (4th) 388 n (S.C.C.).

It is not possible to defame a dead person; however, it is possible to defame a corporation, which is a person in the eyes of the law, and it is possible to defame a product.

When the CBC on their Marketplace program were critical of a particular brand of paint because of its mercury content, they inaccurately implied that it was the same kind of mercury as that which had been associated with disastrous pollution problems in Japan. Color Your World Corp. was able to successfully sue and was awarded $85 000 for their damaged reputation.[14]

For the false statement to be actionable, it must be published. In this sense, "to publish" means that the statement had to be communicated to a third party. Publication could have occurred in a newspaper, in the broadcast media, on the Internet, or simply by word of mouth. It is sufficient publication if just one other person hears or reads the defamatory statement.

Statement must be published

Another important factor to consider is that statements often contain **innuendo**, which is an implied or hidden meaning. A statement may appear perfectly innocent on the surface but, when combined with other information, it may take on a different meaning. It is no excuse to say that the person making the statement thought it was true or did not know of the special facts that created the innuendo. Such a mistake is no defence, and the offending party can be held liable for the defamatory remark.

Innuendo

Mistake no excuse

In the case of *E. Hulton & Co. v. Jones*,[15] a newspaper published a fictitious story lampooning the double standards of the English upper-middle class. They created a fictitious character called Artemus Jones, who led a pious life in England but an immoral one when he vacationed in France. Unfortunately for them, there really was an Artemus Jones who fit the description and sued. Even though the author and publishers had no idea of Mr. Jones' existence, he succeeded in the action against them.

Libel and Slander

Defamation can be either libel, which is written defamation, or slander, which is spoken defamation. The significance of finding a defamatory remark to be libelous rather than slanderous is that libel is easier to prove because there is no requirement to show that out-of-pocket losses have been sustained. Libel is seen to be more deliberate, more premeditated, and also more permanent than slander, thus causing more harm. While defamation is primarily governed by common law, most provinces have passed statutes modifying those common law provisions to satisfy the needs of a modern society. It is becoming apparent, however, that these statutes will need even more modification to take into account the new problems associated with libel and slander on the Internet. The first is to determine what broadcast means and whether Internet publications should be considered as written libel or spoken slander. Messages on the Internet are text based but often produced spontaneously and are temporary in nature. It is often difficult to trace the original source of the defamation because it is so easily copied and transferred by intermediate parties. Nevertheless, the injury caused by such transmission of defamatory information can be extensive. Another problem is that in a traditional communication environment, there is usually a broadcaster or publisher that can be held responsible for the damaging words, but in online communication, there is often no intermediary who checks and authorizes material, nor is there any clear way of determining just how far the message has been spread.

Libel written/slander spoken

Legislation and the Internet

14. Color Your World Corp. v. Canadian Broadcasting Corp. 17 O.R. (3d) 308 (Ont. Gen. Div.); reversed on appeal (1997) 41 C.C.L.T. (2d) 11 (Ont. C.A.)

15. [1910] 26 T.L.R. 128 (House of Lords)

Untangling the WEB

In an Ontario case, a university professor's claim for wrongful dismissal was complicated by the fact that his supervisors sent their highly critical performance evaluation and termination letter to all the professors in the institution via e-mail. The court found that the plaintiff had grounds for a defamation suit as well against his superiors.[16] Electronic messaging does provide a media for disseminating defamatory remarks, and it presents the added difficulty of allowing the originator of the comments to remain anonymous by using a name other than his or her own. This raises the question of whether Internet service providers should be held liable for the part they play in transmitting such messages. As these problems continue to manifest themselves, we expect to see changes in legislation and our courts' decisions influenced by cases being heard in the United States, where such claims are being exercised more quickly and frequently.

Defences

Truth is an absolute defence

Once it has been established that a defamatory statement has been made, several defences are available to the defendant. Truth, sometimes called the **defence of justification**, is an absolute defence. But even when a statement is technically true, it can still be derogatory if it contains an innuendo or if it is capable of being interpreted as referring to another person about whom the statement is false.

Absolute privilege

The second defence is called **absolute privilege**. Anything discussed as part of parliamentary debate on the floor of the legislature, parliament, or in government committees and statements made in a trial cannot give rise to a defamation action, no matter how malicious, scandalous, or derogatory they are. The most significant defence for business people is called **qualified privilege**. When a statement is made pursuant to a duty or special interest, there is no action for defamation so long as the statement was made honestly, without malice, and only circulated to those having a right to know. A manager reporting to a superior about the performance of a worker and members of a professional organization discussing the performance of an officer of that organization would be instances protected by qualified privilege. When a manager sends a defamatory e-mail specifically to one interested party or a limited group of interested addressees, there can still be qualified privilege if the other requirements are met. But where the same message is sent to a web site or chat line that anyone has access to, the publication would likely be too broad and the defence of qualified privilege would be lost.

Qualified privilege, requires duty

Fair comment

The final defence available in the field of defamation is the defence of **fair comment**. When people put their work before the public, as with movies, plays, artwork, books, and the like, they invite public criticism and run the risk that the opinions expressed may not be complimentary. Even where these opinions amount to a vicious attack and may be unreasonable, they cannot sue for defamation. The defence raised here is fair comment. Public figures are also open to such criticism. To successfully use this defence, the critic or editorial writer must be able to show that what was said was a matter of opinion, drawn from true facts that were before the public, and it was not motivated by malice or some ulterior motive. A food critic expressing a negative opinion of a restaurant and a theatre critic attacking a play or movie are examples of fair comment. The same defence should apply where a play, photograph, or musical performance is put on the Internet and made available to a wide audience.

16. Egerton v. Finucan (1995) 55 A.C.W.S. (3d) 1089 (Ont. Gen. Div.), cited in *Canadian Business Law Journal*, Vol. 32, No. 1, p. 24

As mentioned above, many jurisdictions have passed legislations summarizing and, in many cases, significantly modifying common law as it relates to defamation. When the defamatory statement is made in the media, most jurisdictions significantly reduce the damages that can be recovered if an adequate apology is made soon after the defamation was published or broadcast.

Apology reduces damages

In those situations where the act does not apply, when defamation is proven, the damages can be substantial because the courts will not only compensate the victim for actual losses as well as for a damaged reputation but will, in fact, go farther, awarding damages to rehabilitate the victim's reputation. For this reason, the Supreme Court of Canada upheld a decision to award a government employee defamed by a church $1.6 million in damages, far in excess of what would be awarded for general damages in a normal tort action.[17]

Significant damages available

Untangling the WEB

The Internet provides direct and inexpensive access to a massive audience and with it the opportunity to defame. Most often, there is no intervention (editor or publisher) to monitor the communication. The question again is which rules will apply. If the Internet is a broadcaster, then such defamation would be subject to the rules of libel, since in Canada, most broadcast defamation has been made libel by statute. If the information is in the form of a newspaper or journal, the rules of libel will still apply, but if the communication is verbal and between two individuals, as in a phone conversation, the defamation may only be treated as slander. In fact, many argue that Internet communications ought to be the subject of specialized rules or no rules at all. Another question is raised as to whom an injured party can sue. If the author is known, he or she may be in another jurisdiction. If the author of the defamatory comment is unknown or uses a false name, can the service provider be sued for defamation? Even though the court can force the service provider to identify the author, this may not be helpful where they are in a different jurisdiction or without resources. But others may also be responsible for the dissemination of the information. It may have originated as an e-mail message to a specific person and been intercepted. It has been established that a service provider who fails to remove offensive material after it has become apparent can be held responsible. American cases suggest that when the service provider has no editorial control and is merely the distributor of the information, they will not be held liable. It is likely that these intermediaries will be liable for the defamation only if they encouraged the offending behaviour or they knew or ought to have known of it and failed to remove it once they knew of its existence.

Privacy

The laws relating to intentional torts generally protect people who are harmed by another's deliberate actions, and the courts have been willing to expand common law to include new technologies, even when the method of committing the tort was not in existence when the common law principle was established.[18] We can expect that the general body of tort law will also be expanded to include new forms of wrongs committed over the Internet.

Breach of privacy, however, is an area not recognized as a common law tort, and it is likely that protecting such violations of a person's or business's privacy will be beyond common law to provide a remedy. Private information that is exchanged in a commercial transaction over the Internet and then without consent is used again or sold to another company for another purpose is just one of the ways this problem is manifested. The new *Personal Information Protection and Electronic Documents Act* regulates the collection and use of personal information, requiring

Privacy protection found only in statutes

17. Hill v. Church of Scientology of Toronto [1995] 2 S.C.R. 1130
18. Motherwell v. Motherwell [1976] 6 W.W.R. (Alta. S.C.) p. 551.

organizations to account for their activities, identify the purposes for which it the information is being collected, inform and get the consent of the individuals involved, and limit the use, disclosure, and retention of the information. They would have to ensure the accuracy of the information, protect it with security safeguards, and be open about its policies and practices relating to the management of the information. The act requires that organizations make available to individuals, upon request, the nature of the information and how it is being used. It also outlines how an individual would proceed to have a complaint reviewed and empowers a privacy commissioner appointed for the purpose to impose fines for violations.[19]

The Ontario Ministry of Consumer and Commercial Relations has seen the number of consumer complaints in e-commerce increase exponentially and have acted on a number of recommendations to help protect consumers.[20] Governments still face the seemingly insurmountable challenge of enforcing new regulations because of the borderless nature of the Internet. The challenge is to encourage retailers to regulate themselves because if one country makes the rules too harsh, businesses will simply set up elsewhere to avoid those rules. This is another area where international treaties may make an important contribution.

The *Personal Information Protection and Electronic Documents Act*[21] has attached as part of the act and given statutory standing to the Code of the Canadian Standards Association (CSA), entitled the Model Code for the Protection of Personal Information. It sets out 10 privacy protection principles. The CSA Code was approved as a national standard by the Standards Council of Canada and was published in 1996. The act applies to federal agencies initially, then after three years to provinces as well, unless the provinces have similar legislation already in place. A federal privacy commissioner will enforce the provisions of the act. The European Community enacted legislation to protect privacy in this area some time ago, and the passage of this act provides similar protection here, removing a major barrier that threatened to interfere with international business.

Another problem relating to privacy is the unauthorized interception of communications between individuals. While most sites where important information is transferred have encryption devices, determined hackers can break those codes. If the codes become too sophisticated, then governments which make use of this information in their surveillance activities cannot decode the information and so are reluctant to allow advanced encryption. This creates a serious dilemma.

Computer users often insert links to a competitor's web site that then can be made to appear as their own. They also can employ "cookies," which are embedded devices that allow the tracking of a user's Internet activities, allowing them to read private information. When an individual's browsing on the Internet is tracked in this way, the information may be used by the service-provider to improve their service, but it may also be sold to retailers for marketing purposes or used to incriminate a person who has been downloading and inappropriately using sites.

The new act will require that notice and consent be given before private information can be collected as well as disclosure as to how the information will be used. Individuals will also gain the right to check for accuracy of the information collected and to determine that the information is secure and not being used for other purposes. Again, the problem is enforcement. Studies have shown that voluntary privacy protection has been poor, with many businesses secretly collecting

19. Bill C-6 S.C (2000)
20. *National Post*, Aug. 11, 2000, p. A2.
21. Bill C-6 S.C (2000)

and using personal information. Secret surveillance of computer users is a major problem, especially in the work environment, where it seems that employers have the right to read employees' e-mails and monitor their use of the Internet on their office computers.

Negligence

Crocker v. Sundance Northwest Resorts Ltd.[22]

Mr. Crocker and his friend went to Sundance Resorts, and one evening, after a day of skiing, they were at a bar, where they saw a video of an inner-tube race that was part of the activities associated with an event called the Sundance Spring Carnival. The race was run on the regular ski slopes in a section where there were "moguls" that caused the tubes and the people on them to bounce around like "rag dolls." A videotape of the event showed the contestants "falling off these tubes, being bounced off, releasing their grip, chasing after the tubes," and generally having what was described by another contestant as a "blast." The event was put on by the defendants, the operators of the ski slope.

The plaintiff, Mr. Crocker, signed up for the race, and in the process, he signed, without reading, a release absolving the ski slope operators of all responsibility for any injuries he might suffer as a result of the race. Mr. Crocker and his friend, in a festive mood, went down the slope once, with only minor injury, and won their heat. By the second heat, it was clear that Mr. Crocker had been drinking, and the manager of the facility suggested that he not go down the hill. In fact, Mr. Crocker had not only had a couple drinks at the bar but also had been given two large swallows of brandy by the driver of a beer van. In the next race, Mr. Crocker fell off the tube and broke his neck, which rendered him a quadriplegic.

The Supreme Court had to decide whether Sundance should be responsible for Mr. Crocker's foolish conduct and, if so, to what extent. It had to determine just what nature of duty was owed by Sundance to Mr. Crocker and the other contestants. The court determined that a clearly dangerous competition was established for commercial gain. There was a duty of care towards visibly intoxicated participants, who are obviously susceptible to more damage and more potential injury than the normal person. Sundance had an obligation to take all reasonable steps to keep Mr. Crocker from competing in his inebriated state. Although Mr. Crocker was told he should not proceed, not only did Sundance fail to prevent him from competing but also, when he dropped his inner tube, they provided him with another. This clearly breached their duty of care towards Mr. Crocker, and so negligence on the part of Sundance was established.

The court then determined that Mr. Crocker had contributed to his own loss by his own negligence, and under the statute in place in Ontario, the court apportioned the blame assessing Mr. Crocker at 25 percent responsible, reducing the judgment accordingly.

The case not only illustrates the requirements of a duty of care and the reasonable person test in determining the nature of that duty but also illustrates the defence of contributory negligence and voluntary assumption of risk. In this case, it was argued that Mr. Crocker put himself voluntarily into a position of danger and, in the process, assumed the risk, which would completely bar the negligence action on his part. The court pointed out that the principle of voluntarily assuming

22. [1998] 1 S.C.R. 1186

the risk has been restricted in recent times to such an extent that it had to be clear that Mr. Crocker not only assumed the physical risk but absolved Sundance of any legal responsibility for anything that happened. In fact, Mr. Crocker had signed a waiver to that effect, but the court said it was meaningless, since he had not read it.

Negligence—careless conduct causing another injury

Negligence is by far the most important area of tort liability for business people and professionals. It involves inadvertent or unintentional careless conduct causing injury or damage to another person or their property. The main problem for the court is to determine what standard of care was required of the defendant and whether there was a failure to meet that standard.

The Reasonable Person Test

Reasonable person test establishes standard

The reasonable person test is used by the court in many areas of law to establish standards of socially acceptable behaviour. Faced with the problem of having to decide if certain conduct is socially acceptable, the judge or members of the jury simply ask themselves, "What would a reasonably prudent person, in possession of all the facts of the case, have done in this situation?"

Reasonably prudent is better than average

It is important to understand that the standard determined using the reasonable person test is not what would be expected of an average person. A reasonable person is expected to be particularly careful, a level of behaviour considerably better than average. On the other hand, the conduct is not required to be perfect.

An analogy can be made to par in a golf game. A standard score is set for each hole on the course called par. If par for a particular hole is three, the average golfer would likely score 4 or 5. On the other hand, 3 is not the best possible score. Rather, par is the score you would expect from a good golfer playing well. Similarly, the reasonable person test represents the standard of care expected from a prudent person who is being careful. The reasonable person test has a particularly important role to play in negligence.

Determining the Existence of a Duty

Negligence involves a failure on someone's part to live up to a duty to be careful to someone else. We do not have a duty to be careful to everyone. The court must determine whether a duty of care was owed by the defendant to the plaintiff. The court uses the reasonable foreseeability test, a variant of the reasonable person test, to determine the existence of such a duty. If it were reasonably foreseeable that the conduct complained of would cause harm to the plaintiff, a duty to be careful exists. It seems almost self-evident today that we should act carefully towards people that we can see are put at risk by our behaviour, but this was not always the case.

Reasonable foreseeability test establishes duty

Donoghue v. Stevenson[23]

The reasonable foreseeability test was developed in *Donoghue v. Stevenson*, one of the most significant cases of the 20th century. Two women went into a café where one ordered a bottle of ginger beer for her friend, Mrs. Donoghue. After consuming some of it, Mrs. Donoghue discovered part of a decomposed snail at the bottom of

23. [1932] A.C. 562 (H.L.)

her bottle. She became very ill as a result of drinking the contaminated beverage. In the process of suing, she discovered that she had some serious problems. She could not successfully sue the café that had supplied the ginger beer for breach of contract; she had no contract with the establishment, as her friend had made the purchase. Similarly, she could not successfully sue the café for negligence, since they had done nothing wrong, the ginger beer having been bottled in an opaque container and served to her in the bottle. Her only recourse was to sue the manufacturer for negligence in producing the product, but the bottler claimed they owed her no duty to be careful. The court had to determine whether a duty to be careful was owed by the manufacturer to the consumer of their product. In the process of finding that such a duty was owed, the House of Lords developed the reasonable foreseeability test. Lord Atkin, one of the judges in the case, made the following classic statement when discussing how to determine to whom we owe a duty:

> "The rule that you are to love your neighbour becomes in law, you must not injure your neighbour; and the lawyer's question 'Who is my neighbour?' receives a restricted reply. You must take reasonable care to avoid acts or omissions which you can reasonably foresee would be likely to injure your neighbour. Who, then, in law, is my neighbour? The answer seems to be—persons who are so closely and directly affected by my act that I ought reasonably to have them in contemplation as being so affected when I am directing my mind to the acts or omissions which are called in question."[24]

We owe a duty, then, to anyone we can reasonably anticipate might be harmed by our conduct. The reasonable foreseeability test has been further refined in the British *Anns* case[25] The *Anns* case created a two-stage test for determining the existence of a duty of care. The first question to ask is whether there was a degree of neighbourhood or proximity between the parties such that if the person being sued had thought of it, he or she would have realized that his or her actions posed a risk of danger to the other. Essentially, this question restates the *Donoghue v. Stevenson* reasonable foreseeability test. The second set of questions probe deeper, providing for exceptions or modifications to the principal test. Was there any reason that the duty should not be imposed? Should the scope of the duty be reduced? Should the class to whom the duty is owed be limited, or should the damages be reduced? These questions allow the court to consider social policy, rather than strict legal rules when looking at special situations and relationships. Essentially, the courts try to avoid situations where a defendant may be exposed to "liability in an indeterminate amount for an indeterminate time to an indeterminate class."[26] The British have abandoned the principles set out in the *Anns* case, but the Supreme Court of Canada has made it clear that it is good law in Canada (the *Jervis Crown* case[27]). In Canada, then, the existence of a duty of care is established by the reasonable foreseeability test set out in the *Donoghue v. Stevenson* case and as refined in the *Anns* case.

Duty owed to anyone who could foreseeably be harmed

Scope of duty can be reduced where appropriate

24. *Ibid*. p. 580
25. Anns v. Merton, London Borough Council [1977] 2 All E.R. 492 (H.L.)
26. Ultramares Corp. v. Touche, (1931) 174 N.E. 441 at 444 (N.Y.C.A.)
27. Canadian National Railway Co. v. Norsk Pacific Steamship Co. [1992] 1 S.C.R. 1021

Ryan v. Victoria (City) et al.[28]

This is a recent case where the Supreme Court of Canada applied the *Anns* case to determine whether a duty of care existed. In this instance, a railway company with the approval of the City of Victoria widened to four inches the flange area beside the railroad tracks running down the middle of a city street. The tracks "meandered … in a lazy S shape" down the street, and Mr. Ryan, a motorcyclist was forced to cross them at an angle that forced him into oncoming traffic. He was injured when his motorcycle tire was caught in the widened gap beside the track. The problem here was that legislation permitted the railroad to widen the gap. The city and the railway argued that because they operated within the legislated standard, there was no negligence. The court was careful to point out that the policy consideration that were to be taken into consideration when applying the *Anns* case test related only to the determination of the existence of a duty, not to the determination of whether the appropriate standard was breached. The court found that it was foreseeable that the gap could cause injury to users of the street. They also concluded that there were no policy considerations to remove or limit the duty. The railway argued that their compliance with the statutory standard was good enough. The court disagreed and said, "They owed a duty of care to the appellant with respect to the flangeways on Store Street, and that duty required them to exercise reasonable care in the circumstances. Their compliance with regulatory standards did not replace or exhaust that obligation." A reasonable person would have foreseen the danger inherent in the wider gap and kept it to a narrower dimension. The railway was liable for breaching that reasonable standard and was found negligent. This case is important in that it shows us how the *Anns* case has modified our approach to the determination of the existence of a duty but also how that test is limited to that purpose. It is also interesting in that it shows that merely adhering to a legislated standard, or for that matter common practice in a profession or trade, may not be good enough to avoid liability.

In most negligence cases, the existence of a duty is obvious and the court need not deal with the problem. Still, it is a requirement and important in those cases where the existence of a duty of care is brought into question.

Misfeasance and Nonfeasance

When discussing duty of care, it is also important to note that the law imposes a duty on people to carry out their activities carefully so as to not cause harm to others. This

Unacceptable action— misfeasance

involves misfeasance or wrongful conduct. But the courts are very reluctant to provide a remedy in a case of nonfeasance (when a person fails to do something), unless it can be established that a particular relationship existed, such as in the case

Failure to act—nonfeasance

of a swimmer and a lifeguard, or a child and a guardian. People who see a child drowning have no duty in tort law to rescue that child, unless they happen to be lifeguards. Doctors have no legal duty to come to the aid of an accident victim when

Usually no duty where nonfeasance

they pass a car crash. But once someone does start to help, they have an obligation to continue to do so in a reasonable way. When someone attempts to repair a car, a friend has no legal duty to help, but if he does, he is responsible for any damage caused by his carelessness. These rules discourage people from coming

Once started, a person must give reasonable care

to the aid of others. In an attempt to alleviate such harsh consequences, some ju-

28. [1999] 1 S.C.R. 201

risdictions have introduced legislations either creating a duty to assist or at least protecting rescuers from liability for injuries arising out of their rescue efforts.

Standard of Conduct

The existence of a duty to be careful is usually apparent. Normally, the main problem for the court is to determine just how careful the defendant should have been. Here, the reasonable person test is used to determine what level of care should have been exercised. The court asks what a reasonable person would have done in the same circumstances. If the conduct of the defendant is found to have fallen below this standard, he is negligent and liable for any injury or loss resulting. What is reasonable conduct will vary with the circumstances. For example, the court will take into account the risk of loss.

Reasonable person test determines standard of care

In *Blyth v. Birmingham Water Works, Co.*,[29] the plaintiff's home was flooded when a water main serving a fireplug froze and burst during a severe winter cold spell. The court rejected the plaintiff's claim that the water works company was negligent for not having placed the pipes deeper. The great costs of doing so would not have been reasonably justified considering the risk, this being the coldest winter in 50 years. The judge in the case said:

Risk of injury affects standard

> "Negligence is the omission to do something which a reasonable man, guided upon those considerations which ordinarily regulate the conduct of human affairs, would do, or doing something which a prudent and reasonable man would not do.[30]

Similarly a person driving a truck or car must be more careful than a person driving a hay wagon because of the greater risk of more significant injury.

Greater costs will also be taken into consideration in determining the required standard of care. It may be possible to design and build an automobile that would suffer minimal damage in a high-speed accident, but the costs involved would be prohibitive. No one could afford such a car: therefore, it would be unreasonable to hold a manufacturer to such a standard. But here, care must be taken because saving money will not excuse the production of a defective or dangerous product. A balance must be struck.

High costs affect standards

What constitutes reasonable behaviour will also vary with the expertise of the person being sued. A doctor is expected to function at a higher level than a normal person, at least as far as medical matters are concerned, and so is held to a higher standard. The test asks: Was the person's conduct up to the standard expected of a reasonable person in the same circumstances? Did he or she conduct himself or herself as a reasonable doctor, reasonable lawyer, reasonable accountant, reasonable plumber, or reasonable driver? This has special implications for professionals and other experts and will be discussed below as a special topic.

Standard depends on expertise

The opposite is true when children are involved. The courts recognize that a 13-year-old cannot be expected to act at the same level of responsibility as an adult. Children are liable for their torts, but the standard required of them is the level of conduct that would be expected of a reasonable child of the same age. Thus, a small child playing with matches may not be liable for a resulting fire, whereas a teenager doing the same thing could very likely be held responsible. At this point, attention usually turns to the parents. Although many people do not realize it, parents are not, as a general rule, vicariously liable for the torts committed by their children. In

Liability varies with age

29. (1856) 156 E.R. 1047 (Ex. Ct)
30. *Ibid.*, p. 1049

the absence of a statute to the contrary, and these are becoming much more common, parents are only liable if it can be established that they were negligent in their own right by failing to properly train, control, or supervise their children.

Parents Not Liable for Torts Committed by Their Children

A child was caught shoplifting in the defendant's store, and the store, through their lawyers, sent a letter to the child's mother demanding payment to compensate them for the losses and threatening to start a civil action against her if she did not pay. The amount demanded was more than the amount stolen; the store justified this by suggesting that it was designed to offset the cost of security people the store was forced to employ. The mother paid the money,

but after receiving legal advice, she brought this small claims action, demanding return of the money. She was successful. The judge found that parents ought not to be held liable for torts of their children. Unless some personal liability on the part of the mother could be shown, such as negligence, there was no liability and no right to demand payment from her.

B. (D.C.) v. Arkin (1996) 138 D.L.R. (4th) 309 (Man. Q.B.)

Carelessness can be assumed from circumstances

It is not always necessary for the plaintiff to show that the defendant was careless. This can sometimes be implied from the surrounding circumstances. For example, if a piano were to fall into the street from a fourth-floor apartment, injuring a passerby, those facts by themselves seem to say more eloquently than anyone could that the people who were handling the piano were careless in the way they moved it. From the evidence of the falling piano, the court can conclude that the handlers were negligent.

This type of situation used to be dealt with under a special provision of the law of negligence called *res ipsa loquitur*, but the Supreme Court of Canada has said that it is better approached as matter of circumstantial evidence.[31] The new approach is somewhat more flexible, but the effect is similar. The court can find that the circumstantial evidence establishes a *prima facie* (on the face of it) **case** and then turn to the defendants to produce evidence that they were not negligent. Without such evidence from the defendants, the plaintiff will be successful.

Untangling the WEB

Online retailers are liable if their product or the information they provide is defective and causes injury under the law of negligence. Professionals dispensing information should include disclaimers, specific instructions for use, and restrictions, e.g., "for adult use only." Liability may be avoided by developing a process for creating a contract with listed restrictions and disclaimers. People using the information should be required to indicate their agreement with the instructions and restrictions. But there is an expectation that the information will be accurate and kept current, or the purveyors may be held liable for damages when people are misled by inaccurate information. It is likely though in cases of negligence that the common law principles can be applied if the problems of jurisdiction can be sorted out.

31. Fontaine v. British Columbia (Official Administrator) [1998] 1 S.C.R. 424

Special Situations

The court deals with some special situations in unique ways. In common law, people who occupy property have a special obligation to people who are injured on their property. Note that this obligation rests on the occupier, not the owner; thus, where the property is leased, the duty falls on the tenant, not the landlord. The obligation to look out for the welfare of visitors varies with their status. A person coming on a property for a business purpose is referred to as an invitee. A person on the property with permission but for a non-business purpose is a licensee, and a person there without permission is a trespasser. In common law, the occupier has to act more carefully towards the invitee. They are required to take reasonable steps to protect such visitors from unusual dangers. This may extend to putting up a fence around an elevator shaft or providing a hard hat. The duty towards licensees is less, only to take reasonable steps to warn of hidden dangers on the property. Here a sign would suffice. The only duty to a trespasser is not to willfully or recklessly cause him harm.

Occupiers owe special duty

These different standards have caused problems, especially where children are involved. Most provinces enacted legislation in the form of occupiers' liability acts, which eliminated the distinction between invitees and licensees, imposing just one standard of care for visitors and their property on the premises of others. In Ontario, for example, the *Occupiers' Liability Act*[32] imposes a duty on occupiers to take reasonable care of all people and their property coming onto the premises.

Invitee/licensee distinction may no longer be important

> 3(1) An occupier of premises owes a duty to take such care as in all the circumstances of the case is reasonable to see that persons entering on the premises and the property or brought on the premises by those persons are reasonably safe while on the premises.

In the case introducing this chapter, the garage proprietors were liable for the injuries the boy suffered because they had failed to take reasonable steps, as required by the provincial act, to protect him from the danger of the open cesspool.

As for trespassers, the legislation usually retains the common law minimal obligation not to willfully or recklessly cause the trespasser injury. This minimal duty is extended to other visitors when they have come on the property in such a way as to voluntarily assume the risks of being there or they are there for a criminal purpose.

Houle et al. v. Calgary (City)[33]

This case involved an abandoned supermarket in a suburban area of Calgary. Located in the parking lot of that supermarket was an electrical transformer surrounded by a 10-foot fence. Sean Houle was an eight-year-old child, who managed to climb over the fence and was injured by an electrical shock from the transformer. He was seriously burned and his arm had to be amputated. While at first there was some dispute about who was responsible for the property, the court held that because the City of Calgary had built the enclosure and had the only keys to it, they were responsible for it. The judge then applied the *Occupier's Liability Act* to the situation and found that Sean was a child trespasser under the act. This was a suburban neighborhood with lots of children, and the city should have known that the parking lot had become a children's playground. In addition, the electrical

---

32. *Occupier's Liability Act*, R.S.O. (1980) c.322 (p. 79)
33. (1985) 20 D.L.R. (4th) 15 (Alta. C.A.); leave to appeal to S.C.C. refused (1985) 20 D.L.R. (4th) 15 n

power represented a substantial danger to the children. As a result, the court applied Section 13 of the act, which summarized the duty of an occupier towards such trespassing children as "the occupier owes a duty to that child to take such care as in all the circumstances of the case is reasonable to see that the child will be reasonably safe from that danger." The city clearly failed in this duty and was, therefore, liable for the child's injuries. People must take care to ensure that the property they are responsible for is safe for all those using it. This applies to businesses as well as private residences.

Special duties of innkeepers

An even more onerous duty is imposed on occupiers when an inn or hotel is involved. In common law, innkeepers owe a duty to their guests to provide protection from the wrongful acts of others, even when the innkeeper or servant is not at fault. This is a much higher duty than normal, and it is only when the damage or loss to a guest's property is caused by that guest's own negligence that the innkeeper is relieved of responsibility. Most provinces have reduced the common law liability of innkeepers through legislation so that they are only liable where they or their employees are negligent. It is important to note, however, that their liability is only reduced where they have carefully complied with the statute by placing notices at designated locations.

The appropriate section of the British Columbia *Hotel Keepers Act* is as follows:

3(1) No innkeeper is liable to make good to his guest loss of or injury to goods or property brought to his inn, except where the goods or property have been

(a) stolen, lost or injured through the wilful act, default, or neglect of the innkeeper or his servant;

(b) deposited expressly for safe custody with the innkeeper, except that in case of the deposit, the innkeeper may require as a condition of his liability that the goods or property be deposited in a box or other receptacle, fastened, and sealed by the person depositing the goods or property.

Subsection 2 imposes the duty of a bailee for reward on the hotel where a car has been left in their keeping. Bailments will be discussed in Chapter 15. Section 5 requires the posting of notice, or the liability reverts to the higher common law standard.

5(1) Every innkeeper shall keep conspicuously posted in the office and public rooms and in every bedroom in the inn a copy of Section 3, printed in plain type.

(2) An innkeeper is entitled to the benefit of Section 3 for the goods or property brought to the inn only while the copies are posted. [34]

A special problem arises when alcohol is served. The courts are willing to hold commercial dispensers of alcoholic beverages at least partially responsible when a patron becomes intoxicated and is injured, as the Supreme Court of Canada made clear in the *Crocker* case used to open this section. Following this trend, we can expect companies and even individual hosts to be liable when private parties or gatherings lead to similar results.

34. *Hotel Keepers Act,* (1996) R.S.B.C. c. 206

Jacobsen v. Nike Canada Ltd.[35]

Mr. Jacobsen was an employee of Nike Canada and was working for them setting up a display at a trade show in the B.C. Place Stadium. Because of the nature of the job, he was required to work for a long period of time, and the employer, through its representative, supplied the workers with food and considerable amounts of beer, which they were allowed to drink while on the job. At 11:30 p.m., they finished, and Mr. Jacobsen along with some of the other employees went to two clubs where they consumed more beer. The plaintiff consumed about 10 beers while working and more at the clubs. Driving home that night, he was involved in a serious single-vehicle accident that left him a quadriplegic.

There was no question that the employer owed a duty of care to their employee having put him in this position. The problem was the nature of that duty and whether the duty had been breached. The court held that the employer should have known that he would likely drive home drunk and had a duty to ensure that he did not. The employer had required him to drive his car that day, and they had supplied the beer. They were in breach of their duty to provide a safe place of work. "I find that Nike failed to meet the standard of care required of an employer by providing alcohol in the workplace in the circumstances in which it did so on September 6, 1991, not monitoring the plaintiff's consumption and taking no steps to ensure the plaintiff did not drive while impaired." Even though Jacobsen had consumed more alcohol at other establishments later, Nike had breached their duty and were liable for his injuries. This case not only shows how careful employers have to be towards their employees but also indicates the direction the law is going towards imposing liability on hosts who provide alcohol to their customers and guests. Note that Mr. Jacobsen was found to be contributorily negligent and 25 percent responsible for his own injuries.

Legislation

Although the reasonable person standard discussed here is extremely important, there are many situations where this has been changed by statute. Examples are the occupiers' liability acts and innkeepers acts discussed above. The motor vehicle acts of the provinces also create special categories of duty that make people responsible for the condition of their car even if they were not aware of a defect. As a general rule, however, these statutes do not create new categories of tort unless they specifically say so. Thus, human rights acts and privacy legislation may impose new obligations on people, but violations of these obligations do not amount to a tort unless the act says they do. Some jurisdictions have also changed tort law with respect to automobile collisions. Because of the devastating losses and injuries associated with this area, many provinces have turned to compulsory insurance schemes. Some jurisdictions have gone further, instituting "no fault" programs, where people are treated the same and compensated for their injuries whether they were at fault or not. There is much debate with respect to these schemes, but it is generally agreed that it is necessary to ensure that all are covered and distribute the losses as broadly as possible among all the driving public.

Modifications imposed by statute

The trend away from fault

35. (1996) 133 D.L.R. (4th) 377 (B.C.S.C.).

Negligent Misstatement

Until relatively recently, liability for negligence was thought to be limited to conduct which fell below an acceptable standard of care. In 1963, the House of Lords in the United Kingdom indicated their willingness to expand this liability to careless words causing economic loss.[36]

Negligent words causing economic loss actionable

The Supreme Court of Canada adopted a similar approach in the case of *Haig v. Bamford et al.*[37] An accounting firm negligently prepared financial statements for a company, knowing that the statements would be used to encourage investors. Mr. Haig purchased a number of shares but found the company to be considerably less profitable than the incorrect financial statements had led him to believe. As a result, he suffered a financial loss.

There was no direct relationship between Mr. Haig and the negligent firm. The accountants were negligent in the performance of its services to the company at the time Mr. Haig was a potential investor. Previously, the imposition of liability depended on the negligent conduct causing physical injury or damage. Here, there was no physical contact and or loss. Mr. Haig lost money when he relied on the financial statement.

Negligent words may create liability

This case is significant because for the first time in Canada, liability for the tort of negligence was extended to pure economic loss caused by negligent words spoken by experts. As a result, such experts may find themselves responsible not only to their immediate clients but also to others who suffer loss because of their careless statements. This has had a considerable impact on all those claiming professional expertise. The liability of professionals and other experts will be discussed as a special topic below.

Strict Liability

As mentioned above, the commission of a tort involves wrongful conduct. This requires fault, and in a negligence action, that fault usually takes the form of conduct falling below the standard of a reasonable person in the circumstances. It must be noted, however, that there are some situations where the courts will impose liability even when the defendant has acted completely reasonably.

Liability even when conduct was reasonable

The case of *Rylands v. Fletcher*[38] established a rule applicable in such instances. The defendant had built a reservoir on his property, but under the surface, there was a shaft from a coal mine leading to his neighbour's property. The water escaped, flooding his neighbour's mine. Rylands was in no way negligent, having no knowledge of the underground shaft. His conduct was well within what would have been expected of a reasonable person. Still, the court held him liable for the damage. The principle applied was that if a person brings something inherently dangerous, such as stored water or explosives, onto his property and it escapes, the occupier is liable for any damage. The House of Lords supported Justice Blackburn's decision, which said, "The true rule of law is that the person who, for his own purposes, brings on his land and collects and keeps there anything likely to do mischief

When dangerous things escape

36. Hedley Byrne & Co. v. Heller's Partners Ltd. [1963] 2 All E.R. 575 (H.L.)

37. (S.C.C.) [1977] 1 S.C.R. 466

38. (1868) L.R. 3 H.L. 330

Strict Liability for Dangerous Substances

The tenant, Skrow's Produce, owned a truck that had propane tanks built into it. One of the tanks leaked when the truck was parked in front of the plaintiff's place of business during a sale. The fire department ordered evacuation of the premises until the gas dissipated, causing considerable loss of business. The plaintiffs sued under the principle of strict liability. The court agreed that storing propane on the truck was a danger-

ous and unusual use of property and applied the precedent from *Rylands v. Fletcher*. The court also found that the defendant had caused a nuisance and that the case was actionable on that basis as well. At the time that the truck was parked alongside the store, the driver knew it was discharging propane. That made it an abnormal use.

Ira-Berg Ltd. v. Skrow's Produce (1971) Ltd., (1990) 76 D.L.R. (4th) 431 (Ont. Gen. Div.)

if it escapes, must keep it at his peril; and if he does not do so, is *prima facie* answerable for all the damage which is the natural consequence of its escape."[39]

It must be noted that strict liability will not be imposed unless the use of the property is unusual. Today, electricity and plumbing are part of a normal operation of modern buildings, and damage caused by these modern conveniences will normally not support a claim of strict liability. To succeed in such situations, nuisance or negligence must be established.

Must be unusual use of property

A form of strict liability, that is, liability without fault, is also imposed on employers when they are held liable for torts committed by employees during the course of their employment. This is referred to as vicarious liability. The employer is without fault and yet is held liable for the wrongful acts of employees. This is justified by the fact that the employer profits by the employees conduct and, therefore, ought to bear responsibility. This will be covered in Chapter 11 under "Liability of Employer."

Vicarious liability of employer

Only in these rare circumstances will liability be imposed strictly. But there are other situations where the standard imposed is extremely high. Negligence is normally determined by finding that there was a failure to live up to the standard of a reasonable person. Where dangerous products, processes or animals are involved, the standard of care required is very high because the risk of injury is great. The obligations of persons in control in such situations approach strict liability. Food handlers, for example, find themselves in this unenviable position.

Material Loss and Causation

Unlike intentional torts that may be actionable even without any specific damage, negligence requires that some sort of loss to person or property has been suffered. When a customer slips and falls on a wet floor in a store but suffers no injury, there is no right to sue, even though the store employees have been careless. However, if the customer breaks a leg, this would be a tangible, physical injury, which would provide grounds for an action.

Damage or injury must be present

In the past, there had to be some actual physical damage or injury for the person to successfully sue for negligence. Today, the courts are willing to provide a

39. *Ibid.* p. 339–340

remedy even in cases of pure economic loss or where the negligence has caused a recognized mental disorder, such as depression or an obsessive-compulsive disorder.

Canada Trust Co. v. Sorkos et al.[40]

Mr Sorkos owned property that he offered for sale through Canada Trust. The purchase price was based on a per-acre basis, but because of an error on the part of the employees of Canada Trust, the size of the parcel of land was not the 5.72 acres they calculated but only 5.66 acres. Because of this, the actual price paid was almost $50 000 less than Mr. Sorkos had expected. Considering he lost money on the sale because of this mistake, he refused to pay the $24 000 of the commission still outstanding. Canada Trust sued. The court found that there was negligent misstatement here but was not convinced that it made any difference to the price. Mr. Sorkos claimed that he wanted a set price for the total of the land and because of the mistake he was forced to sell for less. The court, however, was not convinced that he could have achieved the higher price, given the land that had been excluded from the sale. The price was already considerably higher than the estimated market value of the land, and at the time the offer was accepted, Mr. Sorkos made no objection to the fact that the price was less. In effect, the court found that although there was negligent misstatement on the part of Canada Trust and their agents, this caused no damage or loss to Mr. Sorkos, and so there was no liability. Mr. Sorkos had to pay the remaining commission. There was negligent misstatement with relation to the size of the property, but there was no indication that this had caused a loss. Mr. Sorkos was unable to show that he would have received a higher price had the true facts been known. This case illustrates the very important principle that in order for an action in negligence to succeed, it must be demonstrated that the conduct complained of actually caused a loss or injury.

Conduct must be cause of injury

Not only must there be damage. That damage must be a direct result of the careless conduct. If the operator of a motor vehicle knowingly drives at night without tail lights, the driver can be said to be careless. However, if the vehicle is involved in a head-on collision, the driver of the other car could not rely on the first driver's failure to have tail-lights to support a negligence action. The test usually applied in such situations is called the "**but for**" test. The plaintiff must prove to the court's satisfaction that but for the conduct complained of, no injury would have resulted. In this illustration, the plaintiff cannot say that but for a failure to have properly functioning tail-lights, no collision would have occurred.

Kauffman v. Toronto Transit Commission[41]

In this Ontario case, two boys were scuffling on an escalator and bumped into a man causing him to fall against the plaintiff, who, in turn, fell down and was injured. She sued the Toronto Transit Commission, claiming that they had been negligent in not supplying proper handrails. The court found that the Toronto Transit Commission had not been negligent. Mrs. Kauffman failed to prove that the lack of a handrail had anything to do with her injuries. The court was satisfied that she would have been injured whether or not the handrail had been supplied. The plaintiff was unable to establish that but for the negligent conduct of the Toronto Transit Commission, she would not have suffered an injury.

40. (1996) 135 D.L.R. (4th) 383 (Ont. C.A.)
41. (1959) 18 D.L.R. (2d) 204 (Ont. C.A.); aff'd [1960] S.C.R. 251

Defences

Once the plaintiff has established that the defendant owed a duty to be careful to the plaintiff, that the defendant's conduct fell below the standard of care required in the situation, and that the conduct complained of caused some injury or loss to the plaintiff, negligence is established. Still, there may be some matters the defendant can raise in defence. These are summarized below.

Remoteness

Problems sometimes arise when the connection between the conduct complained of and the injury seems tenuous or where the nature of the injury suffered is unusual or unexpected. For example, if a careless driver were to damage a power pole causing an interruption of power to a business resulting in considerable economic loss, should the driver be held responsible for such an unexpected result? The suggestion is that the connection between the conduct complained of and the actual damage suffered is too remote. There has been great confusion over the years, but in Canada today, our courts only allow a defence of remoteness when the defendant could not have reasonably anticipated the general nature of the injury or damage suffered. Mr. Justice Dickson in *The Queen v. Coté* explained: "It is not necessary that one foresee the precise concatenation of events; it is enough to fix liability if one can foresee in a general way the class or character of injury which occurred."[42]

Problem of remoteness

This is often confused with the test to determine whether a duty of care exists, since both are based on the reasonable foreseeability test. But with duty, the test is used to determine whether danger to the plaintiff should have been anticipated, whereas with remoteness, it is the type of injury itself that must have been foreseen. As was explained, duty is now determined by an application of the *Anns* case test, and it is likely that the problem of remoteness is also dealt with by applying the second half of that test. The second part of the *Anns* case test asks the following questions: Was there any reason that the duty should not be imposed? Should the scope of the duty be reduced? Should the class to whom the duty is owed be limited, or should the damages be reduced? It is the application of these principles then that will determine whether the injuries or damages suffered were too remote.

***Anns* case now applied**

Although there is much confusion in the application of these principles, there is one area of certainty: where the nature but not the extent of a personal injury was reasonably foreseeable. The rule is simply *that we take our victims as we find them.* If a person has a weak heart or a tendency to a particular disease or physical condition, we cannot avoid responsibility by claiming that we could not reasonably be expected to foresee the special condition. If a person experiences greater injury from our conduct than would be expected because of a unique physical condition, there is nonetheless a responsibility to compensate for all consequences of the injury. This principle is often referred to as the **thin skull** rule.

We take our victims as we find them

In the case of *Smith v. Leech Brain*,[43] the defendant's employee was hurt when he was struck on the lip by a drop of molten metal. Because of a pre-cancerous condition existing in the employee, this burn developed into cancer, which eventually killed him. Although this consequence of the injury was in no way reasonably foreseeable, the employer was held liable for the death of the employee because the original accident was caused by the employer's negligence.

But we must be careful in applying the principle. If the aggravated injury was inevitable and the conduct of the defendant simply determined the timing, the

---

42. [1976] 1 S.C.R. 595 S.C.C. at 604
43. [1961] 3 All E.R. 1159 (Q.B.)

defendant will not be responsible for the additional loss. If a worker has one eye and loses the other in an accident, the damage is much more devastating than the loss of a single eye. Under the thin skull rule, the defendant will be responsible for the greater damages resulting from the total blindness. But if that one-eyed worker had a deteriorating condition in his remaining eye that would have eventually caused its loss, the defendant's conduct is not responsible for the worker's blindness; the deteriorating condition is, and the worker will receive considerably less compensation. This has been dubbed the **crumbling skull rule** and must be used in conjunction with the thin skull rule.[44]

Not responsible for inevitable loss

Contributory Negligence

Historically, when a defendant could show that the plaintiff was also careless, contributing to his own loss, it was a complete bar to recovery. This was an all-or-nothing result and was clearly unfair. For example, if a driver fails to stop at a light and a second driver fails to notice the car coming into his path because he is adjusting his radio, he will not be able to recover for any injuries suffered in the accident. In this case, it is clear that the second driver was being careless by not being fully aware of what was happening on the road; this conduct at least contributed to the accident and completely bars him from recovery of damages. Because this approach is rather harsh, it was somewhat modified by the **last clear chance doctrine**, which made the person who had the last opportunity to avoid the accident responsible. This was still an unfair all-or-nothing approach, and legislation was enacted to alleviate the problem. The *Negligence Act* in Ontario[45] is a typical example because it abandons the all-or-nothing approach and permits the court to apportion responsibility between the two parties. Compensation must be paid in proportion to that assigned responsibility. In the example above, the first driver was at fault for driving through the stoplight, and the second driver contributed to the accident through lack of attention. The courts would apportion liability and require each to bear a percentage of the responsibility for the losses suffered.

Negligence of victim may reduce or eliminate award

Act allows apportionment of responsibility

Spiewak et al. v. 251268 Ontario Ltd. et al.[46]

Mr. Spiewack and Ms. James purchased an apartment building, using the services of Clements and MacKenzie, two experienced people in the real estate business. Before purchasing, Mr. Spiewack made it clear to the agents that the property had to be self-sustaining, as he was in a "tight financial spot." Clements and MacKenzie made an estimate of what the income would be from each suite, and based on this, an offer was made that the vendor accepted. This involved a small deposit and the vendor providing mortgage financing for the remainder. In fact, the actual rental income was about $100 per unit less, making the transaction not financially viable. The purchasers were unable to make the payments and had to surrender the property back to the vendor. They brought this action to recover their loss from Clements and MacKenzie. Because they no longer had the property, the remedy of rescission was not available, and the purchasers sought a remedy of damages for their negligent misrepresentation. The court found that it was clear that the plaintiffs had relied on the incorrect information supplied by the defendants, that this information had been supplied negligently, and that it had caused their loss. However, the judge also found that the plaintiffs were experienced business people and

44. Athey v. Leonati (1996) 140 D.L.R. (4th) 235
45. *Negligence Act*, R.S.O. (1980) c. 315
46. 43 D.L.R. (4th) 554 (Ont. H.C.)

should have sought legal advice for this transaction. Their failure to do so was contributory negligence, and their damage award was reduced by 20 percent because of that negligence. It cannot be overemphasized that in business, people are expected to have a certain amount of business acumen. They must seek the advice of professionals and not simply trust the information they receive from others. When they perform below that standard and are less than vigilant, they may find themselves responsible for at least a portion of their own losses.

Voluntary Assumption of Risk

A plaintiff in a negligence action may also lose the right to receive compensation where he has voluntarily assumed the risk. The principle being applied is that the law does not assist a volunteer (*Volenti non fit injuria*). If a person knowingly gets into a car with a driver who is obviously intoxicated, should he be able to sue if injured? Historically, the answer would be no, and it was a complete bar to recovery. Today, the principle is much more restrictive. To escape liability, not only must the defendant show that the victim voluntarily put himself in danger but also that he did so in such a way as to clearly absolve the plaintiff of responsibility. If a person puts himself or herself in harm's way like this, they are completely barred from recovering any damages. It is difficult to establish this waiver of legal responsibility, and so only rarely will a claim of voluntary assumption of risk be successful.

The law will not assist volunteers

But assumption of legal risk must be clear

The courts now usually deal with such foolhardy behaviour under the heading of contributory negligence, and this, in turn, permits the courts to apportion the loss between the parties—a much more satisfactory result. This was done in the *Crocker v. Sundance* case used to introduce the section on negligence: the court rejected voluntary assumption of risk and found contributory negligence instead.

Some jurisdictions have included provisions in their occupier's liability acts absolving responsibility where the visitor has voluntarily assumed the risk. Although the legislation does not say it, the Supreme Court of Canada has interpreted this in the same restrictive way, and so this provision will only absolve the occupier of responsibility where it is clear that the visitor has assumed the legal risk as well as the physical risk.[47] This will happen in only the rarest of circumstances.

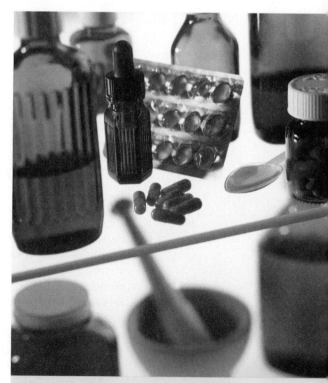

When a rescuer is involved, he or she cannot be said to have voluntarily assumed the risk. A father who is injured when he jumps in front of a train to save his child can hold the railway responsible for failing to have proper barriers. If the rescuer is injured, the author of the danger cannot escape liability by claiming the rescuer voluntarily assumed the risk. If the potential danger was reasonably foreseeable, so was the potential need for a rescue. The person who caused the danger must pay compensation to both the victim and the injured rescuer.[48] Similarly, the principle does not apply to work-related accidents, even if the work being performed is inherently dangerous.

Pharmaceutical companies must give appropriate warnings and instructions.
First Light/The Sbrookes

47. Waldick v. Malcolm [1991] 2 S.C.R. 456
48. Videan v. British Transport Commission [1963] 2 All E.R. 860 (C.A.)

Product Liability

Nicholson et al. v. John Deer Ltd. et al.[49]

The Nicholsons purchased a second-hand riding lawnmower manufactured by John Deere Ltd. Before using the mower, one day, Mrs. Nicholson opened the hood to fill up the gas tank. She took off the cap and placed it on the tank and started to pour in the gas. She had to stop to retrieve the gas cap when it rolled off the tank. She again placed it on the hood and continued to pour gas into the tank. The cap rolled away again; this time it hit the battery and caused a spark that ignited the gasoline fumes. As the fire started, she spontaneously dropped the gasoline can she was holding, spilling the gas. The resulting fire destroyed both the garage and her home. Mrs. Nicholson sued the manufacturer for compensation for the losses she had suffered. The court found that the design was defective and that the manufacturer was aware of the problem, since there had been several incidents and lawsuits over this and the previous models. In fact, John Deere recognized the danger associated with their product and had manufactured a battery-covered safety kit to solve the problem. They also took steps to warn the users of their mower of the danger and of the availability of the safety kit. There was a decal on the gas tank warning of the danger of spark. There were several warnings of the danger in the operating manual, and they had a program in place whereby their dealers and agents were encouraged to tell the customers about the safety kit and have it installed. The Nicholsons did not receive a manual with their used mower and were not aware of this safety kit, which had not been installed on their mower. When they had it serviced, the dealer did not tell them of the safety kit. The court held that these efforts on the part of John Deere were inadequate and that they should have taken much more positive action to make sure the defects were corrected. In addition, the dealer, who failed to tell the Nicholsons about the danger and the safety kit, was also liable for negligence. This case is interesting in that it shows the great responsibility placed on a manufacturer when such a defective and dangerous product is produced. Once it had been established that the design is defective and dangerous, it is very difficult, if not impossible, for the manufacturer to show that they were not negligent, despite their stringent efforts to correct the situation.

Injury and loss are often caused indirectly. When products are manufactured, those products are sometimes dangerous because of their inherent nature, such as chemicals or explosives, or because they are defective. The American approach to product liability is somewhat different from that in Canada. In the United States, by statute and case law, a much greater responsibility has been imposed on manufacturers, where injured consumers are only required to demonstrate that a defect in the product caused the injury. There is no need to establish negligence by demonstrating a failure to live up to a standard of care. This is based on either contract, where the principle of **privity** has been abandoned, or strict liability. In either case, once the defect and injury have been established, liability falls on the producer of the product.

This **strict liability** approach to product liability has not yet been adopted in most provinces in Canada. Here, it is not enough to show that the defective

---

49. 34 D.L.R. (4th) 542; varied 57 D.L.R. (4th) 639 (Ont. H.C.) (1986) 34 D.L.R. (4th) 542 (Ont. H.C.); aff'd (1989) 57 D.L.R. (4th) 639 (Ont. C.A.)

product caused injury. In this country, it is still necessary for a plaintiff to establish that the defendant was negligent. Not only is it necessary to establish that there was a duty to be careful but also that there was a failure to live up to that duty. Either the manufacturer or an employee must be shown to have been "careless." *Donoghue v. Stevenson,* the case involving the snail in the ginger beer discussed earlier, had a significant impact on product liability in tort law. Historically, because there were usually several intervening steps between the manufacturer and the ultimate consumer of a product, it was thought that the manufacturer owed no duty of care to the ultimate consumer. This case established that if a product was designed in such a way as to get into the hands of the consumer without intervening inspection or modification, a duty of care did exist. Now, as we deal with more complicated manufactured goods, there is even less likelihood that any intermediate inspection would have disclosed the problem. As a result, today, it is much more difficult for a manufacturer to deny the existence of a duty of care. This duty along with evidence of a breach of that duty will impose liability on the producer of the product.

Breach of duty must be shown for product liability

A particularly difficult problem in product liability cases is to show that someone was "careless" in the manufacturing process. In Canada, the courts are willing to draw a conclusion, from the circumstantial evidence of the injury or loss, that someone must have been negligent, leaving it to the defendant to then produce evidence to the contrary. As discussed above, this "**circumstantial evidence**" method replaces the *res ipsa loquitur* approach used in the past and also seems more appropriate for product liability cases.

Breach of duty can be implied from circumstances

This creates difficulty for the manufacturer in these situations. Where policies and procedures are in place such that if followed no injury could happen, then they must not have been followed. If they were followed and injury still happened, the policies were not adequate. Either way negligence is established. Once the court has drawn the inference of negligence from the circumstances of the injury, the manufacturer will have to show that they were not careless in order to avoid liability. The snail in the bottle will be enough for the court to draw an inference of negligence on the part of the defendant.

Varga v. John Labatt Ltd., Highgate and Hurse[50]

In this case the plaintiff complained of illness after consuming a bottle of beer determined later to contain chlorine. The bottle was purchased by a friend; thus, no action in contract could be brought against the seller. Following *Donoghue v. Stevenson,* the court had no difficulty finding that a duty to be careful existed on the part of the producer, but they then had to determine whether that duty had been breached. Once it was established that the beer had been contaminated with a significant amount of chlorine at the point of production, the court was willing to presume negligence on the part of the manufacturer on the basis of this circumstantial evidence. The bottler then tried to rebut this presumption of negligence by showing that they only used a weak solution of chlorine when cleaning the bottles. They also stressed that they had a very thorough process to stop such contamination from taking place. Because of this and the fact that the chlorine solution was much stronger than what they used, they could not be responsible. The court held that since it was clear that the chlorine had entered the bottle at the point of production, clearly someone at the plant had veered from the procedures and policies in place, acted negligently, and caused the producer to be liable. If the policies and procedures had been followed, there would have been no injury.

50. (1956) 6 D.L.R. (2nd) 336 (Ont. H.C.)

Manufacturers must warn and act reasonably to make dangerous products safer

Where the products are inherently dangerous, as is the case with chemicals, explosives, tools, and pharmaceuticals, the requirements are a little different. The manufacturer must do all that he can to make the product as safe as reasonably possible, given the risks, and to give appropriate warnings and instructions. In Canada, the defendant must still show negligence on the part of the manufacturer, but the focus is on whether the warnings and instructions are clear and whether everything reasonably possible has been done, given the considerable risk. For example, there have been great strides made in making pharmaceutical products safe for children by sealing the products and providing child-proof caps. Power tools generally have a double switch mechanism or a locking device to prevent children or even adults from accidentally turning on the power. Where this has been done effectively, the manufacturer will likely escape liability. That is why such great care is now taken to place warnings on dangerous goods. To say that the misuse of a knife or table saw might result in injury seems self-evident. Warnings to that effect appear on such products nonetheless.

It must be emphasized that liability for damage or injury caused by products is not always based on negligence. When a **contract** exists between the injured party and the seller, and the product is defective or dangerous or otherwise causes injury or damage, that seller may be liable for a breach of the contract of sale even when there is no fault on the part of the seller. In the case of *Donoghue v. Stevenson*, had Mrs. Donoghue been the one to purchase the ginger beer instead of her friend, she could have sued the café for breach of contract, the product not being fit to consume. But because she was not the purchaser, she had no action against the seller. Some provinces have removed this privity of contract restriction in product liability cases, thus imposing a contractual duty on the manufacturer, the wholesaler, and the seller to protect the ultimate consumer even when no fault is involved. For a more complete discussion of contractual product liability, refer to Chapter 9 under "Consumer Protection Legislation."

Liability for breach may be set out in contract for sale or statute

Finally, it should also be noted that it is becoming increasingly rare, especially when a civil jury is involved, for the manufacturer not to be found liable when its product causes injury. Whether this reflects a rising standard, a move towards adopting strict liability, or a decision to place the liability on the party likely to have insurance remains to be seen.

Liability of Professionals and Other Experts

For business students who are planning to enter professions or who intend to do consulting work, the subject of **professional liability** may be one of the most important covered in this text. Experts are simply people who hold themselves out to have some specialized knowledge or skill not generally available. Professionals are usually experts who belong to professional organizations and practise in a specific area of service. The definition is obviously imprecise and, for the purposes of this discussion, should be viewed as expansive rather than restrictive. Whether we are talking of medical malpractice or the responsibilities of accountants, litigation over the quality of their work by disgruntled clients has become an important aspect of their practice. Not only have the occurrences of such malpractice actions increased dramatically in recent years, so also has the amount of damages awarded by the courts. Today, an important consideration for any professional is the amount of **liability insurance** they must retain at a very high cost. The liability of professionals

Professional liability and insurance costs important aspects of business

may be founded in contract law or based on fiduciary duty, but the expansion of liability that has taken place recently has been in the area of tort law, specifically negligence. Professionals may also face their own governing bodies that set rules and standards that must be adhered to by the members. Failure to comply with the rules or complaints from unhappy clients may result in disciplinary action with the potential consequence of losing the right to practise.

Liability must be based on contract, fiduciary duty or tort

Contract

In the past, the liability of accountants, bankers, lawyers, business consultants, and other professionals was based on the contract they had with their clients. Contract will be discussed in the next chapters, but briefly, the parties could make whatever arrangement they wanted, either expanding or limiting their liability. In theory, the risk borne by the professional in each agreement would be reflected in the price agreed to. The contracts spell out exactly what is expected of the professional, not only setting out what is to be done but also setting out limitations on what is expected. Such contracts may contain exemption clauses or disclaimers that limit the liability of the professional for any mistakes made and damages incurred. If the client does not like this, he can go elsewhere or insist that the clause be removed, usually resulting in a higher fee to be paid. The fee negotiated should reflect the risks and duties agreed to by the parties. The courts have always been reluctant to interfere in this bargaining process, and in fact, there often is no written contract, and terms have to be implied from the relationship and the normal practices of the profession. Implicit in such contracts is that the professional perform the service requested with due diligence. Thus, the requirement to adhere to a **reasonable standard of performance**, which is the basis of tort liability, is incorporated into the contractual obligations as well. But it is important to remember that the presence of a disclaimer, waiver, or other limitation cannot be overcome by suing in tort instead.

In past, contractual risk determined price

Tort standard implied in contract, but note disclaimer

Privity of contract is also extremely important when exploring the limits of the liability of professionals. The contract is between the professional and the client, and outsiders would generally have no rights under the agreement. Thus, an accountant would have a contract with the company for which he prepares financial statements. If a mistake is made, the shareholders and investors would have no recourse against the accountant for damages suffered in contract law, only the company itself. The court's willingness to expand tort liability beyond these immediate parties has had an important impact on the risks faced by accountants and other experts.

Tort liability extends beyond parties to contract

Negligence

The expansion of tort liability has introduced considerable uncertainty into the area of professional liability. The standard of care expected of a professional is reasonably straightforward and will be discussed below. What has changed in recent times and expanded the liability of most experts far beyond what it has been is just who can sue. Is an architect liable to a person injured in a collapsed building designed by her when errors are found in her designs? Is an accountant liable to shareholders or investors because of erroneous financial statements prepared for a specific client, the company? The extension of liability to these third parties has greatly expanded the risks faced by professionals who provide these services. The discussion that follows will take a closer look at a professional's liability for negligence.

Extension of liability to third parties

Standard of Care

The standard of care expected from an expert is a little different from that expected from a non-expert. The expert must live up to the standard of the reasonable person *in the circumstances*. There are two problems here: first, the level of skill they must have and, second, how they exercise that skill. Essentially, these people are required to have the skills and abilities that one would of expect from an expert or professional in that field. If a person professes to be a medical doctor, he had better have the training and skills of a medical doctor. If he claims to be a specialist, such as a plastic surgeon, he must be able to demonstrate that he has gone through the specialized training required for that designation. The same applies to a chartered accountant or investment counsellor. They have to have the training and skills expected of someone in that profession. It will be no excuse for them to claim they are not familiar with that standard or theory if it can be shown to be part of the normal knowledge or skill expected of an expert in that field.

The accounting bodies, for example, have established standards of practice for their members. GAAP (generally accepted accounting principles) and GAAS (generally accepted auditing standards). Where it can be shown that an accountant has failed to live up to these standards, that will generally be enough to establish negligence.

The second problem relates to how that skill is exercised. In assessing liability, the court determines what a reasonable person, possessed of the same skills and abilities as the defendant, would have done in the circumstances. For a doctor, the test is that of a reasonable doctor; for an accountant, a reasonable accountant; for a lawyer, a reasonable lawyer. It must be emphasized that a client or patient is not required to tolerate ineptitude on the part of professionals because of inexperience. It may be true that a doctor or mechanic in the first month of employment is more likely to make a mistake, but these people have represented themselves as proficient members of their profession. They must, therefore, live up to the level of competence one would expect of a normal member of their profession functioning in a reasonably prudent manner.

It can be very helpful to the defendant to show that what he did was common practice among his colleagues. Such common practice in the profession is generally an indication of competent professional service. But this is not always the case. Simply showing the conduct complained of was common practice among professionals will not necessarily absolve the defendant of liability for negligence. The test is that of a reasonable person, not an average person. Although one hopes that the average standard of practice in the skilled professions and the practice one would expect from a reasonable person would coincide, this is not always the case. When it is obvious that the common practice is dangerous or careless, then such sloppy practice will not be tolerated. The court, in such circumstances, is not reluctant to declare that the common practice falls below the standard of a reasonable person and is, therefore, negligent. This principle has recently been reinforced by the Supreme Court of Canada in the *Waldick v. Malcolm* case, where Iacobucci Justice, quoting Linden, states: "Tort courts have not abdicated their responsibility to evaluate customs, for negligent conduct cannot be countenanced, even when a large group is continually guilty of it." In short, no amount of general community compliance will render negligent conduct "reasonable ... in all the circumstances."[51]

Standard is that of a reasonable member of the profession

What should a business consider?

Common practice may not measure up to reasonable standard

51. Waldick v. Malcolm, [1991] 2 S.C.R. 456 at 473

It is clear, however, that to find such negligence in the face of common practice in a profession would only happen in extraordinary circumstances.

In *Kripps v. Touche Ross*,[52] the British Columbia Court of Appeal held that even where accountants follow GAAP, they cannot be sure they are acting reasonably. In that case, the company involved had invested funds raised from investors in mortgages. In fact, over $4 million of those mortgages (about one-third of their entire investment portfolio) were in default, and this was not disclosed in the 1983 financial statements, even though the auditors were aware of the situation. The court held that the investors were misled by the accounting statements, and the accountants were held liable, even though they had carefully followed GAAP. They did not disclose this information because the GAAP rules then in place did not require such disclosure. The court said, in effect, that the accountants could not hide behind the GAAP standards to escape liability.

To Whom Is the Duty Owed (the Problem with Words)

In the past, professionals and other experts only faced liability to their clients for shoddy work on the basis of contract law and to their colleagues and clients on the basis of a breach of a fiduciary duty. Only medical practitioners causing physical injury and experts, such as architects and engineers, whose services produced physical structures which would cause injury if they failed, might be subject to liability to strangers. If those injured were not immediate parties and their loss, whether caused by physical acts or words, was purely economic, there was considerable reluctance on the part of the court to extend the professional's liability to them.

Today accountants, bankers, lawyers, business consultants, and other professionals giving financial advice may be sued when their negligent words cause **economic loss**. As mentioned above, under "Negligent Misstatement," it is only in the past few years that courts have been willing to grant compensation for this kind of loss.

Modern standards recognize economic loss caused by negligent words

The case of *Haig v. Bamford et al.*[53] was the first in this country, in which accountants were found liable to third-party investors for their negligence in preparing audited financial statements. As a result, accountants and other experts now find themselves responsible not only to their immediate clients but also to others who suffer loss because of their careless statements.

Once the court decided to provide liability for economic loss caused by such negligent words, they then had to decide just how far this liability would extend. Should the same test be used to determine the existence of duty as when physical conduct was involved? As you will recall, when conduct causing injury was involved, the test to determine whether a duty existed came from the case of *Donoghue v. Stevenson*. A duty to be careful was owed to anyone you could reasonably foresee might be harmed by your conduct. Should careless words be treated the same as careless conduct, or should a narrower test to determine duty be adopted? Many argue vigorously that the **reasonable foreseeability test** is much too broad for determining liability when mere words are involved and only economic damage has been suffered. They argue that words are much more volatile and that the adoption of the reasonable foreseeability test would expose professionals and other experts to considerably greater liability than would be appropriate.

Liability may extend beyond immediate parties

52. [1997] 6 W.W.R. 421 (B.C.C.A.); leave to appeal to S.C.C. refused 102 B.C.A.C. 238 (note)
53. [1977] 1 S.C.R. 466

In fact, the judges in the *Haig* case stopped short of adopting the reasonable fore-seeability test but said that a duty of care was owed only when the person making the misleading statement knew it was to be used by an individual or a limited class of people. There have been several subsequent cases involving accountants or auditors preparing incorrect financial statements and being sued by third parties (investors) who suffered loss when they relied on them. In these cases, the lower courts have followed the example of the Supreme Court in the *Haig* case and imposed liability only where the accountants knew that investors were likely to rely on the statements.

What should a business consider?

Thus, an accountant preparing financial statements to be included in a prospectus would owe a duty to investors because he knew they would rely on them. But where the statements were just being prepared as part of the company's annual report and they were relied on by an investor without the specific knowledge of the accountant, there would be no duty.

Anns case applies to careless words causing loss

The *Anns* case discussed above has been welcomed in Canada because it retains this general reasonable foreseeability test, so much a part of our law of negligence, but provides a framework for dealing with negligent misstatement and mere economic loss on a more restrictive basis. As you will recall, the *Anns* case deals with such difficult situations by taking a two-stage approach. The first question in the *Anns* case established duty on the basis of the injury being reasonably foreseeable, but the second question allowed for this duty to be diminished or limited when considerations warranted the duty to be restricted to a specific class or the damages to be reduced. The *Haig* case clearly established that we can be held liable for our careless words, but there has always been a question of where to draw the line, and the *Anns* case provides a better method of drawing that line.

As indicated above, the *Haig* decision and subsequent cases have limited liability to those situations where we knew (or should have known) that our words would be relied on by an individual or by someone who was a member of a group we knew would be relying on the statement. Although it was not formulated that way, this approach is consistent with the *Anns* case, being an application of the second principal restricting or narrowing the duty where appropriate to do so.

Duty determined by reasonable forseeability

In *Hercules*,[54] the Supreme Court of Canada further refined accountants' liability. There, the shareholders of a company relied on incorrect financial statements to make further investments in that company. The shareholders were clearly a group that the accountants could expect to rely on the statements, and so, using the *Haig* case, a duty was owed. But these financial statements, were prepared not to encourage further investment but to evaluate the capabilities of the management team at the shareholders' meeting. Should accountants' liability extend beyond the purpose for which the statements are prepared? Applying the *Anns* case, the Supreme Court found there was a *prima facie* duty owed by the accountants. But applying the second part of the test developed in the *Anns* case, the court also decided that the duty of the accountants should only impose liability for the purpose for which the financial statements were prepared, in this case to evaluate management and not to be used by shareholders for investment decisions. The accountants, therefore, escaped liability.

but

Scope of duty may be reduced where appropriate

It seems clear that the *Anns* case is very important in Canadian law, allowing the courts to apply social policy to limit duty and liability where it seems appropriate to do so. From this, it should be apparent why the Supreme Court of Canada has retained the *Anns* case as an important part of our tort law, refusing to follow the House of Lords' lead to abandon it.

54. Hercules Management Ltd. v. Ernst & Young [1997] 2 S.C.R. 165

From the point of view of a professional or any other person professing expertise, it is vital to understand that a duty to be careful exists not only to their clients but also to others who may be affected by the advice or service they give. This liability may result from careless conduct or careless words. With any luck, that duty may be reduced or restricted by the application of the test set out in the second part of the *Anns* case.

Tort liability of professionals extends beyond clients

Finally, as discussed above, it should be emphasized that in order to succeed in any negligent action, the plaintiff must show that the **negligent conduct** (or words) caused the loss. If the professional can show that the negligent words were not relied on, that the investment or action involved would have taken place in any case, there is no liability. Also the liability of the defendant will be reduced by any contributory negligence that might be present on the part of the plaintiff.

Avoiding Risk

It has been suggested that risk avoidance is the most appropriate course for business people to reduce the likelihood of being sued. Professionals should examine not only the condition of their premises, tools, cars, and other physical objects used in the course of the business but also the habits and practices that may give rise to a complaint. Medical professionals, such as doctors, nurses, podiatrists, chiropractors, and the like, run some limited risk of malpractice based on the tort of **assault** (trespass to person). Since the nature of their practice depends on physical contact with their clients and patients, ensuring consent is a vital component of risk avoidance. A much greater problem arises when physical injury is caused by an error in judgment or mistake in practice. People involved in sports, education, training, and recreational activities face a similar risk. The main thing to remember is that the level of care demanded of such experts is that of the reasonable person in the circumstances.

Risk avoidance is key

For other business professionals, there is limited risk of being held liable for physical injury resulting from assault or negligence because of the lack of physical contact. Only when dealing with irate clients or colleagues might a confrontation result in physical injury, exposing the professional to liability for assault (trespass to person). Obviously, such confrontations should be avoided at all costs. Still great care should be taken to ensure that premises are safe for the public, clients, and employees. The best method of risk avoidance is to carefully inspect the premises and examine the practices of the business, anticipating what might go wrong, and taking the steps to correct the problems.

Practices should be adapted to avoid risk

When false or inaccurate information is unintentionally conveyed by an expert who should have known better and a client suffers economic loss because they relied on that information, this is a form of negligence for which a professional can be held liable. If misleading words are said knowingly or without belief in their truth, this is **deceit,** and the person committing the fraud is liable for any damages suffered by someone relying on those words. Professionals are expected to be experts in their areas and should be certain that the information they provide is truthful and accurate. Even disclaimers will not protect the professional from liability if the court determines that he or she should have been aware of the fault.

Fiduciary Duty and Breach of Trust

When a person places trust in a professional, the professional has a fiduciary obligation to act in the client's best interests. In the past, it was thought that this duty arose in only narrow circumstances where the fiduciary was in a position of power to

Fiduciary duty extended

make decisions affecting the client and where the client was peculiarly vulnerable or at the mercy of the fiduciary. However, the Supreme Court in *Hodgkinson v. Simms*[55] seems to have extended this duty to any situation where one person advises another, and reliance is placed on that advice. This is, in effect, a relationship built on the trust placed in the professional by the client, and when this is the case, the duties on the fiduciary are significant. A fiduciary duty requires loyalty and good faith. It also requires the fiduciary to avoid any situation where their self-interest conflicts with that duty and to otherwise act in the best interests of the person to whom the duty is owed. Any opportunity to acquire property or some other business interest or benefit that arises as a result of that relationship belongs to the client. Even when taking advantage of the opportunity will not harm the client, the fiduciary cannot do it. Any information coming to the fiduciary because of his or her position must remain confidential and not be disclosed. Nor can the fiduciary use such information for his or her own benefit. Fiduciaries must always put the interests of their clients ahead of their own. Perhaps the most difficult and common violation of a fiduciary duty is the conflict of interest.

Loyalty and good faith required

Information must be disclosed

A classic example of a conflict of interest is where an accountant advises a client to invest in a real estate development while also acting for the developers. Such a conflict requires the accountant to fulfill his fiduciary duty by at least disclosing his role in the development to the investors. This was the *Hodgkinson v. Simms* case, where the defendant's failure to do so resulted in a judgment against him for over $350 000. People acting as agents sometimes have the opportunity to take a commission from both the seller and the buyer. This also is a breach of fiduciary duty.

Real estate agents, travel and insurance agents, professionals giving advice, as well as bankers and financial planers are all likely to find themselves in such a fiduciary relationship. Even within organizations, **fiduciary duty** is common. Directors, officers, and managers owe a fiduciary duty to the company. Any situation where a person puts their affairs in the hands of a trusted advisor or employee can give rise to a fiduciary duty. Generally, ordinary employees are not fiduciaries but may assume such an obligation, depending on the function they assume. A purchasing agent, for example, will owe a fiduciary duty to her employer. Even where no fiduciary duty exists, specific aspects of it, such as the obligation to keep information confidential, may rest on the employees.

Fiduciary duty owed by directors and officers to company

Even though duties and obligations based on the duty of reasonable care in negligence are expanding at a considerable rate and to some extent overlap more traditional sources of duty on the basis of contract and the fiduciary relationship, it is vitally important not to forget about the fiduciary duty. The fiduciary duty goes far beyond the avoidance of negligence and can be the greatest potential risk to a business if it is not taken seriously. The subject of fiduciary duty will be discussed again in the chapters devoted to employment, agency, and business organizations.

Trust funds

The fiduciary duty discussed here is obviously founded on a relationship built on trust, but professionals often will find themselves in a much more specific trust relationship. Often, funds from transactions or property are left in the hands of professionals for periods of time. Real estate agents, accountants, lawyers, and financial planners, for example, often find themselves in possession of large amounts of their clients' money. Any misuse of such property or funds is actionable as a breach of trust. Struggling professionals may be tempted to borrow from such funds, with every intention of paying the money back. No matter how sincere the intention, this is a very serious violation, and the professional is not only liable for

---

55. [1994] 3 S.C.R. 377

any loss but certainly subject to disciplinary action within his professional organization. Criminal penalties may also be imposed.

Insurance

Brief mention should be made here of the problems of insurance. Professionals find themselves in the position where it is vitally important to have **liability,** sometimes called **errors and omissions insurance**. The premiums associated with such insurance can be a significant cost of carrying on business and, where possible, some may be tempted to avoid the cost.

Insurance reduces risk

A new area of professional business practice, for example, is in the area of alternative dispute resolution (ADR). Professional negotiators, mediators, and arbitrators are expanding their services from labour and family disputes to all areas of business conflict. Because this is a new and quickly growing area, standards and certification have been slow to follow. It also may not be apparent to the practitioners just what kind of risk they face. Whatever the reason, a survey of ADR practitioners in the family field showed that 77 percent of them carry no liability insurance.[56]

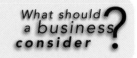

Lawyers and accountants may require such insurance as a condition of practice. Law societies often arrange for their own coverage for their members, and a lawyer cannot practice without it. Problems often arise as to the type of coverage acquired. Insurers will cover negligence on the part of the insured but often will not cover fraud or breach of trust. This can cause great difficulties when a person is responsible for the frauds committed by his or her partner. The type of policy might also be important. Some policies only cover claims that have been made during the period of coverage. If the coverage is allowed to lapse and claims are then made, even if for events that happened during the period of coverage, the insurer will likely not be required to pay.

Professionals often require insurance

As a general comment, this kind of insurance has become much less attractive to insurance companies. The courts have been stricter in their interpretation of the insurer's obligations, and with the increased risk caused by the expansion of liability to third parties for negligent words and for economic loss, it is not surprising that the premiums have been rising at an accelerated rate. This, coupled with the fact that the reserves of the insurance companies have become seriously depleted because of these claims, has caused the insurance industry to become somewhat reluctant in providing this type of coverage. As a result, liability insurance premiums for all types of professionals are going up at a disturbing rate. Insurance will be covered as a general topic in Chapter 15.

Problems have increased significantly

One of the services provided by the insurer is to arrange for legal representation for the insured professional when litigation does arise. This is normally done to ensure that the interests of the insurance company are protected, not those of the insured, since they will have to pay if liability is established. Because of the significant costs of litigation, malpractice actions involving professionals require the commitment of significant resources, even if the professional wins. All parties, including the insurance companies, risk considerable losses. It has been suggested that professional malpractice is an ideal area to be handled by the ADR mechanisms discussed in Chapter 2.

56. M. Conrad, "Family ADR providers come from all walks of life: survey." *The Lawyers Weekly,* 15:35 (26 January 1996) 13.

Professional Disciplinary Bodies

One feature associated with professionals is their membership in governing professional bodies. Examples are the law society, the medical association, the teachers' federation, the various accounting organizations, as well as administrative bodies over optometrists, chiropractors, and other groups of experts offering services to the public. Most of these bodies are created under provincial legislation that gives them varying degrees of control over the practice as well as the individuals claiming to offer that kind of service. The highest degree of control is found in such organizations as the law society or medical association. This is a licensing function, and therefore, no one can carry on the activities associated with the practice of law or medicine without being a member in good standing of those associations. The accounting bodies have somewhat less control, being able to restrict, for example, who can call themselves a Chartered Accountant (CA) or a Certified General Accountant (CGA) but have somewhat lesser control over people who do not claim to be part of those organizations performing accounting services. Some organizations are completely voluntary and have no authority over their members. Practising professionals should determine just how important it is to belong to their organization and the kind of power that body has over them. For our discussion of professional liability, it is important to look at the licensing and disciplinary powers of these bodies.

All these organizations, even the voluntary ones, have the power to determine who can join them. They also have the power to suspend or expel members, if the situation warrants. Where membership in the organization determines a person's right to practise, as is the case with the law society, suspension or expulsion can destroy that person's career. This poses a greater threat than a malpractice lawsuit. As part of this process, the professional bodies set standards of conduct both ethical and relating to quality of practice. They also typically set educational qualifications and continuing training requirements that must be met in order to maintain that membership.

When these bodies find a problem, either as the result of a complaint against a member or through their own auditing process, a disciplinary process may be initiated. These are self-governing bodies, and so, the actual process will vary, but there are several requirements that must be met, or the member subject to the discipline can challenge the decision in court. These bodies are administrative tribunals, and even those organizations that do not acquire their power through government statute must adhere to the requirements (set out in Chapter 3) relating to administrative tribunals, or their decision will be subject to judicial review.

Basically, what is needed is a fair hearing. This requires clear notice to the member of when and where the hearing is to be held and notice as to the nature of the complaint and the charge that must be answered. There must also be sufficient time provided for the member to prepare that answer.

At the hearing, certain requirements must be met. The member must be given a chance to face his accusers, if that is necessary to determine the matter. He must be given the opportunity to hear all the evidence against him and answer it. He must be able to put his side forward. The decision makers must be bias free, must hear all the evidence presented, and must base their decision only on that evidence. Usually, the member has the right to be represented by counsel, although this is not always the case. Any statutory provisions must be adhered to. Where internal procedural practices have been established, they also must be adhered to. Where legislation is involved, the statute must be in compliance with the *Charter of Rights and Freedoms,* and the process and decision of the disciplinary body must not

Some professional bodies exercise significant control

Power of suspension

Must act fairly or decision can be challenged

***Charter* may apply**

violate any human rights legislation in place in that jurisdiction. Finally, the penalty itself must be within the power of the disciplinary body to administer. Because these bodies (except for the law society) are typically made up of non-lawyers, they often fall short of these requirements, and the disciplined member may have the right to have the decision overturned.

Compliance with human rights statutes

The penalties that can be imposed by these bodies are limited usually to suspension or expulsion from the professional organization, possibly with upgrading requirements or some other qualification, such as supervision by a colleague before practice can be resumed. Suspension or expulsion can be devastating to the practitioner, much more significant than a large damage award in a malpractice action. To the public, however, this is often just seen as a minor penalty. It is a difficult part of the governing body's responsibilities to balance these different perceptions of the severity of the penalties imposed. Even the question of limiting the civil liability of professionals to pay damages by allowing them to incorporate or other means is being considered in some provinces.

Penalties, suspension, expulsion

The governing bodies may also find themselves the object of a professional malpractice action. It is their function to ensure that a certain level of competency and ethical practice is maintained among the members. When someone is cheated or is the victim of the incompetence of a member of that society, they sometimes turn to the society itself, claiming that it has failed in its duty to protect the public from the wrongdoer.

Schilling v. Certified General Accountant Association of British Columbia[57]

In this case, a member of the Certified General Accountants Association was under disciplinary review for misconduct when he resigned from the organization. Prior to this time, the plaintiffs had placed their entire life savings in his care. About a year after his resignation as a CGA, he absconded with these funds, leaving the plaintiffs with nothing. They sued the CGA Association, claiming that the body had failed to protect the public and themselves specifically by failing to provide notification of the resignation and that the accountant was no longer a member in good standing. They claimed as well that the association had failed do anything to ensure that he was no longer claiming to be a CGA even after they were aware that he was. The court agreed and the CGA Association had to reimburse the plaintiffs for their losses.

In addition to establishing licensing, certification, training, and disciplinary standards, these organizations also typically play a significant role in public education and arranging for the on-going training of their members. Arranging for the malpractice insurance discussed above can also be a major responsibility of the organization. Of course, all this costs money, and belonging to these professional organizations typically requires the payment of significant annual fees.

Other Business Torts

People involved in business activities can find themselves faced with tortious liability for their conduct in all the categories of torts listed above. Businesses that deal directly with the public, especially in the service industries, such as restaurants, hotels

57. Schilling v. Certified General Accountant Association of British Columbia, [1995] 2 W.W.R. 115 (B.C.S.C.); reversed on appeal [1996] 7 W.W.R. 268 (B.C.C.A.); leave to appeal to the S.C.C. was refused.

and retail merchandising, are often faced with their employees becoming involved in altercations with customers in the course of their work. Such altercations can result in actions against the business on the basis of vicarious liability for assault and battery, negligence, trespass, and even false imprisonment. When business premises visited by customers or the public are involved, there can be actions for negligence based on occupiers' liability.

Much more likely, depending on the nature of the business, are actions for negligence for injury or damage caused by improper performance of the service supplied or product sold. As discussed above, even if only careless words are involved and the business is restricted to giving advice and opinions, there can now be liability to both clients and third parties who suffer financially from relying on those words. And if those words are false and cause damage to someone's reputation, the business can be sued for defamation. Those providing consulting services to businesses and private individuals, such as bankers, accountants, auditors, lawyers, financial advisors, engineers, and architects, are only a few of the professionals who find themselves increasingly vulnerable to damage actions for both tort and breach of contract.

In addition to the categories of torts discussed in this chapter, there are other unique ones that can be important to businesses: inducing breach of contract; deceit; conversion; passing off; and defamation with respect to a product, called injurious falsehood. Most of these are associated with unfair or overaggressive competition.

Inducing breach of contract usually involves an employer persuading an employee of another business to leave that employment and work for him or her. This practice is common when that employee has special knowledge about trade secrets or customer lists or has a special relationship with customers enabling him or her to bring them to the new job. If the employee is contractually committed to stay in that position of employment for a period of time or not to disclose the secret information, they will breach that contractual obligation if they do so. For the other employer to persuade the employee to commit such a breach, usually with financial incentives that make it worth the risk, violates a duty not to intervene in that relationship. The new employer may face the tort action of inducing breach of contract as a result. For the victim to sue for inducing breach of contract, they must be able to establish that there was a contract that was breached and that the person being sued knew about the contract and intentionally induced the breach. This type of tort can also be committed when one business induces another to breach contractual relations with someone else, as when a supplier is persuaded to abandon one customer in favour of another or a customer is persuaded to breach their contract with a competing supplier. The victim likely has the right to sue the employee or supplier for breach, but it is often preferable to sue the other employer because they have deep pockets (the funds to make the action worthwhile), whereas it is likely that suing the employee is not worth the effort.

A related problem exists when one business intentionally interferes with the operation of a competitor. When this is done through ordinary competition, there is no complaint, but sometimes that competition becomes unfair. Examples of unfair competition are one business seeking confidential information from the employees or another; intimidation to discourage someone from opening a business in an area or to sell a particular product at a lower price; or even where one restaurant sends employees to the door of another to redirect customers to the first. These are all examples of improper interference in business. Most of these kinds of

Intentional torts important in some businesses

Negligence more common

Inducing breach of contract actionable

problems are dealt with by the federal *Competition Act,* and this will be discussed in Chapter 9.

The tort of **deceit** involves the fraudulent and intentional misleading of another person, causing damage. This is where one person lies to another, causing loss. It is an intentional tort and one of the few situations where the court will entertain an application for punitive damages. As mentioned, this is an order that the defendant pay money to the plaintiff, not to compensate the victim but to punish the wrongdoer and to discourage that kind of conduct. The case of *Derry v. Peek*[58] established that deceit did not require actual knowledge that what was stated was incorrect. It was enough that the person making the statement did not believe it to be true. This is a common wrong committed in business and will be dealt with in Chapter 7 under "Fraudulent Misrepresentation."

Conversion involves one person intentionally appropriating the goods of another person for his or her own purposes. Theft of goods, in addition to being a crime, is also actionable under the tort of conversion. Conversion also takes place when someone sells or otherwise wrongfully disposes of goods belonging to someone else, or when a person acquires possession of goods through deceit and the goods are damaged or destroyed to the extent that they are no longer of any value to the rightful owner. The courts, in such circumstances, will usually award damages as a remedy, the person converting the goods in effect being forced to purchase them. The courts also have the power to order the return of the goods if that is a more appropriate remedy. Of course, any direct intentional interference causing damage to the goods of another is a trespass to chattels, and other remedies may be available as a result. When someone "keys" the paint on a new car or kicks the door in, they have committed trespass to chattels and are liable to pay compensation and possibly punitive damages to the victim.

A **passing off action** is appropriate when a business or product is presented to the public in such a way as to lead the public to believe that the product is being provided by another. When imitation Rolex watches are sold as the real thing or when a restaurant adopts the golden arches logo leading the public to believe it is part of the McDonald's chain, when it is not, the tort of passing off has been committed. The court can award damages in these circumstances, but an injunction or an order that the offending product be delivered to the plaintiff for destruction may be a more appropriate remedy. This will be discussed in more detail in Chapter 16 under "Intellectual Property."

The tort of **injurious falsehood** will also be discussed under that heading. This tort takes place when one person attacks the reputation of another's product or business. When a person spreads a false rumour that the wine manufactured by a competitor is adulterated with some other substance or that his business is about to become bankrupt, they have committed an injurious falsehood. Although this tort is often called trade slander or product defamation, it must be distinguished from the tort of defamation that involves injury to the personal reputation of the injured party. Injurious falsehood deals with the reputation and value of a person's property. It may reflect negatively on the quality of the product, or it may relate to title. When a person falsely claims that the seller does not own what he is selling or that the product is in violation of patent or copyright, he has uttered an actionable injurious falsehood.

Fraud or deceit actionable

Conversion actionable

Passing off actionable

Injurious falsehood actionable

58. (1889) 14 App. Cas. 337 at 374 (H.L.)

Procor Ltd. v. United Steelworkers of America et al.[59]

Procor Ltd. is a manufacturer who exports much of their product to the United States. They were involved in a serious and difficult labour dispute with their employees. In the air of hostility created by the labour dispute, members of the union accused the company of customs fraud, saying that they were exporting Japanese products into the United States without disclosing the fact. This caused an intensive and disruptive investigation into the operations of the company, even stopping production for a time. In addition, there was considerable negative publicity. The investigation exonerated the company, showing the union members to be wrong and the accusations to be unfounded. Procor then sued the union and the members who had made the accusations for injurious falsehood. These defendants had made statements that they knew or should have known to be false to the customs agents, instigating the investigation. In addition to the presence of a false statement made to a party causing damage, it is also necessary to establish malice to succeed in an injurious falsehood action. Malice is usually described as a dishonest or improper motive. While the judge did not find that they lied outright, he did find that the union officials were "willfully blind to the truth" when they made these false statements to the customs officials, and that was enough to establish malice. In addition, their motive was not to act as good citizens but to further their labour dispute and vent their frustrations and hostility towards the company. This was an improper purpose and also supported the finding of malice. The judge also found that the defendants had participated in a conspiracy to accomplish these goals and were as a result liable to pay $100 000 general damages and a further $100 000 punitive damages. In a society like ours, we have to be so careful about what we say about others. This case is an example of the difficulties that a few misplaced words can cause. Remember, although this instance involved a labour dispute, torts, such as injurious falsehood and defamation, can arise in all our business relations.

A particular problem that arises in business is the problem over **privacy**. Invasion of a person's privacy may take the form of a physical intrusion, surveillance, misuse of an image or name, or access to information. Businesses often use information that people would like to keep private. They sometimes use images or likenesses to promote products without permission. In common law, there is no tort of invasion of privacy, but several provinces have made interfering with a person's privacy a tort. Others, including the federal government, have passed statutes restricting the use of private information with the penalties limited to those set out in the statute. The federal government has appointed a privacy commissioner to enforce its statute. Even where there is no privacy tort, the action complained of may qualify as another kind of tort. For example, where a business uses a person's image, name, or likeness to promote their product without permission, there is an innuendo communicated that the person has endorsed the product. That is a false statement and is actionable as defamation.

Protection of privacy legislated

Businesses are often tempted to extract private information from their employees or even to use surveillance techniques to obtain information about them. Telephones and electronic mail are sometimes monitored. Medical information, political or religious affiliations, treatment for alcohol- or drug-related problems, even mental conditions, all may be of considerable interest. Surveillance to detect

59. (1990) 65 D.L.R. (4th) 287 (Ont. H.C.).

theft and for other security concerns are also common. This is dangerous territory, as it may violate statutory rights to privacy in place in that jurisdiction, and it
may also be a violation of human rights legislation, depending on the kind of information being sought and the methods used to obtain it.

Finally, it must be noted that particular problems arise through the use of the
Internet. Because the Internet is uncontrolled, people can say whatever they want.
All sorts of salacious, mischievous, defamatory, and obscene material appears on the
Internet every day. Many of the problems already discussed arise in this particular
format. Confidential information may be involved. Defamation and injurious falsehood may take place. Privacy may be invaded. Fraud and negligent misrepresentations may be made. What can the victim do? The person who made the offending
comment is liable for what they say, but often, this is a useless remedy because either the wrongdoer has no money or it is not possible to determine who is responsible. Can the online service provider, the people who operate the Internet or
the operators of the particular web site or chat-line, be sued for allowing their facilities to be used in this way? Probably, the people who have direct control will
have some responsibility, but the larger service providers, such as Compuserve,
may be treated more like a telephone company that does not have direct responsibility for the calls, unless they have been directly asked to intervene. These questions have yet to be clarified in Canadian law.

Privacy and the Internet

Braintech, Inc. v. Kostiuk[60]

A case heard in the British Columbia Court of Appeal and refused leave to appeal
at the Supreme Court of Canada helps to clarify some of the problems regarding
jurisdiction in Internet-related disputes. In this case, a Vancouver firm sued a
Vancouver investor for defamation over comments he made about the company in
a chat room at Silicon Investor. The lawsuit was filed in a Texas court, even though
both litigants were in Vancouver, and there was no active presence of the plaintiff
in Texas, primarily because the court in that jurisdiction has a reputation for making huge damage awards. The defendant did not defend himself, believing that
the court had no jurisdiction in the case. The plaintiff was awarded $400 000 (US)
in damages. When the successful plaintiff took the judgment to the British Columbia
court to have it enforced, the defendant argued that the Texas court had no jurisdiction in the matter and was not the appropriate forum to hear the case. He lost
at the trial level but had that decision reversed at the appeal level. It was argued that
the case should have been heard where there was a "real and substantial connection"
to the matter in dispute. Because of the nature of the Internet, the only connection
with Texas was that a Texas resident could have dialed into an out-of-state Internet
site and read the alleged liable. But that was true of any location in any country, and
to allow any location to have such jurisdiction would have a "crippling effect" on the
Internet and freedom of expression. The danger is having several different paral-
lel actions going on at the same time. The action should be brought according to
American law in a jurisdiction where there was a "real and substantial presence" or
in Canadian law a "real and substantial connection." That was British Columbia
and not Texas. Although the Supreme Court will not hear the appeal, the decision is important because it is "the most significant ruling yet in Canada about the
Internet, primarily because it spells out under what conditions a given jurisdiction

60. (1999) 171 D.L.R. (4th) 46 (B.C.C.A.); leave to appeal to S.C.C. refused (March 9, 2000) Doc.
    27296

can rule on an Internet dispute and, by extension, which set of laws ought to apply to cyberspace behaviour."[61] Note, however, that the use of the Internet here was passive. Where the parties are using the Internet to communicate back and forth, negotiating and engaging in commercial activities, this is an active use of the Internet, and the outcome would likely be quite different.

Summary

Tort law

- Protects people from intentional or careless interference with their person, property, or reputation

Intentional torts

- Assault and battery—defences are consent or self-defence (reasonable force)
- Trespass—temporary or permanent intrusion on someone else's property
- False imprisonment—a person falsely restrained by someone without authority
- Defamation—a false statement that discredits a person
  - Libel is written defamation and slander is spoken
  - Defences—absolute privilege, qualified privilege, truth, and fair comment

Negligence

- Inadvertent conduct falling below an acceptable standard of behaviour
- Plaintiff must establish:
  - that a duty of care was owed using reasonable foreseeability test
  - that conduct fell below level expected from a reasonable person
  - that material damage resulted from the conduct
  - that the injury or damage was not too remote
  - that they had not voluntarily assumed the risk
- If there is contributory negligence, courts may apportion the losses

Product liability

- Based on negligence. Manufacturers owe a duty to consumers of their products.

Professional liability

- Also usually based on negligence
- Professionals may be liable for:
  - false or inaccurate information that causes economic loss and breaches of fiduciary duty or contractual obligations
  - inducing breach of contract, deceit, conversion, passing off, and injurious falsehood

61. *Ibid*, p. C6

QUESTIONS

1. Explain what is meant by the statement: "A tort is a civil wrong."

2. How do the courts usually determine what standard people must meet to avoid being declared negligent?

3. Distinguish between assault and battery.

4. How do doctors avoid liability for the tort of assault and battery when operating on or otherwise treating patients?

5. What limitations are there on the right of self-defence when people are defending themselves against an attack?

6. Describe the situations in which battery may be justified.

7. What are the necessary elements that must be present for a person to be classified as a trespasser?

8. What may the proprietor of a business do when faced with an unruly patron?

9. Imprisonment can take the form of confinement, arrest, or submission to authority. Explain.

10. What must be established to sue successfully for false imprisonment?

11. Distinguish between libel and slander and explain the significance of the distinction.

12. Define the terms "innuendo" and "qualified privilege."

13. List and explain what a plaintiff must establish to succeed in a negligence action.

14. What remedies are available when a tort is committed intentionally that may not be available when the conduct is unintentional?

15. What test do courts use to determine whether the defendant owed a duty to be careful to the plaintiff?

16. What problem normally faced in product liability cases was overcome by the decision made in *Donoghue v. Stevenson*?

17. Distinguish between misfeasance and nonfeasance and explain the significance of the difference in tort law.

18. Explain how the test used to determine the standard of care required from professionals is different from the test used to determine the standard of care required generally.

19. Explain how the standard of care that an occupier must exercise to a person using the property has changed in recent years.

20. How does the "but for" test help to satisfy the requirements of causation?

21. Explain how the effect of the presence of contributory negligence has been modified in recent years.

22. Why is the case of *Haig v. Bamford* considered important in the recent development of tort law?

23. Identify the legal principles related to professional liability established by the British *Anns* case.

24. Discuss the tort implications of making false claims against another person or company.

25. Privacy concerns are becoming more problematic in the technological age. What tort principles protect the rights of individuals in this area?

26. Consider the problems related to jurisdiction where the Internet is the means of communicating a defamatory message.

CASES

1. Edwards v. Tracey Starr's Shows (Edmonton) Ltd.

In this case, a man and his friend went to a nightclub for dinner and a few drinks and to see the show. Towards the end of their visit, both men went to the washroom. When they returned, the plaintiff tripped over a step that protruded into the aisle from the stage, fell, and was seriously injured. It is likely that had he been watching where he was going, he would have seen the step and avoided it, though there was some dispute about the lighting. The judge in this case said that the plaintiff was distracted by an exotic dancer on the stage and that was why he fell. Explain the liability of the nightclub in these circumstances and any defences they might have. Would your answer be different in a jurisdiction where there was no occupiers' liability act?

2. Kovacs v. Ontario Jockey Club

Mr. Kovacs tried to use a credit voucher that he had obtained from one racetrack at another, both owned and operated by the Ontario Jockey Club. Because of some misunderstanding, he was identified as a person who had committed a fraud on the racetrack. He was approached by two security guards and was asked to go to the office to discuss the matter. Mr. Kovacs felt that he had no choice, and he accompanied them. The matter was straightened out in about 20 minutes, and he went on his way. Mr. Kovacs sued for false imprisonment. What is the likely outcome?

3. Conrad v. Snair

Mr. Snow operated and owned a 10-metre sailboat which he had built by hand and which he moored along with several other boats in Echo Bay. Mr. Snair was visiting his former girlfriend, who owned property in Echo Bay, in his 4.6-metre Boston Whaler runabout. Mr. Snow's vessel was already in the bay when Mr. Snair arrived. Dinner was served overlooking the bay containing the various boats, and later that night, Mr. Snair took Ms. Conrad in the Boston Whaler over to the yacht club, in the process of which he had to pass by Mr. Snow's boat. Shortly after midnight, on returning from the yacht club, Mr. Snair operated his boat at high speed and collided with Mr. Snow's sailboat. Ms. Conrad suffered severe brain damage. The Canadian collision regulations require that sailboats moored in this fashion hang a white light from the mast. Mr. Snow had failed to post such a light. Several other vessels in the bay had also failed to post such lights, and it seemed to be the practice in that area not to bother. Ms. Conrad sued Mr. Snair as well as Mr. Snow for negligence. Explain who would be held responsible for the accident.

4. Van der Zalm v. Times Publishers, Bierman, McClintock, and Underhill

The plaintiff was the Minister of Human Resources for the Government of British Columbia and had been responsible for initiating some significant changes in the province's welfare programs. Many people in the province were very critical of what they perceived to be a restrictive and retrogressive approach to welfare. The defendants published in their newspaper a cartoon depicting the plaintiff "gleefully pulling wings from flies." The defendants claimed that since the plaintiff had carried on his duties as cabinet minister in a way that inflicted suffering on those who could not protect themselves, their depiction of him as cruel and thoughtless was fair comment. The evidence before the court, however, indicated that the minister had carried out his duties in good faith and that there was no evidence to show that he was a person of cruel or sadistic character who enjoyed inflicting suffering. The court was left with the problem of deciding whether the message contained in the cartoon was fair comment. Discuss the probable outcome.

5. Dixon v. Deacon Morgan McEwan Easson

Mr. Dixon was an investor, who chose to invest $1.2 million in National Business Systems when the share price was $12.89 per share. These shares went up in price somewhat, but before he could sell, the Securities Commission suspended trading. When trading resumed, the shares sold at about $3. Dixon had invested on the strength of financial statements, including one marked "Consolidated Statements of Income and Retained Earnings (Audited)," which had been audited by the defendants. In fact, these statements were based on fraudulent information supplied by the management of National Business Systems to indicate annual profits of $14 million, when the company had lost $33 million. There is no question that the accounting firms involved in the audit were negligent for not detecting the inaccuracy. Mr. Dixon sued the accounting firm for negligence. Nothing on the document indicated who the auditors were, and the statements had been prepared without the auditors knowing that they would be used by an investor, such as Mr. Dixon. The question the court had to determine was whether the auditor owed a duty to Mr. Dixon to be careful. If the auditors had known that the statements were being prepared to attract investors, would this affect your answer?

CHAPTER 5

Formation of Contracts

CHAPTER HIGHLIGHTS

- The requirements of a valid contract
- Offer and acceptance—the necessary conditions
- Consideration—essential ingredient in a valid contract
- The principles of promissory estoppel and *quantum meruit*
- When a contract requires a seal

The law of contracts is the second and most significant area of private law affecting business people. The world of commerce is based on contracts, and they are at the heart of most business relationships. In this and the following three chapters, we will discuss how a contract is formed, various factors that affect them, and how contracts can come to an end. This chapter introduces the first two of the five essential elements necessary for valid contracts, and the other three will be discussed in the following chapter.

McIntyre v. Pietrobon[1]

Mr. and Mrs. McIntyre decided to purchase a house being offered for sale by the Pietrobons. They signed an interim agreement and paid a deposit of $10 000. The interim agreement contained a standard provision, which stated, "Subject to purchaser obtaining satisfactory personal financing." The McIntyres did not obtain financing; they did not even try. They simply changed their minds and wanted their $10 000 deposit back. The Pietrobons would not return the money because they claimed that the McIntyres had breached their contract and had forfeited their right to it. The McIntyres sued. The judge held that since the clause was so vague, there was no agreement, and ordered the return of the money.

On the other hand, in a subsequent and similar British Columbia case, the sale of the house was made conditional on the sale of the purchaser's house by a certain date. This is a common provision in real estate transactions where purchasers have to sell their old houses before purchasing a new one. In this case, the vendor cancelled the contract before the sale was made, but the purchaser did sell his house by the specified date and sued to enforce the contract. The same argument was made, that the provision was too vague making the contract uncertain. In this case, however, the Court of Appeal found that the purchaser was obligated to make a reasonable effort to sell the house and, given that, the contract was sufficiently certain and was, as a result, binding on the parties.[2]

1. (1987) 15 B.C.L.R. (2d) 350 (B.C.S.C.)
2. Wiebe v. Bobsien 20 D.L.R. (4th) 475, (B.C.C.A.)

These cases affirm that the terms of a contract must be certain and that people working in the real estate industry and most other commercial activities must be well versed in the law relating to contracts and very careful when drawing up such agreements, making certain that what the parties have agreed to is clear and nothing left to be agreed upon later.

The Contractual Relationship

Knowledge of contract law is vital to all business people because most commercial transactions have contracts at their base. A **contract** is a voluntary exchange of promises, creating obligations, which, if defaulted on, can be enforced and remedied by the courts. It is important to understand that when drawing up a contract, people create and define their own rules and obligations as opposed to other areas of the law, such as torts, where the rules and obligations are imposed on them. A valid contract creates a situation that enables parties to the contract to predict with some certainty their future relationship because each party knows that the courts will hold them to their agreement. In spite of this willingness to enforce a valid contract, the courts do not generally get involved at the formation stage of a contractual relationship, creating an environment often referred to as freedom of contract. People can enter into almost any kind of contractual agreement they want to, as long as the contract meets the common law requirements that will be discussed in this and the following chapters. It should be noted, however, that the courts have interfered where there is a clear imbalance between the parties, usually in response to consumer protection legislation. The law of contract is found primarily in the common law or case law, but in specialized areas, such as the sale of goods, partnerships, corporations, real property, legislation, which will be the subjects of later chapters, has been enacted that modifies, restricts, or replaces these common law principles. When we study contract law, the focus is on the problems, and there is a danger of concluding that most contracts go bad. In fact, most contractual agreements are honoured or resolved to the mutual satisfaction of the parties. The courts only become involved when a conflict arises. The law has been shaped by the courts' resolution of those disputes.

Exchange of promises enforceable in court

Importance of statutes

Ingredients of a Contract

Not all agreements are contracts. To qualify as a valid contract, an agreement must meet certain basic qualifications. They are:

1. **Consensus**. Parties to a contract must reach a mutual agreement to commit themselves to a certain transaction. They are assumed to approach the agreement from equal bargaining positions, free to enter it as they choose. The process by which this agreement is reached usually involves an offer and an acceptance, although consensus can be inferred.

2. **Consideration**. There must be a commitment on the part of both parties to do something or to abstain from doing something. The consideration is the price each is willing to pay to participate in the contract.

3. **Capacity**. Parties to a contract must be legally capable of understanding and entering into the bargain. Limitations in contracting capacity have been placed on infants, insane or intoxicated persons, aliens, and, in some instances, native peoples and corporations.

4. **Legality**. The object and consideration involved in the agreement must be legal and not against public policy.

5. **Intention**. Both parties must be serious when striking the bargain, and both must intend that legally enforceable obligations will result from it.

It should be noted here that although the general rule is that an agreement reached verbally between parties is every bit as binding as a written one, legislation has been passed requiring that certain types of contracts be supported by evidence in **writing** before they can be enforced in the courts. For convenience, this limited requirement of writing will also be discussed along with the five essential ingredients of contract.

Terms and Definitions

Before addressing these elements of a contract in more detail, it is necessary to outline some basic terminology used in the discussion of contractual obligations.

Formal and Simple Contracts

The use of a seal

A formal contract is one that is sealed. A modern seal is usually a paper wafer affixed to a document by the party to be bound, but any mark or impression will do. Simple contracts, sometimes called **parol contracts**, may be verbal or written but are not under seal.

Express and Implied Contracts

Contracts may be inferred

An express contract is one in which the parties have expressly stated their agreement, either verbally or in writing. An implied contract is inferred from the conduct of the parties. When people deposit coins in vending machines, it can be inferred that they intend to create a contractual relationship, and thus, an implied contract is in force. Portions of an express contract may also be implied.

Valid, Void, and Voidable Contracts

A void contract is no contract

A valid contract is one that is legally binding on both parties. A void contract does not qualify as a legally binding contract because of some missing ingredient. If the parties to a void contract thought they were bound and followed the agreement, the courts would try to put the parties back to their original positions. A voidable contract does exist and has legal effect, but one of the parties has the option to end the contract. This distinction between void and voidable can have important implications for outsiders to the contract who have acquired an interest in the subject matter. If the original contract is void, the goods must be returned, but if it is only voidable, the outsider has acquired good title and can keep the goods.

Unenforceable and Illegal Contracts

An example of an unenforceable contract is one that is required to be in writing under the *Statute of Frauds* and is not. It may be good and valid in all other respects, but the courts will not help either party to force the other to perform such a contract. As well, once it has been performed, the courts will not help either party get out of it.

Illegal contract is void

An illegal contract is one that involves the performance of an unlawful act. It is void, and the parties to such an agreement cannot be required to perform it. If the contract has been performed or partially performed, the court, because of the moral taint, normally will not assist either party to undo it by returning them to their original positions, as would usually be the case in a void contract. For example, when a deposit has been paid, the court will not order its return, nor will it require property to be returned, even when one of the parties has been enriched at the other's expense. Of course, the courts will intervene on behalf of a party who is innocent of any wrongdoing.

The status of these two types of agreement, then, is quite different. The unenforceable contract is valid, and the illegal contract is void. The two are handled in a similar fashion by the courts; however, the courts are more sympathetic where an unenforceable contract is involved and are more likely to help the parties when disputes arise than is the case with an illegal contract.

Bilateral and Unilateral Contracts

A bilateral contract is one in which both parties assume obligations to be performed. There is no exchange of promises in a unilateral contract. One party requests some conduct, and it is the performance of what has been requested that causes the contract to come into effect. A reward is an example of a unilateral contract. It is not until the lost item is returned that the offer is accepted and the contract created. Thus, a bilateral contract involves an exchange of promises, whereas a unilateral contract involves a promise and an act.

Unilateral contract performance is acceptance

Consensus

Dickinson v. Dodds[3]

One of the best cases to illustrate how offer and acceptance work is an old case from the latter part of the 19th century. Mr. John Dodds owned property and made an offer to sell it to Mr. Dickinson for £800, saying specifically, "This offer to be left over until Friday, 9:00 am." On the Thursday afternoon prior to that time limit, Mr. Dickinson learned that Mr. Dodds had been trying to sell or indeed had sold the property to someone else. This prompted Mr. Dickinson to make sure that the acceptance was received before the stated deadline.

He went to Mr. Dodds' home and left a written acceptance at that location. The next morning, Mr. Dickinson went down to the train station to intercept Mr. Dodds as he arrived in town. When Mr. Dickinson located him, he handed him a written acceptance. Mr. Dodds replied that it was too late and that he had already sold the property. This took place before the stated deadline.

The case is important because it illustrates the nature of an offer. The offer is a tentative commitment on the part of the person making it and until the other party accepts it, there is no obligation on the person making the offer. In this case, Mr. Dodds was free to withdraw his offer any time before it was accepted. The real question was whether or not the offer was still open and able to be accepted at the time of the purported acceptance—that is, when the letter was left at his residence or at the train station the next morning. There was no longer an offer open that could be accepted at those times. Mr. Dodds was free to change his mind and had done so. But he had to make it clear to the other party that he had revoked the offer. In this case, there was no question that Mr. Dickinson knew Mr. Dodds had changed his mind, since he admitted it in his pleadings. Because Mr. Dickinson knew that Mr. Dodds had changed his mind before he tried to accept, there was no contract. But if Mr. Dickinson had not been aware that Mr. Dodds was no longer of a mind to sell, there would have been a valid contract.

3. (1876) 2 Ch. D. 463 (C.A.)

The essence of a contract is, at least in theory, the **meeting of the minds** of the contracting parties. The two parties must have a common will in relation to the subject matter of their negotiations, and they must have reached an agreement. They must share an understanding of the bargain struck and be willing to commit themselves to the terms of the contract.

Agreement reached— bargain struck

However, if people were bound only to the terms of contracts they fully understood, there would be few enforceable contracts. Few people thoroughly read the major contracts they enter into, such as insurance policies, leases, and loans, and of those who do, few fully understand the specific meaning of the documents. The law does not recognize the excuse that one of the contracting parties did not read the contract or that he or she did not understand it.

Terms must be clear and unambiguous

Both parties must have had an opportunity to read and understand the contract for it to be valid, that is, the terms of the contract must be unambiguous so that if they are read with the help of a lawyer, a reasonable person could understand their meaning. It is only when the terms themselves are ambiguous that the court may decide that there has been no consensus between the parties, and the contract will be declared void. This was the problem with the agreement in the case used to introduce this chapter. Because of the vague nature of the terms, the would-be purchasers were successful in getting back their deposit. There was no contract.

Obviously, mistakes happen, and some very complex rules, which we will discuss later, have been developed to handle them. Nevertheless, contract law is based on the assumption that the culmination of the bargaining process is when one party states its position in the form of an offer in the expectation that the other party, through acceptance, will make a similar commitment to be bound by the terms of that offer. It should be stressed that a valid offer and an acceptance are not always obvious, and yet, from the conduct of the parties or other factors, it is clear that the parties have a mutual understanding between them. In such circumstances, the courts are willing to imply the existence of a contract, and no evidence of a specific identifiable offer and acceptance is required.

Offer

The offer contains all the terms to be included in the contract; all that is required of the other party is to give its consent or denial. The offer is a tentative promise on the part of one party to do something if the other party is willing to do whatever the first party requests. When a sales person offers to sell a car to a customer for $5000, the offer is a tentative promise by the seller to deliver the car contingent on the customer's willingness to pay the $5000. The process of making an offer is the communication of a willingness to be bound by the terms and conditions stated in that offer.

Offer—tentative promise

This aspect of the offer often confuses those involved in commercial activities. People borrowing money, acquiring insurance, and so forth frequently have a form placed before them by a salesperson who says, in effect, "This is our contract; sign here." In fact, the document is not a contract at all but only an offer. Once accepted and signed by the customer, the document embodies the terms and conditions of the contract. The offer must contain all significant terms of the proposed contract. The courts do have the power to imply into contracts many of the insignificant terms the parties may not have considered, such as time of delivery, time of payment, and so on. Such terms must be incidental to the central agreement but consistent with the apparent intention of the parties. Courts will often turn to the common practice of the trade or industry to help them imply such terms. When

Offer—must include all important terms

goods are sold, the *Sale of Goods Act* sets out the terms to be implied when missing in the contract of sale. The sale of goods is a major topic discussed in Chapter 8. As mentioned, it is possible for the courts to infer the entire contract from the conduct of the parties, but if it is clear that important terms have been left out or are to be negotiated later, there is no contract, and it will be declared void.

Some terms can be implied

Bawitko Investments Ltd. v. Kernels Popcorn Ltd.[4]

Kernels Popcorn Ltd. sold popcorn products in a number of specialty stores franchised in Canada and the United States. Anthony Passander, who represented Bawitko Investments Limited, negotiated with Kernels to open such a franchise at a particular location in Ontario. He was given an information package, including a complicated draft franchise agreement. The negotiations went well, and at one stage, the parties shook hands, and the representative for Kernels said, "You've got a deal." It was clear from the dealings that the parties intended to formalize their obligations in a written document. Subsequently, the relationship deteriorated, and Kernels cancelled the deal. Passander still wanted to have the franchise, however, and sued to enforce the original oral contract. The judge made it clear that it was quite possible for the parties to agree to a contract orally, expecting it to be put into a formal written document later, and such an oral contract could be binding. In this case, however, there was still much left to be determined, and there was not sufficient agreement between the parties as to the terms to create an enforceable contract. The judge found that "at all relevant times the appellant plainly considered that the terms of the intended formal agreement were not yet settled." In his decision, the judge said, "… when the original contract is incomplete because essential provisions intended to govern the contractual relationship have not been settled or agreed upon; or the contract is too general or uncertain to be valid in itself and is dependent on the making of a formal contract; or the understanding or intention of the parties, even if there is no uncertainty as to the terms of their agreement, is that their legal obligations are to be deferred until a formal contract has been approved and executed, the original or preliminary agreement cannot constitute an enforceable contract. In other words, in such circumstances, the 'contract to make a contract' is not a contract at all."

This principle must be distinguished from two other situations that appear similar. If a document refers to an intention to create a more formal document later, such as where a letter of intent or understanding is given, if all the requirements for a contract are met, the transaction may be binding at the earlier stage. Thus, an **interim agreement** may be binding, even though a formal contract will be created later. When a person does not want to be bound by such a letter, they should clearly state that in the document. The common practice of a particular industry will also affect just what constitutes a contract and at what stage it is considered binding.

The second situation involves **subject-to clauses**. An offer may include a term making the contract conditional on some future event. A person may offer to purchase a house "subject to" the sale of their house. These types of provisions are not necessarily uncertain or ambiguous, unless the subject-to clause itself is uncertain, as would be the case if the sale were made "subject to my satisfaction." If the terms of the offer are clear and nothing is left to be negotiated or agreed upon, the parties are bound to perform as agreed, once the subject-to term has been satisfied.

Contract not binding until condition satisfied

4. 79 D.L.R. (4th) 97 (Ont. C.A.)

Note exception for service

Some types of contractual relationships, often referred to as **quasi-contracts**, must be viewed as exceptions to the rule that important terms must be clear. These contracts involve requests for goods and services and will be discussed under the heading of *quantum meruit* below.

Invitation to Treat

An offer is usually made to an individual or a group of people, but it is also possible to make an offer to the world at large, such as a notice offering a reward for information or the return of a lost item. Generally, however, newspaper, radio, and television advertisements are called invitations to treat. They have no legal effect but are simply invitations to potential customers to engage in the process of negotiation.

Invitation not an offer

It is sometimes difficult to distinguish between an offer and an invitation to treat. When a tire store puts an ad in the newspaper that says, "Automobile tires for sale, two for the price of one," this is not an offer at all. The potential customer must go to the shop, look at the tires, and determine the value of the deal. The ad is simply an invitation to the reader to visit the place of business and make an offer to purchase some tires. Catalogues and personal ads in the classified section of a newspaper are also invitations to treat. It is important that people engaged in the bargaining process not be exposed to legal liability before they are ready to be serious.

Goods displayed on the shelves of stores, even though the prices of items are clearly marked, are only an invitation to the customer to pick up the desired item, take it to the checkout counter, and make an offer to purchase it at the price marked.

A customer makes an offer to purchase when she takes an item to the checkout.

PhotoDisc

There is still some controversy over this point, but most jurisdictions have accepted the principle established in *Pharmaceutical Society of Great Britain v. Boots Cash Chemists (Southern), Ltd.*[5] In this case, the British Court of Appeal was faced with the problem of deciding whether a statute controlling the sale of certain types of drugs had been violated. The court had to determine whether clearly priced goods displayed on the shelf of a self-service merchandising operation were being offered for sale. The court determined that such a display was an invitation to treat and not an offer.

Because of this, there may be a temptation to switch the prices on items displayed for sale in a store. To do so, however, is a crime.[6] Although the display of the goods is only an invitation, the customer is only being invited to make the offer designated.

Offer by Conduct

A customer in a self-serve store brings the goods to be purchased to a cashier and places the goods and money on the counter. This is an offer implied by conduct. When a person hails a cab, the gesture of raising a hand and calling "Taxi!"

---

5. [1953] 1 All E.R. 482 (C.A.); aff'g [1952] 2 All E.R. 456 (Q.B.)

6. Obtaining goods by false pretences, *Criminal Code*, R.S.C. 1985, c.C-46 s.

constitutes an offer. An auctioneer's comment, "Do I hear $50?" is merely an invitation to the customer to make an offer. When a person in the audience raises a hand or makes some other acceptable gesture, that is the offer, and the auctioneer is free to accept or reject it. A further question, "Do I hear $60?" is an invitation for more offers. The statement "Sold" is an acceptance of the customer's offer.

Offer may be implied by conduct

Communication of an Offer

Before an offer can be accepted, it must first be communicated to the offeree. People cannot accept offers they know nothing about. If a lost dog is returned by someone who is unaware that a reward had been offered, that person has no right to claim the reward, since the offer has not been communicated.

Offer must be communicated

Another situation in which the communication of an offer can present a problem occurs when two offers cross in the mail. If one party sends a letter to another offering to sell a car for $500 and the person to whom the offer is sent, unaware of the first letter, sends another letter offering to purchase the car for the same price, there is no contract. Even though the parties are of a similar mind, neither is aware of the other's offer when the letters are sent, and so, neither could be called an acceptance. If the owner of the vehicle sells it to a third party, the other party would have no complaint.

Similarly, if a person fails to bring all the terms of the offer to the attention of the offeree, the undisclosed terms do not form part of the contract and are not binding on the offeree. A merchant will often try to include an **exemption clause** in a contract. This is an attempt to limit liability for improper performance.

At a parking lot, for example, there is usually a sign disclaiming responsibility for theft or damage to cars or contents left on the lot. A ticket granting admission to a tennis court or to use a ski lift often includes a term disclaiming responsibility for injury, damages, or loss of personal property by theft. In both cases, the term is only binding when it has been reasonably brought to the attention of the patron at the time the contract is made. The sign in the parking lot must be placed in a well-lit, strategic spot where the driver will see it before or at the time the contract is made. When a ticket machine is involved, the practice is to place the notice of the terms on or near the machine so that the person parking cannot avoid seeing the notice. If a ticket is involved and the terms are listed on the back, there must be a reference on the front of the ticket drawing the patron's attention to the back for it to be binding. The ticket must be given at the time the contract is made, not afterwards. When a business regularly depends on such exemption clauses in its contracts, it is vital, especially where it is involved in consumer transactions with the public, that it takes care to draw the customers' attention to this provision at the time of the creation of the contract.

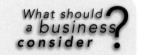

Exemption clauses are more commonly found in written contracts. When people sign contracts, they are generally taken to have read the entire document. Even then, where an exemption clause is unusually restrictive, the court may hold that there was a requirement to specifically bring the clause to the attention of the other contracting party and that the obligation was not met. Even then, if the merchant's failure to perform amounts to a fundamental breach, he or she still may not be able to rely on the exemption clause for protection. The topic of fundamental breach will be discussed in Chapter 7.

Only the person to whom the offer is made can respond to it and, then, only if the offer has been communicated to the offeree or an agent. If the offer is made generally, anyone fulfilling the terms can respond. If the offer is made to a group, anyone in the group satisfying the terms can respond to the offer. But if the offer is made to a specific person, no one else can accept it.

Only person(s) to whom the offer is made can accept

The End of an Offer

For the acceptance of an offer to be effective, the offer must be in force at the time of the acceptance. There are several ways for an offer to come to an end before acceptance.

Offer ends
- **when specified**

1. **End of a specified time**. If the offer contains a term specifying when the offer will come to an end, the expiration of that time will end the offer. Note that the offeror is still free to revoke the offer before this time expires, unless an option has been purchased. Option agreements will be discussed below.

- **at a reasonable time**

2. **The expiration of a reasonable time**. If no time is specified for the offer to end, it will expire at the end of a reasonable time; thus, an offer to sell a ship would likely last longer than an offer to sell a load of ripe peaches.

Mitchell v. Bennett, Cole Adjusters Ltd. et al[7]

The day after a fire in her house, Mrs. Mitchell made a claim on her insurance. In February, three months after the fire the insurance adjusters offered her $9000, less her $100 deductible, to settle the claim. There was some considerable delay in communication between the adjusters, Mrs. Mitchell, and her lawyers, but it was clear in September, because of a telephone conversation between her lawyer and the adjuster, that the company was still willing to stand by its February offer. Finally, she signed the appropriate proof-of-loss form and sent this to her lawyer, who then attempted to accept the offer to settle on her behalf on December 16. The adjusters refused to honour the settlement, claiming the offer had lapsed. Where there is no specific time limit set for the offer to expire, it will expire after a reasonable time. The judge found that because of the nature of this matter, the offer could be outstanding for a longer period. If the sale of a commodity had been involved, the offer would have lapsed after a much shorter period. This was supported by the willingness of the adjusters to still settle on the basis of the offer in September. But in this case, the court found that the offer had expired on November 9, one year after the claim was initiated. There was a one-year limitation period in place, requiring any action from such a claim to be commenced by writ no later than one year after the fire. After that time, the insurance company would no longer have any obligation to her, and so, the judge found that any offer to settle would, by inference, not extend beyond the expiration of this limitation period. We always have to be vigilant to deal with matters in a timely manner. We cannot expect such offers to continue indefinitely. This case illustrates the dangers of inaction.

- **at death of offeror**

3. **Death or insanity of offeror**. If the offeror dies or becomes insane to the extent of being incapable of understanding what he or she is doing, the offer automatically ends and cannot be accepted. This is the case even if the offeree is unaware of the death or insanity.

- **when revoked**

Revocation must be communicated

4. **Revocation of offer**. The offeror may revoke an offer any time before acceptance. For such revocation to be effective, it must be communicated to the offeree. The offer ends when the offeror tells the offeree that he has changed his mind. When letters are used, the revocation is only effective when received. Until that time, an offeree can still accept the offer. Until the offeror is sure that the message has been received by the offeree or her agent, he should not offer

7. (1986) 33 D.L.R. (4th) 398 (B.C.S.C.)

or sell the subject matter of the contract to anyone else. While it is possible for the revocation to be communicated indirectly, reliance on such a method would be foolish in the extreme.

In the case of *Dickinson v. Dodds* used to introduce this section, Dodds was extremely lucky. Although there was no attempt to revoke, Dickinson admitted that he knew, "beyond a shadow of a doubt," of the sale before he tried to accept. Had Dickinson not learned of the sale or not admitted he knew, Dodds would have been bound by both contracts to sell the same land.

5. **Rejection and counteroffer**. During the bargaining process, several different proposals may be put forward, rejected, and then followed by counterproposals. To avoid confusion, whenever an offer is put forward and rejected, or a counterproposal is put forward, which by implication is a rejection, the first offer is brought to an end. For example, where a salesperson offers to sell a car to a customer for $5000 and that person replies, "I'll give you $4500," a counteroffer has been made and, by implication, the original offer has been rejected. If the seller rejects the counteroffer, it is too late for the purchaser to reconsider and accept the original offer; it no longer exists. Under such circumstances, an attempt to accept the original $5000 offer constitutes a new offer, which the seller is free to accept or reject.

Rejection or counteroffer ends offer

Request for information is not a counteroffer

Sometimes, it is difficult to tell what constitutes a rejection or a counteroffer. When the offeree is merely requesting information or clarification, that does not constitute a counteroffer or a rejection, and the offer remains in force. If the purchaser in the preceding example had asked, "Does the car have white-wall tires?" the courts would interpret the question as a request for information that would have no effect on the original offer. On the other hand, if the purchaser had asked, "Will you take $4500?" even though it was worded as a request for information, it would likely be a treated as a counteroffer, and the original offer would have ended.

The existence of an offer can be affected by other factors as well. For example, the offer will be ended if the activity contemplated by the contracting parties becomes illegal before acceptance or if the goods forming the subject matter of the contract are destroyed without the parties being aware of it.

Offers That Cannot Be Revoked

Often, business people find the uncertainty associated with the offeror's right to revoke any time prior to the point of acceptance very inconvenient, especially when they are arranging their business affairs in order to take advantage of the offer.

A typical problem involves land accumulations. When developers wish to build a hotel, mall, or other large projects, they normally have to acquire the land to be used from several different owners, but they do not want to make any commitments to those owners, until they are sure they can get all the parcels of land necessary for the project. They will get offers to sell from each of the landowners, but if those owners are free to revoke, there is no certainty for the developers.

In these circumstances, a separate, subsidiary contract is entered into, called an **option agreement**, wherein consideration is given by the offeree specifically to keep the offer open for a given length of time. The developer now has the certainty necessary to accomplish his goal. Such arrangements are quite common and found in all areas of finance and business. Options can also be put under seal; the use of the seal will be discussed later under "Consideration."

Where option exists, offer cannot be revoked

Subsidiary contracts may be implied

Sometimes the courts are willing to imply such a **subsidiary contract**. As discussed, unilateral contracts involve offers that are accepted by performance. What is to stop the offeror from revoking at the last minute? In the United States, when performance of such a unilateral contract has started, the courts will imply a subsidiary contract and not permit the offeror to revoke after performance has started. Thus, if an employer promises to give her business to an employee if he stays until she retires, the acceptance is made simply by his staying on. With such an implied subsidiary contract, the employer could not wait until just before retirement and then revoke the offer. It is likely that the problem would be dealt with in the same way in Canada. In Canada, the courts have adopted a similar attitude in tendering situations. It is common business practice to put out a request for bids in order to get the best possible price on a required product or service. This is the normal practice in the construction industry. The request for bids is an invitation to treat and the submitted bid the offer. The problem is that there is nothing to stop the offeror from withdrawing his offer if he realizes he has made a mistake or upon seeing the other bids realizes his is too low. The Supreme Court of Canada has decided that in some circumstances such tendered bids cannot be revoked. Where the original request for tenders made it clear that bids would only be considered where the offeror agrees that the offer cannot be withdrawn once submitted, a subsidiary contract exists, and the offer then cannot be revoked. As above, the problem is also avoided when the tendered bid is made under seal.

Standard Form Contract

Bargaining difficult with standard form contract

Statutes and attitude of court mitigate this

The law assumes that the two parties to an agreement are in equal bargaining positions and that both will negotiate the terms of the agreement until a consensus which represents a fair bargain is reached. In actual fact, most large businesses do not negotiate with their customers. Rather, they present a contract with fixed terms, which the customer is invited to accept. A passenger purchasing an airline ticket is an example. These are called standard form contracts and contain one-sided terms favouring the business. The exemption clauses, discussed above, that attempt to limit the liability of the business are examples of such one-sided terms. To correct the imbalance and alleviate some of the unfairness, consumer protection legislation has been enacted in most jurisdictions controlling the worst abuses. Consumer protection is one of the subjects covered in Chapter 9. When the courts deal with these clauses, they interpret them strictly so that any ambiguity is read in favour of the disadvantaged party. Thus, a business that includes in its contracts terms disclaiming responsibility for "damage" to goods left on the premises would still be held responsible for goods that were stolen. Even where the exemption clause is clear, the courts are showing a willingness to set them aside on the basis of fairness.

Acceptance

Entores Ltd. v. Miles Far East Corp.[8]

In this case, an American company was dealing with a British company through a Dutch subsidiary for the purchase of electronic components. The British court was being asked by the British company for permission to sue the American company in the United Kingdom. The British court would have jurisdiction only if the

8. [1955] 2 All E.R. 493 (C.A.)

contract came into existence in the United Kingdom. It was argued that since the Dutch company made the acceptance, applying the postbox rule, the contract came into existence where the acceptance originated, in Holland. The court rejected this argument. The parties were using the telex, which uses the phone lines much like a fax machine today, to communicate. The court found that because telex was instantaneous, like the telephone, there was no need to extend the postbox rule exception to this kind of communication. Therefore, the general rule of acceptance, whereby the acceptance was effective only when and where communicated to the offeror, applied. Since the British company made the offer, and they were in the United Kingdom when they received the acceptance, the contract came into existence in the United Kingdom, and the court there had jurisdiction.

This case not only illustrates what happens when the postbox rule comes into play but also shows that when new, instantaneous methods of communication are involved, the postbox rule does not apply. This will be expanded on below.

At the heart of contract law is the concept of consensus and mutual commitment. The manifestation of an intention to commit on the part of the offeror is found in the offer; the offeree's intention to commit is found in the acceptance. The contract is formed, and the parties are bound by it at the point of acceptance. The key to understanding acceptance is that the commitment must be total. If a condition or qualification is put on the acceptance, it then becomes a counteroffer, not an acceptance. If a salesperson offers to sell a car to a customer for $5000 and the response is, "I accept, provided you include new tires," the response is a counteroffer, and the seller is now in a position to accept or reject the new offer. Nor is it possible to accept only part of an offer. If a person offers to sell a house and its furnishings at a stipulated price for each, the purchaser cannot say, "I accept your offer, but I only want the furniture." For an acceptance to be valid, it must be an all-or-nothing proposition.

Acceptance must be unconditional

A serious problem can arise in business where customers and suppliers exchange order forms. Often, the customer, instead of filling in the supplier's order form, simply sends their own which may include different terms. This is not an acceptance but a counteroffer. If the supplier simply sends the product in response, they have accepted and are bound by the new terms often not realizing the difference. Such a mistake is easily made, and care should be taken to watch for such substituted forms.

Even a clear acceptance cannot correct an incomplete offer. When the wording of an offer is unclear, the courts will apply the reasonable person test to determine what was meant but will not go so far as to strike a bargain on behalf of the parties. As mentioned, there is no such thing as a contract to enter into a contract.

Halifax (County) v. Giles[9]

In 1963, John and Hazel Giles conveyed certain property to Halifax County to be used for a fire hall. The deed contained a covenant that if the property was no longer used as a fire hall at any time over the next 50 years, the Gileses or their heirs would have "first right or option to purchase" the property. A fire hall was constructed on the property, but that use ended in 1987. The sole heir of the Gileses demanded that the covenant be honoured. Negotiations took place, but no price could be agreed upon. The court, in this case, had to determine what interest, if

9. (1994) 111 D.L.R. (4th) 614 (N.S.C.A.)

any, Ms. Giles had with respect to the property. After examining the deed carefully, the judge determined that the deed purported to create an option but that no price or method to determine a price had been set out. The court could not create a contract for the parties, and so, there was no contractual right in this instance. When the parties fail to create a contract between themselves, the court will not do it for them. No matter how definite the acceptance, it will not overcome the defect of an incomplete or otherwise defective offer.

Communication of Acceptance

Offer may be accepted by conduct, where specified

Usually, acceptance of an agreement is accomplished by communicating it to the offeror. However, it is possible for an offer to be accepted by conduct. If the offeror has indicated particular conduct to specify acceptance, the offeree must comply with that stipulation for it to be effective. If a homeowner offers $1000 to a contractor to paint a house and specifies that if the painter wants the job, he is to get the keys from a neighbour and do the job while the homeowner is away on vacation, full compliance with those directions amounts to acceptance, and a contract is created.

Communication of Acceptance May Be Indirect

This dispute involves a tender made by Lanca to the Board of Education for the construction of a school building. The provisions of the tender required that a formal contract be executed within seven days of the notification of the acceptance of the tender. A board meeting was held, at which a resolution to accept Lanca's tender was passed. The president of Lanca was present, to the knowledge of the board. Some members of the board, as well as the board's architect and controller, all spoke at the meeting in terms that implied that the plaintiff was going to be building the school. Two days later, the board rescinded its resolution and awarded the contract to someone else. The question facing the court was whether notice of the acceptance had been given to the plaintiff sufficient to create a binding contract. The answer was yes, and the board was liable for the breach.

Lanca Contracting Ltd. v. Brant (County) Board of Education, (1986) 26 D.L.R. (4th) 708 (Ont. C.A,)

Unilateral contract accepted by completion of performance

A **unilateral contract** is accepted by performance of the act specified in the offer. A firm in the United Kingdom offered a large sum of money to the first human-powered aircraft to fly across the English Channel. It would not be necessary for a person making the attempt to submit a formal acceptance before making the try. Starting the flight would not constitute acceptance either. For an acceptance to be effective, the cross-Channel flight would have to be completed. As discussed above, this poses a problem, because in theory at least, there is nothing to stop the offeror from withdrawing the offer after the performance has started but before completion. This may now be handled by finding a subsidiary contract requiring that once the performance starts, the offer cannot be revoked. In any case, where acceptance is by conduct, there is no requirement to communicate the acceptance to the offeror, although there may still be a need to notify the offeror that the required conduct has taken place where this is not self-evident.

A selling practice has developed, in which a merchandiser, without asking, sends a product to the home of a potential customer with an invoice stating that if the goods are not returned within a specified time, the customer will have purchased them. Silence, as a general rule, will not constitute acceptance. When goods are supplied in this way, you can normally ignore them. Just put them away. If you use the goods, you are receiving a benefit and have accepted the offer. This is another example of an unacceptable practice curbed by consumer protection legislation in many jurisdictions. But this may not be the case where you had prior dealings with the supplier.

An important exception to silence not being an acceptance is where there is an ongoing business relationship between the parties. It is quite common for a supplier to send materials used by a business on a regular basis with the understanding that they will continue to be sent unless the supplier is informed otherwise. A relationship of trust has developed, and the business now has a duty to inform the supplier when they change their mind. When a person joins a book-of-the-month club, a similar duty is created, and return of the book may be required to escape obligation.

Unsolicited offer not accepted by silence—but note exception

This is often abused, as when a cable TV supplier decided to supply more channels at an increased fee. They simply changed the service and charged their customers the higher fee, informing them that if they did not want the added service, they had to notify the cable company. Silence was to be taken as acceptance. Because of the ongoing relationship, they would have been successful, had it not been for the public outcry.

Such negative option schemes are now controlled by many jurisdictions in their consumer protection legislation.

Where acceptance is not by conduct, the general rule is that it is not effective until it has been communicated to the offeror. The result flowing from this general rule is that a contract comes into existence when and where the offeror learns of the acceptance, rather than where it is made by the offeree. If a supplier of lumber products in Halifax makes an offer to a customer in Winnipeg and the offeree accepts over the telephone, the contract comes into existence in Halifax, since that is where the offeror heard the acceptance. This can have quite an impact where businesses are communicating at a distance; it may determine that the law of one jurisdiction applies rather than another. In addition, the acceptance becomes effective and a contract is formed at the time the acceptance is communicated.

Acceptance must be communicated to be effective

The Postbox Rule

R. v. Commercial Credit Corp. Ltd.[10]

This case deals with a conditional sale agreement, and the court had to determine whether the contract came into existence inside or outside the province in order to determine which creditor had first claim with respect to the goods used as security. Such conditional sales agreements have to be registered with respect to sales that take place within the province. If the contract was created within the province, and there was no such registration that creditor would lose any claim to the assets. In fact, the original offer had been made by a finance company (Commercial Credit Ltd.) within the province and sent by courier to the offeree outside the province. This offer was then accepted and the acceptance returned also by courier. The problem for the court was whether the postbox rule applied to this form of communication. The judge based his decision on the principle of commercial convenience, which establishes that where the offeror chooses to use the postal service "or some similar organization," the acceptance is effective when and where sent. The

10. (1983) 4 D.L.R. (4th) 314; (N.S.S.C.[A.D.]) aff'd (sub. nom. Nova Scotia v. Weymouth Sea Products Ltd.) (1983) 149 D.L.R. (3d) 637 (N.S.S.C. [T.D.])

judge said, referring to the finance company, "They were the ones that chose the method of communication, and having done so on behalf of both parties, the mailbox doctrine was brought into play. Its extension to a courier service was sound in principle and, in my opinion, the contracts were therefore made outside of Nova Scotia when their acceptances were sent back to Commercial Credit." This is one of the few cases where the postbox rule has been extended beyond communication by mail or telegram. The conclusion that such an important concept should be extended to what is essentially the same type of service offered by private courier services is very attractive, but it remains to be affirmed by a higher-level court, and there is still some question if it will apply beyond Nova Scotia.

Mailed acceptance effective when and where dropped in postbox

Difficulties arise when parties deal with each other over long distances using non-instant forms of communication. Because neither party can be absolutely sure of the other's state of mind at a given time, there can be no certainty of the contract's status. The postbox rule, mentioned above, was developed to solve this problem. When an acceptance is mailed and the use of the postal service is a reasonable means of communication in the circumstances, that acceptance is effective when and where it is deposited in the mailbox. This is a clear exception to the general rule discussed above, where an acceptance is not effective until the offeror learns of it. One problem—determining the point of consensus—is solved, but another is created. For a period of time, while the letter of acceptance is still in the mail, the offeror is bound in contract but unaware of that fact. Where this is a problem, it can be overcome by the offeror stipulating the use of a different means of communication. Otherwise, the court will determine the most reasonable means of responding and, if that is by mail, apply the post box rule accordingly. Where a different means of acceptance is used other than appropriate or specified, the acceptance will be effective only when received, even where the method chosen was faster.

Only applies where response by mail appropriate

When determining whether the postbox rule applies, if the original offer is sent by mail, there is usually little question about a response by mail being appropriate. Difficulty arises when a different means of communication is involved, as is illustrated in *Henthorne v. Fraser*.[11] The plaintiff, Mr. Henthorne, went to the defendant's office, where he was offered some property, with the offer to be left open for 14 days. He took the offer home to think about it and, after several days, posted a letter of acceptance. In the meantime, the defendant, Mr. Fraser, sold the property to another party and wrote a letter to Henthorne revoking the offer. The two letters crossed in the mail. The court had to decide when, if at all, the acceptance was effective. It decided that a reasonable person would have responded by mail, even though the offer had been handed to him in person, and therefore, the acceptance was effective when it was placed in the mailbox.

Postbox rule extended to telegrams

The postbox rule has been extended to include telegrams but not to instantaneous forms of communication, such as telex, as illustrated by the *Entores* case. Today, it is becoming much more common to use electronic means of communication, such as electronic mail and fax, rather than the postal service, and the question arises whether the postbox rule will be extended to these methods of doing business. In the *Entores* case, Lord Denning found that it was not appropriate to use the postbox rule, where instantaneous means of communication, such as the telephone or telex, are used. Since these new electronic communications are also instantaneous, it is not likely that the postbox rule will be extended to them. The

11. [1892] 2 Ch. 27 (Eng. Ch. D.)

problems caused by communication delay, which the postbox rule was meant to solve, are no longer present. This conclusion is confirmed at least with respect to communication by fax in *Eastern Power Limited v. Azienda Comunale Energia and Ambiente*,[12] where the Ontario Court of Appeal found that an acceptance sent by fax was effective only when it was received by the offeror.

It should be noted that there are still significant advantages to using the mail. The use of the mails involves the exchange of a permanent tangible record of the transaction and its terms.

Untangling the WEB

Electronic communication, such as e-mail, may be convenient, but it suffers from a lack of permanency or certainty. These records can be lost with the crash of a system or simply altered in an undetectable way, and while there are methods in place to overcome these problems, careful thought should be given before abandoning the use of paper.

A more significant impact of the operation of the postbox rule may be the determination of *where* the offer was accepted as opposed to *when*. If the offeror, trying to sell lumber products in Halifax, had been communicating with the offeree in Winnipeg by mail, the postbox rule would likely apply. The letter of acceptance would have been effective in Winnipeg, where it was sent from rather than in Halifax where it was received, thus making it more likely that Manitoba law would apply. Had the communication been over the telephone, Nova Scotia law would more likely apply. Of course, other factors, such as where delivery of the product is to take place and where the goods are to be used, will also be taken into consideration by the court in determining what law to apply to the transaction.

It must be stressed that the postbox rule is an exception to the requirement that an acceptance must be communicated to be effective. It does not apply to the offer or to a revocation of that offer. In the *Henthorne v. Fraser* case discussed above, there was both a letter of revocation posted as well as the letter of acceptance. The courts found that the postbox rule applied to the acceptance, and it was effective when sent but that the revocation had to be received by the offeror before it could have any effect on the transaction.

Postbox rule does not apply to revocation

Untangling the WEB

The question of when an offer is accepted becomes very problematic when contracts are created online. Is the acceptance effective when and where made, or does it have to be received and read by some person before a contract is created and enforceable? While the actual transmission of the message may be instantaneous, there may be some considerable delay before the message is actually read by a real person. One of the few cases dealing with the problem was an American case, *Corinthian Pharmaceutical Systems Inc. v. Lederle Laboratories*,[13] where the judge found that when the customer sent an acceptance online, that acceptance was not effective until communicated, and that was not until someone actually read the message. This is consistent with the *Entores* case but leads to very difficult problems for businesses, not the least of which is how consumer protection legislation applies to these contracts. It is likely that these difficulties will not be resolved until specific statutes are enacted to control electronic commerce.

12. (1999) 178 D.L.R. (4th) 409 (Ont. C.A.); leave to appeal to S.C.C. refused (June 22, 2000) Doc. 27595

13. (1989) 724 F. Supp. 605 (S.D. Ind.)

A great danger exists, especially in business when the offeror is dealing with several potential prospects with respect to the same transaction. People in such circumstances often think that they can make offers to several different people and that when a deal is struck with one, that ends the matter with relation to the rest. That is normally not the case, and care should be taken to revoke any other outstanding offers before another is made to someone else. In such circumstances, the offeror should keep in mind not only the possibility that the offer has been accepted by mail and he is not yet aware of it but also that his letter of revocation will not be effective until received. A way to avoid the problem is to make any subsequent dealings subject to the original offer lapsing without acceptance.

Untangling the WEB

Contracts are agreements between two parties, and it seems that the medium in which the contract is made should make little difference to the validity of the contract. But Internet transactions do create some special problems. Advertisements are not usually considered offers, but if an advertisement posted to your e-mail box includes terms of purchase that are specific and complete and the site provides the means for you to click through to eventually accept the terms set out by the retailer in exchange for the goods or service, it would seem to qualify as an offer. If the retailer wants to retain the right to modify or reject your order, then it should be made clear in the advertisement that it is merely an invitation to treat. An offer can be accepted by e-mail or on a web site, as long as the basic requirements of acceptance are met. Another problems relates to the application of the postbox rule. If it applies, then the acceptance is effective when sent. This suggests that the jurisdiction of the acceptor will apply. But after the *Entores*[14] case, it is likely that the postbox rule will not be extended to these modern means of communication. Still, some argue that the postbox rule should apply because Internet communication is not as instantaneous as it first appears. It may not even involve communications between people, given the sophisticated software in place in retail marketing today. This is another reason why retailers might want to stipulate that an advertisement is merely an invitation to treat, making it more likely that the law in their own jurisdiction will be in force.

The purchaser of a product, whether in a store or online, must have access to the terms of the agreement. When purchasing software, it is common to have the actual product sealed in shrinkwrap which, when opened, indicates acceptance of the terms. When a person buys software online or purchases the license to use it, the purchaser is usually required to indicate that they have read and accepted the seller's terms and conditions. Clicking the "I accept" button is the equivalent of removing the shrinkwrap. This is called "clickwrap" or "webwrap." The process protects the seller, providing a remedy if the purchaser misuses the product, but it does not allow the buyer to test the product to be sure it meets their needs and return it if it does not. The buyer needs to be aware that opening the product or downloading it binds them to the terms of the licensing agreement and to be careful to read and understand the terms before accepting them. It is important that all the terms of the agreement be made available to the purchaser before they have an opportunity to click the "I accept" button.

It may be difficult to determine just who the parties to the contract are and if they have authority to enter into the contract. Is the owner of the computer bound or the user? Can computers contracting with each other bind their owners? Sometimes online offers are automatic, and once the purchaser's inventory level has dropped to a certain level, the computer sends an order to the supplier's computer, which acknowledges receipt of the request. Are the parties bound in such circumstances? These are among the questions that are yet to be resolved.

14. Entores Ltd. v. Miles Fareast Corp. [1955] 1 All E.R. 493

Consideration

Gilbert Steel Ltd. v. University Construction Ltd.[15]

This case illustrates not only the nature of consideration, but also the principle of promissory estoppel, which will be discussed below. Gilbert Steel had supplied construction steel to University Construction on a number of their projects. For one particular project, they had a contract for a specified amount of steel to be provided at a set price and of set quality. Unfortunately for Gilbert Steel, their supplier increased the price of steel during the project. Gilbert Steel turned to University Construction and sought a new agreement with them to increase the cost of steel. University Construction agreed to pay the higher price.

The steel was delivered, and payments were made, but the payments were never enough to cover the extra cost so that at the end of the project, a balance was owing to Gilbert Steel. When Gilbert demanded payment, University refused to pay the extra over the price originally agreed on, taking the position that they did not receive anything in exchange for their promise to pay a higher amount. Prior to that agreement, Gilbert Steel had been obligated to supply the steel at a set price, and subsequent to that agreement, the only change was that University Construction had committed to pay more. Such a one-sided agreement was not a binding contract. In order for a contract to exist, there must be an exchange of promises or commitments between the parties—a one-sided agreement is not enforceable.

The lawyers for Gilbert Steel made several attempts to convince the court that there was benefit on University's side, that is, there was "consideration." They argued first that at the time of the promise to pay the higher price, Gilbert Steel had agreed to give University Construction a "good price" on a subsequent project. The court found that this was not specific enough and that there was no commitment involved. Gilbert also argued that because University did not have to pay for 60 days, they were getting free credit for whatever they owed during that period of time. They also argued that because the increase in price made the amount owing more, the free credit was worth more than it was before, and this qualified as consideration. The judge's response was "I cannot accept counsel's contention, ingenious as it is, that the increased credit inherent in the increased price constitutes consideration." Finally, Gilbert argued that since the promise to pay the higher price was relied on and steel was delivered, an estoppel was created, and therefore, the higher amount should be paid.

As will be seen from the discussion below, promissory estoppel can arise in situations where an agreement is one-sided and there is no consideration to support it, but such a promise in Canada and the United Kingdom can only be used as a defence when the person making the promise is for some reason suing the other. In this case, the person making the promise is University Construction and it is Gilbert Steel, the recipient of the promise, that is suing for breach of contract; promissory estoppel, instead of being used as "shield," is being used as a "sword," and that is not permissible in Canada. Had University Construction made the higher payments and sued Gilbert Steel to get them back, then promissory estoppel may have been available to Gilbert Steel as a defence.

15. (1976) 67 D.L.R. (3d) 606 (Ont. C.A.)

Consideration—the price one is willing to pay for a promise

Consideration—not necessarily money

Central to contract law is the bargaining process in which people trade promises for promises and all parties derive some benefit from the deal. That benefit, essential to the existence of a contract, is called consideration and is defined as the price one commits to pay for the promise of another. Consideration is not restricted to the exchange of money. A bargain may involve the exchange of anything the parties think is of value. For example, where Brown purchases a computer from Ace Computers Ltd. for $2000, there is valid consideration on both sides. The promise to deliver the computer is valid consideration as is the promise to pay $2000. Thus, before the parties actually exchange the computer for the cash, they are still bound in contract because the consideration given is the exchange of commitments or promises. If one of the parties fails to honour that commitment, the other can successfully sue for breach of contract.

Because it is sometimes difficult to determine the value a person is getting from a deal, it is often better to look at what the parties are giving or paying. For example, if a public-spirited business agrees to pay someone to clean up a public park, the commitment is still binding, even though it might have been made out of a sense of civic responsibility and may result in no actual benefit to the business. Both sides have exchanged promises or commitments. Normally, the promise to make a charitable donation is not enforceable, it being a promise to make a gift, but when the charity at the request of the donor agrees to use the money in a certain way, it has made a commitment, and both parties will be bound.

Similarly, the contract is just as binding if the consideration involved is a commitment not to do something as opposed to a promise to do something. For example, if a business promises to pay its employees $500 to quit smoking, such an arrangement is a valid, binding contract. The consideration on the one side is the promise to pay $500, and the consideration on the other side is the promise to refrain from doing something the party has a legal right to do, that is, smoke.

Consideration can be benefit or detriment

Courts will not enforce one-sided agreement

Consideration is a benefit or a detriment flowing between the parties to an agreement as the result of a bargain being struck. If the agreement is one-sided and only one of the parties is getting anything from the deal, it is called a **gratuitous promise** or a gift, and the courts will not enforce it. It may well be that such gratuitous promises ought to be honoured from an ethical point of view, but there is no legal obligation to do so. Once the gift has been given, however, the courts will not assist the giver in getting it back. Also, when services are performed gratuitously, there is still an obligation to do a proper job. If through the negligence of the person performing the gratuitous service, damage or injury results, he or she can be sued in tort. For example, if a skilled carpenter out of the goodness of his

Consideration for Promissory Note Was Rearranging Obligations

A woman was indebted to the Bank of Nova Scotia, and in the process of the renewal and rearrangement of those debts, her husband signed a promissory note to the bank. Before that time, there was no indebtedness on his part. Eventually, the husband and wife separated, and upon the wife's default, the bank came after the husband for payment on the promissory note. The husband claimed that he had received no consideration in exchange for his promise to be responsible for his wife's pre-existing debts. The court found that because pursuant to the husband's signing the promissory note, the bank had given up its rights or claims under the old arrangement, which would not have happened without the husband's promise, consideration did exist.

Bank of Nova Scotia v. Hallgarth (1986) 2 D.L.R. (4th) 158 (B.C.C.A.)

heart helps his neighbour repair a roof and because of his negligence the roof leaks and causes damage to furniture and belongings, the neighbour can sue in tort for compensation.

Adequacy of Consideration

It is not necessary that the consideration be fair to both parties. Contract law rests on the foundation that both parties are free to bargain. Once they reach an agreement, the court will assist them in enforcing the resulting contract but will not release either of them from a bad deal. If a person agrees to sell someone a brand new Cadillac for $100, this becomes a valid, binding contract. This does not mean that the courts will never look at the adequacy or fairness of the consideration. When businesses deal with each other, the value of a particular deal to the parties is not always apparent, and the wisdom of the courts not reviewing the fairness of the consideration is clear. But when businesses deal with the public in the form of consumers, the courts are much more concerned with fairness and are much more willing to rescue consumers where they have been taken advantage of by the business. This power to intervene is now usually found in statute, but the courts themselves have developed such concepts as **unconscionability**, fraud, or mistake (to be discussed below), which give them power to review these transactions. The courts will also look at the fairness of consideration when one of the parties claims insanity, drunkenness, or undue influence. Although the consideration paid does not need to be fair, it must have some legal value. In the case of *White v. Bluett*,[16] a father agreed to give his son money if the boy would stop bothering him. It was held that such a promise had no intrinsic value and, therefore, was not consideration. Similarly, if a person agrees to give love and affection in return for a promise of money, that is not sufficient consideration. Whatever the parties have bargained for must have some material value for the courts to enforce the bargain.

When two parties strike a bargain, they must agree to a specific consideration or price. Suppose someone agrees to exchange a car for another's promise to "do some work around the house." Such a promise would not be enforceable because the work to be done is not specified. This problem becomes acute whenever a monetary consideration is involved. It is not sufficient to promise to give "some money" as payment for the promise of another. Such a commitment must refer to a specific or calculable amount of money. When the parties agree to pay the "market value" of an item or where some other objective method or formula for pricing a product at some time in the future is used, the consideration is calculable and is thus sufficiently specific to be binding. Even then, great care must be taken to make sure the price at that time will be clear.[17]

Inadequate consideration may indicate fraud, insanity, etc.

Consideration—

- **need not be fair but must be specific**
- **particularly, if money is involved**

Watson v. Moore Corp.[18]

Ms. Watson was hired by Moore Corporation Ltd. in 1963. After several years of employment, she was required to sign a document stating that if she were dismissed, she would be entitled to the minimum notice required by statute plus one week. In 1993, after 25 years of employment, she was dismissed with only 20 weeks' pay as required by the agreement. This was based on the minimum notice set out in the *Employment Standards Act* of 18 weeks for this period of employment. The

16. (1953) 23 L.J. Ex.36 (C.E.)
17. Folley v. Classique Coaches (1934) 2K.B. 1 (C.A.)
18. (1996) 134 D.L.R. (4th) 252 (B.C.C.A.)

Employment Standards Act only sets out a minimum, but the normal requirement of reasonable notice under common law when greater, as in this case (18 months), will prevail. However, this common law requirement of reasonable notice can be modified by agreement, and the question for the court in this case was whether the documents signed by Ms. Watson years after she was hired shortened the notice period to 20 weeks as argued by Moore Corp. For this to be the case, there had to be a contract to that effect between the parties. The documents showed that there was an agreement to that effect, but for it to be enforceable, there had to be consideration present on both sides. What consideration did Moore Corp. give in order to persuade Ms. Watson to give up her common law right to reasonable notice? Moore Corp. claimed that the fact that it continued to employ her after she signed the agreement was sufficient consideration. But the appeal judge found that such continued employment was not consideration, unless there was some evidence that she would have been dismissed if she had not signed. There was no indication that her employment would have been ended had she not signed this document, and therefore, there was no consideration to support the new agreement. As a result, she was entitled to the higher standard of notice as required by common law, in this case 18 months' notice

This case shows how easy it was to miss the requirement of consideration in what appeared to be a normal adjustment of the employment relationship. It also shows how significant such an error can be for the business.

Existing Duty

A new bargain requires new consideration

The adequacy of consideration becomes important whenever there is an existing duty to do the thing contracted for. For example, Olsen operated a small painting business and agreed to paint Chang's house for $1500 and then said to Chang when the painting was three-quarters finished, "I will not finish unless you promise to pay me another $500." Even if Chang were to agree to this extra payment, it would not be binding because Chang would receive nothing in exchange for the promise to pay the extra $500. Olsen was obligated to finish painting the house before the promise to pay the extra $500 was made. After the promise to pay the extra amount was made, the obligation remained the same. Olsen's legal position did not change; therefore, there was no consideration. These types of problems often arise in the construction industry, where unforeseen factors may increase the costs significantly. It is vitally important for the parties to take great care to predict all costs that are likely to arise and to build into their agreement provisions for resolving conflicts over these unexpected eventualities.

When a duty to act exists but that duty is owed to a third party, a promise to do the same thing for someone else is enforceable. In the situation above, if Adams, a potential tenant, realized that Olsen's reluctance to finish the job would delay possession of the premises, and thus cause greater expense, and Adams promised to pay Olsen the extra $500, that agreement would be binding. Before Adams' promise to pay the extra $500, Olsen was legally obligated to Chang to finish painting the house. After the promise to Adams, Olsen is now legally obligated to Adams as well as Chang to paint the house. Olsen's legal position has changed because Olsen now runs the risk of having to pay Adams' damages as well as Chang's if the contract is breached. There is a valid consideration here and the contract is binding.

Whenever the existing duty involves a police officer, firefighter, or other public servants, there can be no further promise to do what they are already legally obligated to do. A firefighter cannot arrive at a blaze and extract a promise from the victim to pay an extra $500 to put out the fire. Such a contract would be against public policy and unenforceable. Paying police personnel in their off-duty hours to provide security at a rock concert or celebration is valid, because they are on their own time and not otherwise obligated to help.

Past Consideration

There are situations when consideration appears to be present but, in fact, is not. One of these is when the consideration was given in the past, that is, the bargain is struck after the price agreed on has been paid. Where an employer promises to pay an employee a bonus because of all the good work that employee has done in the past, there is no bargain. The work has already been done. Although it may appear that both parties have given something (the employer the promised bonus and the employee the good work), such a promise is not enforceable. The key to this problem is in the timing. When the promise to pay the bonus was made, the work had already been performed, so where is the bargain? In fact, the employer is in exactly the same legal position before the promise as afterwards. Thus, it is often said, "past consideration is no consideration."

Past consideration is no consideration

Paying Less to Satisfy a Debt

Another situation in which consideration appears to be present, but often is not, is when people who are obligated to pay a certain sum of money (where the amount is not in dispute) negotiate with their creditors to accept lesser amounts in full payment of the debt. Suppose a debtor who owes a moneylender $5000 payable on or before June 10 approaches the creditor on June 11 and says, "I can't pay you the $5000 I owe you. If you will take $3000 in full satisfaction of the debt, I will pay you that instead." What is the position of the creditor who takes this money? Can the creditor still sue for the remaining $2000? In fact, the reduction of the debt is gratuitous. The creditor has received nothing for his promise to take less in full satisfaction of the debt. Under common law, it was quite clear that such a one-sided promise was not binding. Even when the partial payment was actually taken, the creditor could then turn around and sue for the remainder.[19] But as a practical business matter, in many situations, such an arrangement to take less is beneficial to the creditor as well as the debtor. The creditor might otherwise have to sue to recover and get nothing. Today, many Canadian jurisdictions have passed legislation providing that when a creditor has agreed to take less in full satisfaction of a debt and has actually received the partial payment agreed on, the creditor is bound and cannot sue for any deficit.[20] When the creditor has only agreed to take less, however, and the payment has not yet been made, the creditor is still free to change his or her mind and insist on the entire amount being paid. Of course, when the debtor has agreed to pay the lesser amount early or do something in addition to the payment, such as pay a higher rate of interest, there is consideration on both sides to support the new arrangement, and the creditor is bound by the promise to take less.

When there is no consideration, there is no bargain

Note statutory exceptions

Settlement out of Court

The parties to a dispute are encouraged to settle the matter without going to court. Are such settlements binding? When one party learns later that had he persisted he

19. Foakes v. Beer (1884) 9 App. Cas. 605 (H.L.)

20. *Law and Equity Act,* R.S.B.C. (1996) 253 s.43

**Consideration not a factor
in out-of-court settlements**

would have won more than he settled for, where is the consideration supporting the settlement? In fact, both parties have given up their right to have the court determine the matter, and so, there is an exchange of consideration, both having paid a price. The release signed in such situations is binding, and so, great care should be taken before signing such a release.

Illegal Consideration

**Illegal or impossible
consideration is no
consideration**

There are some policy restrictions on what constitutes good consideration. If a drug company were to agree to produce an illegal, prohibited drug in exchange for a large payment, such an agreement would not be enforceable, since the consideration given for the promise of payment was a commitment to perform an unlawful act. Contracts between businesses to interfere with free competition and restrain trade may also be invalid due to illegality.

In addition, for consideration to be valid, it must be possible to perform the consideration promised. If a company were to agree for payment to change lead into gold, such a promise would be unenforceable due to the impossibility of performance (at least at this time).

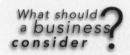

The old adage that you cannot get something for nothing has been enshrined in the law of contract in the form of the requirement of consideration. In all contracts, except those under seal, there must be a bargain where both parties make some commitment to each other. The lack of such consideration is often difficult to see especially in business deals where pre-existing obligations are being modified. In such circumstances, business people have to be especially vigilant in their dealings to ensure that the deals that they do come up with are legally enforceable and not simply one-sided gratuitous arrangements that can be ignored by the other party.

Request for Services

**Must pay reasonable
amount for services**

Where services are requested from providers, such as lawyers or mechanics, the parties often do not agree on a specific price before the service is performed. A mechanic might be asked to fix a car without reference to price. In these circumstances, the courts will impose an obligation to pay a reasonable price.

This is an application of the principle of **quantum meruit,** sometimes called quasi contract. *Quantum meruit* means "as much as is deserved," and the courts use this principle to impose an obligation to pay a reasonable price when services are requested. The courts will also use *quantum meruit* to determine what should be paid when a person providing the services is not allowed to finish by a breaching party. For example, when a person has agreed to paint a house and before the job is finished and payment due the other party refuses to allow completion, the courts use the *quantum meruit* principle and order that the breaching party pay a reasonable price for the benefit he has received. The same is not true if the breaching party is the one seeking payment. In the example above, if the painter was the one who refused to finish the job, he could not demand partial payment for what had been done. The requirement to pay a reasonable price when no specific price has been agreed upon has also been applied to the sale of goods by provincial statute.

Promissory Estoppel

Another exception to the rule that a promise is only enforceable if consideration is present is on the basis of the principle of promissory estoppel, sometimes referred to as equitable estoppel. The more common or ordinary use of the term estoppel occurs when a person makes a statement of fact, such as "the property line is here" or "Jones is my agent," and another person relies on that statement, the person who made it cannot later deny its truth. He must live with what he has led the other person to believe. The apparent authority of agents to be discussed in a subsequent chapter is based on this principle of estoppel. Promissory estoppel, in contrast, does not deal in statements of fact. Instead we are talking about situations where a person makes a promise to do something in the future. As we have discussed, such promises or commitments are consideration, and if there is an exchange of such promises, that is the definition of a contract, and the promises are enforceable. But where the promise is one-sided and the other person relies on it, is such a one-sided promise ever binding on the promisor? Gratuitous promises are not normally enforceable. But there are situations in which the promisee incurs expenses or other obligations in anticipation of the promise being performed. In the presence of such reliance, unique remedies have been developed to compensate for significant loss.

Gratuitous promises usually not enforceable

In the United States, it is possible to sue for compensation when a person relies on such a one-sided promise and suffers a loss, but in the United Kingdom and Canada, such an unfulfilled promise can only be used as a defence to an action initiated by the person who made the promise.

In London, England, just before the war, High Trees House, Ltd. rented an apartment building from Central London Property Trust, Ltd. under a 99-year lease with the intention of renting out the individual flats in that building.[21] The two parties agreed to a set yearly rent of £2500. Because of the outbreak of World War II, it soon became apparent that High Trees would not be able to rent out all the flats, and so in 1942, the property owners agreed to lower the yearly rent to £1250. After the war, they changed their minds and demanded payment of the entire rent, including back rent for the portion that had not been paid since 1942. The court agreed that for the period after the war, High Trees had to again pay the full rent, but as far as the back rent was concerned, the property owners were bound by their promise to take the lower amount. High Trees was not suing to enforce the promise; rather, the property owners were suing for the higher amount in spite of their promise. High Trees used the plaintiff's promise as a defence to its claim.

Thus, in Canada and the United Kingdom, the principle of promissory estoppel is remedial in nature. In another significant British case, *Combe v. Combe*, Lord Denning made it clear that "it does not create new causes of action where none existed before,"[22] and Lord Asquith, in his concurring judgment, said that promissory estoppel could only be used as "a shield but not as a sword."[23] Although there is some dispute about it, the use of promissory estoppel as a defence is effectively limited in Canada, which is why in the case of Gilbert Steel used to open this section, the argument of promissory estoppel failed. They were suing to collect the higher price promised, thus using the promise as a sword. In fact, in almost every case where promissory estoppel has been successfully used as a defence, there was an existing legal relationship, usually contractual, that was modified by the promise. The promisor was attempting to enforce the original terms of the agreement, ignoring the relied upon promise to alter the terms. The disappointed promisee

Promisory estoppel can only be used as a defence

21. Central London Property Trust Ltd. v. High Trees House, Ltd. [1947] 130 (K.B.)

22. [1951] 1 All E.R. 767 at 769 (C.A.)

23. *Ibid* at p. 772. British Columbia legislation may have the effect of allowing a person to sue for compensation (use as a "sword") when such promises are relied on as found in that province's *Law and Equity Act*, R.S.B.C. (1996) c. 253 s. 59, ss. 5.

then was using the promise as a shield or defence to the action. To raise this defence successfully, the victim must also demonstrate reliance on the promise and injury suffered as a result of that reliance.

Re Toronto College Street Centre Ltd. and City of Toronto et al.[24]

The use of promissory estoppel is not limited to contract. An example of the use of promissory estoppel in a non-contract case involved the owner of a building that was recognized as an important heritage site. The owners entered into a development agreement with the city but with the understanding that a restaurant and auditorium on the seventh floor would be retained. When this proved uneconomical, the owners applied for a building permit to change the use of the seventh floor to rental units. The permit was refused, and that decision was challenged by way of judicial review of administrative action, as discussed in Chapter 3. The court based its decision partly on promissory estoppel. The owners of the building had promised to maintain the seventh floor as a restaurant and auditorium, and the city had refused to grant a permit to do otherwise. The owners were estopped by their promise. Note that the promise of the owners of the property was being used as a defence by the city and that it was clear that the city had relied on the promise when allowing them to do other things with the building. The case is interesting in that it involves the enforcement of the doctrine in a non-contract situation and to the benefit of a government entity rather than an individual. There are many other non-contract cases where promissory estoppel is raised, often where some time period or statutory limitation period has expired but where an understanding has been encouraged to the effect that the time limit or limitation period would not be enforced.

Sealed Documents

Sealed documents do not require consideration

The last major exception to the requirement of consideration is the use of the seal. Seals were originally made by placing some melted wax on a document and impressing a signet ring in it, thus lending authenticity or authority to the document. When the parties went to so much trouble to indicate they were serious, they were bound by their commitment. This practice of being bound by sealed documents, which was in place before modern contract law, was retained and so must be viewed as an exception to the rule that consideration is required for a contract to be binding. A paper wafer is now normally used instead of the formal seal and signet impression, although the seal can be almost any form of marking on the document that the parties have identified as a seal. These types of contracts are now considered formal contracts or deeds, and the court will not entertain any suggestion that the promise contained in the document is not supported by consideration. Although it is not necessary to look for consideration when a seal is present, it is important to realize that the existence of the seal does not do away with the other requirements of a valid contract.

In general, there must be some form of valid consideration in the form of a benefit or detriment flowing between the parties for a court to enforce a promise. Only when the document embodying the agreement is sealed, or on those rare occasions when the promise of the promisor is being raised as a defence by the promisee will the court not require consideration to be established.

24. 31 D.L.R (4th) 402 (Ont. C.A.)

Summary

Contract

- A contract is an exchange of promises or commitments enforceable in court
- There are two essential ingredients of a contract: consensus and consideration

Consensus

- Offer—a tentative promise by the offeror contingent upon an acceptance by the offeree
    - All the essential terms of the contract must be contained in the offer
    - Non-essential terms will be implied
    - The offer will end at a specified time, but it may be revoked earlier simply by notice to the offeree, unless an option agreement has been entered into
    - In the absence of a specified time limit, the offer will lapse after a reasonable time
    - A counteroffer, rejection, or the death or insanity of the offeror will also cause an offer to lapse
- Acceptance—an indication of a willingness to be bound
    - Must be communicated
    - Postbox rule—an acceptance by mail is effective when and where it is dropped in the mailbox

Consideration

- The price paid for the promise of another
- Both contracting parties must have experienced some benefit
- Gratuitous promises are not enforceable
- Must be both specific and legal
- Past consideration is no consideration
- Promissory or equitable estoppel—a one-sided promise is generally not enforceable, but the promise may be used as a defence
- *Quantum meruit*—when there is a request for services with no agreement as to the amount, a reasonable price must be paid under this principle
- Seal—when there is a seal, there can be no question about the presence of consideration

---

QUESTIONS

1. What is meant by "freedom of contract"? Explain the impact of this principle on the development of contract law.

2. List and explain the elements that must be present for an agreement to qualify as a contract.

3. At what stage in the process of forming a contract are the terms of the contract clearly set out?

4. Explain what is meant by an implied term in a contract.

5. What circumstances might prompt a court to imply terms into a contract?

6. Distinguish between an offer and an invitation to treat.

7. List and explain the various ways an offer can come to an end.

8. What is the effect of the offeror stating in an offer that the offer will remain open for acceptance until a specific date?

9. Give examples of offers that cannot be revoked and explain why.

10. What risks are faced when a person offers to sell certain goods to A and then sells them to B? How can this problem be avoided?

11. What qualities must an acceptance demonstrate to be effective?

12. Explain how a unilateral offer is accepted.

13. Explain the effect of the postbox rule on the principles governing acceptance.

14. How do the courts determine when the postbox rule should be applied?

15. Define consideration and explain what is meant by the term "the exchange of consideration."

16. What difficulty might be faced by a person who has already agreed to do a specific job and then extracts a promise of more pay from the other party?

17. Explain why a contract dispute settled out of court is considered binding even though one party would have obtained more if the action had been taken to court.

18. Explain a person's obligation regarding payment when he or she has requested a service without specifying a particular fee.

19. Describe what is meant by promissory estoppel and the circumstances in which it will arise in contract disputes.

20. How does the presence of a seal affect the requirement that consideration must be present in a contract?

21. Explain under what circumstances a person who fails to properly perform a gratuitous promise can be held legally liable for that failure.

CASES

1. Regina v. Dawood

Mrs. Dawood had been shopping in a department store and came to a display rack containing children's jumpers and blouses. On some of the hangers, the jumpers and blouses were combined to make an outfit on sale for a single price, while some of the hangers contained individually priced jumpers and blouses. Mrs. Dawood took a blouse from one of the two-piece outfits and put it on its own hanger with a jumper from one of the individual hangers and took the outfit she had made to the cash register. She had removed any indication of price from the blouse so that the clerk was led to believe that the price from the jumper was the price for the whole outfit. The cashier charged her the lower price which she paid. It is important to note that there was no attempt to hide the blouse in any way but the effect was that she paid for only the jumper. Mrs. Dawood was subsequently charged with theft, and the problem for the court was to determine if a crime had taken place. Discuss.

2. DIS, Data Wiz Information Systems Inc. v. Q. W. Page Associates Inc.

Both the plaintiff and the defendant were in the software development business. The defendant manufactured accounting software, and the plaintiff, Data Wiz, developed a data-based information system and sold it through a telemarketing scheme. Data Wiz wanted the exclusive distributorship rights to sell the defendant's accounting software in the United Kingdom and entered into negotiations with the defendant to that effect. These negotiations resulted in a memorandum of understanding and an international distribution agreement being executed by both parties. However, an important provision of the contract, namely, the discount that the distributor was to get, was left blank. There was some delay in obtaining the financing, and the defendant refused to go ahead until the financing was in place, insisting on some significant changes to the memorandum of understanding. What arguments could the defendant bring forth to escape liability under the contract? How could these be countered by the plaintiff?

3. Calgary v. Northern Construction Ltd.

The city of Calgary advertised for tenders for a construction project. One of the terms of the advertisement was that once submitted, the bid could not be revoked. Northern Construction submitted the low bid on the job. They then examined their bid and realized they had made an error in their calculations. They showed these documents to Calgary's representatives, who agreed that they had made an error. Northern Construction then requested that they be released from their bid. Calgary, however, would not release them from the bid and accepted it as the winning one. Since Northern Construction refused to honour the contract, Calgary was forced to go with the second-lowest bid, and they sued. Explain the legal arguments available to each side and the likely outcome of the action.

4. Francis v. Canadian Imperial Bank of Commerce

After several interviews with the bank, Mr. Francis was offered a position of employment in a letter dated June 9, 1978. He responded on June 15 accepting the offer, by which he was to start work on July 4. When he showed up for work, he was presented with a number of documents that required his signature, including one entitled "Employment Agreement," which he signed along with the others. One of the terms of that employment agreement was that if he should ever be terminated, he was entitled to only three months' notice. After working for the bank for a number of years, his employment was terminated with only three months' notice, and he sued for wrongful dismissal. There was no finding in these circumstances that Mr. Francis had done anything wrong, and so the court assessed that under normal circumstances, he would be entitled to 12 months' notice or pay in lieu of notice upon termination, given the length of service and surrounding circumstances. Discuss the arguments available to Mr. Francis to support his claim for the higher amount of notice and the arguments available to the bank in response.

5. Re 6781427 Holdings and Alma Mater Society of U.B.C.

The holding company in this case leased an area from the Alma Mater Society in the Student Union Building, where it operated a cookie shop with a three-year lease containing an option to renew. The renewal provision of the lease required that notice of renewal be given to the landlord in writing before midnight, July 31, 1986. In fact, the holding company approached the general manager of the Alma Mater Society to see if they could expand the area that they were using. The manager could not give a response right away but said he would probably know by September. When September came, the manager said he would not know until December. As a result, the holding company missed the July 31 deadline while waiting for a response to their request. In September, the Alma Mater Society ordered it to vacate the premises. Explain the arguments available to both parties to explain their positions.

CHAPTER 6

Formation of Contracts (Continued)

CHAPTER HIGHLIGHTS

- Capacity to contract
- Illegal contracts and contracts against public policy
- Intention to contract
- Forms of a contract
- The requirement of writing

Non-competition covenants are valid only if they are reasonable and not against public interest; otherwise, they are void. That the terms of the contract be legal is only one of the requirements of a legally binding contract that will be discussed in this chapter. The other elements that must be present are capacity, legality, and intention. There is, in addition, the requirement that some contracts be evidenced in writing for them to be enforceable. Although, as a practical matter, putting a contract in writing is very important, the general principle is that an oral contract is as binding as a written one.

Misasiv v. Guzzo[1]

When Mr. Guzzo sold his retail fruit market, he signed a written agreement that included the term that he would not become involved in a similar business within five miles of the one he sold for a period of five years. Within a year of the sale, a similar business was opened up by Mr. Guzzo's son within the prohibited five-mile radius. The purchasers suspected that it was really Mr. Guzzo's new business and sued for breach of the non-competition clause in the purchase agreement. The question was whether the non-competition clause was valid, since it was an attempt to limit competition. The judge decided that the clause was valid, that the arrangement for the new business was no more than a "sham," and that Mr. Guzzo himself was at least indirectly involved in it in violation of the non-competition covenant. The plaintiff was awarded damages of $20 000.

1. Misasiv v. Guzzo (1984) 78 C.P.R. (2d) 70 (Ont. H.C.)

Capacity

Our lawmakers have always recognized that some people are more vulnerable than others and, thus, require special protection. Over the years, several categories of people have been protected by having their freedom to enter into contracts severely restricted or, in some cases, eliminated completely.

Infants

The age at which a person becomes an adult in Canada is controlled by statute and varies (either 18 or 19 years) from province to province. The general principle in all jurisdictions is that infants (persons under the age of majority) who enter into contracts are not bound by the agreements, although the adults with whom they contract are bound. The courts try to balance protecting the infant against the objective of not imposing undue hardship on the party with whom the infant contracts. It is important to distinguish between the artificial incapacity imposed on a youth who is a functioning member of society and the actual incapacity of a child who is incapable of understanding what is happening. Most problems arise when dealing with young people who are approaching the age of majority. The test for infancy is objective. When an adult deals with a customer who is under the age of majority, it makes no difference to the court that the adult was under the impression the other party was an adult or that the infant clearly understood the terms of the contract. The court is only concerned with the fact that the person was under the statutory age of majority at the time the contract was created. As a general rule, whenever an infant enters into a contract with an adult, the adult is bound by the contract, but the infant can escape. The contract, therefore, is **voidable**. For example, where a car dealership offers to sell a car for $2500 to a minor who accepts the offer, the dealership will be bound by the contract. The young person, however, would be free to either honour the agreement and purchase the car or refuse to go through with the deal. In British Columbia, which has unique legislation governing infants, such contracts are said to be **unenforceable**. Although the difference between voidable and unenforceable may be subtle, it can be important. The courts will not assist someone to enforce the contract against the infant, but if that infant has performed, the courts will not assist the infant to get out of it, since the unenforceable contract is valid. Unenforceable contracts are discussed below under the requirement of writing.

Age of majority varies with provinces

Infants not bound by contracts, but adults are

Necessaries and Beneficial Contracts of Service

Infants are bound by contracts for the acquisition of necessaries and for contracts of service that benefit the infant. **Necessaries** are things required to function in society, such as food, clothing, transportation, or lodging. What constitutes a necessary will vary with the particular needs of an infant and his or her status. If the young person is purchasing clothing and already has a sufficient supply, that clothing is not a necessary. It has been determined that for a young person in a higher social status, an item that would normally be considered a luxury, such as fine jewelry, may be determined to be a necessary.[2] Although this type of distinction is less likely to be made today, it is clear that where infants are married or living on their

Infants bound by contracts for necessaries

---

2. Peters v. Flemming (1840) 6 M & W 42

own, what constitutes a necessary will be broader when they are single and dependent on their parents. The courts have held that medical, dental, and legal services, toiletries, uniforms, and even a house can be necessaries in different situations, but it is unlikely that they will find that a car qualifies, since other alternative forms of transportation are generally available. Even when the subject of the contract is determined to be a necessary, it does not guarantee that the merchant will get paid full price as the infant is only obligated to pay a reasonable price for such necessaries.

The question arises as to whether an infant can refuse delivery when necessaries have been ordered. It is clear that when educational, medical, or legal services are the subject of the contract, it will be binding on the infant, even if the services have not yet been delivered. But it is likely that where goods or other necessary services are involved, there will be no obligation on the infant until the infant has received the goods or services. When an infant borrows money to buy necessaries, there is only an obligation to repay the debt if the funds advanced are actually used for necessaries. For this reason, money loaned to an infant to pay for school tuition cannot be recovered by the creditor if it is used for gambling. Government student loans are exceptions because they are supported by legislation requiring repayment regardless of what the money is used for and regardless of the age of the borrower.

Infants must pay money borrowed and used for necessaries

A contract in which an infant agrees to do something for someone else is binding, if it can be demonstrated that, taken as a whole, the contract is for the benefit of the infant. These are usually contracts related to employment or apprenticeship. Such contracts are only binding where it is clear that taken in their entirety, they benefit the infant. If it becomes apparent that the infant is being taken advantage of or the contract is not in the infant's best interests, the infant will not be bound. Today, these kinds of relationships are usually controlled by legislation.

Infants bound by contracts of service which substantially benefit them

In the British Columbia statute, all contracts, including necessaries and beneficial contracts of service, are unenforceable against an infant. Only student loans and other contracts made specifically enforceable by statute will be binding on infants in that province.

Note B.C. exception

Infants' Voidable Contracts

The voidable nature of an infant's contract means that the infant can get out of the contract. But when the infant reaches the age of majority, he or she can ratify the contract, either in writing or by implication. (In some provinces, written ratification is required by statute.) The process of ratification breathes new life into old agreements, making them binding. For example, if an infant agrees to pay $5000 for an automobile in a series of installments, this contract is voidable. If, however, on coming of age, the infant makes a written statement or indicates by actions that he or she intends to be bound by the contract, such as paying a further installment, it is binding.

Infant can ratify contract at age of majority

Some types of continuing contracts are voidable at the option of the infant. These contracts require positive steps on the part of the infant to overcome their effects. The infant must take action shortly after reaching majority to indicate that he or she will no longer be bound by the agreement if the subject of the contract is a continuing benefit. These continuing agreements include acquired interest in land through lease arrangements, partnership agreements, or holding shares in a company. There are some types of contracts, however, that are not binding on the infant under any circumstances. If a contract contains a clause amounting to a penalty against the infant or if the contract, taken as a whole, can be said by the court to be prejudicial to the interests of the infant, the contract is simply void.

Bayview Credit Union Ltd. v. Daigle[3]

In most jurisdictions, an infant who enters into a contract that is not binding on him will be bound if he ratifies that agreement after coming of age. Daigle was a minor when he borrowed money from the Bayview Credit Union for the purchase of a car and a motorcycle. The loan arrangement went through several stages of renegotiation, and finally he owed just over $5000. A chattel mortgage was registered against the motorcycle to partially secure the loan. He made a number of payments but none after September 10, 1981. Daigle turned 19 years (the age of majority in New Brunswick) on February 26, 1982. After several conversations with the manager of the credit union, and six months had passed, Daigle told them where the motorcycle was, and it was repossessed. It was sold, and after applying the proceeds to the debt, deducting the costs of repossession and sale, and adding the accrued interest, Daigle still owed just over $4100. The credit union sued, and Daigle claimed that as he had been an infant at the time of making the contract, the contract was voidable in his favour. The credit union argued that his action of telling them where the motorcycle was and agreeing to its being repossessed amounted to a ratification of the agreement. Since this ratification took place after his 19th birthday, it revived the debt, and he had to pay the whole outstanding amount. The court held that Daigle's action of assisting in the repossession was nothing more than what he was required to do in any case and that this by itself did not amount to ratification. The judge commented, "Surely the acts of the defendant here, in co-operating as he did to the benefit of the plaintiff, should not place him in a worse position than a person who would refuse cooperation to reduce the plaintiff's loss." In this case, Daigle was lucky, but the case does illustrate the danger of business people dealing with minors as if they were adults. While it is true that if the merchant can get the infant to ratify or acknowledge their debt after he or she reaches majority, the debt can be enforced. But such ratification must be clear and not simply assisting to collect the collateral security. To contract with infants for such non-necessaries is dangerous, but to rely on such ratification after they reach majority is foolhardy.

Although these principles may seem reasonably straightforward, their application has created a good deal of confusion. To appreciate the reasons for this, it is necessary to think of the contractual relationship progressing through prescribed stages. At the first stage, when the parties have entered into the agreement, but the infant has not yet obtained any benefit from it and has not yet paid, the infant can get out of the agreement. This is an **executory** contract. If the infant has received the goods but has not yet paid for them, he or she is not necessarily bound by the agreement. This is a **partially executed contract.** When the goods are in the infant's possession, the infant will be required to return them or pay for them and, upon return, is entitled to the return of any money already paid. If the infant has passed those goods on to a third party or the goods have been destroyed, the merchant will not be entitled to repayment, nor can the merchant insist that the party to whom the goods have been given return them.

Conflict may arise when the contract has been **executed**. Can infants change their minds once they have obtained the benefit under the contract and insist on

3. (1983) 3 D.L.R. (4th) 95 (N.B.Q.B.).

the return of their money? In Canadian law, the conclusion seems to be that infants are bound by the agreement unless it can be demonstrated that what was received was of no value at all. An infant can insist that payment be returned if there is total failure of consideration where the infant gained nothing from the deal.

Where contract bestows no benefit, infant can escape even executed contract

Parents' Liability

There is a popular misconception that liability will rest with the parents if a child fails to pay a debt. Parents are not usually responsible for the torts of their children, nor are they responsible for their contractual obligations in the absence of specific legislation creating such a responsibility. If an infant enters into a contract, it is that infant's responsibility alone. The adult contracting with the infant cannot turn to the parents if the infant does not live up to the contract. The parents are in no way obligated to honour the infant's defaulted promises, whether or not those promises are binding on the infant, except in those circumstances where liability is imposed by statute. Many jurisdictions have passed legislation making parents liable for the torts and contracts of their children, often in specific situations, such as school-related activities. But in the absence of such legislation, only when the infant is acting as an agent of the parents will the parents be liable for the contracts of their children. This is a simple question of agency and the infant's authority to bind parents as agents will be dealt with in a subsequent chapter. Merchants can overcome this difficulty by having the parents guarantee the infant's obligation at the time the contract is entered into. A guarantee is a written commitment, whereby the guarantor agrees to pay the debt if the debtor does not. Since the very purpose of the guarantee is to encourage the merchant to go through with the contract, these guarantees have been held to be binding on the parents in Canadian law. Because parents are responsible to provide for their minor children, they can be held responsible by the merchant for contracts entered into by their children for necessaries.

Parents not responsible for infant's contracts, except where authorized

Infant's Liability for Torts

It is true that an infant cannot be sued for breach of contract when non-necessaries are involved. However, sometimes a breach of contract will qualify as negligence under tort law. As a result, merchants have tried to get around the protection afforded to infants in contract law by suing for tort instead. It is a basic tenet of tort law that an infant is as liable as an adult for torts committed, although the standard of behaviour expected may differ. Thus, in negligence, once it has been established that an infant failed to live up to the level of responsibility that society deems appropriate, the infant will be held responsible for those inappropriate actions, but the courts will not allow adults to change to a tort action just to get around the incapacity problem in contract law. If it is appropriate to sue for breach of contract, the plaintiff must do so, and if the infant is protected by the defence of incapacity, that is the end of the matter.

On the other hand, if the infant used the subject matter of the contract in some way completely beyond the contemplation of the contract and carelessly caused injury or damage to those goods, the adult would be able to sue for negligence, since the act complained of was not anticipated in the contractual relationship. For example, if an infant rents a two-wheel drive automobile and then damages it while off-roading, the merchant would be able to sue the infant for negligence, since the use to which the automobile was put was outside what was anticipated in the contract. However, if the infant had an accident while driving the rented automobile on the

Infant may be liable in tort

**Adults cannot avoid
protection given to infants
by suing in tort**

highway, the adult could not sue for tort, even if the infant was clearly negligent, because that activity could have been anticipated by the contract. In short, the adult cannot circumvent the protection afforded to the infant in contract law by suing for tort instead. This explains why rental car agencies will not rent to minors, but when an infant misrepresents himself or herself as an adult and contracts to rent a vehicle, the agency may be able to get redress from the infant on the grounds of the fraudulent misrepresentation. As explained above, parents are not liable for the torts of their children, unless they can be said to have been negligent in their own right or where there is a statute in place imposing such liability.

**Except where tort arises
independent of contract**

**Untangling
the
WEB**

In any contract where the parties do not meet face to face, there is difficulty in determining whether the parties have the capacity to contract. This is equally problematic in electronic communication. Children have access to computers; criminals use it to transact their schemes. It is very difficult to determine precisely whom you are dealing with, and so, it is particularly important that buyers beware and sellers include appropriate restrictions and disclaimers.

Insanity and Drunkenness

Hardman v. Falk[4]

Nora Falk and her sister, Ethel Swenson, lived with their 87-year-old mother on her farm located on Annacis Island in the Fraser River. They were approached by a real estate agent to purchase the farm, and after negotiating a complex deal involving a generous price for the land and an option agreement for $1, the sisters finally explained that they did not own the property, their mother did. The deal was then explained to the mother who nodded her understanding. They then explained that she was too old and feeble to sign her name, and they assisted her to mark the document with an X beside her name.

In fact, the real estate agency was assembling land for the Annacis Island Industrial Estates and had acquired similar options on various farms in the vicinity. Once they exercised those options, they were committed, and only then did the sisters refuse to go through with the deal. They claimed that their mother's mind was gone and the agreement was not worth the paper it was printed on.

It was clearly established through evidence that the aged mother did not have the mental capacity to form a contract and was incapable of understanding what was going on. But the court held that there was nothing in the circumstances that should have alerted the plaintiffs to that fact, and although the daughters claimed to have told the plaintiffs about their mother's mental condition, the court rejected that testimony. The court decided that because the plaintiffs were not in a position where they knew or ought to have known of the insanity of the person that they were contracting with, the contract was valid and binding. Age, by itself, does not prompt a person to enquire as to that person's mental capacity. The court also looked at the $1 that was paid for the option and concluded that because the

---

4. [1955] 3 D.L.R. 129 (B.C.C.A.); aff'd [1955] 1 D.L.R. 432 (B.C.S.C.)

dollar was being paid for the privilege of paying more for the property than what it was worth, there was no problem with the consideration paid for the option.

Remember that there are two contracts here. The first is the option to hold the offer open, and the second the actual agreement to purchase the land. Once the courts determine that some consideration was paid, they normally do not enter into a debate as to whether it was adequate or not. However, when a mentally disabled person is involved, the court will ask whether that person has been taken advantage of. In this case, because a higher price was paid than should be expected, there was no question of the mother being taken advantage of. The daughters were attempting to use the courts to get an even higher price for the property, and the court was not sympathetic to their position.

This case illustrates the two things that must be established to get out of a contract when one of the parties claims insanity: first, that the person was so mentally incapacitated that they did not know or understand what they were doing; and, second, that the other contracting party knew or ought to have known of the insanity.

Insanity applies if person did not understand and if other party knew or ought to have known of incapacity

The law extends its protection to those incapacitated because of insanity in a way similar to the protection given to infants, and as with infants, the insane or intoxicated person is also required to pay a reasonable price for necessaries. To qualify for this protection, it must be shown that the insane person could not understand the nature of the act being performed. For example, if a man thinks he is Napoleon and is selling his horse when, in fact, he is selling his car, he would be declared insane because he does not understand the nature of the transaction. To escape contractual liability on the basis of insanity, the insane person or a representative must prove not only insanity but also that the person he or she was dealing with knew or ought to have known of the incapacity. This is the point illustrated in the case discussed above.

Once a person has been committed to a psychiatric institution, all contracts entered into are considered void and are not binding on either party. A trustee is appointed to handle their affairs. To understand the precise rights and obligations of such patients and the care and use of the patient's property, the appropriate provincial legislation should be carefully examined.

Provincial legislation applies to people committed to institutions

People who lose their ability to reason through intoxication, whether from alcohol or drugs, are treated in the same way as the insane. For a defence of intoxication to be considered, it must be demonstrated that the person was so incapacitated that he or she could not understand the nature of the transaction and that the other person knew or ought to have known of the incapacity. The person trying to escape a contract on the basis of drunkenness must also be able to show that, on reaching sobriety, the contract was repudiated. An intoxicated person who purchases shares is not permitted, on becoming sober, to wait and see whether the stocks go up or down before repudiating the contract. Hesitation to repudiate makes the contract binding. This requirement of **repudiation** also applies to insane people who regain their sanity. A person who is of weakened intellect, or otherwise vulnerable but not insane, is still to some extent protected. Unconscionable transactions, the legal principle providing this protection, will be discussed below.

Drunkenness treated like insanity

Must repudiate upon becoming sober

Others of Limited Capacity

Limited companies have their capacity to contract determined by the legislation under which they are incorporated. In some jurisdictions, companies can limit

Corporate capacity—usually no longer a problem

their capacity to contract by so stating in their incorporating documents. Otherwise, all companies incorporated under these general statutes have "all the power of a natural person" to contract. Even in those jurisdictions where the capacity of a corporation can be limited, people dealing with those companies are only affected by that limitation if they have notice of it.

Capacity of government bodies and Crown corporations limited by legislation

Other corporate bodies are created by special legislation. These include some private companies, crown corporations and other government bodies that have been created to accomplish a particular government purpose. The Canadian National Railway, Canada Post, Petro-Canada, Air Canada, and Canada Mortgage and Housing Corporation are some examples. The normal rules of contract law apply to these bodies, but their powers are often limited by specific legislation, and outsiders dealing with them must be alert to the possibility of their limited capacity. In the absence of such statutory provisions, the merchant is free to assume that the government body or corporation in question has the power to do whatever it has agreed to do. Legislation will override any common law contractual principle, so anyone dealing with a crown corporation or government body in any unusual way is well advised to check the legislation that created it.

Capacity of enemy aliens limited in times of war

Dealing with aliens and representatives of foreign governments also gives rise to capacity issues. Any contract with a citizen of a country against which war has been declared is void under common law if it can be shown to have a detrimental effect on Canada. If the effect of the contract with such a person is not detrimental to the country in any way, the contract is merely suspended for the duration of the hostilities; otherwise, it is void. The Canadian government usually passes legislation to cover this area of law, which overrides or supplements these common law provisions whenever hostilities break out.

Contracts with foreign governments may or may not be enforceable

Contracts with foreign governments or their representatives were traditionally thought to be unenforceable even in times of peace because of a foreign government's immunity from prosecution in Canadian courts. This immunity is based on the fact that the sovereignty of the foreign government would be lost if subjected to the jurisdiction of our courts. This provision was particularly important when dealing with matters of state that were of diplomatic importance. However, since foreign governments are now more frequently involved in simple commercial enterprises that have nothing to do with matters of state, the courts have been willing to treat them as any other party to commercial transactions. These principles are now embodied in legislation.[5] Representatives of foreign governments, such as ambassadors and their families, have traditionally been immune from prosecution in our criminal courts and continue to be. In a civil matter, a court will not issue a writ against such a person, and their property is immune from seizure. Of course, these representatives can waive this immunity, if they wish, but anyone dealing with people with diplomatic immunity ought to be aware of the protection they have been given.

Cargo Ex the Ship "Atra" v. Lorac Transport Ltd.[6]

Domtar sold a shipload of utility poles to the government of Iran (through Satkab Co.). The poles were to be shipped on the Atra, with Satkab designated as the owner in the bill of lading. The poles were loaded onto the ship, but before it left St. John's harbour, hostilities broke out in the Persian Gulf, and because of these conditions, the cargo could not be unloaded where specified. After some

5. *State Immunity Act*, R.S.C., 1985, c. S-18.
6. (1986) 28 D.L.R. (4th) 309 (F.C.A.).

negotiations, no other destination could be agreed upon, and the poles were off-loaded. The shipping company sued Satkab (the Iranian government) for the extra costs involved, and the cargo was arrested (seized). The Iranian government claimed they were not liable for the debt because of the principle of sovereign immunity. The Federal Court of Appeal considered that argument but pointed out that such sovereign immunity was not absolute. In recent years, what was once considered an absolute principle is now quite restricted. When the activity involves a governmental function, there is still immunity, but where it is only commercial or trading in nature, that immunity is lost. In this case, the court held that the activity was strictly commercial in nature and, as a result, there was no sovereign immunity. The Iranian government had to pay the extra costs incurred by the shipping company. Today, this principle is embodied in the *State Immunity Act.*[7]

Trade unions in many jurisdictions are, with some qualifications, considered legal entities, much like corporations, and can sue or be sued in their own capacity. Legislation in all provinces has given trade unions the capacity to enter into contracts relevant to their union responsibilities.

Trade unions have capacity to contract for union activities

People who have filed for, or been placed in, bankruptcy also have their contractual capacity significantly limited before they are discharged. Bankruptcy will be discussed in a subsequent chapter.

Finally, the capacity of Native people living on reserves (Status Indians) is still limited to some extent by the *Indian Act.*[8] Although they may seem discriminatory, these provisions remain because they are viewed as protections exempted from the operation of the *Charter of Rights and Freedoms* by Section 35, which recognizes and affirms existing aboriginal and treaty rights.

Status Indians still protected under *Indian Act*

As a general rule, the capacity to enter into contracts is not a problem facing most business people. Still, in those few situations listed, it is vital to be aware of the problem and alert to the possibility that the law may protect the person being dealt with, especially where merchants are dealing with under-age customers. As a practical matter, the difficulty is usually avoided where cash is involved and no credit is extended to the under-age customer. The problem of capacity may come up in the other types of transactions as well, and the businessperson should be aware of the potential for difficulties so that steps can be taken to avoid the problem.

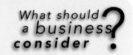

Legality

The objectives of an agreement must be legal and not contrary to public interest, for the agreement to qualify as a binding contract. It is easy to understand that a contract to commit a crime would be void, but there are many other types of activities that, while not illegal, are considered immoral or contrary to public interest. The courts have taken several different approaches when faced with the problem of immoral or illegal contracts.

Illegal and Prohibited Contracts

Contracts to commit illegal acts are not only void but illegal as well. The distinction is important because the court, when faced with a void contract, will restore the

7. *Supra* note 6
8. *Indian Act*, R.S.C. 1985, c. I-5.

Illegal contracts—courts will not assist parties

parties to their original position ordering the parties to return any deposits advanced and property that has been transferred. When a contract is illegal, it involves unacceptable or immoral conduct. Under such circumstances, the contract is still void, but the courts will not assist the parties by restoring them to their original position, unless one of them is innocent of any wrongdoing. An illegal contract usually involves the commission of some prohibited conduct, such as the sale of a controlled substance or the commission of some violent or anti-social act. The conduct may be identified as wrongful and specifically prohibited by the *Criminal Code* or some other statute. Or it may simply be inconsistent with the provisions of such a statute. Common law actually goes further and labels some types of immoral conduct as unacceptable and against public policy, and even though they are not crimes or violations of statute, when people attempt to create bargains in such circumstances, they are treated as illegal contracts. Prostitution is an example.

Response of court varies according to violation

Statute may set out consequences

Where the contract involves clear moral wrongdoing, the contract is illegal. But many federal and provincial statutes are more regulatory in nature. These statutes often contain provisions declaring any agreement in violation to be void or to incur specific consequences. But often, these statutes are silent as to what will happen in the event of a violation. When there is a violation that involves no moral wrongdoing, the courts simply treat the contract as void but not illegal. If the unacceptable term can be separated from the main agreement, only that part will be void. In circumstances where it is clear that the purpose of the contract is to generate income and the violation is more one of procedure than of substance, the courts will actually enforce the contract allowing the parties to correct the procedural defect.

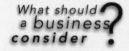

For example, most cities have legislation requiring that trades people, such as roofers and painters, acquire licenses to practise. When work has been performed by a tradesperson who does not have a license and the courts determine that the object of the bylaw is merely to generate revenue, they may enforce the contract and simply require that the tradesperson acquire the license after the fact. But where the purpose of the bylaw is to protect the public from unqualified or unethical tradespeople, the unlicensed tradesperson will not be able to enforce the contract. If the legislation itself sets out the consequences of an infraction, this will override any discretion available to the court.

Examples

The following is a list of some of the types of contracts that have been determined to be illegal and against public policy.

Examples of contracts against public policy

1. **Contracts to commit a crime or a tort**. For example, if Mullins offers Nowak $100 to falsely claim that Abercromby did a poor job of repairing his house, that would be defamation, and the contract to pay Nowak to do it would be illegal.

2. **Contracts involving immoral acts**. For example, although prostitution is not illegal in Canada, a prostitute could not expect the courts to enforce a bargain made with a client because the act is considered immoral.

3. **Contracts that obstruct justice**. If the effect of the contract is to interfere with the judicial process, it is against public policy. An agreement that encourages criminal activity by providing to pay a person a salary when he gets caught and is in jail would involve such an obstruction of justice.

Re Royal Bank of Canada and Newell[9]

In this case, a woman forged her husband's signature on 40 cheques totalling over $58 000. When the husband, Mr. Newell, discovered his account short and approached the bank, they had him sign a letter, whereby he assumed "all liability and responsibility" for the cheques forged by his wife. It was found by the appeal judge that he did this only because the bank officers told him that if he did not, his wife would be prosecuted. In the judge's words, "In view of the way in which the bank presented the situation to Mr. Newell, the only reasonable inference, as was found by the trial judge, was that he accepted responsibility solely to protect his wife from prosecution. This was, then, an agreement to stifle a criminal prosecution which is an illegal contract and unenforceable." Because the contract was illegal, his agreement to accept responsibility for the cheques was void, and he was entitled to his money back. Such an arrangement may seem very attractive to a merchant or creditor who is the victim of such illegal conduct, but this kind of arrangement smacks of blackmail. Certainly, it interferes with and covers up a criminal act avoiding proper prosecution, which is against the interests of the public, and thus is both void and illegal.

4. **Contracts that injure the state**. An example of this would be a contract to sell secret defence information.

5. **Contracts that promote litigation**. An agreement whereby one person, for some ulterior motive, pays another to sue a third would be void as promoting litigation. An exception is the lawyer's contingency fee. In this arrangement, the lawyer agrees to proceed with the action without payment, in return for a share of the judgment often amounting to 30 or 40 percent. This agreement appears to be permissible because it does not promote litigation but serves to make the courts more accessible to those who normally could not afford to proceed. At the time of writing, Ontario still prohibits contingency fee arrangements, except in class action suits.

Contingency fee arrangements permissible because they make courts accessible

6. **Contracts injuring public service**. Bribing a public official to vote a particular way is an example of such an illegal contract.

7. **Contracts in restraint of marriage**. Any contract that has as its object the prevention of marriage is against public policy. An agreement to pay someone $100 000 in return for a promise never to marry would not be binding.

8. **Contracts that are bets and wagers**. In common law, all gambling activities were considered either illegal or against public policy, and so, the courts would not enforce any contracts related to them. Now, this area is covered by statute, and the rules vary from province to province. These statutory provisions are designed primarily to limit and regulate gambling activities, and the courts will only enforce contracts where the activities have statutory approval or are licensed.

Insurance is like a wager. A person owning property pays for insurance against the destruction or loss of the property. If the property is destroyed, the insurer compensates the owner for the loss. This requirement of loss is called

Insurance contract is valid where there is an insurable interest

9. 147 D.L.R. (4th) 268 (N.S.C.A.).

an insurable interest and must be present for the insurance to be valid. Insurance will be discussed in a subsequent chapter.

Contracts for the sale of shares have the same difficulty. If the contract merely requires the parties to pay each other the difference if the share price goes up or down, it is void as a wager. To avoid this problem, the contract must provide that the share will actually change hands. Commodities traded in a similar fashion suffer the same problem.

9. **Contracts that unduly restrain trade.** When a business is sold, the parties often include a clause prohibiting the seller from opening another business in competition. If such a provision is reasonable and necessary to protect the interests of the parties, it is enforceable, but if the provision is unreasonably restrictive or against public interest, that provision of the contract is void. For example, Beaudoin purchases a barbershop from Ahmed for $50 000. A considerable portion of the purchase price may be for the customer relations established by Ahmed. This is called good will. If Ahmed then opens another barbershop next door, it would destroy the goodwill aspect of the contract. It would be reasonable for the buyer to include a provision in the contract prohibiting the seller from carrying on a similar business for a specified time (for example, three years) and within a specified geographical area (for example, five kilometers). If the time and distance restrictions agreed to are not excessive, this would be classed as a reasonable restraint of trade, and the contract would be valid.

In the example used to introduce this chapter, the agreement prohibiting Mr. Guzzo from opening a similar business within five years was held by the court to be a reasonable restraint of trade. His violation of this clause cost him $20 000.

Restrictive covenants must be reasonable

Essentially, some interests must need protection; the restrictions must be no greater than necessary to protect those interests; and the restrictions must not be against the interests of the public. The agreement is against public interest when it interferes with free trade, driving up prices, decreasing service, or having any other effect whereby the public may be harmed. If it is possible to separate the restrictive covenant from the rest of the agreement, then only that part of the contract will be void, when it unduly restrains trade. The purchase price and all other terms of the agreement would be the same, but the seller would have no restrictions at all and would be free to open a similar business anywhere. In the example above, if the provision in the contract for the purchase of the barbershop prohibited Ahmed from opening another shop anywhere in Canada or imposed an unreasonably long period of time, such as 10 years, this provision of the agreement would likely be void. Ahmed would then be free to open a new barbershop wherever he wanted.

Bassman v. Deloite, Haskins, and Sells of Canada[10]

Mr. Bassman, an Ontario accountant, entered into a partnership to carry on that profession in the city of Windsor. A term of that agreement prohibited him, upon termination of this relationship, from competing with the firm for five years. This was stated to mean that he was prohibited from doing business with anyone who was a client or had been a client of the firm within a five-year period preceding his

10. (1984) 4 D.L.R. (4th) 558 (Ont. H.C.)

separation. This clause was clearly in restraint of trade and therefore void, unless it could be shown to be reasonable in the sense that it was in the interests of the parties and the public. The question the court had to deal with was whether the restriction went farther than necessary to protect the business. The problem was the prohibition against doing work for former clients. These people had already left and were no longer paying fees to the partnership. Therefore, there was no need to restrict Mr. Bassman from doing business with them. The provision was, therefore, an unreasonable restraint of trade and void. It should be noted that the court will not rewrite such a clause, and if it cannot be separated from the rest of the agreement, the whole agreement will be void. In this case, the definition of competition as dealing with current and former clients could not be untangled, and this whole non-competition clause was void. Business people should be careful to avoid the temptation to make these clauses any broader than necessary.

An employer will often impose a similar restrictive covenant requiring employees to promise not to compete during or after their employment. Although the same test of reasonableness is used, the courts are much more reluctant to find such restrictive covenants valid. It is only where the employee is in unique position to harm the company that these provisions will be enforced. This will be discussed in more detail in Chapter 11.

Provincial statutes regulate gambling activities such as video lottery terminals.
The Canadian Press/Jeff McIntosh

10. **Contracts between businesses to fix prices or otherwise reduce competition.** These are controlled by the federal *Competition Act.*[11] This statute specifically prohibits agreements that have the "undue" restriction of competition as their primary purpose or objective. Thus, if two merchants agreed not to sell a particular commodity below a certain price, or not to open up branches that would compete with each other in specified communities, and they were the only ones selling the products in that community, such agreements would likely be void. Such a conspiracy may be punishable as a criminal act. This is another example of a contract in restraint of trade. The *Competition Act* prohibits a number of other unacceptable business practices, some of which will be discussed in a subsequent chapter.

Undue restriction or competition prohibited

32.(1) Everyone who conspires, combines, agrees, or arranges with another person

(c) to prevent or lessen, unduly, competition in the production, manufacture, purchase, barter, sale, storage, rental, transportation, or supply of a product, or in the price of insurance upon persons or property, is guilty of an indictable offence and is liable to imprisonment for five years or a fine of one million dollars or both.

These are some of the categories held to be against public policy. This list is neither complete nor exhaustive, and it may well be that new types of activities made possible by changing technology could also be declared as being against public policy.

11. *Competition Act,* R.S.C. 1985, c.C-34

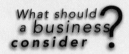

What should a business consider?

There is a great temptation for business people to restrict the right of people they have done business with or their former employees from competing with them by including non-competition clauses in their contracts. This is a dangerous road and should be taken with caution. Former employees can take business away when they leave, and this amounts to unfair competition that can be restricted by properly drawn non-competition clauses. But those clauses must not go too far. They must be reasonable in the circumstances and not be against public interest. There is a tendency for the person who is advantaged by such a clause to make it much broader than is necessary to prevent unfair competition. But such clauses are only reasonable, and therefore binding, if they restrict competition no further than is necessary to prevent unfair competition. They should have a geographical limit and a time limit to their operation. A clause restricting competition within a 500 km radius when 50 km would be sufficient is void. So would a clause with a five-year restriction when one year would be enough. Great care should be exercised in drawing these non-competition clauses, and legal advice should be obtained to make sure that the resulting clause will be enforceable.

Intention

Osorio et al. v. Cardona[12]

Osorio and Cardona were friends who had recently come to Canada from Colombia and often went to the horse races together. On July 10, a wagering scheme, known as the Sweep Six, was offered at the racetracks. This wager involved betting on six races and predicting the winners. Both Osorio and Cardona had tickets on the Sweep Six, and after the third race, they discovered that both their tickets were still in the running. This meant that they had a significant chance of winning.

They entered into an agreement to the effect that if either of them won, the winner would pay the other 30 percent (this was later modified because of the odds involved: if Cardona won, Osorio would only receive 20 percent, but if Osorio won, Cardona would receive 30 percent). In fact, Osorio's horse was knocked out in the next race but Cardona's went on to win $735 403.

After several days of trying to avoid Osorio, Cardona finally told him that he would have to take $60 000 or nothing (the 20 percent share would have been $147 000). There was also some threat involved that Cardona would leave the country and go back to Colombia and Osorio would get nothing. Osorio agreed to take the $60 000. This was given to him, but then he sued for the remainder.

12. (1984) 15 D.L.R. (4th) 619 (B.C.S.C.).

There is no question about the fact that the parties had agreed to split the money in the way outlined. The problem is whether such an agreement is binding on the parties.

The first point to note is that the contract between the parties is not a bet or a wager; rather, it is an agreement to pool the winnings, so there is no problem with legality. The problem is whether the parties intended to be legally bound and intended legal consequences to flow. This has to be determined from the conduct of the parties. The courts try to give effect to the reasonable expectations of the parties in such an agreement, and so, the test of whether there is an intention to be legally bound or not is objective, and it does not matter what the actual state of mind of the parties was.

Cardona had always acted towards Osorio in a way that led Osorio to believe that he was serious and that he intended the agreement to be in force. The renegotiation of the split from 30 percent to 20 percent indicates that they were in serious negotiations, and so, the court decided that there was an intention to be legally bound and, therefore, a contract existed between the parties.

The final question that arises is whether the agreement to accept $60 000 actually paid over to Osorio ended the obligations between the parties; while this might be so under normal circumstances, it was the threat of Cardona leaving and giving Osorio nothing that had forced him to take the lower payment. Such an agreement, extracted by threat to pay nothing, was unconscionable, and therefore, the agreement to take less was unenforceable. Osorio was able to collect the other $87 000.

This case illustrates not only what is meant by the requirement that the parties intend to be legally bound by their agreement but also that the test to determine the presence of intention is an objective rather than a subjective test whereby the court seeks to enforce the reasonable expectations of the parties.

Another element necessary to establish the existence of a binding contract is the requirement that the parties must have intended that legal obligations and rights would flow from their agreement. If a person invited a friend over for dinner and the friend failed to show up for some reason, the delinquent guest would probably be quite surprised if the would-be host were to sue for breach of contract. In such a social relationship, neither party intended to create a legal obligation.

Parties must have intended legal consequences from agreements

When determining intention, the courts do not look to the state of mind of the person making the promise. Rather, they look to the reasonable expectations of the promisee. The test is objective. If the court finds that it was reasonable for the promisee to think that the promisor was serious and that their agreement was legally binding, it is not going to help the person making the promise to say he was only kidding. The contract is binding unless it is clear that the promisee should have known that the person making the offer was not serious.

Courts will enforce reasonable expectations

The following situations illustrate instances in which this problem arises and indicate the courts' probable responses.

1. **Stated intention of the parties**. If the parties clearly state that they do not wish to be legally bound by their agreement or that the agreement is not to be enforceable in any court, that instruction will be honoured. Such a statement must be embodied in the terms of the contract and be very clear as to the intention.

Courts will accept stated intention

Courts will presume intention in commercial transactions

2. **Commercial relations.** If the relationship between the contracting parties is primarily commercial in nature, the courts will presume that the parties intended to be legally bound by their agreement. The contract will be binding on them in the absence of any evidence or clear instructions to the contrary.

Courts will presume no intention in domestic and social relations

3. **Domestic and social relations.** When an agreement is between members of a family or friends involved in domestic (non-business) activities, there is a presumption that the parties do not intend legal consequences to flow from the agreement. If members of a family informally agree to make payments to each other, such as a child agreeing to pay room and board or parents to pay an allowance, the courts would assume that there is no intention to be legally bound and would not enforce the agreement. However, if the parties had gone to the trouble of having a lawyer draw up a formal contract, then the court would be satisfied that the parties did intend that legal consequences would flow from their agreement and would enforce the contract.

Reasonable person test applies where social and business relations mix

4. **Social and business relations.** Problems arise when the relationship involved is a mixture of social and commercial relations, such as when people jointly enter a contest and dispute over the distribution of the prize. This problem could become more prevalent in Canada with the proliferation of lotteries with large prizes. In such cases, the court must treat each situation on its individual merits. In fact, the courts turn to the reasonable person test to determine whether it is reasonable for the parties trying to enforce the agreement to think that a legally binding contract had been created. This was the problem in the Osorio case used to introduce this section, and the court had to use the reasonable person test to determine whether they were serious in their agreement to share the winnings.

—and when dealing with exaggerated claims

5. **Exaggerated claims.** Merchants often exaggerate the qualities of their products in advertisements or as they talk to customers claiming their product to be "the biggest" or "the best." To some extent, this enthusiasm is expected and is not taken seriously by the public or the courts. The problem is where to draw the line, and the courts again apply the reasonable person test to determine whether in the circumstances the customer should have taken the exaggerated claim seriously.

Carlill v. Carbolic Smoke Ball Company[13]

In this case, the manufacturers, the defendants, made a product that they claimed would protect users from influenza. They offered £100 to anyone who used their product as prescribed and still contracted influenza and stated in an advertisement that £1000 had been deposited in the Alliance Bank, Regent Street, which showed their sincerity in the matter.

Mrs. Carlill used the product, got influenza, and claimed the money; but the company reneged, stating that the advertisement was an advertising puff that merely indicated some enthusiasm for the product and was not meant to be taken seriously by the public. The court held that depositing money to back up the claim had taken it out of the category of an advertising puff. It was determined that a reasonable person would have thought the advertisement was serious, so the offer was valid. There was intention, and Mrs. Carlill's use of the product and contracting the illness were appropriate forms of acceptance; thus, there was a valid contract.

13. [1892] 2 Q.B. 484; [1893] 1 Q.B. 256; aff'g [1892] 2 Q.B. 484

Untangling the WEB

Today, in consumer transactions, these exaggerated claims are usually controlled by statute.

Commercial transactions over the Internet may require that parties to the contracts stipulate what will constitute a binding agreement. Because parties endeavour to make their own law when they develop a contract, they can also determine what records of their intention to be bound in an online agreement will be admissible. When a software product is sold to a consumer, the intention to be bound by the contract is assumed when the client installs and uses the software, and this alone would likely constitute evidence of intention.[14] The parties will also often specify the law of the jurisdiction which will govern the transaction, thus avoiding jurisdictional and conflict of law problems that might otherwise arise.

Form of the Contract

We have established that the essential ingredients of contracts are consensus, consideration, capacity, legality, and intention. Nevertheless, the courts must sometimes consider an additional factor before they will enforce a contract. Historically, the form of the contract was very important. Promises were enforceable because they were contained in sealed documents or deeds. The seal is still significant because it eliminates the need to show consideration. Today, as a general rule, in the common law system there are no requirements with respect to the form a contract must take to be enforceable, although many jurisdictions still require that in specific situations, the documents used must be sealed. Deeds to transfer interests in land in some provinces are an example.

People are often surprised to find that verbal agreements are every bit as binding on them as those in writing. While there is some truth in the old saying that a promise is worthless if it is not in writing, it cannot be overemphasized that most verbal agreements have the same legal status as written ones, as long as they meet the requirements described in this and the previous chapters. The courts are even willing to imply that a contract exists by looking at the conduct of the parties.

The importance of the written document is practical, not theoretical. It is always a good idea to put the terms of an agreement in writing so that if a dispute arises there is something permanent that establishes the terms to which the parties agreed. In the absence of such a document, it is surprising how differently even well-intentioned people remember the terms of their agreement. If the dispute between the parties does end in litigation, the parties will be in a better position to prove their case if they can produce written evidence to support their claim. Of course, all this will be modified either by statute or practice, as the use of electronic communication and data storage replaces the use of paper. It will be interesting to see how these developing technologies will respond to the need for certainty and permanency now served by the use of paper records in business.

Verbal contracts binding but writing advised

14. For more information on contracts on the Internet, see *Canadian Business Journal*, Vol. 32 1999.

Statute of Frauds

Writing required to enforce some contracts

In some limited circumstances, a contract is required by statute to be evidenced in writing for it to be enforceable.

During the reign of Charles II in the 17th century, many unscrupulous land dealers cheated others out of their property by perjuring themselves in court. To prevent this abuse, parliament enacted the *Statute of Frauds*, which required that certain types of transactions be evidenced in writing before the courts would enforce them. The *Statute of Frauds* has remained in force in the United Kingdom over the years and has become part of the law of most of the common law provinces in Canada. Significant modifications to the *Statute of Frauds* has been made in many jurisdictions. British Columbia has repealed its *Statute of Frauds* altogether and included some of its provisions in the *Law and Equity Act*.[15] Manitoba has similarly repealed its *Statute of Frauds*; there is no general writing requirement in that province.[16] It must be emphasized that failure to comply with the *Statute of Frauds* does not invalidate the contract; it merely prevents the parties from using the courts to enforce it.

Statute of Frauds requires writing for enforcement in courts

Writing Still Needed in Manitoba

Two parties were negotiating by telephone, and at the conclusion of the conversation, a deal was struck. But before any documents were drawn up, the vendor changed his mind, and the purchaser sued. The court held that despite the fact that the *Statute of Frauds* had been repealed, there was the usual expectation of the parties that the contract dealing with the sale of land would not be effective until put into writing and, therefore, that expectation was honoured.

Megill-Stephenson Co. v. Woo, 59 D.L.R. (4th) 146 (Man.C.A.)

The following is a discussion of the types of contracts generally included under the *Statute of Frauds* in Canada. The actual wording varies between provinces.

When contract cannot be performed in one year

1. **Contracts not to be performed within one year**. When the terms of the agreement make it impossible to perform the contract within one full year from the time the contract is entered into, there must be evidence in writing for it to be enforceable. For example, if Sasaki Explosives Ltd. agrees in March 2000 to provide a fireworks display at the July 1 celebrations in Halifax in the summer of the year 2001, that contract must be evidenced by writing to be enforceable. Failure to have evidence in writing will make it no less a contract but the courts will refuse to enforce it. British Columbia and Ontario have eliminated the requirement of writing in this area.

When an interest in land is involved

2. **Land dealings**. Any contract that affects a party's interest in land must be evidenced in writing to be enforceable. It is often difficult to determine just what types of contracts affect interest or ownership in land and what types do not. Any sale of land or part of it, such as the creation of a joint tenancy in land, must be evidenced in writing. Any creation of an easement or right of way or estate, such as a life estate, is also covered by the *Statute of Frauds*. But contracts for services to the land that do not affect the interest to the land itself are not covered. For example, if a carpenter agrees to build a house, such an agreement may

---

15. R.S.B.C. (1996) c. 253, s. 59.

16. *An Act to Repeal the Statute of Frauds*, R.S.M. 1987, c.F 158

affect the value of the land but not the interest in the land itself and so need not be evidenced in writing to be enforceable. This provision of the *Statute of Frauds* has also been modified in some jurisdictions. In British Columbia, a lease for three years or less is exempt from the legislation, but longer leases are treated just like any other interest in land and must be evidenced in writing to be enforceable.

3. **Guarantees and indemnities**. When moneylenders are not satisfied with the creditworthiness of a debtor, they may insist that someone else sign as well. This means that the creditor wants another person to add his or her credit to the transaction and assume responsibility for the repayment of the debt. The arrangement can be in the form of a guarantee or an indemnity. If the third party incurs a secondary liability for the debt, it is called a **guarantee**. The guarantor promises that if the debtor fails to pay the debt, he or she will assume the responsibility and pay. Note that in this type of transaction, the obligation is secondary or contingent; there is no obligation on the guarantor until the debtor actually fails to pay the debt.

When guarantee is involved

An **indemnity** describes a relationship in which the third party assumes a primary obligation for the repayment of the debt or other obligation along with the debtor. As a result, both owe the debt, and the creditor can look to either for repayment. When a third party says, "I'll see that you get paid," there is an assumption of a primary obligation, and the promise is an indemnity. The distinction between the two is important because, in most provinces, the *Statute of Frauds* requires that a guarantee be in writing but not an indemnity. If the court classifies the nature of the third-party agreement as an indemnity, there is no requirement of writing. The distinction can be vital when a person has made only a verbal commitment to pay the outstanding loan to the debtor. In British Columbia, the *Law and Equity Act* requires that both indemnities and guarantees be evidenced in writing to be enforceable. In some jurisdictions, this requirement of writing extends to promises to be responsible for the torts (miscarriages) of others as well.

4. **Promises in consideration of marriage**. It is not necessary that a promise to marry be evidenced in writing to be enforceable. This provision covers those situations in which a promise is contingent on another's commitment to marry. Thus, a parent's promise to give a child a new car upon marriage would have to be evidenced in writing to be enforceable. This provision has been abolished in Ontario and British Columbia. In those provinces where the provision is still in place, its operation must be viewed as subject to overriding family law legislation.

When promise is given in consideration of marriage

5. **The promise of an executor**. The executor of an estate (the person named in the will to act as trustee) is often called on to pay the debts or other obligations of the deceased out of his own pocket usually to avoid the delay normally associated with probate. Under the *Statute of Frauds,* the executor is only bound by such a promise where it is evidenced by writing.

When an executor promises to meet the debts of an estate out of own pocket

This provision has also been abolished in British Columbia.

6. **Others**. The original *Statute of Frauds* required that whenever the purchase price of goods sold exceeded a specified minimum, there had to be evidence in writing for the sale to be enforceable. This provision has been included in the *Sale of Goods Act* in many jurisdictions in Canada but not in British Columbia. It is usually sufficient evidence in writing if a receipt or sales slip has been

When goods sold over specific value

given or if delivery of the goods has been accepted. The definition of goods and the sale of goods generally will be discussed in Chapter 9. Parliament and the provincial legislatures have passed many statutes that require the transaction itself to be in writing to be valid. Some examples are the *Bills of Exchange Act*, insurance legislation, consumer protection legislation, some of the legislation dealing with employment relations, and the carriage of goods and passengers.

What Constitutes Evidence in Writing

Writing must contain all essential terms

It is not necessary that the entire contract be in writing to satisfy the *Statute of Frauds*; the courts have held that only the main or essential terms must be evidenced in writing. This usually means a description of the parties to the agreement, a description of the property involved, and a statement of the price paid. It must be remembered that if the parties have included any other unusual or essential terms in their agreement, those terms must also be evidenced in writing. Care has been taken throughout this discussion to avoid saying that the contract itself has to be in writing. It does not. The only thing that the act requires is that there be some evidence in writing.

—and may arise after agreement

—and be signed by party to be charged but need not be in the same document

This evidence can come into existence after the contract. If someone tries to avoid responsibility under an agreement because it is not "in writing," it would be unwise to write a letter to the other party to that effect. Such a letter may qualify as the required evidence in writing and thus defeat the objective of getting out of the deal. The *Statute of Frauds* also requires that the evidence in writing be signed but only by the person who is trying to deny the existence of the obligation. The written evidence need not be in a single document but can be contained in a compilation of documents, the whole of which indicates the existence of the contract. For example, if a person agreed to sell a house to another for $100 000 and the seller then refused to go through with the deal, it would be necessary for the purchaser to produce a document signed by the seller which identified the property, the purchaser, the amount of money involved, and any other unique or essential terms. It is only when all these requirements are satisfied that there is sufficient evidence in writing to satisfy the *Statute of Frauds* and thus make the contract enforceable in the courts.

Untangling the WEB

With the movement of commerce away from a paper-based towards an electronic-based environment, there has been a pressing need to determine what constitutes writing under the terms of the *Statute of Frauds* and the use of electronic signatures. While many contracts do not require printed documentation or signatures, it is often in the best interests of the parties to have a record of the transactions. Electronic records can be easily altered, and methods have been created to try to ensure the authenticity of electronic signatures and evidence. Many jurisdictions have amended their *Statute of Frauds* to accommodate electronic evidence, and processes for providing electronic identification have been adopted. This area is now regulated in Canada by the *Personal Information Protection and Electronic Documents Act*.[17] This act pertains to the use of electronic signatures between individuals and government. Private sector use of digital signatures is addressed in a proposed act called the *Uniform Electronic Commerce Act*.[18]

The United States passed a federal law in the summer of 2000 to legalize electronic signatures. It is still important to keep printed copies of documents providing evidence of a commercial transaction completed online, although because there is the possibility of altering such documents, their validity may be questioned by the court if the contract is disputed.

17. S.C. 2000 c.P-8.6, some not yet proclaimed.

18. A copy of the proposed *Uniform Electronic Commerce Act* can be found online at <http://www.law.ualberta.ca/alri/ulc/current/evecatin.htm>

Effect of the Statute of Frauds

It is vital to remember that under the *Statute of Frauds*, if a contract is not in writing that does not make the contract void, it is merely unenforceable. This means that the contract is still binding on the parties, but the courts will not assist them to enforce it. If the parties have already performed, or if there is some other remedy available that does not require the court's involvement, the contract will still be binding, even in the absence of evidence in writing. The courts will not assist a person who has performed to get out of a contract. Nor will the court order the return of money even when there is no evidence in writing of the contract. In effect, the party only did what was required under the contract. Similarly, when there is a lien (a right to seize property) or when there is a right to set off a debt against the obligations established within the contract, the parties themselves may be in a position to enforce it without the help of the courts. In that sense, such a contract is binding, even though there is no evidence in writing.

Contract still valid even where no writing, just unenforceable

Part Performance

Part Performance Satisfies Statute

In this case, the Crown expropriated some land and built a highway. They agreed to allow the owner of the land to move people, livestock, and equipment across that highway, and the government department even helped by producing fencing and ramps to accomplish it. This arrangement continued for 27 years. The result was that the owner of the property acquired a right of way across the highway that was an equitable interest across the property. The court held that even though the *Statute of Frauds* required evidence in writing, this was not a necessity here because the 27 years of crossing the highway with the help of the government constituted part performance.

Hill v. Nova Scotia (Attorney General) 142 D.L.R. (4th) 230 (S.C.C.)

The court will waive the requirement of writing if the parties can produce evidence to show that a contract dealing with an interest in land has been partially performed. There are some important limitations to this principle. The part performance must be evidence of the existence of the contract and consistent only with the existence of the contract. The payment of money owed under the contract will not usually be acceptable as proof of part performance because the payment of money is consistent with any number of different obligations. In British Columbia, by statute, the payment of a deposit is sufficient part performance with respect to land transactions to make such a contract enforceable.[19] A good example of acceptable part performance when land has been sold is the starting of construction. The permission to enter onto the land and start building is consistent with the sale of the land, and so, the part performance will be accepted by the courts as sufficient evidence to support the contract.

When part performance consistent with contract, writing not required

There are only a few situations where a contract must be evidenced in writing for it to be enforceable. Still, from a practical business point of view, such contractual arrangements should always be put into writing or, as technology develops, some other permanent form. Even people with the best of intentions will remember things differently as time passes. It is vital, therefore, to have a permanent memorandum that can be referred to later so that the terms are certain and the

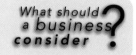

What should a business consider?

19. *Law and Equity Act*, R.S.B.C. 1996, c. 253, s.59 (4)

good will between the parties retained. Where relations have broken down, there is nothing better than a written document to resolve a dispute that arises over a soured business transaction. Chances are that the existence of the document by itself may prevent litigation, and if it does not, at least there is evidence as to what the parties agreed to that can be used in the action. And so, while in law it may be true that an oral contract is as binding as a written one, it is poor practice, indeed, to rely on such oral arrangements in business.

Summary

Parties to a contract must meet certain conditions in order to be able to create a binding agreement. The first has to do with the legal capacity of the parties; the second is their legality; and third, the parties must have an intention to be bound. The *Statute of Frauds* in most jurisdictions requires that some contracts also be evidenced in writing.

Capacity

- Infants
  - Contracts with infants in most provinces are voidable, except for contracts for necessaries and beneficial contracts of service.
  - In British Columbia, by statute, all contracts with infants are unenforceable, except those that are specifically made enforceable by legislation, such as government student loans
- Insanity and drunkenness
  - A contract will be rendered invalid only when the person was so insane as to not know what he or she was doing and the other contracting party knew or ought to have known of that incapacity
- Other
  - Corporations, enemy aliens in times of war, trade unions, government agencies, bankrupts, and status Indians on reserves have their capacity to enter into contracts limited to some extent

Legality

- Contracts that are illegal or against public policy may also be invalid or unenforceable
- Agreements to commit crimes or immoral acts, to obstruct justice, to injure the state, to promote litigation, to injure public service, and to restrain marriage and, in some circumstances, bets or wagers may be held to be illegal or against public policy
- Contracts that unduly restrain trade, such as price fixing, are generally prohibited, but contracts in which one party agrees not to carry on business in competition with another are valid, if they can be shown to be reasonable in terms of the interests of the parties and the public

Intention

- Both parties must intend to be legally bound by their agreement

- In family and other social relationships, there is a presumption of no intention, but this can be challenged by evidence that shows an intent to be bound. In commercial relationships, intention is presumed
- In unusual situations, the reasonable person test is used to determine intention

Statute of Frauds

- Contracts dealing with interests in land, contracts that will not be performed within one year, and contracts involving guarantees, in consideration of marriage, and by the executor of an estate to personally pay a debt are examples of contracts that, under the *Statute of Frauds*, must be evidenced in writing to be enforceable
- The *Statute* has been repealed or modified in many jurisdictions
- When part performance is established, such agreements are enforceable

QUESTIONS

1. Explain the circumstances in which an infant may escape liability for a contract and the circumstances in which an infant is bound by a contract.

2. What is the significance of an infant's contract being designated as a beneficial contract of service?

3. What is the responsibility of parents for the actions of their infant children in both tort and contract law?

4. What are the rights and obligations of the parties involved when an infant makes a contract with an adult for non-necessaries?

5. Explain the circumstances in which an infant can be sued for tort even though a contract between the parties is involved.

6. What must an insane or drunk person establish to escape liability under a contract?

7. Explain four other situations where business people must be careful that those they deal with have the capacity to contract.

8. Explain what care business people must exercise when entering into contracts with Crown corporations or government bodies.

9. Describe how the courts treat a contract to commit a crime.

10. Give five examples of contracts deemed by the courts to be against public policy and describe the effect of such a designation.

11. Are all contracts that restrain trade unlawful? Explain.

12. Explain how the courts' treatment of domestic agreements differs from their response to commercial transactions when the question of intention arises.

13. Describe tests the courts will use in determining whether the parties were serious in their statements.

14. What is the significance of a written document in contractual relations?

15. Explain why some people have suggested that the *Statute of Frauds* has led to more frauds than it has prevented.

16. Give examples of the types of contracts currently included under the *Statute of Frauds*.

17. What must be evidenced in writing to satisfy the requirements of the *Statute of Frauds*?

18. Under what circumstances will a contract falling under the jurisdiction of the *Statute of Frauds* be enforceable even though it is not evidenced by writing?

CASES

1. Re Collins

Mrs. Collins was divorced from a famous rock star and living in Vancouver with his two children. As part of the divorce, she received a substantial payment along with a support payment for each child. She persuaded Mr. Collins to purchase a large house in the city, which he did, but he arranged that the house be held in trust for the two minor children. Mrs. Collins became concerned about her financial position and persuaded the two children to transfer the title of the house to her. At the time of the trial, the oldest child who had reached the age of majority confirmed the sale, but the youngest child was still under age. Evidence was presented that this contract was for the benefit of the children, giving the children the security they needed until they reached the age of 25 years. Evidence indicated that the minor child had received independent legal advice, and a psychiatrist testified that this was truly the desire of the child to make sure the mother had financial security. Explain the arguments that support the transfer of the house and the arguments against it.

2. Lenson v. Lenson

The father owned a farm in Saskatchewan and his son, the plaintiff, lived on that farm with his wife. For a number of years, they had a crop-sharing arrangement, which was essentially a lease on the property paid for by the son sharing the crop with his father. This arrangement had been going on for some time, when the son alleged they had entered into an oral agreement whereby he would buy the farm for $100 000 and be given the land immediately around the farmhouse as a gift. According to the son's testimony, he and his wife gave up several opportunities to buy surrounding property and made considerable improvements on the land in question, but eventually there was a falling out between the parties, and the father denied that any agreement existed. Explain what difficulties the son will face in trying to establish his claim to the land and how those difficulties can be overcome.

3. Ouston et al. v. Zurowski et al.

A number of plaintiffs including Ouston were persuaded to invest in a scheme run by the defendant, "Kulnan Investment Corp.," which was a pyramid investment scheme. Such a scheme is similar to a chain letter, where one person higher on the chain makes money on the basis of others being persuaded to join the chain for a fee. The idea is that the person joining the chain will get higher in that chain as others join and make a considerable amount of money on those they recruit. The problem with such schemes is that the people last to join lose all their money.

The plaintiffs testified that they were told when they were brought into the scheme by Zurowski that if the board should stop, Zurowski would make sure they got their money back, that is, if the pyramid scheme failed, he would reimburse the defendants. The scheme did fail because of local publicity that discouraged any further meetings and the attraction of any further investors. Pyramid schemes are illegal under the *Criminal Code*. In this action, Ouston and the other plaintiffs seek to have their money returned. Explain what arguments they can put forward to support this request and the likely attitude of the court in granting remedies.

4. Canadian American Finance Corp. v. King

The Canadian American Finance Corporation markets a registered scholarship savings plan for profit. King was employed to market the plan as director of agencies. King set up a separate company to market the plan. The agreement between the Canadian American Finance Corporation and King included a non-competition clause that said that once the relationship was terminated, King could not enter into competition with the corporation for a period of two years in Canada or Bermuda. King eventually quit and went to work for a rival company in Alberta and British Columbia. Comment on the arguments available to both parties as to the validity of this non-competition clause.

5. Performance Systems Inc. v. Pezim

The defendant was involved in promoting a restaurant chain in Canada that required buying a franchise from a similar American company. The American company loaned the Canadian company $50 000 on the strength of a promissory note guaranteed by the defendant. There was some dispute about whether the agents who consented to the guarantee on behalf of the defendant were authorized to do so, but it was held that the defendant could not deny that he had guaranteed the promissory note despite the fact that the guarantee had not been signed until several months after the $50 000 was advanced. When the Canadian company ran into difficulties and was unable to repay the loan, the American company demanded that the defendant honour the guarantee. What arguments would the defendant raise in defence of this action? Explain the likely outcome.

Factors Affecting the Contractual Relationship

- The nature and effect of a mistake in a contract
- Misrepresentation and its consequences on a contract
- The implications of duress and undue influence
- The rules governing privity and assignment

The two previous chapters examined the process of forming contracts. This chapter will discuss the extent of the responsibilities and obligations of the original parties to an agreement, what happens when the parties disagree as to the nature and effect of the contract, and how those obligations are affected when an innocent third party or a stranger to the contract becomes involved.

Hoy v. Lozanovski[1]

Mr. Hoy purchased a 50-year-old house from Mr. and Mrs. Lozanovski after having a builder friend inspect it and indicate that it was sound. Soon after he moved in, he discovered that the house was infested with termites; it had to be completely renovated at a cost of $25 000 before he could live in it. Mr. Hoy sued the Lozanovskis, claiming damages in this amount for fraudulent misrepresentation. The judge held that there was no fraud, since the Lozanovskis did not know of the termites when they sold the house. Even if they had, the judge said, they would not be liable, since they were silent (they had made no statements that the house was free from such infestation) and the purchaser had not relied on any representations from them and had his own builder inspect the house. To obtain damages, Mr. Hoy not only had to demonstrate that the misrepresentation was fraudulent rather than innocent but also that he had relied on the representation in question. In this case, not only was there no reliance on the representation, there was no representation at all. Misrepresentation is just one of the factors to be considered in this chapter that can affect the rights of the parties to a contract.

1. Hoy v. Lozanovski as reported in *The Lawyers Weekly*, April 3, 1987.

Mistake

In limited circumstances, the courts will provide a remedy where one or both of the parties has made a mistake with respect to a contract. This is especially true when it is clear that because of the mistake, the parties have failed to reach a consensus and there is no complete agreement between them.

Misunderstanding that destroys consensus results in void contract

Mistakes in contract involve a person's mind being at odds with the terms, surrounding circumstances, or other factors relating to the contract. Such a mistake can relate to the terms of the contract, including the identity of the parties. It can relate to an assumption upon which the contract is based, whether as to a matter of fact, some future event, or the law surrounding the contract. And it can also concern an expected result or consequence of the agreement. The mistake can be made by only one of the parties or by both. Where both parties are making a mistake, it can be a **shared mistake,** where both are making the same mistake, or it can be a misunderstanding, where each party has a different idea as to the meaning of the terms of the contract. Not all these errors are reviewable by the court.

Mistake must be part of agreement, not just affect agreement

When such a mistake has been made, the courts are reluctant to relieve a person of their obligations when this would interfere with the reasonable expectations of the other party or where some other injustice would result. Therefore, the courts will not assist a person who has simply misjudged the effect of the contract. When a person buys shares or other property expecting the price to go up and it goes down, that is his problem. But when the mistake relates to the terms of the agreement itself, such as the identity of the parties or the subject matter of the agreement, the courts are more willing to provide a remedy. The courts also will not interfere with contractual obligations unless the demonstrated mistake is significant or material with respect to the agreement. If a person ordering a new car is delivered one that is a slightly different colour than the one he had in mind when he chose it, that will not be enough to allow him to avoid the contract. Finally, where the mistake is caused by the negligence of one of the parties that party will normally be held responsible for the error.

Careless party responsible when mistake is result of negligence

The courts are less likely to remedy a mistake in law

While a mistake, in fact, may justify the court questioning the contract, it is not so clear when the mistake is one of law. In the past, there was no remedy if the mistake made was one of law based on the principle that ignorance of the law is no excuse. Recently, however, in *Canada v. British Columbia*, the Supreme Court of Canada expressed a reluctance to continue this distinction.[2] In that case, money had been paid under a mistake in law, and the court was reluctant to let the payment stand, causing one of the parties to be unjustly enriched. As a result, at least where a payment has been made on the basis of a mistake in law and one party receives money he is not entitled to, the court will order those funds returned on the basis of **unjust enrichment.**

The area of mistake in contract law is very confusing, and it has not been uncommon over the years for the courts to reverse or modify their position. The discussion below is an attempt to summarize the important aspects of the law in this area. The approach taken concentrates on three different ways that a mistake can be made. It should be remembered that if a contract is found to be void, it is not a

2. (1989) 59 DLR (4th) 161

contract at all, but if it is voidable, the contract does exist, but one of the parties has the option of getting out of it. When an innocent third party has acquired goods that are the subject of a voidable contract, that party gets to keep the goods, but if the contract was void—that is, there never was a contract—the person who sold the goods to the third party never had title to them, and those goods must be returned to the original owner.

Shared Mistake

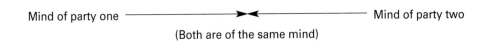

Mind of party one ————————►◄———————— Mind of party two

(Both are of the same mind)

Fundamental shared mistake about subject matter—void

A shared mistake takes place when the two parties are in complete agreement, but they have both made the same mistake regarding a fundamental aspect of the subject matter of the contract. The most common example of such a shared mistake resulting in a void contract is where the subject matter of the contract no longer exists at the time the contract is made. Thus, where the parties enter into an agreement for the sale and purchase of the cargo of a ship without knowing that the cargo was destroyed the night before, the contract is void because of the shared mistake. The courts have also found a contract void because of a shared mistake when, unknown to the parties, the property being sold was already owned by the purchaser. In both these instances, the parties have together made the same significant mistake with respect to a factual aspect of the contract that has destroyed the basis of the contract. As a result, the contract is void, for lack of consensus.

When the parties make a mistake about only the value of what they are dealing with, it normally will not affect the enforceability of the contract. For example, if both vendor and purchaser think that they are dealing with an ordinary violin when, in fact, they are dealing with a rare and valuable Stradivarius, the contract would be binding nevertheless.

Rectification

Courts will correct an improperly recorded agreement

If the written document does not reflect the common intention of the parties to the contract, the courts are willing to correct or rectify the document. For example, if two parties had agreed to the sale of land for $500 000 and a clerical error made the document read $50 000, the court would add the missing zero and require the parties to perform the corrected agreement. The courts will only do this where it is clear that both understood what they were agreeing to and what was written was different from that understanding. If in the above example both parties intended to write $50 000 on the basis of a shared error about how much land was included, the court will not rectify this, as they both intended to put down that amount in the written document. The fact that it was based on an error will not support rectification. It is important to remember that the courts are not rewriting the agreement during rectification. They are simply correcting a written document so that it corresponds to the demonstrated intention of the two parties. Rectification of the contract may be available as a remedy in other situations as well, such as where a unilateral mistake is caused by the fraud of the other party.

Downtown King West Development Corp. v. Massey Ferguson Industries Ltd.[3]

Lochan Ora Investments Ltd. entered into an agreement with Massey Ferguson Industries Ltd. by letter for the lease of certain property. This agreement included a provision giving the lessee a right of first refusal over the 10-year period of the lease and the right to purchase the property first if Massey Ferguson decided to sell it any time during the term of the lease. This agreement anticipated the drawing up of a formal lease to be executed by the parties. Before this was done, the position of Lochan Ora Investments Ltd. was taken over by Downtown King West Development Corporation, involving many of the same individuals. After some further negotiation and the exchange of several drafts, a formal lease was eventually completed between Massey Ferguson and Downtown King West. Unfortunately, the right of first refusal in the formal lease had been changed and only applied to the *last five years* of the 10-year lease period. Massey Ferguson did, in fact, sell the property, but it was during the first five years of the lease, and this action was brought to determine whether the right of first refusal was for the whole lease period and, if it was, to enforce it. Downtown King West claimed that both parties had intended the right of first refusal to extend for the entire length of the lease, not just the last five years as evidenced by the original letter agreement and asked the court to "rectify" the agreement so that it would read that way.

The lower court did, in fact, rectify the agreement, but this was overturned on appeal. Rectification is only permitted when the written document does not reflect the clear intention of both parties. This is a case of unilateral mistake. Massey Ferguson wanted the term changed, and this was written into the formal lease. They had included the change in each of the seven draft versions of the lease. They were not aware that Downtown King West was not aware of the change or that they still wanted the right of first refusal to extend over the entire period of the lease. Rectification is not permitted unless both parties were of the same mind and only the recording of that shared intention was in error. This is not the situation in this case. Massey Ferguson clearly wanted one thing, and Downtown King West intended another. This case is helpful in showing the limited power of the court to rectify and the restricted situations where rectification can be used.

Misunderstanding

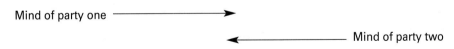

Mind of party one ⟶

⟵ Mind of party two

(Parties have different understanding of contract)

A different type of mistake occurs when the parties have a misunderstanding about the terms of the agreement itself and neither party is aware of the other's different understanding. When one party to an agreement thinks that the agreement is to do

Mistake must be serious

3. (1996) 133 D.L.R. (4th) 550 (Ont. C.A.); leave to appeal to S.C.C. refused (1996) 138 D.L.R. (4th) vii (note)

**Court will enforce
reasonable interpretation**

something else, the courts will usually apply the reasonable person test to determine which interpretation of the contract is more reasonable. The court will then adopt the more reasonable position as the correct interpretation of the contract. This point is discussed below in more detail under the heading "Rules of Interpretation." Only if the error is a serious one and the court cannot choose between the two positions because both are equally reasonable will the contract be declared void.

**Where equally reasonable
and serious—void**

The case of *Raffels v. Wichelhaus* is a good example of such a dilemma. In this case, the contract concerned a cargo being transported on a ship called the Peerless. It happened that there were two ships by this name, both leaving the same port but at different times. The seller intended one of these two ships, and the purchaser had in mind the other. There was no way of applying the reasonable person test to this case, and since the disagreement was fundamental, the contract was declared void.

Meaning of "Sale" Clarified

In a listing agreement, a vendor agreed to pay a real estate agent a commission on the sale of property if that sale or exchange, however affected, was procured by the agent. The agent procured an offer, including a deposit, and requested payment according to the agreement. Unfortunately, the deal fell through, giving the vendor the right to keep the deposit. But the agent who was holding the deposit refused to pay it over to the vendor, claiming that they were entitled to their commission because a sale had been made. The Supreme Court of Canada had to decide whether the agent was still entitled to the commission. The court, after looking at the practice in the industry and the various contracts involved, concluded that the completion of a contract of sale was not enough; the sale itself had to go through, despite the fact that the vendor obtained compensation in the form of a deposit from the reluctant purchaser.

Leading Investments Ltd. v. New Forest Investments Ltd. [1986] 1 S.C.R. 70; application for reconsideration refused (sub. nom. H.W. Liebig Co. v. Leading Investments Ltd.) (1986) 18 O.A.C. 80 (S.C.C.).

One-Sided Mistake

Mind of party one

(Where only one party is mistaken)

Moss v. Chin[4]

In this case, Mrs. Moss was a pedestrian in a crosswalk when she was struck by a car driven by Mr. Chin. She was severely injured and became unconscious. A government official, called a public trustee, was appointed to act on her behalf and start a legal action against the person causing her injuries. Since the defendant was insured by the Insurance Corporation of British Columbia (ICBC), they defended the action. Her claim was for $300 000 in damages, most of which was for pain, suffering, and future care. In the process of negotiations between the parties, Mrs.

4. 120 D.L.R. (4th) 406 (B.C. S.C.)

Moss suffered a seizure, and it became apparent that she would not live long. When the lawyer for the public trustee learned of this, he got permission to settle the matter right away with ICBC, for if she died her right to sue would die with her. An offer to settle was made by ICBC the day after the plaintiff died. The public trustee and the solicitor, while failing to inform ICBC of her death, accepted the offer on her behalf. ICBC paid out the money but eventually learned about what had happened and brought an application to the court to have the settlement set aside.

The court found that the agreement had been entered into on the basis of a unilateral mistake. Normally, a unilateral mistake is simply the problem of the person making it and will not affect the rights of the other parties. In effect, the person making the mistake has misled himself, and there is no remedy. If there is fraud involved, however, or, as in this case, where one party deliberately sets out to make sure the other does not discover a mistake, the court has the power to interfere. The court ordered that the contract be rescinded.

This case is interesting because it illustrates the difference between a unilateral mistake and other forms of mistakes and shows that even when such unilateral mistakes are made, under some limited circumstances, there may be a rescission of the contract.

A one-sided or **unilateral mistake** takes place where one of the parties makes a mistake in relationship to the contract and the other party is aware that this mistake is being made. This was the situation in *Moss v. Chin* above. As a general rule, there is no recourse for a person who makes such a one-sided mistake. Thus, when the manager of a business buys a computer by name and model, thinking it will do a specific job and it turns out that it does not have the required capacity, a mistake has been made by the purchaser, but there will likely be no remedy. This is a one-sided mistake, and if there was no reliance placed on the salesperson and no misrepresentation or misleading information supplied in the documentation and brochures, there will be no remedy. In effect, the purchaser has misled himself, and the principle of *caveat emptor* ("Let the buyer beware") applies. It should be noted, however, that when the offeror makes an obvious error in relation to his or her offer, the purchaser will not be allowed to take advantage of this obvious error and snap up the offer. Thus, if the merchant selling the computer misquoted it and agreed to sell it at $25 instead of the $2500 normal price, the purchaser would not be able to ignore such an obvious error and "snap it up" at the bargain price. When a one-sided mistake takes place, the person making the mistake usually only has a remedy when he or she has been misled, and then the normal course of action is to claim for misrepresentation with its associated remedies. Even when there has been misrepresentation, it may be important for the victim to establish that the misrepresentation led to a mistake with respect to the contract. If goods are involved and they have been resold to an innocent third party, the remedy of rescission for misrepresentation will not be available. However, if a mistake sufficient to affect consensus has taken place, the contract may be void, allowing recovery of the goods involved, even from an innocent purchaser.

One-sided mistake—"Let the buyer beware"

Such a one-sided mistake can occur when there is incorrect identification of one of the parties to a contract. If the person claiming that a mistake has taken place actually thought the deal was with someone else and can demonstrate that identity was an important aspect of the agreement, the court will declare the contract to be void. However, if the party using mistaken identity as a defence was just in error about some attribute of the other party, this will not affect the existence of the contract.

If mistake about identity—void contract

For example, if a vendor thought that jewellery was being sold on credit to Ms. Paré, a wealthy movie star, and in fact, the Ms. Paré the merchant was dealing with was a waitress and not associated with the movie industry at all, the contract would be binding and title would go to the purchaser. He knew he was dealing with a specific woman, Ms. Pare, but was mistaken in terms of one of her attributes; her wealth. If the jewellery is resold, the ultimate purchaser would acquire good title. Of course, the seller would still have recourse against Ms. Paré if she did not pay for the jewellery. But if the seller thought that the purchaser was Ms. Paré, a wealthy and well-known movie star and, in fact, the purchaser was Ms. Capozzi, a waitress, a mistake has been made about the identity of the person with whom the seller is dealing, and there would be no contract. In this case, the mistake is not as to the woman's attributes but as to her very identity. He thinks he is actually dealing with someone else entirely, and there is no contract.[5]

Contract may be void when one party makes mistake sufficient to affect consensus

For a contract to be declared void because of a one-sided or unilateral mistake, usually the person making the mistake has been misled by the other party. Misrepresentation will be discussed below, but here, it is important to note that where misrepresentation causes a person to make a mistake that is so significant that it destroys consensus, the court may declare the contract to be void, whereas normally, the victim is limited to the remedies associated with misrepresentation.

Non Est Factum

If misled about nature of document signed—void

Where one of the parties is unaware of the nature of the document being signed, the courts will, in rare circumstances, declare the agreement void on the basis of **non est factum** ("It is not my act"). If a person was led to believe he was guaranteeing a note and was, in fact, signing a mortgage agreement on his home, he could argue that there was no consensus between the parties and no contract. This might be a valid defence even against an innocent third party who had acquired rights under the agreement. For this defence to succeed and the contract to be void, it must be shown that the mistake about the document went to the very nature of that document rather than merely to its terms. In the example above, if the mistake was only that he thought the document involved a mortgage requiring 10 percent interest when it was actually for 15 percent, he would still be bound. The mistake being made was with respect to some aspect of the document, not the document itself.

—but not where negligence present

Today, negligence, such as failure to read the document before signing, can defeat the defence of *non est factum* in the absence of wrongdoing by the plaintiff. It is unlikely, therefore, that such a defence will be successful, unless it can be shown that the error was caused by misrepresentation. The remedies that are available for misrepresentation are discussed below, but in those limited situations where the misrepresentation has led to a fundamental mistake, the contract may be void as well.

Deraps v. Coia et al.[6]

Mr. Deraps was a labourer for some 20 years before he discovered he had lung cancer in 1990. During that time, he paid into a pension fund, and when he could no longer work, he talked to the union representative Ms. Hickey about his options. It was explained to both Mr. and Mrs. Deraps that he was eligible for a disability pension and that he would receive a higher pension payment if his wife signed a

5. Cundy v. Lindsay (1878) 3 App. Cas. 459 (H.L.)

6. (1999) 173 D.L.R. (4th) 717 (Ont. C. Gen. Div.); rev'd on other grounds (1999) 179 D.L.R. (4th) 168 (C.A.)

waiver of spousal benefits. Mrs. Deraps signed the waiver, and within a year, he died. Mrs. Deraps brought this action to have the waiver declared void on the basis of *non est factum*. She claimed that she did not understand that the effect of the waiver was that she would receive no pension at all after Mr. Deraps died. The trial court agreed and found that the information given by Ms. Hickey was confusing and that Mrs. Deraps did not understand what she was signing. This was appealed, and the decision of the trial judge was overturned. The court held that the document was explained to her "in as simple terms possible." Even though there was no indication that she had ever been specifically told that she would get nothing after her husband died, it was clear that was the effect of signing the waiver. They also held that she read and wrote English and that the document she signed was not fundamentally different from what she thought she was signing. These factors defeated the claim of *non est factum*. In addition, the fact that she did not bother to read the document before signing disqualified her from claiming *non est factum*. This case shows how difficult it now is to succeed in claims for *non est factum*. The judge clearly was not convinced that she did not understand what she was signing, but even if she was confused, the mistake has to go to the whole nature of the document, and it did not. In addition to that reason, her carelessness in failing to read the document made the claim of *non est factum* unavailable to her. It is this last factor of negligence preventing the claim of *non est factum* that has reduced the use of *non est factum* to such a significant extent.

Rules of Interpretation

The test to determine whether a mistake has taken place is objective. The courts are not concerned with what the parties thought they were agreeing to but rather with what the parties should have been aware of and expected when they made the agreement. In such instances, the courts use the reasonable person test. Instead of declaring the contract void because one of the parties has made a mistake about the meaning of a term, the courts will look at the wording to determine what a reasonable person would have understood the term to mean. In those rare circumstances in which there is no reasonable interpretation of the agreement or the positions taken by the two parties are equally reasonable, the courts can declare the contract to be void.[7]

Reasonable person test applies when there is a misunderstanding

Whenever there is a dispute involving the meaning of a specific term, the courts have a choice of applying the literal meaning of the term or adopting a more liberal approach by trying to determine the parties' intent. The courts will apply the literal meaning of the wording chosen by the parties if there is no ambiguity. If the term is ambiguous, the court will look at what was behind the agreement and apply the most reasonable meaning of the term to the contract.

Courts apply literal meaning to specific wording

Ambiguous wording interpreted liberally

Determining the literal meaning of the words is not as simple as it might first appear. Even dictionaries often have several different meanings for particular words. Determining the intention of the parties may also be difficult because of the conflicting positions taken by the parties to the dispute. The court will often look at how the terms are normally used in the particular industry involved. The court will also look at past dealings between the parties as well as their dealings at the time the contract was formed to determine what they intended by the words they used. The key to the court's approach to such ambiguous terms in an agreement is to choose the most reasonable interpretation. Another rule courts use in these situations is the **parol evidence rule**. Where the terms used in an agreement are clear and unambiguous, the courts

Courts will not permit outside evidence to contradict clear wording

7. Raffels v. Wichelhaus (1864) 2 H. & C. 906 (E.D.)

will not allow other outside evidence to be introduced to show a different meaning was intended. "What you see is what you get." If you state in your agreement that the contract is for the sale of a "1984 Chrysler automobile," you cannot later try to introduce evidence that a Chrysler sailboat was intended. Of course, if the contract only referred to a "1984 Chrysler," it is ambiguous, and evidence then could be introduced to show that a car or sailboat was intended.

Exceptions to the parole evidence rule

The courts will also override the parol evidence rule when the evidence to be introduced is of a fraud or some other problem associated with the formation of the contract, such as duress or undue influence. Other exceptions to the parol evidence rule include evidence of **a condition precedent** (a condition that has to be met before the obligations set out in the contract are in force); evidence of a **collateral contract** (a separate contractual obligation that can stand alone, independent of the written one); evidence of a subsequent agreement entered into by the parties after the written one; or the absence of an intention that all of the contract would be embodied in the written document. When the evidence contradicting the terms of the agreement falls into one of these categories, the court can be persuaded to hear it, despite the parol evidence rule.

Courts will imply terms, where appropriate

The courts are also willing to imply terms into an agreement, when necessary. It does not occur to most contracting parties to provide terms in their agreement for every possible eventuality, and the courts are willing to supply these missing terms. Where the parties agree to the purchase of a car, for example, they might not specify the time of delivery or when the price is to be paid. The courts will imply what is reasonable in the circumstances, likely that delivery must take place within a reasonable time, and that the price is to be paid upon delivery. What is reasonable will often be determined by looking at past dealings between the parties or the normal practices and traditions found within that specific industry or trade. Some terms may be implied automatically by statute. The *Sale of Goods Act* has set down in rule form the terms that are implied in a contract for the sale of goods when the parties have not addressed them. As well, some consumer protection legislation imposes terms in contracts whether or not the parties have agreed to them. The courts themselves have been known to impose contract terms on the parties and modify obligations, using the principle of fairness[8] and unconscionability discussed below.

Statutes may imply terms into contract

Equity may be used to settle mistakes in contracts

Term Implied into Contract

Two parties entered into a joint venture agreement for the development of computer software. Unfortunately, nowhere in the agreement did they make any provision for the termination of the relationship. One of the parties terminated the relationship without notice, causing significant damage to the other, who sued. The court held that although there was no termination provision, termination by either party on reasonable notice should be implied into the contract, for clearly, the parties should not have expected their agreement to be perpetual. But then again, the notice was not given at all, so the terminating party was responsible for at least some of the damages.

Rapatax Inc. v. Cantax Corp. (1987) 145 D.L.R. (4th) 419 (Alta. C.A.)

---

8. Cooper v. Phibbs (1867) L.R. 2 H.L. 149 (H.L.)

This is one of the areas where the greatest confrontation takes place and where business people would be wise to review their practices. There may be great value in establishing the trust associated with a deal made on a handshake, but this examination of mistake and misrepresentation shows the downside. Even the most sincere businessperson can forget just what they have agreed to or they can recall the terms quite differently even when they had the same understanding of the terms of the agreement in the first place. And that does not even consider the instances of wilful blindness and convenient memory loss. Putting an agreement into some permanent form, such as writing, is only the first step. Great care should be taken to ensure that the words used are clear and unambiguous so that there can be no question later of what has been agreed upon. Using this approach will usually contribute to the good will between business people rather than threaten it. Conflict is reduced and confidence increased on the basis of good business practices.

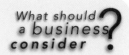

Misrepresentation

Metropolitan Stores of Canada Ltd. v. Nova Construction Co.[9]

Metropolitan Stores had occupied space in the Antigonish Mall for seven years, when the owners of the mall sold it to Nova Construction. Metropolitan and Antigonish had entered into a verbal agreement, but a lease had never been signed, and Nova, upon taking over, tried to evict Metropolitan, resulting in litigation between the two parties.

In the process of attempting to reach a settlement, a new lease was negotiated for a 20-year term. One of its provisions was that no stores in competition with Metropolitan would be allowed to be located in the mall; but the clause would not apply if there were any expansion to the existing shopping centre.

When questioned about this, the representative of the mall explained that the only expansion that would take place would be within the present boundaries of the mall and that another clause in the agreement protected Metropolitan from competition within those boundaries. The representative knew that this was false, and seven years later, the mall purchased surrounding property, expanded into that area, and leased property to another department store similar to Metropolitan, in direct contravention of the intent of the lease. They claimed that the exemption clause permitted this.

In the original lease agreement between Metropolitan and Nova, the area of the present mall was specifically covered by the non-competition clause. So when Metropolitan was told that any expansion was going to take place within the present boundaries of the mall, they did not worry about a competing department store moving in because they were protected by the provision setting out the mall boundaries. In effect, Metropolitan was tricked into signing a lease that did not protect them the way they thought it would. Metropolitan claimed that the lease had been breached and stopped paying rent; again, Nova tried to evict them.

Metropolitan first tried to claim that the lease ought to be interpreted so that this expansion and leasing to the other department store would be considered a violation of it. The judge looked at that and found that the wording of the lease was clear. There was no ambiguity, and so he was not free to do that. However, he did find that a fraudulent misrepresentation had taken place, which induced Metropolitan to enter into the contract. Although the parol evidence rule restricts

9. (1988) 50 D.L.R. (4th) 508 (N.S.C.A.)

any outside extrinsic evidence which conflicts with the plain meaning and unambiguous wording of the contract from being considered, there are several exceptions, one of which is evidence of fraud inducing the parties to enter into the contract. Such fraud was found in these circumstances.

This case is unusual because the normal remedies for misrepresentation are either rescission or, when fraud is present, rescission and/or damages. In this case, however, Metropolitan asked for rectification of the contract, that is, for the contract to be rewritten to include the terms as they understood it, making the expansion with the inclusion of the rival department store a breach of their lease. The trial judge thought this was going too far, but the Court of Appeal was willing to rectify the agreement, added the appropriate words to the lease, and declared Nova in breach of that lease. **Rectification**—the rewriting of a contract on behalf of one of the parties at the expense of the other—is a drastic remedy, but because of the fraud, it was appropriate.

Misrepresentation is a misleading statement that induces a contract

When one person misleads another, inducing that person to enter into a contract, an actionable misrepresentation has taken place. **Misrepresentation** is a false statement of fact that persuades someone to enter into a contract. The false statement can be made fraudulently, when the person making the statement knew it was false; negligently, when the person should have known the statement was false; or completely innocently, when the misrepresentation is made without fault.

Allegation of Fact

Misrepresentation must be fact, not opinion—nor promise

The statement that forms the basis of the misrepresentation must be an allegation of fact. Only statements made about the current state of things which prove to be incorrect can be considered misrepresentation. A promise to do something in the future will only qualify as a misrepresentation when it can be clearly shown that person making the promise had no intention of honouring that promise at the time it was made. Such promises of future conduct have to be enforced under general contract law. Thus, where a person gratuitously promises to help a person move and then changes his mind, such a failure is not actionable because there is no contract between them. Where the misleading statement being complained of was an expression of opinion rather than fact, it, too, is not actionable, unless the person making the statement was an expert. When a person declares that the car he is selling is a "good car" or a "good deal," he is entitled to have that opinion, and the statement is not actionable if the car later breaks down. But if a mechanic makes the same statement, and it proves false, it can be actionable as misrepresentation because he is an expert.

Opinion by expert may be misrepresentation

Silence or Non-disclosure

For a misrepresentation to take place, there also must be some positive misleading form of communication. Silence or non-disclosure by itself is not usually actionable. There are, however, some special situations, where the person contracting is required to disclose certain information. For example, insurance contracts require the parties acquiring insurance to disclose a great deal of personal information that affects the policy. People who apply for life insurance are required to disclose if they have had heart attacks or other medical problems. The sale of new shares involves a similar obligation of disclosure to an investor in a prospectus. If the terms require that the parties disclose all information to each other as a condition of the agreement, the contract can be rescinded if they fail to do so. Professionals also have an obligation to disclose certain information at their disposal that might affect the actions of their clients. These are often referred to as **utmost good faith** contracts. The requirement of good faith is being expanded into most contractual relationships, and it is now much more common for the courts to find that a misrepresentation has taken place where one party withholds information from the other.

Silence not misrepresentation, unless there is duty to disclose

Where a person actively attempts to hide information that would be important to the other contracting party, this also might qualify as misrepresentation. A person anxious to sell a car might be tempted to hide a noisy transmission by using a heavier grade of oil, and such an act might well invite a claim of misrepresentation. It is not necessary that the statement be written or verbal; misrepresentation can occur even if the method of communicating it is a gesture, such as a nod of the head.

Misrepresentation is normally only available as a cause of action when an actual representation has been made. When individuals mislead themselves, *caveat emptor* applies, and there is no cause for complaint. It is for this reason that in the example used to introduce the chapter the action against the vendors of the property infested by termites failed. Mr. Hoy, the purchaser, went to considerable trouble to inspect the property and so, in effect, misled himself about its condition. The vendors had made no representation in relation to it.

False Statement

It is not only necessary to demonstrate that the misleading comment qualifies as an allegation of fact, but it must also be shown that the statement is incorrect and untrue. Even when a person technically tells the truth but withholds information that would have created an entirely different impression, this can amount to misrepresentation. For example, if a used car salesperson tells a potential purchaser that the transmission of a particular car has just been replaced but fails to say it was replaced with a used transmission, this partial truth can be misrepresentation.

Partial disclosure may be misrepresentation

Misrepresentation must have misled the victim

Statement Must Be Inducement

A victim of misrepresentation must show that he or she was induced into entering a contract by a false statement. If the victim knew that the statement was false and entered into the agreement anyway, either because he or she did not believe the statement or it did not make any difference, the misrepresentation is not actionable. Similarly, if the person thought the statement was true but would have entered into the contract even if he or she had known it was false, there is no misrepresentation. The false statement must affect the outcome of the agreement, and the victim must have been misled into doing something that he or she otherwise would not have done for there to be an actionable misrepresentation. In the *Hoy v. Lozanovski* case, used to open the chapter, even if the court had found that Mr. Hoy had made a misleading statement, it likely would not have qualified as an actionable misrepresentation because the

A salesperson who hides faults in a used car may be guilty of misrepresentation.
PhotoDisc

purchaser did not rely on it. We know this because Mr. Hoy was careful to have the house inspected by his builder friend before it was purchased.

Beer v. Townsgate I Ltd.[10]

Townsgate I Ltd. was a developer and, in 1989, set out to develop a luxury condominium site containing 220 units. The realty company hired to sell the units ran a grand opening sale, generating an atmosphere of frenzy and hype that created the impression that there was a scarcity of these units and that people ought to buy right away. People lined up for hours in the freezing cold to get their deal. Only some of the units were sold, and after several months, the bottom fell out of the market, requiring the remainder to be advertised and sold at a much-reduced price. Those that had already purchased were upset. Some were allowed to pay a reduced price but some wanted out of the deal and their money back. In this case, we are interested in the two buyers that were able to successfully rescind the agreement on the basis of negligent misrepresentation. They claimed that in the frenzied atmosphere around the sale, the purchasers were given a false sense of scarcity, that they were told that it was "risk free," and that it was a "guaranteed" investment. The trial judge and appeal judge agreed that there was negligent misrepresentation but then had to consider whether that misrepresentation was relied on by the purchasers. One purchaser when asked why he purchased responded, "Because, as I told you, I didn't see that there was nothing to lose here; only to gain." This clear lack of sophistication helped the judges to find that the misrepresentation was relied on and that without it, there would have been no purchase.

The remaining problem was a provision in the contract that read, "It is agreed that there is no representation, warranty, collateral agreement, or condition affecting this agreement or the real property or supported hereby other than as expressed herein in writing whether contained in any sales brochures or alleged to have been made by any sales representatives or agents." The parol evidence rule discussed above states that where the terms of an agreement are clear and unambiguous, no outside evidence can be introduced to contradict it. This rule did not apply in this case for two reasons. First, an exception to the rule is where there has been a misrepresentation inducing a person to enter a contract as in this case. Secondly, the clause was buried in fine print and was not only not brought to the attention of the purchasers, but they were not even given the time to read it. For these reasons, the purchasers were able to get their money back. This is a very interesting case, and it illustrates how a contract can be rescinded on the basis of misrepresentation if that misrepresentation is relied on and induces the person to enter into the contract. It also illustrates the operation of the parol evidence rule and the exceptions to it.

As a Term of the Contract

The law of misrepresentation discussed here applies where the misleading statement induced or persuaded the victim to enter into a contract. These special remedies are needed because the misleading statement usually does not become a term of the agreement itself. If the misleading statement complained of has become a term of the agreement, the normal rules of breach of contract apply, providing

10. (1997)152 D.L.R. (4th) 671 (Ont. C.A.); reversing in part on other grounds (1995) 25 O.R. (3d) 785 (Gen. Div.); leave to appeal refused (1998) 112 O.A.C. 200 (note) (S.C.C.).

much broader remedies that are easier to obtain. If Osterman agreed to sell Nasser a 1957 Ford Thunderbird for $10 000 but the car turned out to be a 1957 Ford Fairlane, Nasser is free to sue Osterman for breach of contract. But if Osterman bought a particular property because the vendor Nasser said that the municipal council had voted to build a new highway nearby, it would be a rare contract that would include such a provision as a term of the agreement. Because the statement is an inducement to buy, not a term of the contract, the victim must rely on the rules of misrepresentation to obtain a remedy. The remedies available will depend on whether the statement was made inadvertently, fraudulently, or negligently.

Breach of contract action may be appropriate if misleading term in contract

Even so, the courts today are more open to the suggestion that such representations have become terms of the contract. Even statements in advertisements now can be taken to be part of the contract. Many provinces in their consumer protection legislation not only have provisions controlling misleading and deceptive trade practices but also state that the representations of salespeople are specifically made part of the contract. The topic of consumer protection legislation will be discussed in a subsequent chapter.

Innocent Misrepresentation

An innocent misrepresentation is a false statement made honestly and without carelessness by a person who believes it to be true. Where a heavy-duty equipment supplier sells a truck claiming it can haul five tons of gravel but its actual capacity is only three tons, this is misrepresentation, even where the seller believed what he was saying was true. If the person making the misrepresentation is in no way at fault, the misrepresentation is innocent, and the remedies are limited. The only recourse available to the victim is to ask for the equitable remedy of rescission. As soon as the victim realizes what has happened, he or she can either choose to ignore the misrepresentation and affirm the contract or rescind the contract.

Unintentional misrepresentation—remedy is rescission

Rescission

Rescission attempts to return both parties to their original positions; the subject matter of the contract must be returned to the original owner, and any monies paid under the contract must also be returned. The courts will also require the party who is returning the subject matter of the contract to return any benefit derived from the property while it was in his or her possession. Similarly, a person can be compensated for any expenses incurred. Damages are not available as a remedy because both parties are innocent. Although rescission is an important remedy, because it is equitable, it is quite restricted in its application. Rescission is not available in the following situations:

Monetary benefit and expenses

1. **Affirmation**. Victims of misrepresentation who have affirmed the contract are bound by the affirmation and cannot later insist on rescission. Thus, where a person uses the proceeds of a contract knowing of the misrepresentation, he has affirmed the contract.

Rescission not available if contract affirmed

2. **Impossible to restore**. The remedy of rescission is not available if the parties cannot be returned to their original positions because the subject matter of the contract has been destroyed or damaged. Since neither party is at fault, with innocent misrepresentation, the court will not impose a burden on either one of them but will simply deny a remedy.

—restoration impossible

—or it will affect third party

3. **Third-party involvement**. Rescission will not be granted if it will adversely affect the position of a third party. When the subject matter of the contract has been resold by the purchaser to a third party who has no knowledge of the misrepresentation and otherwise comes to the transaction with clean hands, the courts will not interfere with that person's possession and title to the goods.

4. **Failure on the part of the victim**. Where the victim comes without "clean hands," rescission will be available. Where the victim has also misled or cheated, rescission will be denied. Where the victim has caused unreasonable delay, rescission will be denied. These principles apply to all equitable remedies, and these will be discussed in the next chapter.

Equitable remedy

Rescission and/or damages for torts for intentional misrepresentation

Fraudulent Misrepresentation

If a misrepresentation of fact is intentional and induces another person to enter into a contract, the victim of the fraud can sue for damages under the tort of deceit in addition to or instead of rescission. The problem with fraudulent misrepresentation is to determine just how intentional the false statement has to be. In the case of *Derry v. Peek*,[11] it was established that fraud has taken place when the false statement was made "(1) knowingly, (2) without belief in its truth, or (3) recklessly careless, whether it be true or false."[12] There have been some difficulties over the years in interpreting just what these words mean, but essentially, it is fraud if it can be demonstrated that the person who made the false statement does not honestly believe it to be true. The persons making the statement cannot avoid responsibility by claiming they did not know for sure that what they said was false or because they did not bother to find out the truth. Even if the victim of the misrepresentation could have found out the truth easily but relied instead on the statement of the defendant, there is still fraud.

When a person innocently makes a false statement and later discovers the mistake, he or she must without delay inform the other person of the misrepresentation. Failure to do so will turn an innocent misrepresentation into a fraud. A person who, during the process of negotiating the terms of a contract, makes a statement which was true but later becomes false because of changing circumstances must correct the statement upon finding out the truth.

Once it has been established that the false statement was intentional and thus fraudulent, the courts can award rescission or damages:

Recission

1. **Rescission or avoidance**. The victim of fraudulent misrepresentation retains the right to have the parties to the contract returned to their original positions and to be reimbursed for any out-of-pocket expenses.

Damages

2. **Damages for deceit**. The victim of fraudulent misrepresentation can seek monetary compensation as well as rescission for any loss incurred as a result of the fraud. When damages are awarded, the courts try to put the victim in the

11. (1889) 14 App. Cas. 337 (H.L.).
12. *Ibid.*, p. 374.

position he or she would have been in had the contract not been entered into. Note that no property is being returned and that the courts are not attempting to return both parties to their original positions, as with rescission. Rather, the courts try to compensate the victim financially for the loss suffered; this payment is made at the expense of the person who is at fault. A victim of fraud can seek damages even after the contract has been affirmed. The victim does not lose the right to demand monetary compensation simply by giving up the right to claim rescission. On rare occasions, the victim of a fraudulent misrepresentation can seek punitive damages, that is, damages intended to punish the wrongdoer rather than compensate the victim.

The major problem with fraudulent misrepresentation is the need to establish that the person being sued knowingly misled the victim. This is often difficult to do and not necessary if only rescission is sought. If rescission will suffice as a remedy, the person suing will usually claim innocent misrepresentation even where fraud is apparent.

Negligent Misrepresentation

An important recent development in tort law is the granting of the remedy of damages for negligent misrepresentation (sometimes called negligent misstatement as discussed in Chapter 4). Today, if it can be shown that the parties should have known what they said was false, even though they honestly believed it was true, the remedies of damages as well as rescission will be available. Even when the negligent statement becomes a term of the contract or arises out of a contractual relationship, the plaintiff may have a choice about whether to sue in contract or sue in tort for negligence. The Supreme Court of Canada made it clear that such "concurrent liability" may exist, although with some important limitations, such as not permitting the plaintiff to circumvent the protection provided in an exemption clause by suing in tort instead.[13]

Negligent damages may be available in cases of misrepresentation

If the misrepresentation has become a term of the contract and there is a breach, where the misrepresentation is fraudulent, and when it is negligent, damages are available as a remedy.[14] Thus, it appears that only when the misrepresentation is truly innocent and without fault is the victim restricted to the remedy of rescission.

Untangling the WEB

The principles of contract law dealing with mistake and misrepresentation will apply to electronic transactions just as they do to other contracts. These principles are also embodied in provincial consumer protection legislation, and the recommendation is to amend that legislation so that Internet shoppers have the right to cancel a contract if they change their minds within a certain time or where the goods are not delivered within a specified time.

13. Central & Eastern Trust Co. v. Rafuse (1988) 1 S.C.R. 1206; varying [1986] 2 S.C.R. 147, and B.C. International Ltd. v. British Columbia Hydro & Power Authority [1993] 1 S.C.R. 12; application for rehearing refused (1993) 5 C.L.R. (2d) 173 (note) (S.C.C.)
14. Beaufort Realties v. Chomedey Aluminum Co. (1981) 116 D.L.R. (3d) 193 (N.B.C.A.)

Duress and Undue Influence

Duress

Through a complicated series of transactions, a family made arrangements to develop several hectares of land owned by the parents. Serious difficulties arose between the parties, and a son threatened physical harm to one of his siblings. Fearing that threat, the parents conveyed certain properties and created other advantages for that son. When an action was brought to enforce the agreement made by the parents and the defence of duress was raised, the trial court found the contract void on that basis. However, the Court of Appeal reversed this, finding the contract voidable. The distinction is important: a void contract is no contract, and nothing done by the parties can give it life afterwards; if a contract is voidable, however, the con-duct of the victims can revive it if they continue to perform its terms after the duress has passed. This is called affirming the contract. In this case, although the court found the contract voidable rather than void, it did not find affirmation of the contract in the conduct of the parents. Although the parents continued to perform after the threat was passed, they were not aware of their right to rescind the contract and so could not be said to have affirmed it. This case also points out the fact that when duress is involved, the force or threat does not have to be directed at the other party in the contract; it can be directed at some other person.

Byle v. Byle, 65 D.L.R. (4th) 641 (B.C.C.A.)

Duress involves threats of violence or imprisonment—contract voidable

When people are forced or pressured to enter into contracts against their will by threats of violence or imprisonment, duress is present, and the contracts are voidable. Today, duress includes not only threats of violence and imprisonment but threats of criminal prosecution and threats to disclose embarrassing or scandalous information.

In Canada, duress also includes threats to a person's goods or property. If O'Rourke threatened to vandalize Tong's store unless Tong agreed to purchase his vegetables from O'Rourke, this would qualify as duress in Canada, and the contract with O'Rourke would be voidable. To succeed, it is necessary to show that the threat was the main inducement for entering into the agreement.

Economic advantage not enough

Even though the threat of loss of employment and other financial losses can amount to economic duress and be actionable, it is important not to mistake the normal predicaments in which we all find ourselves for improper pressure or duress. If a person has no choice except to use a particular taxi because it is the only one on the street or has to deal with the only airline or telephone company that services a particular area, these accepted conditions of the marketplace do not amount to duress. Likewise, where a person has to pay a high rate of interest because no one else will loan money at a lower rate is not duress. Even the threat of suing when the person doing so has a legitimate right to sue is not duress. Rather, it is the legitimate exercise of the rights of that person.

Voidable contracts cannot affect third parties

A third party's position cannot be jeopardized if the victim of duress seeks a remedy. Thus, if a purchaser improperly pressures someone into selling a gold watch and then resells that watch to an innocent third party, the watch cannot be retrieved. Because a voidable contract is still a contract, the title is passed on to the third party. Had the watch been stolen from the original owner and then sold to an innocent third party, the original owner would not have given up title to the watch and could, therefore, retrieve it.

Undue Influence

The types of pressure brought to bear upon people are often more subtle than those described by duress. When pressure from a dominant, trusted person makes it impossible to bargain freely, it is regarded as undue influence, and the resulting contract is voidable.

Undue influence involves undue pressures—contract voidable

In the case of *Allcard v. Skinner*,[15] a woman entered a religious order and gave it all her property. The court determined that there had been undue influence when the gift was given, even though there was clear evidence that there had been no overt attempt on the part of the religious order to influence this woman. The court would have set the gift aside, except that she had affirmed it after leaving the relationship.

The court may find undue influence in the following situations:

1. **Presumption based on a special relationship.** In certain categories of relationships, the courts will presume the presence of undue influence, and if the presumption is not rebutted, the contract will be set aside. These categories are:

   Undue influence presumed in certain relationships

   (a) Adult contracting with infant child or adult contracting with parent with mental disability
   (b) Solicitor contracting with client
   (c) Doctor contracting with patient
   (d) Religious advisor contracting with parishioner (as in the case of *Allcard v. Skinner* discussed above)
   (e) Trustee contracting with beneficiary
   (f) Guardian contracting with ward

Note that in contracts between parents and adult children and between spouses, undue influence is not automatically presumed.

Undue Influence Presumed

Barney was a friend and client of John Farlow, a solicitor, and in the past had lent him money. In this transaction, Farlow persuaded Barney to guarantee a loan of $50 000 he was getting from the Rochdale Credit Union. Barney did so reluctantly. Farlow died, and the credit union demanded payment from Barney. The Ontario Court of Appeal found undue influence on the part of Farlow in persuading his client to guarantee the loan, and because Farlow represented both parties, the credit union was also responsible for that undue influence, and Barney did not have to pay the debt. The case illustrates how in transactions between solicitor and client, undue influence is presumed, but it is also interesting because the third party, Rochdale Credit Union, is affected by that presumption.

Rochdale Credit Union Ltd. v. Barney (1984) 14 D.L.R. (4th) 116 (Ont. C.A.); leave to appeal refused (1985) 8 O.A.C. 320 (S.C.C.)

---

15. (1887) 36 Ch.D. 145 (C.A.)

Undue influence pressure from circumstances

2. **Presumption based on unique circumstances**. If the relationship involved does not fall into one of the protected classes listed above, there can still be a presumption of undue influence on the basis of unique circumstances. The courts then attempt to determine whether the surrounding circumstances cast doubt on the voluntariness of the agreement, in which case, the court may still presume undue influence where it is just and reasonable to do so. A husband or a wife signing a guarantee for the indebtedness of their spouse might be such a situation. If the court makes that presumption, it falls on the party trying to enforce the contract to show that there was no domination or unfair advantage taken of the other party.

Where undue influence must be proven

3. **Undue influence determined from facts**. In the absence of a relationship that gives rise to the presumption, it is still possible for a victim to produce actual evidence to satisfy the court that undue influence was, in fact, exerted and that there was coercion. This can be difficult to prove, since the victim must show that a relationship of trust developed because of the relationship between the contracting parties and that that trust was abused. When it can be shown that the person trying to enforce the contract took advantage of the fact that he or she was being relied on for advice, the courts may find that there was undue influence.

Even when undue influence has been established, the contract will be binding if the person trying to enforce the contract can show that the undue influence was overcome and that the victim either affirmed the contract, which was the situation in the *Allcard* case, or did nothing to rescind it after escaping the relationship. The courts may also refuse a remedy if the person trying to escape the contract is not altogether innocent of wrongdoing.

Independent legal advice desirable, but contract must be fair

Of course, if the party accused of undue influence can convince the court that in fact, there was no such influence, any presumption is rebutted and the contract is binding. It is advisable, therefore, for contracting parties who are concerned with this problem to ensure that the other party get independent legal advice before entering into an agreement. This is especially true for professionals who are contracting with clients for matters outside that professional relationship. When it can be demonstrated that the potential victim followed independent legal advice, it is very likely that the courts will enforce the agreement. It must be stressed that the terms of the agreement must be reasonable in such circumstances. The courts will resist enforcing a contract that conveys great advantage to one of the parties, whether or not independent legal advice has been taken.

Bank's Special Interest Leads to Undue Influence

Three men entered into a deal with the Bank of Montreal to take over a failing business, the bank being the primary creditor. The bank required that all three men and their wives sign personal guarantees securing the loan. The wives were under pressure from their husbands, who were much more experienced in matters of business, to sign; they were not informed of the business risk and did not receive independent legal advice. Because of this, the court relieved them of any obligations under those guarantees, citing undue influence. The bank was under a special obligation because the business was already failing, and they had a unique interest in trying to get the men to take over the debt. Because of the ignorance of the wives and the pressure they were under, the bank should have known that independent legal advice was required.

Bank of Montreal v. Featherstone et al. 35 D.L.R. (4th) 626 (Ont. H.C.)

Unconscionable Transactions

Woods v. Hubley[16]

This is a case dealing with an insurance company and a person injured in an automobile accident. Mrs. Woods was a passenger in a car driven by her mother when it was struck from behind and extensively damaged by a car owned by Brenda Hubley and driven by Michael Hubley. There was no question that the Hubleys were responsible. Mrs. Woods suffered pain in her back and neck area, for which she eventually had to have surgery to repair the spinal injury.

About a week before the surgery, the insurance adjuster contacted her by telephone offering her a $3500 settlement. "Take it or leave it." She agreed, signed a release, and was paid the $3500. Unfortunately, even after the operation, her condition got worse, and she brought an application to the court to have the release set aside. This was done, and she was awarded damages of over $500 000.

Several problems faced the court, but we will limit the discussion to unconscionability, the basis on which the appeal court set aside the contract. Mrs. Woods had been taken advantage of. In fact, the trial judge found that the adjuster had deceived and misled Mrs. Woods and prevented her from having a fair opportunity to consult a lawyer. "He effectively dissuaded her from seeking the services of a lawyer, thereby taking advantage of her ignorance and her need." The trial judge quoted Justice Hallet from the case of *Stevenson v. Hilty (Canada Ltd.)*, where he found that a transaction can be set aside as unconscionable where the evidence shows (1) that there is an inequality in the bargaining positions of the parties arising out of ignorance, need, or distress of the weaker party; (2) where the stronger party has consciously used the position of power to achieve an advantage; and (3) the agreement reached is substantially unfair to the weaker party. These elements were established in this case, and therefore the settlement agreement was set aside.

This case illustrates the direction that the courts are moving in and that many transactions found to be unfair and prejudicial to one of the parties are now set aside on the basis of "unconscionability," as discussed below.

The concept of unconscionable transactions has received a greater acceptance by courts in recent years. This is an equitable doctrine that permits the court to set aside a contract in which one party has been taken advantage of because of such factors as desperation caused by poverty and intellectual impairment that falls short of incapacity. To escape from such a contract, it must be shown that the bargaining positions of the parties were unequal, that one party dominated and took advantage of the other, and that the consideration involved was grossly unfair.

In fact, the courts are showing a willingness to expand this concept and apply it in situations where they feel an injustice has been done or where the results of the agreement are simply unfair, as was the case in *Woods v. Hubley*. It must be remembered that simple economic advantage will not qualify. If a person having limited assets cannot get a loan from anyone else and must pay 20 percent interest, that in itself will not make the contract unconscionable. There must be evidence that the debtor was taken advantage of because of some problem, such as lack of

16. (1995) 140 N.S.R. (2d) 180 (S.C.); varied on other grounds (1995) 130 D.L.R. (4th) 119 (C.A.); leave to appeal refused (1996) 136 D.L.R. (4th) vii (note) (S.C.C.).

sophistication, age, or desperation, and then it must be shown that the resulting deal was not reasonable. If the 20 percent interest charged was reasonable, given the risk, the contract is not unconscionable.

There is some overlap in the principles of unconscionable transactions and undue influence. Although legislation has been passed in most common law provinces prohibiting unconscionable transactions, in most instances, the statutory provisions are limited to loan transactions. The recent acceptance of this equitable doctrine developed by the courts makes the defence of unconscionability available even when the contracts in question do not involve the loan of money.

Both common law and statute

Bertolo v. Bank of Montreal[17]

One of the lessons that comes from this case is that business people should be careful not to put too much confidence in their lawyers. Eric Bertolo wanted to open an Italian restaurant but had no funds. The Bank of Montreal agreed to supply 100 percent financing on the basis of a guarantee from Eric and his wife and a mortgage on his mother's home. The problem was that Mrs. Bertolo, Eric's mother, was not fluent in English and did not know what was going on. All she knew was that her son was opening a restaurant and she was helping him.

It was clear to the bank that Mrs. Bertolo was in need of independent legal advice. Factors such as her age and lack of business experience, the considerable risk involved, the lack of any benefit to her, and her relationship to the real borrower of the money, her son, required that she receive independent advice. They sent her to the bank's lawyer, who was also Eric's lawyer. He had his partner advise her of her legal position. The question here was whether the advice she received was sufficiently independent or whether the mortgage and promissory note could be set aside on the basis of unconscionability. In fact, there was no evidence of just what advice she did receive or that she was told that her house was at stake. To make things worse, before leaving the office, the bank's lawyer assured her that she should not worry and that all would be fine. The bank manager later gave her similar assurances.

The lawyer for the bank could not give her independent legal advice, being in a conflict-of-interest position representing the other parties. The court held that the partner was also in the same conflict-of-interest position. Therefore, the advice she received was not given independently. Both the lawyers and the bank manager should have known better. In short, because of her circumstances, this is a situation that required her to be given independent legal advice to ensure that she understood the nature and implications of the transaction she was entering into. The bank knew that and undertook to ensure that she was given such independent advice. They failed to do so. Thus, to enforce the security would be unconscionable, and she was successful in this action. Here, the lawyers failed the bank, but also the bank manager should have known better when dealing with such a person. Great care must be taken to ensure that in these kinds of circumstances, there is no undue influence and that when dealing with such vulnerable people, every effort is made to ensure that they are not being taken advantage of and receive proper independent legal advice.

17. (1986) 33 D.L.R. (4th) 610 (Ont. C.A.)

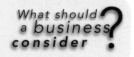

Business people, especially professionals in service industries, such as lawyers, bankers, and accountants, should be careful when dealing with their clients to avoid situations where an accusation of undue influence or unconscionability can arise. Business arrangements other than those related to the profession should be avoided and even those related to the profession should be guarded so that conflicts of interest do not arise. When in doubt, the transaction should be avoided or care should be taken to ensure that the client obtains independent legal advice. The problem is that if the deal goes well, no one will complain, but if a loss takes place, the client may have grounds to seek compensation from the professional for any losses suffered.

Privity of Contract and Assignment

Privity

When two parties enter into a contract, they create a world of law unto themselves. Contracting is a bargaining process, and only those participating in the bargain can be affected by it. It is a fundamental principle of contract law that the parties to a contract do not have the power to impose benefits or obligations on third parties or outsiders who are not parties to the contract. The contracting parties have created a private agreement, and outsiders to it can neither enforce it nor be bound to perform its terms. This principle is called **privity of contract**.

Contract only affects parties to it

The case of *Donoghue v. Stevenson*[18] referred to in Chapter 4 illustrates the application of the privity principle. In that case, a woman bought for her friend a bottle of ginger beer in which a decomposed snail was found. Because the person who bought the ginger beer was not the person who consumed it, the victim could not sue the owner of the café for breach of contract, since there was no contract between them. Under normal circumstances, merchants can be sued by the purchaser for breach of contract for selling faulty products, even though they are unaware of the problem. If there is no contract, the victim must sue the manufacturer in tort for negligence, not for breach of contract.

Exceptions

There are several exceptions and apparent exceptions to the operation of the privity rule. First, it must be emphasised that while a third party upon whom a benefit is bestowed cannot enforce the contract, the original parties still have the right to insist on performance. Thus, if Aguilar, who operates a landscaping company, contracts with Balzer to mow Carriere's lawn, Carriere cannot enforce the agreement, but Balzer certainly can. The court may provide either damages or money compensation calculated on the basis of what it would cost to have somebody else mow the lawn.

Original party to contract can enforce it where benefit to be bestowed on outsider

Where land is involved, the rights of the parties are said to run with the land. If a person leases a suite in a house and the owner sells the house, the new owner must honour the lease, even though the lessee was not a party to the contract of sale.

Where interest in land involved, rights run with the land

When an agent acts on behalf of a principal in contracting with a third party, the actions of that agent are binding on the principal. When a clerk in a store sells

18. [1932] A.C. 562 (H.L.)

a magazine to a customer, the storeowner is bound. This may seem inconsistent with privity, but in fact, the contract is between the storeowner and the customer, the clerk merely acting as a go-between. Agency will be discussed in detail in a subsequent chapter.

The concept of the **trust** is a little more complicated. This involves one person transferring their property to a second person obligated to use it to the benefit of a third. This is often done in estate planning, the beneficiaries being the family of the person creating the trust. In order for this to work, the third-party beneficiary must be able to enforce the contract between the original parties. Since the person creating the trust is often dead and unable to enforce the original contract, it would be an affront to allow the trustee to ignore the obligations set out in the agreement and take the benefits for himself. The Courts of Chancery developed the equitable principle of the trust to overcome this problem, and the beneficiary now can enforce the terms of the original trust agreement.

Insurance is handled in a similar fashion, the beneficiary of an insurance contract having the power to enforce it after the death of the insured. Sometimes, when a contract bestows a benefit on a third party, the courts will imply a trust, even though parties did not specifically create one. This is called a **constructive trust** and provides an important method for the third party to obtain the benefit promised.

Finally, when the parties themselves agree to change or end their agreement, there is no problem with privity. Where the parties to an existing contract agree to substitute someone new into the relationship in place of one of the original parties, the new contract is binding. This is called a **novation**. If Jones has a contract to provide janitorial services to a college and he sells his business to Brown, there is no problem with Brown taking over that service contract, provided the college agrees. A new contract has been substituted for the old one, and no privity problem arises, since all parties have agreed to the change.

In fact, there are signs that the doctrine of privity may be breaking down. Contracting parties often protect themselves from contract and tort liability by including exemption clauses in contracts that limit that liability.

In the case of *London Drugs Ltd. v. Kuehne & Nagel International Ltd.,*[19] the Supreme Court of Canada has extended the protection of such a properly worded exemption clause, not only to the employer but to the employee as well. In this case, a clause in the contract limited liability to only $40 maximum. Kuehne & Nagel had contracted with London Drugs to store a large transformer, and because of mishandling by their employees, that transformer suffered significant damage. Since London Drugs could get only $40 from Kuehne & Nagel, they sued the employees who caused the damage, claiming they were not protected by the exemption clause. The Supreme Court, however, found that the protection of the exemption clause extended to the employees, even though they were not party to the contract. The departure of the Supreme Court from the privity rule in this case may indicate a willingness to do so in other circumstances as well.

Agents create contract between principal and third party
—but limited by authority

Trust allows a third party to benefit from the property of another

Beneficiary can enforce trust agreement against trustee

Beneficiary can enforce insurance contract

Novation involves new agreement

Employees protected by exculpatory clauses

Tony and Jim's Holdings Ltd. et al. v. Silva[20]

Norman Silva was the creator and primary shareholder of Mamma Mia Pizza (Kingston) Ltd., which was located in a strip mall owned by James Zikovelis and Antonio Sarris (the landlords). The tenancy agreement required that the landlord provide insurance and that the tenant pay the premium. The landlord took out

19. [1993] 1 W.W.R. 1 (S.C.C.).
20. (1999) 170 D.L.R. (4th) 193 (Ont. C.A.).

insurance on the premises with the Canadian General Insurance Company. Mr. Silva caused a fire on the premises, when he negligently left a pot of butter on a gas fire set too high while he went next door for a coffee. Considerable damage took place, and the landlord made a claim to the insurance company. That claim was honoured, but when an insurance company pays out on a claim, they normally take over the right of the claimant to sue the person who caused the loss. This is called the right of subrogation. In this case, when the insurance company paid out on the claim, they assumed the right to sue the person who caused the loss, that is Mr. Silva, the president of the tenant corporation. In this policy, however, there was a clause whereby the insurance company had given up their right to subrogation "... all rights of subrogation are hereby waived against any corporation, firm, individual, or other interest with respect to which insurance is provided by this policy." The insurance company took the position that this was a contractual right between their insured and themselves and that, under the principle of privity, the clause did not and could not bestow any rights on an outsider (Mr. Silva) not party to the contract. Because of privity, they claimed to still have the right to sue Mr. Silva despite the non-subrogation clause. The Court of Appeal had to decide whether the principle of privity of contract gave the insurance company the right to sue, effectively overriding the non-subrogation clause in the contract. The court held that privity did not apply in this situation. In effect, they created another exception to the privity rule and said that to do otherwise would allow the insurance company to circumvent the provision of the contract. To give effect to the reasonable expectation of the parties to the contract, this waiver of the right to subrogate included in the contract had to be enforced even to the benefit of the third party, Mr. Silva. This is another example of how the principle of privity of contract is being abandoned. For good reason, the courts are moving away from this restrictive and, in many situations, inappropriate legal principle.

Another area where the rule of privity of contract may be weakening is in the field of product liability. In *Donoghue v. Stevenson*,[21] the consumer of the ginger beer could not sue the merchant because she was not the one who purchased it and there was no contract between them. Some provinces have passed legislation allowing the consumer of such products to sue the seller in contract law where the defective product causes injury, even when the injured person is not the purchaser and not party to the contract. The courts have also extended the right to sue in contract law in product liability cases by finding collateral contracts created by advertising brochures giving the purchaser a right to seek redress in contract law back past the retailer to the manufacturer. These topics will be discussed in Chapter 9, under "Consumer Protection Legislation."

Assignment

Just as a person buying goods under a contract is then free to resell them, so can a person entitled to receive a benefit under a contract transfer that benefit to a third party. This is called the **assignment of contractual rights,** and the benefit transferred is known as a **chose in action**. While the practice of transferring such rights was originally not permitted because of privity, it is now a common practice. The essential principle is that a person who has acquired a right or a benefit under a contract has the right to assign that benefit to another. Where Jung does carpentry work for Simons and is owed money for those services, Jung is free to assign (sell)

Contracting party can
assign rights

21. Donoghue, *supra* note 38

that claim to Green. Jung is referred to as the assignor, a party to the original contract, and Green as the assignee, a stranger to it.

The ability to make such assignments has become a vital component in our commercial world. There are, however, some important qualifications to keep in mind. First, only the benefit can be assigned, not an obligation. In the example above, if Jung has done poor work or failed to do the job, Jung is still obligated to Simons, despite the assignment. Jung cannot say that it is no longer his problem, as he has assigned the contract to Green. Jung has only assigned the benefits, not the obligations.

Of course, if Green tried to collect those benefits (the money owed) in face of the defaulted contract, he would fail. While its true that the assignment of the benefits of the contract between Jung and Simons was valid, Green can be in no better position to collect that benefit than was Jung, and Jung has no claim, since he has defaulted. The principle is that an assignee is subject to the equities between the original parties. Jung transferred only what claim he had against Simons to Green, and that claim was tainted. If the debtor, then, has a good defence against the assignor, he also has a good defence against the assignee.

Assignee in no better position than assignor

First City Capital Ltd. v. Petrosar Ltd[22]

Petrosar Limited was a manufacturing company in Ontario and needed a CAD (computer-assisted design) system to help in their business. After investigating a number of different sources, they decided to get a system supplied by TDC Graphics, but to facilitate financing, at the recommendation of TDC, they arranged to lease the computer from Casselman Financial Underwriters Limited (CFUL).

TDC sold the computer equipment to CFUL, and CFUL, in turn, leased that equipment to Petrosar. A vital part of the deal from the point of view of Petrosar was that at the end of one year, they could terminate the lease surrendering back the computer or purchase that computer for the residual amount left owing. This was not set out in the lease agreement itself but was contained in a purchase order and a schedule attached to the lease, and the court found this provision to be an essential part of the lease agreement. To facilitate this, TDC agreed in their agreement of sale with CFUL that in the event the lease was terminated by Petrosar and the computer returned to CFUL, they would, in turn, buy it back from CFUL.

CFUL then assigned this lease agreement with Petrosar to First City Capital Ltd. without informing them of Petrosar's right to terminate or to purchase the computer at the end of the first year. Although notified of this assignment, Petrosar continued to make their payments to CFUL, and at the end of a year, they opted to purchase the computer. When a reasonable price could not be agreed upon, they stopped making any further payments and put the computer in storage. The main problem for the court was to determine whether First City was bound by the right to purchase or to terminate. The court held that even though they did not know of this provision it was part of the original lease agreement, and since that agreement was assigned to them and they took "subject to the equities," this right bound First City as well. What First City got was only what CFUL had to give, and that was a lease subject to this right to purchase or terminate. It was argued that the price was not sufficiently clear and therefore that provision would have to be void for uncertainty. But the court held that since it was stated as the "residual amount owing"

22. 42 D.L.R. (4th) 738 (Ont. H.C.)

that could be calculated and was sufficiently clear to be part of the contract. First City's failure to convey them the computer for the residual amount owing, as agreed, entitled Petrosar to stop paying, and First City failed in their action. This action shows us not only how careful we have to be in setting out the agreement we have reached but also the position of an assignee. That assignee can be in no better position than the assignor, and so, the assignee not only acquires the benefits assigned to it but also the liabilities. The assignee only gets what the assignor has to give.

Although only the benefits can be assigned, that does not mean the original party to the contract always has to be the one to perform. Often, it is understood that the actual work or service involved will be performed by an employee or subcontractor. This is called **vicarious performance**. The point is that the original party to the contract remains responsible for the work, no matter who does it. But in many cases, the service must be performed by the person so contracting. If a famous artist agreed to paint a portrait, it is likely that the customer would not be satisfied if the actual painting were subcontracted to another.

Only benefits can be assigned

Because of the restrictions of privity, the method used for an assignee to enforce an assignment was to bring an action against the original contracting party through the assignor. This is referred to as "joining" the assignor in the action. This can be a cumbersome process, and it has been modified by statute. If the assignment meets certain qualifications, it qualifies as a **statutory assignment**, and the assignee can enforce the claim directly without involving the assignor. In the earlier example, if the assignment qualifies as a statutory assignment, instead of Green having to collect by bringing an action in the name of Jung against Simons, thus joining Jung in the action, Green can now simply sue Simons directly for the money.

The qualifications that have to be met to establish a statutory assignment are as follows: first, the assignment must be absolute, meaning that it must be both unconditional and complete. The full amount owed must be assigned without any strings attached. Second, the assignment must be in writing, with the parties identified. And, third, the original party obligated to pay must be notified of the assignment. Only when all these requirements are met will the assignee be able to sue directly; otherwise he must still join the assignor in any attempt at collection.

Qualifications for statutory assignment

Some things, such as the right to collect support payments or the right to sue another in a tort action, cannot be assigned. Certain statutes, such as the *Workers Compensation Act* (in some jurisdictions) prohibit the assignment of benefits provided under them. While it is true that the right to sue cannot be assigned, there is no such restriction on the assignment of the proceeds from such a lawsuit once awarded.

Some things cannot be assigned

—the right to sue

Sometimes, an assignor may be tempted to assign the same claim to two assignees. This, of course, is fraud, and the victim has the right to seek redress from the assignor. Often, however, that assignor has fled or has no funds. The original debtor against whom the assignment is made is only obligated to pay once, and one of the two assignees will be out of luck. In such circumstances, it is the first assignee to give the debtor notice of the assignment that will collect. The other assignee will be left to remedies against the assignor, which may be worthless. It is, therefore, vital in business to take such assignments with care and then to immediately notify the debtor. It is only when the debtor makes the mistake of ignoring such notice and paying either the other assignee or the original assignor that they may have to pay twice.

Debtor must pay first who gives notice of assignment

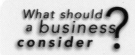

Business people should never ignore a notice of assignment and continue paying the original party. There is no problem so long as the payment is passed on, but you cannot be sure that this will be done. Also, business people often assume that once they have assigned the debt, they no longer have anything to do with the transaction. If a product has been sold and the financing arrangements have been assigned to a finance company, the merchant vendor is still responsible with respect to the performance of the product. If it is defective or dangerous, causing injury or loss, it is the vendor that is responsible, not the finance company. You can only assign the benefits, not your obligations under such a contract.

The principles discussed so far relate to voluntary assignments. There are some circumstances in which the assignment of rights can take place involuntarily. For example, rights and obligations are automatically transferred to the administrator or executor of the estate when a person dies. This representative steps into the deceased's shoes and is not restricted by the privity of contract rule, unless the terms of the contract require personal performance by the deceased. The second situation of **involuntary assignment** is when a party to a contract goes bankrupt. Under bankruptcy legislation, the bankrupt's assets are transferred to a trustee, called the receiver, who will then distribute them to pay the creditors as much as possible.

Involuntary assignment in cases of death and bankruptcy

Negotiable Instruments

Negotiable instruments true exceptions to privity

Another exception to the privity of contract rule recognizes the commercial realities of modern business. As commerce developed, it became necessary to devise a method to freely exchange and pass on claims for debt that had been incurred in the process of business. When these claims met certain qualifications, they were defined as **negotiable instruments,** and through them, unique rights were bestowed on the parties. Cheques, promissory notes, and bills of exchange are examples of negotiable instruments. While the use of cheques as a method of paying in personal or consumer transactions has significantly decreased as direct debit cards gain popularity, cheques are still an important method of transferring funds in business. Promissory notes retain their popularity where credit is involved because of the unique advantages they bestow.

Negotiable instruments give better rights to holder than is the case with assignment

These rights will be discussed in detail in Chapter 10. Briefly, the negotiable instrument could be freely passed from one person to another, conveying with it all the rights associated with the original agreement between the parties, and no notice of the transaction would be required. This flexibility is completely inconsistent with the doctrine of privity of contract and the law of assignment discussed above. The most significant innovation of negotiable instruments was that better rights or claims than those held by the initial parties could be passed on. As discussed under "Assignment," it was clear that even when it was possible to assign contractual rights, the assignee was subject to whatever equities existed between the original two parties. Thus, if a defence, such as fraud, was available against the original party to the contract (the assignor), it was available against the assignee as well. This is not the case with negotiable instruments. Even when a defence of fraud is available against the initial party to a transaction, a third party to a negotiable instrument who satisfies the qualifications to be a "holder in due course" can require payment despite the existence of the fraud.

Summary

Mistake

- Must go to the nature of the agreement or the existence of the subject matter, not just to the effect of the agreement when performed

Types	Remedy
Both parties making a common error	There is no contract
An error in recording the terms	Can be corrected by rectification
A misunderstanding between the parties	Most reasonable interpretation of the contract
A one-sided mistake	*Caveat emptor* applies unless the mistake is so fundamental as to destroy consensus between the parties or there is existence of fraud

Misrepresentation

- A false statement that induces a person to enter a contract

Types	Remedy
A false statement inducing contract	Misrepresentation is actionable
Innocent misrepresentation	The remedy is rescission
Fraudulent misrepresentation	The victim may sue for damages for the tort of deceit and/or rescission
Negligence	Damages may also be available

Duress or undue influence

- Contract is voidable if made under duress or undue influence
- Unconscionability may cause court to set aside or modify contract

Privity of contract

- Only the original parties to the contract are bound. Any benefit going to a third party must be enforced by the original party to the agreement
- The **trust** is a true exception to the privity rule because the beneficiary can enforce it, even though he or she is not a party to the original agreement

Assignment

- Only the benefits, not the obligations, in a contract can be sold (assigned) to a third party, and those benefits must be enforced through the original contracting party, the assignor
- Only when it qualifies as a statutory assignment can the assignee enforce the assigned rights directly
- Negotiable instruments also may be enforced by third parties without notification to the original drawer of the instrument, sometimes conveying better rights than existed between the original parties

QUESTIONS

1. Distinguish between a mistake about the effect of a contract and a mistake about its nature. Explain the significance of this distinction.

2. Distinguish among mistake, mutual mistake, and unilateral mistake.

3. What approach will the courts usually take when the mistake involves disagreement about the meaning of the contract?

4. How will the courts respond to ambiguous wording in a contract?

5. Explain the parol evidence rule.

6. What must a party to a contract show to obtain rectification of a document?

7. When will a misunderstanding as to the terms of a contract cause that contract to be void?

8. Under what circumstances would a person raise a claim of *non est factum*? What restrictions are there on its availability?

9. Explain what is meant by *caveat emptor*. What is this principle's significance in relation to unilateral mistake?

10. What happens when a misrepresentation becomes a term of the contract?

11. What is the distinction among fraudulent, negligent, and innocent misrepresentation? Why is the distinction important?

12. Under what circumstances can silence or a statement of opinion become misrepresentation?

13. What factors may affect the availability of the remedy of rescission?

14. Describe the relationship between misrepresentation and mistake.

15. What is the significance of determining whether a contract is voidable rather than void?

16. Distinguish among duress, undue influence, and unconscionability and give examples of each.

17. What is meant by privity of contract?

18. Explain what is meant by the term "novation."

19. Explain the relationship of the privity principle to land transactions, agency, trusts, assignment, and the position of employees.

20. What qualifications must be realized before there can be a statutory assignment?

21. What limitations are placed on the rights and obligations of the assignee when a contract is assigned?

22. What is meant by "the assignee takes subject to the equities"? When is it appropriate to determine these equities?

23. What is the significance of a negotiable instrument in terms of the rights conveyed to third parties?

CASES

1. Corporate Properties Ltd. v. Manufacturers Life Insurance Co.

In this case, Bloor West leased property from Manulife and, in turn, sublet that property to Corporate Properties Ltd. The arrangement was that Bloor West would pay Manulife a certain set percentage of its gross revenues that was earned from the property. Corporate Properties, which initially owned Bloor West but eventually sold their interest through refinancing, had agreed to a different calculation for paying rent to Bloor West. But Corporate Properties, instead of paying their rent to Bloor West, paid it directly to Manulife. Instead of basing the rental payment on what Bloor West earned from the property, they based it on what they earned from the property, which was considerably more, thus, from their perspective, creating an overpayment for a considerable period of time. When they discovered this in 1983, they demanded repayment of the overages paid. While the matter was in dispute, they, under protest, made further payments for the period between 1984 to 1986. The ambiguity is whether the term "gross annual income" refers to that received by Bloor West or the income from the properties obtained by Corporate Properties. Certainly Corporate Properties treated it for years as if it referred to their gross income from the properties. Explain the arguments available to all the parties and whether Manulife will have to repay these overpayments.

2. Hayward v. Mellick

Mellick had 94 acres of land that he wanted to sell. In the process of negotiations with Hayward, he represented to Hayward that the farm had approximately 65 acres of workable farmland. Relying on this representation, Hayward purchased the farm and later learned that the farm had only 51.7 workable acres. In fact, Mellick had never measured the farm, and it was only his own personal belief that it had 65 workable acres. But he never told Hayward that he was not sure. Hayward sued for compensation. Discuss the legal position of the parties. How would your answer be affected by the knowledge that the written contract included an exemption clause that stated, "It is agreed that there is no representation, warranty, collateral agreement, or condition affecting this agreement or the real property or supported hereby other than as expressed herein, in writing"?

3. Pettit v. Foster Wheeler Ltd.

Roderick Ashley Ltd. was supplying materials for Foster Wheeler Ltd. at a project at the University of Alberta in Edmonton. Mr. Pettit had supplied financing worth $14 000 to Roderick Ashley Ltd. Pursuant to that agreement, Pettit took an assignment of all accounts of Roderick Ashley. Notice of this assignment was given to Foster Wheeler Ltd., who was told to make all payments to Mr. Johnston, Pettit's lawyer, who would hold the money in trust for him. Some payments were made, but on December 27, the Bank of Nova Scotia sent a letter to Foster Wheeler Ltd., stating that it had received a general assignment of book debts of Roderick Ashley as collateral security for a debt and that any payments to be made to Roderick Ashley should now be paid to the Bank of Nova Scotia. Accordingly, Foster Wheeler Ltd. immediately paid the $7345 outstanding to the Bank of Nova Scotia instead of paying to Pettit and Johnston. Pettit and Johnston then sued Foster Wheeler Ltd. for this amount, claiming that it should have been paid to them. Explain the likely outcome.

4. Re Royal Bank of Canada and Gill et al.

The younger Mr. Gill was fluent in English and a sophisticated businessman who had worked in a credit union for a number of years as well as managing his father's berry farm. To take advantage of a business opportunity, he arranged with the Royal Bank to borrow $87 000. During the negotiations, it became clear that he could get a more favourable rate of interest if his father guaranteed the loan. In fact, the son had done a considerable amount of banking on behalf of his father, who was also a customer of the same bank. The elder Mr. Gill could not read, write, or speak English and relied on his son in all his business dealings. The documents were prepared, and the son brought his father to the bank to sign. At no time did he explain to his father that he was signing a personal guarantee, and the evidence is clear that the father had no idea what he was signing other than that it was a document associated with a loan transaction. Mr. Gill, Sr., had implicit faith in his son's handling of his business affairs. Mr. Gill, Jr., on the other hand, was so excited about the deal that he apparently never explained the nature of the documents to his father. It is clear in this situation that at no time was there any misrepresentation to the father or the son on the part of the bank. When the loan was defaulted, the bank turned to the father for payment. Explain the arguments of the father and the bank as to whether Mr. Gill, Sr., should be held responsible for this debt and the likely outcome.

5. Stott v. Merrit Investment Corp.

Stott was a sales representative working in the securities business for the defendant. He was approached by a customer who wanted to start an account to speculate in gold futures, a very risky business. The account was started, and some successes were achieved, but then the market reversed itself and the customer lost heavily. The customer ended up indebted to the company for $66 000. Stott was called into his supervisor's office and asked to sign an agreement stating that Stott would be fully responsible for that amount if the customer could not pay. He suggested that he should have legal advice and was told, "You are probably right, but if you don't sign, it won't go well with you at this firm, and it would be very difficult for you to find employment in the industry." Stott signed the document and continued to work for Merrit. Deductions were taken off his income for this debt over the employment period. Several months later, he said that he had received legal advice and offered to settle the debt for 25 percent of the outstanding amount. Even when he resigned two years after the event, it was clear that he felt some obligation under the agreement.

Some time later, he left and obtained other employment; he refused any further responsibility and sued Merrit for the amount that had been deducted from his income to pay this debt. Merrit countersued for the amount still outstanding. What are the legal arguments to support each position? Would your answer be different if you were to learn that it was the practice in the industry to hold sales representatives responsible to some extent for such bad accounts?

CHAPTER 8

The End of the Contractual Relationship

Contracts can come to an end or be discharged by performance, breach, agreement between the parties to end or modify, and frustration. This chapter will examine each of these.

Standard Precast Ltd. v. Dywidag Fab Con Products Ltd.[1]

Standard had an agreement to supply 133 pre-cast concrete panels for Dywidag, which were later to be erected at a building site by a general contractor within a limited time period. Unfortunately, the first nine of these concrete slabs failed to meet the specifications set out in the contract. Dywidag cancelled the contract, on 24 hours' notice, against Standard's protests. The Supreme Court of British Columbia had to decide whether the breach committed by Standard in failing to produce the first nine panels properly was a breach sufficient enough to justify the termination of the whole agreement. This is a problem that often arises when performance of the contract is being done in installments and there is a failure of all or some of those installments. At what stage is the other contracting party entitled to treat the contract as ended and make other arrangements?

The trial judge found that the contract had been repudiated through conduct. Standard's failure was significant enough for Dywidag to lose confidence in them, treat the contract as discharged through breach, and turn to another source. However, the decision was overturned on appeal—the court decided that because the panels could be replaced or corrected, the breach did not destroy the commercial purpose of the contract and so was not fundamental enough to justify the termination.

Performance

Contractual obligations are discharged and a contract is ended when each party satisfactorily performs or completes its part of the bargain. The importance of finding that a contract has been discharged by performance is that the other party must still

1. 56 D.L.R. (4th) 385 (B.C.C.A.)

perform their obligations under the agreement. But the question arises, will anything short of exact performance satisfy the requirement? Where the failure to perform involves a minor term or **warranty,** the contract will be considered discharged by performance. The other party will be required to perform subject to a claim for compensation for whatever loss was caused by the breach of warranty.

Where warranty breached, contract still considered performed

When a **condition** or major term of the contract is breached, the contract is normally considered discharged, and the other party is relieved of performing their obligations under it. This will be discussed in more detail below. But when a major term of the contract is breached in some minor inconsequential way, the court will usually treat it like a breach of warranty and will still require the other party to perform their obligations, subject to a claim for the loss caused by the shortfall. This is called discharge by **substantial performance**. For example, if a contractor has agreed to build a warehouse of 12 000 square feet and it turns out to be only 11 975, the contract is substantially performed, and the contractor is discharged from further performance. The customer must still pay for the building but has the right to deduct the value of the shortfall from the payment. Note, however, that there are some types of contracts where only exact performance will suffice.

But some contracts must be performed exactly

Contract discharged when contract substantially performed

Sail Labrador Ltd. v. Navimar Corp.[2]

Sail Labrador Ltd. leased a ship from Navimar Corp. Ltd. This kind of arrangement is called a charter party. A provision in the lease included an option to purchase the ship at the end of the lease period. This option was only available if every payment set out in the schedule of payments was properly made. Although the contract required cash, the parties agreed that a series of post-dated cheques would be given as payment. Unfortunately, because of a bank error, one of the later cheques in the series was dishonoured for insufficient funds. This was immediately corrected, but the owner of the ship took the position that the option to purchase was no longer available because of this failure to properly perform as required.

The Supreme Court of Canada decided that this was a minor or inconsequential breach and that the owner of the vessel had assumed the risk of such an error when they agreed to take post-dated cheques. Since the error was immediately corrected and the contract had been substantially performed, the option was still available to Sail Labrador to exercise and purchase the ship. This case illustrates two important points. It illustrates how an option works and that the terms upon which the option is based must normally be carefully followed. It also illustrates the doctrine of substantial performance, which provides that where a contract is essentially performed except for some minor unimportant variation, the other party must treat it as properly completed and live up to their side of the agreement.

Tender

The general rule in common law is that when a person has tendered performance of a contract, it counts as if the contract had been performed. This means that if a person is ready, willing, and able to perform a contractual obligation and attempts to do so, but the other party refuses to accept it or prevents it, the first party is taken to have completed the contractual obligation and is discharged from it.

2. [1999] S.C.R. 265

Tender of performance discharges obligation

Tendered performance means that the person performing must actually attempt to deliver the specified goods or attempt to perform the specified service. The person who has attempted performance is then in a position to sue the other party for damages, and it is no defence for that other party to claim that the service was not actually performed.

Where goods and services are involved and tender of performance is refused, the person so tendering will normally only be entitled to compensation for losses, not the original price agreed to. If Chan's Renovation Service contracted with Smith to install new gutters on his house and when Chan shows up to do the job on the specified day he is refused entrance, he has discharged his obligation. But when he sues, he will only be entitled to the lost profit, not the total price, since he has not incurred the expenses associated with actually doing the job, such as the cost of the gutter material, nails, and brackets that he can return or use on another job.

The effect of tendering proper payment of debt is different. It does not extinguish the debt but simply relieves the debtor of the obligation to seek out the creditor to make payment. It thus becomes the creditor's responsibility to ask the debtor for payment and to bear the cost of doing so. Even if it becomes necessary for the creditor to sue, the costs of the court action are the creditor's responsibility, if it can be shown that the debtor properly attempted to pay the debt.

Where debt owed and money refused—money still owed, but creditor bears expense

Proper payment of a debt requires legal tender. Cheques, even certified cheques, are acceptable only when the parties have agreed to allow cheques to be used to pay debts. This may be an actual agreement between the parties, or it may be implied from accepted business practice.

Untangling the WEB

As we move to a cashless society, with electronic transfer and credit and debit cards becoming even more common, it has become much more important to specify methods of payment to be used in business transactions.

Payment must be in legal tender

If there is any question about the acceptable form of payment, it is advisable to present cash and then only the exact amount in proper legal tender. When coins are used, under the *Currency Act*[3] creditors can refuse to take over 25 pennies, five dollars' worth of nickels, 10 dollars' worth of dimes and quarters, 25 one-dollar coins, and $40 of the larger coins. There is no limit on what qualifies as legal tender when paper money is offered, as long as official Canadian bank notes are used.

Delivery must be at a reasonable time and place

The delivery of money, goods, or services must be tendered at a reasonable time and place. Usually, this means during normal business hours at a person's place of business, unless it has been otherwise specified in the contract. Thus, if Jones has a contract to deliver five tons of ripe tomatoes to Sharif by July 10, Jones would be expected to make that delivery to Sharif's packing house rather than to his home or office. The delivery should also take place during the usual working day. Sharif would not be obligated to accept delivery at 6:00 p.m. on Saturday, unless such a time was permitted in the contract.

When the parties specify a time for performance in the contract, normally, that time must be strictly adhered to. Even just a few seconds can make a difference.

---

3. *Currency Act*, R.S.C. (1985) c. C-52

This was the case in *Smith Bros. & Wilson (B.C.) Ltd. v. British Columbia Hydro and Power Authority,*[4] where a bid was submitted for a job just a few minutes after the time specified in the tender for the bidding to close. Even a bid tendered that close in time could not be considered.

When no time is specified, the parties must perform within a reasonable time, to be determined by the circumstances.

Even when the contract has been properly performed by both parties, there may be some continuing obligations. For example, where a product is sold and the purchase price has been paid, title has transferred to the purchaser. Even then, if the product is dangerous or fails to meet the specifications of the agreement, the purchaser can turn back to the seller and seek compensation for the breach.

Continual obligations

Breach

Breach of contract involves the failure of the breaching party to properly perform its contractual obligations. Such a breach can take place in two ways: (1) by improper or incomplete performance of the obligations set out in the agreement, and (2) by refusal to perform. Refusal, also called repudiation, will be discussed below. In the example used to introduce this chapter, the failure to deliver the appropriate concrete panels was serious enough so that it was treated as a breach of the whole contract. Such a breach may be either a major or a minor infraction.

Breach may involve failure to perform or repudiation

Cameron Auctioneers & Appraisers Ltd. et al. v. G.R. Galbraith Supplies[5]

Galbraith Supplies was involved in the business of supplying tools and equipment and, while in some financial difficulty, entered into a contract with Cameron Auctioneers to sell a portion of their inventory. Under the contract, Galbraith was to supply a list of the goods to be sold along with the invoiced value of each, adding to a total invoice price of "approximately $175 000." This book value was considerably less than what the goods would be expected to sell for, but the detailed listing was necessary so that Cameron could price the goods to be sold and properly advertise the auction. In fact, Galbraith had used these goods to secure a loan with the bank, and so, in order for the creditor to allow the sale, the contract also guaranteed that they would be sold for at least $175 000. Cameron was to keep 20 percent of the proceeds, and Galbraith was to pay for the expenses associated with the sale.

In fact, no list was provided, and the total invoiced value of the goods supplied was only about $140 000. Also, many of the goods were delivered late. The actual sale only brought in $51 000. Galbraith sued for the guaranteed minimum. At trial level, the court recognized that only goods worth $140 000 had been delivered and so simply reduced the guarantee proportionally, awarding $100 000 damages.

On appeal, the judge determined that Galbraith's failure to deliver the proper amount of goods properly invoiced and in a timely manner amounted to a breach of a condition that discharged the contract. Cameron's promise to pay a minimum was contingent on Galbraith supplying the proper goods to sell and the appropriate information. This failure to supply enough goods and the information to sell them contributed to the failure by preventing Cameron from properly pricing the goods and adequately advertising the auction. As a result of this breach of condition, Cameron was excused from performing its side of the deal (the guarantee), and

4. B.C.S.C. February 24, 1997, reported in *The Lawyers Weekly*, Vol. 16, No. 42.
5. 47 D.L.R. (4th) 141 (N.B.C.A.)

therefore, no damages other than the payment of the price obtained were awarded. After Cameron's 20 percent portion, Galbraith got only 80 percent of the actual proceeds of the sale (approximately $40 000). This case is valuable in that it illustrates in strong terms the effect of a breach of condition in a contract. When one party fails to perform an important part of a contract, the other party can be discharged from performing any obligations they have under that contract.

Conditions and Warranties

Terms essential to the substantial performance of a contract are called conditions. Terms that are minor, insignificant, or peripheral to the central obligation of the contract are called warranties. The failure to perform a condition of the contract generally permits the other party to treat his or her obligation as ended and to sue for breach of contract. But the improper performance of a warranty does not relieve the other party of the obligation to fulfill his or her side of the agreement. The victim of such a breach of warranty has the right to sue the other party for whatever it costs to overcome the deficiency in performance but still must perform his or her part of the agreement.

Breach of condition—party relieved

Breach of warranty—performance required

Although the breach of a condition will normally allow the victim of the breach to treat the contract as discharged, they can treat the contract as still binding if they choose. If they take some benefit under the agreement knowing of the breach, they lose the right to discharge and must perform their obligations.

If Beaman had agreed to provide a sculpture of flying geese for the foyer of Singh's new office building in Regina and instead delivered a sculpture of a moose, this would normally be a breach of a condition, and Singh would not have to pay. However, if he liked it, Singh could choose to accept the moose; but if he did so, he would have to pay for it. At best, Singh might be able to reduce the payment by whatever reduced value it has.

Breach accepted—performance required

A breach of condition in a contract that has been accepted by the other party is treated as a breach of warranty.

Warranties can become conditions and vice versa

What is important to one person might seem unimportant to another. Therefore, terms can be designated as either conditions or warranties in the agreement. Normally, when a person orders a new car, the particular shade of red ordered would be a minor term, and if the car of a slightly different shade was delivered, the purchaser would still have to take it. But where the exact shade is important to the purchaser, which might be the case where it is used as a trademark for a business, they can designate the required shade to be a condition and refuse to take the car if a car of any other shade of red is delivered. Similarly, the person supplying goods or services will often designate a term that would normally be a condition as a warranty in the agreement. The *Sale of Goods Act* states that in transactions governed by the act, the court has the option of treating a term specified as a warranty or as a condition, no matter what it is called.[6]

It should also be noted that in some cases, the obligations set out in the contract are independent of each other. For example, a landlord's obligation to repair in a lease and a tenant's obligation to pay rent may be independent, preventing the tenant from withholding rent when faced with a landlord's failure to make proper repairs.

Exemption Clauses

Exemption clauses attempt to limit liability

Exemption clauses, sometimes referred to as exculpatory clauses, are an attempt by a party to significantly limit or eliminate their liability under an agreement. The

6. *Sale of Goods Act*, R.S.B.C. (2996) c.410 s. 15

courts will generally enforce exemption clauses because the object of contract law is to carry out whatever the parties have freely bargained to do. But they do so reluctantly. If there is any ambiguity in the terms of the exemption clause, the narrow or restrictive meaning will be used.

Exemption clauses strictly interpreted

If a restaurant has a sign above the cloakroom stating, "Not responsible for lost or stolen clothing," bringing this term to the customer's attention would make it part of the contract of bailment, in which goods are being cared for by someone else. If clothes left there are damaged by fire or water instead of being stolen or lost, the proprietor would not be able to rely on the sign to avoid liability because the courts would interpret the exemption clause narrowly. Similarly, if a briefcase left with the proprietor were stolen, the proprietor would not be able to rely on the exemption clause because it was not clothing that was stolen.

Exemption clauses are intricate and involved because the people who draft them try to cover all possible eventualities, knowing that the courts will take a restrictive approach in their interpretation. They usually form a part of the written document, but they could be included in a sign or notice. In any case, the terms cannot be unilaterally imposed and must be brought to the attention of the customer at the time the contract is made. If the clause is on the back of the ticket or receipt, there must be a reference on the front directing the holder to read the back. Where a sign limiting liability is involved, as at a car park or train station, it must be in clear view so that a reasonable person would notice it when entering the premises or undertaking a contractual obligation. Even when the exemption clause is part of a written contract, if it is in any way unique or unusual, it must be brought to the attention of the other contracting party. If it is buried in other insignificant writing or so small it cannot be read, it is doubtful that it will have any legal effect.

Must be brought to attention of party at time of contract

When goods or services are sold in consumer transactions, these exemption clauses are usually embodied in terms referred to as "limited warranties." The term is unfortunate, since these are major terms of the contract or conditions, not minor ones. The courts are likely to be much more sympathetic to the plight of a customer in a consumer transaction who has not read the exemption clause than to the more sophisticated parties in a business transaction. It is important to note that under the *Sale of Goods Act* and other consumer protection legislation, the sellers' right to restrict their obligations in such sales may be extremely limited.

Effect of legislation

Exemption Clause Strictly Interpreted

A Purolator employee delivered an expensive medical machine meant for Meditek to the wrong address. As a safeguard, Purolator employees fill out delivery sheets indicating where the goods have been delivered to and the signature of a recipient so that missing goods can be traced in the event of misdelivery; in this case, however, the delivery sheets had been falsified, and it was impossible for Purolator to trace the goods. It was only after a prolonged delay, during which Meditek acquired a different machine, that the goods were found, but Meditek refused delivery and sued Purolator for damages, including the cost of the extra machine. Purolator claimed their liability was limited by an exemption clause in the Meditek contract that limited Purolator's liability, "whether or not from negligence or gross negligence." The court found that Purolator was not protected by the clause, since the actual damage was caused by a willful act of the employee to falsify the delivery sheets. Such exemption clauses are strictly interpreted against the breaching party, and although this one covered even gross negligence, it did not cover willful or fraudulent conduct.

Meditek Laboratory Services Ltd. v. Purolator Courier Ltd., 125 D.L.R. (4th) 738 (Man. C.A.)

Fundamental Breach

Suppliers of goods or services try to limit their liability as much as possible. Sometimes, they try to limit their liability to such an extent that it affects the entire nature of the contract or it eliminates their obligation entirely. When a contract fails at this basic level, the problem for the court is to determine whether an exemption clause can exempt liability for such a fundamental breach. The courts have shown a reluctance to interfere in the parties' freedom to bargain and so have indicated that it is possible to word an exemption clause to cover even such fundamental obligations. But they also take the position that unless it was absolutely clear to the parties that the exemption clause covered such a basic failure to perform, there will be no protection. Since it is unlikely that the other party would have knowingly agreed to a term that relieved the breaching party of these fundamental obligations, the courts usually have no difficulty finding that an exemption clause, even a carefully worded one, does not apply. This is called the **construction approach** to fundamental breach. It is important to remember, however, that the Supreme Court of Canada, in *Hunter Engineering*,[7] has made it clear that a properly worded exemption clause can overcome even a fundamental breach.

Exemption clauses usually ineffective in cases of fundamental breach

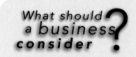

In business dealings, people often think that they are only bound by the narrowest interpretation of the words they have used in their contract. In fact, the courts often take a more expansive view even implying obligations that may not be stated. Such a commonly implied obligation is the duty to act in good faith towards the other contracting party. The significance of such a finding is illustrated by the following case.

MDS Health Group Limited v. King Street Medical Arts Centre Limited[8]

A group of Ontario doctors owned a building and agreed to let a medical lab (the MDS Group) lease a part of that building. The lease included a restrictive covenant that the landlord, King Street Medical Arts Centre Limited, would not permit any other tenant to provide medical lab services at the site, although the doctors would not be restricted from doing their own medical lab work. During the term of the lease, the landlord requested MDS to pay a much higher rent, and the lab refused, insisting that the terms of the lease be honoured.

In retaliation, a number of the doctors who were shareholders in the landlord company then took one of the rooms in the facility and used it as a collection point for sending samples to another lab. This did not violate the terms of the lease, as no lab work was actually done there nor were samples taken from patients. The doctors also encouraged their patients to have other lab work done elsewhere and effectively destroyed the business of MDS, the first lab.

The court held that the doctors had a duty to act in good faith in performing their contractual obligations, and an injunction was granted stopping the practice. While they might not have been technically in violation of the strict wording of their agreement, they certainly had breached their implied obligation to act in good faith in relation to the MDS group.

7. Hunter Engineering Co. v. Syncrude Canada Ltd., [1989] 1 S.C.R. 426; see also Beaufort Realties v. Chomedey Aluminum Co. Ltd. [1980] 2 S.C.R. 718

8. MDS Health Group Ltd. v. King Street Medical Arts Centre (1994) 12 B.L.R. (2d) 209 (Ont. Gen. Div.)

Repudiation

Fletton Ltd. v. Peat Marwick Ltd.[9]

Peat Marwick Ltd., acting as a receiver, came into possession of 2797 washer/dryer units from an import company that had become insolvent and entered into an agreement to sell these units to Fletton Ltd. One of the conditions of the agreement was that Fletton, the purchaser, would obtain product liability insurance on the units or an unqualified legal opinion that there could be no liability to Peat Marwick. Peat Marwick was aware of some electrical problems in the units with the potential to cause a fire and wanted to make sure they would face no liability.

Fletton could not arrange for the insurance, and in August, Peat Marwick repudiated the contract, having found another purchaser at a considerably higher price. Fletton sued for breach of contract, asking for an order of specific performance, which would require Peat Marwick to perform their side of the contract and deliver the units.

The problem was to determine who had breached the contract. Peat Marwick had repudiated, and that would have entitled Fletton to treat the contract as discharged by breach. But Fletton continued to insist on performance and continued to look for appropriate insurance coverage. They did not accept the repudiation and so could not rely on it as a breach. They never did find insurance coverage, and so, the court found that Fletton had breached the contract, not Peat Marwick.

This case illustrates the nature of anticipatory breach. You have a right to demand performance or to sue for breach, but if you do demand performance, you had better be prepared to perform your side of the agreement, or you may be the one that is in breach.

Repudiation occurs when one of the parties to a contract indicates to the other "an intimation or an intention to abandon and altogether to refuse performance of the contract."[10] Repudiation that takes place after performance is due is just one more way that a contract can be breached, but if this refusal occurs before performance is due, it is called **anticipatory breach** and is treated somewhat differently. In the face of such an anticipatory breach, the victim has a choice. The courts allow the victim to immediately treat the contract as breached, to sue or otherwise make different arrangements, and to refuse to go through with any further performance on their part. Alternatively, the victim of the repudiation can ignore the breach, demand performance, and continue to perform their side of the agreement. If the repudiating party then fails to perform, the innocent party can then sue for breach of contract, and the party repudiating will be held responsible for damages incurred even after the repudiation. If the choice is made to discharge the contract, the repudiation must relate to an important term of the contract and be a clear refusal to perform, not just a disagreement as to the nature of the contractual obligations.

Once made, the choice is binding. This can have serious consequences, and if the victim chooses to insist on performance and then cannot perform itself, it is the one in breach of contract, as happened in the *Fletton* case discussed above.

Repudiation is refusal to perform

Victim is discharged and can sue if repudiation occurs before due date—or demand performance and wait

Victim is bound by choice

9. (1988) 50 D.L.R. (4th) 729 (B.C.C.A.)
10. Comment of Lord Coleridge, C.J. in Freeth v. Burr (1874) L.R. 9 C.P. (C.C.P.) 208 (Eng. C.P.) at 213

Changing circumstances may affect repudiation

When repudiation in the form of an anticipatory breach does take place, the innocent party also runs the risk of being affected by changing circumstances.

In the case of *Avery v. Bowden*,[11] the defendant chartered the plaintiff's ship and agreed to supply it with a cargo at the Russian port of Odessa. However, when the ship arrived, because of the strained relations between the United Kingdom and Russia at the time, the defendant refused to supply a cargo and insisted that the boat leave. The captain stayed in port hoping that the supplier would change his mind. Before the expiration of the specified time for the cargo to be delivered, the Crimean War then broke out, making it impossible to go through with the contract, whether the parties wanted to or not. The owner of the ship sued for breach of contract.

Although the court agreed that the plaintiff would have had the right to treat the contract as discharged by breach once the defendant had clearly indicated that he was not going to go through with the agreement, the defendant had chosen not to acknowledge the repudiation. Therefore, the contract had not been breached, since the time specified for performance had not yet expired when the war broke out. The contract was discharged by frustration, not by breach. Frustration will be discussed later in the chapter.

Repudiation may be implicit by conduct

Repudiation can be expressed or implied from the conduct of the parties. Where the goods to be sold are sold to someone else, such repudiation will be implied. Also, repudiation may be implied from the failure to properly perform a term of the agreement. For example, where there is an ongoing obligation and one part is breached, such as the failure to deliver an important installment, repudiation may be implied. Just missing one delivery will normally not be serious enough, but where that failure is delivery of the first installment or of several installments, it may be serious enough to cast doubt on the proper performance of the rest of the agreement. This may discharge the contract. This was the dilemma faced by the court in *Standard Precast Ltd. v. Dywidag Fab Con Products Ltd.* used to introduce this chapter.

Untangling the WEB

The same rules that control performance of contractual obligations generally will apply to Internet transactions, but the problem is with breach and jurisdiction. Not only will it be difficult to bring an action to enforce the transaction where the seller or purchaser resides in a different jurisdiction, but it may actually be next to impossible to even identify whom to sue. It is clear that even if international treaties are set up to provide protection and unified rules, there will still be some jurisdictions that will provide a haven for questionable activities, and it will take little effort to route transactions through these havens to minimize risk for even legitimate businesses.

Discharge by Agreement

Gregorio v. Intrans-Corp.[12]

Gregorio, a truck driver, ordered a truck from the dealership Intrans for $100 000. It was purchased from the supplier Paccar, who obtained it from the American manufacturer. This agreement was entered into on May 12, 1984. Financing was

---

11. (1855) 5 E. & B. 714; aff'd (1856) 6 E. & B. 953 (Ex. Ct)

12. (1994) 115 D.L.R. (4th) 200 (Ont. C.A.); additional reasons (1994) 15 B.L.R. (2d) 109 (note) (Ont. C.A.)

arranged on July 3 removing the only condition on the sale, and so, there was a binding contract as of that date. On August 2, when the truck was delivered, Gregorio was required to sign certain documents, including a warranty which purported to give a one-year limited warranty but excluded all other implied warranties and other liability for consequential damages for failure to perform.

The *Sale of Goods Act* will be discussed in the next chapter, but it should be noted that this statute implies certain warranties and conditions into such contracts that protect the purchaser, unless the parties specify otherwise in their agreement. This is what the August 2 warranty signed by Gregorio purported to do.

The truck turned out to be a lemon. After several attempts to fix it, Gregorio sued to get his money back in 1987. He succeeded in doing so because the contract for the purchase was entered into on May 12, 1984, and the August 2 warranty was an attempt to modify that agreement. Since Gregorio received no consideration for the changes, he was not bound by the agreement to modify. The contract for purchase was the May 12, 1984, agreement, which did not exclude the implied conditions and warranties supplied by the *Sale of Goods Act,* and so, they were part of that agreement. Gregorio was entitled to rescission because of the implied condition that the goods be fit for their purpose. A contract can be modified by agreement, but it is vitally important that all the elements be present. In this case, consideration was missing, and Gregorio was not affected by the changes.

Just as the parties to a contract can agree to the creation of contractual obligations between them, they can also agree to end or modify those obligations. This is referred to as **discharge by agreement**. Whether the intention of the parties is to merely modify the old agreement or to end it and substitute a new one, all the ingredients necessary to form a contract, including consensus, must be present. The importance of determining that a new agreement has been substituted for the old one, rather than just a modification, relates to whether other terms in the old agreement are included in the new one. Exemption clauses and penalty clauses, for example, may not be carried over. Whether a new agreement has been created or the old one modified will be determined by looking at the intention of the parties and what has been changed. The more important the provision changed, the more likely it is that a new agreement has been substituted for the old one. When the new agreement involves a new party being substituted for one of the original parties to the agreement, it is called a **novation**. Whether the terms of the agreement or the parties to it are being changed, there must be complete agreement among all these parties before the new agreement becomes binding. It should be noted that if the original agreement needed to be evidenced in writing, then any modifications to it must also be evidenced in writing. A verbal agreement to discharge such a written contract would be valid, but the new contract must be evidenced in writing.

A contract requires consensus; thus, one party cannot unilaterally impose modification or termination on the other. It may be tempting for a merchant to abandon a contractual relationship with one tradesman when he finds someone else who will do the job at a lower price. If there is a binding contract, he cannot escape it just because he no longer likes the deal even where the job has not yet been started. To make this type of change, he must have the agreement of the original tradesman.

Consideration is also necessary to support a new agreement to discharge or modify the first contract. If both parties have something left to do under the original contract and the agreement to modify relieves them of their obligations, there

Contracts can be modified or ended by agreement

Must have consensus

Novation involves new party

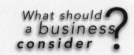

What should a business consider

Must have consideration

is valid consideration on both sides to support the change. This is called **bilateral discharge** or mutual release. In the example above, if the merchant can get the first tradesman to agree to let him off the hook, there would be no problem with consideration, neither party yet having performed. The problem arises where the discharge or modification is one-sided. Where one party performs their side, allowing the other out of all or part of their obligations, the discharge may not be binding because of lack of consideration. The original contract may still be enforceable. When a significant change is introduced that favours only one party, there may also be a problem with consideration. This was the reason the limited warranty provision agreed to later did not bind Gregorio in *Gregorio v. Intrans-Corp.*, discussed above. Of course, the consideration problem can be avoided by doing some extra work or by putting the agreement under seal. Even when the discharge is entirely one-sided, the person being relieved of their obligation may be able to raise the defence of promissory estoppel if sued under the original agreement. Such one-sided discharge or modification of contractual obligations is primarily where the principle of promissory estoppel arises, as was discussed in Chapter 5.

Unilateral discharge requires accord and satisfaction

When the parties discharge the contract on the payment of some substituted consideration, they have reached an **accord and satisfaction,** and the change is binding. The accord is the agreement reached, and satisfaction refers to the additional consideration given to support the discharge. To illustrate this point, consider the situation in which Aiello agrees to paint Newcombe's house for $500 to be paid in advance. After payment, Aiello tells Newcombe that she is no longer able to paint the house. If Newcombe were to tell Aiello, "Don't worry about it," would he be bound by those words? Normally, such a release would not be binding because of the lack of consideration. But if they Aiello were to agree to do something extra, such as paint Newcombe's fence instead, there would be a new agreement (an accord) with added consideration (satisfaction), and the new arrangement would be binding. Airlines often find themselves in this position when they have overbooked a flight. They will usually ask for volunteers to give up their seats and go on a later flight. Inducements, such as free flights and deluxe accommodation, are offered. Those that volunteer have reached an accord and satisfaction with the airline and cannot complain later.

Vandekerkhove v. Litchfield[13]

Mr. Litchfield had a business operating heavy equipment and ran into financial difficulty in 1982. At that time, he entered into an agreement to borrow $150 000 from a relative, Mr. Vandekerkhove. This agreement involved repayment at a reasonable rate of interest but also required the payment of a bonus of another $75 000 if it was repaid within 6 months and $150 000 if it took longer. This made the agreement illegal under Section 347 of the *Criminal Code*,[14] but neither of the parties was aware of this.

Mr. Litchfield was plagued by further problems and borrowed a further $145 000 from Mr. Vandekerkhove. In 1986, it was decided to bring these two debts together, and it was agreed in a new contract, referred to as "this restated loan agreement," that Litchfield should repay $318 250 at 12.5 percent interest. This represented the original $150 000 plus the agreed upon interest without the bonus, which amounted to $23 250, and the additional $145 000 borrowed.

13. (1995) 121 D.L.R. (4th) 571 (B.C.C.A.); leave to appeal refused (1995) 126 D.L.R. (4th) vii (note) (S.C.C.)

14. R.S.C. 1985, c. C-46

Mr. Vandekerkhove then tried to enforce the original bonus that was secured by a mortgage on Mr. Litchfield's house. In this action, that contract was set aside because it was an illegal agreement, and in this action, Mr. Litchfield was seeking the return of the $23 250 portion of the new agreement claiming that because it was originally based on an illegal contract which was set aside, it too ought to be set aside. The trial judge agreed, but this was overturned on appeal. Both parties were unaware of the illegal nature of the 1982 contract when they entered into the 1986 contract. They both had acted in good faith, and no illegal interest had, in fact, been paid. Their renegotiated agreement involved a change of consideration on both sides and so was binding on them. This is an example of an accord and satisfaction where a new agreement with new consideration is reached. The interest that was eventually paid was fair and reasonable, and this new agreement was binding on them. This case is a good example of how the principle of accord and satisfaction works and that such renegotiated agreements can be binding even when the original contract was illegal. It also illustrates that the courts' attitude is much more lenient towards illegal contracts where both of the parties are innocent or act in good faith.

As was explained in Chapter 5, a problem arises where a creditor agrees to take less than is owed in full satisfaction of a debt. Such an arrangement is very tempting to creditors, as they would rather have partial payment rather than nothing. So long as the payment is made before the due date, there is consideration, but where it is made after, the case of *Foakes v. Beer*[15] has established that there is no consideration to support the change, and the creditor, even after the partial payment, can still sue for the shortfall. This result is not very desirable from a business point of view, since arriving at such accommodation makes for more efficient business relationships. Creditors would often prefer to be able to take such a partial payment rather than get nothing, and debtors must be certain of the discharge before they are willing to make the payment. As a result, several provinces, including Ontario and British Columbia, have adopted legislation that largely overrules the precedent set in *Foakes v. Beer*. In these jurisdictions, if partial payment is offered and, in fact, taken as full payment of a debt, the creditor cannot sue for any deficit. Nothing forces the creditor to accept the lesser amount, but if it is taken, the creditor must be satisfied with it.

Partial payment of debt acceptable, if actually taken

Contractual Terms

Most contracts, by their nature, will end upon proper performance. However, sometimes they involve ongoing relationships, with no provision to bring that relationship to an end. In these circumstances, the parties can usually terminate the contract simply by giving the other reasonable notice. Often, the contract will provide for its own termination, usually by specifying a particular period of notice that must be given, and that provision will be binding subject to contrary legislation. In employment relationships and residential tenancy arrangements, for example, such termination provisions must comply with the governing statutes.

Contract may provide for its own discharge

When the contract itself specifies that some event or requirement must be satisfied before the parties are bound by it, this is properly referred to as a **condition precedent** but is more commonly called a **"subject to" clause.** For example, if Nishi were to agree to buy Fafard's house, subject to the sale of her own house, the contract is conditional on that event. Thus, if Nishi fails to sell her house, she is not obligated

Condition precedent

15. (1884) 9 App. Cas. 605 (H.L.)

Conditions subsequent

to go through with any agreement for the purchase of Fafard's house. When a condition precedent is not satisfied, there is no contractual obligation on either party. **Conditions subsequent** are terms that bring the obligations of the parties to an end upon some event or condition taking place. Whereas conditions precedent determine when the obligations between the parties begin, conditions subsequent determine when they end. For example, if Agar agreed to pay Nguyen $400 per month for janitorial services "until Nguyen ceases to be a full-time student," this term is a condition subsequent. Agar will be obligated to pay only until Nguyen finishes school.

Sometimes the contract anticipates some catastrophic event, such as a riot or flood, that will interfere with the performance of the contract and specifies discharge when such an event takes place. This is referred to as a *force majeure* **clause**. Such terms might provide for discharge but might also set out the consequences, such as which party will bear the risk of loss. Of course, the parties can always agree to end, modify, or substitute obligations with a new agreement, as discussed above.

Contracts can also end by operation of law, as would be the case when of one of the parties dies or becomes insane or bankrupt. Bankruptcy will be discussed in Chapter 10.

Frustration

British Columbia (Minister of Crown Lands) v. Cressey Development Corp.[16]

Cressey bought land from the British Columbia government, which was conveyed to him upon payment of $2 million in September 1988. This was all done on the expectation that the municipality would rezone the property so that it could be developed. In fact, the rezoning did not take place, and since this was not the fault of either party, the court held that it frustrated the contract. The contract was ended, and the title retransferred to the British Columbia government, which was ordered to return the money.

An unexpected event beyond the control of either party led to frustration of the contract. In cases like this, the contractual obligations cease to exist. A further question arises, however, as to what then ought to happen between the parties. In the present instance, the British Columbia government had the use of the money for a considerable time, so the court held that they should be required to pay interest to Cressey for the use of that money. Cressey also argued that they had done a considerable amount of work in preparation for the development of the property, for which they wanted compensation.

Under legislation dealing with frustrated contracts in place in most jurisdictions, where one party does work and it confers a benefit on another, even though the contract is frustrated, compensation must be paid by the benefiting party. In this case, however, the court held that although the work had been done and the effort expended, the government had received no benefit, and therefore, Cressey was not entitled to compensation. Note that the British Columbia legislation permits the payment of compensation for such expenses, even when the other party received no benefit, but since this was not claimed, no such order could be made. The case illustrates not only how a contract can be ended by a frustrating event but also the rights of the parties once such frustration has taken place.

16. (1992) 97 D.L.R (4th) p. 380 (B.C.S.C.)

Sometimes some unexpected event out of the control of the parties makes the performance of the contract impossible. For example, where a construction firm agrees to repair a bridge but the bridge is destroyed in a storm before they can perform, performance has become impossible. In such circumstances, the contract is considered discharged through frustration. Frustration occurs when some unforeseen, outside event interferes with the performance of the contract, making the basic object of the agreement unobtainable.

Frustrating event may end contract

It is easy to understand frustration when performance of the contract is made impossible, such as when a person agrees to paint a house that is destroyed in a fire before the job is done. The difficulty arises because the courts have expanded the principle to cover situations where the foundation of the contract is destroyed. Performance may still be technically possible, but the whole nature of the relationship has changed, making performance something essentially different from what the parties anticipated.

In the case of *Krell v. Henry*,[17] the parties agreed to the rental of an apartment to view the coronation parade of Edward VII. A small deposit was paid at the time the contract was entered into, but the coronation parade was cancelled before the balance was paid because of the King's sudden illness. It was still possible for the parties to go through with the performance of the contract and for the tenant to occupy the flat, but to do so with no coronation parade to watch would be something essentially different from what the parties had in mind when they entered into the contract. Although performance of the contract was possible in a literal sense, it was no longer possible to obtain the purpose or object of the contract itself. Thus, the contract was said to be frustrated.

The destruction of a building may lead to frustration of a contract for janitorial services.
The Canadian Press/AP Photo/ Jeff Zelevansky

Care should be taken not to confuse frustration with shared mistake, discussed in the preceding chapter. With shared mistake, there is no contract because the subject matter had been destroyed before the contract was entered into. Frustration deals with situations where the problems arise after the formation of the contract. If a ship that is the subject of a contract is destroyed before the contract is made, the parties are making a mistake assuming the ship to still be as expected. But if the ship is destroyed after the contract is made, the contract is discharged through frustration.

Shared mistake not the same as frustration

Frustration commonly arises in the following circumstances:

1. Performance of a contract becomes impossible because the subject matter of the agreement is destroyed or is otherwise unusable. Contracts may be frustrated when a person who has agreed to supply personal services becomes ill or dies, or when the specific article that formed the object of the contract is destroyed before the agreement can be performed.

Circumstances constituting frustration

In the case of *Taylor v. Caldwell*,[18] there was an agreement between the parties to rent out a music hall. The hall burned down six days before the performance was to take place. The court held that the contract was discharged through frustration.

2. An event that forms the basis of a contract fails to take place. An example of this is found in *Krell v. Henry* cited earlier.

17. [1903] 2 K.B. 740 (C.A.)
18. (1863) 3 B. & S. 826 (Q.B.)

3. Acts of the government interfere with performance. Government policy can interfere with the performance of a contract in several different ways. A contract with someone in another country may become unlawful through a declaration of war; contracts involving the manufacture and production of particular drugs or foodstuffs may become illegal by statute. A contract may anticipate the acquisition of a licence or permit, which the government does not grant, as happened in the *British Columbia v. Cressey* case discussed above. Note as well that all levels of government have the power to expropriate the property that may form the basis of a contract.

Circumstances Not Constituting Frustration

Self-induced frustration involves one of the parties to the agreement causing the interfering event. It may appear to be frustration, but self-induced frustration is simply treated as a breach of contract. For example, if Moser has a contract to build an apartment building for Wu but the city refuses to grant Moser a building permit, we would expect the contract to be frustrated. However, if the building permit is refused because Moser failed to submit the appropriate plans as required by city bylaw, the frustration is self-induced. Moser is responsible for the misfortune; the refusal of the city to grant a permit will not provide an excuse for Moser's failure to perform the contract.

As well, where the parties have anticipated the frustrating event or have provided for one of the parties to bear the risk of such an eventuality, these contractual terms, often called *force majeure* clauses, will prevail. The parties will not be able to claim that their agreement has been frustrated. It is only when the event is an unforeseen interference, not caused by either party, that the courts are willing to find frustration.

Finally, the contract is not frustrated if the unforeseen outside event only makes the performance of the contract more costly or more difficult.

In the case of *Tsakiroglou Co. v. Noblee & Thorl GmbH*,[19] the defendant agreed to sell and deliver a cargo of Sudanese groundnuts from a port in the Sudan to Hamburg. But the Suez War broke out, closing the Suez Canal, and the cargo was not delivered. The purchaser sued for breach of contract, and the seller claimed frustration. The court held that although it was more difficult and costly to ship the cargo around Africa, the essential nature of the contract remained intact and frustration did not apply. The seller was held liable for breach of contract, although the result would likely have been different had they specified delivery through the Suez canal.

Similarly, if a farmer agrees to sell 50 boxes of Golden Delicious apples to a buyer and then his crop is destroyed by hail, this is not frustration unless the terms of the contract specifically stated that the apples were to come from his trees. The source of the apples was not a term of the contract, and the farmer can simply obtain them from another farmer or on the open market and thus fulfill his contractual obligation.

Self-induced frustration is breach

Must be unanticipated to be frustration

Increase in costs is not frustration

Increased difficulty is not frustration

Dinicola et al. v. Huang & Danczkay Properties[20]

Huang & Danczkay Properties sold certain condominiums before they were built, in fact, even before they had finalized the purchase of the property. There was a clause in the contract providing that the developers could terminate the agree-

19. [1962] A.C. 93 (H.L.)
20. (1998) 163 D.L.R. (4th) 286 (Ont. C.A.)

ment and return deposits paid without further liability up to June 30, 1988, if municipal approval was not obtained. There was another clause permitting major design modifications, where necessary, but the purchasers had no such flexibility. Although things looked like they were going well, on June 30, 1988, negotiations deteriorated, and the permit to build was eventually refused. This action for damages was brought by a number of the purchasers against the developers for breach of contract. The developers argued that the contract was discharged by frustration because of the failure of the municipality to grant the permit to build.

The courts at both the trial and appeal levels rejected this position for two reasons. The clause referred to above makes it absolutely clear that the contract anticipated the possibility that the development might not be approved and provided for an escape for the developer, at least until June 30. Frustration must be an outside event that was not anticipated by either party. Here, the developers not only anticipated that this might take place but provided for it in the contract. Because the failure to approve took place after the June 30 date, it only put the risk of this happening onto the developer; it did not discharge the contract.

The second reason frustration did not apply was because the developer had caused the situation that led to the refusal of the permit. In the final stages of the negotiations, the representative of the developer wrote to the municipal council declaring that they would not negotiate further. As a result, the permit was refused. Because the letter precipitated the refusal, the court found that this was an example of self-induced frustration. For a contract to be discharged through frustration, it is not only necessary to show that the frustrating event was unforeseen but also that it was not within the control of either party. Self-induced frustration is simply breach of contract. The doctrine of frustration was never meant to give one of the parties an advantage, but it provides for those unexpected and uncontrollable events that disrupt our lives and our business dealings. This case nicely illustrates not only what frustration is but also what it is not.

Effect of Frustration

The major problem associated with frustration is to determine who shall suffer the loss when the contract is discharged. Under common law, the general principle was, "Let the loss lie where it falls." In other words, the party who had done work or provided services before the frustrating event would bear the loss and could not seek compensation from the other party. Similarly, money already paid was lost. Note, however, that any money that should have been paid before the frustrating event still had to be paid.

Let loss lie where it falls under common law

This position was considered unsatisfactory and the House of Lords modified this position in the *Fibrosa* case,[21] which required the return of a deposit paid by a Polish company to a British manufacturer after the outbreak of war frustrated their contract. Because the Polish company had received no benefit, they were entitled to the return of their deposit. This represents the common law position today but still leads to some unsatisfactory results. The whole deposit or nothing has to be returned, depending on whether any benefit was received.

Problems with deposits

Legislation in most jurisdictions, in the form of the *Frustrated Contracts Act,* now permits the court, where a benefit has been obtained by one party prior to the frustrating event, to order that party to pay the other for it. This position was advanced in the *British Columbia v. Cressey* case, discussed earlier, but failed because the court was not convinced that the British Columbia government actually received a benefit.

---

21. Fibrosa Spolka Akeyjna v. Fairbairn Lawson Combe Barbouk Ltd. [1943] A.C. 32 (H.L.)

Legislation allows deposits to be split

Where a deposit has been paid, the legislation usually allows the court to take into consideration the costs that have been incurred in preparation to perform the contract, whether or not the other party has received a benefit. The court can now apportion that deposit on the basis of the costs incurred and the benefits received. In British Columbia and the Yukon, the statutes go further and allow the courts to assess the costs both parties have incurred and to apportion those costs (whether or not a deposit has been paid), requiring one party to make payment to the other. In the *Cressey* case, this did not happen because the plaintiff failed to make the appropriate claim.

Other statutes also modify the common law application of the frustration principle. In common law, frustration does not apply to leases, but most jurisdictions have clearly stated that in residential leases, frustration will apply. British Columbia extends the application of frustration to commercial leases as well. When goods are being sold, the *Sale of Goods Act* provides that if the goods, through no fault of the parties, perish before the risk passes to the purchaser, the contract is voided. This means that the contract is not binding on the purchaser, and any moneys paid have to be returned.

Reimbursement for Expenses Where Contract Frustrated

The plaintiff's truck was sent to the defendant for repairs after an accident. Repairs worth some $28 000 were completed when a fire destroyed both the shop and the truck, thus frustrating the repair contract.

The *Ontario Frustrated Contracts Act* provided that when funds were paid (as with a deposit) or were payable before the frustrating event took place,

they could be used to reimburse for expenses incurred. The court found that such funds for the repair work done prior to the fire were payable before the fire and ordered that the company be reimbursed for the expenses they incurred in repairing the vehicle from that amount owing.

Can-Truck Transportation Ltd. v. Fenton's Auto Paint Shop Ltd., (1993) 101 D.L.R. (4th) 562 (Ont. C.A.)

Remedies for Breach of Contract

It takes both parties to end a contract by breach

A breach of a condition in a contract does not automatically end all obligations of both parties to that contract. The victim of the breach has the right to ignore the breach and continue to treat the contract as if it were in force. If Mouzakis agreed to sell Smith a car and delivered a boat, Smith can choose to take the boat. It takes both parties to discharge a contract by breach of condition. Even if the victim of the breach elects to treat his or her obligations under the contract as discharged, this does not end the obligations of the breaching party. The nature of those obligations is changed; the breaching party becomes liable for the remedies that are discussed below.

It should be noted that the following remedies are obtained though the litigation process and, as such, represent a failure not a victory. Disputes are much better resolved through negotiation or even with the help of third parties, as with mediation and arbitration. Suing should be viewed as a last resort and the remedies that follow as a poor consolation.

Rescission and Rectification

The equitable remedies of rescission and rectification available to victims in con-tractual relationships were discussed in Chapter 7. Rectification was available where a mistake had taken place in recording the terms agreed to and is not normally considered to be a remedy for breach. The court will sometimes rectify or correct those terms to properly reflect the agreement. Rescission involves the court putting the parties back into the position they were in before they entered into the contract. This remedy also is more associated with problems involved with the formation of the contract, such as misrepresentation, mistake, duress, fraud, or failure of one of the required elements, such as consensus, consideration, capacity, legality or in-tention. Rescission may be available as a remedy for breach where the other party has repudiated the contract.

Remedies available where formation of contract was defective

Remedies Provided in Contract

It is possible for a contract to set out the consequence in the event of breach. The consequences may be quite varied. The contract may call for mediation or arbi-tration to resolve disputes and determine compensation. The contract might also delineate the maximum amount of compensation to be paid by the breaching party. Businesses often post signs indicating that they are not responsible for losses over a specified amount. Failure to make an installment payment will often trig-ger an **acceleration clause,** which makes the entire outstanding debt due and payable immediately. Where the contract involves a consumer transaction, the op-eration of acceleration clauses are often restricted by legislation, one of the subjects of the next chapter.

Remedies set out in contract

Liquidated Damages

Often, the contract will specify the amount of damages that must be paid in the event of breach. These are called liquidated damages, and the courts will normally enforce such terms once liability has been determined. Where the amount is actually pre-paid with the provision that the funds are to be forfeited in the event of a breach, it is called a deposit. For example, the vendor of an automobile will usually require the buyer to pay a substantial deposit when ordering to secure the purchase. If the purchaser fails to go through with the deal when the car arrives, the vendor can re-tain the deposit.

Liquidated damages are specified in contract

It is important to distinguish between deposits and down payments. **Deposits** are to be forfeited in the event of a breach, whereas a **down payment** is just the first pay-ment and may have to be returned. Of course, when the victim of the breach has the down payment in hand, it may be used as a lever to force performance. But when it comes to trial, the court will order its return, usually setting off the actual damages to be paid against the down payment. As a rule it does not matter what the term is called, but it is the presence of a term requiring the forfeiture of the pre-payment that will cause the court to treat it as a deposit.

Deposits to be forfeited upon breach

Deposit is forfeited—down payment is not

The temptation to take a large deposit entails significant risk. To qualify as liq-uidated damages, a deposit must be an honest attempt by the parties to estimate the damages that would be suffered if the contract were breached. Too large a pre-payment becomes an unreasonable penalty rather than liquidated damages and must be returned. A $1000 deposit on a new car might be fair in view of the cost of advertising, the time lost, the extra interest payments, and so on. But a $10 000

Deposit must not be penalty

deposit on a $15 000 car is no longer an attempt to compensate for possible loss or injury but becomes an attempt to punish the breaching party for failure to go through with the contract. Such a penalty clause, being excessive, is unconscionable and void. Such a penalty would have to be returned subject to an action to establish the actual loss.

Even when no pre-payment is involved, a liquidated damages clause is held to the same standard and may be challenged if the object is to unreasonably punish rather than to compensate and the amount involved is exorbitant.

Meunier v. Cloutier[22]

Cloutier sold his hotel in Timmins, Ontario, to Meunier in 1977. The contract of sale included a non-competition clause, whereby Cloutier agreed not to participate in the hotel business in Timmins for five years. If this covenant were breached, Cloutier was to pay Meunier $50 000 as liquidated damages. Cloutier then went to Florida and there remarried. Later, he returned to Canada, and about four years after the sale, his wife purchased another similar establishment only a block and a half away. The court held that although Cloutier did not have a direct interest in this new establishment, he participated in its operation sufficiently to have breached his covenant not to compete. This action was brought by Meunier for the $50 000 set out as liquidated damages in the event of such a breach.

The court had to determine whether the requirement to pay $50 000 was enforceable as liquidated damages or was void as a penalty. The court, after finding that the appropriate time to determine reasonableness was at the time the contract was made, determined that the time involved and the geographical limitation were both reasonable, nor was the public interest offended by this provision. The problem was whether it was unreasonable to require the payment of $50 000, no matter what the breach. The Supreme Court of Canada, in *H.F. Clarke Ltd. v. Thermidaire Corp. Ltd.*,[23] determined that when such lump-sum payments are involved, as opposed to the use of some formula for calculating damages, the court had to ascertain whether the amount to be paid was "reasonable in the circumstances." This required the court to look at the nature of the breach itself as opposed to what the parties had in mind when they entered into the contract. Where the breach is minor and enforcing the lump-sum payment gives the other a windfall, such an award would be unconscionable and would, therefore, be an unreasonable penalty. In this case, the breach was minor in that the competition was only for a short time towards the end of the five-year period, and there was no proof that the plaintiff suffered any damages at all. Requiring Cloutier to pay the $50 000 in these circumstances would be unconscionable, and therefore the non-competition clause was a penalty and unenforceable.

This case shows the problems associated with such liquidated damages/penalty clauses in contracts. It is the court's function to punish, and so unreasonable penalty clauses, which, by definition punish, are prohibited. Note that in this case, the non-competition clause was valid; it was the damages portion of that provision that was unacceptable.

22. (1984) 9 D.L.R. (4th) 486 (Ont. H.C.)

23. [1976] 1 S.C.R. 319

Damages

The most common remedy for a breach of contract is an order that the breaching party pay damages. Damages are amounts of money assessed by the court and designed to compensate victims for their losses. The object is to put the victim, as near as monetary compensation can, into the position he or she would have been in had the contract been properly performed. For example, if a person bought defective paint from a supplier which blistered when put on the walls, necessitating repainting, the court would not only award the cost of the paint as damage but also take into consideration the amount it would cost for a painter to scrape the blistered paint off and repaint the house. The courts will then order the vendor to pay a sum sufficient to put the purchaser in the position he or she would have been in if the paint had not been defective.

Damages in contract law designed to compensate

Victim of breach compensated as if contract had been properly performed

Ed Learn Ford Sales Ltd. v. Giovannone[24]

Giovannone traded his Lincoln car in for a truck at Ed Learn Ford Sales Ltd. The Lincoln was then resold to a purchaser before any of the parties discovered that the car had been stolen. In order to ensure that their customer could keep the car, the dealer paid off the insurance company which had paid out on the stolen vehicle claim of the original owner of the vehicle. This cost Ed Learn Ford Sales Ltd. $6175.50. Since they had allowed Giovannone $9200 trade-in on the Lincoln, they sued him for breach of contract claiming this amount. The court, however, looked at what the dealer had lost, which was only the $6175.50 they had put out to satisfy the insurance company, and judgment was granted for that amount. In his judgment, the judge quoted from the Privy Council decision in *Wertheim v. Chicoutimi Pulp Co.*, "…it is the general intention of the law that, in giving damages for breach of contract, the party complaining should, so far as it can be done by money, be placed in the same position as he would have been in if the contract had been performed."[25]

The dealership also argued that Giovannone had made other misrepresentations with respect to the mileage and year of the Lincoln but the court held that the dealers, as experts, were in the best position to determine those things.

The case demonstrates how damages are assessed in a breach of contract action and also is valuable in reviewing that for a misrepresentation to be actionable, the victim must have relied upon it.

Limitations on Recoverable Damages

Although damages are designed to compensate a person for injuries suffered, not all losses are recoverable. Remoteness and mitigation are two limitations on the recoverability of damages.

Not all losses can be recovered

The important case of *Hadley v. Baxendale*,[26] involved the shipping of a broken crankshaft from a steam engine to be used as a pattern for the manufacture of a new one. The shipper was asked to send it quickly but failed to do so. Unknown to the shipper, the plaintiff's entire plant was shut down while waiting for the crankshaft.

24. (1990) 74 D.L.R. (4th) 761 (Ont. Gen. Div.)

25. [1911] A.C. 301 at 307

26. (1854) 156 E.R. 145 (Ex. Ct)

This caused great expense to the plaintiff, who sued the shipper for lost profits. The shipper claimed that he could not be responsible for the unusual damage because he had no knowledge of it. The court used the reasonable person test to determine the extent of the shipper's responsibility for damages and held that the shipper was only responsible for the usual damages that could be expected if the contract were breached and therefore not liable for the plaintiff's lost profits.

Remoteness

Must pay reasonably anticipated losses

The principle that has developed from this and other cases is essentially that a breaching party is only responsible for those damages, which, at the time the contract was entered into, seem a likely outcome if the contract were breached. Thus, the breaching party is responsible not only for the normally expected damages that flow from a breach but also for any unusual damages resulting from special circumstances which were communicated to him or her at the time of the contract. In short, the breaching party is responsible in contract law for any damages that can be reasonably foreseen at the time the contract is entered into.

One area where the problem of remoteness often arises is in a claim for damages to compensate for lost profits. The breaching party must be aware of the details of the other person's business at the time the contract is entered into for a claim of lost profits, to be considered especially if the lost profits are unusually large. Goods purchased for some unusual or specialized purpose may have a greater-than-normal potential to cause injury, but it is only when that unusual or specialized purpose is communicated to the vendor that the vendor can be held responsible for all the damages suffered. If Seto bought from Mishra a sealant normally used for another purpose to waterproof the foundation of his house, Mishra would not be liable if it failed to do the job, unless he knew what the sealant was to be used for at the time it was purchased.

When a contract is breached, damages are awarded in order to compensate for monetary losses. It is only recently that courts have shown a willingness to award monetary compensation for mental distress. These situations are generally limited to cases where some non-monetary benefit was the subject matter of the contract, such as a disrupted vacation or cruise.[27] Punitive damages are generally not available for breach of contract in the absence of a tort, such as deceit.

Victims must mitigate their losses

Mitigation

Victims of breach have an obligation to mitigate their losses, that is, to keep them as low as is reasonably possible.

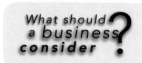

If a business were to purchase computers that were not up to the task for which they were purchased, it could not simply watch them fail causing huge losses. It must take steps to upgrade, replace, or repair those computers so as to minimize its loss. Even where the seller has assured it they can do the job, when it becomes obvious that they cannot, it must mitigate their losses.

The failure to mitigate is a common problem in wrongful dismissal actions. A person who has been wrongfully dismissed has a right to sue but must make a reasonable effort to find other employment. Damages in such actions are based on the difference between how much notice the employee should have been given as opposed to how much they actually received. If the employer can show that the dismissed employee failed to look for another job, the damages will be reduced by the amount he would have earned during that notice period. He should have mitigated by trying to find another job.

27. Jarvis v. Swan Tours Ltd. [1973] Q. B. 233. (C.A.)

Note also that the obligation to mitigate means simply that the victim of the breach must take all reasonable steps to minimize losses suffered. That person is not required to take personal risks or to incur unreasonable expense in the process.

Equitable Remedies

The following are examples of remedies that have been developed by the Courts of Chancery to deal with special situations in which the ordinary remedy of damages would not be adequate for the injuries suffered in a breach-of-contract situation. Note that these remedies are discretionary and will only be granted when the judge thinks it right and fair to do so.

Specific Performance

Specific performance occurs when the court orders the defaulting party to live up to the terms of the contract. Where a development company acquires a number of properties to build a new shopping mall and one property owner refuses to go through with the deal, it would be appropriate to obtain a court order for specific performance, ordering that property owner to transfer the property at the agreed upon price. But if the same developer ordered a number of new trucks from a dealer who then refused to deliver them, specific performance would not be appropriate, as equivalent vehicles could be obtained elsewhere. The appropriate remedy would be damages, and they would be assessed on the basis of the extra cost of getting the vehicles from another dealer. Only if the trucks were unique and not available from some other source might specific performance be available.

Courts can order performance of contract

—but only where damages would be inappropriate

The courts will not order the defaulting party to perform a contract that requires personal service. If our developer were to contract with a famous performer to sing at a concert celebrating the opening of the shopping mall and the performer then refused to perform, finding a more lucrative engagement elsewhere, the court would not order specific performance and require the performer to sing in these circumstances. Similarly, the courts will not award specific performance as a remedy in any situation that would require close supervision to ensure that the contract is properly performed. Nor will specific performance be available where it would hurt a third party.

Courts will not force performance of contracts for personal services

Since all land is unique, the courts in the past have been willing to award specific performance whenever the parties to the purchase of land breached their contract. The Supreme Court of Canada has indicated, however, that now contracts dealing with the purchase of land will be treated like any other contract, limiting the availability of specific performance to those situations where damages are inappropriate.[28]

Injunction

Specific performance involves a court order to do something (to perform the contract), whereas an injunction usually involves an order to refrain from some offensive conduct. In our example above, the court would not order the performer to fulfill the contract by singing at the concert but may well order her not to breach the agreement by performing somewhere else. The injunction is not limited to breach of contract; it may be available in any situation in which wrongful conduct is involved.

Courts may order breaching conduct to stop

28. Semelhago v. Paramadevan [1996] 2 S.C.R. 415

In rare circumstances, the courts may issue a mandatory injunction when a person does something to violate a contractual term and thereby creates an ongoing problem. Striking workers involved in an illegal work stoppage are often ordered to stop breaching their contract and return to work. Another example might involve our developer above if he were to place a sign above his shopping centre that exceeds the permitted height limit set out in a restrictive covenant or a municipal bylaw. He would likely be ordered to remove the sign or reduce it to the permitted height. Such mandatory injunctions are not common.

—but not where person can no longer earn a living

As with specific performance, there are many instances in which the courts will refuse to issue an injunction. The courts will not order an injunction that would make it impossible for the person defaulting on the contractual agreement to earn a living any other way. A professional football team might be able to require one of its players to agree not to play for any other football team, but it would not be able to enforce by injunction a requirement that the football player not be employed by any other person at all. Similarly, the courts will not issue an injunction when damages provide a sufficient remedy. An injunction is not designed to punish someone for breaching a contract but to prevent further injury. An injunction will also not be awarded where it will cause harm to a third party.

—but not where damages more appropriate

Accounting

Court may order accounting and require profits to be paid over

It is often difficult for the victim of the breach to determine just what kind of injuries he or she has suffered, especially when the offending party has taken advantage of some opportunities or rights belonging to the victim. This can happen when there is a fiduciary relationship between the contracting parties, that is, a relationship in which the person dishonouring the contract has a duty to act in the best interests of the other party. In these circumstances, the court can order that the defaulting party disclose all financial dealings and records so that the injured party can determine what he or she is entitled to claim. The court will then order the offending party to pay over any profits made from the wrongful conduct to the injured party. So the court, instead of awarding damages on the basis of what has been lost by the victim, awards damages on the basis of what has been wrongfully obtained by the breaching party.

Quantum Meruit

Court may order payment for part performance

In some situations, the contract is breached before the amount agreed to in the contract is due and payable to the injured party. The courts have the power to award compensation for the value of work performed on the basis of *quantum meruit*, if the injured party has done a considerable amount of work towards earning that payment. This is the same principle that allowed the supplier of a service to collect a reasonable fee, even when no price was agreed upon. Care must be exercised because the same does not apply if the breaching party has done some work but payment for this work is not due at the time the breach takes place. The courts are extremely reluctant to grant any compensation for the breaching party's partial performance of the agreement, unless the contractual obligations have been substantially performed. Sometimes partial payment is payable before completion, and in that case, even the breaching party can collect.

If a contractor has agreed to build a house with payment due upon completion of the job and refuses to continue after completing half, he will not be successful in claiming compensation for what he has done. He should finish the job. But if he has finished half the project and the other party refuses to let him continue, the contractor, being the innocent party, will be able to claim compensation for what has been done under the principle of *quantum meruit*. Only where the contract called for partial payments at different stages of completion will the breaching party be able to collect for those payments due before the breach.

Some general requirements must be met before the courts will grant an equitable remedy. If there has been **laches**, an undue delay on the part of the person seeking the equitable remedy, the courts can refuse to grant the remedy. The plaintiff will still be able to pursue any common law remedy, such as damages without penalty for delay, provided the action is brought within the limitation period in place, as discussed in Chapter 2. The courts can refuse to award an equitable remedy in any situation in which it would cause hardship to the parties or to some other person or would be inappropriate for any other reason. A person seeking equity must come to the court with clean hands. The remedy will be denied when the person seeking the equitable remedy is also guilty of some wrongdoing. These requirements apply to all equitable remedies.

Undue delay

Hardship

Clean hands

Island Properties Ltd. v. Entertainment Enterprises Ltd. et al.[29]

Entertainment Enterprises Limited and Denis Galway (referred to as Galway below) owned 83 acres in Newfoundland and arranged to sell it through Craig Williams of Central & Eastern Trust Real Estate. The property was first offered through the agent Williams to Islands Properties Ltd, but when it appeared that they had not responded by the specified time, 11:59 p.m. on July 9, 1980, and the deal had fallen through, the property was offered to another purchaser, Pegasus, by Miller, one of the other agents involved. This offer was accepted. Unfortunately, the first purchaser Island property had sent an acceptance before the deadline to the agent Williams that had not been passed on to Galway. The court found that this also was a valid acceptance and that the property had been sold to both purchasers. Galway transferred the property to Pegasus, and Island property sued for breach of contract asking for the remedy of specific performance.

At trial, the judge expressed disappointment at the behaviour of the real estate agents and ordered that the property be returned by Pegasus and transferred to Island Properties, the only party with "totally clean hands."

On appeal, the judge ordered that the property be returned to Pegasus. Pegasus was an innocent third party, and an equitable remedy cannot be given where it will cause harm to such an innocent party. There was some suggestion that the trial judge also thought the conduct of Pegasus was tainted, but the appeal court could find no basis for that, and, in fact, Pegasus had just taken advantage of a good deal when they became aware of it.

Specific performance is an equitable remedy and because of that, there are several restrictions on its availability. Undue delay in bringing the action and wrongdoing on the part of the person seeking the remedy are examples. Also, when a third party becomes involved, the courts will not award an equitable remedy that will cause them harm. Although it was clear here that the property had been sold to two different buyers and that the first was Island Property; because the property had been conveyed to the innocent Pegasus, it could not be taken back from it. Specific performance was not available, only damages could be given as a remedy. Had there been evidence to support the finding that Pegasus was also part of the improper dealing, there would have been no hesitation in awarding specific performance to Island Properties.

29. (1986) 26 D.L.R. (4th) 347 (Nfld. C.A.)

Time limits

Another factor that may affect the right of the victim of a breach of contract to obtain any remedy is the limitations legislation, discussed in Chapter 2. The limitation periods outlined in such statutes also apply to the field of contracts, thus limiting the availability of the remedies discussed after the passage of specified time periods.

Contempt

Finally, it should be noted that when a judgment or an equitable remedy has been awarded and a defendant refuses to comply, the defendant may be held in contempt of court and can be jailed, although this is extremely unlikely. The remedies to enforce a judgment, outlined generally in Chapter 2, are available to the victim of a breach of contract as well.

Summary

Contracts

- Can come to an end through performance, breach, agreement, or frustration

Performance

- When properly tendered but refused, contract is discharged
- When money is still owed, the creditor must bear the cost of its collection

Breach

- The victim may treat the contract as discharged and sue
- Breached warranty—contract is still binding but the victim can sue for damages
- Anticipatory breach—victim can treat the contract as discharged immediately or wait for performance

Agreement

- Contract provides for its own end

Frustration

- Contract impossible to perform as expected
- Monies advanced may be apportioned to compensate for expenses or losses incurred
- Self-induced frustration is breach of contract

Remedies

- Damages reasonably within the contemplation of the parties, after all has been done to mitigate the loss
- Damages set out in contract must be reasonable
- Deposit cannot be a penalty
- Specific performance requires the breaching party to fulfill agreement
- Injunction—a court order stopping breaching party
- Accounting and *quantum meruit* also available

QUESTIONS

1. Describe the various ways in which a contractual relationship can come to an end.

2. Under what circumstances would a breaching party who had partially performed the terms of the contract be entitled to receive part payment?

3. Describe the differences between a condition and a warranty. What is the significance of the distinction?

4. How may the victim of the breach of a condition lose the right to rescind the contract?

5. What constitutes adequate tender of performance?

6. What recourse is available to one party to a contract when performance is made impossible by the other party's conduct?

7. What options are available to the victim of an anticipatory breach? Explain the advantages, disadvantages, and risks associated with these options.

8. How do the courts approach an exclusionary or exculpatory clause in a contract?

9. What is meant by fundamental breach, and how does the court deal with the problem?

10. What two factors are most likely to be absent when a claim that a contract was discharged or modified by agreement is challenged in court?

11. Explain what rule the case of *Foakes v. Beer* established. How has it been modified by statute since then?

12. Distinguish between contractual terms that are conditions precedent and those that are conditions subsequent.

13. Define frustration. List three ways in which frustration can take place.

14. What is the significance of a court's determination that a contract was frustrated through the fault of one of the parties?

15. Explain how the *Fibrosa* case and subsequent statute law have modified the previously accepted common law rule on the obligations of the parties in the face of a frustrating event.

16. Distinguish between a deposit and a down payment. What is the significance of this distinction?

17. What must be the demonstrated intention of the parties for money paid under a term of a contract to be categorized as a deposit?

18. Explain what limitations on the recovery of damages were developed from the case of *Hadley v. Baxendale.*

19. Describe what is meant by mitigation. Explain how the obligation to mitigate damages limits the ability of the victim of a breach to obtain damages.

20. Distinguish between specific performance and injunction. Explain the restrictions on their availability.

CASES

1. Sumpter v. Hedges

The plaintiff agreed to erect certain buildings for the defendant for a lump-sum payment to be made upon completion. The plaintiff failed to finish the work and asked for reimbursement for the amount he had done. The defendant refused. The plaintiff then sued for payment for the work he had done. What factors would the court need to determine before they decided the case? Explain the likely outcome.

2. Betker v. Williams

Mrs. Williams owned property in Cranbrook and listed the property for sale with Mr. Klinkhammer, a real estate agent. It was advertised as a residential lot in the local newspaper, with a clear indication that a house could be built on it. Mr. Betker bought the property after specifically asking Mr. Klinkhammer if it would be appropriate for a solar home and receiving a positive reply. Four years after the sale, they discovered that a house could not be built on the property because it was too small for a septic tank and had no access to the city sewer line.

It turned out that neither the Williams nor the realtors were aware of this problem. The Betkers learned that they could not build a house on the property, and they brought an action against the realtors and Mrs. Williams. There was a term in the agreement stating that there were no representations other than those contained on the written agreement itself, but this provision had not been specifically brought to the attention of the purchasers. Explain the arguments available to both parties and the appropriate remedies that might be sought.

3. Bell v. St. Thomas University

Bell was enrolled at the defendant university in a four-year program leading to a bachelor of social work. The program required the successful completion of a field practice course called Social Work 410. He took this course but failed it in 1987. The university calendar contained a provision about the repeating of courses that stated, "Students may without special permission register for a course already taken in order to meet a prerequisite or other degree requirement or in order to improve their grade." But in this case, before allowing Bell to repeat Social Work 410, the department required him to fulfill certain conditions. He made several attempts to comply, but these attempts were rejected, and he was not permitted to retake the course.

Explain what options were available to Mr. Bell in these circumstances. Would your answer be any different if you understood that the course required Mr. Bell to interact with the community, including people at risk, and that his failing grade, and the terms and conditions imposed, related to making sure that no damage was done to the people he was dealing with?

4. Capital Quality Homes, Ltd. v. Colwym Construction Ltd.

The plaintiff paid a $13 980 deposit to the defendant for some undeveloped land in Windsor, Ontario. The agreement involved the conveyance of 26 separate building lots, and the defendant was required to deliver 26 individual deeds of conveyance, one for each building lot. After the contract was entered into by the parties but before it was executed, legislation was passed bringing planning consent for the land in question under the control of a designated committee. The parties disagreed about who bore the obligation to get the required consents.

At the closing date, the defendant was unable to deliver the individual deeds required, even though the plaintiff was ready to pay the required funds. It should be noted that this change of law took place only 33 days before the closing date for the transfer of the property, and it is questionable whether it was possible to obtain the required consent in time.

The plaintiff sued for the return of the $13 980 deposit paid. Explain the likely outcome. Would your answer be affected if the reason consent was not obtained was that the defendant had made no effort to obtain the required consents?

5. Strata Corp. NW 1714 v. Winkler

Winkler was a contractor who agreed to erect a building on behalf of Strata Corporation according to certain specifications. When it was built, it failed to meet those specifications. There was insufficient depth of fill under the concrete floor; the floor itself was not of sufficient thickness; and Winkler had also failed to properly waterproof the walls. Strata Corporation claimed damages in the amount of $170 000, the amount it would take to rebuild the building to the stated specifications. The judge made a finding of fact that if the court awarded the $170 000, it would far exceed any reduction in value caused by the work that had been done improperly. Explain the arguments available on both sides and the likely outcome.

6. Computer Workshops v. Banner Capital Market Brokers

Banner, the defendant in this action, was in the brokerage industry and was developing a computer software network to handle his business. The plaintiff, Computer Workshops Ltd., entered into an agreement with Banner to provide him with the necessary hardware and software equipment to do the job. After 25 of the 100 computers agreed to were delivered, Banner discovered that Computer Workshops was negotiating with Banner's competition to provide them with a similar system with similar capabilities. Banner learned that in those discussions, certain confidential information that he had given to Computer Workshops had been disclosed to their competitor. Banner refused to take the rest of the computers.

Computer Workshops sued for breach. Explain the arguments on both sides and any defence that might be available to Banner in these circumstances.

Commercial Transactions

The world of commerce involves myriad individual transactions which, taken together, create markets that establish the economic structure of our society. Whether these transactions are associated with complex commercial activities or simple purchases, they are all controlled by an involved set of rules embodied in both common law and legislation. This section examines that complex body of rules. Chapter 9 examines transactions involving the sale of goods, the *Sale of Goods Act,* and the various statutes that are now in place intended to protect the consumer. Chapter 10 looks at secured transactions and the legislation controlling activities involving the use of personal property as security and the other means used by creditors to ensure that they get paid first by a debtor. This chapter also covers negotiable instruments and bankruptcy.

First Light

Sales and Consumer Protection

The preceding four chapters were devoted to a general examination of the law of contracts. It should be apparent that this body of law has been developed by the courts rather than enacted through legislation. Although some incidental statutes modify particular aspects of contract law, it is still accurate to say that the law of contracts is based primarily on case law. There are, however, two particular areas where legislation has been enacted that profoundly affect the contractual relationship. The first part of this chapter is devoted to legislative statutes relating to the sale of goods. The second part of the chapter deals with consumer protection legislation.

Dominion Home Improvements Ltd. v. Knuude[1]

Mrs. Knuude was an 80-year-old homeowner who was approached by a door-to-door sales representative for a home improvements company. The representative told Mrs. Knuude she had a problem with her windows that needed fixing. After four hours of extremely-high-pressure selling, which included a refusal to leave unless the contract was signed, the sales representative left with a contract signed by her for repair and installation of an aluminum soffit, eavestroughs, flashing, repairing a damp wall, and weatherstripping all the doors and windows in the house. Mrs. Knuude signed a $300 cheque as a deposit but stopped payment on it immediately after the salesman left.

The next day, workers from the firm came to do the work and she insisted they leave. This brought the sales representative back, who, by devious means, persuaded her to reinstate the contract. The work was done. She again refused to pay, and the company sued for the money owed under the contract.

The judge determined that this was a clear case of fraud, that the contract was not binding on her as it was unconscionable, and that it did not conform to the requirements set out in the provincial consumer protection act. This is an example

1. (1986) 20 C.L.R. 192 (Ont. Dist. Ct)

of the unscrupulous business practices engaged in by some people that have led to the increase in legislation designed to protect consumers, the subject matter of this chapter.

The Sale of Goods

The *Sale of Goods Act*

The *Sale of Goods Act* is another example of the summation and codification by the British parliament of the case law in place in the 19th century. This statute was adopted with only minor variations by every common law province in Canada.

The primary purpose of the act is to imply the terms that the parties to sale-of-goods transactions often leave out. For example, the parties may not specify a date for payment or time of delivery, and the act will imply the missing terms into the contract. Note that the act only provides missing terms, and so, the stated intention of the parties will override the provisions of the act. Note as well that the *Sale of Goods Act* not only applies to retail and consumer transactions but also to all situations where goods are bought and sold, even significant commercial transactions involving large machinery, such as railway locomotives or earth-moving equipment.

Sale of Goods Act implies terms into contract

Parties can contract out of provisions of the act

The *Sale of Goods Act* should be viewed as a supplement to the common law rules of contract, as set out in the previous four chapters. Those rules apply to sale-of-goods transactions as well, the act complementing rather than overriding them. Thus, offer and acceptance, as well as consideration, capacity, legality, and intention, must be present for the contract to be formed. Also the rules with respect to mistake, misrepresentation, privity, and breach apply to the contract.

All other contract rules must be complied with

Goods and Services

The *Sale of Goods Act* only affects those contracts involving goods. Goods are tangible items, such as watches, televisions, books, and so on. The term "goods" does not include real estate but does include crops still growing on land. Buildings and building materials are subject to the *Sale of Goods Act* until they become attached to the land, and then, they are treated as part of the real property and not subject to the act. Contracts for intangibles, such as services or the exchange of negotiable instruments, stocks, bonds, and other documents representing rights or claims (referred to as a **chose in action**), are not covered by the act. Transactions involving both goods and services can pose a problem. When a lawyer makes a will or an artist paints a portrait, the client gets a physical item, the will or portrait, but the main component of the transaction is the service provided, and so, the *Sale of Goods Act* will not apply. Note that if the client were to then resell the portrait, the act would apply. Sometimes, the service and sale of goods components of a transaction can be separated, as when parts are installed to repair an automobile. Then, the *Sale of Goods Act* will apply to the goods portion of that contract. Note as well that when only services are involved, the court may still be willing to imply terms, such as the requirement of a certain level of quality, even though the *Sale of Goods Act* does not apply.

Act applies only to sale of goods

Gee v. White Spot Ltd. and Pan et al. v. White Spot Ltd.[2]

In July 1985, Mr. Gee went to the White Spot restaurant and ordered a meal. Unfortunately, the food was contaminated, and Mr. Gee suffered botulism poisoning. He sued White Spot, claiming compensation for the serious damages he suffered. The judge first had to determine whether the *Sale of Goods Act* applied to this transaction. He decided that since the primary purpose of the transaction was to obtain the food, a chattel, and that the service component was incidental, the *Sale of Goods Act* applied to the purchase. The judge then looked at Section 18(b) of the act that required the goods to be of merchantable quality. This meant that the food had to be fit for the purpose it was normally used, that is, fit for human consumption. He also looked at Section 18(a), which provides that when the skill of the seller is relied on and it is in the normal course of the business to supply the goods, those goods have to be fit for the purpose for which they are purchased. The goods failed these tests, and Mr. Gee was successful in his action, the contract of purchase having been breached.

Note that even though there was some service element involved, the court had no problem finding that this was the sale of a good. This case is also instructive in that it shows how the court dealt with the quality requirement as it applies to food and the liability faced which went far beyond the cost of the meal.

Transfer of Goods

Goods must be transferred

The *Sale of Goods Act* only applies when it can be demonstrated that the parties intended that the actual possession and property of the goods would transfer to the buyer. Often, goods are used to secure a loan, and although a **bill of sale** is sometimes used to create that security, there is no expectation that the goods will actually change hands, and the *Sale of Goods Act* does not apply. Where a conditional sale is involved, however, the act does apply, since a true sale does take place, with title eventually passing to the buyer after the appropriate payments are made. These secured transactions will be discussed in the following chapter.

Monetary Consideration

Act does not apply to barter

It is also necessary that monetary consideration be given for the goods for the *Sale of Goods Act* to apply. Money must change hands. The act does not cover barter transactions but where goods are traded in and some money is exchanged, the *Sale of Goods Act* does apply.

Requirement of Writing

Some provinces require evidence in writing

Originally, the *Statute of Frauds* required that contracts involving the sale of goods over a certain value be evidenced in writing. Today, these requirements are included in the *Sale of Goods Act* of some provinces, where goods exceeding $30 to $50 (depending on the jurisdiction) must be evidenced in writing for the contract to be enforceable. Of course, part payment or performance will also make the contract enforceable. Sometimes, the buyer will give something in earnest (anything of value) to make the contract binding. Some provinces, for example, British Columbia, Ontario and Manitoba, have eliminated any writing requirement in sale of goods transactions.

2. (1986) 32 D.L.R. (4th) 238 (B.C.S.C.)

Title and Risk

When the title to the goods does not transfer immediately upon the sale agreement being concluded, it is called an **agreement to sell**. Determining who has title at any given time is important because under the *Sale of Goods Act,* whoever has title bears the risk of damage or destruction to the goods, unless the parties have agreed otherwise. There are three common methods whereby the parties override the *Sale of Goods Act* by specifying when title transfers or who will bear the risk.

Distinction between sale and agreement to sell

Normally risk follows title

Exceptions for assumptions of risk

1. **C.I.F. contracts (cost, insurance, and freight).** In this type of contract, the buyer may obtain title at an early stage in the transaction, but the seller has assumed responsibility to pay for the costs involved in the shipping of those goods as well as arranging insurance to a specific point in the process, such as to the transport service or the destination.

2. **F.O.B. contracts (free on board).** With F.O.B. contracts, the parties have specified that the seller will bear the risk until a specified point in the transport process. This might be when the goods are placed on board the carrier chosen to transport them to the buyer or when the carrier delivers the goods to the designated destination or at any other designated point in the process. At that point, the buyer assumes the risk.

3. **C.O.D. contracts (cash on delivery).** This type of contract entitles the seller to maintain both the proprietary rights or title as well as control over the possession of those goods until they are delivered to the buyer's premises and paid for. The risk stays with the seller until delivery at the specified location is complete.

Bills of lading are also often used by the seller to maintain control over the goods during shipment. A **bill of lading** is a document given by the transporter or carrier of the goods to the shipper as a form of receipt. The person designated as the consignee on a bill of lading has the right to take delivery of the goods at their destination. A straight bill of lading usually names the buyer as the consignee on the document; the shipper/seller no longer has control, and the risk shifts to the buyer during shipping. When **order bills of lading** are used, shippers name themselves as consignees and retain the right to receive the goods at their destination or to designate that right to someone else. Sellers who have maintained control in this way bear responsibility for the goods until they have reached their destination subject to any other provisions that may be in the contract of sale itself. It should be noted that the use of order bills of lading provides sellers with maximum flexibility and facilitates such arrangements as financing, in which the goods are used as security.

Bills of lading may determine title

George Smith Trucking Co. Ltd. v. Golden Seven Enterprises Inc. et al.[3]

Intercontinental, the seller, was a meat-packing business in Saskatchewan that sold meat products to Golden Seven Enterprises, the buyer. These goods were to be resold by the buyer to certain customers in Japan. George Smith Trucking Co. Ltd., the trucker, a Manitoba trucking company, was engaged by the buyer to transport the meat from Saskatchewan to Vancouver, where it would then be shipped directly to Japan. These shipments were to be made in a series of installments, each to be paid for separately.

3. (1989) 55 D.L.R. (4th) 161 (B.C.C.A.)

Unfortunately, the buyer ran into financial troubles. Two installments had been shipped and the third completed for shipping, but none had been paid for. The seller claimed to still have title to the goods because they had retained certain documentation from the buyer until payment. The seller then arranged to resell the goods directly to Japan, bypassing the buyer. The trucking company, which had not been paid, brought this action to stop that sale, realizing that it would only have a claim for its transport fee against the goods if its title were still in the hands of their customer, the buyer.

The court held that the withholding of the documents was not for the purpose of controlling title but to pressure payment and so had to look to the *Sale of Goods Act* or the terms of the contract of sale to determine when title transferred. In fact, the contract provided for the goods to be shipped to the F.O.B. point of shipping. This meant that title in the goods transferred when they were loaded on the trucks in Saskatchewan. Risk also transferred at that time. Because title had transferred to the buyer, the trucking company was entitled to its lien against the goods and its fee for transporting the goods to Vancouver. Although there are very specific rules set out in the *Sale of Goods Act* determining when title transfers, those rules can be overridden by the agreement. Using the F.O.B. designation is an example of the stated intention of the parties overriding the act. The implications can be significant, determining not only who bears the risk but also, as in this case, determining who has first claim on the goods and whether the transporter can recover the shipment fee.

Transfer of Title

Remedy may depend on who has title

The timing of the transfer of the property or title of the goods can control more than risk. Whoever has the proprietary interest will determine whether the seller can sue for the entire price of the goods or merely for damages upon default by the purchaser. The time of the transfer of title and risk will be implied according to the following rules when the parties do not indicate otherwise.[4]

Rules for determining title

Rule 1

> Where there is an unconditional contract for the sale of specific goods in a deliverable state, the property in the goods passes to the buyer when the contract is made, and it is immaterial whether the time of payment or the time of delivery or both are postponed.

Title transfers immediately

This rule states that when the contract involves the sale of a specifically identified and finished item, the proprietary interest transfers to the buyer at the time the contract is made. For example, if Lynch walked into Amann's TV store on Thursday night, pointed to a television set and said, "I want to buy that one," the property in that television would transfer to Lynch as soon as Amann accepted the offer. If the TV is destroyed by fire before it is picked up, Lynch will bear the risk. Note that who actually pays will often be determined by the nature of the insurance coverage.

Rule 2

> Where there is a contract for the sale of specific goods and the seller is bound to do something to the goods for the purpose of putting

---

4. These provisions are taken from Section 21 of the *Sale of Goods Act*. References to the act throughout this chapter refer to the *Sale of Goods Act*, R.S.O. (1990 c.S.1). Every province has a similar act, although the wording of the provisions may vary.

them into a deliverable state, the property does not pass until such thing is done and the buyer has notice thereof.

When some modification or repair must be made to the goods, title does not transfer until that is done and the buyer notified. This notice usually comes in the form of delivery of the goods, but it would probably be sufficient notice for the seller to telephone the buyer and say, "Your goods are ready." In the example used earlier, if Lynch required that Amann repair a scratch on the television set before taking delivery, the title and risk would still be with Amann at the time of the fire, unless Lynch had been informed that his TV was ready for pick-up.

Rule 3

Where there is a contract for the sale of specific goods in a deliverable state, but the seller is bound to weigh, measure, test, or do some other act or thing with reference to the goods for the purpose of ascertaining the price, the property does not pass until the act or thing is done and the buyer has notice thereof.

The provisions of this rule are similar to those set out in Rule 2, but the goods must be weighed, measured, or tested and notice given before title and risk will pass to the buyer. For example, if Schmidt agreed to purchase a particular truckload of potatoes from Naslund, it would probably be necessary to weigh the load to determine the exact price. Title to the potatoes would only transfer to Schmidt after the weighing was completed and notice given.

Rule 4

When goods are delivered to the buyer on approval or on "sale or return" or other similar terms, the property in them passes to the buyer:

(a) when he signifies his approval or acceptance to the seller or does any other act adopting the transaction, or

(b) if he does not signify his approval or acceptance to the seller but retains the goods without giving notice of rejection, then if a time has been fixed for the return of the goods on the expiration of that time, and if no time has been fixed on the expiration of a reasonable time and what is a reasonable time is a question of fact.

This rule covers situations in which goods are taken by the buyer to test for a trial period before deciding to keep them. Here, title transfers when the buyer indicates acceptance to the seller or does something indicating he has accepted the goods, such as installing them in his home or car. If a time for trial has been specified, title transfers after the expiration of that time period or in the absence of that after a reasonable time.

In our earlier example, if Amann had allowed Lynch to take the television home and try it for four days, title and risk would not transfer to Lynch until the expiration of those four days, unless Lynch notified Amann before that time that he was happy with the goods. Title would pass earlier if Lynch resold the TV or built it into the wall of his den.

Rule 5

(a) When there is a contract for the sale of unascertained or future goods by description, and goods of that description and in a deliverable state are unconditionally appropriated to the contract, either by the seller with the assent of the buyer, or by the buyer with the assent of the seller, the property in the goods thereupon passes to the buyer. Such assent may be express or implied and may be given either before or after the appropriation is made.

(b) If pursuant to the contract the seller delivers the goods to the buyer or to a carrier or other bailee (whether named by the buyer or not) for the purpose of transmission to the buyer and does not reserve the right to disposal, he shall be deemed to have unconditionally appropriated the goods to the contract.

The goods covered by Rule 5 are those that have not been manufactured at the time the contract was entered into or that exist but have not yet been separated out and identified as the particular goods to be used in a given transaction. Normally, in the example above, Lynch would not be given the TV set on display but would be given one like it from storage. Rule 5 would apply because no specific goods have yet been appropriated to the contract at the time of the sale. Rule 5 also applies when a person orders something that has not yet been manufactured, such as an order for a new car.

Only when the goods have been manufactured or separated out and unconditionally committed to the buyer with the buyer's assent does title pass. While notice to the buyer that the goods are ready may be the most common method of satisfying the assent or approval provision, assent is often implied from the circumstances. Thus, if a person were to leave her car with a dealer for the installation of a new stereo cassette player, she will be taken to have assented to the selection of the stereo when it is installed, since she left her car there for that purpose.

It must always be remembered that the parties can specify a contrary intention in the contract, overriding these rules with respect to title and risk. Great care should be used in examining the terms of the contract to determine whether this has been done.

When goods are not manufactured or identifiable as goods in question, unconditional appropriation and assent needed

Re Royal Bank of Canada and Saskatchewan Telecommunications [5]

Tritec built pre-fabricated buildings and was in the process of building several for Saskatchewan Telecommunications. When finished, the buildings were to be transported to northern Saskatchewan and bolted to timbers in the ground. During the construction, the Royal Bank of Canada put Tritec into receivership and seized the unfinished buildings.

The court had to decide who was entitled to the buildings upon completion, and in order to do that, they had to determine whether the *Sale of Goods Act* applied. Was this a contract for the sale of a chattel or of the construction of a building? Because the degree of connection to the ground was slight and the buildings were essentially portable, the situation was covered by the *Sale of Goods Act* and there being no provisions in the contract otherwise, the provisions of the act relating to the transfer of title applied.

Since the goods were in the process of being built, this was an agreement for sale and covered by Rule 5. Title only transfers when the goods have been unconditionally appropriated to the contract with the assent of the other party and as this had not yet happened, the Royal Bank had first claim on the buildings.

5. (1985) 20 D.L.R. (4th) 415 (Sask. C.A.)

When title passes can be very important, not just when the goods are destroyed or damaged but also in situations like this, where the seller, or buyer for that matter, goes into receivership or becomes bankrupt. Who has title will not only determine who bears the risk but also who has first claim to the goods in the event of default.

Rights and Obligations of the Parties

Hunter Engineering Co. v. Syncrude Canada Ltd.[6]

As part of its tar sands extraction project in Northern Alberta, Syncrude used a large conveyor belt to carry sand over long distances. Syncrude contracted with two different American firms to supply a number of gear-boxes for the system. Both companies, Hunter Engineering and Allis Chalmers, went to the same subcontractor to manufacture these gears, and they were all made to the same design and specifications. Unfortunately, several failed, and the others were examined and found to have cracks suggesting that all the gearboxes supplied by both companies would fail in the future. Syncrude had to expend considerable funds to repair the defects and sued both Hunter Engineering and Allis Chalmers seeking compensation. Both companies admitted that the gears were defective, but both claimed that they were protected by clauses in their contracts restricting their liability to a limited period of time, which had expired.

The court found that this was a transaction covered by the *Sale of Goods Act* and that the provision requiring the manufactured goods to be fit for the purpose for which they were used when the skill of the supplier was relied on was an implied term of the contract. The court then had to determine whether the exemption clauses contained in the contracts overrode the operation of the act.

The court found that although the Hunter Engineering contract had a provision limiting the time they were liable, it did not contain a clause specifically exempting the operation of the *Sale of Goods Act* provisions. Therefore, they were still in force, and Hunter was liable to Syncrude. The Allis Chalmers contract, on the other hand, did contain such a clause specifically excluding any statutory warranties or conditions other than those specifically included in the contract, and since the time limit for the warranty had expired, there was no liability. It was also argued that if the breach was fundamental, this exemption clause could not stand. The Supreme Court of Canada held that even in the face of such a fundamental breach, it is possible for the parties to exempt themselves from liability, and this was what Allis Chalmers had effectively done in this instance.

The above case not only illustrates that the *Sale of Goods Act* applies to business as well as consumer transactions even where massive machinery is involved, but also that the parties can contract out of the provisions, if they wish, and that even the principle of fundamental breach can be overcome by a very careful and specifically worded exemption clause. Fundamental breach was discussed in more detail in the previous chapter.

The *Sale of Goods Act* implies both conditions and warranties into the contract. The difference is important. An implied warranty is a minor term, and its breach does not discharge the victim from the rest of their contractual obligations, whereas the breach of an implied condition allows the victim to treat the contract as ended.

Conditions and warranties under *Sale of Goods Act*

6. [1989] 1 S.C.R. 426

Note that the parties can designate a term that would normally be a warranty as a condition and vice versa, but the court always retains the power to make the final determination, no matter what the term is called in the contract.

A breach of a condition does not always bring a contract to an end. The victim of a breach of a condition has the option to ignore it or treat it as a breach of warranty. The victim of a breach may also lose the right to have a contract discharged by a breach of condition by accepting the goods. In our example of the television set purchased from Amann's television store, Lynch would be entitled to return the set and demand a refund if he had specified as a condition of the contract that the television had a remote control device and he did not discover until he got it home that his set did not have one. But if he set up the TV knowing that there was no remote and watched it over the weekend anyway, he has accepted the goods and cannot return the set, although he could still sue for damages for the reduced value.

Acceptance causes victims of breach to lose right of discharge

Title

The *Sale of Goods Act* implies several terms into sales agreements that cover a seller's right to sell goods to a buyer. Section 13(a) of the Ontario *Sale of Goods Act* makes it a condition that the seller has the right to sell the goods or will have the right at the time title is to be transferred. Thus, Amann breaches a condition of the contract if he does not own and has no right to acquire the television set he tries to sell to Lynch. Lynch would be free from any further obligation under the contract.

Seller must convey good title

Section 13(b) requires that the seller provide quiet possession of the goods as a warranty of the contract. This means that the goods must be delivered in such a condition that they can be used and enjoyed by the buyer in the way they were intended, free from any interference. This is broader than Section 13(a) in that it goes beyond problems with title to cover such things as the infringement of copyright or patent. Since the buyer would be prevented from using the product, this would interfere with his right to quiet enjoyment.

—and quiet possession

Section 13(c) of the act specifies that it shall be an implied warranty of the contract that the goods shall be free from any charge or encumbrance that has not been disclosed to the buyer. These are referred to as **liens** and give the lien holder a prior claim on the goods for the amount owed. Secured transactions will be discussed in the next chapter. The purchaser should do a title search at the appropriate registry office before buying, but even if this is not done and a lien is present, because of Section 13(c), the purchaser has the right to claim against the seller for any losses.

—and goods free from charge or encumbrance

Description

Goods are often sold on the Internet and by catalogue, mail order, or other forms of distance shopping. In such circumstances, the goods are sold by description that involves text often accompanied by a picture or illustration. Section 14 of the Ontario *Sale of Goods Act* provides that when the sale is accomplished by description, there shall be an implied condition in contracts that the goods delivered must match the description or illustration provided. If Afsari based her order on the Internet for a new camera from an illustration showing a Nikon F100 camera and the camera that Afsari eventually received was a Nikon F80, there has been a breach of the implied condition that the goods match the description.

Goods must match description

Most sales of manufactured goods are by description

Sale by description includes the sale of all manufactured goods even when sold in self-service situations. Because one manufactured item is virtually indistinguishable from another of the same make and model, the purchaser is relying on the general description provided by the manufacturer. Even when a sample is inspected, the item must match the manufacturer's description whether that description is found on the box or in a specification sheet, brochure, or catalogue.

Goods bought on-line must match the description or picture provided.
Stone/Andreas Pollok

Fitness and Quality

Another condition the *Sale of Goods Act* implies into a sale by description is that the goods provided must be of a merchantable quality (Section 15 of the Ontario act). This means that the goods must be free of any defect that would have persuaded the purchaser not to buy them at the agreed-upon price if the purchaser had known of the defect at the outset. If a sample has been inspected, the defect must not have been readily apparent upon examination. This provision has become much more important in modern times because of the broader approach taken by the courts as to what qualifies as sale by description. It is now clear that this provision applies to virtually all sales of mass-produced goods.

Goods must be of merchantable quality

A similar provision requires that if the purchaser has relied on the skill and ability of the salesperson to advise on the suitability of a particular product for an intended purpose, there is an implied condition that the product will be reasonably fit for that purpose. This applies when the goods are being used for some unique purpose but also applies when they are being used normally. This is the section applicable to the *Hunter* case discussed above.

Goods must be suitable for purpose of purchase when sales person relied upon

When goods are asked for by trade name, this section does not apply; however, it must be clear that when this is done, the skill of the seller is not being relied on.[7] Also, if it is not in the seller's course of business to sell the product, this provision does not apply.

If Florio were to buy a particular kind of paint from McGregor's paint company after asking if it were suitable for concrete and later found that the paint peeled, Florio would be able to sue McGregor for compensation because of the breach of the implied condition that the goods would be reasonably suitable for their intended purpose, but if he bought it by trade name, disregarding any recommendations from the sales staff, he would only have himself to blame.

British Columbia has recently expanded this part of their *Sale of Goods Act*, making these provisions apply to leased goods as well and also adding a provision that the goods be "durable for a reasonable period of time."[8] While these provisions do not relieve the purchaser of the obligation to be cautious, they do provide for a certain minimum level of protection and quality.

Goods must be durable in B.C.

7. Baldry v. Marshall [1925] 1 K.B. 260 (C.A.)

8. *Sale of Goods Act*, R.S.B.C. (1996) Chapter 410, Section 18(c)

Product Liability Where Seller Relies on Manufacturer's or Retailer's Instructions

Eli Lilly Canada sold a herbicide to the Caners, who applied it to their crop. In the first year this was done, the crop grew with large areas of weed infestation, the herbicide having failed to do the job. The next year, after consulting with Eli Lilly, they treated the field with the herbicide again and the result was essentially that the crop did not grow at all. Eli Lilly claimed that in the first year, the Caners did not follow the instructions properly and failed to apply the herbicide evenly and that in the second year, Mr. Caner sowed his crop too deeply. The court found that the instructions provided were imprecise, and therefore under the *Sale of Goods Act*, the warranty as to fitness and quality was breached. It is interesting that at the trial level, the court found contributory negligence and reduced the award accordingly, but at the appeal level, the judge specifically said that contributory negligence, as found in the *Tortfeasors and Contributory Negligence Act* of Manitoba, did not apply to sale of goods actions.

Caners v. Eli Lilly Canada Inc., 134 D.L.R. (4th) 730 (Man. C.A.).

Sample

Goods must match sample and be free of significant hidden defects

The act uses a similar approach for the purchase of goods after examining a sample. When an order for goods is placed after inspecting a sample, the bulk of the goods delivered must correspond to that sample. The goods must also be free from any hidden defects that would have persuaded the purchaser not to buy them at that price if he or she had been aware of the defects when inspecting the sample. For example, if the load of bricks Tsang bought from Cashin after first inspecting a sample brick looked fine but, in fact, had not been baked properly and disintegrated after being used in Tsang's building, the bricks would be of unmerchantable quality, a breach of an implied condition of the contract.

Parties free to contract out

It must be re-emphasized that, under the terms of the *Sale of Goods Act*, the parties are generally free to include clauses that override the provisions set out in the act. Most sales contracts for manufactured goods contain "warranties," including exculpatory clauses, which try to reduce or exclude these obligations relating to fitness and quality. If such clauses are carefully worded, they can override these provisions unless prohibited by statute. In the Hunter case discussed above, the exemption clause was effective with respect to Allis-Chalmers, but not with respect to Hunter, which had not excluded the implied conditions of the statute. Most jurisdictions in Canada have enacted legislation prohibiting the seller from excluding or limiting these provisions relating to fitness and quality in consumer sales transactions. In B.C., this prohibition is found in the *Sale of Goods Act*. Elsewhere, it is included along with a specific list of the warranties in the consumer protection acts of the respective provinces. Consumer protection legislation will be discussed below.

Other Implied Terms

Where price omitted— reasonable price

Time, payment, and place for delivery implied terms

There are several other terms that are implied by the *Sale of Goods Act* unless otherwise specified by the parties. Where no price is stated, a reasonable price must be paid for goods. Delivery must take place within a reasonable time, and payment is due upon delivery. The time of payment will be treated as a warranty, but whether the time of delivery will be treated as a condition or a warranty will be implied from the conduct of the parties. When bulk goods, such as grains, lumber, and ore, are involved, if significantly too little or too much is delivered, the buyer is free to either reject the goods or keep them and pay for them at the contracted rate. The provisions affecting delivery, place, time, and quantity of the goods are usually made conditions by the parties.

Remedies on Default

When the buyer defaults, the seller has an unpaid seller's lien against the goods, giving the seller the right to retain the goods until appropriate payment has been made, even though title may have transferred.

Unpaid seller's lien and ***stoppage in transitu***

Similarly, when the goods are en route to the buyer, upon default, the seller has the right to intercept them and retake possession from the transporter, so long as the goods have not yet reached the buyer. This is referred to as the seller's right of *stoppage in transitu.*

Normally, in the absence of any secured credit arrangement, if the goods get into the hands of the buyer, they become part of the buyer's estate and may be claimed by other creditors. Recent changes in the *Bankruptcy and Insolvency Act,* however, allow a supplier of such goods to retake those goods if, within 30 days of delivery, the debtor has become bankrupt or a receiver has been appointed and, of course, provided the debtor or trustee still has them.

Seller protected in case of bankruptcy

In the event of a breach, the seller retains all the normal breach of contract remedies that were discussed in the previous chapter. And in some special circumstances where the sale of goods is involved, the seller may be able to sue for the entire purchase price rather than just damages in the event of a breach. For example, when title has transferred and payment is in default, in effect, the buyer is refusing to take his own goods. But the seller must be careful and do nothing inconsistent with his continued willingness to perform. If he tries to sell the goods to someone else, for example, he will no longer be able to sue for the whole price, just for what he has lost on the sale. These losses will normally include the costs involved in restocking and resale, and where the goods are resold at a lower price, that loss will be included as well. The seller also has an obligation to mitigate losses, which usually requires the seller to take steps to resell the goods immediately. When a deposit is involved, the seller can keep the deposit. This is not the case where the pre-payment is a down payment only. In fact, it may well not be worth the effort if it is not possible to sue for the actual price of the goods.

Seller still entitled to sue for damages for breach

Seller can sue for price in cases of default or refusal of delivery once title has passed

9. Geist, Michael. *Internet Law in Canada,* (Toronto, Ont: Captus Press Inc., 2000) p. 475.

Purchaser's remedies those of contract law

The remedies available to the buyer if the seller defaults are those of general contract law. Where misrepresentation is involved, the purchaser may be able to rescind the contract or seek damages when there has been fraud or negligence. Where a condition of the contract is breached, the buyer may refuse to perform or demand return of any money paid; but if only a warranty is breached, the buyer must go through with the deal, subject to a right for damages. The damages usually are determined by what it costs to bring the goods up to the specifications in the original contract or their reduction in value because of the breach. But when there are additional injuries suffered because of the delay in obtaining the goods or the defect involved, the buyer will be able to claim them as well.

Extent of damages depends on circumstances

Defective goods sometimes cause physical injury, and these damages can also be claimed as long as they were reasonably within the contemplation of the parties at the time the contract was entered into. Thus, someone who suffers food poisoning because of poor-quality food at a restaurant, as in the *Gee* case discussed above, can seek compensation for their injuries under the *Sale of Goods Act* provisions, and those damages can be substantial. When unique goods are involved, the buyer may also be able to claim a remedy of specific performance and force the seller to go through with the sale rather than pay damages in compensation.

Finally, it should be mentioned that most provinces have enacted an international sale of goods act. The federal government is a signatory to a United Nations convention along with many other nations, and the provincial legislation is intended to implement that international treaty. A great deal of trading today is done in the international arena, and these statutes are intended to bring the same kind of structure and certainty to import and export dealings as the *Sale of Goods Act* provides domestically.

What should a business consider?

Business people should always be aware of the operation of the *Sale of Goods Act*, especially the provisions related to fitness and quality. Even in large commercial transactions, it is important to specify the nature and limits of the obligations of the parties where the sales of goods are involved to avoid unwanted terms from being implied into the contract. This is true even where heavy-duty machinery is involved, as was the case in the *Hunter Engineering* case discussed above. In that case, one of the suppliers included an exculpatory clause specifying the limits of their liability, and the other supplier did not. The *Sale of Goods Act* provisions relating to quality applied to that transaction making them responsible for defects in their product in a way that they had not allowed for. Such unexpected and unplanned for responsibility can have devastating results not anticipated in the price charged. And so, whether buyer or seller, it is important to keep in mind that the *Sale of Goods Act* applies in any circumstances where goods are being transferred for money.

Untangling the WEB

The United Nations has created a Model Code on Electronic Commerce, and its terms have been largely incorporated into the *Uniform Electronic Commerce Act* drafted by the Uniform Law Conference of Canada. Although this has not been passed as formal legislation in Canada, it has been approved for distribution to all Canadian jurisdictions as a guideline for the creation of new provincial legislation and to encourage compliance with a common set of goals and practices. You can view the entire act at <http://www.law.ualberta.ca/alri/ulc/current/euecatin.htm>

Consumer Protection Legislation

Rushak v. Henneken[10]

Mrs. Rushak went with a friend to purchase a used car. She had a look at a very attractive 1982 Mercedes sports model. (The trial judge later said that the car was "of such peerless beauty that ... she appears to have cast a hypnotic spell upon all who had dealings with her.") The salesperson was Mr. Henneken, who was also the owner of the car lot.

The car had been imported from Germany, and Mr. Henneken knew that cars from Germany often had a problem with rust. He told her that he knew the owner, that the car was one of the best of its kind in Vancouver, and that it was generally a very nice car, a "good vehicle." Some minor rust was pointed out to her, and she was advised to have the car checked out by a Mercedes dealer. In fact, the car was taken to a mechanic who reported only minor surface rust but also suggested it be taken to a Mercedes dealer. It was put on a hoist and her friend and others, including Mr. Henneken, looked at it, and all thought it looked pretty good.

Mrs. Rushak bought the car but could not get used to driving the standard transmission, so she let it sit for a year. When she tried to sell it, she discovered serious mechanical and rust problems. The estimate was $10 000 just to fix the rust. When she sued Mr. Henneken, she found that there was no remedy under common law or the *Sale of Goods Act* because they had maintained all along that the car should be inspected by a Mercedes dealer. But the court also found that Mr. Henneken's statement that the car was "the best in Vancouver" and that it was a "good vehicle" was a violation and actionable under the *Trade Practices Act,* even though Mr. Henneken was acting honestly and was not intentionally misleading the purchaser. This illustrates how important and extensive consumer protection legislation is. The judge in this case said, "While it used to be said that what is described in general terms as 'puffery' on the part of the salesman does not give rise to legal consequences, I am not satisfied that the same can necessarily be said today, in light of the provisions of the *Trade Practices Act*; 'puffery' cannot, in my view, excuse the giving of an unqualified opinion as to quality when the supplier has factual knowledge indicating that the opinion may, in an important respect, very well be wrong."

The second major area where legislation has been introduced that has a major impact on contractual relations is in the area of consumer transactions. Consumer transactions involve goods or services purchased by individuals rather than corporations, for personal use and not for resale or for business purposes.

> **Consumer transaction involves purchases for personal consumption rather than business use**

Although consumer protection statutes vary greatly, they do have common objectives. They impose standards and responsibilities on manufacturers and suppliers of goods. They control the use and disclosure of information, and they control unethical or otherwise unacceptable business practices. The rest of this chapter will examine these areas and consider the regulatory bodies created to enforce these statutes. Although provincial statutes predominate, there is also considerable federal legislation in the field.

> **Statutes impose standards**

10. (1991) 84 D.L.R. (4th) 87 (B.C.C.A.)

Although the main purpose of the *Sale of Goods Act* is to imply terms into a contract, which the parties have omitted, some provisions have a consumer protection aspect to them. A form of consumer protection legislation has been present in our legal system for centuries, but in the past several decades, statutes which have significantly expanded and modified the law in this area have been passed.

Until recently, the common contractual themes of *caveat emptor* and freedom of contract dominated consumer transactions. But because of the vulnerability of consumers to abuse and their weakened bargaining position with respect to those they deal with, limits have been placed on those principles. In most provinces, this legislation is found in one *Consumer Protection Act,* although some jurisdictions have added another, referred to as the *Trade Practices* or *Business Practices Act.* Canada has recently released consumer protection guidelines for Internet transactions and they can be found at the Office of Consumer Affairs Canada web site: <http://strategis. ic.gc.ca/SSG/ca01185e.html>.

Statutes prevent abuse

Responsibility for Goods Sold

The *Sale of Goods Act,* in different provinces, has provisions that require that the seller convey good title, and that the goods correspond to their description and sample, and are fit and of merchantable quality. In commercial transactions, these can be contracted out of exemption clauses, but in most provinces in Canada, legislation is in place, removing the right to contract out of these provisions in consumer transactions. New Brunswick, Saskatchewan, and British Columbia have imposed conditions requiring goods to be durable. Pre-contractual statements made by salespeople also become terms of the contract.

Effect of exemption clauses limited by statute

As a result, merchants can no longer rely on exemption clauses to relieve themselves of the obligation to deliver quality goods to the purchaser. Purchasers can now sue for breach of contract and receive significant compensation for their losses when products are unfit even after the expiration of a stated warranty period. This applies to online consumer transactions as well, depending on what state or province has jurisdiction.

When an unsafe product causes injury, not only can the victim sue in tort for negligence, but if they are the buyer, they can also sue the seller for breach of contract under the *Sale of Goods Act.* The damages awarded in such cases can go far beyond a refund of the purchase price, as was the case in *Gee v. White Spot* discussed earlier.

Tort liability requires fault but contract does not

The advantage of suing in contract is that it is only necessary to establish that the contract was breached. It is no help for the defendant to show that " it wasn't his fault." Unfortunately, only the actual buyer can sue for breach. In the case of *Donoghue v. Stevenson* discussed in Chapter 4, Mrs. Donoghue consumed a contaminated bottle of ginger beer given to her by a friend. She could not sue the seller for breach, not being "privy" to the contract, and had to sue the manufacturer for negligence instead. Had Mrs. Donoghue purchased the beer, the seller would have been liable, even though they had no idea that the ginger beer was defective. This case establishes a victim's right to sue the manufacturer in tort. But it is important to understand that in Canada, when suing in tort, it is still necessary to establish that there was fault or negligence on the part of the manufacturer.

Contract liability limited to immediate parties

This is a significant obstacle because often the person who consumes the product is not the purchaser and cannot sue the seller for breach. Some provinces have extended the requirements of fitness and quality to anyone the seller could reasonably foresee might use the product. Others have eliminated privity as a defence where warranties of fitness are implied through their consumer protection acts. The right to sue for breach is thus extended beyond the original parties to the contract, making the seller liable, even when there is no indication of fault on their part. The courts have also shown a willingness to get around the privity problem. In the case of *Murray v. Sperry Rand Corp.*[11] the manufacturer was found liable to the consumer in contract, even though the purchase was made from a retailer. Because false claims were included in the advertising brochures produced by the manufacturer, the court found that there was a subsidiary or collateral contract between manufacturer and purchaser that allowed the consumer to sue the manufacturer directly in contract. This is consistent with the tendency of the courts to abandon the privity principle.

Liability extended by statute

and by collateral contract

Kelly v. Mack Canada Inc. et al.[12]

Mr. Kelly purchased a used White truck from a Mack dealership (Maughans) after being assured by the president of that firm that it had a rebuilt engine, was in good shape, and would be able to do the logging for which it was being purchased. It turned out to be so defective that it could not do the job and required substantial repair. He took the truck back and traded it on a new "Mack" truck for the same purpose. It also proved defective and had to be returned. In this case, he was suing both the dealer as well as the manufacturer for compensation. The first problem was whether he had any right to sue the manufacturer other than in tort. The judge found that the manufacturers warranty created a separate supplemental contract between Mr. Kelly and the manufacturer according to the terms of that contract. Since it only provided for the repair or replacement of the truck and not for its return, the manufacturer had no liability to Mr. Kelly in these circumstances. The provisions of the *Sale of Goods Act*, however, bound the dealer. Since the breach was "fundamental," any exemption clause could not be relied upon and the implied warranty with respect to quality applied to the transaction.

This case is instructive in that it shows that there can be a contract between the manufacturer and the customer, even though there is a retailer in between and also that the liabilities of the manufacturer will vary according to how that contract comes about. Where the contract is part of the agreement of sale, both manufacturer and seller will be liable and the *Sale of Goods Act* will apply to both. Where the manufacturer's warranty is obviously supplemental, as it is here, the liability will be limited to that set out strictly in that agreement, and the *Sale of Goods Act* provisions will not apply. It is also interesting in that both the trial and appeal judges found that exemption clauses set out in the sales contract did not apply because of fundamental breach. Today, because of the *Hunter Engineering* case, it is likely that the expression "fundamental breach" would not be used, but if it were found that the exemption clause was not intended to cover such a basic breach, the exemption clause would still not apply.

The case also shows how the courts determine damages. Here the judge decided that the breach was ongoing from the start, and so no deduction for use or depreciation was awarded. The court also looked at the amount of downtime and lost wages that Mr. Kelly suffered.

11. (1979) 23 O.R. (2d) 456 (Ont. H.C.)
12. (1988) 53 D.L.R. (4th) 476 (Ont. C.A.)

Duty to warn when product hazardous

Some useful products, by their very nature, are hazardous. The obligation of the manufacturer and seller of such products is to make them as safe as possible, warn the potential user of the dangers, and provide information on their proper use. An injured consumer can sue the manufacturer for negligence when these steps are not followed. Except where the danger is obvious, a warning incorporated into the product label must alert the consumer to the hazards associated with the product. If the warning is inadequate, the manufacturer and seller are liable for the injuries that result. Even where the dangers are obvious, as with a sharp knife, the practice is growing for manufacturers to include such a warning, out of an abundance of caution. Federal legislation dealing with the merchandising of dangerous products will be covered later in this chapter. Note that many provinces have extended these consumer protection provisions to cover not only sales but the increasingly common practice of creating long-term leases as well.

Unacceptable Business Practices

Another area of unacceptable abuse involving consumer transactions is where the seller or their representative makes misleading or false statements to persuade people to buy a product. Under common law, these statements would not form part of the contract, and the purchaser would have little recourse. Further, contracts of sale often contain clauses stating that there are no other representations other than those contained in the written document, making any false or misleading claims by salespeople not actionable, unless they are included in the contract.

Legislation incorporates misleading statements into contract

Most provinces have passed legislation making merchants and their agents more responsible for their statements by incorporating these statements into the contract and making any attempt to override them void. Thus, any statements made by salespeople or contained in advertisements become terms of the contract and are actionable as breaches if they prove incorrect or are not honoured. If Mrs. Holberg, the purchaser of a used car from Affleck's Fine Car Co., was informed by the salesperson that the car had only been driven to church on Sundays. That statement would, under these provisions, be incorporated into the contract even if it were not contained in the written document. If Mrs. Holberg could convince the court that a false statement had been made, she could sue for breach of contract when the statement proved false.

This type of provision is included in the New Brunswick and Saskatchewan legislation dealing with consumer product warranties. Other provinces have incorporated similar provisions into unfair business practices legislation, variously referred to as *Trade Practices Act*, *Unfair Trade Practices Act*, and *Business Practices Act*.

Motor Vehicle Manufacturers' Assn. v. Ontario (Ministry of Consumer and Commercial Relations)[13]

The Motor Vehicle Manufacturers' Association (representing the Canadian divisions of Ford, Chrysler, and GM) set up a promotional scheme, whereby certain purchasers of specified cars could choose between two alternative purchasing methods. Under the financing option, they could purchase the car at the stated sales price at a favourable rate of interest, or under the cash-back option, they could purchase the car at a reduced price for cash. An application was made to the court which found that there was no attempt to mislead or hide anything and that in all the association's advertising and promotion, it was made clear that both these choices were available. There was, therefore, no violation of the *Business Practices Act*.

13. (1988) 49 D.L.R. (4th) 592 (Ont. H.C.)

But under Section 24 of the *Consumer Protection Act* of Ontario, they were required to disclose the true cost of borrowing. When the scheme was examined, the court found that Section 24 had been infringed in that the true cost of borrowing had not been disclosed. When the seller is the lender, as in this case, the correct way to calculate the interest rate would have been to calculate it on the reduced price of the car when the purchase was for cash. This would increase the declared interest rate considerably.

These statutes do not just catch disreputable business people who out to cheat their customers. In this case, there is no question of the association attempting to defraud or confuse their customers by these options. While the cost of borrowing as disclosed was not in compliance with the *Consumer Protection Act*, nothing was hidden, and there was no attempt to mislead.

Typically, this type of statute lists several different kinds of misleading and deceptive statements deemed unfair practices. The consumer is given the right to have the contract rescinded or to sue for damages. As mentioned above, contracts will often contain terms stating that there are no other representations other than what appears on the written document, but these statutes make such clauses void, leaving the purchaser free to sue.

Unfair practices identified in statute

This is true even when the parties involved have been relatively innocent, as in the Rushak case discussed above. No one in that case faulted Mr. Henneken's honesty, but the statements he made still qualified as a deceptive practice, and he was required to pay damages to Mrs. Rushak.

The government department involved is also given considerable powers to investigate complaints and to deal with complaints against offending merchandisers, including the powers to impose fines, to suspend licenses, and, in some provinces, even to pursue a civil action on behalf of the consumer. Ontario, Newfoundland, British Columbia, Prince Edward Island, and, to a lesser extent, Manitoba have versions of business practices statutes. There are also many other federal and provincial statutes that contain provisions prohibiting deceptive and misleading statements. The common law provisions concerning false and misleading claims in consumer transactions have been considerably strengthened by these statutory provisions.

Government bodies have been given significant powers

Director of Trade Practices v. Ideal Credit Referral Services Ltd. et al.[14]

This case involves some serious misleading and deceptive practices requiring the court to deal with the interpretation and application of the act. Ideal Credit was a British Columbia company involved in a scheme where they advertised to the United States market that they would guarantee the loan of money even to customers who had a bad credit rating. The advertising included such phrases as "Good or Bad Credit!" "Bankruptcies O.K.!" and "Guaranteed Results!" When the customers responded, they were required to pay a non-refundable $300 "processing fee." In fact, after paying the fee, a credit check was made costing another $15, and the vast majority of the applicants were turned down, with Ideal Credit keeping the $300. The director of trade practices in British Columbia brought an application to the court for a declaration that Ideal was engaged in "deceptive or unconscionable acts" and for an injunction to restrain the practice. Ideal argued that since advertising was directed at people in the United States, an injunction under the British Columbia *Trade Practices Act* could not be granted. This argument was accepted at the trial court level, but the Court of Appeal overturned the decision. The court refused to interpret the act in such a way that allowed a deceptive and misleading practice to take place in British Columbia just so long as the victims were in the United States. The court held that the act prohibited deceptive and misleading practices that take place in British Columbia no matter where the victim was, and that the act was meant to control unethical business practices within British Columbia. In fact, this argument had been raised as an initial objection, and so, the matter still had to be sent back to the trial court to determine whether the practice complained of was misleading and deceptive.

The case is instructive for us because it shows the extent of the provincial legislation emphasizing that it applies even where the effects of the unacceptable practices are felt outside the province and may be very important with respect to Internet transactions. It also is an example of the director, a provincially appointed official, exercising his power to prosecute a complaint and gives an indication of the kinds of unacceptable practices that the director will attack as deceptive and misleading.

Unconscionable Transactions

Unconscionable transactions or unfair bargains controlled

Consumers sometimes are taken advantage of because of some vulnerability, such as desperation, poverty, or mental weakness. Legislation in the form of the *Unconscionable Transactions Relief Act* or *Unconscionable Transactions Act* has been enacted to prevent unscrupulous merchants from taking advantage of such vulnerable individuals. These statutes are restricted to situations involving the borrowing of money, and for the transaction to be found unconscionable, the actual cost of borrowing must be excessive in the circumstances. If the risk justifies the high rate of interest, even where the consumer was of weak intellect or in desperate straights,

Creditor's risk considered

it is not an unconscionable transaction. When such unconscionability is demonstrated, the courts can set the contract aside, modify its terms, or order the return of money paid.

McHugh v. Forbes[15]

Gwen Forbes owned a key-punch business, in which she employed a number of people, when she ran into financial difficulties and had to borrow a significant amount of money from Mr. McHugh. The funds were loaned to her in a number of separate transactions involving promissory notes. The first two were repaid, but several more had not been, when a final promissory note, which represented a consolidation of all the other unpaid loans, was made. In each case, the interest rate was stated as a monthly rate, but a yearly equivalent had also been set out, which ranged from 28 to 36 percent. For the last consolidation loan, Mr. McHugh threatened that if she did not sign the promissory note, he would go to Mrs. Forbes' husband who was not aware of the indebtedness. This action was brought to collect on the note when Mrs. Forbes defaulted. She claimed that because the transactions were unconscionable, violating the provincial *Unconscionable Transactions Relief Act*, she ought to be relieved of the high rate of interest charged. The court found that in saying that he would go to her husband, Mr. McHugh was simply trying to get that money from another source and this did not make the transaction unconscionable. The court also held that although the rate of interest charged was high, it was not excessive or unreasonable, given the risk, and so did not make the transaction unconscionable. It was also argued that Section 4 of the *Canada Interest*

Act was infringed by these notes because the interest payable was calculated monthly. This argument was also rejected because the notes included the yearly equivalent of the monthly rate.

For our purposes, the case illustrates what is needed for a transaction to be unconscionable. The rate of interest normally charged varies with the risk faced by the lender, a high risk justifying a higher rate of interest. If the borrower cannot get money from anyone else at a lower rate because of the risk, then a high rate of interest is to be expected and is not unconscionable. While threats to disclose such a debt may at first seem like blackmail, in circumstances like these, where Mr. McHugh was turning to the husband simply to get repaid by him, not as a method of coercing the wife, it is just what one would expect in these circumstances and does not create an unconscionable transaction.

In the provinces of Ontario, Prince Edward Island, and British Columbia, the statutes go further, extending the concept of unconscionability beyond loan transactions to also cover unacceptable business practices. In these provinces, the courts can look at such factors as physical infirmity, illiteracy, inability to understand the language of an agreement, undue influence, a price that grossly exceeds the value of the goods, and the lack of reasonable benefit to the consumer as factors in establishing unconscionability. Remedies, such as rescission, damages, and exemplary damages, are available, and in some provinces, the government agency may assist in or even initiate an action on behalf of the consumer.

In some provinces, government can initiate action

In addition to these legislative provisions, the common law doctrine of unconscionability in contract law, as discussed in Chapter 7, has become much more accepted and can also be applied in these consumer situations. In the case introducing this chapter, Mrs. Knuude was able to escape her contractual obligations because she was taken advantage of and unreasonably pressured by the sales representative. This made the contract unconscionable.

Common law developments

Controlled Business Practices

Consumer protection legislation also places controls on several specific kinds of business activities. All provinces restrict **door-to-door** or **direct sales**. The main method of doing this is by imposing a **cooling-off period**, which allows purchasers a given period of time, in most provinces up to 10 days, to change their minds and rescind the contract. In some jurisdictions, when these contracts require performance at some future date, they must be in writing, and an extended cooling-off period is imposed, usually from the time that the customer actually receives the written contract.

Door-to-door sales controlled

Untangling the WEB

Such protections are not necessarily extended to online transactions because they were passed before electronic commerce had become common. The legislation often includes terms that would render their application to Internet vendors impractical or make it difficult for courts to stretch their interpretation to include online selling.

Provisions to allow for a cooling-off period for Internet transactions, although very desirable, are not yet in place in most jurisdictions. Consumers may also find jurisdiction a problem, as unscrupulous vendors may locate in an area that does not have protective legislation in place and where courts are not required to enforce the judgments of courts in other provinces or territories.

Referral selling is another activity controlled or prohibited by consumer protection legislation because of the potential for abuse. This practice involves a customer making a list of friends that the seller then approaches. The customer providing the list is given some benefit, such as a portion off the purchase price of the item sold, on the basis of the number of friends who make a similar purchase.

Other types of potentially abusive business activities that are prohibited or controlled in various jurisdictions are food plans sales, unsolicited goods and services or credit cards, discounting income tax returns, selling training courses and prearranged funeral services, and inappropriate debt collection activities.

Methods of Control

Several methods used to control abusive activity

Controlling these unacceptable activities through legislation is accomplished by several methods. One effective method requires people supplying these goods and services to be licensed, which gives the government additional control, allowing suspension or revocation of the license and even the imposition of fines or imprisonment in the event of abusive behaviour. In addition to the power to investigate and seize records, often, these government bodies are given the power to initiate actions on behalf of the victimized consumer or to help them start their own action.

Loan Transactions

True cost of borrowing must be disclosed

Along with the unconscionable transactions legislation discussed above, every province has enacted legislation requiring that the true cost of borrowing be disclosed, thus prohibiting excessive rates of interests and costs in loan transactions. The federal *Interest Act* has similar requirements. The *Criminal Code* also prohibits the charging of excessive rates of interest.

Proper Disclosure of Interest Rates Required

The defendant law firm drew up certain promissory notes on behalf of Elcano Acceptance that they used in their business. The notes stated interest calculated at the rate of 2 percent per month. Section 4 of the *Interest Act* provides that any contract where interest is payable must be stated at an annual rate; otherwise, it is not permissible to collect more than 5 percent interest. Because of this, Elcano was not able to collect the interest due and payable from the customers pursuant to the promissory notes and successfully sued the law firm for negligence.

Elcano Acceptance Ltd. v. Richmond, Richmond, Stambler & Mills, (1991) 79 D.L.R. (4th) 154 (Ont. C.A.)

These provisions prevent the practice of hiding excessive interest rates in the payment of a bonus or through some other subterfuge. For example, Abrams borrows money at a rate of 10 percent on a $20 000 loan but also agrees to pay a $5000 bonus. Abrams walks out of the office with $20 000, but when the time comes to repay the money, he discovers that the 10 percent interest quoted was on the $25 000 now owing, not the $20 000 that was borrowed. These statutes are designed to have all this information fully disclosed to the borrower at the outset. They usually prohibit misleading information in advertisements about the cost of borrowing and require moneylenders to be registered, which makes them subject to suspension by the government body for misbehaviour or incompetence.

Legislation is also in place controlling credit-reporting agencies. While providing a valuable service to the lender, these businesses sometimes cause great harm to the borrower through carelessness or indifference. It varies with the jurisdiction, but these statutes usually require such bodies to be registered, limit the type of information that can be disclosed, make it an offence to knowingly include false information, give the individual the right to inspect the file and to correct or remove erroneous information, and, in some jurisdictions, prohibit the agency from making any report to the creditor without the written permission of the borrower.

Credit reporting practices controlled

Excessive Interest Charges Prohibited

Mrs. Banks needed a short-term loan and arranged through her accountant for a loan from Mrs. Milani. The terms were that she would borrow $32 000 but repay $35 000 one month later and pay interest on the $35 000 at 18 percent. It was clear that neither party intended to break the law, but this amounted to an annual rate of interest of 250 percent because of the $3000 bonus involved. The court held that this rate of interest violated Section 347 of the *Criminal Code*. The court also found that the 18 percent interest charged was, by itself, unconscionable. As a result, Mrs. Banks was required only to repay the $32 000 she actually received and the interest payable on that was established at the rate normally charged litigants on money due, called the "pre-judgment interest rate." Had the parties been aware they were breaking the law, they would have been subject to criminal penalties.

Milani v. Banks, 98 D.L.R. (4th) 104 (Ont. C. Gen. Div.)

Debt Collection Processes

Unpaid creditors often turn to debt collection agencies to assist in the collection process. The practices used by such agencies are sometimes abusive, and legislation has been enacted to control their activities. Common law remedies for abusive debt collection practices, such as defamation, assault and battery, trespass, and even false imprisonment, are usually ineffective. The legislation enacted requires these agencies to be licensed, adding the threat of a suspended or revoked license in the event of infractions. These statutes set out specific unacceptable collection practices, such as excessive phone calls, calls at unreasonable hours, collect calls, threats of legal action with no foundation, issuing letters of collection that resemble official court documents, deceptive or misleading statements, communicating with employers, friends, or relatives, and putting pressure on innocent relatives to pay the debt.

Abusive debt collection practices controlled

Some provinces require that debt collection agencies use only previously approved form letters in their demands for payment. In British Columbia, any practice that involves the use of "undue, excessive, or unreasonable pressures on debtors or any member of his family or household or his employer" is prohibited.[16] The punishment for parties engaged in such activities may range from the loss of their license to prosecution and a fine. Manitoba and British Columbia have also given debtors the right to civil action for any damages suffered because of the abusive practices.

16. *Debt Collection Act*, R.S.B.C. (1996) c. 92 s. 14(1)

The threat of criminal prosecution to pressure a debtor to pay is a violation of the *Criminal Code* and can result in prosecution against the person making the threat.

Consumer Service Bodies

Most of the consumer protection statutes referred to in this chapter empower a government body or agency to implement the legislation. The authority given to such departments usually includes the right to hear and investigate complaints, seize records, search premises, suspend licenses, impose fines or some other corrective action, and initiate civil actions on behalf of the consumer.

Role of government agencies

In some jurisdictions, these bodies have become clearing houses of consumer information, with a mandate to collect and disseminate that information to the public. Consumer bureaus can collect information on dangerous products, consumer business scams, or unacceptable practices. They may get involved in advertising to educate the consumer.

Also private agencies

Private organizations, such as the Better Business Bureau, are also designed to be clearing houses for such information. It must be remembered, however, that the bureau is supported and sustained by the business community and, thus, has a vested interest in serving that community. The theory is that it is in the best interests of the business community to maintain high standards by weeding out disreputable businesses. The Better Business Bureau and similar organizations serve that function for members of the business community who join them.

Federal Legislation

Regina v. Clarke Transport Canada Inc. (and four other corporations)[17]

This case is interesting because it indicates what must be established to prove a violation of the *Competition Act* in the form of price fixing. Here, five corporations were involved in providing pool car freight-forwarding services. This business involved arranging of boxcars filled with mixed commodities for various customers for transportation by rail. They charged a price by weight and were charged a fee per boxcar by the railroads. The skill involved and the profits were determined by arranging the most weight per boxcar possible. It was clearly established in this action that representatives of these five corporations had attempted to keep the price high for this service by agreeing among themselves not to attract customers away from the other firms by undercutting the price they were charging. They also exchanged information and documentation so that they were all aware of what was being charged so that no undercutting would take place. These five corporations were charged with conspiring to unduly limit competition in the market place in violation of the *Competition Act*. Although this seems to be as clear an example of price maintenance as we could have, the court found the five corporations not guilty of the charges. A necessary element of the charge is that competition be unduly limited in the market. Here, the court said, the market was broader than just the pooling of freight-forwarding services. The customers could have shipped their goods by trucking services or through intra-modal rail services (involving the shipping of trailers on flatcars). When the court defined the market on this broader scale, the Crown had failed to show that the conspiracy resulted in unduly limiting competition, and a verdict of not guilty followed.

17. (1995) 130 D.L.R. (4th) 500 (Ont. Gen. Div.)

The *Competition Act* is designed to ensure that competition remains and restricts any attempt to unduly lessen that competition. To determine whether that competition has been unduly limited, the extent of the market must be determined. Here, because there were alternatives, competition was maintained, and there was no violation of the provisions of the *Competition Act.*

This case is presented as an example of how the *Competition Act* works and to show that not all situations where parties enter into agreements restricting competition will be illegal or in violation of the act.

Although the most dramatic developments in consumer protection legislation have taken place provincially in recent years, there are some significant and effective federal statutes as well. The Department of Consumer and Corporate Affairs was established under the *Department of Consumer and Corporate Affairs Act* with a mandate to enforce legislation and provide service to consumers. The act establishes that the department is to be concerned with consumer affairs and restraint of trade and bankruptcy, as well as provide systems to educate and protect consumers. The department has established extensive research facilities to identify unsafe products. It has also become active in consumer matters at the local level, hearing and investigating complaints and communicating with consumers and merchants.

The *Competition Act*

One of the most important federal acts related to the protection of consumers is the *Competition Act.*[18] The act is primarily intended to prevent business activities that interfere with the operation of the free market system, and so, it indirectly protects the public from unfair pricing.

A competition tribunal has been set up to enforce the provisions of the *Competition Act.* The tribunal functions much like a court, with prosecution of violations and imposition of significant fines and imprisonment up to five years.

Competition Act controls abuses in free market

One of the main purposes of the *Competition Act* is to control mergers. Mergers are no longer treated as inherently bad; the tribunal just reviews them to determine whether they will have the effect of substantially limiting or lessening competition. **Horizontal mergers** take place when one competitor buys out another . The tribunal must weigh the increased efficiency gained against the loss of competition. **Vertical mergers** involve the merger of a supplier and retailer, the danger being that the supplier will squeeze out the competition by favouring their own retailer as explained below. **Conglomerate mergers** involve companies not in direct competition. The tribunal will look to determine if the overall effect is to unreasonably limit competition.

Mergers controlled

The *Competition Act* has specific provisions prohibiting certain anti-competitive, abusive trade practices. This act seeks to prevent one company that is dominant in a particular market from using its position to impose anti-competitive forces in that market. For example, suppose a dominant company in a market has a sale or uses loss leaders in such a way as to drive its competitors out of business. This is known as predatory pricing, which is prohibited.

Abusive trade practices prohibited

Other, more indirect activities that have a similar effect are also prohibited. For example, the vertical price squeeze involves a vertically integrated supplier raising prices so that other retailers purchasing from them have to sell the goods at a higher price, thus reducing their profit margin. This price increase affects the supplier's own

18. *Competition Act,* S.C. (1984-85-86) c. 91

retail operation as well; however, its profit is made at the wholesale level at the expense of the retail level. A similar prohibited practice involves a newly vertically integrated company that refuses to supply other retailers as it has in the past in order to enhance the competitive position of its own retail operation. A third variation used where one of the related companies is a railroad or other transportation company involves manipulating freight prices to give an advantage to its own retail operation at the expense of the competition.

The act also contains provisions restricting agreements between merchants that unduly restrict competition. Thus, if two merchants agree not to sell specific goods in the other's area and they are the only source of those goods, this would likely violate this portion of the act. In the *Clarke Transport* case discussed earlier, their non-competition agreement was not in violation of the act because there was no evidence that the arrangement in question had any impact on the overall market situation.

Undue restriction of competition prohibited

Other examples of prohibited activities are bid rigging (a group of bidders agreeing ahead of time who will be the low bidder); blacklisting someone in professional sports; agreements among banks controlling interest rates; and suppliers discriminating between customers with rebates and special discounts for only some.

The *Competition Act* also prohibits such offensive practices as misleading advertising in any form; double-ticketing, which means that more than one price ticket is displayed on an item (goods must be sold at the lowest price); and bait-and-switch advertising by which customers are enticed into a store by unreasonably low advertised prices and when the goods are not available, the customers are switched to higher-priced items. The act also controls referral selling schemes, pyramid selling schemes, and selling for higher prices than advertised and requires that when promotional contests are involved, the chances of winning be clearly stated.

Misleading advertising and abusive sales tactics prohibited

Effective penalties available

Previously, one of the most common complaints about both federal and provincial consumer legislation was that it was toothless. Ineffectual enforcement provisions often made it more profitable to break the law than to follow it. Many provincial consumer protection statutes have been significantly strengthened through increased maximum fines and the introduction of other methods of enforcement, such as allowing consumers to sue in their own right for violation of the legislation. The provisions of the *Competition Act* have also been enhanced. Jail sentences of up to five years and significant fines of up to $10 million strengthen the act. Other provisions allow consumers the right to sue offending parties directly for damages suffered due to misleading or deceptive sales practices.

Other Federal Legislation

Food and Drug Act carries strict penalties

Several other federal statutes have the effect of protecting the consumer. The *Food and Drug Act*[19] is intended primarily to control the sale of food, drugs, and cosmetics unfit for consumption or use. The legislation also prohibits misleading or deceptive claims associated with the sale, labelling, and advertising of these products. Several categories of drugs are created. **Unsafe drugs,** such as thalidomide, are prohibited from sale in Canada. Certain **dangerous drugs** that are useful are allowed to be sold under controlled conditions, and the act makes it an offence to traffic in certain **controlled drugs,** such as amphetamines and steroids. Strong and effective enforcement provisions are included.

19. R.S.C. 1985, c. F-27

The *Hazardous Products Act* [20]similarly controls the manufacture, importation, and sale of products inherently dangerous. Some particularly dangerous products, such as inflammable clothing or dangerous toys, are prohibited from sale in Canada, while the sale of other potentially dangerous products is allowed, provided that they comply with certain enacted regulations. Examples of the latter are such products as cradles, cribs, carpets, kettles, toys, and pacifiers. The act also contains important inspection, analysis, and enforcement provisions. Some hazardous products are covered by their own legislation, such as the *Explosives Act*[21], the *Pest Control Products Act*,[22] and the *Motor Vehicle Safety Act*.[23]

Hazardous products

The *Weights and Measures Act*,[24] the *Consumer Packaging and Labelling Act*,[25] and the *Textile Labelling Act*[26] are intended to force proper disclosure of information and thus help consumers make comparisons between products. There are other federal and provincial statutes that are not primarily designed for consumer protection but have some provisions that serve that purpose. The provisions added to the *Bills of Exchange Act*[27] dealing with consumer bills and notes, which will be discussed in Chapter 10, are an example.

For business people, it is important to understand that the operation of the consumer protection legislation has shifted the balance and now puts the merchant in a vulnerable position and the consumers in a position that is much more favourable. The old principle of *caveat emptor* that required the consumer of products or services to be careful in their dealings seems to have gone by the board, while the onus on the merchant to be careful and be responsible for whatever goes wrong seems to have taken its place. The only hesitation in coming to this conclusion is the criticism that even though these consumer protection statutes seem strong, they often are ineffective because of poor enforcement provisions. Still, merchants must be aware that the nature of their responsibility has changed, becoming much more onerous in the process.

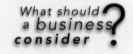
What should a business consider?

Summary

Sale of Goods Act

- Implies certain terms of a contract unless the parties have agreed otherwise
- Only applies when goods are being sold
- Risk follows title, except where there is agreement otherwise, and supplies five rules to determine when title is transferred
- Seller must convey good title and quiet possession
- Goods must be free of any lien or charge and be of merchantable quality
- Goods must match the sample or description
- In the event of a default, where the goods are not yet in the hands of the purchaser, the seller has an unpaid seller's lien and has the right of *stoppage in transitu*

20. 1985, c. H-3
21. R.S.C. 1985, c. E-17
22. R.S.C. 1985, c. P-9
23. S.C. 1993, c-16
24. R.S.C. 1985, c. W-6
25. R.S.C. 1985, c. C-38
26. R.S.C. 1985, c. T-10
27. R.S.C. 1985, c. B-4

Consumer Protection

- A number of statutes are in place to protect consumers, including *Consumer Protection Acts*, *Trade Practices Acts*, *Unconscionable Transactions Acts*, and *Direct Sellers Acts*
- These statutes control unacceptable business practices, such as misrepresentation and other forms of misleading advertising; unconscionable transactions (that is, when a merchant takes advantage of a weak-willed or otherwise unequal customer); and specific activities, such as door-to-door and referral selling.
- Moneylenders are required to disclose the true cost of borrowing to their customers
- Abusive debt collection practices are restricted
- The federal *Competition Act* controls inappropriate practices
- *Hazardous Products Marketing Act* controls and restricts dangerous products
- Many other federal statutes protect customers

QUESTIONS

1. Explain the purpose of the *Sale of Goods Act* in relation to the obligations of the parties to a sale-of-goods transaction.

2. What three qualifications must be met before the *Sale of Goods Act* applies to a transaction?

3. What is the distinction between a sale and an agreement to sell? What is the significance of that distinction?

4. When does the risk transfer to the buyer in a sale-of-goods transaction? Explain the exceptions to this general rule.

5. What is a bill of lading? How can it affect who bears the risk in a sale-of-goods transaction?

6. Indicate when title transfers in the following situations:

   a. When the contract for sale is unconditional and the goods involved are in a deliverable state at the time the purchase is made

   b. When the subject of the contract involves specific goods to which the seller is obligated to do something, such as repair, clean, or modify, to get them into a deliverable state

   c. When the contract for sale involves specific, identified goods, which must be weighed or measured before being given to the buyer

   d. When the goods are delivered to the buyer on approval

   e. When goods purchased by description have not been selected, separated out, or manufactured at the time the sales contract is entered into

7. The *Sale of Goods Act* imposes terms relating to goods matching samples or descriptions, and meeting standards of fitness, quality, and title. Explain the nature of these implied terms and their effect on the parties. Indicate which

terms are conditions and which are warranties. Explain the significance of the distinction.

8. Explain what merchantable quality means.

9. Explain the effect of an exculpatory clause included in a contract that is inconsistent with the terms set out in the *Sale of Goods Act*.

10. Explain the rights of the seller when the buyer of goods

    a. becomes insolvent;

    b. defaults on the contract of sale while the goods are still in the hands of the seller; or

    c. defaults after the goods have been given to a third party to deliver but before they are received by the buyer.

11. Explain why it might be more difficult for a seller of goods to sue for damages than for price.

12. Under what circumstances may a buyer refuse delivery of goods?

13. The *Sale of Goods Act* in each province implies certain terms into contracts of sale relating to the fitness and quality of the product. What are the approaches used in various Canadian jurisdictions to make these provisions mandatory in consumer transactions?

14. How does the concept of privity of contract limit the effectiveness of many consumer protection provisions? How have some jurisdictions overcome this problem?

15. What common law provisions are available to protect consumers from unscrupulous business practices? Describe the limitations inherent in these provisions and the steps that have been taken to overcome these limitations.

16. Explain the object of the *Unconscionable Transactions Relief Act* and the limitations to its application. In your answer, discuss significant variations between provinces.

17. What statutory provisions have been introduced throughout Canada to control door-to-door selling, referral selling, and the practice of purchasing tax refunds?

18. Describe the methods outlined in federal and provincial consumer protection statutes to control businesses with a tendency to abusive practices. Discuss the effectiveness of these tactics.

19. What services are provided to consumers through organizations set up by the federal and provincial governments? Discuss whether these services are adequate.

20. Describe the practices controlled by the *Competition Act* and explain how that control is accomplished.

CASES

1. Lasby v. Royal City Chrysler Plymouth

Mrs. Lasby, after considerable dealing with the defendants, through their salesperson, Mr. MacDonald, decided to purchase, on Mr. MacDonald's recommendation, a Dodge 600. She had been given the impression that the car had a big engine and that it was executive-driven. After getting it home, she found out the engine had four cylinders, not six as she thought, but did not do anything about this since she was assured by Mr. MacDonald that it was the largest four-cylinder engine made. A few months later, when she was having it serviced, Mrs. Lasby mentioned to her mechanic that it had the big engine. He told her that it had, in fact, the smaller engine and that there was a much bigger engine than hers. She asked Royal City for her money back, but the dealership refused to either return her money or take the car back.

Under these circumstances, explain Mrs. Lasby's options. What would be the appropriate remedy? How would your answer be affected by learning that by the time of the trial, the car was 22 months older and had been driven a further 40 000 kilometres?

2. Harry v. Kreutziger

Harry was a Native Indian with a grade 5 education, a hearing defect, and a retiring manner. He owned a fishing boat worth very little, except for the fishing license that went with it. With the license, the boat was worth about $16 000. Kreutziger persuaded Harry to sell the boat and license to him for $4500, saying that as a Native Indian, Harry would have little trouble getting another license. Harry sued to have the contract set aside. What would be the nature of Harry's complaint against Kreutziger? What defences would be available to Kreutziger in response to Harry's action? Predict the outcome.

3. W.W. Distributors & Co. v. Thorsteinson

A salesman and his manager approached a young engaged girl and her mother at their home one evening and, after using some very-high-pressure sales tactics, sold them some cooking utensils. The mother was persuaded to sign the contract after being told that it was not really important. By so doing, the mother became a party to the agreement, even though it had been made clear to the salesman that her only involvement was to lend her daughter $50 towards the purchase. The daughter was led to believe that she was getting very good value for her money, but experts clearly established that the price was over 75 percent more than the maximum value of the goods involved. The next day, unable to contact the plaintiff, the mother stopped payment on the cheque. When this was discovered, the salesman went to her home and was informed that the mother and daughter were repudiating the agreement. The company immediately commenced an action to recover the purchase price and the various penalties and service charges built into the agreement.

Explain the arguments that could be raised on both sides and the likely outcome. What effect would it have on your answer to learn that the engaged girl was under the age of majority? What legislation provisions have been put into place in most jurisdictions to curb this type of abuse?

4. Regina v. Birchcliff Lincoln Mercury Sales Ltd.

Birchcliff operated a car dealership with a service centre, where a sign was posted stating "Customer labour charges are based on $38 per hour flat rate." The sign was there because Ford, the manufacturer, insisted that such notices be posted in clear sight at their dealerships.

In fact, a flat rate of $38 per hour was not charged for the services given; rather, for each job, reference was made to a standard industry guide that set out the number of hours the job ought to take, and the charges were based on that guide. Even if the time spent on a particular job was less than that set out in the standard guide, the amount stated in the guide was charged.

Explain the nature of the complaint in these circumstances and the likely consequences that Birchcliff would face.

5. Sumner Sports Inc. v. Pavillon Chasse & Peche (440) Inc.

Sumner and Pavillon were in the business of selling hunting and fishing gear in their respective areas. They entered into an agreement that for a specific period of time, Sumner would not retail specific products in or around the city of Laval but only sell their goods to Pavillon and that Pavillon would not sell their products in the lower St Lawrence area or City of Ottawa and only sell products purchased from Sumner. In effect, the two companies agreed not to carry on business in competition with each other. Pavillon violated this agreement, and Sumner sued. Pavillon claimed that the contract was illegal, being a violation of the *Combines Investigation Act* (which was repealed and replaced by the *Competition Act*) and therefore could not be enforced. Explain the arguments that can be raised by both parties supporting their positions and the likely outcome.

Priority of Creditors

CHAPTER HIGHLIGHTS

- Securing debt—the methods and processes
- Security transactions—rights and obligations
- Builders' liens
- Negotiable instruments
- Bankruptcy

A considerable industry has developed around the practices of lending money and granting credit. This chapter will examine the various methods that have been developed to ensure that money owed is properly repaid and the legislation that has been created to control such transactions. Although there is some overlap, this area is primarily under the jurisdiction of the provinces. Provincial legislation varies considerably from province to province, but the many common principles, along with some significant variations, will be examined in this chapter. This chapter will also explore the related topics of negotiable instruments and bankruptcy.

Toronto Dominion Bank v. Calderbank et al.[1]

Mr. Calderbank was the driving force in Skyhook Operations Ltd., a company incorporated to carry out helicopter logging. He held 50 percent of the shares, and two investors, Mr. Rodenbush and Mr. Rooke, held the other 50 percent. The Toronto Dominion Bank had granted Skyhook Operations a $25 000 line of credit as well as a fixed loan of $112 000; the investors had signed a personal guarantee for this debt.

Mr. Calderbank approached the bank manager to extend the line of credit explaining that the other two shareholders of Skyhook would invest a further $20 000 and would also agree to the extended line of credit. He also confided that he was going to start another company to compete with Skyhook so that he could keep all the profits for himself. In effect, he told the bank manager that he was going to get his partners to invest more money and then turn his back on them. After being assured that the additional investment and the extended line of credit would stay with Skyhook, the bank manager agreed to the extension.

When Mr. Rooke and Mr. Rodenbush came to the bank to guarantee the extended line of credit, the bank manager was careful not to tell them anything of Mr. Calderbank's plans, thinking they were to be confidential. Mr. Calderbank then

1. (1983) 3 D.L.R. (4th) 716 (B.C.C.A.)

exhausted Skyhook's funds and formed his new company; after Mr. Rooke and Mr. Rodenbush learned of this, they informed the bank that they would not be responsible for any further Skyhook debt. Skyhook failed, and when Mr. Rooke and Mr. Rodenbush learned that the bank manager had known all along of Mr. Calderbank's plans, they refused to honour their guarantee, and the bank brought an action to enforce it.

Personal guarantees are a common and vital aspect of doing business in Canada today. Corporations are separate legal entities, and a creditor needs the assurance that someone, usually a shareholder, will be responsible for the debt if the corporation fails. It is vitally important that people understand that when they sign such a personal guarantee, there is a real possibility that they will be called on to pay back the debt.

In the above case, however, the court found that the investors were not bound by the guarantee they had signed. Because a guarantor's position is so vulnerable, the law has imposed an obligation on the creditor not to make new arrangements with the debtor that will put the guarantor at greater risk without first obtaining the guarantor's permission for the change. In the process, they must inform the guarantor of any unusual factors that persuade the guarantor not to agree to the change. The bank manager's failure to disclose that Mr. Calderbank was about to start another company in competition with Skyhook amounted to misrepresentation, and therefore, Mr. Rooke and Mr. Rodenbush were not required to pay the guarantee. The personal guarantee is one of the important topics discussed in this chapter.

Methods of Securing Debt

When a debtor borrows money, the creditor is at risk if the debtor cannot repay. Usually, the debtor is required to take steps to reduce this risk and ensure that there will be enough assets available to the creditor to cover the debt. To persuade a creditor to lend money, a debtor must do something to ensure that the creditor will be paid before the others, even in the event of insolvency. Several methods have been developed to satisfy this requirement. When the parties are successful in creating a priority system of one creditor over the others, the party with priority is said to be a **secured creditor**.

Security helps assure creditor of repayment

Personal Property

Both real and personal properties have been used to create security. **Real property** includes land and any buildings or items attached to the land, called **fixtures,** and **mortgages** are the common method of using real property as security. Non-real property is called personal property, and such **personalty** is also used extensively to secure the payment of money owed. Personal property can be divided into **chattels**, which are tangible, movable things, and intangible rights called **choses in action**. A creditor has a right to claim against the debtor for the amount owed, a claim that can be enforced in the courts in the event of default. This right or claim is a chose in action. A cheque or a promissory note is actually a chose in action because the paper merely represents an obligation to pay and a right to sue for failure to do so. Both a chattel and a chose in action can be used to secure a debt. The most common method in consumer transactions is to take real property or chattels as security.

Real property includes land and buildings

Personal property can be used as security

The oldest system for using personal property as security is a **pledge** or a **pawn,** in which a creditor (pawnbroker) takes possession of a particular item as security and holds it until repayment. The creditor has possession of the goods, but the debtor still has title and remains the owner. Only when there is no repayment does the pawnbroker acquire the right to sell the goods to recover the amount lost.

In most circumstances, it is inconvenient and contrary to the intention of the parties for the creditor to take possession of the goods to be used as security. If a person were to purchase a new car on credit, it would be silly for the car to remain in the possession of the creditor until the debt was paid off. Now, like real property mortgages, when personal property is used as security, the goods stay with the debtor, and the creditor has the right to seize the goods upon default. Only when the debtor fails to repay the loan can the creditor take possession of the personal property. Such a transaction often takes the form of the creditor being given title to the goods used as security, but the primary purpose is to create a security by giving the creditor first claim on the goods, not the transfer or sale of the goods themselves.

> **Personal property security involves right to take possession upon default**

The Traditional Approach

Historically, conditional sales agreements, chattel mortgages, and the assignment of accounts receivable were the common methods of using personal property as security. Each method was regulated by its own statute, and so, there was a considerable variety of legislation governing these transactions in the various provinces. Some maritime provinces still use this approach.

> **Conditional seller retains title until payment is completed**

A conditional sales agreement, governed by the *Conditional Sales Act* of the province, involves the seller of the goods, who is also the creditor retaining title to those goods until the final payment is made. In our legal system, ownership (or title) and possession of the goods can be separated, and this is the key to understanding how chattels can be used as security. In effect, a conditional sale takes place in a two-staged process. First, possession is given to the purchaser, and finally, after the last payment is made, title to the goods follows. It should be noted that the *Sale of Goods Act* applies to this transaction even though the sale takes place over a protracted period of time.

Goodfellow Inc. v. Heather Building Supplies Ltd.[2]

Goodfellow Inc. supplied lumber to Heather Building Supplies Ltd. At the time that lumber was supplied, it was made clear that title was to remain with the seller until payment in full was received. The packing slips and invoices contained the following declaration. "RESERVE ON OWNERSHIP: GOODFELLOW INC. WILL REMAIN THE RIGHTFUL OWNER OF ALL GOODS SOLD TO THE BUYER AS LONG AS THE PURCHASE PRICE HAS NOT BEEN PAID IN FULL."

Heather building suppliers defaulted on the payment for the lumber, and Goodfellow Inc. had it seized. The process required that an order for repossession be obtained, that the sheriff seize the lumber, but that a three-day waiting period be observed before the sheriff could, in turn, deliver the lumber back to Goodfellow Inc. During that time, Heather made a proposal under the *Bankruptcy and Insolvency Act* that stopped the lumber from being returned to Goodfellow. Heather eventually became bankrupt, and the trustee claimed the lumber for the other creditors claiming that Goodfellow Inc. had not properly registered the secured transaction as required under the *Conditional Sales Act* and had lost their claim to the goods. In

2. (1996) 141 D.L.R. (4th) 282 (N.S.C.A.)

effect, the court determined that this was a conditional sale under the *Conditional Sale Act*, and as such, it had to be properly registered to maintain its priority against third parties and other creditors. Since it was not, Goodfellow had no further claim to the lumber, and the court ordered that it be delivered to the trustee so that it could be sold for the benefit of the other creditors.

This case illustrates in a very straightforward way the effect of not properly following the procedural requirements, such as registration under this legislation. It also illustrates the effect of a proposal under the *Bankruptcy and Insolvency Act* to temporarily stop any action proceeding against the debtor and the important role of a trustee in bankruptcy. Bankruptcy will be a major topic discussed later in the chapter.

A chattel mortgage is similar, but instead of title being retained by the seller/creditor in a sale transaction, the debtor has gone to a creditor, such as a bank, and borrowed money. To secure the loan, that debtor has transferred title to some good, such as a car or boat, to the bank as "collateral security." The end result is the same so that throughout the duration of the loan transaction, the creditor has title to the goods, and the debtor has possession. When the last payment is made, the creditor surrenders title to the goods to the debtor. Because title used as security is usually transferred by a document called a **bill of sale**, the legislation governing this form of security is generally called the *Bills of Sale Act*. But it is important to note that because no actual sale of the goods is contemplated, the *Sale of Goods Act* will not apply to this transaction.

Chattel mortgage

—title to goods transferred to secure loan

The assignment of book accounts does not involve using goods as security. Rather, the creditor is given the right to collect money owed to the business in the event of a default. This is an example of a chose in action being used as a security. Often, a business will have few tangible assets but still have considerable funds owed to it in the form of accounts receivable, which are monies owed to the business for goods or services provided. To secure the loan, then, the right to collect these outstanding debts is conditionally transferred to the creditor, who, in the event of a default, has the right to intercept them and collect the amounts owing directly. This method of providing collateral security is governed by the *Assignment of Book Accounts Act*.

Accounts receivable can be used as security for a loan

Redi-Mix Ltd. v. Hub Dairy & Barn Systems Ltd.[3]

Both Redi-mix and the Toronto Dominion Bank had claims against Hub Dairy & Barn Systems. Hub Dairy had made an "assignment of accounts" to the bank to secure a loan, and Redi-Mix had a judgment against Hub Dairy for $10 552.50.

Farm & Garden Centre of Saskatoon Ltd. was a customer of Hub Dairy and owed a considerable amount to them for services that had been supplied after the assignment to the Toronto Dominion Bank had been made. Farm & Garden had made a series of regular payments to Hub Dairy, when they were served notice of the judgment by Redi-Mix, demanding any further payments be made to them. Shortly afterwards, the Toronto Dominion Bank also served notice on them of the assignment and demanded that all payments be made to them. The Farm & Garden Centre wisely paid the money into court so that the court could sort out who was entitled to the payment.

The court held that this was a valid assignment of book accounts under the *Personal Property Security Act*, that the secured transaction had been properly attached

3. (1987) 41 D.L.R. (4th) 360 (Sask. Q.B.)

and perfected under that act, and therefore the bank was entitled to the payment. It was only necessary that the bank properly register the assignment, and this was sufficient notice to others. It did not matter that Farm & Garden did not know of the assignment or that they continued to make their payments to Hub Dairy. There was no reason why the bank could not rely on the debtor to collect the funds and redirect them to the bank. It was also not necessary for the bank to serve notice of the assignment on each debtor of Hub Dairy, as this would create chaos in the banking world. By their nature, assignment of accounts include future debts, and so no further notification is needed other than the registration of the assignment of accounts.

This case not only illustrates the nature of the assignment of accounts receivable and the priority established by proper registration, but also shows how the assignment of accounts receivable has been incorporated under the personal property security legislation now in place in most jurisdictions.

In this case, Farm & Garden was unaware of the problems of Hub Dairy or of the assignment to the Toronto Dominion Bank. When they were notified, they paid the money into court. As was indicated in Chapter 6, it could be a serious error had they ignored the notice of assignment and continued to pay Hub Dairy or if they had made the mistake of responding to the wrong notice and paying to the wrong claimant. In that case, they might have to pay twice.

An essential feature of these secured transactions is the right of the creditor to take back the goods or intercept the debt owing in the event of default. This has to be the case even where those goods have been resold to an innocent third party (which would be unfair to the innocent third-party purchaser). Not to allow it, on the other hand, would defeat the whole process and the nature of secured transactions. Thus, where Lee has purchased a car under a conditional sale agreement and defaults on his payments, the seller has to be able to retake the goods, even when Lee has resold the car to an innocent purchaser (Chan). To overcome this problem, all jurisdictions require the security to be registered with a designated agency. The potential buyer (or another creditor interested in taking those goods as security) then searches the registry to determine the status of the goods. If a lien has been registered, they are warned. If they fail to search the registry, it is their failure, and they are subject to the registered lien. The creditor will have the right to retake the goods even from this now less-than-innocent third party. If the car dealership had properly registered their security against the car, they would have the right to repossess it even against Chan, who should have searched the registry before buying.

Registration protects parties

This traditional approach towards secured transactions has some significant drawbacks. Because several different statutes were involved, there was confusion and sometimes injustice due to the different provisions.

A New Approach

Many of these statutes had different conditions under which registration must take place, different time limits, different places for registration, different remedies, and no unified system of enforcement. To remedy this situation, most provinces now have, or are preparing to put in place, legislation adopted from the United States, called *Personal Property Security Acts*. The significance of these acts is that one set of rules controls all types of personal property used as security. There can still be con-

Personal property security acts rationalize the area

tractual differences between conditional sales, chattel mortgages and the other types of secured transactions covered by this legislation, but the formal requirements and procedures for all these types of securities are the same. As well, the *Personal Property Security Act* allows other, less common forms of personal property, such as licenses, shares, and bonds, to be used as security and treated in a uniform way.

The *Personal Property Security Act*

Re Foster[4]

Mr. Foster obtained his license to drive a taxi in the city of Mississauga. One of the conditions attached to the license was that it was not transferable until three years from the date it was issued. But Mr. Foster needed money and made arrangements for four loans with four different creditors using the taxi license as security in various forms.

Mr. Foster did not recover from his financial problems and made an assignment in bankruptcy just 11 days before the restriction on the license that prohibited him from transferring it expired. All four creditors claimed a right to the license, and in this action, these claims were put forward.

The court first had to deal with the question of whether a license could be a form of property under the *Personal Property Security Act*. The court held that although there were some limitations on the license, including the possibility that it might be suspended or revoked, it still represented a valuable asset, and therefore qualified as property under the act.

The next problem for the court was to decide which of the four creditors had priority in their claim. In the first transaction, the license was simply treated as a security for the loan. In the second, the agreement between the parties purported to lease the license to the creditor with an option to purchase. The third purported to be a sale to the creditor of an interest in the license, with the creditor to get the whole thing in the event of default. The fourth was the sale of the license to the creditor for its stated value, which was then leased back to Mr. Foster.

The court held that the first three transactions, where money was loaned and the license was used as security, fell under the *Personal Property Security Act* and the provisions of that act had to be complied with in order to establish priority. Only the first creditor properly registered his security interest. The second and third creditors made a minor but fatal mistake when registering their interest by leaving Mr. Foster's middle initial off the registration document. The whole purpose of a personal property security act is to provide for a method to alert people to secured interests in property, and in order to do that, the interest must be properly registered. Ontario's act specifically required that the middle initial be included in the registration. Since it was not, those two secured interests were not valid. The fourth transaction, where the license was sold with a lease back, was a simple sale and did not require registration, so this claimant was entitled to the license, subject to the interest of the first creditor who had properly registered his claim. It is interesting that before the trial, the first and fourth creditors got together and made a settlement between themselves, in which the first creditor got the license, and so the court did not have to decide between them.

4. (1992) 89 D.L.R. (4th) 555 (Ont. Gen. Div.)

This case illustrates several important points concerning secured transactions. First, something as intangible as a license can be used to secure a loan and is covered by the *Personal Property Security Act.* The act, therefore, is much more flexible than the old method. Second, various different kinds of transactions in relationship to property are caught as security transactions under the act, providing greater flexibility. It also illustrates the importance of properly following the procedures for registration of secured interests and how claims can be lost due to minor mistakes.

Most provinces in Canada have replaced or are about to replace their *Conditional Sales Act, Bills of Sale Act,* and *Assignment of Book Accounts Act* with one statute called the *Personal Property Security Act.* The agreement between the parties may still take the form of a chattel mortgage, conditional sales agreement or a general assignment of book accounts, but in these jurisdictions, it is the *Personal Property Security Act* that governs the transaction. The act is designed to cover any situation in which a creditor is given a secured interest against the personal property assets of a debtor to ensure repayment of a loan or obligation.

Act creates one cohesive process

Because the act is broader in its application and because now by this statute, title does not actually change hands, there is much more flexibility as to what can be used to create such a security. Security is created when the creditor is given assurance that they will have first claim against some asset in the event of a default The act permits a security interest to be created in all types of tangible and intangible personal property of the debtor. In addition to the traditional chattel mortgages and conditional sales, the act covers assignment of contracts and debts and leasing arrangements intended to create a security. This flexibility is illustrated in the *Foster* case used to introduce this section. Still the content of the original contract is important. A primary purpose of the statute is to give effect to the contractual obligations entered into by the parties.

Contract prevails

The method of creating a secured relationship under this statute is unique. There are three stages. First, the parties must enter into the contractual agreement; second, the secured interest must attach to the collateral which has been identified to provide the security; and third, the secured interest must be perfected.

For **attachment** to take place, the parties must have performed or partially performed the contract, with the debtor receiving some value or benefit from the agreement, that is, if a person requiring a business loan makes an agreement with a bank to that effect and uses a car as collateral for the loan, that security does not attach until the debtor has actually received the money from the bank. The contractual agreement must create a security arrangement that gives the creditor a preferred position in relation to the collateral. These contracts usually take the form of the more traditional conditional sale, chattel mortgage, or assignment of book accounts discussed above, but they need not be restricted in this way. The attachment process will give the secured party (the creditor, in this instance, the bank) certain rights and remedies in relationship to the car, such as the right to retake the goods upon default. But those rights and obligations apply only in the relationship between those two parties (creditor and debtor). The car could not be retaken from an innocent third party, such as a subsequent buyer.

Security must attach to collateral

Perfection required to prevail against outsiders

For the creditor to obtain priority over third parties, the secured transaction must also be **perfected**. This perfection can be accomplished in one of two ways. The first is by registering the security obligation as was done under the old legislation. This process has been simplified so that a single form is used. The form and required content of the financing statement varies to some extent from province to province, but in general, the form requires the complete name and address of the parties, and the type and description, including the serial number of the security used. Where a motor vehicle is used as security, its year, make, model, and vehicle identification number must also be set out. In Ontario, when consumer goods are involved, the financing statement must give the amount owed and the date of maturity of the agreement.

Perfection through registration

Re Telecom Leasing Canada (Re Giffen)[5]

Telecom Leasing Canada (TLC) Ltd. leased a 1993 Saturn to the British Columbia Telephone Company, and as permitted under that agreement, they, in turn, leased the car to their employee, Carol Giffen. This lease agreement allowed Ms. Giffen the option to buy the car, but was not registered under the *Personal Property Security Act* of the province. Unfortunately, Ms. Giffen found it necessary to make an assignment in bankruptcy. The car was repossessed and sold, and this case was brought by the trustee in bankruptcy representing the other creditors to determine who had the right to the proceeds.

The trustee argued that this was a secured transaction and had to be properly registered under the *Personal Property Security Act* in order to perfect it and preserve rights against third parties and other creditors. Because it was not, the trustee had claim to the proceeds. The leasing company argued that a lease does not convey any proprietary interest in the car to the lessee. Since it was not the "property of the bankrupt," it could not be assigned in the bankruptcy process to the trustee.

The Supreme Court of Canada found that the *Personal Property Security Act* redefined the traditional rights in property and that since the bankrupt had the right to use the car during the time she had it and had the option to buy it, she did have a proprietary right in the vehicle. Telecom had a secured interest in the vehicle, but they had to perfect that security under the act to protect their rights. Their failure to do so resulted in the trustee having the right to the proceeds of the sale.

This case illustrates the operation of the *Personal Property Security Act* and how it interrelates with the *Bankruptcy and Insolvency Act*. It also shows how the *Personal Property Security Act* has expanded what can be taken as security and how that security can be structured far beyond the traditional chattel mortgage, conditional sale, and assignment of book debts transactions. In this case, leasing arrangements where there is an option to buy are clearly caught by the act.

The second way the transaction can be perfected is by the creditor obtaining physical possession of the collateral used. Whether possession or registration is used depends on the nature of the security. Where shares or a promissory note are used as security, it would be appropriate for the creditor to take possession of the certificate or note. But where a physical item is involved, such as a car, a truck, or other type of equipment that is required for use by the debtor, registration is the more appropriate process. The whole purpose of requiring registration is to provide a method whereby a third party will not be misled by the debtor when he or she is in possession of the collateral property. This, of course, is not a problem if the property used as collateral is in the possession of the creditor, and in those circumstances, registration is not required for perfection or to protect the rights of

Perfection through possession

5. [1998] 1 S.C.R. 91

innocent third parties. If more than one secured interest is perfected by registering different financing agreements against the same collateral, the priority between those secured parties is generally determined by the date registration takes place.

Re Bank of Nova Scotia and Royal Bank of Canada et al.[6]

Farm Rite Equipment Ltd. gave the Royal Bank an assignment of all their property, including after-acquired property, to secure their indebtedness to the bank. This was registered pursuant to the *Personal Property Security Act*. A few years later, Farm Rite acquired two Chevrolet Silverado trucks on conditional sale contracts from Dahlen Chev. Olds. Ltd., and these conditional sales agreements were assigned to the Bank of Nova Scotia. These conditional sales transactions were not properly registered pursuant to the *Personal Property Security Act* of the province until after Farm Rite Ltd. went into receivership. In 1985, a receiver acting for the Royal Bank was appointed and took over the property of Farm Rite Ltd. They also took physical possession of the two trucks and sold them. The question in this case was who was entitled to the proceeds of the sale of the trucks.

The problem here was that the act in force required that all motor vehicles be registered by their serial numbers, and the Royal Bank had not done this. Because of this oversight, the Bank of Nova Scotia had priority by their registration subsequent to the receivership.

For our purposes, what is interesting is that the Royal Bank argued that since they had repossessed the vehicles, they had been perfected by possession and that established their priority over the Bank of Nova Scotia. The court held, however, that perfection by possession required not just legal possession, as in the case of a receivership, but actual possession of the goods. More importantly for our purposes, perfection by possession also required that the possession of the goods be taken as collateral not for the purpose of realizing on that security. This means that possession of the goods must take place at the time of the transaction in order to create the secured interest in the collateral. When a default has taken place, it is too late to repair any defects by repossession of the property used as security. The point is that when there are such conflicting claims, they are not going to be settled by a race to see who can repossess the goods first.

Rights and Remedies upon Default

Royal Bank of Canada v. J. Segreto Construction Ltd.[7]

Two corporations borrowed money from the Royal Bank and executed promissory notes to ensure repayment. As part of the agreement, each corporation put up certain construction equipment as security for the loan, and financing statements were properly registered under the *Personal Property Security Act* to that effect. The debtors defaulted on the loan, and the Royal Bank seized the construction equipment that had been put up as security. This equipment was then sold at public auction but did not bring in enough to cover the amount owing. The bank then sued the two corporations for the shortfall.

Unfortunately for the bank, when they seized and sold the construction equipment, they failed to notify the debtor when and where it was to be resold as required under the *Personal Property Security Act*. The court held that this failure

6. (1987) 42 D.L.R. (4th) 636 (Sask. C.A.)
7. (1988) 47 D.L.R. (4th) 761 (Ont. C.A.)

completely prohibited the bank from claiming any deficit, and they had to be content with the proceeds of the sale.

This case is reasonably straightforward, but it illustrates how important it is to follow the designated procedures. When a default takes place, it is normal to repossess and resell the goods used as security. But the legislation requires that the debtor be notified about the resale and be given time to reclaim the goods. Since this did not happen in this case, there was no right to sue for a shortfall. The provisions of the statute are designed to protect both the rights of the debtor and the rights of the secured creditor and must be carefully followed.

Repossession. In the event of a default by the debtor, the creditor has the normal contractual rights and remedies based on the original contract and common law. The provisions of the *Personal Property Security Act* only come into play when the creditor attempts to exercise his rights against the collateral security. This normally involves taking possession of the goods and reselling them to recover the amount owed. This right to repossess should be specified in the original contract, and then the repossession has to take place without otherwise violating the law. The creditor, usually acting through an agent called a bailiff, can come onto the property of the debtor and repossess the goods, provided no force is used. No threats or violence can be used, and the bailiff is not permitted to force open windows or break down doors.

All normal contract remedies available upon default

Upon default, creditor can take possession and dispose of collateral

Suppose Wizinsky has lent money to Barbosa and taken security in the form of a chattel mortgage against Barbosa's car, and Barbosa defaults. Wizinsky would be able to tow the car away from Barbosa's open carport. But if the car were in a locked garage, Wizinsky would not be able to seize the vehicle without the court's assistance because then it would be necessary to force open the garage. Nor could the creditor or bailiff remove Barbosa forcibly from the vehicle to take possession of it. In such circumstances, the appropriate procedure is to get a court order and then get the local judicial officer, usually a sheriff, to enforce the order. Such officers can use whatever force is necessary to fulfill their duties and enforce court orders.

Court order and sheriff necessary when force required

There are other restrictions on the creditors right to take action. When consumer goods are involved, in British Columbia, the *Personal Property Security Act*[8] requires that when two-thirds of the debt has been paid, consumer goods cannot be retaken unless there is a court order. The *Consumer Protection Act*[9] of Ontario has a similar provision.

Whether commercial or consumer goods are involved, while they are in the possession of the creditor, "commercially reasonable" care must taken to protect the goods and keep them in good repair. If the goods require repair to sell them, such "commercially reasonable" expenses will be added to the amount the debtor owes.

Creditor must care of collateral in his or her possession

Once repossession has taken place, the goods are normally sold to satisfy the debt. This may be done by private sale, public auction, or any other means that is commercially reasonable. Before they are resold, however, the creditor must give 15 days' notice to the debtor and other interested parties, setting out such information as a description of the goods, the amount owing, that they are going to be sold, and that the party receiving the notice has the right to redeem them by paying what is owed to the creditor. The notice also must state that failure to redeem the goods will result in them being sold and that the debtor will continue to be responsible for any deficiency when the amount realized from the sale is not enough to cover the amount owed plus any interest and expenses that have accumulated.

Seized goods can be sold to satisfy debt

Any deficit may be repaid by the debtor

8. R.S.B.C. 1996, c. 359
9. R.S.O. 1990, c. C-31

Note that while there is a requirement to pay any deficiency, the debtor also has the right to any surplus over and above what is realized from the sale.

Failure to strictly adhere to the provisions of the act can result in the creditor losing the right to be repaid for any deficiency, as happened in the *Segreto* case discussed above. The creditor may also be responsible for any loss caused by their failure to properly look after the goods while in their possession or for failure to obtain a fair price because of an improper sale.

Keeping Goods to Satisfy Debt. An alternative available in most jurisdictions is for the creditor taking the goods and keeping them in satisfaction of the debt, instead of taking and reselling the goods. This ends any claim the debtor may have to a surplus and any claim the creditor may have to a deficiency. Again, the creditor must serve notice of this intention, and the debtor and other interested parties then have 15 days to file an objection. If no one objects, the creditor can keep the property; otherwise, the creditor must sell it in the normal way within 90 days.

Where consumer goods are involved, if the procedures are not properly followed, the debtor may be able to recover not only the interest paid but also a portion of the actual price paid for the goods. This is true even when the debtor has not suffered any damages. In British Columbia, when consumer goods are involved, the debtor has no obligation to pay for a deficiency.

These procedures may appear very cumbersome, and the legislation itself is very complex, but in actual practice, it is quite straightforward and works quite well. For example, where a personal property security act is in place and a person goes to a bank or credit union with a car as security, the security becomes attached to the car once the contract has been entered into and the monies advanced. The credit union then perfects the security by registering the financing statement with a central registry. Thereafter, if the debtor tries to sell that car, the buyer may search the registry and should find the registered security against the vehicle. If the third party buys the car anyway, and there is a default, the creditor will be able to recover the vehicle even from the innocent third party. This is the essence of the creditor's security.

Once there is a default, the credit union has the option of either pursuing its normal breach of contract remedies or taking possession of the vehicle. If it chooses the latter, it cannot use force to do so, and once the vehicle is repossessed, it must keep it in good repair; but thereafter, it can choose to dispose of the car (sell it) to recover the amount of money owing.

Right to Redeem. First, notice of such disposition must be given to the debtor and any other interested parties, that is, the creditors, so that they have a chance to redeem it by paying off any money owing. If they fail to redeem and the goods are sold, any surplus after paying off the principal, interest, legal fees, repair expenses, and so on will go to the debtor, and in most cases, any deficiency (shortfall) can be recovered from the debtor. Alternatively, the credit union can choose to retain the car by serving notice of its intention of so doing. If the credit union chooses this route and there is no objection, it can do whatever it wants with the car, but the debtor's obligation ends. If there is a deficiency, the creditor will not be able to claim it against the debtor.

In those provinces where a personal property security act is not yet in force, very similar rights exist at a practical level. A creditor can use an item of personal property, such as a car, a boat, or even accounts receivable, as security for a loan.

Option to retain the collateral

Defaulting debtor has right to redeem

The creditor must register the transaction and, in the event of default, has the right to repossess the goods even from an innocent third party and resell them. The problem is that these provisions are found in separate bills of sale, conditional sales, and assignment of book accounts acts. The purpose of the *Personal Property Security Act* is to overcome this duplication and confusion and bring all such uses of personal property as security under one system and one statute and to allow more flexibility as to what can be used as security.

Personal property security acts unify and simplify process

The *Bank Act*

Prior to the passage of personal property security acts, there was considerable restriction on what could be used as security when conditional sales and chattel mortgages were involved. A solution to the problem was found in the federal *Bank Act,*[10] which allows growing crops, inventories, and goods in the process of manufacture to be taken as security by the banks. Because of the nature of manufacturing, merchandising, and the growing process, it was also necessary that these goods be allowed to be sold in the course of business without affecting the nature of that security. Sections 426 and 427 of the *Bank Act* allows this to happen.

Anticipated crops can be used as security

As can goods before manufacture

The *Bank Act* is still an important federal statute, but now, in those jurisdictions that have a personal property security act, other lenders have the same flexibility. There is now also more overlap with the *Bank Act* and, as a result, more potential conflicts. People also must worry about two different sets of rules. One important feature of the act is that the loan is registered with the local branch of the Bank of Canada.

This banking legislation also permits banks to continue to use the normal types of secured transactions available to everyone, such as chattel mortgages, guarantees, real estate mortgages, assignment of debts, and so on.

Kawai Canada Music Ltd. v. Encore Music Ltd.[11]

Encore operated a retail music store where they sold pianos, organs, and other musical instruments and equipment. Kawai Canada Music Ltd. supplied a series of pianos and other musical equipment to Encore under a series of conditional sales agreements. These were all properly registered under the appropriate legislation in place in that province.

Before these transaction took place, Encore borrowed money from the Royal Bank, which had taken as security an assignment of "all pianos, organs, and miscellaneous parts and accessories held for repair or resale" under Section 178 of the *Bank Act* (R.S.C. 1985, c. B-1). When Encore defaulted on their payments to Kawai, they repossessed the instruments they had supplied, but the bank intervened, claiming they had priority under the Section 178 security. The court had to decide whether the *Bank Act* prevailed over the provincial legislation. The court held that although the *Bank Act* prevailed and the interests of the bank came first, because of the nature of a conditional sale, Encore never did have title to the instruments that Kawai supplied. They could not give as security what they did not have, and so Kawai had first claim under the conditional sales agreements.

10. S.C. 1991, c. 46

11. (1993) 101 D.L.R. (4th) 1 (Alta. C.A.)

Note that this case illustrates the nature of the *Bank Act* security and the ability to take changing inventory as security, the pianos being after-acquired property. But it also shows the limitations of such security and the essential nature of a conditional sale agreement where title remains with the seller. This transaction took place before there was a personal property security act in place in Alberta, and there is some question whether the case would be decided the same today after the *Re Telecom Leasing Canada (Re Giffen)* case in the Supreme Court of Canada discussed above.

Floating Charges

Floating charges are used by creditors when dealing with corporations that must be free to purchase and sell the assets used as security without interference. When a corporation makes a bond or a debenture issue, it is often secured by such a floating charge.

Bonds and debentures

A corporation's debt can take several forms, including a **bond** or **debenture**. Bonds are usually secured and, in effect, involve a mortgage of company assets, whereas debentures are usually unsecured. The terms are confusing because in the United Kingdom, a debenture is secured, whereas in the United States and usually in Canada, it is not. A bond or debenture issue usually involves more than one creditor, and such bonds or debentures are commonly sold on the open market.

Floating charge not fixed on goods until default

The security granted often takes the form of a floating charge against the general assets of the corporation as with inventory and goods in the process of manufacture. This allows the corporation to continue to purchase new goods and sell its inventory in the normal course of business, and customers take the goods they purchase free and clear of any encumbrance. It is only upon default or some other crystallizing event as set out in the agreement, such as the payment of unauthorized dividends or the sale of a valuable asset, that the floating charge descends, attaches to the specific goods, and becomes a fixed charge. Any other fixed charge, such as a chattel mortgage against specific property will take priority over the floating charge, assuming both have been properly registered (unless this has been changed by statute). The advantage of a floating charge is that it can be used against inventory or goods being manufactured without interfering with the ongoing business and still provide a priority against unsecured general creditors.

Since the personal property security acts in place in most jurisdictions allow inventory and other changing assets to be used as security, in those jurisdictions, the floating charge is of diminishing importance.

Other Legislation

Creditors protected when merchant sells bulk of business

Other legislation has been enacted to protect creditors against frauds committed by debtors. The *Bulk Sale Act* in place in some provinces is designed to prevent merchants from selling all or almost all of the business's assets before a creditor can take action to stop them. Creditors expect a business to sell inventory in the normal course of business, but when all or most of the inventory or other assets or equipment needed for the ongoing operation is sold, this indicates that the merchant is going out of business, and the *Bulk Sale Act* operates in these circumstances to protect the creditors. This is done by requiring that the purchaser obtain a list of creditors, that they be notified of the sale, and that, if they wish, the proceeds be paid directly to them.

Bulk sale acts regulate sale of large portion of assets

Sometimes, desperate debtors are tempted to hide property or otherwise protect it from the claims of creditors. Giving or selling property to a friend or relative to avoid the debt becomes a void transaction. The creditor can seek out the fraudulently transferred property and get it back from the purchaser. This does not apply to a proper sale involving an arm's-length transaction, where a fair price is paid and the purchaser is unaware of any debts owing. In these circumstances, the third party is called a *bona fide* **purchaser for value**. Another way in which a debtor might attempt to cheat a creditor is by paying one creditor in preference over another. This is often done where the defaulting debtor hopes to again deal with the preferred creditor sometime in the future. The unpaid creditors can challenge this type of **fraudulent preference**.

Fraudulent conveyance void

Fraudulent preference void

Legislation embodying these provisions varies from province to province; the statutes are variously called *Fraudulent Conveyances Act, Fraudulent Preferences Act, Assignment and Preferences Act,* and *Fraudulent Creditors Act.* They are designed primarily to prevent debtors from unfairly making payments or transferring property in such a way as to keep it from the just claims of creditors. The Saskatchewan *Fraudulent Preferences Act* reads as follows:

> 3. ... every gift, conveyance, assignment or transfer, delivery over, or payment of goods, chattels, or effects or of bills, bonds, notes, or securities or of shares, dividends, premiums, or bonus in a bank, company, or corporation, or of any other property real or personal, made by a person at a time when he is in insolvent circumstances or is unable to pay his debts in full or knows that he is on the eve of insolvency, with intent to defeat, hinder, delay, or prejudice his creditors or any one or more of them, is void as against the creditor or creditors injured, delayed or prejudiced.[12]

The federal *Bankruptcy and Insolvency Act* discussed below also has provisions prohibiting settlements (fraudulent transfers) and preferences (provisions that apply uniformly throughout Canada). The wording used in the federal and provincial acts vary considerably, which may make it more effective in any given situation to proceed under one statute than another.

Similar restriction in federal bankruptcy

Guarantees

Another method creditors use to ensure the repayment of a debt is the guarantee. When corporations are involved, the use of guarantees is very common as a means of circumventing the limited liability characteristic of incorporation, making the principals of a corporation directly responsible for loans and other obligations. In consumer transactions, they are a frequently used method of putting a more substantial debtor under obligation to ensure the repayment of a loan or other debt, as when parents are asked to guarantee the loans of their children.

The essential nature of a guarantee is that the creditor can turn to some third party who assumes the obligation to ensure the debt is repaid. The borrower produces a relative, friend, or business associate who is willing to take responsibility for the debt.

Guarantor must pay when debtor defaults

A guarantee involves a secondary obligation that arises only in the event of a default. It is not a guarantee when a third party agrees to be directly responsible for paying a debt or to indemnify the creditor for any loss; such an obligation is not secondary but primary, the debtors sharing the responsibility, and is referred to as an **indemnity**.

12. *Fraudulent Preferences Act,* R.S.S. (196=78) c. F-21 s. 3

Evidence in writing of guarantee required

The distinction, although subtle, can be important. As we discussed in Chapter 5, the *Statute of Frauds* requires that certain types of contracts be evidenced in writing to be enforceable in the courts. In most provinces, only the guarantee must be evidenced in writing, but in British Columbia, both indemnities and guarantees must be evidenced in writing. And in Alberta, personal guarantees other than those for land transactions must be entered into in the presence of a notary public, and a certificate to that effect must be produced, which states that the lawyer or notary is satisfied that the guarantor understands the nature of the obligation entered into, and when this is not correct, the guarantee is unenforceable.[13]

Contractual requirements must be met for guarantor to be bound

Since a guarantee is a separate contract, all the elements of a contract, including consensus (offer and acceptance) and consideration, must be present. There is seldom a difficulty with consensus, as the advancement of the funds is a good indication of acceptance, but consideration can sometimes be a problem. The consideration requirement is usually satisfied when the funds are advanced to the debtor. It may not look like the guarantor gets anything from the deal, but the creditor would not have advanced the funds without the guarantee, and so, there is consideration on both sides. Where the guarantee is obtained because the debtor is in default, the consideration is the creditor's refraining from exercising his right to take action against the debtor.

—including consideration

Sometimes, however, the funds are advanced before the guarantee is given. If Kotsalis borrows money from the Business Bank and the manager of the bank fails to obtain a guarantee as required by bank policy, he will be in trouble if tries to get it later. If the manager gets a third party to sign a guarantee after the fact, it would likely fail because of the lack of consideration, the funds already having been advanced. To avoid any problem with consideration, these institutions usually require all guarantees be placed under seal. As we discussed in Chapter 4, when a seal is present, consideration is conclusively presumed.

Rights and Obligations of the Parties

The creditor has significant duties to protect the interests of the guarantor. At the outset, it is important for the creditor to ensure that the guarantor understands the full nature of the guarantee he or she is signing. Guarantors often escape their obligation by claiming misrepresentation, *non est factum,* or undue influence. When in doubt, the creditor should insist that the guarantor obtain independent legal advice.

Creditors must not weaken the position of the guarantor

After the guarantee has been created, the creditor is obligated to do nothing to weaken the position of the guarantor; therefore, the agreement must be strictly adhered to. Subsequent dealings between the creditor and debtor without involving the guarantor are the most common grounds for ending a guarantor's obligation. The principle is that any substantial change in the nature of the contract between the creditor and debtor without the guarantor's consent will relieve the guarantor of any obligation. If the creditor simply delays bringing an action to give a defaulting debtor a chance to pay, this will not be considered a substantial change in the relationship but just a gratuitous forbearance on the part of the creditor in enforcing his legal rights. If this is done formally with a change to the agreement, the creditor should take care to include a statement reserving rights against the guarantor. The effect will be that the guarantor will continue to be bound by the original agreement. Generally, when the creditor and debtor without the guarantor agree to changes, such as more debt, a higher interest rate, different sized installments, such changes can release the guarantor from obligation.

Significant changes may release guarantor

Creditor can reserve rights against guarantor

13. Bank of British Columbia v. Shank Investments et al. [1985] 1 W.W.R. 730

Guarantor Released Because of Change

Farries Enterprises owned certain property and gave Royal Trust a mortgage on it to secure a loan. Reid also guaranteed the loan. Afterwards, Farries sold the property to a third party, who agreed to assume the mortgage and the responsibilities under it. Unfortunately, they ran into financial troubles and got Royal Trust to extend the loan for a year at higher interest. But they still defaulted on the loan, so Royal Trust seized the property and had it sold. In this action, Royal Trust sued Reid for the difference between what was owing and what the property was sold for, claiming Reid was still responsible as guarantor. The court held that Reid was no longer responsible, since the nature of the agreement changed when the time was extended and the higher rate of interest agreed to, and Reid had not consented to this.

Reid et al. v. Royal Trust Corporation of Canada, (1985) 20 D.L.R. (4th) 223 (P.E.I. C.A.)

The guarantor is also released from obligation when other forms of security, such as chattel mortgages, are released. For example, if Kotsalis were to go to the Business Bank requesting a loan and the bank required that Bruno guarantee the loan in addition to taking a chattel mortgage against Kotsalis's car as security, such an arrangement would cease to be binding on Bruno if the bank subsequently allowed Kotsalis to sell the car without the consent of Bruno. Similarly, Bruno would be released if the bank advanced Kotsalis more money or agreed to a change in the nature of the repayment terms without Bruno's consent. However, the guarantor is still bound if the agreement between the guarantor and the creditor permits such modification. It is becoming common practice for such transactions to contain a clause creating a **continuing guarantee,** allowing the creditor to continue to advance funds up to a pre-set limit without affecting the obligation of the guarantor to pay in the event of default.

Releasing security

First City Capital Ltd. v. Hall[14]

Karsha Holdings Ltd. was a company whose sole shareholders and officers were Hall and deHaan. The company entered into seven lease agreements for word processing equipment with First City Capital and Hall and deHaan signed personal guarantees for the indebtedness. Karsha Holdings Ltd. also owed money to the Royal Bank secured against the assets of the corporation. A few years later, Hall sold her interest in Karsha Holdings to deHaan, and shortly after, Karsha Holdings defaulted on its payments to First City Capital for the seven leases and on the indebtedness to the Royal Bank. First City Capital had failed to perfect their lease agreements through registration as required, and so, the word processing equipment went to the Royal Bank, which had properly perfected its security.

First City Capital turned to Hall on the personal guarantee for payment. Did First City's failure to register release Hall from her guarantee? The court decided that First City owed the guarantor an obligation to ensure that the security was perfected so that it could be returned to that guarantor upon payment of the guarantee. Their failure to do so prevented them from seeking redress from Hall. The court found that in the absence of any provision in the contract relieving them of this obligation, First City was prohibited from suing. Interestingly, there was a provision in the guarantee that attempted to relieve them of such obligations. It stated that the guarantee would be enforceable, "notwithstanding that the lease or any

14. (1993) 99 D.L.R. (4th) 435 (Ont. C.A.)

other arrangements shall be void or voidable against the lessee ... including ... by reason ... of ... failure by any person to file any document or take any other action to
make the lease ... enforceable."

But the court responded to this by pointing out that the failure to properly register the leases did not make those leases void or voidable, just ineffective against third
parties. This provision of the guarantee agreement said nothing about ineffective
leases, and so, First City was still prohibited from suing Hall on the guarantee.

This case nicely illustrates the operation of the guarantee, and the obligations
placed on the creditor to preserve and protect the position of the guarantor doing
nothing to weaken it. It also illustrates how any provisions in the guarantee agreement that purports to change these obligations are strictly interpreted in favour
of the guarantor.

Withholding information

The guarantor may also be released from this obligation where the creditor
has important information that has been withheld from the guarantor. Because
there is a duty to disclose such information, withholding it can amount to misrepresentation. This is what happened in the *Calderbank* case discussed at the beginning
of the chapter. To be considered misrepresentation, the withheld information
must be of some substantial and unusual nature and not simply the normal kind of
information that would pass between business associates. In the *Calderbank* case,
the information that the driving force behind the company, Calderbank, intended
to start another company in competition was of such significant and unusual nature
as to void the guarantee.

**Guarantor assumes rights
of creditor upon payment**

When a default occurs, the creditor is not required to demand payment from
the debtor or take steps to seize any other security before seeking payment from the
guarantor, unless this has been agreed to in the contract. A guarantor who pays
the debt is **subrogated** to the rights of the creditor, which means, in effect, that
the guarantor steps into the creditor's shoes. Any remedy or right available to the
creditor after payment is available to the guarantor, including the right to seize a
chattel used as security for the debt and to sue the debtor and take advantage of the
proceedings available to assist in collecting the debt.

**Defences of debtor are
available to guarantor**

Also, any defences that are available to the debtor are also available to the guarantor. If breach of contract, fraud, or misrepresentation on the part of the creditor
has barred an action by the creditor against the debtor, the creditor cannot instead look to the guarantor for payment because the guarantor is entitled to those
same defences. Note, however, that if the reason the guarantee was required was because of the infancy of the debtor, the guarantor will normally not be allowed to use
that infancy as a defence against the creditor.

Because the basic obligations of the guarantor are determined by contract, they
can be modified by contract as well. Today, it is common for creditors to include provisions that attempt to exempt the creditor from the basic obligations discussed
here, but like all exemption clauses, they are interpreted very carefully by the courts
against the party they advantage. Great care should be taken when entering into a
guarantee to determine the extent of such exemption clauses and how they modify the obligations of the parties.

Builders' Liens

A person who supplies goods or services that will be incorporated into another
person's property faces two potentially significant problems in common law. First,
when the contract is with the owner, the only recourse is to sue the owner, not to

take action against the property. Second, if the contract is with someone working for the owner of the property, such as a general contractor in construction situations, there is no contractual remedy against the owner because of the principle of privity. Subcontractors and wage earners in these circumstances must look to the general contractor for satisfaction.

To alleviate these difficulties, the *Mechanics' Lien Acts*, the *Builders' Lien Acts* and, in Ontario, the *Construction Liens Act*, were passed. The resulting liens are variously called mechanics' liens, builders' liens, or construction liens. These acts allow the contractor, subcontractor, wager, earner, or supplier, or lessor of goods or equipment, to register a lien against that property in order to force payment. If necessary, this extends to selling the property to satisfy the debt.

Privity overcome with builders' lien

Registration

The registration of the lien must take place within 30 to 60 days of the work done (or completion of the project depending on the province). Registration only creates a claim against the property. To realize on the claim, the lien holder must commence an action in court to enforce contractual obligation.

Registration establishes claim

In Ontario, the process is similar to that used under the *Personal Property Security Act*. The lien is created when the work is done or the goods are supplied; but in order to enforce the lien, it must first be preserved and then perfected. The lien is preserved by registration within 45 days of the substantial completion of the job (or in some situations, by serving notice on the landowner). Perfection takes place when the lien holder initiates a court action to enforce the contractual claim.[15]

Holdback

It should be obvious that this process places a heavy burden on the landowner, who is liable to pay the contractor, but is also liable for that contractor's obligations to his suppliers' employees and subcontractors. The holdback provision was created to relieve this burden. The statutes require that the landowner (or anyone else paying funds to others working on the property) hold back a certain percentage (from 10 to 20 percent, depending on the province), and that these funds be retained to satisfy any liens that may be filed against the property. The holdback is retained slightly longer than the period in which a lien must be filed, and if there is no lien within the specified period, the amount held back is then paid out pursuant to the contract.

Holdback fulfills obligation

For example, Brough, a land owner in British Columbia, has a contract with Soland to build a house for $100 000. Soland hires several subtrades and contracts with suppliers to do the job. If not paid, those suppliers and subcontractors have the right to file a lien against the property within 45 days. Brough, instead of paying Soland the $100 000 contracted for, would withhold 10%, or $10 000. At the end of the specified time (55 days in British Columbia), Brough would search to ensure no liens had been filed. If none were filed, Brough would pay Soland the remaining $10 000, knowing that it was too late for any liens to be filed. If Brough discovered that a lien had been filed, he would retain the $10 000 and apply to the court to have the lien removed. Brough would pay the $10 000 into court, leaving himself and the lien claimant to fight over the money. Even if there were several liens filed, and the claims were for more than the 10% holdback, it would be the end of Brough's obligation and the court would remove the lien from his property upon payment of the $10 000 into court. Alternatively, Brough could simply wait

Court will remove lien upon payment of holdback in court

15. *Construction Liens Act*, R.S.O. (1990) c. 30

to see if any of the lien claimants commenced an action to enforce their claim in court. If they failed to do so, the lien would automatically end after one year in British Columbia (180 days in Alberta and 90 days in Ontario). In British Columbia, Brough could actually demand that an action commence within 21 days, and failure to do so on the part of the lien holder would extinguish the lien.

The only circumstances under which Brough might have to pay more than the 10% holdback would be if he were aware of the disputes, and that liens were filed before he paid the $90 000 to Soland. Many provinces now require that a certificate of substantial completion is made when the job is finished. The times discussed here will run from the creation of that certificate.

Priorities

As mentioned above, if not paid, sale of the property can be forced by the lien claimant. This seldom happens, however, because the presence of the lien puts great pressure on the landowner to pay to have it removed. When registered against the property, it takes priority over other interests, including new mortgages (which include any further advances on existing mortgages) or transfers. Thus, the owner can't sell the property or mortgage it without removing the lien. Of course, in the unlikely event that the property is sold to satisfy the lien claimants, any pre-existing mortgages have to be satisfied before the lien claimants are paid out of the proceeds.

Funds paid constitute trust

A problem often arises when a landowner or contractor pays funds for a job to someone he has contracted with, and the recipient, instead of paying his subtrades, diverts that money to other debts he has owing. To ensure that the funds paid out by one party are used to pay others with respect to that project, several provinces, including Ontario and British Columbia, have declared that any funds paid pursuant to the job constitute a trust fund with the suppliers of goods and services as beneficiaries of that trust. This designation is significant because it provides both civil and criminal remedies (when any of the parties breach that trust) by diverting the funds for another purpose. The funds are also insulated against claims levied against them by outside creditors, giving priority to the claims of those who contributed directly to the job, such as wage earners, subcontractors, and suppliers.

Harding Carpets Ltd. v. Saint John Tile & Terrazzo Co. Ltd.[16]

This case deals with the construction of the Hilton Hotel in Saint John, New Brunswick. The General contractor was Rocca Construction Ltd., and Rocca subcontracted for both the supply and installation of the carpeting to Saint John Tile & Terrazzo. It is important to note that Saint John Tile owed Rocca Construction $50 000 for a deficiency in another project.

In this hotel job, a string of subcontractors and suppliers were involved, the carpeting eventually being purchased from Harding Carpets.

Rocca Construction paid Saint John Tile the $80 000 agreed but insisted that Saint John Tile pay them back the $50 000 owing on the outstanding debt. This they did. The remaining $30 000 did not make it through all the subcontractors and Harding got nothing. Although there was no direct contract between Harding Carpets and Rocca, they claimed that the original $80 000 paid to Saint John Tile constituted a trust under the provincial *Builder's Lien Act* and that it could not be diverted to another debt. The court agreed, and Rocca had to pay the money owing to Harding. This case illustrates the problems created because of privity of contract

16. 49 D.L.R. (4th) 311; leave to appeal to S.C.C. refused November 3, 1988 (N.B.C.A.)

in the construction industry and the legislated solutions in the form of trust provisions now included in most builder's liens statutes.

It is important to point out that in this case, the money was paid to the subcontractor and then returned creating the trust. In *Re P. Nicholls Enterprises Ltd.,*[17] the money to cover the prior debt was simply withheld from the subcontractor. The Ontario Court of Appeal held that where the contractor simply withholds the money owed, there is no trust created, and the right to set off one debt against the other old debt remains. The Ontario legislation has been changed since this case with the *Construction Liens Act,* and so, now even funds "not yet paid" would be part of the trust funds and likely not available for set off in that province.

Negotiable Instruments

Toronto Dominion Bank v. Jordan[18]

Mrs. Jordan was a bank clerk who had convinced her husband and Mr. Courage, the manager of the local branch of the Toronto Dominion Bank, that she was a wealthy and successful business executive. In fact, she was using the bank accounts of several relatives to move money from account to account to support her speculation in the stock market. Such a practice is known as "kiting" and involves drawing cheques on a succession of accounts to cover funds drawn from those accounts. Because there is a time delay in clearing the cheques and the final cheque covers the deficit caused by the first cheque, it is difficult to detect that there is an amount outstanding.

Mrs. Jordan gave Mr. Courage gifts and involved him in some of her profitable speculations. When two other bank managers became suspicious and warned him that she might be kiting cheques, he ignored their warnings. Mr. Courage did become nervous, however, and pressed her to cover a $350 000 overdraft that he had allowed her to accumulate. Mrs. Jordan covered this with a blank cheque she had obtained from her husband drawn on the Teacher's Credit Union, which she filled in for $359 000. She gave the cheque to Mr. Courage, but when it was dishonoured, it brought her "kiting" scheme to an end.

The Toronto Dominion Bank branch, of which Mr. Courage was the manager, then sued Mr. Jordan for the face value of the cheque drawn on his account. Normally, the bank would be in no better position than Mrs. Jordan and would not be able to collect because of her fraud. But when a negotiable instrument is involved, the situation can be quite different. If an innocent third party acquires a cheque in good faith, it can be enforced against the drawer, even if the intervening party has been fraudulent.

This raised the question of whether Mr. Courage had acted in good faith. The court looked at his involvement with Mrs. Jordan and decided that while he may not have been directly dishonest, he certainly had not acquired the cheque in good faith and, therefore, the bank could not enforce it against Mr. Jordan.[19]

This complicated set of transactions illustrates the most significant characteristic of negotiable instruments—that is, their enforceability in the hands of innocent third parties and the corresponding extreme vulnerability of those who make such negotiable instruments and allow them to be circulated.

17. 17 D.L.R. (4th) 301 (Ont. C.A.)
18. (1985) 61 B.C.L.R. 105 (C.A.); leave to appeal to S.C.C. refused (1985) 62 B.C.L.R. xii
19. *Ibid* at p. 105

Another tool often used in credit transactions is a negotiable instrument. **Negotiable instruments** are primarily cheques, promissory notes, and bills of exchange, and they have some very unique characteristics. Their origins are founded in common law, with a history that can be traced back to the Law Merchant discussed in Chapter 1. Today, negotiable instruments are controlled by federal statute—the *Bills of Exchange Act*.[20] They are used primarily as a convenient method of transferring funds (cheques), or as an instrument of credit where they are made payable at some future date. They can be made to bear interest and be paid by installment. The feature that makes them so unique is their characteristic of negotiability. Negotiable instruments can be transferred from one person to another without notice to the original debtor and still be presented by the holder with the assurance of payment independent of any problems associated with the original transaction. While the use of negotiable instruments has fallen because of the growing use of credit cards, debit cards, and the electronic transfer of funds, they still play a significant role in commercial transactions and consumer credit.

The principle of privity of contract (discussed in Chapter 7) normally would dictate that any third party being assigned rights in a transaction would be in no better position than the person they obtained those rights from. Thus, if the claims of that original party to the transaction were defective, the claims obtained by any assignee would also be defective. In other words, if the debtor had a good defense against the other party to the transaction, they would also have a good defense against any assignee. However, with negotiable instruments, even though the position between the original parties is no better, once that instrument gets into the hands of a third party who qualifies as a **holder in due course**, that party can collect on the instrument, despite any problems with the original transaction and any defenses the debtor may have had against the original party to whom the negotiable instrument was originally given.

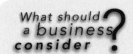

Business people often use negotiable instruments with no thought of the implications. When they use a cheque to pay a debt, they usually assume that if there is a problem, they can stop payment; while this may be true with respect to the original payee, if that cheque is passed on to an innocent third party (a holder in due course), they will be obligated under the cheque, even if it turns out that the goods purchased were defective or the services below standard. The same applies with promissory notes and bills of exchange. Often, business people are asked to sign a promissory note along with other documents where a credit transaction is involved. What they do not realize is that the note or bill can be negotiated to an innocent third party and that they will be obligated to honour it, no matter how dissatisfied they are with the goods or services provided. Business people must be very cautious when dealing with negotiable instruments and appreciate that when they sign them they will likely have to honour them, no matter what problems arise.

To qualify as a holder in due course, that person must have **received it through negotiation**, and not be one of the original parties to the instrument. It must be taken **complete and regular on its face**, without any indication of alteration. A person cannot be a holder in due course of a "blank cheque." The holder in due course must have acquired it before it became **due and payable**; otherwise, the question arises why a previous holder didn't present it for payment. Where the instrument is payable on demand, it must not be overdue, which means in circulation for an "unreasonable length of time." If you know it has been **dishonoured**, you

Negotiable instruments are freely transferrable and used as substitutes for cash

Holder in due course acquires better rights

Holder in due course must have acquired instrument

—through negotiation

—before due and payable

---

20. *Bills of Exchange Act*, R.S.C. 1985, c. B-4

cannot be a holder in due course. Also, the instrument has to have been acquired in **good faith** without **notice of any problems** associated with the original transaction, called "**defects of title**." Such defects of title may be viewed as problems, such as fraud, undue influence, duress, illegal consideration, or incapacity associated with the original transaction. Finally, someone (not necessarily the person claiming to be a holder in due course) must have given valid consideration for the instrument. Where the instrument has been forged or altered, or where it has been discharged by payment or otherwise so that the holder has notice of it, is called **real defenses**, and the maker of the instrument will not have to pay even when the person presenting it for payment qualifies as an innocent holder in due course.

—in good faith

—with no defects

—valid consideration

Real defenses allow maker to not pay out on instrument

Thus, if James sold Sandoval some phony stocks, paid for with a promissory note, Sandoval would be perfectly within his rights to refuse to pay James when the note became due on the basis of the fraud. However, if James were to pass that promissory note on to an innocent third party (that gave consideration for it and had no notice of the fraud, such as James' bank or another creditor who qualified as a holder in due course), Sandoval would have to pay and could not use James' fraud as a defense. This characteristic makes such promissory notes extremely attractive in commercial transactions, since the person receiving the note, cheque, or bill has to worry less about the validity of the original transaction and concentrate instead on the credit worthiness of the person committed to pay on the instrument. Of course, if the holder presenting it for payment knows about the fraud of "defect of title," they would not qualify as a holder in due course and Sandoval would not have to pay.

Royal Bank of Canada Ltd. v. Pentagon Construction Maritime Ltd.[21]

Maramichi Glassworks Ltd. was a customer of the Royal Bank. It was in financial difficulty when it assigned any benefits flowing under a contract it had with Pentagon Construction Maritime Ltd. (Maritime) to the Royal Bank. Maritime was informed of this arrangement and made two cheques totalling approximately $20 000 payable to Maramichi Glassworks. Maritime made it clear to Maramichi that unless Maramichi performed the appropriate services contracted for, the cheque would not be honoured. Maritime made this clear to the Royal Bank as well. Maramichi Glassworks did not live up to its contractual requirements, and Maritime put a stop payment on these two cheques. The Royal Bank tried to collect, but the cheques were dishonoured. The Royal Bank sued Maritime claiming to be a holder in due course. The court found that because the Royal Bank knew that payment of the cheques was qualified, being payable only if the payee performed the work contracted for, the bank could not qualify as a holder in due course and could not enforce payment against Maritime because the condition had not been met.

This case illustrates that in order to qualify as a negotiable instrument, the cheque or any other negotiable instrument must be unconditional. Since the promise to pay was qualified, and the bank knew it, the bank didn't qualify as a holder in due course and could not enforce payment.

21. (1983) 45 N.B.R. (2d) 148 (Q.B.)

Types of Negotiable Instruments

The subject of negotiable instruments is governed by the *Bills of Exchange Act*, which was originally passed in 1890, with very little modification since. The *Bills of Exchange Act* is federal legislation, and so, its provisions apply uniformly throughout Canada.[22] Although the statute basically codified the existing common law, there were some important changes, and the current act makes it clear that common law principles apply except when specifically contrary to the provisions of the act. One of the effects of leaving the door open to the operation of common law in this way is that the types of negotiable instruments are not limited to promissory notes, bills of exchange, and cheques as set out in the act. Thus, bonds payable to order and share certificates can also share the characteristics of negotiable instruments.[23]

Bills of Exchange

With bill of exchange, drawee orders drawer to pay payee

A bill of exchange, sometimes referred to as a **draft**, involves three people. The **drawer** draws up the instrument and orders the **drawee** to pay a third party, the **payee**, when the instrument is presented for payment. Although the bill is addressed to the drawee, it is physically transferred to the payee, who is entitled to collect on it. Usually, the drawee is a financial institution with which the drawer has made prior arrangements, to ensure that the instrument will be honoured. Although the same form is used, sometimes a bill of exchange is used as a means of collecting a debt, and then, the drawer orders the drawee/debtor to make payment to a third party. The idea is that when the payee presents the instrument to the drawee/debtor for payment, it will be honoured; if it is not, there will be damage to the debtor's credit standing.

Bills of Exchange

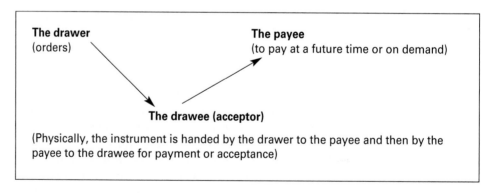

The drawer
(orders)

The payee
(to pay at a future time or on demand)

The drawee (acceptor)

(Physically, the instrument is handed by the drawer to the payee and then by the payee to the drawee for payment or acceptance)

Bill paid upon maturity

The bill of exchange may be payable immediately, but often is made payable at some future time, thus creating a credit relationship. When this happens, the payee will often bring the instrument to the drawee to see if it will be honoured at the maturity date. In these circumstances, the drawee will give assurance of future

22. *Bills of Exchange Act*, R.S.C. 1985, c. B-4
23. *Business Corporations Act*, S.Q. 1982

payment by writing "accepted" across the instrument with the appropriate time, date, and signature. Before this acceptance, the payee has no claim on the drawee, relying only on the drawee's obligations to the drawer to pay the instrument. The drawer could order the drawee not to pay if for some reason the transaction it was based on went bad. The payee could not force the drawee to pay, and if the bill was dishonoured, has to look to the drawer for redress. However, after the drawee has accepted, the drawee becomes the acceptor and is primarily liable under the instrument. As a result, the drawer loses all control over the instrument and can no longer countermand payment.

Once accepted, drawee primarily liable

Drawee has no obligation to payee before acceptance

For example, if Garcia buys a boat from Saito and gives Saito a bill of exchange, payable three months later, drawn on Ace Trust Company, where Garcia has an account or line of credit, it is quite likely that Saito would go to Ace Trust Company as soon as possible to find out whether Ace would honour the bill three months hence. Ace Trust Company would indicate their willingness to honour the instrument at maturity by their representative writing "accepted" across the instrument, accompanied by the date and the signature of the appropriate signing officer. If they refuse to do this, the bill would be dishonoured, and Saito would then turn to Garcia, the original drawer of the instrument, for satisfaction. But if Ace does accept the bill, Garcia can no longer issue any instructions to Ace in relation to it. In effect, the primary debtor is now Ace Trust Company. Since they have assumed the debt and the obligation to pay, Garcia has lost control of the situation. Even if Garcia were to discover that there had been some fraudulent misrepresentation on the part of Saito, Garcia could no longer countermand the order to Ace Trust Company once the bill has been accepted and Ace has become the primary debtor. Garcia has the right to sue Saito for compensation, but he cannot prevent Ace from paying out on the accepted bill of exchange.

Although the bill of exchange was traditionally the most significant type of negotiable instrument, its use in modern times has dwindled because of business people's increased reliance on cheques and, more recently, the move to electronic methods of banking. However, the bill of exchange is still a valuable tool of commerce, and there are many circumstances in which, because of tradition or the need for the unique qualities of this instrument, the bill of exchange is still important today.

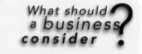

Cheques

The most common form of negotiable instrument is the cheque, which most people use in their regular financial dealings. It is defined as a bill of exchange drawn on a bank and payable on demand (and so, shares the general characteristics of the bill of exchange discussed above). Since it is payable on demand, it is primarily used to transfer funds, rather than as an instrument of credit. Post-dated cheques are sometimes used but, technically, are not negotiable instruments before the specified date. A cheque involves three people. The drawer makes out the cheque and is obligated to it; the bank (or credit union) is ordered to pay it when presented; and the payee, the person it is made out to, is entitled to the payment. Like the bill of exchange, the bank has no obligation to honour the instrument, and so it can be countermanded by the drawer any time before payment. In this event, the payee must look to the drawer for redress. To avoid this, the practice of certifying the cheque either before or after it has been delivered to the payee has been

Cheque is a bill of exchange drawn on the bank payable on demand

developed. When this happens, the bank has given assurance that the cheque will be honoured, and it is then treated like an accepted bill of exchange (the drawer loses the right to countermand). Many banks now issue a separate bank draft instead of going through this certification process.

Cheques

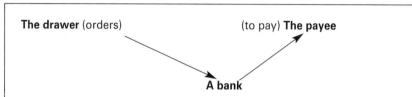

The drawer (orders) (to pay) **The payee**

A bank

(Physically, the instrument is handed by the drawer to the payee and then by the payee to the bank. Certification can be requested by the drawer before delivery or by the payee after delivery)

A Certified Cheque Is Like Cash

Office Plus Interiors entered into an agreement to purchase office furniture from Centrac for $48 000. Centrac demanded payment by certified cheque. Mr. Stanway, a principal of Office Plus, deposited a cheque for $76 000 from another source in their account at the Canadian Imperial Bank of Commerce (CIBC). He then asked the bank to certify an Office Plus cheque for $48 000 to Centrac, which they did without checking to see if the deposited cheque would be honoured. Centrac took the cheque and delivered the furniture to Office Plus. When it was learned that the $76 000 cheque deposited earlier would not be honoured, the representatives of the CIBC phoned Centrac and told them not to bother trying to negotiate the $48 000 cheque, as they had stopped payment on it. But Centrac did present it for payment, and when it was dishonoured, Centrac sued CIBC for payment. The court held that when the bank had certified the cheque, it was giving Mr. Stanway something equivalent to cash, and therefore CIBC was required to honour it. "Once certification was made, any attempt made by the bank to avoid payment was too late." The bank, in this case, may have made an error in not checking out the first $76 000 cheque, but they could not hide behind that error.

Centrac Inc. v. Canadian Imperial Bank of Commerce, 120 D.L.R. (4th) 765 (Ont. C.A.)

Promissory Notes

Promissory notes are promises to pay

The easiest form of negotiable instrument to understand is the promissory note. This involves only two people: the maker, who promises to pay a specified amount (often with interest and in installments), and the payee, to whom the payment is due (at a specified time or on demand). Where installments are involved, the payment should be noted on the instrument so that any subsequent holder has notice. The main function of promissory notes is to advance credit; they are commonly used by financial institutions, especially in consumer loan transactions. The position of the maker of such a promissory note is the same as the acceptor of a bill of exchange—they are simply obligated to honour the note. As with other negotiable instruments,

Main function is to advance credit

when the note gets into the hands of an innocent third party, the third party can enforce it, even if there are problems with the original transaction.

It is this characteristic that makes the use of promissory notes so attractive to merchants and financial institutions arranging consumer credit. The merchant will often arrange a sale on credit and then transfer the credit aspect of the transaction to a separate financial institution. Even if there has been fraud or some other form of questionable conduct on the part of the merchant, the financial institution to which the instrument is transferred does not have to worry, because it is an innocent third party. This practice is subject to abuse, and because of this, the *Bills of Exchange Act* was amended in 1970, requiring such transactions to be stamped as "consumer purchase." With this notification, the advantages of being an innocent third party are lost, and the debtor on the instrument can raise the same defenses against a holder in due course that they could against the original merchant, who was the payee on the instrument.

Promissory Note

The maker   (promises to pay a certain sum, on a date or on demand to)   **The payee**
──►
(The maker gives the note to the payee who later can collect as promised)

Negotiation

To qualify as a negotiable instrument, the cheque, bill of exchange, or promissory note must meet certain qualifications. The negotiable instrument must be **unconditional**—a note made payable "if the car is properly repaired" would not qualify as a negotiable instrument. The instrument must be in **writing and signed** by the maker or drawer (or authorized agent). It must also be **payable at some fixed time or on demand**. By definition, a cheque is payable on demand, and that is why a postdated cheque does not qualify as a negotiable instrument until the specified date arrives. Promissory notes, on the other hand, are usually made payable at some specified future date and are thus instruments of credit. They can also be made payable after some uncertain but inevitable date, such as "90 days after the death of Jones." The instrument must also be made out for a **fixed amount of money** specified on the face. A promise to pay inheritance will not qualify, as the amount is not certain. Note that the instrument can bear interest, provided the amount is specified and it can be paid by installments. When the installments are made, it should be noted on the instrument so that a subsequent holder has notice. It should also be noted that the instrument only becomes negotiable after the maker has **delivered** it to the payee for the first time. However, if a completed instrument gets into the hands of an innocent holder in due course, such delivery is "conclusively presumed." Finally, it should be noted that as the instrument is passed from person to person, the **whole instrument must pass**. For example, you cannot take a promissory note made out for $1000 and transfer half of it to a subsequent holder

Instrument must be in writing and signed

—specified time for payment

—or on demand

—must be for a fixed sum

—must be delivered to payee

Cannot transfer only part of claim

and retain the other half for yourself. (You can sell the note at a discount, say for $800, but here the subsequent holder acquires the whole claim for $1000 even though he has only paid $800 for it.)

A key to understanding negotiable instruments is to remember that they are freely transferable from holder to holder without notice to the original maker. This process, negotiation, is accomplished in one of two ways. If it is a bearer instrument that is made out payable to bearer, then it need only be delivered from one person to another. If it is made payable to a specific person, it is called an order instrument and it must be endorsed (signed on the back by the person it is made payable to) and transferred. Once endorsed with a simple signature, called a **blank endorsement**, it becomes a bearer instrument. In fact, there are other ways of endorsing the instrument leading to different consequences. A **special endorsement** is where the endorser specifies to whom it is payable. Further negotiation requires a second endorsement of that person, just as with an order instrument. These are the most common forms, but others are also possible. A **restrictive endorsement**, "for deposit only," stops further negotiation. A **qualified endorsement**, "without recourse," protects the endorser from liability. Normally, if the negotiable instrument is not honoured, the holder can turn to any endorser for payment. This insulates the endorser from such an outcome. An **accommodation endorser** is not usually a holder of the instrument, but simply adds their credit to it through endorsement. Finally, a **conditional endorsement**, "Pay to Jones only if car repair acceptable," specifies who is to receive payment and places some condition on that right. Note that while a negotiable instrument must be unconditional, the same is not true of an endorsement.

When making such a negotiable instrument, remember that if it gets into the hands of an innocent holder in due course, which includes the payee's bank, the maker will have to honour it. When they pay by cheque, most people think they can stop payment if something goes wrong, and while that is true, that may only delay the inevitable. The bank usually requires a personal order to dishonour in writing, and when that is done, it will not pay (but the holder in due course will have the right to seek redress from the maker directly). The maker will then have to sue the payee for redress and, at this stage, that is often a hollow remedy.

Letters of Credit

Similar to negotiable instruments, the letter of credit is used in commercial relationships, especially in international trade. The **letter of credit** is a guarantee from the importer's bank that the price stated will be paid upon presentation of appropriate documentation confirming delivery, thus giving assurance from the financial institution to the seller that they will be paid by their customer. This letter of credit is normally delivered to the exporter by the importer, who, upon delivery of the goods, submits the appropriate documentation to the importer's bank and receives payment. Sometimes, especially when the importer's bank is in a foreign country, the exporter will require that a bank that they have confidence in, usually in their own country, becomes involved as a confirming bank. The exporter's chosen confirming bank then receives the letter of credit directly from the importer's bank and commits to the exporter that they will honour it upon receiving the appropriate documentation. The confirming bank plays a role very much like that of endorsing a negotiable instrument in that they add their guarantee to the letter of credit. The exporter then simply submits the appropriate documents indicating performance to their bank and receives payment.

Instrument must be endorsed and delivered

Holder must give notice of dishonour in writing

Letters of credit used in international trade

Role of confirming bank

If Chan were exporting pianos from Hong Kong to Weiss in Canada, to satisfy Chan, Weiss might ask the Royal Bank to generate a letter of credit to support this transaction. The letter of credit would guarantee payment to Chan of a specific amount (for example, $200 000) upon the production of certain documentation. This required documentation might include a proof of insurance, bill of lading, customs declaration, and invoice. It might even require a certificate of inspection from some third party to indicate that the goods are as expected. The letter of credit would be given to Weiss by the Royal Bank, and Weiss would deliver it to Chan, who would, upon shipping the goods, present the appropriate documents, including the letter of credit, and collect the money from the bank.

More likely than not, however, Chan would want his own bank involved in the transaction. If he only involves his bank in an advising capacity where it assumes no liability, it is referred to as an advising bank, but where Chan wants his bank to guarantee payment, it is called a confirming bank. If he were to choose the Hong Kong Bank as the confirming bank, he would inform Weiss of this requirement at the outset, and when making arrangements for the letter of credit with the Royal Bank, Weiss would also provide the Royal Bank with the particulars of the Honk Kong Bank as the confirming bank. The Royal Bank contacts the Hong Kong Bank directly, making arrangements for the confirmed letter of credit. The Hong Kong Bank then sends a confirmed letter of credit to Chan, who then ships the pianos. Chan then submits the appropriate documents confirming delivery to his bank, the Hong Kong Bank, which, after careful inspection and if satisfied, makes the appropriate payment. These documents are then sent to the Royal Bank, which pays the Hong Kong Bank and appropriately debits the account of Weiss.

This may seem like a very complex process, but it is really quite simple in that the two traders choose banks that they trust to hold and transfer the funds. The effect is quite similar to that of a bank draft, but this process is often more convenient and more flexible.

Often, drafts are used in conjunction with this process, the letter of credit authorizing the creditor to obtain payment by drawing a draft on the issuing or confirming bank. In the above example, Chan, upon presenting the appropriate documentation showing that the pianos were shipped, would then draw a bill of exchange (a draft) naming the Royal Bank as the drawee and himself or his bank as the payee, which he could then give to his bank for collection.

Drafts used in conjunction with letters of credit

Letters of credit are primarily used in international trade, but they are very flexible and because of this quality, it is not uncommon to find them being used in domestic business transactions as well. Letters of credit are also used in other ways, for example, to guarantee, in effect, that one party to a contract will properly perform. If there is a breach, the victim has recourse to the bank that has issued the letter of credit. This is referred to as a standby letter of credit.

Also used in domestic transactions

Bankruptcy

Both secured and unsecured creditors are affected when a debtor becomes bankrupt. An unsecured creditor, sometimes called a general creditor, has no priority claim against the assets of the debtor and, in the event of bankruptcy, is entitled only to a share of what is left after the secured creditors and others who have a prior claim have been paid. Even the secured creditor may become a general creditor for the outstanding amount where the sale of the item used as security does not bring in enough to pay all the debt. Such general creditors have no special claim to assets and must look to the normal debt collection processes discussed in Chapter 1.

General creditor has right to sue

A growing number of businesses face bankruptcy.

The Slide Farm/Al Harvey

These include the right to seek judgment and then take the appropriate steps to have that judgment enforced through the garnishee of bank accounts or the seizure of property. This may be a waste of resources, however, if there are many creditors and insufficient assets. In these circumstances, the debtor often is forced to or voluntarily becomes bankrupt.

The *Bankruptcy and Insolvency Act*[24] is a federal statute uniformly applicable throughout Canada. Its purpose is to preserve as much of the debtors assets as possible for the benefit of the creditors and also to rehabilitate such debtors by forgiving the unpaid debt, thus removing an insurmountable burden and restoring them as productive members of society. In 1992, the act was the subject of significant amendment and introduced a further objective to help viable businesses survive restructuring. It should be noted that some people and bodies are exempt from this legislation; banks, trust companies, and railways, for example, are not covered by the *Bankruptcy and Insolvency Act*.

Insolvency simply means that a person is unable to pay his or her debts. **Bankruptcy**, on the other hand, is the process by which a debtor's assets are transferred to a **trustee in bankruptcy** who then deals with them for the benefit of the creditors. Where the transfer is done voluntarily by the debtor, it is called an **assignment in bankruptcy**, but where it is forced on the debtor, the process is done by obtaining a **receiving order** from the court. A creditor who is owed more than $1000 can petition the court to force the debtor into bankruptcy. When the court grants a receiving order, this results in a statutory assignment of the debtor's assets to the trustee, ensuring that the assets will be preserved and distributed fairly so that the creditors will get paid at least some of what they are owed. The relevant section is Section 71(2):

> 71(2) On a receiving order being made or an assignment being filed with an official receiver, a bankrupt ceases to have any capacity to dispose of or otherwise deal with his property, which shall, subject to this act and to the rights of the secured creditors, forthwith pass to and vest in the trustee named in the receiving order or assignment. ...

To obtain a **receiving order**, the creditor must show that the debtor has committed an **act of bankruptcy**. Significant acts of bankruptcy include the voluntary assignment of assets to a trustee in bankruptcy, fraudulent transfers of money or assets to keep them out of the hands of the trustee, a fraudulent preference given to one of the creditors, trying to leave the jurisdiction without paying debts, and general insolvency.

The *Bankruptcy and Insolvency Act* provides an alternative to bankruptcy. Two separate procedures are involved. For commercial debtors, the process involves the filing of a notice of intention to file a reorganization proposal; the filing of a statement of projected cash flow within 10 days; and then, within 30 days, the reorganization proposal itself. This is followed by a meeting of the creditors, of whom

Bankruptcy involves transfer of assets to trustee

—by voluntary assignment

—by receiving order

Alternatives to bankruptcy

24. S.C. (1992) c. 27

two-thirds by value and a majority by number must approve the proposal. If they do, all are bound by it, including secured creditors who have approved the proposal. If the creditors reject the proposal, the insolvent debtor is deemed to have made an assignment in bankruptcy from the day the notice of intention was filed, and the normal bankruptcy procedures follow. An important effect of filing the notice is that creditors, including even secured creditors, are prevented from taking action against the debtor or the assets, until the vote takes place about two months later, and this time may be extended. In effect, the insolvent debtor is protected from the creditors, and if the proposal is accepted, that protection continues.

Consumer debtors are similarly protected when they make a consumer proposal. The insolvent debtor goes to a professional administrator who examines the debtor's finances, prepares the proposal and any reports required, and provides counselling for the debtor. With the administrator's help, the insolvent debtor files a consumer proposal. No actual meeting is required unless demanded by the creditors. The proposal must contain a commitment by the debtor to make a payment to the administrator, at least once every three months, which is then distributed to the creditors. As long as the debtor lives up to the obligations in the proposal, action cannot be taken against him or her by unsecured creditors, public utilities, landlords, and so on. Even those supplying ongoing services, such as power, gas, and telephone, must continue supplying them. But if the debtor defaults, the proposal is annulled, and the debtor will then face the normal bankruptcy procedures. Once the trustee has been given the assets of a bankrupt debtor, it is the trustee's responsibility to distribute them fairly to the creditors.

Priority among Creditors

Secured creditors retain a prior claim at least to the value of the asset used as security. The trustee may sell the asset and use the funds to pay off the secured creditor or, if they can agree on a value, surrender the asset to that creditor. When there is a shortfall, the secured creditor becomes a general creditor for any outstanding amount. If the goods are sold for more than is owing, the excess will be paid out to the other creditors.

A significant change under the new *Bankruptcy Act* allows a supplier of goods to demand the return of those goods upon learning of the bankruptcy, provided this is within 30 days of delivery of those goods and the debtor or trustee still has them.

Even suppliers of goods, such as crops, produce, fish, and so on, that become commingled and lose their identity have a prior claim with respect to those goods. They become a secured creditor with respect to their value, provided the products were delivered within 15 days and the claim filed within 30 days of the bankruptcy.

The trustee must evaluate the various claims of the creditors. Some may be rejected if there is no legitimate basis, although this may be challenged in court. After the secured creditors have received what they are entitled to, the trustee distributes the remaining assets, or the proceeds from the sales of those assets, to the other creditors. Next to be paid are preferred creditors as follows: funeral expenses, costs associated with the bankruptcy process, claims for arrears in wages for a limited amount and time period, municipal taxes, arrears in rent for a limited period, some direct costs incurred by creditors in the execution process, amounts owed to Workers' Compensation, employment insurance, and income tax which should have been deducted from salaries, and other claims of the Crown. General creditors are paid only after these obligations have been met.

Re Speedy Roofing Ltd.[25]

In this case, Mr. Pompeo and Mr. Gaggi were the sole shareholders of Speedy Roofing Ltd., and through years of operation, Speedy Roofing became indebted to one of their suppliers, Roofmart. Eventually, Roofmart became concerned and insisted on security for the indebtedness, and mortgages were provided on the homes of the wives of Mr. Pompeo and Mr. Gaggi.

In 1983, the financial problems of Speedy became insurmountable, and the Royal Bank forced the company into bankruptcy. Shortly before this, however, Speedy Roofing paid Roofmart over $80 000 to have the two mortgages discharged. In this action, the Royal Bank is claiming that the payment from Speedy to Roofmart amounted to a fraudulent preference.

The *Bankruptcy Act* specifically prohibits payments that favour one creditor over another, and the court has the right under the act to order the funds repaid if they are made within three months of the bankruptcy. The court in this case did make such an order, and Roofmart was required to repay the $80 000 paid for the discharge of the mortgages over to the trustee in bankruptcy, who then made it available to all the creditors.

The case illustrates that the purpose of the bankruptcy legislation is to obtain as much as possible for all the creditors. It may be in the best interests for the bankrupt to make sure one of the creditors gets paid in preference to another, but under the act, such payment is an offence that can be reversed.

Fraudulent transfers and preferences prohibited

As discussed above, debtors often attempt to keep their property out of the hands of creditors by transferring it to friends or relatives, or they sometimes try to pay off one preferred creditor and not others. This happens in bankruptcy situations as well and the trustee in bankruptcy can reverse these **fraudulent transfers** (or **settlements** as they are called in the act).

The relevant sections for the *Bankruptcy and Insolvency Act* are as follows:

91. (1) Any settlement of property made within the period beginning on the day that is one year before the date of the initial bankruptcy event in respect of the settlor and ending on the date that the settlor became bankrupt, both dates included, is void against the trustee.

95. (1) Every conveyance or transfer of property or charge thereon made, every payment made, every obligation incurred, and every judicial proceeding taken or suffered by any insolvent person in favour of any creditor or of any person in trust for any creditor with a view to giving that creditor a preference over the other creditors is, where it is made, incurred, taken, or suffered within the period beginning on the day that is three months before the date of the initial bankruptcy event and ending on the date the insolvent person became bankrupt, both dates included, deemed fraudulent and void as against the trustee in the bankruptcy.

Limitations on undischarged bankrupts

When a payment is made to one creditor in preference to the others, the trustee can force the return of those funds so that they can be fairly distributed to all the creditors. This was the situation in the *Speedy Roofing* case discussed above. As part of the bankruptcy process, the debtor is required to file an affidavit setting out all debt, creditors, and assets. Once the assets have been transferred to a trustee by voluntary assignment or through a receiving order, the debtor is an **undischarged bankrupt**. While in that state, if the bankrupt is involved in any transaction or

25. (1987) 45 D.L.R. (4th) 142 (Ont. S.C.)

Settlement and Fraudulent Conveyance by Bankrupt Prohibited

On March 6, 1980, a successful business person transferred his interest in his matrimonial residence to his wife and continued to live there with her. One of his corporations, Textile Industries Ltd., ran into financial difficulty. He had signed a guarantee for the indebtedness of this corporation and so was personally responsible for its debts. In 1977, an action was commenced against the corporation that eventually led to the businessman claiming bankruptcy. It was clear at the time of transfer to the wife that the matter was going to go to trial and that the businessman was facing substantial loss. In May 1980, judgment was given against Textile Industries and the businessman as guarantor. The question that the court had to decide here was whether the transfer of the interest in the matrimonial home amounted to a prohibited settlement under the provisions of the *Bankruptcy Act*. A settlement occurs when a person transfers property to another in order to preserve some benefit for himself or herself. The court held that this was exactly what had happened and voided the transaction. The court was also asked to determine whether, under the provincial *Fraudulent Conveyances Act*, this was a fraudulent conveyance—that is, a case of a debtor conveying property to another in order to defeat or defraud creditors. This also was found to have taken place and was additional grounds on which the transaction was set aside.

Re Fancy, 8 D.L.R. (4th) (1984) 418 (Ont. Bktcy.)

borrows over $500, they must disclose their status or face fine or imprisonment. Also they cannot be a director of a corporation until discharged.

Once the process is completed and the creditors have received all they can from the assets, the bankrupt may apply to the court to be discharged. This application is automatic where an individual is involved, and where it is the person's first bankruptcy, the discharge is generally automatic.

Eventually a bankrupt may be discharged

Discharge of Bankrupt Not Always Unconditional

A lawyer became bankrupt because a business enterprise he was involved in failed. He maintained a very high lifestyle while going through the bankruptcy process and looked forward to a reasonable income after his discharge as well. The court, on determining that, in fact, no payments had been made to the trustee in bankruptcy, ordered that under these circumstances he should not be entitled to an unconditional discharge and required him to consent to a judgment for $80 000, in effect, make a commitment to pay back a significant amount to his creditors. The court has the discretion to place such conditions on the discharge of a bankrupt.

On the other hand, the same court dealt with another lawyer who ran into financial difficulties at age 53 years. But this person did all he could to repay his creditors, including significantly reducing his lifestyle. Only after these honest efforts to repay failed, because of matters out of his control, was he forced to make an assignment in bankruptcy. In these circumstances, the court had no hesitation in finding that he was entitled to an unconditional discharge. The judge found that this was an appropriate situation where the bankrupt should be given a fresh start, even though his assets were not sufficient to pay back 50 cents on the dollar. In reaching this conclusion, the court considered his honesty, his struggle for nine years to pay back his creditors, and at his age his need to be free to prepare for his retirement so that he could support his wife and family.

Re McAfee, 49 D.L.R. (4th) (1988) 401 (B.C.C.A.)
Re Irwin, 112 D.L.R. (4th) (1994) 164 (B.C.C.A.)

Effect of discharge is to end most debts

Upon discharge, the debtor is freed from most previous claims by creditors and is in a position to start over. Any assets subsequently obtained by the discharged bankrupts are theirs to do with as they wish and unpaid creditors cannot claim against them. By statute, some obligations do survive the discharge, such as family maintenance payments and outstanding fines. Student loans are also still payable, although there is considerable controversy over these provisions.

Discharge not granted if bankruptcy offence is committed

Debtors who commit bankruptcy offences will not be discharged and are liable to be imprisoned. In addition to settlements, such as fraudulent preferences and fraudulent transfers, the *Bankruptcy Act* sets out several other bankruptcy offences: lying while under examination by the trustee in bankruptcy, hiding or concealing property, misleading or falsifying records, or otherwise trying to cheat the creditor. The court will also be reluctant to discharge bankrupts who have paid creditors less than 50 cents on the dollar. Under such circumstances, the court can put conditions or restrictions on the bankrupt, such as requiring that they make additional payments to the creditors, thus granting only a conditional discharge. In the Supreme Court of Canada, Justice Estey commented on the purpose of the bankruptcy process and said,

> "The purpose and object of the *Bankruptcy Act* is to equitably distribute the assets of the debtor and to permit his rehabilitation as a citizen, unfettered by past debts. The discharge, however, is not a matter of right, and the provisions of Sections 142 and 143 plainly indicate that in certain cases the debtor should suffer a period of probation."[26]

Note that this reference relates to a prior act, but similar provisions are in the current statute.

Bankruptcy proceedings also apply to corporations; but unless the corporation can pay back the full amount owed or has completed the "proposal" process outlined above, it cannot receive a discharge from the bankruptcy. Instead, it faces dissolution. It should be noted that other statutes, both federal and provincial, such as the *Winding Up Act, Company Creditor's Arrangement Act, Bulk Sale Act,* and *Construction Liens Act,* are available to disgruntled shareholders and creditors of corporations.

Bankrupt corporations are dissolved

Receivership may be based on contract

Corporations that go into receivership are often not involved in bankruptcy at all. When a creditor loans such a corporation significant funds, they usually include in the agreement the right, in the event of default or some other triggering event, to appoint a receiver to take over the business without the necessity of going through the bankruptcy procedure. Such an assignment of assets to a receiver is not actually a bankruptcy, but the effect can be every bit as devastating to the business. The rights of creditors to appoint such receivers have been limited to some extent by the recent revisions to the *Bankruptcy and Insolvency Act* discussed above.

Orderly payment of debt set out in legislation

Legislation also exists to assist in the orderly payment of debt. If the account owed is less than $1000 or if the debtor obtains the consent of the creditors, the debtor can make arrangements to consolidate all the debts and pay all the creditors back at one rate with one payment. Government agencies available to assist in this process can be helpful to both the debtor and the creditor. It must be remembered that the creditor is in the business of making money, not destroying the debtor. If the debtor cannot pay, the creditor gains nothing by harassment. The two main purposes of the *Bankruptcy and Insolvency Act* and the other legislation discussed in this section are to ensure that the creditor realizes as much of the amount owed as possible and to rehabilitate the debtor. The legislation also provides punishment for fraudulent activities by the debtor and provides a uniform system of laws throughout Canada. The idea is to restore the debtor as a productive working member of the community as soon as possible.

26. Industrial Acceptance Corp. v. Lalonde [1952] 2 S.C.R. 109 (S.C.C.) at 120

Summary

Security

- Gives a creditor some assurance that he or she will be paid even when other creditors are not
- Conditional sales agreement—the creditor retains title while giving the debtor possession of the goods
- Chattel mortgage—the debtor gives up title to the creditor while keeping possession; in the event of default, the creditor may retake the goods
- Assignment of book accounts can also be used as security

Personal Property Security Act

- Allows both chattels and intangible forms of personal property to be used as security
- The security must first attach, but the priority is usually established by perfection (involving registration or taking possession of the property)
- In the event of default, the creditor can retake the goods and resell them and/or sue for the debt. In some situations, the creditor must choose one or the other but cannot do both
- Floating charge allows a debtor to bring new goods into the security group and dispose of others out of it; it is only with default that the charge attaches and prevents further dealing with the goods
- Guarantee—a contingent liability in which someone agrees to be responsible when a debtor fails to pay
- Indemnity involves a co-responsibility for the debt; if a guarantor pays the creditor, he or she steps into the shoes of the creditor and can seek redress from the debtor
- Builders' lien gives the supplier of services or materials (when not paid) the right to register a lien against the building in which the materials or services were used; owner of the property, when paying the general contractor, must hold back a certain amount to make sure all debts are paid

Negotiable instruments

- Freely transferable
- Effective substitute for money
- Method of advancing credit
- Regulated by *Bills of Exchange Act*

Holder in due course

- Innocent holder of a negotiable instrument acquires better rights than the immediate parties

  Types
  - Promissory notes—a maker promises to repay a payee
  - Bills of exchange or drafts—a drawer orders a drawee to pay a payee
  - Cheques—bills of exchange drawn on a bank, payable on demand
  - Certified cheque—similar to an accepted bill of exchange

Negotiation

- Accomplished by endorsement and delivery if it is an order instrument but by delivery alone if it is a bearer instrument

Qualifications

- Instrument must be signed and contain an unconditional commitment to pay a fixed amount of money at a fixed time or on demand
- Instrument must be delivered, and the whole instrument must pass

Holder in due course qualifications

- A person must have received the instrument for value
- Instrument must be complete and regular on its face; received through negotiation, before it was due and payable; and received in good faith and without knowledge of any defect of title or notice of dishonour
- Only real defences can be used against a holder in due course, whereas real defences and defect of title defences can be used against other holders

Endorser

- Liable on default by the original drawer only if properly notified of the default

Bankruptcy

- Can take place voluntarily through assignment or involuntarily through a receiving order
- Involves the transfer of the debtor's assets to a trustee in bankruptcy who sells the assets and distributes the proceeds to the creditors
- After meeting certain qualifications, the debtor can apply to be discharged
- Absolute discharge relieves responsibility for these prior debts

----

QUESTIONS

1. Distinguish between the following:

    a. A chattel mortgage and a mortgage on real estate

    b. A chattel mortgage and a conditional sale

    c. Real property and personal property

    d. Chose in action and a chattel

2. What significant problem associated with the practice of taking goods as security is alleviated by the registration requirements introduced by legislation? Describe the resulting obligations on all parties.

3. What obligations are imposed on the secured creditor who retakes goods used as security when a debtor defaults?

4. Why is the security allowed banks under the *Bank Act* significantly different from other forms of secured transactions? How are the registration requirements different?

5. In what ways was the passage of the *Personal Property Security Act* a significant departure from the traditional treatment of secured transactions?

6. Distinguish among security contract, attachment, and perfection, and explain the significance of each step. Explain how it is accomplished.

7. In the event of a default, explain what the rights of a secured party are and what limitations there are on those rights.

8. What kinds of property can be used as collateral under the *Personal Property Security Act*?

9. Explain the rights of debtors after they have defaulted and the secured party has taken possession of the collateral.

10. What happens upon default when a floating charge has been used to secure a debt? How does this form of security affect the priorities between types of creditors?

11. Explain the position of the secured creditor in relation to the debtor and other creditors in the following situations in which assets have been used as security. Indicate provincial variations in your response.

   a. The amount still owing to the secured creditor is less than the value of the asset used as security.

   b. The amount still owing to the secured creditor is greater than the value used as security.

12. What obligations does the guarantor of another person's debt incur? What protection is available to guarantors in subsequent dealings between the creditor and debtor?

13. When a debtor defaults on a loan and the guarantor is required to pay, what rights does the guarantor have in relation to the debtor?

14. What significant difficulty facing the supplier of goods and services in the construction industry is overcome by the creation of the builders' lien? Include an explanation of the significance of the declaration that any money paid by the owner to the contractor is held in trust.

15. What remedies are available to a supplier of goods and services who has filed a builders' lien?

16. What is the difficulty associated with the assignment of contractual rights that is overcome when a negotiable instrument is used?

17. What is the difference between a bill of exchange, promissory note, and cheque? Give an example of when each would be used, and give examples of two other kinds of instruments that sometimes qualify as negotiable instruments.

18. When a payee presents a bill of exchange for acceptance to the drawee (and it is accepted), how does this acceptance affect the position of the drawer and drawee of the instrument?

19. Define what is meant by a holder in due course, the characteristics this person must have to qualify, and the significance of being so designated.

Explain how the knowledge of a holder of a negotiable instrument can affect his or her right to claim to be a holder in due course.

20. Distinguish between a standby letter of credit and a normal letter of credit.

21. Define the objectives of bankruptcy legislation and explain how these objectives are accomplished. Explain what role the process of discharge and the function of the trustee in bankruptcy have in the realization of these goals.

22. Explain what is meant by a settlement under the *Bankruptcy and Insolvency Act*, and how such a settlement is dealt with.

CASES

1. Re Purschke and Avco Financial Services Canada Ltd.
Sandra Harris entered into a chattel mortgage with a bank in 1985. The bank registered this chattel mortgage, but the serial number was recorded incorrectly. Ms. Harris then granted another chattel mortgage to Avco in 1986, which was properly registered. Before Avco registered the mortgage, they contacted the bank for a credit check on Ms. Harris and were told that the bank had a chattel mortgage already on the vehicle. After Avco registered their chattel mortgage, they contacted the bank telling them that they had done a search, found the incorrect number, and had registered their mortgage ahead of the bank. Avco seized the motor vehicle, and after correcting the serial number, the bank challenged Avco's right to the car. Explain the arguments available on both sides.

2. Red Deer College v. W.W. Construction, Lethbridge, Ltd.
Red Deer College owned property and hired W.W. Construction as the general contractor to complete certain buildings on that property. W.W. Construction then hired several subtrades to continue with the work. A number of liens were registered against the project, and Red Deer College not only held back the 15 percent required by law but also refused to pay out any further money to the defendant. W.W. Construction then failed to complete the project and abandoned it. Red Deer College had to get other subcontractors to finish the job. In this action, W.W. Construction claimed for money owed less the 15 percent holdback. Explain the legal obligations of Red Deer College.

3. Eastern Elevator Services Ltd. v. Wolfe
Wolfe was dissatisfied with his employment and discussed the possibility of working with another employer, Pace. An agreement was reached whereby a separate company, Eastern Elevator Services Ltd., would be incorporated and employ Wolfe. But Wolfe had to give Eastern a $5000 cheque to show how sincere he was, the understanding being that the cheque would not be cashed unless Wolfe failed to honour the agreement and did not take up his new position of employment. The deal fell through, and Wolfe did not become an employee. He stopped payment on the cheque. Eastern sought a court order that required Wolfe to pay out on the cheque.

Explain the arguments available to Wolfe as to why he should not be required to honour the cheque and, moreover, why he should not be required to pay the $5000. Would your answer be any different if the cheque had been placed in the hands of an innocent third party that was a qualified holder in due course?

4. A. E. LePage Real Estate Services Ltd. v. Rattray Publications

In 1985, Rattray agreed to lease certain premises from A. E. LePage on Yonge Street in Toronto. Pursuant to that agreement, Rattray delivered a cheque to LePage for $20 825.89 as a deposit. It was drawn at a branch of the CIBC. A. E. LePage was acting for London Life, the owner of the property. The offer was taken by LePage to London Life for their signature. Rattray changed his mind and stopped payment on the cheque, but because of a mistake at the CIBC branch, the stop payment order was ignored when the cheque was brought in for certification by a representative of LePage. The cheque was subsequently deposited in LePage's trust account at the Toronto Dominion Bank, but when it was sent to the CIBC branch, they refused to honour it.

Indicate the arguments on both sides of this case as to whether A. E. LePage should be able to require the bank to honour this cheque. Explain Rattray's position. Would your answer be any different if the cheque had been certified by Rattray in the first place and then presented to LePage?

5. Finning Tractor and Equipment Company Limited v. Mee

In April 1976, Morrill and Sturgeon Lumber Company signed a conditional sales agreement with Finning Tractor to purchase a new caterpillar wheel loader. The agreement was guaranteed by Mee. The purchaser defaulted after some payments were made. Finning chose to seek payment from the guarantor instead of seizing the tractor under the conditional sales agreement. Explain the liability of the guarantor in these circumstances. Would your answer be any different if you learned that Finning had neglected to register the conditional sales agreement and therefore had lost its priority against other secured creditors?

Employment and Agency

Business activity, in addition to the production of products or services, normally involves interaction with customers, suppliers, creditors, and others. These activities are carried out by employees or other representatives, and the legal rules and principles associated with these relationships are the subject of this section. Chapter 11 deals with the master-servant relationship or employment. It looks at the responsibilities that employees and employers have to each other, statutes which set standards and establish the rights of such workers, and the special labour legislation controlling the collective bargaining process. Chapter 12 examines the agency function, where one person represents another in transactions with a third. The law of agency is much more significant than is sometimes appreciated, since in the corporate environment, all transactions must be entered into by such representatives.

Photo by PhotoDisc

CHAPTER 11

Employment

CHAPTER HIGHLIGHTS

- Distinctions between employees and contractors
- Employment relationships
- Collective bargaining and labour unions

A contract for employment is one of the most important in which a person will become involved. This chapter is devoted to exploring the different legal ramifications of the employment relationship.

Dishonesty Justifies Dismissal[1]

Jack Gibson was 67 years old when he was hired by a food distribution company on a two-year contract that included $3000 a month, car expenses, and a membership at an exclusive golf and country club. As the sales manager, he was required to supervise other sales staff and telephone and visit various supermarkets in the area to see that they were properly stocked with the company's products. Gibson's employer went away for two months, and when he returned, he discovered that certain stores were not properly stocked and that the company had lost the account of a major customer. When asked about this, Gibson told his employer that the stores were being regularly called, visited, and serviced.

The employer doubted this and hired a private detective to follow Gibson. From the reports of the detective, the employer learned that Gibson regularly visited the golf club. When called into the office, Gibson at first lied about the number of calls he made and then, when confronted with the evidence, admitted his failure for health reasons. Gibson was fired and sued for wrongful dismissal. The court said that while Gibson's failure to perform his duties may have supported his dismissal, it was his dishonesty that caused a fundamental breach of the employment contract.

What Is Employment?

Not all work is employment

Employment involves one person doing work for another, but not all such relationships are classed as employment. The work of independent contractors, such as doctors, lawyers, plumbers, and the like, must be distinguished from employment. Such independent contractors work for themselves and act independently, providing a specific service for the person they contract with, whereas an employee is said to be in a master-servant relationship, acting under the direction of the master.

1. *The Lawyers Weekly*, November 6, 1987, p. 6.

Agency is a third type of business relationship, where one person acts as a go-between in relationships between others, and will be discussed in detail in the next chapter. Each of these relationships imposes different legal rights and obligations on the parties; understanding which body of rights governs a particular relationship can be of vital importance.

Jaremko v. A. E. LePage Real Estate Services Ltd.[2]

Mr. Jaremko was a real estate salesman, paid by commission, working for A. E. LePage, when he was discharged without notice for failing to disclose to his employer that he had agreed to contribute his commission to assist in the purchase of a building. In fact, Mr. Jaremko had sent a letter disclosing this fact to the seller and was about to do the same with his employer. Note as well that A. E. LePage was guilty of the same thing, having failed to disclose to the seller that they were going to lease back a large portion of the building for their offices.

When he sued A. E. LePage for wrongful dismissal, their first argument was that Mr. Jaremko was not an employee. The court took pains to point out that although Mr. Jaremko was paid by commission and was in control of his own time, he was an integral part of the organization, subject to company discipline, had to adhere to company policy, had offices supplied by LePage, worked exclusively for them, and otherwise was generally under their control. The judge found that a master-servant relationship did exist.

They also argued that he was discharged for cause, but the court found that his minor interest in the transaction was properly disclosed and found it somewhat ironic that A. E. LePage would complain under these circumstances, when they had failed to disclose their interest to the seller and the purchaser had made no complaint.

LePage also relied on a previous incident in which Mr. Jaremko had received a secret commission, but because that had been dealt with at that time, it could not be revived here.

For our purposes, this case illustrates the distinction between an independent contractor and an employee or servant and how each case must be considered independently. You cannot simply say that if a person is paid by commission, the person is an independent contractor. You must look beyond that. It also illustrates just cause and how the conduct of both parties has to be examined in determining whether there is justification for dismissing an employee.

The Control Test

The traditional method of determining whether an employment relationship exists is to assess the degree of control exercised by the person paying for the service. A person who is told not only what to do but how to do it is classed as an employee. But if the person doing the work is free to decide how the job should be done, the position is more likely that of an independent contractor. For example, if Fong hires Kirk to paint a house, Kirk could be either an independent contractor or an employee. If Fong tells Kirk what tools to use, when to work, and how to perform the job, then Kirk is an employee. If Kirk supplies the tools, and determines what time to start work, and the best way to perform the job, then Kirk is probably an independent contractor. Whether the person is paid a wage or salary or is paid by the job is also taken into consideration in determining employment. Courts will also look

Employee controlled by employer

2. (1987) 39 D.L.R. (4th) 252 (Ont. H.C.); affirmed (1989) 60 D.L.R. (4th) 762 (Ont. C.A.)

at who owns the tools used and who profits or runs the risk of loss from the work performed.

The employment relationship involves a contract in which the employee agrees generally to serve the employer, that is, the person acquiring that service has the right to supervise and direct. On the other hand, an independent contractor agrees to do a particular job not to enter a general service relationship. In other words, employees work for their employer, whereas independent contractors work for themselves. In the case discussed above, it was clear to the court that Mr. Jaremko was working for A. E. LePage and not for himself.

Independent contractor works independently

The Organization Test

Organization test supplements control test

In recent years, the courts have supplemented the control test with the organization test. Even if there is little direct control, where the individual is an integral part of the organization working only for that company and subject to group control, that person is likely an employee.[3] It was the application of the organization test that determined Mr. Jaremko was an employee of A. E. LePage.

Definition of employment broadened

It is important to note that at least for the purposes of establishing vicarious liability, a person can be an independent contractor for most purposes but an employee or a servant in some specific instances.[4] This ruling has prompted the courts to find employment relationships in areas that were traditionally considered purely independent. Joe could be a plumber acting as an independent contractor for Smith for most of the job, but while digging a drainage ditch at Smith's direction, he could be considered an employee for that purpose. If someone was hurt, Smith could be found vicariously liable for Jones' careless conduct in digging that ditch.

B. (W.R.) v. Plint[5]

This is one of several recent cases in which a person in the care of another suffers sexual abuse at the hands of the caregiver. The United Church of Canada operated a residential school, where a dormitory supervisor sexually assaulted several resident children. This action was brought by those children, now adults, against the dormitory supervisor, the United Church, and the Government of Canada, for compensation for the damage they suffered because of that abuse.

Once it was established that the employee was responsible for the abuse, the court had to deal with whether the employer was vicariously liable and just who the employer was. Where the wrong committed is closely connected with the nature of the job or where the employee has been given the authority or power to do the offensive acts, vicarious liability will be imposed. The court determined that the offensive conduct was closely connected with the nature of the dormitory supervisor's job and that he had been given the power and authority to act in the position of a parent. Vicarious liability was therefore imposed on the employer. But who was the employer?

The principal of the school determined the pay and was responsible for hiring and firing dormitory supervisors. The principal was an employee of the United Church and could be hired and fired under its direction. The United Church managed the school and was therefore the employer and vicariously liable. The

3. John G. Fleming, *The Law of Torts*, 8th ed. (Sydney, Australia: The Law Book Co. Ltd., 1992), p. 372.

4. Cooperators Insurance Assn. v. Kearney [1965] S.C.R. 106

5. (1998) 161 D.L.R. (4th) 538 (B.C.S.C.)

Government of Canada paid the salaries of the employees and could also determine whether an employee at the school was to be fired. The principal testified that he felt like he had two bosses. He reported to both the United Church and the Government of Canada.

The court found that this was a joint venture, that both the Government of Canada and the United Church were employers, and that both were vicariously liable for the sexual assault of the dormitory supervisor. This case illustrates that when there is intentional wrongdoing, vicarious liability can be imposed if the employer has put the employee in a position of power where he can commit the offending action. It is also shows that there may be more than one employer. The court looked both at the degree of control and the organization test and concluded that the residential school was "the business" of both the Government of Canada and the United Church, and therefore, both were vicariously liable.

Individual statutes may provide a definition of employment for the purposes of that statute but there is no general legislated definition. And so, when a court is dealing with vicarious liability or wrongful dismissal, it must turn to the principles discussed above in determining whether an employment relationship existed.

An employee can be an agent

It is also important to note that while a person cannot be an independent contractor and an employee at the same time, the same is not true of an agent. **Agents** can be independent contractors or employees. A sales clerk in a store is both an employee and an agent, and a person selling insurance is likely an independent contractor but is also functioning as an agent for their client. Its important to keep these categories separate, as the liability of the parties will likely be determined by the relationship between them.

An agent can be independent

The legal principles governing the independent contractor are embodied in the general rules of contract law already covered in Chapters 5 to 8. This chapter will examine the law of master and servant, the federal and provincial legislation, the trade union movement, and collective bargaining. The law of agency will be discussed in the following chapter.

The Law of Master and Servant

Over the years, the common law courts developed special rules to deal with the unique problems associated with employment, which was then referred to as a master-servant relationship. Today, employment law is governed primarily by the general provisions of contract law, supplemented by these special rules, as well as a number of statutes that further define the responsibilities and obligations of the parties.

The main responsibility of the employer, in addition to wages, is to provide a safe workplace and good working conditions for the employee. Some types of jobs are inherently dangerous, as in construction, and the employer is obligated to minimize the danger usually by promoting safe work practices, erecting protective fences, barriers, and nets, and requiring the use of proper safety equipment. The employer must hire competent people. If it can be shown that the employer hired a careless or incompetent worker who caused injury to others, the employer may be held accountable. Jobsite health and safety requirements and injuries caused by other workers are specialized areas covered by workers compensation legislation and will be discussed below.

Employer must provide safe working conditions

Other obligations of employer

The contract of employment usually includes a commitment by the employer to pay a specific wage or salary. That agreement will often also set out bonus arrangements, benefit packages, and the repayment of reasonable expenses incurred.

Obligations of employee

The employee also has obligations to fulfill. The employee must possess the skills claimed and exercise them in a reasonably competent and careful manner. The employee has an obligation to follow any reasonable order pertaining to the employment and must treat the property of the employer carefully. The employee must be honest, loyal, and courteous; an employee who does the work required but acts in an insubordinate or disloyal way can be fired. Similarly, an employee must be punctual and work for the time specified in the contract. With some types of jobs, there may also be an obligation to act in the best interests of the employer. An employee who becomes aware of financial opportunities in the course of performing his job, must offer them first to the employer. In the same way, if the employee uses company time or facilities without permission, he or she may be disciplined. This is referred to as a **fiduciary obligation** and is usually only imposed on senior level employees.

General contract law applies to employment

Although employment contracts are often not formal or written documents, it is always good advice to put the contract in writing, clearly stating the provisions that are important for the parties. These provisions may include the rate of pay, hours of work, and a description of what services are required and for what period. As with other contracts, all the ingredients necessary for a contract to exist must be present. Employers often try to impose new one-sided employment contracts on their employees well after the commencement of employment. These contracts often include terms adverse to the employee, such as restrictive covenants or terms limiting the period of notice to be given upon termination. When imposed after the fact, these provisions are often not binding because of a failure of consideration. When **restrictive covenants** are included in the original contract, committing the employee not to work in a particular geographic area or in a particular industry after leaving the position, it has to be for a reasonable time and area, be the most appropriate way of protecting the employer's interests, and not be against the public interest. For example, if an employer invents a special production method, the secrecy of which could only be maintained by requiring that the employees commit themselves not to work in a similar industry for a reasonable period of time, a restrictive covenant in the contract of employment to that effect would likely be valid. But in general, the courts are much more reluctant to enforce restrictive covenants in employment contracts because of the danger of denying the employee the ability to earn a livelihood and because of the normally weaker bargaining position of the employee.

Restrictive covenants must be reasonable

Scantron Corp. v. Bruce[6]

Bruce was the sales manager for Scantron Canada, a corporation selling scannable forms and optical equipment to read those forms. He and another employee, Burrows, left that employment in December 1995 and shortly thereafter started another company, Scanforms Canada, also selling scannable forms. They sent out a mailing to the categories of businesses that included Scantron's customers and solicited sales from those customers in direct competition with Scantron.

By doing this, they were in breach of an agreement they had signed that they would not compete with Scantron by soliciting their clients for a period of 12 months

6. (1996) 136 D.L.R. (4th) 64 (Ont. Gen. Div.)

after their employment was terminated. Scantron, by this application, was asking for an interlocutory injunction. This was an application before the trial for an injunction to stop the offending conduct until the matter could be determined at trial. To obtain such an injunction, the applicant had to establish a strong *prima facie* case, evidence of irreparable harm, and that the balance of convenience favoured the applicant. The court first looked at the restrictive covenant and determined that it was reasonable and did not go further than necessary to protect the employer's interest. The court found that while Bruce and Burrows had resisted signing the agreement, they were not coerced into it and that the restrictive covenant was therefore valid on the face of it and had been breached by their solicitation of the clients of Scantron. Irreparable harm was present because of the permanent reduction of Scantron's market share. The balance of convenience issue presented some difficulty, but the court decided that since Bruce and Burrows were aware of the restrictive covenant and took a calculated risk in breaching it, the interlocutory injunction was granted. Note that the court also found that Bruce and, because of his association with him, Burrows were also in breach of a fiduciary duty not to use confidential information obtained from Scantron in unfair competition with them.

In contrast in an earlier case, *Mercury Marine Ltd. v. Dillon et al.,*[7] where the employee quit to work for a competitor, thereby breaching a restrictive covenant not to compete for 18 months, the court refused to grant an interlocutory injunction. The term went further than necessary to protect the business, there being no geographical limitation, and so no strong *prima facie* case against the employee. Also, since damages would have sufficed as a remedy and to grant the injunction would have deprived the defendant of employment altogether, the balance of convenience was with the defendant, and the injunction was refused.

These cases show us not only when a restrictive covenant is valid but also when an interlocutory injunction will be granted. There must be a strong *prima facie* case demonstrated, there must be evidence of irreparable harm and the balance of convenience must be in favour of the employer.

Termination

An employment contract may provide for its own discharge, or the parties can mutually agree to bring it to an end. However, most contracts of employment are for an indefinite period of time with no reference to notice requirements. In general, such contracts of employment can be terminated by either party giving reasonable notice, by the employer giving the compensation that should have been earned in that notice period (pay in lieu of notice), or immediately with just cause.

Reasonable notice of termination required of both employer and employee

Just as the employee is not bound to the job and can leave after giving reasonable notice, so also is the employer free to terminate the employment relationship for any reason as long as sufficient notice is given. A restriction on the employer's right to terminate even with proper notice is found in provincial and federal human rights legislation, including the *Charter of Rights and Freedoms,* which prohibits such action when it amounts to discrimination on the basis of gender, religion, colour, physical disability, or age.[8]

But note human rights violations

---

7. 30 D.L.R. (4th) 627 (Ont. H.C.)

8. *Constitution Act* (1982) Part 1; *Canadian Charter of Rights and Freedoms*, Sections 15, 16, and 28 and, for example, *Human Rights Code*, R.S.O. (1990) c. H.19 s. 5.

Reasonable Notice

What constitutes reasonable notice varies with circumstances

The problem for employers is that what constitutes such reasonable notice in Canada, especially where long-term employees are involved, can be quite significant. Today, the practice is for the courts to impose lengthy notice periods on the basis of such factors as length of service, the type of job, the employee's qualifications and age, and the nature of the job market.[9] In some cases involving long-term senior managers, the required notice period may be as long as two years. Even short-term or probationary employees may be entitled to extended notice periods if the employee has not been informed of the basis on which his performance will be evaluated or was persuaded to leave another job.

Trade unions generally include terms in their collective agreements as to when an employee can be terminated and what notice is required. Also minimum statutory notice periods are set out in employment standards statutes and will be discussed below.

Reasonable Notice Can Be Significant Even for New Employees

Mr. Isaacs had a good education and a successful career with another company when he was persuaded to move to MHG International to be its purchasing agent. He was hired in anticipation of a large project involving the construction of a petrochemical plant. That project was abandoned, and seven months after he was hired, Mr. Isaacs was terminated. He sued for wrongful dismissal. The question facing the court was how much notice should have been given. Although Isaacs had only been working for the company for seven months, the court held that he was entitled to nine months' notice or pay in lieu of notice. This was upheld at the appeal level on the basis that he was persuaded to leave secure employment for this new job.

Isaacs v. MHG International Ltd., (1984) 7 D.L.R. (4th) 570 (Ont. C.A.).

Just Cause

Notice not required when there is just cause

Where there is just cause, there is no requirement upon an employer to give any notice. An employee can be dismissed without notice for such things as serious absenteeism, consistent tardiness, open disobedience, habitual negligence, incompetence, harassing other employees, drinking on the job, or immoral conduct on or off the job that reflects badly on the employer. Even swearing at the employer has been determined to be serious misconduct sufficient to justify dismissal. In rare circumstances, such wrongful conduct may be used to defend a wrongful dismissal action, even if it is discovered after the employee has been dismissed. In the example used to introduce this chapter, it was the employee's dishonesty in lying to his employer about how many calls he had made that justified the dismissal. Such dishonesty need not be tolerated by the employer, no matter what the plight of the employee is. When dismissing employees for such dishonesty as fraud or theft, great care must be taken to ensure that the accusations are accurate and the evidence firm. The courts have awarded significant damages for wrongful dismissal, including punitive damages, when such charges have proven false. Also, care should be taken to ensure that when a person is dismissed, the real reason for the termi-

---

9. Bardal v. *The Globe and Mail* Ltd. 24 D.L.R. (2d) 140 (H.C.).

nation is not discrimination. The human rights tribunals of the various jurisdictions are very active in prosecuting such violations.

Just Cause Can Be Learned and Advanced After the Fact

Mr. King's employment was terminated because the transport company was being reorganized, and he was offered a year's pay in lieu of notice. He sued for wrongful dismissal. Shortly after he had been given notice of his termination, he had informed his employer that another employee who was his subordinate had theft and alcohol problems and that he had not reported this as required. The court in this case had to decide whether this failure on the part of Mr. King amounted to cause and whether the company was allowed to raise it after giving him notice of termination and the offer of a year's severance pay. The court held that Mr. King's failure to report did constitute cause and could be used as grounds for his dismissal. Therefore, his action for wrongful dismissal failed, and he got nothing.

King v. Mayne Nickless Transport Inc., 114 D.L.R. (4th) 124 (B.C.C.A.)

Disabled Workers

In the past, employees who became seriously ill, even though not at fault, could be discharged without notice if they could no longer perform their job. The employer did not have to pay for work not done. In effect, the employment contract was frustrated. Today, however, there is a legislated duty to accommodate disabled workers that are still able to work, and human rights commissions are very willing to rule against employers who fire workers because of illness or disability too quickly. The employer must take great care to comply with the provisions of both the *Human Rights Code* and the *Workers' Compensation Act* designed to protect disabled or injured workers. Today, most businesses have some form of illness and long-term disability insurance or policy as part of their benefit package to deal with this problem.

Frustration

Incompetence

Although an employee is entitled to refuse to work because of dangerous working conditions, failure to perform a reasonable order is also grounds for dismissal without notice. Incompetence is just cause for dismissal; however, employers are well advised to let employees know when the level of performance is unacceptable as soon as it becomes apparent and provide an opportunity for improvement. It may appear to be easier to let the matter go, but the employer may then be faced with the argument that the employer's conduct and acceptance of the employee's performance led that employee to believe that the level of performance was appropriate. This argument will be especially difficult to overcome if bonuses or wage increases were given to the employee in the past despite the poor performance.

Problem where incompetence tolerated

Layoffs

When an employer simply runs out of work for the employee to do, that is not just cause for termination, and reasonable notice is still required. Even when the layoff is only temporary, the employee is entitled to treat it as termination and demand the appropriate notice and compensation. In the absence of such reasonable notice

Layoff or termination

or just cause, the employee can sue the employer for wrongful dismissal. Provisions in collective agreements often cover layoffs and recalls, and several provinces have included provisions covering temporary layoffs in their employment standards legislation.[10]

Wrongful Leaving

Employees are also required to give reasonable notice upon leaving, although what constitutes reasonable notice is usually considerably less. Unless the employee is in a key position, such as senior executive or salesperson, it is usually not worth the effort to sue when an employee leaves without giving proper notice. But key employees may be required to give substantial notice just like employers. Employees are entitled to leave without notice if the employer gives an unreasonable or dangerous order, if the working conditions are dangerous and the employer refuses to correct them, or if the employer involves the employee in illegal or immoral activities.

When employees can leave without notice

But in most cases, where former employees are sued, it is for breach of fiduciary duty or for disclosing confidential information. Ordinary employees do not have a fiduciary duty, and unless there is a valid restrictive covenant in their employment contract preventing them from doing so, they are free to compete with their former employer as soon as they leave. That competition, however, must start after they leave. Employees cannot gather information, copy customer lists, or solicit customers before termination. If they do, they can be sued. Similarly, if the departing employee takes confidential information and misuses it, that conduct is also actionable. Managers and other executives do have a fiduciary duty to their employer and may find themselves somewhat restricted in what they can do even after they leave their employment. It is much preferable for the employer to set out such restrictions clearly in the original employment contract.

Employees may be sued for breach of duty

Even Employees Can Be Required to Give Lengthy Notice

Savoy and Deringer were employees of Tree Savers, a relatively small company working in the oil industry. After giving Tree Savers' management two weeks' notice, they left and incorporated a company in competition with Tree Savers. Savoy and Deringer had been key employees at Tree Savers—Savoy was described as the whole sales arm of the company—and when they left, they took some documents with them, including lists of contacts. Ducharme, who gave them financial aid and advice, and the company they created, Trojan, were also defendants. The court had to decide whether Savoy and the others were in violation of their fiduciary duty to their former employer. The answer was yes, and an injunction was issued ordering them to stop their offending conduct. Ducharme was also found liable for inducing them to breach their contract. The court decided that because the two men were senior key employees, they should have given their employer 18 months' notice, and the damages awarded were calculated on this basis.

Tree Savers International Ltd. v. Savoy (1992) 87 D.L.R. (4th) 202 (Alta. C.A.)

10. For example, *Employment Standards Act*, R.S.O. 1990, c. E.14 s. 57 ss. 17

Constructive Dismissal

When an employer demotes the employee or otherwise unilaterally changes the nature of the job, this may constitute constructive dismissal, and the employee can sue for wrongful dismissal. Sometimes, this is done inadvertently, but often, it is done in order to humiliate or make an employee uncomfortable so that he or she will voluntarily leave. Even where the problems are caused by other employees, as with sexual harassment, the employer is still responsible, and this may constitute constructive dismissal. Where there is constructive dismissal, the employee has an obligation to mitigate possibly to the extent of accepting the new position offered by the employer. Of course, the employee is not obligated to accept such a position where it would cause undue humiliation or otherwise create an impossible working situation, especially if bad relations have been created because of the way the termination took place.

Constructive dismissal—employer breaks contract when nature of job is changed without consent

Greaves v. Ontario Municipal Employees Retirement Board[11]

Mr. Greaves had been working for the defendant for about 12 years as a money manager, eventually becoming a vice-president in charge of various financial and investment areas. In 1993, the employer was reorganized. The court found that the reorganization was appropriate for business purposes, but as a result, Mr. Greaves' overall responsibilities were reduced. Finally, two vice-presidents junior to Mr. Greaves were promoted to positions higher than Mr. Greaves'. He resigned, even though he was asked to stay on at the same salary. He sued for wrongful dismissal. The court found that the reorganization amounted to a demotion of Mr. Greaves and that this demotion constituted a fundamental breach of a major aspect of his contract of employment and amounted to constructive dismissal. However, the court also determined that he had a duty to mitigate his loss and that since he was offered alternative employment at the same salary and refused, he failed to mitigate that loss. He received nothing in his action for wrongful dismissal because of that failure to mitigate.

In another case, a manager was demoted to a non-managerial position after eight years, and she resigned. This also amounted to constructive dismissal, and she was awarded damages based on the 15 months' notice she should have received. In this case, however, there was no reduction because of a failure to mitigate. The court found that the work environment had been poisoned by hard feelings between the employee and her supervisor unrelated to the job, and the demotion was the result of vindictive action by that supervisor. Taking the alternative employment offered was not a viable alternative, and so there was no failure to mitigate the loss.[12]

In a wrongful dismissal action, the damages awarded are usually based on what the employee would have received had proper notice been given. If a person is fired and is given only one month's notice when he should have received five months' notice, he will be awarded the difference, including any benefits and pension rights to which he would have been entitled. But the employee also has an obligation to mitigate and so must try to find another job. Any damages awarded will

Compensation based on notice that should have been given

11. (1995) 129 D.L.R. (4th) 347 (Ont. Gen. Div.)

12. Vanderleest v. City of Regina, 91 D.L.R. (4th) 538 (Sask. Q.B.)

Obligation to mitigate losses

be reduced by what is earned from that other employment. In rare circumstances, the court will also take into account a person's damaged reputation or mental distress and sometimes even award punitive damages, where appropriate. It is normally the employer, usually a company, that is sued for wrongful dismissal, but the individual manager implementing the decision may also be sued where defamation or some other actionable wrong has taken place.

Damages are the appropriate remedy for wrongful dismissal, and it is rare for the court to order that an employee be given back the job. Reinstatement is more common when collective agreements are involved, where the decision is made by an arbitrator rather than a judge. Some statutes, such as the *Canadian Labour Code,* provide for reinstatement in non-union situations as well, but this is still quite rare.

Great care must be exercised when dismissing an employee for incompetence or misconduct. An employer must have the clearest evidence of the misconduct or incompetence and with the latter must demonstrate that the employee has been

Employer must have clear evidence of misconduct

given a reasonable opportunity to improve. Failure to substantiate just cause will likely result in a successful action by the employee for wrongful dismissal and may include an award of punitive damages and compensation for mental distress.

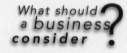

Employers, especially those from the United States, are usually surprised to learn of the lengthy notice requirements for termination in Canada. Including specified notice entitlements in the contract of employment will go a long way to solving the problem. But when this is done, it is vital not to make that contracted notice period less than the minimum specified in the employment standards legislation of the province. Otherwise, the contract clause may be void and the employer required to pay a much higher amount calculated on the common law notice period.

Employers must avoid the temptation to manufacture reasons to justify dismissal without notice or to make the employee so uncomfortable they will quit. The courts today are much more willing to find constructive dismissal and assess higher damages if there is evidence of false statements, defamation, a poisoned work environment, and damage to the employee's reputation. The sensible way to approach the problem is to negotiate with the employee. Typically, the employee will settle for less when he realizes that he will avoid significant legal costs.

Liability of Employer

Employer liable for torts committed by employee while on the job

Although not directly at fault, an employer can be held liable for the tort committed by an employee during the course of employment. This is the principle of vicarious liability discussed in Chapter 3. Because the employer benefits, the employer is responsible. The employer's liability is limited to those activities that take place during the course of employment. This not only includes incidents arising during working hours but also any conduct that takes place as part of the employment activity. If Pawluk injures a pedestrian while delivering a letter to Caron on his way home from work, both Pawluk and his employer would be liable. The negligent act occurred during the course of employment, even though it did not happen during working hours. But if Pawluk injures the pedestrian when he goes out to do his personal banking during working hours, the employer would not be liable. In this case, Pawluk is "on a frolic of his own," and the injury has not taken place in the course of his employment.

As a general rule, there must be an employment relationship for vicarious liability. This is why the tests discussed above for determining if an employment relationship exists are so important. (Some exceptions to the requirement that employment is needed for vicarious liability will be discussed in the next chapter.) Some jurisdictions have legislated vicarious liability in special situations. For example, in British Columbia and some other provinces, the owner of a motor vehicle is vicariously liable for any torts committed by someone else driving their car as if that person were an employee "driving and operating the motor vehicle in the course of his employment."[13] Although the employer has the right to turn to the employee for compensation when found vicariously liable, this is usually a hollow remedy, the employee being in no financial position to pay such compensation.

Vicarious liability and motor vehicles

Employers often try to separate portions of their operations from the actual business they conduct. Cleaning, office management, as well as sales and product service, may be contracted out. This is done to reduce the number of employees thereby reducing administrative costs, leaving the organization free to concentrate on what it does best. It may also reduce the risk of the employer being found vicariously liable when injuries take place. This is much more likely to be successful when great care is taken to make sure the people doing those jobs are truly independent. But even then, the courts may still find a sufficiently close relationship to impose vicarious liability on the employer for the wrongful acts committed by these supposedly independent workers. The risk of such liability should be planned for in the operation of the business.

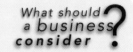

Legislation

As a consequence of the relatively weak position of individual employees in the employment relationship, employees have tended to band together to exert greater pressure on the employer. Such collective action is now governed by legislation and will be discussed under "Collective Bargaining," later in this chapter. A considerable amount of legislation has also been passed which is designed to protect employees, whether unionized or not, by setting minimum standards of safety, remuneration, hours of work, and other benefits. Conditions of employment normally fall under the provincial jurisdiction, but there are a number of activities, such as banking, the military, activities on Indian reserves, the post office, telephone and broadcast companies, and airlines, railroads, and steamships that fall under federal jurisdiction. Most provinces have concentrated their employee welfare legislation into one statute, generally called the *Employment Standards Act* or *Labour Standards Act*. Ontario's act is typical of such legislation and will be used as an illustration.[14]

Both federal and provincial legislation apply

Untangling the WEB

Employment standards legislation varies with each jurisdiction and you should read the legislation that applies in your province. You can gain access to employment standards legislation for most provinces on the Internet. Go to the *Access to Justice* web site at www.acjnet.org and then to "Legislative Materials," click on to your provincial link, and then search for employment standards legislation.

13. *Motor Vehicle Act*, R.S.B.C. 1996, c. 318 s. 86
14. *Employment Standards Act*, R.S.O. 1990, c. E.14

Employment Standards

Machtinger v. HOJ Industries Ltd.[15]

This case involves two employees, Mr. Machtinger and Mr. Lefebvre, who were terminated from their employment with only four weeks' notice, despite the fact that they both had been employed for a number of years. The notice given corresponded with the statutory minimum under the *Employment Standards Act*, even though their actual contracts required even less notice to be given. By the courts determination, if common law applied, they would be entitled to over seven months' notice. Both employees brought a wrongful dismissal action against the employer, demanding compensation. The problem for the court was to decide whether the four weeks' notice was enough.

The Supreme Court of Canada held that any contractual term that did not comply with the minimum standards set out in the act was a nullity, and therefore, the minimal notice provisions found in the contract were void. The court then observed that although the notice given satisfied the requirements of the *Employment Standards Act*, that was merely a minimum standard. Since common law required over seven months' notice in such circumstances, that longer notice requirement prevailed. Complying with the statutory minimum was not good enough in this case.

Notice periods less than the common law standard can be set out in employment contracts, but they must be more generous than the minimum statutory period, or they will be void. The employer will then have to comply with the longer "reasonable notice" provisions found in common law. Remember that the *Employment Standards Act* or its equivalent sets minimum, not maximum, standards.

Statutes set out minimum standards

It must be emphasized that statutory provisions set a minimum standard only. Where the parties have agreed to a higher standard or where a higher standard is imposed by common law, that higher standard will normally prevail (as set out in Section 4.1 of the *Ontario Act*).

Wages

Minimum wage is legislated

Every province has passed legislation that sets minimum wages within its jurisdiction. In Ontario, the minimum wage is to be set by regulation, giving the government more flexibility to make adjustments. In many jurisdictions, such legislation also contains provisions that set standards of payment for piece work, tips, or gratuities, and restrict the amounts that can be deducted from wages to pay for meals, accommodation, and other expenses. In many provinces, the minimum wage will vary among industries and, in most provinces, some categories of employment, such as domestic workers and farm workers, are exempted from minimum wage requirements altogether. Ontario now requires that an employer obtain a permit before a home worker can be hired. Legislation also requires that the employer keep proper records and that a statement of wages earned be supplied to the wage earner. This requirement is contained in Part II of the *Ontario Act*, which also specifies that an employer cannot fire an employee simply because the employee has had his or her wages garnished.

---

15. [1992] 1 S.C.R. 986

Hours of Work

The Ontario *Employment Standards Act,* along with similar statutes in other jurisdictions, protects employees from working excessive hours without appropriate
compensation. In Ontario, the maximum amount to be worked in one day is eight
hours and in a week no more than 48 hours (Part IV). The employer is obligated
to pay a premium for overtime (usually one-and-a-half times the normal rate of
pay) (Part VI). These provisions also typically set out minimum break periods, such
as lunch and coffee breaks, and a minimum period free from work, such as one day
off in seven. Part VIII of the *Ontario Act* states that a vacation of at least two weeks
must be given after a year of employment and that the pay for that vacation period must equal at least 4 percent of the wages earned. This requirement is typical
of other jurisdictions as well. In some provinces, the amount of vacation entitlement increases with the length of employment, as with British Columbia's *Employment
Standards Act.*[16] Most jurisdictions have provisions for paid statutory holidays, such
as New Year's Day and Christmas, although the specific holidays vary from province
to province. Overtime must be paid to a person who works on a statutory holiday.

Hours of work legislated

Termination

Because the common law dealing with termination was considered inadequate in
many situations, legislation was passed to supplement it. In
Ontario, employees having worked between three months
and one year must be given at least one week's notice, and
over one year but less than three years, two weeks' notice
upon termination. This period increases after three years
by one week each year up to a maximum of eight weeks (Part
XIV of the *Ontario Act*). Most jurisdictions have passed similar legislation, but the provisions vary substantially from
province to province. Ontario also provides that when a person has been temporarily laid off for a period longer than 35
weeks of the year, he or she can treat this layoff as a termination. Note that these statutes set minimum standards that
do not override the common law requirements of reasonable notice. This was the main reason for the decision in the
case used to introduce this section. That case also illustrates
how careful employers must be to make sure they are in
compliance with the legislation. As well, collective agreements can usually override these minimum standards.

Employers have an obligation to take steps
to accommodate employees with disabilities.
PhotoDisc

Human Rights

An area of employment law that is becoming much more
significant is the area of protection of employee rights.
With the passage of the *Charter of Rights and Freedoms* as well
as federal and provincial human rights legislation, employers are required not only to ensure that they do not
discriminate in their hiring and employment practices but
also to take active steps to ensure that these basic rights
are protected. Although the *Charter* does not apply directly

16. R.S.B.C. 1996, c. 113 s. 57

Federal and provincial human rights legislation prohibit most forms of discrimination in employment

to most employment situations, it does have an important indirect effect, since the *Canadian Human Rights Act* and the various provincial human rights acts and codes must be consistent with the provisions of the *Charter*. Indeed, as mentioned in Chapter 1, the courts have gone so far as to read into human rights statutes protection for homosexuals, where no such provision was originally included.[17] These statutes vary, to some extent, from jurisdiction to jurisdiction and apply in many social activities but their main impact is in the field of employment. They contain provisions prohibiting discrimination on the basis of race, national or ethnic origin, colour, religion, gender, and in some cases age, marital status, physical or mental disability, including stature, and pardoned criminal convictions.

Tribunals hear complaints

Where violations occur, human rights tribunals have been established to hear complaints. These tribunals have the power to investigate, levy fines, and even order reinstatement of employees if they find that they have been terminated in violation of some human rights provision or forced to quit because of harassment.

Even when the harassment comes from other employees and the employer has failed to take steps to protect that employee, the employer can be responsible.

Harassment also covered

Such **harassment** usually takes the form of sexual harassment, but it may also take the form of harassment on the basis of race, colour, religion, and so on. For this reason, it is vital for employers to be proactive and take positive steps to develop a harassment and discrimination policy that makes it clear that such conduct will not be tolerated and spells out what disciplinary steps might be taken. Many organizations also include prohibitions against harassment on the basis of abuse of power.

In *Robichaud et al. v. The Queen*,[18] the Supreme Court of Canada had to determine whether the employer was responsible for the sexual harassment by another employee. Mrs. Robichaud worked as a lead hand in a cleaning operation for the Department of National Defence, and a supervisor subjected her to unwanted sexual attention. The court concluded that this kind of unwanted sexual harassment amounts to discrimination on the basis of gender because it differentiates adversely against her in her employment on the basis of her gender.

The court also found that the employer, under the *Canadian Human Rights Act,* was liable for the discriminatory acts of their employees that were committed in the course of their employment, much like vicarious liability in common law. Although this is a matter of statutory interpretation and the statute in question has been amended, it does indicate the approach taken by the court when faced with sexual harassment.

This positive obligation on the employer to protect employees from wrongful conduct of others in the workplace has been taken further. Employers now have an obligation to take steps to accommodate employees with disabilities and special

Duty to accommodate

needs. This may extend to changing the physical work environment to accommodate the visually impaired or wheelchair-bound or to allow workers with chronic illness, such as AIDS, or partial disability, to do lighter work or work only part-time. Schedules may require adjustment to accommodate different religious holidays.

Where religious regalia, such as a turban, must be worn, rules should be changed to allow this. Only where there is a *bona fide* occupational requirement that a person be of a particular stature, wear a hardhat, and so on, that occupational requirement will prevail, especially, if it is safety related. But it is vital that that requirement be a necessary part of the job. And even then when such a rule

17. Haig v. Canada (1992) 94 D.L.R. (4th) 1 (Ont. C.A.)

18. [1987] 2 S.C.R. 84

adversely impacts a particular group, the employer must take reasonable steps to accommodate the disadvantaged employee.

Emrick Plastics v. Ontario (Human Rights Commission)[19]

This is a classic case defining the duty to accommodate. Here Mrs. Heincke, who worked as a paint sprayer, became pregnant and wanted to be reassigned to a portion of the plant where there were less paint fumes. She was allowed to work in the packing area for a short time, but the company then changed its mind and would only let her continue if she produced a letter from her doctor absolving the employer of any liability for any damage to her or her baby caused by fumes. This was not something the doctor could do and so she could not work. Because of the company's rule that a paint sprayer could only work as a paint sprayer and since a pregnant woman could not work as a paint sprayer, this amounted to **adverse effect discrimination** against Mrs. Heincke. This type of discrimination involves a generally applicable rule that had a particular adverse effect on her because of her gender. In these circumstances, the employer has a duty to take reasonable steps to accommodate. They could do this by letting her work in the packing room. Their failure to do this after receiving a medical note saying this would be appropriate was a breach of their obligation to accommodate. Their position that they required the doctor to exempt them from liability for any injuries suffered being beyond his role and power was unreasonable in the circumstances. This case involved the court reviewing the decision of a human rights tribunal that had found a failure in the duty to accommodate. The court upheld that decision.

This case shows that even where a rule can be justified for safety or other reasons, when it adversely discriminates against one group of employees, there is a duty to take reasonable steps to accommodate that displaced worker. This is not an absolute duty and will not apply when it forces undue hardship on the employer, but there is a duty to take reasonable steps to reach such an accommodation.

Some jurisdictions have gone further especially in the public sector passing **pay equity** statutes requiring equal pay for work of equal value.[20] These provisions usually benefit women who have traditionally been paid less than men for similar jobs, but they place considerable hardship on the organization that must bear the extra expense.

Pay equity

In some jurisdictions, organizations are permitted to take steps to correct employment situations where there has been a tradition of racial or gender imbalance, such as nursing and engineering. This usually means giving preferential treatment to those job applicants or candidates for advancement who belong to under-represented minority groups. The resulting **reverse discrimination** directed at individuals in the over-represented group is also distasteful, and Ontario has repealed these provisions of its *Employment Equity Act*. Programs that are intended to correct these historical imbalances in the workplace are sometimes called **affirmative action** and are specifically authorized under Section 15, Subsection 2 of the *Charter of Rights and Freedoms*.

Correction of past imbalance

Mandatory retirement also raises human rights issues. Forced retirement at 65 years is usually justified as good social policy, opening up new jobs for the youth and getting rid of less productive employees. But from the point of view of the retiree,

19. (1992) 90 D.L.R. (4th) 476 (Ont. Div. Ct.)
20. *Employment Standards Act*, S.N.B. 1982, c. E-7.2, as amended by S.N.B. (1986) c. 32 s. 4

Mandatory retirement at 65 permitted

it can be a disaster. Although discrimination in employment on the basis of age is usually prohibited, retirement at 65 years is generally exempted in provincial employment standards or human rights statutes. The Supreme Court of Canada has held that where such a mandatory retirement policy is allowed under provincial human rights legislation, it does not violate the provisions of the *Charter of Rights and Freedoms* being a reasonable exception under Section 1.[21]

What should a business consider?

As the rules with respect to discrimination in employment change, employers should be particularly vigilant in developing policies that give same-sex couples the same benefits as others, that accommodate disabled workers, and that prevent the various forms of harassment that can take place in the workplace.

Maternity leave

In addition to the human rights legislation discussed above, all the provincial governments and the federal government have legislation ensuring that a woman can get time off without pay for maternity purposes and be guaranteed that she will have a job to come back to without losing seniority. Many provinces have extended this to providing paternity leave for fathers, but the time allocated is usually less. Whether the leave involved is maternity, paternity, or adoption, most statutes require a minimum time of employment before becoming eligible, usually one year. The Ontario *Employment Standards Act* also prohibits discrimination in benefits on the basis of age, marital status, or gender (Part X).

Child Labour Regulations

Use of children in work force tightly regulated

Child labour is controlled in all jurisdictions in Canada, but the federal government does not set a minimum age for work. It does, however, prevent abuses by restricting the hours a child can work and setting a minimum wage level.[22] Most provinces set a minimum age to work, although it may vary depending on the industry. In Ontario, a person under the age of 18 years cannot work underground in the mining industry, and a person needs to be 16 years to work in the construction industry. In hotels, restaurants, and shops, the minimum age is 14 years, provided the work does not interfere with school hours. Related legislation deals with the statutory requirement that children stay in school until reaching a certain age. All provinces have such statutes, with the age varying from 15 to 16 years, but most provinces also provide for some exceptions to this rule.

Workers' Compensation

Worker's compensation compulsory insurance coverage

Common law was often unable to provide an appropriate remedy for an employee injured on the job. This was especially true when the accident resulted from the employee's own carelessness. All provinces and the federal government have enacted workers' compensation legislation that provides a compulsory insurance program covering accidents that take place on the job. The legislation sets rates of compensation to be paid for different types of injuries and establishes a board that hears and adjudicates the claims of injured employees. The system is essentially a no-fault insurance scheme, in which benefits are paid to injured workers, or to their families in the event of death, and careless conduct on the part of the worker will not disqualify an injured employee from receiving compensation. The program is financed by assessments levied by the provincial workers' compensation boards against the employers; the amount levied varying with the risks associated with the industry involved. Some employees, such as casual workers, farmers, and small

21. Harrison v. University of British Columbia, [1990] 3 S.C.R. 451

22. For example, under *the Canada Shipping Act*, R.S.C. 1985, c. S.9 s. 273, the minimum age in that industry is 15 years with exceptions.

business employees are often excluded, but British Columbia has extended workers' compensation coverage to almost all workers in the province.

A significant aspect of workers' compensation legislation in most jurisdictions is that the worker gives up the right to any other compensation. The worker can no longer sue the employer or the employee who caused the injury, being limited to the benefits bestowed by the workers' compensation system.

Budge v. Alberta (Workers' Compensation Board)[23]

In this case, Mr. Budge, while on his job, was driving his car, when it collided with a light-rail transit vehicle, and he was injured. Both he and his spouse sued for compensation for the injuries that were suffered by him as a result of the accident. But the appropriate sections of the Alberta *Workers Compensation Act* limited his remedy to the benefits provided under that act and prohibited him from suing the other driver or his employer, both of whom were also covered by the act.

In this action, the constitutionality of those sections depriving him of his right to sue was upheld by the court that found that they did not violate his Section 7 *Charter* rights.

(7) Everyone has the right to life, liberty, and security of the person and the right not to be deprived thereof except in accordance with the principles of fundamental justice.

The court found that the provisions in question interfered with economic rights, which were not protected under the *Charter of Rights and Freedoms*. The court also rejected the claim that this was an example of discrimination as prohibited under Section 15 of the *Charter*. This had already been decided by the Supreme Court of Canada when looking at similar provisions in the Newfoundland legislation.[24] Because of these decisions, it is clear that workers' compensation statutes, although they vary considerably in what restrictions they place on a person's right to sue employers and others, are constitutionally valid and effective.

Compensation is also limited to injury or disease that arises in the course of the employment. This can sometimes be a problem where it is difficult to establish that a disease, such as emphysema or a heart condition, was caused by the work of the employee.

Health and Safety

Related to workers' compensation legislation are statutes controlling health and safety conditions in the workplace. The objective is to provide a safer working environment and to reduce the claims on the workers' compensation fund. In some jurisdictions, health and safety requirements are embodied in general labour statutes, as in the *Canada Labour Code*. In other jurisdictions, separate statutes are in place dealing with employment and health and safety as in Ontario's *Occupational Health and Safety Act*.[25] The main thrust of these statutes is as follows:

23. (1991) 77 D.L.R. (4th) 361 (Alta. C.A.)

24. Reference re: *Workers' Compensation Act*, 1983 (Nfld.) [1989] 1 S.C.R. 922 D.L.R. (4th) 765

25. *Occupational Health and Safety Act*, R.S.O. 1990, c. O.1

1. Providing safer working conditions, which is done by requiring fencing of hazardous areas, safety netting, proper shielding of equipment, environmental control and so on

2. Ensuring safe employment practices, such as requiring the supply and use of hard hats, goggles, and protective clothing

3. Establishing programs to educate both the employer and the employee on how to create a safer working environment for all concerned

Safety boards ensure regulations are adhered to

These objectives are facilitated through the establishment of a board with the power to hear complaints and enforce correction. Inspectors can enter the work place without a warrant, and when they encounter dangerous conditions (such as lack of fencing or shielding), poor safety practices (such as failure to use hard hats or safety lines), or environmental contamination (caused by hazardous chemicals, fumes or dust) can order the problem corrected or, in serious cases, shut the jobsite down altogether. The offending business can be prosecuted for violations, especially where injury or death results. These provisions are only effective if the fines are significant, and Ontario, for example, has increased the maximum fines levied and extended liability to make directors of corporations personally responsible for harmful and dangerous practices.

Employment Insurance

Employment insurance is federal jurisdiction

The federal government was given jurisdiction over insurance coverage for unemployed workers by an amendment to the *Constitution Act (1867)* in 1940. Under the *Employment Insurance Act,* both employers and employees pay into a government-supplemented fund,[26] and laid off employees are entitled to receive payments for a specific period of time. This is not a fund where the employee is entitled to get back what they have contributed. Rather, the payments are insurance premiums, and an employee is entitled to receive only what is set out in the statute and regulations. This amount is based on the number of weeks worked before the claim and the amount of wages received. Workers who voluntarily leave their employment or are involved in a strike or lockout are generally not entitled to receive employment insurance benefits. Those who cannot work because others are on strike will receive benefits, provided they otherwise qualify. A severance package from the employer will also limit eligibility, and no benefits will be paid until the severance period is over. Benefits are also paid under the act to those who are unable to work because of illness or disability and due to pregnancy and adoption. Workers may appeal any decisions made, such as entitlement to benefits, to an administrative body set up under the legislation. The rights of individuals before such administrative tribunals were discussed in Chapter 3.

Employee must meet qualifications to receive benefits

Other Legislation

Many other statutes affect the employment relationship. Most jurisdictions have legislation controlling the apprenticeship process and trade schools. Pension benefits are established in some cases and are controlled by legislation in all cases. Some jurisdictions have legislation controlling the licensing of private employment agencies and restricting the types of payments they can receive from their clients.

---

26. *Employment Insurance Act,* S.C. 1996, c. 23

And, as has been discussed in other chapters, legislation such as the *Bankruptcy and Insolvency Act* and the *Mechanics' or Builders' Lien Acts* provide security to the worker in the payment of wages. All jurisdictions have legislation dealing with special categories of employees, such as teachers and public servants.

Adhering to the employment standards legislation and dealing with government regulatory bodies can impose considerable hardship on employers straining their management resources. Dealing with health and safety and workers' compensation issues are a fact of life, and enforcement provisions usually put enough pressure on the employer so that there is adherence. The same is true with employment insurance and taxation. But human rights standards, including provisions against direct and indirect discrimination and harassment, especially when caused by other employees, as well as employment standards, such as minimum wage, hours of work, overtime, holidays, maternity leave and so on, are usually only enforced when someone makes a complaint. Such complaints usually are made only after the employment is terminated; employees who want to keep their jobs usually do not make such complaints. These complaints then come after the fact, often after the employee or group of employees have been working in those conditions, sometimes for years. Penalties imposed can be significant and should be factored in as a potential cost of doing business, even where the employer chooses to ignore the rules. Ideally, the employer should develop carefully crafted policies and develop training for all employees, especially those in key decision making positions, to make sure that these pitfalls are avoided. When jobs are advertised and potential employees interviewed, great care should be taken to avoid stating qualifications or asking questions that could be construed as discriminatory. Questions relating to a person's place of birth, race, religion, age, language, arrest history, gender, sexual preference, child care arrangements, marital status, or medications being taken should be avoided. Care should also be taken to avoid practices that could be considered discriminatory in promotions, benefits, and bonuses. Clear policies designed to prevent harassment or discrimination by other employees should be designed and implemented, with the policy and penalties being made clear to all.

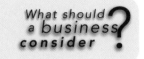

What should a business consider?

Collective Bargaining

A significant portion of the legislation affecting employment relates to the collective bargaining process. But because the percentage of unionized workers in Canada has declined over the past few decades, those laws have changed in response to the diminished political strength of the unions. Trade unions today are in the position of fighting to hold onto what they have gained and resisting the further weakening of their position.

Consequence of weaker unions

Since the time of the industrial revolution in the United Kingdom, workers have banded together in an attempt to overcome poor working conditions and low wages. A considerable amount of confrontation and violence developed between unions and employers, especially at the point where the unions first attempted to organize or unionize the workforce. In North America, governments and courts treated efforts to organize workers as criminal conspiracies, and the activists were severely punished.

Over the years, trade unions gained grudging acceptance, if not respectability, and legislation passed in the first half of the 20th century allowed them to play an increasingly significant role in the economy. The first important piece of legislation passed by the United States Congress in 1935 was known as the *National Labor Relations Act* or the *Wagner Act*.[27] The act reduced conflict by recognizing an employee's right to be a member of a union and eliminating the employer's power to interfere in any way with the organizational process. A trade union successful in persuading over 50 percent of the employees to join was recognized as the official bargaining agent for all the employees in that workforce by the government agency created by the legislation. The employer was then required to negotiate with the trade union in good faith. The primary objectives of the *Wagner Act* were to promote labour peace and to give some stability and structure to the field of labour relations in the United States.

Legislation designed to reduce conflict

Legislation

After a considerable amount of labour strife in Canada, the federal government passed the *Wartime Labour Relations Regulations* by an order-in-council.[28] This order incorporated most of the provisions set out in the *Wagner Act*, and after the war, most Canadian provinces added the provisions of this federal legislation to their provincial statutes. The Canadian legislation, in addition to controlling **recognition disputes** (disputes arising between unions and employers during the organization process), included provisions that reduced conflict in interest disputes and rights disputes. An **interest dispute** is a disagreement between the union and employer about what should be the terms of their collective agreement. A **rights dispute** is a disagreement over the meaning or interpretation of a provision included in a collective agreement. Another type of dispute that can arise is a **jurisdictional dispute,** which is a dispute between two unions over which one should represent a particular group of employees or over which union members ought to do a particular job. For example, should carpenters or steel workers put up metal-stud walls in an office building? The employer is usually caught in the middle in jurisdictional disputes and has little power to affect the situation.

Canada followed example of American legislation

Types of disputes— recognition, interest, rights, jurisdiction

The federal collective bargaining legislation is embodied in the *Canada Labour Code*.[29] This legislation covers those areas over which the federal government has jurisdiction, such as railroads, shipping, air transportation, broadcasting, and dock work. Each provincial government has passed collective bargaining legislation covering areas in which it has jurisdiction. These acts are variously called *Labour Codes, Trade Union Acts, Labour Relations Acts, Industrial Relations Acts,* and *Labour Acts.* The statutes cover most labour relations situations arising within the jurisdictions of the provinces as set out in Section 92 of the *Constitution Act (1867)*. Some types of activities, such as public services, schools, and hospitals, have unique federal or provincial legislation specifically designed to cover labour relations within that industry.

Both federal and provincial legislations cover collective bargaining

In all jurisdictions, special labour relations boards have been established to deal with disputes associated with the collective bargaining process. These bodies take the place of courts. It is important to remember that although they quite often look and act like courts, they are not. Rather, they are part of the executive branch of government, and as such, they can be used as an instrument of government policy. Labour relations boards have the advantage of expertise in labour matters.

Labour tribunals regulate process

27. (1935) 49 Stat. 449

28. 1944, P.C. 1003. (Because of the war emergency, the federal government had the power to pass general legislation for Canada.)

29. R.S.C. 1985, c. L-2

Also, resolution of disputes is usually much quicker than would be the case in the courts. Administrative tribunals are discussed in more detail in Chapter 3.

Important questions arise with respect to union membership, collective bargaining, and the *Charter of Rights and Freedoms*. The Supreme Court of Canada has decided that there is no constitutional right to belong to a union, to strike, or even to bargain collectively. These rights have been created by statute, and the limitations imposed by government do not violate Section 2(d) of the *Charter* guaranteeing freedom of association. However, Section 2(b) of the *Charter* guaranteeing freedom of expression protects picketing to some extent. In short, these rights have been gained politically and not through the courts, and political action must be relied on to retain them.

No constitutional right to belong to a union

Because Canadian labour statutes vary considerably from jurisdiction to jurisdiction, it is impossible to examine them in detail. However, it is possible to make some observations that apply in most areas.

Organization of Employees

Certification

While in some Canadian jurisdictions, it is possible for employers to voluntarily recognize a trade union as the bargaining agent for their employees, the most common method of union recognition in Canada results from the certification process adopted from the *Wagner Act* of 1935. For a union to obtain certification as the **bargaining agent** for a group of employees, referred to as the **bargaining unit**, it must apply to the appropriate labour relations board for certification and satisfy the board that a certain percentage of the workforce are members of the union.

Certification of bargaining unit adopted from *Wagner Act*

In Ontario, if the applicant can show that 40 percent of the workforce has joined the union, it can apply for certification. In most provinces, a certification vote is then held, and a majority vote supporting the union is necessary for it to obtain certification. In some provinces, the labour relations boards have the power to certify without such a vote, but the union must show that it has the support of a greater portion of the workforce. For example, in British Columbia, a union can apply for certification when only 45 percent of the workforce have joined the union, and certification without a vote can take place automatically when over 55 percent of the workforce are members.

Majority of workers must be members of union

Barry's Ltd. v. Fishermen, Food and Allied Workers' Union[30]

This is one of several examples where a labour relations board has exercised its power to certify a union without holding a vote. It also demonstrates the separation of federal and provincial jurisdiction. The employer in this case was a fish processor and because they were subject to the *Federal Fish Inspection Act,* it was argued that they should be within federal jurisdiction and the *Canada Labour Code* as far as labour relations were concerned. That was rejected by the court, which pointed out that just because a business was subject to federal legislation, it did not make it a federal undertaking. Fish processing was within their jurisdiction, and the provincial labour relations board had the authority to determine certification. Second, the case illustrates the power of the board to award certification without a vote. Under the appropriate provincial statute, the board can certify without a vote if they are

30. (1993) 101 D.L.R. (4th) 84 (Nfld. C.A.)

"satisfied that the majority of the employees in the unit are members in good standing of the trade union." The board simply indicated that it was satisfied with the findings of its investigator, who determined that 96 of 130 employees were members of the trade union. It refused to hear evidence that the employees had held a meeting and decided by majority that they wanted to deal with the employer through an employee committee or that the total number of employees was incorrect. The board exercised its power to grant certification without a vote, and the court upheld that decision.

The legislative provision governing the right of labour relations boards to certify even without a vote varies considerably with the jurisdiction, but this case shows not only the power of the board when dealing with labour matters but also that in some circumstances no vote is necessary when certification is applied for.

Bargaining Agent

Only union has right to bargain for employees

Once certified, the trade union has exclusive bargaining authority for the employees it represents, and a unionized employee loses the right to negotiate personally with the employer. The resulting contract between union and employer is binding on all the employees in the designated unit. It is important, therefore, to determine whether the workforce the trade union intends to represent is an appropriate bargaining unit before certification is granted. Labour relations boards discourage bargaining units that are either too small or too large or that contain groups of employees with conflicting interests. Management employees are, thus, excluded. Also to obtain certification, the trade union cannot be guilty of any discriminatory practices. A union that has applied for certification to be the bargaining agent for a group of workers and has failed must wait a specified period before trying again.

Unfair Labour Practices

Canadian Broadcasting Corp. v. Canada (Labour Relations Board)[31]

ACTRA is a union representing writers, journalists, and performers, and in 1988, its president was Dale Goldhawk, a journalist employed by CBC and the host of "Cross Country Checkup" on CBC Radio. The union publishes a regular paper called *ACTRA Scope*, which is distributed across Canada.

As president, Goldhawk wrote an article stating the union's position on free trade, an important issue in the ongoing election debate taking place at that time. Reference was made to this article in several other general publications across Canada. The CBC took the position that they could not have one of their journalists taking such a partisan stand in an election. Journalists were required to be balanced and impartial. Goldhawk was forced to resign from the CBC.

ACTRA responded, claiming that this was an unfair labour practice interfering with the formation or administration of a trade union and prohibited under the *Canada Labour Code*. Both the Canadian Labour Relations Board and, upon appeal, the Supreme Court of Canada agreed, finding against the CBC.

It is interesting to note that as the dispute progressed, Goldhawk and ACTRA presented a compromise proposal that would have had Goldhawk acting as presi-

31. 121 D.L.R. (4th) 385 (S.C.C.)

dent but not as spokesperson for the union. This was rejected by the CBC, and it was the rejection of that compromise position that the Canadian Labour Relations Board found constituted the unfair labour practice.

This case nicely illustrates how important it is to maintain the delicate balance between trade unions and employers and to ensure that the employer in no way interferes with the formation or operation of the trade union. Firing somebody because he became president of a trade union could not be tolerated. The case also illustrates the role played by administrative tribunals in the field of labour relations. This case went first to such a tribunal, and the question the Supreme Court of Canada dealt with was whether the Labour Relations Board had acted within its powers in reaching the decision that it did. The Supreme Court found that they had.

The primary objective of labour legislation is to create an orderly process for the organization and recognition of trade unions eliminating the conflict that often takes place in such circumstances. Prohibited unfair labour practices include threats or coercion of employees by either the union or management. The employer cannot threaten dismissal for joining a trade union or require that an employee refrain from joining a trade union as a condition of employment. Once the organization process has begun in most provinces, the employer cannot change conditions or terms of employment in order to influence the bargaining process. In some jurisdictions, in face of such an unfair labour practice, if the labour relations board concludes that a vote would not reflect the true feelings of the employees, it can grant certification without a vote. This is rarely done and will only take place where there is clear evidence of intimidation interfering with the reliability of the voting process.

Rules of conduct reduce conflict

Threats, coercion, dismissal—unfair labour practices

In some provinces, unfair labour practices can result in certification without vote

Requiring that an employer not coerce or intimidate employees does not eliminate the employer's right to state his or her views during the electioneering process that precedes a certification vote. Freedom of expression as set out in the *Charter of Rights and Freedoms* requires that as long as such statements are merely statements of opinion or fact and do not amount to threat or coercion, they are permitted.

Employer retains right of free speech

Trade unions, even in the process of organizing the workers, do not have the right to trespass on the employer's property or to organize during the employees' work time. However, employers will sometimes allow this so that they can at least know what is going on. Once the trade union has successfully completed the certification process, it becomes the certified bargaining agent for all the employees in the bargaining unit, and the employer must recognize it as such and bargain with it. The trade union can then serve notice on the employer requiring the commencement of collective bargaining.

In some jurisdictions, **employer's organizations** can also be certified, creating bargaining agents that are stronger and better able to negotiate with large unions on behalf of their members. These employer's organizations are usually found where there are a number of small employers, such as in the construction industry. In a similar fashion, local trade union organizations are often affiliated with much larger, parent unions which strengthen the local bargaining units by providing funds to support a prolonged strike and making available research and other expertise to assist in negotiations.

Employer organizations help employers bargain with unions

Unfair labour practices are not limited to the organization process. It remains vitally important to ensure that the union remains independent from employer domination even after certification and to ensure that it can carry on its union activities free from harassment by the employer.

Bargaining

Collective Agreements

Either party can give notice to commence collective bargaining

Any time after a trade union is certified, either party can give notice, requiring bargaining to commence, usually within 10 to 20 days, depending on the jurisdiction. In those situations where the union has been certified for some time and a collective agreement is already in place, this notice cannot be given until shortly before the expiration of the old agreement, usually three to four months.

Parties must bargain in good faith

Once this notice has been given, the parties are required to bargain or negotiate with each other, and in most provinces, the bargaining must be "**in good faith**." Whatever the term means, the parties must at least meet with a willingness to explore compromises and try to find an area of agreement. It does not mean that either party has to agree to the other's terms. Some provinces have adopted the wording used in the federal legislation, requiring the parties to make "every reasonable effort" to reach an agreement.

Employer Must Bargain in Good Faith

The employer operated a mine in the Northwest Territories and put forward an offer to contract with its unionized employees. The offer was rejected, and a bitter 18-month strike followed in which a number of workers died. Some employees were dismissed, and the company, when pressured as part of the eventual settlement package to at least provide for due process in the dismissals, steadfastly refused. After attempts at mediation, an industrial inquiry commission, and intervention by the Minister of Labour, there was still no settlement to the strike. The union went to the Canadian Labour Relations Board, complaining that the employer failed to bargain in good faith.

The board agreed and ordered the employer to renew the original offer made before the strike. The employer refused and appealed the board's decision. The Supreme Court of Canada upheld the Labour Relations Board's right to find that the employer had not bargained in good faith and upheld their right to impose the settlement. The Supreme Court Justices observed that it was not necessary that the Labour Relations Board's finding of lack of good faith be correct, only that it not be patently unreasonable because it was within the board's jurisdiction to make such a finding.

Royal Oak Mines Inc. v. Canada (Labour Relations Board), [1996] 1 S.C.R. 369

Ratification

Once a bargain has been reached, it is presented to the union membership and, where appropriate, to the employer's board or to an employer's council for ratification. When both sides ratify, there is a binding collective agreement. The agreement is a contract, but because of the modifying legislation, it must be viewed as a special form of contract with unique features, such as the method of its enforcement.

Agreement must be ratified

In most jurisdictions, while bargaining is proceeding, the employer is not permitted to change the terms and conditions of the employment, such as wages, benefits, or hours of work. When it is clear that the parties cannot reach an agreement, it is possible in some jurisdictions for the Labour Relations Board to impose a first contract, although this option is seldom used.[32]

32. *Labour Relations Code*, R.S.B.C. 1996, c. 244 s. 55

Mediation (Conciliation)

Mediation, sometimes called conciliation, has been provided for in the various Canadian jurisdictions. When negotiations begin to break down, either party has the right to make application to the appropriate government agency for the appointment of a **conciliator**, sometimes called a **mediator**. This person then meets with the two parties and assists them in their negotiations. The hope is that communications between the two parties will be greatly facilitated by this third-person go-between. The parties are prohibited from taking more drastic forms of action, such as strike or lockout, as long as a conciliator is involved in the negotiations.

Some provinces provide for a two-tiered process of conciliation, with first a single officer and subsequently a conciliation board consisting of three mediators, but the function is essentially the same. It is only after the conciliator or conciliators have removed themselves from the process, by booking out of the dispute and by filing a report, that the parties are allowed to proceed to strike or lockout. In some jurisdictions, conciliation is a pre-requisite to strike or lockout. Although conciliators have no authority to bind the parties, they do have the power to make recommendations that will be embarrassing to an unreasonable party. Note that in many jurisdictions, a conciliator can be imposed on the parties by the Labour Relations Board, even when neither party has requested one.

Mediation assists negotiation process

In Ontario, arbitration can be requested when agreement cannot be reached on a first contract.[33] Arbitration differs from conciliation in that the arbitrator does have the power to make a decision binding on the parties. In other provinces, such as British Columbia and Newfoundland, the boards have the power to impose a first contract in such situations.

Contract Terms

The completed collective agreement must satisfy certain requirements, such as having a term of at least one year. If the parties have placed no time limit on the agreement, it will be deemed to be for one year. The parties often do not reach an agreement until well after the old collective agreement expires. The new one then takes effect retroactively, and so, even with this one-year minimum requirement in effect, the new contract will last only a few months. For example, if Sami is involved in collective bargaining with her employees whose agreement expires on December 31, it is possible that the parties would still be bargaining in the following April. If Sami and her employees finally reach an agreement in June, to run for one year, the agreement would probably be retroactive to the prior January 1 and expire on the following December 31. The agreement would only be in effect for a further six months after the date the agreement was reached. It can be readily seen why every province has taken the approach that any agreement for a period shorter than one year is unworkable.

Contract must be for at least one year

Arbitration

All collective agreements must contain provisions that set out a method for the settlement of disputes arising under the agreement. This is usually accomplished through a **grievance procedure** ultimately leading to arbitration. The contract will set out a process involving a series of structured meetings in which the parties negotiate a settlement. When no settlement can be reached, the matter is submitted to an arbitrator (or panel of arbitrators), who will hold a hearing and make a

Interpretation of contract disputes to be arbitrated through grievance process

33. *Labour Relations Act*, S.O. 1995, c. 1 ss. 43

decision that is binding on both parties. This grievance process is used to resolve disputes not only over the interpretation of the contract provisions but also as a response to individual employee complaints of violations of their rights by the employer.

Decision of arbitrator binding on both parties

While both arbitration and conciliation involve the intervention of an outside third party, the distinction is that the parties are not required to follow the recommendations of a conciliator but the decision of the arbitrator is binding on both parties. Arbitration, therefore, is a substitute for court action. Each party in an arbitration hearing is given an opportunity to put forth its side of the argument and present evidence before the arbitrator makes a decision. Arbitrators are not required to follow the stringent rules of procedure that normally surround judicial proceedings, and their decisions can usually be appealed to the labour relations board and, in some jurisdictions, the courts. The collective agreement replaces any individual contract that may have existed previously between the employer and employee, so all disputes between the parties must be handled by the grievance procedure and arbitration. This method of dispute resolution is compulsory. It is not permissible for the parties to indulge in strikes or lockouts or to use the courts to resolve a dispute over the terms of the contract once it is in force.

No strike when contract is in force

Disputes Arising from Collective Agreement Must Be Arbitrated

Otis Elevator terminated Mr. Bourne, who was in a trade union and subject to a collective agreement between Otis and the union. Bourne sued for wrongful dismissal. This action was brought to determine whether the court had jurisdiction to hear such a case. The judge in this case decided that since Mr. Bourne was a trade union member and there was a collective agreement, the court had no jurisdiction. These types of disputes are determined by the provisions of the agreement, and since it is required under legislation that all collective agreements have arbitration provisions, any dispute arising under that agreement must be settled by arbitration. It is clear that had this matter gone to arbitration, it would have been appropriately resolved there.

Bourne v. Otis Elevator Co. Ltd., 6 D.L.R. (4th) 560 (Ont. H.C.)

Other Terms

In addition to the terms specifically relating to conditions of work, rates of pay, vacations, termination, and the like, which are the main object of the collective bargaining process, there are various other terms which often appear in collective agreements. The federal government and some provinces have passed legislation that requires the contract to cover how technological changes in the industry will be handled. British Columbia now requires that union-management committees be set up to handle such conflicts. Throughout Canada, the parties can agree to terms that provide for union security, such as the **union shop clause**. This clause simply requires that new employees join the union within a specified period of time. In some jurisdictions, particularly in such industries as construction or long shoring, the agreement may require that the employee be a member of the union before getting the job. This requirement is called a **closed shop clause**. In some areas, employees retain the right not to join a union but are still required to pay union dues. This arrangement is referred to as the **Rand Formula**. Many statutes permit the collective agreement to contain a **check-off provision**, which means that the parties have agreed that the employer will deduct union dues from the payroll.

Agreement must provide for technological change

Union and closed shop provisions

Strikes and Lockouts

Some sort of job action will probably result if the parties cannot agree on what terms to include in the agreement. A **lockout** is action taken by the employer to prevent employees from working and earning wages. A **strike** is the withdrawal of services by employees. Although a strike usually consists of refusing to come to work or intentional slowdowns, other forms of interference with production may also be classified as strikes. For example, postal employees announced just before Christmas 1983 that they would process Christmas cards with 10-cent stamps on them despite the fact that the appropriate rate was thirty-two cents per letter. This action was taken to draw attention to the fact that certain commercial users of the postal system got a preferential bulk rate not available to the public. The courts declared that the action was a strike, and since a strike would have been illegal under the circumstances, the union reversed its position. Employees can pressure an employer by strictly adhering to the terms of their agreement or by doing no more than is minimally required. This behaviour is called **work to rule** and will often prompt a lockout. Strikes and lockouts are both **work stoppages** but are initiated by different parties.

Since the main objective of modern collective bargaining legislation is to reduce conflict, the right to strike and the right to lockout have been severely limited. It is unlawful for a strike or lockout to occur while an agreement is in force. Strikes and lockouts can only take place after the last agreement has expired and before the next one comes into effect. Any strike or lockout associated with the recognition process or involving jurisdictional disputes between two unions are also illegal and must be dealt with through the certification process described above. Only when the dispute is part of the negotiation or bargaining process and concerns the terms to be included in the collective agreement (interest dispute) is a strike or lockout legal.

If a collective agreement is in place and a dispute arises as to the terms (a rights dispute), it must be resolved through the grievance and arbitration process described above. Any strike associated with such a dispute is illegal.

Even when the dispute concerns what will go into the new agreement (an interest dispute), there are still some limitations on strike action. The old contract must have expired and the parties must have attempted to bargain in good faith. A vote authorizing strike action must be taken, and a specified period of notice must be given, for example, 72 hours in Alberta and British Columbia. The employer must give the same notice to the employees when a lockout is about to take place. No strike or lockout can take place until a specified period of time has passed after a conciliator has made a report to the Minister of Labour. Even then, in some areas, a further cooling-off period may be imposed. In some jurisdictions, such as Québec and British Columbia, the employer is prohibited from hiring replacement workers during a strike. This restriction puts considerably greater pressure on the employer to settle the dispute and goes some way in reducing the violence associated with such labour-management confrontation. Ontario repealed a similar provision, and the federal government has amended the *Canada Labour Code* to partially prohibit the use of such replacement workers.

Picketing

Once a strike or lockout has taken place, one of the most effective techniques available to trade unions is picketing. But as with striking, the use of picketing is severely limited and controlled. Picketing involves strikers standing near or marching

Job action may involve lockout, strike, work to rule

Strike or lockout can only occur between contracts in an interest dispute

Must bargain in good faith first and vote before strike

Proper strike notice must be given

Right to picket limited by legislation

around a place of business trying to dissuade people from doing business there. Picketing is permissible only when a lawful strike or lockout is in progress. Employees who picket before proper notice has been given or somewhere not permitted under the labour legislation of the province are in violation of the law. A picketer responsible for communicating false information to those who might cross the picket line can be sued for defamation.

When the information communicated does not try to discourage people from crossing the picket line or dealing with the employer, the action may not qualify as picketing. For example, postal employees handing out pamphlets to customers in front of post offices stating the preferred rates charged to bulk users may not be classed as picketing, even though it is embarrassing to the employer.

Violence not permitted

Picketing must be peaceful and merely communicate information. Violence will not be tolerated. A tort action for trespass may follow the violation of private property, and if violence erupts, the assaulting party may face criminal and civil court actions. But if the striking worker keeps his or her conduct strictly within the confines set out in the legislation, in most jurisdictions, no tort action can be taken against that worker or against the union itself. When picketing goes beyond the narrow bounds permitted in common law and legislation, the employer can resort to the courts or labour relations boards to get an injunction to limit or prohibit the picketing. Where the number of picketers used may be excessive, as with mass picketing, this goes beyond simple information communication and becomes intimidation. The employer can then apply to have the number of picketers restricted. Employees face considerable risk of personal liability for damages caused when they involve themselves in illegal picketing.

Strong tradition of union solidarity makes picketing effective

Although picketing limited in this way may seem to be an ineffectual weapon, there is an extremely strong tradition among union members and many others never to cross a picket line. Others simply wish to avoid the unpleasantness of a confrontation. Employers must deal with other businesses, which employ union members, such as suppliers, truck drivers, electricians, plumbers, and telephone service people, and these workers generally will not cross the picket line. Most collective agreements have terms that protect union members from punishment for refusing to cross a valid picket line. It eventually becomes very difficult for an employer to continue in business surrounded by a picket line.

Some provinces permit secondary picketing

Just what locations can be legally picketed varies with the jurisdiction. Employees in every jurisdiction can picket the plant or factory where they work. Only in some jurisdictions, such as New Brunswick, picketing can be extended to any place at which the employer carries out business.[34] Where such **secondary picketing** is allowed, the striking employees are able to picket not just their own workplace but also other locations where the employer carries on business. In any case, unrelated businesses cannot be legally picketed, even if they are located on the same premises as the one struck, as might be the case, for example, in a shopping mall. Of course, whether the picketing is directed towards such an unrelated business in a given dispute is a question for the court or board to decide in each case. But the more extensive the picketing, the more effective the economic pressure placed on the employer.

---

34. *Industrial Relations Act*, R.S.N.B. 1973, c. I-4, s. 104

U.F.C.W., Local 1518 v. Kmart Canada Ltd.[35]

The UFCW represented employees who were locked out from the Kmart department stores in Campbell River and Port Alberni. They decided to escalate the dispute by handing out leaflets to customers in Kmart stores in the Vancouver and Victoria area explaining the nature of their complaints against the company and encouraging them not to shop at Kmart. In British Columbia, the legislation prohibits secondary picketing (picketing at a location other than where the employees work), and the court was asked to decide whether this leafleting qualified as prohibited secondary picketing. The Supreme Court of Canada held that it did not. The court determined that "the distribution of leaflets did not interfere with employees at the secondary sites, nor was there any indication that it interfered with the delivery of supplies. The activity was carried out peacefully, and it did not impede public access to the stores. Neither was there any evidence of verbal or physical intimidation." Some customers may have been persuaded not to deal with the stores, but this was an example of free speech rather than picketing.

The court distinguished between picketing and leafleting and held that **leafleting** was an expression of free speech and guaranteed under Section 2 of the *Charter of Rights and Freedoms*. The prohibition against secondary picketing was also an interference with free speech, but it was justified under Section 1 because of its interference in commercial relations.

Anyone has the legal right to cross a picket line. Customers are free to continue doing business with an employer involved in a strike or lockout; suppliers are free to continue supplying goods and services to the employer if they can persuade their employees to cross the picket line; and the employer has the right to continue normal business activities. Unfortunately, picketers can lose sight of these basic rights when they think their picket line is not being effective. As a result, a considerable amount of intimidation, coercion, violence, and injury still take place despite all the precautions introduced into the labour relations system in Canada.

No legal obligation to honour picket line

Public Sector and Essential Services

The discussion thus far relates to people employed in private industry. However, many people are employed either as part of the public sector or in service industries that are considered essential to society, such as power companies, hospitals, and police and fire departments. Employees falling into these categories are treated differently from those employed in private industry, and special legislation governs their activities. Although labour issues and disputes in these occupations are virtually the same as those in the private sector, the government and the public regard the position of public service employees as quite different. Strikes by police, firefighters, hospital workers, schoolteachers, and other public servants are usually considered inappropriate by members of the public.

Every province has special legislation to deal with these groups. Most provinces permit collective bargaining to some extent, but only a few allow public sector employees to participate in strikes and picketing, the others substituting some form of compulsory arbitration of disputes. Of course, in all labour disputes, including private

Public sector employees have limited rights to job action

35. [1999] 2 S.C.R. 1083

ones, the government retains the right, either by existing statute or by the passage of a specific bill, to impose a settlement or an alternative method of resolving the dispute, such as compulsory arbitration.

Reference Re Public Service Employee Relations Act, Labour Relations Act, and Police Officer Collective Bargaining Act[36]

The *Public Service Employee Relations Act* and certain other Alberta statutes prohibited strikes and picketing among public employees, such as firefighters and police, requiring that any disputes go through a process of binding arbitration. This reference was brought to the Supreme Court of Canada to determine whether these provisions violated the right to freedom of association found in Section 2 of the *Charter of Rights and Freedoms*. The court held that the Section 2 protection of freedom of association did not create the right to bargain collectively or to strike in a labour dispute. These rights are created by legislation and must be carefully balanced against other interests by that legislation. The Alberta prohibition against such strikes in the public sector is valid.

The case is important in that it establishes that the right to bargain collectively and to strike is not protected by the charter and must be fought for in the political arena.

What should a business consider?

One of the most difficult areas that an employer has to deal with is the prospect of a union organizing its workforce. The driving force behind the decisions that are made are often emotional rather than economic, employers not wanting to give up their right to manage or to surrender any control to trade unions. Machismo often seems to reign more than common sense. This is true especially at the organizational stage and is the main reason the employer's role at that level has been minimized. The certification process supervised by government has done wonders to reduce conflict at that stage. Still, a great amount of conflict takes place, and it is vital that managers step back and consider the effect of their dealings with the trade union from a long-term economic view and not be overcome by their own emotions. Managing in a union environment takes a special kind of skill, and not all employers can avoid the pitfalls that arise in this kind of an environment. Still, many successful companies deal with strong unions successfully and great care should be taken, especially in a newly unionized situation, to avoid unfair labour practices and other situations that poison the atmosphere or cripple the position of the employer because of ill-thought-out tactics and strategies.

Union Organization

Unions can expel for misbehaviour

Trade unions must be democratic organizations, in which policy is established by vote and executives and officers are elected. Members can be expelled or disciplined for misbehaviour, such as crossing picket lines after being instructed not to by the union executive. Expulsion can be devastating for a worker, since many collective agreements provide for a **union shop** in which all employees must be members of the union. Some jurisdictions have passed legislation stipulating that a person who loses his or her union membership for reasons other than failure to pay dues will be able to retain employment.[37] There are some employees whose

36. [1987] 1 S.C.R. 313
37. *Canada Labour Code*, R.S.C. 1985, c. L-2 s. 95(e)

religious beliefs prevent them from joining or contributing to such organizations as trade unions, which presents a real dilemma in a union shop situation. Some provinces have passed legislation exempting such individuals from the operation of this provision of the collective agreement, although the other terms of the collective agreement still apply.

Trade unions are subject to the human rights legislation in place in their jurisdiction. In some jurisdictions, the labour legislation provides that they can lose their status as a trade union if they discriminate. Unions have an obligation to represent all their members fairly. Employees who feel unfairly treated by the union or who feel that the union is not properly representing them in disputes with employers can lodge complaints before the provincial Labour Relations Board, and the union may find itself required to compensate the wronged employees.

Trade unions were once considered illegal organizations with no status separate from their membership and therefore no corporate identity. Most provinces have passed legislation giving a recognized trade union the right to sue or be sued on its own behalf, at least for the purposes outlined in the labour legislation.

Trade unions controlled by labour relations boards and courts

Summary

Employee

- Provides general service to employer
- Must follow directions, be honest, careful, and loyal

Independent contractor

- Contracts to do a specific job

Employer

- Vicariously liable for the acts of the employee during the course of employment
- Must also provide a safe working place, direction, and wages

Termination

- Both parties are obligated to give the other reasonable notice
- Amount depends on length of employment
- No notice required when there is just cause for dismissal, such as dishonesty or incompetence
- Wrongful dismissal—employee must mitigate losses by trying to find other employment

Legislation

- Controls minimum wage, hours of work, termination, child labour, discrimination, employment standards, health and safety standards, employment insurance, and workers' compensation

Human rights statutes

- Prohibit discrimination in its various forms

- Require positive action to accommodate religious beliefs and disabled workers.

Collective bargaining

- Now controlled by legislation
- Certification process controls the organization and recognition of bargaining units
- Job action possible only when that bargaining process breaks down
- Strikes allow persuasive picketing but no physical confrontation
- Once the contract is in place, any disputes arising under it must be dealt with through an arbitration process provided for in the agreement

QUESTIONS

1. Distinguish among an employee, an independent contractor, and an agent.

2. Explain how a court will determine whether a person is an employee rather than an independent contractor.

3. Summarize the employer's obligations to the employee and the employee's obligations to the employer under common law in a master-servant relationship.

4. Explain what is meant by a restrictive covenant and what factors determine whether it is enforceable or not.

5. What is the proper way to terminate an employment contract that is for an indefinite period of time?

6. How is the appropriate notice period to terminate an employment relationship determined?

7. Under what circumstances can an employee be dismissed without being given notice? When can an employee leave employment without giving notice?

8. What risk does an employer who ignores an employee's incompetence over a period of time face?

9. What factors will a court take into consideration when determining compensation in a wrongful dismissal action? Indicate any other types of remedies that may be available to the victim.

10. Explain what is meant by "vicarious liability." Describe the limitations on its application and how vicarious liability will affect the position of the employee.

11. Describe how the *Employment Standards Act* protects basic workers' rights.

12. Explain how human rights legislation applies to areas of employment.

13. Explain what is meant by a duty to accommodate in the field of human rights and how that can affect employers.

14. Explain the object and purpose of workers' compensation legislation and how those objectives are accomplished. Explain what the position of the parties would be if only the original common law applied.

15. What is the significance of the *American National Labor Relations Act (Wagner Act)* in Canada?

16. Distinguish among recognition disputes, jurisdiction disputes, interest disputes, and rights disputes.

17. Explain the difference between mediation and arbitration. Describe how these tools are used in Canadian labour disputes.

18. Once a collective agreement is in place, what effect will it have on the individual rights of employees? How will it affect the employer?

19. What kind of disputes are strikes and lockouts limited to? How are the other types of disputes between union and employer dealt with?

20. Distinguish between a strike and a lockout. Describe the type of job action that can constitute a strike.

21. Explain what steps must take place before a strike or lockout is legal.

22. Explain what is meant by picketing, when it can take place, and the limitations that have been placed on picketing in different jurisdictions.

23. What is the legal position of a person who wishes to cross a picket line?

CASES

1. Clare v. Canada (Attorney-General)

Clare was an employee of the federal government, who was fired from his job for incompetence after 23 years of service. After a number of years of satisfactory service in various capacities with the federal public service, the plaintiff received an unsatisfactory evaluation in his performance appraisals for three consecutive reviews. On the basis of this performance, the plaintiff was fired from his position.

During that time, his wife had suffered from a series of major illnesses and nearly died. He was also having serious problems with his son, including physical confrontation. As a result, Clare was experiencing an extreme amount of stress in his life. In addition to his personal troubles, he had a personality conflict with his immediate supervisor that introduced work-related stress. During this period, Clare was receiving counselling and had asked to participate in a federally sponsored program designed to help employees experiencing these kinds of difficulties. The plaintiff sought reassignment, which was refused; and so, after 23 years of service, he was fired from his position.

Explain the legal position of the parties and whether the dismissal was justified in the circumstances. Would your answer be different if it were established that he had experienced family problems over his entire work history with the department, that several of his transfers from one department to another had been to accommodate a "problem or troubled employee," and that his performance had never been fully satisfactory?

2. DiCarlo v. DiSimone et al.

The plaintiff was in a car owned by his employer and driven by a fellow employee when they were in an accident while in the process of work. They collided with a car driven by Lilian Watson and owned by her husband Alfred. Both drivers were found to be negligent and partially at fault in the accident. The plaintiff sued for damages from both drivers, his employer, and Mr. Watson, the owner of the other vehicle. Describe the arguments that can be used by the employee and the employer and any limitations on the amount that can be collected from the Watsons.

3. Parks v. Atlantic Provinces Special Education Authority

Parks had been employed as a residence counsellor since 1976 at a school catering to physically and mentally handicapped children and students up to the age of 21 years. This job was very physically demanding in that he often had to lift the residents, help them to do exercises, help with their personal care, provide assistance on outings, and cope with medical problems and emergencies. The school was originally just for the blind, but the job became more and more onerous as the function of the school broadened. Mr. Parks' job got progressively more difficult.

After nine years, Mr. Parks suffered a herniated disc in his neck caused by lifting patients. In 1987, he developed problems with his left knee. After some time off work on a disability pension, he wanted to return to work in May 1989, but it was clear that he would not be able to do the same heavy lifting that he had done before. His employment was terminated, and he sued for wrongful dismissal.

Explain the arguments on both sides and how much notice Mr. Parks would be entitled to in these circumstances.

4. United Steel Workers of American L. 7917 v. Gibraltar Mines Ltd.

In this case, a number of truck drivers were suspended because they refused to drive their trucks. One of the truck drivers was a union official. The truck drivers claimed that the conditions were unsafe. They had to drive up a ramp beside an open pit. The weather conditions made the ramp slippery. A protective device, called a berm, which was designed to keep the trucks from falling into the pit, was missing for a stretch of about 130 metres. The company claimed that it was an illegal strike and suspended the truck drivers. The drivers brought an application to be reinstated.

Explain the arguments on both sides and the probable outcome. Would your answer differ with the added information that upon learning that the mining operation was still functioning, a union official set up a picket line and encouraged the entire crew to stay off the job?

5. Amalgamated Clothing and Textile Workers Union (Toronto Joint Board) v. Straton Knitting Mills Ltd. et al.

When the union in question tried to organize the workers at the respondent's premises, the co-owner held three meetings with the employees in an attempt to dissuade them from joining the union. He told them it was not necessary for them to have a union, that it would be divisive, that they would have to pay union dues, that there was the possibility of a strike, and that it might result in the loss of contracts for the company, which would mean less work for the employees. The company also changed the pay scale, which resulted in higher wages. A petition was circulated to oppose the union, but there was some suggestion that the management was behind it. Part of the message that got through to the employees was that the employer did not want a union and that if it came, there would be layoffs, short weeks, and perhaps closure of the business. What course of action would you recommend to the union in these circumstances?

CHAPTER 12

Agency

CHAPTER HIGHLIGHTS

- The agency relationship
- The rights and responsibilities of an agent and a principal
- The implications of a fiduciary relationship

Fraudulent misrepresentation is one of the few circumstances in which a principal will be held vicariously liable for the acts of an agent, even in the absence of an employment contract between them, provided that the agent is acting within the authority he has been given by the principal. Such an agency relationship can have a tremendous impact on the principal. How agency relationships are created and the obligations that arise between the parties are the topics covered in this chapter.

Steinman v. Snarey[1]

Mr. Snarey was a "well-respected agent" working for the Mutual Life Assurance Company of Canada, when he was approached by a customer who wanted to take advantage of one of the investment opportunities offered by the company. Mr. Snarey persuaded the customer to part with $16 000 by way of a cheque made out to Mr. Snarey. The customer was told that his money was going into an "investment vehicle offered to the public by Mutual Life." Actually, the company did not offer this kind of investment plan and never had. This was simply a scheme used by Mr. Snarey to cheat a trusting customer out of a considerable amount of money. When the customer discovered the fraud, he turned to the Mutual Life Assurance Company for compensation. In the resulting action, it was determined that Mr. Snarey had devised and conducted a fraudulent scheme. Because he was an agent of Mutual Life with the actual authority to enter into this general type of transaction with the company's customer, the company was vicariously liable for his conduct and had to pay compensation to the client.

The subject of agency is a vital component in any discussion of business law. The legal consequences that stem from an agency relationship are of utmost concern to business people because at least one of the parties in most commercial transactions is functioning as an agent. Agency law is the basis of the law of partnership, and an understanding of it is essential for coming to terms with corporate law. These subjects will be dealt with in the next two chapters.

Agent represents and acts for principal

An agent's function is to represent and act on behalf of a principal in dealings with third parties. Although, by far, the most common type of legal relationship

1. (1987) 26 C.C.L.I. 78 (Ont. Dist. Ct.); aff'd (1988) 32 C.C.L.I. xliii (Ont. Div. Ct.)

in which agents represent principals is in the creation of contracts, agents also find themselves involved in other types of legal relationships. Real estate agents do not usually have the authority to enter into contracts on behalf of vendors, but they function as agents nonetheless because they participate in the negotiations and act as go-betweens. Other professionals, such as lawyers and accountants, also create special legal relationships that are not necessarily contractual in nature on behalf of their clients or principals. The term **agency** refers to the service an agent performs on behalf of the principal. This service may be performed as an employee, as an independent agent, or gratuitously. When an agent is acting independently, the business performing the service is often called an agency, such as a travel agency, employment agency, or real estate agency.

Agency **refers to service performed by an agent**

The discussion in this chapter focuses on the law of agency, and in most cases, no distinction will be made between people functioning as agents as part of an employment contract and those acting independently. In any case, it is important not to think of the agency function found within an employment relationship as just another aspect of that employment. The duties and obligations imposed on agents go far beyond the employment relationship and must be understood as a separate function or set of obligations.

The Agency Relationship

The agency relationship can be created by an express or implied contract, by estoppel, by ratification, or gratuitously, the key element being the granting of authority.

Formation by Contract

Agency relationship usually created through contract

Usually, an agency relationship is created through a contract, called an **agency agreement contract,** between the agent and the principal, and as such, general contract rules apply. This should not be confused with the contracts agents enter into on behalf of their principals. The agency contract can cover such things as the authority of the agent, the duties to be performed, and the nature of payment to be received. It may be imbedded in a contract of employment or establish an independent agency relationship. Generally, there are no additional formal requirements for the creation of such a contract. Thus, although it is a wise practice to do so, the agency agreement need not be in writing, except in those jurisdictions where the *Statute of Frauds* requires it or where it is to last longer than one year as was discussed in Chapter 6. Under the *Bills of Exchange Act,* the granting of the agent's authority where the agent is to sign cheques or other negotiable instruments must also be in writing. Although there may be other advantages in doing so, it is not necessary that the agency agreement be under seal, unless the agent will be sealing documents on behalf of the principal as part of his or her agency function. An agency agreement in writing and under seal is called a **power of attorney**.

Basic rules of contract apply to agency contracts

All the elements of a contract, such as consensus, consideration, legality, intention to be bound, and capacity on the part of both parties, must be present for an agency agreement to be binding. The lack of any one of these elements may void the agency contract, but that will not affect the binding nature of any agreement the agent enters into on behalf of the principal. Thus, if Clarke is underage and acts as Jiwan's agent in the sale of Jiwan's car to Skoda, the agency contract between Clarke and Jiwan may be voidable because of the incapacity of Clarke. But the contract between Jiwan and Skoda for the purchase of the car is still binding. Only when agents are so young, drunk, insane, or otherwise incapacitated that they do not understand what they are doing does the contract between the principal and third party become doubtful on the basis of incapacity or lack of consensus.

Consent only essential requirement of agency

The actions of an agent may be binding on the principal even when the agent is acting gratuitously. Only consent is necessary which explains why, in the above example, the contract for the purchase of the car is binding between Jiwan and Skoda despite the infancy of the agent, Clarke. Still, most agency relationships are based on contract, either expressly entered into by the parties or implied from their conduct. Often, these are simply employment contracts.

Authority of Agents

Most disputes that arise in agency relate to the extent of the authority of the agent in dealing with third parties. An agent's authority can be derived from the principal in several ways.

Actual Authority

The authority specifically given by the principal to the agent and usually set out in the agency agreement is called the agent's actual authority. This actual authority may be expressly stated by the principal or implied from the circumstances, such as from the position the agent has been given. A person who is hired as a purchasing agent has the authority to carry out the customary and traditional responsibilities of purchasing agents as well as the duties necessarily incidental to that function. Of course, normally, no such authority is implied if the principal has specifically stated that the agent does not have it. Still, there may be apparent authority as discussed below.

Actual authority express or implicit

In the example used to introduce this chapter, the contract entered into by Mr. Snarey was just the kind of contract he was authorized to conclude with his clients. Because of this actual authority, the principal was liable for his fraud.

Any written agency agreement should carefully set out the authority of the agent eliminating as far as possible the need for any implied authority. An agent who exceeds this actual authority may be liable for any injury his or her conduct causes the principal. But no matter how much care is used in drafting an agent's actual authority, the principal may still be bound by the agent's conduct that falls within his apparent authority.

Apparent Authority

When a principal does something by conduct or words to lead a third party to believe that an agent has authority, the principal is bound by the agent's actions, even where there is no actual authority. Even when the principal has specifically prohibited the agent from doing what he did, the principal will be bound because of

Apparent authority presumed from actions of principal

Estoppel applies when principal indicates that agent has authority

the agent's apparent authority. This is an application of the principle of estoppel. **Estoppel** applies when a principal has done something to lead the third party to believe that an agent has authority to act on his or her behalf, such as stating "George is my agent and has my authority." Even if the statement is wrong, when a principal leads a third party to believe the agent has authority in this way, that principal is said to have "held out" that the agent has authority to act on his or her behalf. If a third party has relied on this representation, the principal cannot then claim that the agent had no authority.

The most important example of the application of estoppel is in the field of agency. It is important not to confuse this principle of estoppel with equitable or promissory estoppel, as described in Chapter 5. **Equitable estoppel** involves a promise or commitment to do something in the future. Here, we are dealing not with a promise but with a claim or a statement of fact made by the principal.

Agent acting on apparent authority will bind principal

Although the principal may look to the agent for compensation, so long as that agent has acted within his apparent authority, the principal is still bound in contract with the third party. If Pedersen employed Mohammed as sales manager of his used car dealership, it would be reasonable for customers to assume that Mohammed had the authority of a normal manager to sell cars and to take trade-ins. If after receiving instructions from Pedersen not to accept trades over $2000 without his express approval, Mohammed were to give Kim a $5000 trade-in for a 1995 Mercedes, Pedersen would still be bound by the deal. Pedersen put Mohammed in that position and led Kim to believe that Mohammed had the ordinary authority and power of a sales manager. The agent acted within his apparent authority, and the contract was binding on the principal. If, however, the agent had sold Kim the entire car lot, this would be beyond both his actual and apparent authority and would not be binding on Pedersen.

Previous acceptance of agent's actions

A principal can also be bound by the actions of an agent that would normally be beyond the agent's authority if the principal has sanctioned similar actions in the past. Kim's chauffeur Green would not normally be expected to have the authority to purchase automobiles on behalf of his principal. But if he had done so several times in the past and Kim honoured the deals, the dealer, Pederson, would be entitled to assume that the next purchase was authorized as well and Green had apparent authority. Even if Kim specifically told Green not to buy any more cars, and Green in violation of those instructions purchased another car from Pederson, the contract would be binding on Kim because of apparent authority. The existence of this apparent authority is based on the statements and conduct of the principal, not the agent. When the misleading indication of authority comes from the agent rather than the principal, and the action is otherwise unauthorized, the third party will have no claim against the principal.

Untangling the WEB

We normally think of agency as an interaction between human beings. Computerized machines now seem capable of entering into agreements with each other and with people, and in that sense, these machines become agents. Automatic teller machines conduct fairly sophisticated banking transactions based on simple digitized codes. What happens when the person punching in the numbers is not the person the machine thinks he is? How do you determine if the person punching in the numbers has either the actual or apparent authority to make the transaction?

The **reasonable person test** has a significant role to play in determining the existence of apparent authority. The usual authority associated with the position in which an agent has been placed is based on this test. The reasonable person test is also used to determine whether the third party should have been misled into believing that the agent had authority by the statements and conduct of the principal.

Reasonable person test used to determine existence of authority

Dale v. Manitoba[2]

This is a classic case of apparent authority binding a principal, which took place at the University of Manitoba. The Government of Manitoba initiated a program called ACCESS to encourage disadvantaged students to get post-secondary education. The government provided the funding, set out the rules, and determined eligibility, but the university administered the program. The university staff promised students that the funding supplied would continue until they finished their university program. Unfortunately, the federal government cut back transfer payments to the provinces, causing the Manitoba government to cut off funding to the ACCESS program prematurely. Students affected by the cut sued, claiming that the government was bound by the university's promise to provide funding until their program was complete. The court agreed, finding that the university was functioning as an agent for the provincial government. When the university staff promised that the students would be supported for the duration of their studies, they were acting on behalf of the provincial government. Even though they had not been specifically authorized to make such promises, they were acting within their apparent authority when they did so. Thus, the provincial government was bound by that commitment.

When a principal puts an agent in a position so that it appears to others that they have authority to make certain commitments, they have that authority, even though it has not been actually given. This is the very nature of apparent authority and shows how important it is for public and private institutions alike to carefully define the authority of those acting for them and then take steps to ensure that their agents act within those boundaries.

To determine whether a principal is bound in contract with a third party by the actions of an agent, a person must first ask, "Was the agent acting within the actual authority given by the principal?" If the answer is yes, then there is a contract, provided all the other elements are present. If the answer is no, then the question to ask is, "Did the principal do anything to lead the third party to believe that the agent had the authority to act?" In other words, was the agent acting with apparent authority? If the answer is yes and the third party relied on that apparent authority, there is a contract between the principal and the third party. It is only when the answer to both these questions is no that there is no contract, and the third party must look to the agent for redress.

Was the action of the agent authorized by principal?

Most people find it difficult to understand the difference between implied and apparent authority, and in most cases, the distinction is not important. But to clarify, when a principal has specifically stated that the agent does not have authority, no authority can be implied. In spite of such a declaration, however, there may still be apparent authority because of the principal's comments or conduct in relation to the third party (estoppel). The principal has led the third party to believe that the agent has authority and now cannot deny that fact.

2. (1997) 147 D.L.R. (4th) 605 (Man. C.A.)

Ratification

If principal ratifies unauthorized contract, it is binding

A principal can still ratify a contract even if the agent has acted beyond both actual and apparent authority. The first time Kim's chauffeur bought a car on his behalf, there would likely have been no apparent authority, since this is not normally a chauffeur's job. If Kim liked the car, however, he could ratify the contract and the deal would be binding on the dealer. The effect of such ratification is to give the agent authority to act on behalf of the principal retroactive to the time of the sale. The result can seem unfair because the principal is not bound when an agent goes beyond the authority given, but if the principal chooses to ratify, the third party is bound and can do nothing to change that.

In fact, the power of the principal to ratify must meet the following qualifications.

Third party can set time for ratification

1. The third party has the right to set a reasonable time limit within which the ratification must take place. In the case of a chauffeur buying a car without authority, the dealer cannot simply repudiate the contract but could give the principal a short time to ratify by saying, for example, "You have until noon tomorrow to decide." In the United States, once the third party repudiates, it is too late for the principal to ratify. This may indicate the future direction in Canada, but we are not there yet.

Agent must have been acting for a specific principal

2. The agent must have been acting for the specific principal who is now trying to ratify. A person cannot enter into a contract with a third party while purporting to be an agent and then search for a principal to ratify. The customer would be free to repudiate the purchase, since the would-be agent did not have a particular principal in mind when entering into the contract. There is no one to ratify the agreement.

Principal must be capable of entering into contract

• when it is entered into

3. The principal has to be fully capable of entering into the contract at the time the agent was claiming to act on his or her behalf. A principal who did not have the capacity to enter into the original deal because of drunkenness or insanity does not have the power to ratify upon becoming sober or sane. This can be a problem where pre-incorporation contracts are involved. Often, promoters who are planning an incorporation will enter into contracts, such as the purchase of property on behalf of the proposed company, assuming that once the company is formed, it will ratify the agreements. But because there is no company at the time the contract is entered into there can be no ratification, leaving the promoter personally liable for any losses suffered by the third party. Legislation in some jurisdictions has modified this principle to allow a corporation to ratify such pre-incorporation contracts.[3]

• when it is ratified

4. The parties must still be able to perform the object of the contract at the time of the ratification. For example, if an agent enters into a contract on behalf of a principal to insure a building against fire, the principal cannot ratify the agreement after a fire. There is no building to insure when ratification is attempted, so there can be no contract. The contract the agent enters into must not make any reference to the need for ratification. If the contract includes such terms as "subject to principal's approval" or "subject to ratification," it becomes merely an agreement to enter into an agreement. The contractual requirement of consensus is not satisfied, and there is no contract.

---

3. For example, the *Ontario Business Corporation Act*, R.S.O. (1990) c. B.16 s. 21

Ratification can work against the principal in other ways. The principal can inadvertently ratify by knowingly accepting some sort of benefit under the agreement. If Kim's chauffeur bought a new Rolls Royce on Kim's behalf without the actual or apparent authority to do so, Kim would normally not be bound by such a contract. However, if Kim were to use that car in some way, such as driving it to work before returning it to the dealer, Kim would have accepted some benefit under the contract and thus ratified it. Kim would be bound to go through with the purchase of the automobile, provided that at the time he received the benefit, Kim knew that the purchase was made on his behalf.

Ratification can take place inadvertently

Agency by Necessity

Consent is at the heart of agency law. Both principal and agent must consent to the conduct. Without authority (apparent or actual) or ratification, the principal cannot be bound. Only when there is agency by necessity will the court impose an agency relationship on the principal despite the clear lack of consent.

When communication systems were less reliable than they are now, it might have been important for the captain of a ship to decide to sell a cargo that was spoiling, without waiting for instructions from his principal. The owners of the perishable goods could not later attack the sale as being unauthorized and demand the return of the cargo or compensation from the captain. In this circumstance, the ship's captain was authorized to act by the principle of agency by necessity. Today, communication can be instantaneous, and agency-by-necessity normally would not arise. Note that for agency by necessity to apply, there must be some duty or responsibility placed on the agent to care for those goods. Merely finding another person's property in danger does not, in and of itself, create an agency-by-necessity relationship.

Agency by necessity rarely used today

Exception in Family Relationships

It is common for a spouse to have the actual or even apparent authority to act on behalf of their spouse when dealing with merchants, especially for the purchase of necessities and other household goods. When the marriage breaks down, those merchants who, because of past dealings, have been led to believe a person has authority to act for a spouse, may rely on that apparent authority. In the absence of notice to the contrary, the authority continues, even when the spouse has been specifically prohibited from making such purchases.

• except in some family matters

In some circumstances, authority can be implied by operation of law against the will of the other party. A wife who is deserted by her husband is presumed to have the authority to bind him to contracts with third parties for the purchase of necessities. But this must be viewed in the light of modern family law legislation that usually provides a more satisfactory remedy. In some jurisdictions, this principle has been abolished altogether.

A businessperson who deals through an agent runs a risk of that agent entering into contracts that are not authorized. Whether this is done by mistake or intentionally, the effect on the businessperson can be significant. To avoid the problem, the principal should make the limits of that authority absolutely clear to the agent and include those limitations in a written agency agreement, where practicable. The principal should also, where practical, make the limits of the agent's authority clear to the customers or third parties with whom that agent will deal. Customers should also be notified immediately upon the termination of that agent's authority, otherwise it will continue because of the principle of apparent authority.

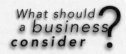

Agents have a duty to act in the best interests of their principals.

Prentice Hall Archives

The Rights and Responsibilities of the Parties

The Agent's Duties

The Contract

When an agency agreement has been created by contract, the agent has an obligation to act within the actual authority given in that agreement. An agent violating the contract but exercising apparent authority can be sued for breach and will have to compensate the principal for any losses suffered. Failure on the part of the agent to fulfill any other obligation set out in the agreement will also constitute an actionable breach of contract. Of course, if the specified act is illegal or against public policy, there is no obligation to perform.

An agent owes a **duty of care** to the principal. The agent must not only have the skills and expertise claimed but must exercise that skill in a reasonable manner. For example, if Khan hires Gamboa to purchase property on which to build an apartment building, Gamboa must not only stay within the authority given but must exercise the degree of care and skill one would expect from a person claiming to be qualified to do that type of job. If Gamboa buys a property for Khan and it turns out to be zoned for single-family dwellings, such a mistake would be below the standard of reasonable performance one would expect from someone in this type of business, and Gamboa would be liable to compensate Khan for any loss.

Agents often have considerable discretion in carrying out agency responsibilities as long as they act to the benefit of the principal. However, an agent cannot go against the specific instructions received, even if it might be in the principal's best interests to do so. If a stockbroker is instructed to sell shares when they reach a specific price, the broker must do so, even though waiting would bring the principal a better price.

Agent owes duty of reasonable care

Agent must perform as required by principal

Volkers et al v. Midland Doherty Ltd. et al.[4]

Mr. Volkers had transferred his RRSP account to the defendant company and was dealing with Mr. Hill. Mr. Volkers was a knowledgeable investor and was assured by the representatives of Midland that he could give instructions to Mr. Hill or any other trader and they would be followed. On February 28, Volkers determined that he wanted to purchase a substantial amount of shares in Breakwater Resources Ltd. After receiving instructions, Mr. Hill made the appropriate purchase. Later that day, Mr. Volkers decided to purchase additional shares in that company and phoned to give instructions to Mr. Gurney to make the purchase first thing the next morning, since Mr. Hill had left for the day.

4. (1995) 17 D.L.R. (4th) 343 (B.C.C.A.).

Mr. Gurney arrived at 7:00 a.m. but because of some doubts about the wisdom of the trade delayed making the purchase until Mr. Hill arrived about two hours later. Unfortunately, trading in Breakwater shares had been stopped before Mr. Hill's arrival, and when it came back on the market, it had doubled in price. Mr. Volkers suffered substantial loss and sued.

It was argued that Mr. Gurney had a duty to act in the best interests of his client, and since this was what he was doing, there should be no liability. This argument was accepted at trial, but on appeal, the decision was reversed. Mr. Gurney had been given specific instructions to purchase the Breakwater shares first thing in the morning, and his duty was to do so or to tell Mr. Volkers that he did not so that Mr. Volkers could make other arrangements. Although the agent was obligated to do what he thought was best for the client, the agent bore an even greater obligation to keep Mr. Volkers informed. Mr. Volkers was the one to make the decision, not Mr. Gurney. This case illustrates that it is an important aspect of the agent's duty to the principal to follow instructions.

Delegation

Generally, the agent has an obligation to perform the agency agreement personally. An agent is not permitted to delegate responsibility to another party, unless there is consent to such delegation, either express or implied by the customs and traditions of the industry. Even then the primary agent has the responsibility to see that the terms of the agency agreement are fulfilled. The authority of an agent is commonly delegated to sub-agents, when that agent is a corporation or large business organization, such as a law firm, bank, real estate agency, or trust company.

Agent cannot delegate responsibility

Accounting

The agent must turn over any monies earned pursuant to the agency function to the principal. If the agent acquires property, goods, or money on behalf of the principal, there is no entitlement to retain any of it other than the authorized commission. Even when the agent has some claim against the funds, he cannot keep them. If the third party owes money to the agent and pays money to the agent intended for the principal, the agent cannot intercept those funds on his own behalf but must pay over any money collected to the principal. To facilitate this process, the agent also has an obligation to keep accurate records of all agency transactions.

Agent must turn money over to principal

Agent must account for funds

Fiduciary Duty

Ocean City Realty Ltd. v. A & M Holdings Ltd. et al.[5]

Mrs. Forbes was a licensed real estate salesperson working for Ocean City Realty Ltd. She was approached by Mr. Halbower to find a commercial building in downtown Victoria. After some investigation, Mrs. Forbes approached the owners of a building to determine whether it might be for sale. The owner of the property, A & M Holdings Ltd., entered into an arrangement with her, whereby they agreed to pay a commission of 1.75 percent if she acted as their agent in selling the building. After some negotiations, the sale was concluded for $5.2 million, but unknown to the seller, Mrs. Forbes had agreed to pay back half her commission to the purchaser, Mr. Halbower. When A & M discovered the secret deal between Mrs. Forbes and Mr. Halbower, they refused to pay any commission.

5. (1987) 36 D.L.R. (4th) 94 (B.C.C.A.)

Mrs. Forbes had a fiduciary obligation to act in the best interests of her principal, A & M, but she argued that they got what they expected and her sacrifice only ensured that the deal went through. That did not hurt A & M but helped them. The court held, however, that one of the key elements in the duty of a fiduciary is to disclose all pertinent information with respect to the transaction that would be considered important by the principal. In this case, the knowledge that she was paying part of her commission back to Mr. Halbower was important to A & M, and it may have determined whether they would go through with the deal or not. In effect, they thought that Mr. Halbower was paying one price, when, in fact, he was paying less for the property. They were entitled to this information, and it may have influenced their decision. Therefore, the fiduciary obligation of the agent had been breached, and the agent was entitled to no commission at all.

One is very sympathetic with the position of Mrs. Forbes. She only paid over part of her commission to Mr. Halbower to preserve the deal. But who was she acting for? If she did not complete this deal, it is quite likely the property would have been sold by another real estate agent to somebody else, and she would have received nothing. And so, it is clear that she was acting in her own self-interest above the interest of the principal. This case strongly illustrates the nature of fiduciary duty where a person owing that duty must submerge personal interests in favour of the interests of the principal they represent.

Agent must act in best interests of principal

The principal is usually quite vulnerable because of the trust put in the agent. This gives rise to a fiduciary duty where the agent has an obligation to act only in the best interests of the principal. The relationship is often referred to as an **utmost good faith relationship**. The agent has an obligation to keep in strict confidence any communications that comes through the agency function. The agent cannot

Agent's Fiduciary Duty Requires Full Disclosure

The plaintiffs listed their home for sale, and Mr. Murray submitted an offer for $29 000 below the list price. His friend, Mr. Charman, a real estate agent (not the listing agent), wrote a letter accompanying this offer, trying to persuade the Baillies to accept this lower offer. They did so, but before the home was transferred, Mr. Murray decided he preferred another home listed by Mr. Charman and bought that. Charman decided he wanted to take over the deal and had a company that he was principal of take delivery of the property from the Baillies. At the time, he substituted the name of the company for his friend Mr. Murray in the transaction. He did not tell the Baillies that he had any interest in that company. When they eventually found out what had happened, they brought this action claiming that Mr. Charman had violated his fiduciary duty to the plaintiffs. The court agreed. Mr. Charman, as the selling agent, would not normally have such a duty to the vendors, but he took on a fiduciary obligation to the Baillies when he wrote that letter persuading them to take the offer by Mr. Murray. After that, he had an obligation to disclose, especially his conflict of interest, when he had his company purchase the house. Because he failed to do so and made personal profit, he had to give up not only the commission he made on the original sale of the Baillies' house to the company but also the commission he made on the resale of the property by the company to the eventual purchaser. Also, he had to hand over the profit the company had made. The standards imposed on a fiduciary in these circumstances are significant.

Baillie v. Charman, 94 D.L.R. (4th) 403 (B.C.C.A.)

take advantage of any personal opportunity that may come to his or her knowledge through the agency relationship. Even if the agent is in a position where some personal benefit will be lost, he or she must act in the principal's best interests. If the agent does stand to benefit personally from the deal, this must be disclosed to the principal. If there is a failure to disclose, the principal can seek an accounting and have any funds gained by the agent in such a way paid over to the principal.

Any information that comes to the agent in the course of duty that could benefit either the principal or the agent must be disclosed to the principal. In the Ocean City case used to introduce this section, it was Mrs. Forbes' failure to fully disclose the special deal she had made with the purchaser that was her undoing. Even though she lost money, she was in breach of her fiduciary duty and lost her commission as a result.

Agent must disclose information

An agent cannot act for both a principal and a third party at the same time. It would be very difficult for an agent to extract the best possible price from a third party on behalf of a principal when the third party was also paying the agent. The common practice of agents accepting gifts, such as holidays, tickets to sporting events, and liquor, is an example of the same problem. If the principal discovers the agent accepting payment from the third party, the principal is entitled to an accounting and the receipt of all such funds and will likely have just cause to terminate the relationship. Only where full disclosure has been made at the outset and permission given can the agent profit personally in this way.

Agent cannot act for both principal and third party without consent of both

In real transactions, the agent usually acts for the seller. This can cause problems for the purchaser who often does not realize this and expects the agent to protect their interests as well. In the western provinces, this difficulty is largely overcome by requiring the purchasers to have their own agent acting for them and splitting the commission.

Agent Owes Fiduciary Duty to Principal, Not Third Party

Adams-Eden was a furniture manufacturer that obtained insurance through the services of an insurance broker who arranged this insurance with Kansa. There was a fire, and Adams-Eden made a claim to Kansa on its insurance. At first, Kansa refused to pay on the basis that they had not been properly informed about prior claims and other material information. Kansa eventually settled their claim and paid Adams-Eden, thinking they would be able to maintain an action for negligence against the insurance broker. The issue before the court was whether the insurance broker owed Kansa a duty to disclose the information. The court held that there was no such duty between the broker and the insurer. The broker was the agent of the furniture company, not the agent of the insurance company. In these circumstances, Kansa's only remedy would have been not to pay out on the claim.

Adams-Eden Furniture Ltd. v. Kansa General Insurance Co., (1996) 141 D.L.R. (4th) 288 (Man. C.A.)

Another problem sometimes arises where an agent who is hired to purchase goods or property sells to the principal property actually owned by the agent as if it came from some third party. This is a violation of the agent's fiduciary duty, even if that property fully satisfies the principal's requirements, and can only be done where there is full disclosure. The reverse is also a breach where the agent buys for himself what he has been hired to sell to others. An example would be where a

Agent must not profit at principal's expense

real estate agent hired to sell a house recognizes it as a good deal and purchases it for himself, usually through a partner or a corporation. The agent then has the advantage of a good price knowing how low the principal will go and getting the commission as well. This is not acting in the best interests of the principal, and the agent would be required to pay back both profits and commission to the vendor of the property.

Agent must not compete with principal

In the same way, the agent must not operate his own business in competition with the principal, especially if a service is being offered. Nor can the agent also represent another principal selling a similar product. Finally, the agent must not collect any profits or commissions that are hidden from the principal paying over all the benefit resulting from the performance of the agency agreement. Such a breach of fiduciary duty on the part of an agent who is an employee will likely constitute just cause for dismissal.

What should a business consider?

The very nature of the job when many professionals and independent business people offer services to others is that of an agent. When a relationship of trust is created, that leaves a client vulnerable, a fiduciary duty is owed, and the person providing the service must put the interests of the client ahead of his or her own and follow the instructions given. It is sometimes difficult to keep personal interests and the interests of customers and clients separate, but failure to do so is asking for trouble. Sometimes, there is temptation to withhold information ("what they don't know won't hurt them") or to take advantage of some deal comes that along because of the position. When someone succumbs to these temptations, they are often found out and are liable to pay any losses suffered. If money is made on the deal, it must go to the person to whom the duty was owed, but if money is lost the agent must bear the loss. It is vitally important that a professional or businessperson in such a position learn the nature of their fiduciary duty and make sure they honour it.

Duties of Principal

The Contract

Principal must honour terms of contract and pay reasonable amount for services

The principal's primary obligation to the agent is to honour the terms of the contract by which the agent was hired. If the contract is silent as to payment, an obligation to pay a reasonable amount can be implied on the basis of the amount of effort put forth by the agent, as well as the customs and traditions of the industry. If the agreement provides for payment only on completion, there is no implied obligation to pay for part performance. Thus, if an agent is to receive a commission upon the sale of a house, even if the agent puts considerable effort into promoting a sale, there is generally no entitlement to commission if no sale occurs. Unless there is agreement to the contrary, the agent is also normally entitled to compensation for reasonable expenses, such as phone bills and car expenses.

Principal must reimburse agent's expenses

Ambiguous authority will be interpreted broadly

If the agency agreement is vague about the extent of the agent's authority, the courts will usually favour an interpretation that gives the agent the broadest possible power. Thus, if Jones is hired as a sales manager for a manufacturing business and is given authority to enter into all sales related to the business, a court will likely interpret it to include authority to sell large blocks of product but no authority to sell the plant itself. When the power to borrow money is involved, however, the courts take a much narrower approach. Thus, if Klassen was hired as a purchasing agent with "all the authority necessary" to carry out that function and he found it necessary to borrow money to make the purchases, the courts would not

• except when power to borrow money is in question

imply an authority to borrow without getting additional approval from the principal. It is necessary for an agent to be given specific authority to borrow money on the principal's behalf in order to proceed.

Undisclosed Principals

In normal circumstances, the agent is not liable to the third party. The contract is between the principal and the third party, and the agent is not a party to it. Sometimes, however, principals do not want a third party to know who they are, and the agent will act without identifying the principal. When an agent makes it clear that they are acting as an agent for a principal who does not want to be identified, the third party can still elect to enter into the agreement, but there will be no recourse against the agent. In the event of a breach, the third party must seek out the identity of the principal and look to that individual for redress. But if the agent fails to state that he or she is acting for someone else and signs the documents as if he or she is the principal, the agent is directly liable to the third party. If an agent acts for an undisclosed principal in a way consistent with either being an agent or the main contracting party, the third party has a choice. For example, when the agent signs a purchase order in a way consistent with being an agent for the purchaser or the actual person purchasing the goods, the third party can sue either the agent or, upon learning the identity, can sue the principal instead. The injured party cannot sue both; once the choice is made, the third party is bound by it.

> **Third party can sue agent or principal if principal undisclosed**

To avoid the problem of undisclosed principal, a person acting as an agent should be extremely careful to make it clear that they are acting in an agency capacity. This is normally done by writing "per" immediately before the signature of the agent. If Sam Jones were acting for Ace Finance Company, he would normally sign:

> Ace Finance Ltd. per Sam Jones

The more cautious approach would be for Sam to state clearly he is acting as an agent for Ace Finance Ltd.

> Sam Jones, acting for Ace Finance Ltd.
>
> or
>
> Sam Jones, acting as agent for Ace Finance Ltd.

No Liability under Contract When Agent Makes It Clear He Is Acting as Agent

Chartwell provided stevedoring services for Q.N.S., which operated a chartered ship. Although Chartwell never mentioned specifically who they were acting for, Chartwell made it clear at all times that they were acting as agents on behalf of others in their dealings with Q.N.S. The deal fell through. Q.N.S. sued Chartwell. The Supreme Court of Canada had to decide whether this was an undisclosed principal situation where the agent could be successfully sued. The court held that because Chartwell had made it clear at all times that they were functioning as an agent, there was no personal liability for that agent on the contract. An agent cannot be held personally liable for a contract that he enters into with a third party if he makes it clear he is acting as an agent, even though he does not disclose the identity of the principal.

Q.N.S. Paper Co. v. Chartwell Shipping Ltd., [1989] 2 S.C.R. 683

Third party can repudiate when identity of undisclosed principal important

Apparent authority does not apply where the principal is undisclosed, since no representations of authority have been made by that principal. A contract binding on the principal and third party only results when the agent is acting within the actual authority given. Even then, not all contracts with undisclosed principals are binding on third parties. An exception is when the identity of the undisclosed principal is important to the third party. In a contract involving personal services, for example, the third party would be able to repudiate upon discovering that the deal had been made with an agent rather than with the principal. In the case of *Nash v. Dix*,[6] a religious group acquired the services of an agent to purchase a church building from another religious organization. They felt that the church building would not be sold to them if they disclosed who they really were. Their fear was justified in that the sale was challenged when the identity of the principal was discovered. The court held that this was not a situation in which the identities of the parties were important, and the sale went through. In the case of *Said v. Butt*,[7] a theatre refused to sell a ticket to someone on opening night because he had caused a disturbance in the past. That person arranged for a friend to acquire the ticket on his behalf but was refused admittance even though he had a ticket. He sued for breach, but the court held that in this situation, the identity of the party was obviously important, and the court did not enforce the contract.

No Apparent Authority with Undisclosed Principal

Sign-O-Lite entered into an agreement with Calbax Properties Ltd., the owners of a Calgary shopping mall, to put up a large outdoor sign there. By the time this agreement expired, the actual ownership of the mall had changed hands, although Sign-O-Lite was not aware of it. In fact, a series of complex dealings had taken place, which left another company controlled by the same principal as Calbax as the managing company of the mall but not the owner, and so Sign-O-Lite thought they were dealing with the same people when they entered into a renewal agreement with the mall management company. The mall management company did not have the authority to renew, and the company owning the property, the defendant in this case, refused to go through with the deal. The court had to decide whether a contract entered into by an agent on behalf of an undisclosed principal was binding on that principal when the agent had gone beyond his or her authority. The court found that in such circumstances, the principal could not be bound; the concepts of apparent authority or ostensible authority did not apply, as they were inconsistent.

Sign-O-Lite Plastics Ltd. v. Metropolitan Life Insurance Co., (1990) 73 D.L.R. (4th) 541 (B.C.C.A.)

Undisclosed principal relationships are often used when well-known companies are assembling land for new projects. Agents approach property owners in the area to obtain options on their properties. The options are only exercised if a sufficient number of property owners are willing to sell at a reasonable price. The undisclosed principal approach is used to discourage people from holding out for higher prices once they find out who is really buying the property.

A third party can choose to sue either the agent or the undisclosed principal, but the third party is only bound by this choice once the identity of the principal has been determined. The principal can enforce the contract, unless the identity of

6. (1898) 78 L.T. 445

7. [1920] 3 K.B. 497

the parties is an important factor in the contractual relationship as discussed above. Similarly, the agent may sue or be sued under the contract when the principal is undisclosed. The agent only loses the right to enforce the agreement when the principal chooses to act like a principal and takes steps to enforce the agreement. Normally, a principal can ratify a contract when an agent has exceeded his authority, but this is not possible when an undisclosed principal is involved. Ratification can only take place when the agent is claiming to act for a specifically identified principal. An undisclosed principal cannot ratify the acts of an agent.

Only identified principal can ratify

The Third Party

Salter v. Cormie[8]

Mr. Salter was employed by a company as treasurer and chief financial officer. He also owned a block of shares in the company. He was fired by the directors, one of whom also acted as the company's lawyer and is the defendant in this case. In the negotiations to settle, the defendant made an offer on behalf of "a group of individuals" to purchase the shares held by Mr. Salter.

The offer was accepted; a deposit was paid, and a few of the shares were transferred, but in general, the contract was not performed. Eventually, the shares were de-listed and became worthless. This action was brought against the company lawyer who negotiated the contract to settle as well as the lawyer's firm. The defendant claimed that despite what was said, he was not representing a specific principal, only that there was an intention to form a group to purchase the shares. The judge said that if the group did exist, they would be liable, and if it did not, the lawyer would be liable on the basis of breach of warranty of authority. Since the lawyer took the position that the group did not exist and that he was an agent acting on its behalf, he and his firm were liable to Mr. Salter.

"An agent who expressly contracts on behalf of undisclosed principals will be liable if, in fact, he has no principals or if they have not authorized this transaction. And, of course he will be liable if he contracts on behalf of a named principal who, in fact, has not given authority."

This case illustrates the most important situation where the agent will be personally liable to the third party he deals with. Not having the authority claimed is inconsistent with the very nature of the agency relationship and flies in the face of the trust placed in the agent by the third party to be what he claims to be.

When an agent does not have the authority claimed, either actual or apparent, that agent may be sued by the third party for breach of "warranty of authority." This action is founded in contract law and is the most common example of an agent being sued directly by the third party. Also, an agent who intentionally misleads the third party into believing that he or she has authority that he or she does not hold may be sued by the third party for the tort of deceit. Furthermore, agents who inadvertently exceed their authority can be sued for negligence.

Third party can sue agent for unauthorized acts

It is important to distinguish between the tortious liability of the agent based on fraud or negligence and a contract action based on breach of warranty of authority. Where a breach of warranty of authority action is brought, the damages will be limited to those that were reasonably foreseeable at the time the contract was

Remedies in tort available for fraud or negligence

8. (1993) 108 D.L.R. (4th) 372 (Alta. C.A.)

entered into or those that flow naturally from the breach. If, unknown to the agent, the goods were to be resold at an unusually high profit which was lost because of the breach of warranty of authority, the agent would not be liable for those losses, since they were not reasonably foreseeable. However, if the third party could establish the agent's fraud or negligence, the lost profits might be recovered from the agent because they are the direct consequence of the tortious conduct.

Liability for Agent's Tortious Conduct

Vicarious liability limited to employment

As discussed in Chapters 4 and 11, an employer is vicariously liable for the acts an employee commits during the course of employment. When an agent is also an employee of the principal, the principal is vicariously liable for any tortious acts committed by the agent in the course of that employment. The difficulty arises when the agent is not an employee but is acting independently. The Supreme Court of Canada has held that the principle of vicarious liability is restricted to those situations in which a master-servant relationship can be demonstrated.[9] Still, it is often argued that a principal can be held vicariously liable for the wrongful conduct of an independent agent. In this text, we have taken the more conservative position that employment must be present for vicarious liability to exist. It must be emphasized, however, that the courts have been expanding the definition of employment. Fleming points out that "the employment of a servant may be limited to a single occasion, or extend over a long period; it may even be gratuitous."[10] Even if the relationship involves a person who is essentially an independent agent, that agent may be functioning as an employee or servant in a given situation and thus impose vicarious liability on the principal. With such a broad definition of employment, judges will have little difficulty imposing vicarious liability on principals when the circumstances warrant. Of course, the principal can then look to the agent for compensation for any losses incurred by having to pay compensation to the person injured by the agent's wrongful conduct.

Vicarious liability where independent agent deceitful

There are some situations in which vicarious liability will apply even if the agent is acting independently. The courts are clearly willing to hold the principal responsible for the fraudulent misrepresentation of an agent, even when no employment exists. The vendor can be held responsible for a fraud committed by a real estate agent in the process of selling a house on behalf of the vendor. In the example used to introduce the chapter, it made no difference whether Mr. Snarey was an employee or was acting as an independent agent; because fraud was involved, the principal was liable for the agent's wrongful conduct. In rare cases, there may be other wrongful conduct, such as negligence, that gives rise to the imposition of vicarious liability on the principal, even for the acts of such independent agents. But clearly, liability will be limited to those situations where the wrongful conduct takes place as the agent performs the specific act they have been employed to do.

Begusic v. Clark, Wilson & Co.[11]

Mrs. Begusic purchased a residence in a cooperative in a very unusual transaction. The cooperative was built on land leased for 66 years, and the lease contained a provision requiring the renegotiation of the rent paid for the lease every 22 years. A set rent was in place for the first period, and at the end of the first 22 years, it was to go

9. T. G. Bright and Company v. Kerr [1939] S.C.R. 63

10. John G. Fleming, *The Law of Torts*, 8th ed. (Sydney, Australia: The Law Book Co. Ltd., 1990), p. 371.

11. 92 D.L.R. (4th) 273 (B.C.S.C.)

up to 7.5 percent of the market value of the property. The tenants were aware that they would have to pay a portion of the rent for the property but had no idea that there was a rent revision provision or that the rent would increase so much (for one tenant the increase was 1700 percent) In fact, several actions were brought by a number of the tenants when the unexpected increases became apparent.

In this particular case, an action was brought against the real estate agent and the lawyer involved as well as their principal, the vendor, on the basis of vicarious liability. When the real estate agents dealt with Mrs. Begusic, they failed to inform her of the unusual nature of the lease provisions or her potential responsibility in relations to them. That information was contained in a prospectus that should have been given to her but was not. At the lawyers office, she did not even see the lawyer; rather, a paralegal made sure she signed all the appropriate documents. Again, she was not given the prospectus, nor was she informed of the unusual nature of the transaction. In neither case was she informed of the rent revision provisions.

The court found that the real estate agents had a duty to give her a copy of the prospectus and to explain the unusual provisions of the transaction, especially the rent review provision. Their failure to do so amounted to negligent misrepresentation. The position of the lawyers was a little more complicated, since they claimed to be only representing the vendor and to have little or no duty to look after Mrs. Begusic's interests. The court concluded, however, that in the circumstances, it was reasonable for the plaintiff to believe that the lawyers were looking after her interests, that as such they had a duty to bring the rent review provisions of the lease to her attention, and that they had failed in this duty. She attended at their office as encouraged by the realtors and was given a bill for their services. Both the lawyers and the real estate agents were liable to Mrs. Begusic. The court, then, had to consider the vicarious liability of the vendor. It was clear that both the lawyer and the real estate agents were acting on behalf of the vendor when they failed to disclose the appropriate information to the plaintiff and to deliver the prospectus to her. The duties they were performing were the specific acts they were authorized to do and so both were acting within their authority when the wrongs were committed. The vendors were, therefore, vicariously liable for these wrongful acts.

This case illustrates the operation of vicarious liability even when there is no employment relationship between the parties. The negligence of the real estate agents and solicitors occurred while actually doing what they had been authorized to do, and so, vicarious liability followed.

Direct liability if principal is origin of fraud

A principal can also be found directly liable for their own tortious conduct. If the principal has requested the act complained of, has told the agent to make a particular statement that turns out to be defamatory or misleading, or is negligent in allowing the agent to make the particular statements complained of, the principal may be directly liable. In the case of *Junkin v. Bedard*,[12] Junkin owned a motel that was sold to a third party through an agent. Junkin provided false information regarding the profitability of the motel to the agent, knowing that the agent would pass it on to the purchaser, Bedard. The agent did so, and Bedard bought the property. Bedard later discovered the falsification and sued Junkin for fraud. Because the agent had innocently passed the information on to Bedard, Junkin alone had committed the fraud, even though the agent had communicated the information. Here, the principal was directly liable for his own fraud. If the agent

Vicarious liability—both parties liable

had fabricated the false information, the principal would have been vicariously liable for the agent's fraud. As is the case with employment law, vicarious liability makes the principal responsible, but it does not relieve the agent of liability for their own tortious conduct. Both can be sued, but the principal can then seek compensation from the agent.

What should a business consider?

Since most business is done through agents, business people must take care to understand the exposure they have to liability for their agents conduct. That liability may be based in contract or tort, and both are derived from the duties and authority given. Whether the agent is independent or an employee, care should be taken to carefully define his or her authority and to make sure that the agent stays within those specified parameters. Even then, liability may be incurred when agents do in a careless manner what they are authorized to do. The key here is to minimize exposure, not to eliminate it. In the end, the best practice is to ensure that agents are reliable and trustworthy. As with most things, there is no substitution for careful selection and training.

Termination of Agency

Termination as per agreement

Since the right of an agent to act for a principal is based on the principal's consent, as soon as the agent is notified of the withdrawal of that consent, that authority ends. When the agent is an employee, the relationship is usually ended with appropriate notice, as discussed in Chapter 11. But even where employment may continue, the authority to act as an agent will end immediately upon notification of the agent. Sometimes, the agency agreement will set out when the agent's authority will end. If the agency relationship was created for a specific length of time, the authority of the agent automatically terminates at the end of that period. Similarly, if the agency contract created the relationship for the duration of a particular project or event, for example, "for the duration of the 2001 Canadian National Exhibition," the authority ends when the project or event ends.

Requirement of notification

When the principal wants to end the agent's authority to act, simple notification is usually sufficient, for there is no requirement that the notice be reasonable, only that it be communicated to the agent. This applies to the termination of authority to enter into new contracts on the principal's behalf, not necessarily to the right to continued payment, which may be based on other contractual considerations. If the activities the agent is engaged to perform become impossible or essentially different from what the parties anticipated, then the contractual doctrine of frustration may apply and terminate the agent's authority. Similarly, an agent's authority to act on behalf of a principal is terminated when the actions the agent is engaged to perform become illegal. If Cantello agreed to act as Jasper's agent to sell products in a pyramid sales scheme, Cantello's authority to represent Jasper would have been terminated automatically when the *Criminal Code* provision prohibiting such activities was passed.[13]

Frustration may terminate agency

Death, insanity, or bankruptcy will terminate agency

An agent's authority to act on behalf of a principal can be terminated in several other ways. The death or insanity of a principal will automatically end the authority of an agent. When the principal is a corporation, its dissolution will have a similar effect. An agent will lose authority when a principal becomes bankrupt, although other people may assume such authority under the direction of the trustee. The third party will normally not be affected in the same way. Certainly, as far as ter-

13. *Criminal Code*, R.S.C. (1985) c. C-46 s. 206

mination of authority on the basis of agreement is concerned, unless the principal notifies the third party of such termination, the actions of the agent may still be binding on the principal on the basis of apparent authority. Though it is not entirely clear, this may also be the case when the principal becomes insane. In the case of bankruptcy or death of the principal or dissolution of the company, the agent's actual and apparent authority ceases. Because of the principle of apparent authority, it is vitally important for a principal to take steps to notify current and potential customers as well as other people and businesses that they may have dealings with regarding the termination of the agent's authority.

Specialized Agency Relationships

Many examples of specialized services offered to businesses and the public are essentially agencies in nature, such as those of travel agents, real estate agents, lawyers, accountants, stockbrokers, financial advisors, and insurance representatives. Some of these agents do not enter into contracts on behalf of their clients but negotiate and act on their clients' behalf in other ways. For example, a real estate agent neither offers nor accepts on behalf of a client. In fact, the client is usually the vendor of property, and the agent's job is to take care of the preliminary matters and bring the purchaser and vendor together so they can enter into a contract directly. Nonetheless, few would dispute that these real estate agents are carrying out an essentially agency function and thus have a fiduciary obligation to their clients. The important thing to remember is that the general provisions set out above also apply to these special agency relationships, although there may be some exceptions. For example, in most of these specialized service professions, the rule that an agent cannot delegate usually does not apply. The very nature of these businesses requires that employees of the firm, not the firm itself, will act on behalf of the client.

General principles apply to specialized agencies as well

Most of these specialized agencies are fulfilling a service function and are governed by special statutes and professional organizations. For example, the real estate industry in each province has legislation in place that creates commissions or boards that govern the industry. The commissions require that anyone acting for another in the sale of property be licensed or be in the employ of a licensed real estate agent. Bodies that license their members often provide training and discipline them when required. It is beyond the scope of this text to examine these professional bodies in detail; students are encouraged to examine the controlling legislation, as well as to seek information directly from the governing professional bodies. Most of them are concerned about their public image and are happy to cooperate.

Special statutes and professional organizations

Often, agencies perform a service to their customers that involves not only representing those customers but giving them advice. Because of the specialized expertise provided, customers are particularly vulnerable to abuse when such agencies try to take advantage of them. The governing bodies hear complaints and go a long way towards regulating the industry and preventing such abuses. But abuses still occur, and victims should know that they have recourse based on the fiduciary duty principles set out here as well as remedies in contract and tort discussed before. Such fiduciary duties, in fact, may be imposed on other professional advisers, even when their duties do not extend to being agents.[14]

14. Hodginson v. Simms [1994] 3 S.C.R. 377

Summary

Agents

- Act for a principal in dealings with third parties

Authority

- Actual authority is defined in the contract
- Apparent authority
  - When the principal has done something to lead the third party to believe that the agent has authority even when such authority has been specifically withheld
  - Even when the agent has exceeded both the actual and apparent authority, the principal may ratify the agreement
  - Ratification works retroactively
  - Only when the agent acts beyond all authority can he or she be sued (breach of warranty of authority)

Agent's duties

- Involve performing terms of contract; providing an accounting of funds, and fiduciary duty
- Cannot be delegated

Principal's duties

- Involve honouring terms of contract and reimbursing agent's expenses

Undisclosed principal

- Third party has a choice to sue the agent or the undisclosed principal to enforce the contract

Vicarious liability

- In the absence of an employment relationship, the principal is not vicariously liable for the acts of the agent, except when fraudulent and negligent misrepresentation is involved

Fiduciary relationship

- Exists between the agent and the principal
- Agent has obligation to act in the best interests of the principal

Termination

- The agency relationship is typically terminated by simple notification or as agreed in the agency contract
- Death or insanity of the principal or, when the principal is a corporation, the dissolution of that corporation will also terminate the agent's authority

QUESTIONS

1. What is the agent's function? Why is it important to understand the law of agency in business?

2. Distinguish among agents, employees, and independent contractors. Describe the relationship between them and the principals.

3. What is the significance of the agency agreement for the parties to it?

4. Explain what effect an agent's limited capacity will have on the contractual obligations created between a principal and a third party. What effect would the incapacity of the principal have on this relationship?

5. Distinguish between an agent's actual, implied, and apparent authority. Explain why this distinction can be important from the agent's point of view.

6. Distinguish among promissory, equitable, and ordinary estoppel. Explain the role estoppel plays in agency law.

7. Explain what is meant by ratification. Explain why the principal's right to ratify might be considered unfair to the third party?

8. Describe the limitations on a principal's right to ratify the actions of his or her agent. How can the principle of ratification be as dangerous to the principal as it is to the third party?

9. What effect does it have on the relationship between the principal and the third party when an agent writes on an agreement "subject to ratification?"

10. Agents owe a fiduciary duty to their principals. What are the requirements of that duty?

11. What options are open to a third party who has been dealing with an undisclosed principal if the contract is breached?

12. Does an undisclosed principal have the right to ratify an agent's unauthorized act?

13. Explain how the doctrine of vicarious liability applies in a principal-agent relationship.

14. How does the function performed by a real estate agent differ significantly from that normally performed in a principal-agency relationship? What governs the real estate agent's conduct?

CASES

1. Kisil v. John S. Stevens Ltd.

Mr. and Mrs. Kisil bought a house through Buckley, an agent for the John S. Stevens firm. In the process of selling the house, Buckley assured the Kisils that there was no problem with the water in the well. They decided to buy the house, but Buckley kept them out of the house until after the deal's closing date. All this time, Buckley maintained that the condition of the well was good and that the water would clear up as soon as it was used a bit. In fact, the well had been improperly constructed and the water it produced was unfit for use. The Kisils sued Buckley and the real estate company. Describe the arguments which would form the basis of their complaint, their likelihood of success and the remedies available. Explain as well the legal position of the vendor.

2. Rockland Industries Inc. v. Amerada Minerals Corporation of Canada Limited

Kurtz was a salesman in charge of bulk sales and the manager of marketing who reported to Deverin, a senior vice-president of Amerada. Kurtz negotiated and concluded a deal with Powers and Leaderman, employees of Rockland Industries Inc., for the sale of 50 000 tons (45 360 tonnes) of sulphur. During the process of negotiation, Kurtz gave no indication of any qualifications on his authority. However, any sale of this magnitude had to be approved by an executive operating committee of Amerada and signed by the chairman of the board. After the deal was completed, Rockland's representative was informed of the limitations on Kurtz's authority but was also told that the operating committee had given approval and that the chairman of the board's signature was merely a rubber stamp. In fact, Amerada refused to deliver the sulphur, and Rockland had to acquire it from other sources. They were able to acquire only 25 000 tons and sued Amerada for damages. Explain the arguments available to both sides and the likely outcome.

3. Alberta Housing Corporation v. Achten and Alberta Housing Corporation v. Orysiuk

The Alberta Housing Corporation embarked on a plan to secretly create a landbank to stabilize residential prices as the city of Edmonton expanded. Orysiuk was the managing director of the Alberta Housing Corporation, who was given the task of making the acquisitions for the landbank. The Housing Corporation acquired the services of Achtem, a lawyer, who was given a commission of 5 percent on the acquisition of lands. Other parties were also engaged to assemble the land, including a real estate company that was given a commission of 3 percent. Achtem acquired a large amount of land on behalf of the Alberta Housing Corporation and earned over $200 000 in commissions. After a number of properties had already been acquired under the relationship between Achtem and the Alberta Housing Corporation, Achtem entered into a separate secret agreement with Orysiuk, whereby he paid back one-half of his commission. When this deal was eventually discovered, the Alberta Housing Corporation sued both parties for the recovery of the Corporation's money.

Explain the arguments available on both sides and the likely outcome. Would it affect your answer if you learned that the Alberta Housing Corporation was not injured by Orysiuk's and Achtem's actions and had paid a fair price for the property including legal fees and commissions? The Alberta Housing Corporation also insisted on the return of over $30 000 they had paid to Achtem in legal fees. Explain the likely outcome.

4. Guertin v. Royal Bank of Canada

Mrs. Guertin worked at a snack bar. The owners of the snack bar owned another restaurant which was located in the same mall as a branch of the Royal Bank managed by Mr. Arcand. Mr. and Mrs. Guertin were good customers of the Royal Bank and went to talk to the bank manager about the possibilities of buying this snack bar. They told him that the price was $30 000, but they also told him they thought they could get it for $22 000 or $23 000. In fact, the Guertins were waiting to see if the price would come down. In the meantime, Mr. Arcand offered $23 000 for the snack bar, which was accepted. The purchase was made through his wife because the bank rules prohibited him from buying it himself. Explain the liability of Mr. Arcand and the bank in these circumstances and any complaints the Guertins might have about his conduct.

5. Raso v. Dionigi

Guerino Sirianni was a real estate agent working for Joseph Leonardis Real Estate Ltd. His sister-in-law Raffaela was looking for some income property, and after some searching, Sirianni entered into a deal with Mr. and Mrs. Dionigi, persuading them to list their property for sale with him and subsequently presented an offer to purchase from his sister-in-law, who used her maiden name (R. Raso in trust) so that the sellers would not know that he was related to the purchaser. Before the deal was to close, the Dionigis discovered the relationship between the agent and the purchaser and refused to go through with the deal. Sirianni sued for his commission and his brother and sister-in-law sued for specific performance.

Explain the arguments that are available to the sellers in response to these claims. How would your answer be affected by the knowledge that the brother and sister-in-law of Sirianni had disclosed to him that they were willing to pay between $250 000 and $300 000 for the property, and in the negotiations that followed, this was not disclosed to the sellers. In fact, the first offer made by his brother and sister-in-law was only $270 000. The sellers eventually took $285 000 for the property, not knowing that the purchasers were willing to go to $300 000. The actual fair market value of the property was determined to be $285 000.

Business Organizations

One important characteristic of our modern commercial world is the effort that has been made by the legal system to facilitate the involvement of large groups of people in various business projects and activities. Partnership is the historical method of people joining together to carry on such business activities, and this, along with an examination of the sole proprietorship, is the subject matter of Chapter 13. Chapter 14 deals with the now-more-common method used, where people come together to participate in business, the corporation. Corporations are artificial persons, and their uniqueness results in a complex world of interaction among the company, shareholders, creditors, managers, and workers, and developing an understanding of these relationships is the objective of that chapter.

Photo by Crown Life Insurance

CHAPTER 13

Sole Proprietorship and Partnership

Partners are responsible for the wrongful conduct of each other, and this case illustrates just how careful people going into business with others have to be. This chapter is primarily devoted to an examination of partnership law, how a partnership is created, and the obligations of the parties involved. Each of the different methods of carrying on a business has specific rules and obligations associated with it. It is vitally important that the parties to such business relationships clearly understand the legal implications of their associations, whether they are the owners of the business, employees, or outsiders involved in commercial transactions with it.

Victoria & Grey Trust Company v. Crawford et al.[1]

One of the partners in a law firm was helping to administer an estate, when he was asked to transfer the amount outstanding in the estate ($60 025) to a bank in California. These funds were on deposit at a local branch of the Royal Bank, and a cheque was drawn up, signed by the executrix of the estate and made out to the California bank as payee. The lawyer, however, made another copy of that cheque, with himself as payee, forged the signature of the executrix, and destroyed the first cheque. He then cashed the cheque at his own bank. When this action was discovered, he was charged and convicted of fraud.

The bank on which the cheque was drawn was required to reimburse the estate, and they turned to the convicted lawyer's partners to compensate them. There was no question that the partners were honest and innocent of any wrongdoing, but they still had to compensate Victoria & Grey for its $60 025 loss.

Types of Business Organization

Sole proprietorship is one person

There are essentially three major types of business organization. The first, the **sole proprietorship**, is an individual carrying on business alone. Employees may be hired and business may be carried on through the services of an agent, but the

1. (1986) 57 O.R. (2d) 484 (H.C.)

business is the sole responsibility of one person, the owner. A second method of carrying on business is called a **partnership,** where ownership and responsibilities, along with both profits and losses, are shared by two or more partners. As was the case with the sole proprietorship, the partnership may also employ others and act through agents. The third type of business organization is the incorporated company. Any type of business organization involving more than one person can be called a company; a **corporation**, however, is a legal entity. By statute, it has been given an identity separate from the individual members who make it up. Thus, contracts with a corporation are dealings with the corporation itself as if it were a person in its own right.

In a partnership, owners share responsibilities

Corporation is a separate legal entity

There are other ways for people to work together to carry on a commercial activity. For example, a **non-profit society** can be set up under the *Societies Act.* This also creates a separate legal entity, but the procedure of incorporation and the obligations of those involved are quite different. There are also several ways in which these various types of business organizations can be combined. A **holding corporation** holds shares in other corporations. A **joint venture** involves several different incorporated corporations that band together to form a special corporation or partnership to accomplish a major project. The discussion in this chapter will be limited to an examination of sole proprietorship and partnership, while Chapter 14 will deal with corporations.

Societies are separate legal entities, but obligations differ

The Sole Proprietorship

Sole proprietorship carries on business in own right

The sole proprietorship is simply an individual carrying on a business activity on his or her own. The sole proprietor makes all the decisions associated with the business and is the only one entitled to the benefits derived from the business. A sole proprietor also bears full responsibility for all the costs, losses, and obligations incurred in the business activity. Thus, there is no distinction between the personal assets of the sole proprietor and those of the business. They are all the assets of the proprietor and are available to creditors if things go wrong.

A sole proprietor has complete control of and responsibility for the business.
PhotoDisc

Government Regulations

The sole proprietor, like all other types of business organizations, must satisfy many federal, provincial, and municipal requirements in order to carry on business. Usually, the name of the business must be registered and a license to operate obtained from the appropriate level of government. This licensing process is used to control or restrict certain types of businesses, such as door-to-door sales, credit information services, moneylenders, hotels, and cabarets. When the handling of food or dangerous commodities is involved, there are further provincial and federal regulations that must be obeyed. Sole proprietors must also satisfy local zoning bylaws, and if they have employees, they are subject to employment legislation, such as workers' compensation, employment insurance, and income tax regulations. They are also required to remit Goods and Services Tax if the business income is more than $30 000 per year.

Must adhere to licensing and governing regulations

Sole proprietor relatively free of outside interference

As a general rule, sole proprietors are subject to fewer government regulations than partnerships and corporations. Only minimal records need be kept, and sole proprietors are usually not required to disclose information about the business to others. They must keep sufficient records to satisfy government agencies, such as Revenue Canada. In essence, the sole proprietor has complete control and complete responsibility for the business activity.

Liability

Sole proprietors do not have accountability to others and alone are responsible for making important business decisions. They can only look to their own resources to finance the business operation; they cannot sell shares and are restricted to their own credit standing when borrowing money to finance the business. The sole proprietor owns all the assets, receives all the profits of the business, and is responsible for all its debts and liabilities. This **unlimited liability** can be the most significant disadvantage of the sole proprietorship. When the liability is incurred for breached contracts or torts or where there is insurmountable debt, the whole burden falls on the sole proprietor. Under the principle of **vicarious liability**, the sole proprietor is responsible for any tort committed by an employee during the course of employment. Although the sole proprietor's entire personal fortune is at risk, much of this risk can be offset by carrying adequate insurance. Any profit derived from a sole proprietorship is subject to personal income tax, while some tax advantages available to partnerships and corporations are not available to sole proprietors. These factors alone are often enough to encourage the businessperson to incorporate.

Sole proprietor has unlimited liability

Sole proprietor vicariously liable for employees' actions

Professionals bound by certain rules

Some individuals, notably professionals, such as doctors, dentists, lawyers, and accountants, cannot incorporate their practice and derive little advantage from doing so in those jurisdictions where professional incorporations are permitted. They carry on business as sole proprietors or band together in a group as partners. These professionals must join the appropriate professional organization, such as the law society or medical association of the province. These **professional associations** are set up under legislation, with extensive power to regulate educational and professional qualifications and standards of behaviour and to establish methods of disciplining members for wrongful conduct or incompetence. Note that it is only the practice of the professional service that cannot be incorporated, and so, these professionals obtain many of the advantages of incorporation by establishing companies that own the building, employ the office staff, and supply the management service and equipment to the professional.

Partnership

Partnership—carrying on business together for profit

Partnership governed by contract laws

The simplest form of business where people pool their resources and carry on business together with the object of making profit is a partnership. This relationship is based on contract, and so, basic contract law applies, with special provisions to deal with this unique relationship. Unlike a corporation, a partnership is not a separate legal personality from those making it up. However, the firm can enter into legal relationships so that it is not necessary to contract with each partner individually. This allows the partnership the convenience of functioning as a single business unit. It can own land, contract with others, and sue or be sued in its own name.

Legislation

In 1890, as part of a similar trend in other areas of law in the United Kingdom, the vast body of case law governing partnership was summarized into one statute, the *Partnership Act.* This legislation was adopted in all the common law provinces of Canada, where it has remained in place to the present day, with only a few alterations, such as the creation of limited partners. With some minor variations province to province, the law of partnership is basically consistent across Canada. For convenience, the Ontario version will be used whenever the *Partnership Act* is referred to, and the sections discussed will refer to that statute.[2]

Partnership Act **still used today**

Creation of the Partnership

Olson v. Gullo[3]

Mr. Gullo entered into a verbal agreement with Mr. Olson to purchase and develop a 1000-acre (405-hectare) tract of land as an industrial park. They were both to contribute equal funding and their special skills—Mr. Gullo in real estate speculation and Mr. Olson in marketing and promotion. The pair had difficulty purchasing the designated land from the owners and eventually abandoned the project.

As it turned out, however, Mr. Gullo was able to maintain part of the deal by purchasing one 90-acre (36-hectare) parcel for himself, which he then sold at a $2.5 million profit. Mr. Olson, who was an employee of Mr. Gullo, found out about the deal, quit his job, and sued. It is interesting to note that Mr. Gullo died before the trial, but not before trying to have Mr. Olson murdered.

Mr. Gullo's son carried on the defence of this action.

The first problem for the court was to decide whether a partnership existed between the parties. The plaintiff relied on the oral agreement, the existence of which was flatly denied by the defendant. The judge found that each was to contribute an equal share of the funds needed to acquire the land; that Mr. Gullo was to negotiate the purchases; and that Mr. Olson was to find interested investors and prepare promotional material. Thus, as they were carrying on business together with a view to making profits, their relationship was one of partnership. Mr. Gullo then had a fiduciary obligation to act in the best interests of his partner. When he secretly purchased the 90-acre parcel for himself, he did so in breach of that obligation.

The court then had to find an appropriate remedy in the circumstances. At the trial level, the court decided that the whole $2.5 million profit should be forfeited to Mr. Olson in order to discourage this kind of wrongful behaviour. If Mr. Gullo were allowed to keep half the profits, he would only be in the position he would have been in had he not committed the fraud in the first place, and there would be no consequence for his wrongful behaviour. This was overturned on appeal, with that court finding that the nature of a partnership required the equal sharing of assets and profits. Mr. Gullo, despite his misconduct, was entitled to half the profits.

The case illustrates not only what is necessary for a partnership to exist and the essential nature of that partnership but also the fiduciary obligation or duty between the partners to act in the best interests of each other.

---

2. R.S.O. 1990, c. P. 5

3. (1994) 113 D.L.R. (4th) 42 (Ont. C.A.); leave to appeal refused (1994) 116 D.L.R. (4th) vii (note) (S.C.C.)

A partnership is not always created by formal agreement between the partners. The *Partnership Act* provides that a partnership is created when two or more people carry on business in common with a view towards profits.[4] A profit does not actually have to be made, only that profit is the object of the exercise. It should be noted that the sharing of gross returns from a business activity does not in itself create a partnership. It is the sharing of the net proceeds after expenses have been deducted (the profits) from the enterprise that gives rise to the presumption of a partnership. The splitting of the commission on a sale by two real estate agents does not create a partnership, but when they split what is left after expenses, the presumption of a partnership will arise.

Partnership Act lists exceptions

The *Partnership Act* sets out a number of other circumstances, which, though they involve the sharing of income, by themselves will *not* establish a partnership.[5]

1. Owning property in common, even when it is rented out for profit

2. When a debt is repaid by the creditor's taking a share of the debtor's profits. For example, Pallas owes Clegg $10 000, and Clegg agrees to let Pallas pay it back by paying 20 percent of the profits of Pallas's furniture store per month until repaid

3. When the payment of an employee is based on a share of sales or profits, such as commission selling or profit-sharing schemes

4. When the beneficiary of a deceased partner receives the deceased partner's share of the profits

5. When a loan is made in relation to a business and payment of interest varies with the profit. For example, Pallas loans Clegg $10 000 to start a furniture business, and Clegg pays interest on that $10 000 principal by paying 10 percent of the store's profits per month

Partnership exists when profits shared

When a business is sold and the payment of the goodwill portion varies with the profitability of the business. For example, Pallas sells Clegg a furniture business for $10 000 for the assets and 50 percent of the first year's profits for goodwill.

The question remains: What constitutes carrying on business together with a view to profit? When evidence indicates that there has been one of the following, a partnership will be presumed:

1. Joint contribution of capital to establish a business

2. Intention to share expenses, profits, or losses

3. Joint participation in the management of a business

Partnership must carry on continuing business

If two people operate a restaurant together by sharing the work and expenses and jointly making decisions, the relationship is a partnership. It should be further noted that the *Partnership Act* requires that the parties carry on a continuing business together. A single joint project, for example, a school dance put on by two university students who combine their resources, would probably not be classed as a partnership. (If the students put on several dances, they would be in the "business" of providing this type of entertainment and, thus, would be in legal partnership, whether they looked at it that way or not.)

---

4. supra note 2, s. 2

5. *Ibid.* s. 5

Co-owning Property Does Not Create Partnership

In this case, a number of people owned an apartment building together under the name of one of them, "M. Kalmykow in trust," that is, in trust with the other owners as well. A corporation was created to control the property called Kamex Developments Ltd. The co-owners met monthly to discuss the property and what should be done including the possibility of sale. One of these parties, Mr. March, took it upon himself to list the property for sale under an exclusive listing agreement. He was not authorized to do so by the others. The property was eventually sold by a different agent, and under this agreement, A. E. LePage claimed their commission of $45 000 on the basis that Mr. March was in partnership with the rest and therefore bound the partnership to the exclusive listing agreement. Looking at the nature of the agreement, the court found that although all these people owned the property together, this was not enough to constitute a partnership and so the others were not liable for the commission.

A. E. LePage Ltd. v. Kamex Developments Ltd. (1977) 78 D.L.R. (3d) 223 (Ont. C.A.); aff'd [1979] 2 S.C.R. 155

Creation by Inadvertence

It is important to realize that the existence of a partnership relationship is a question of fact that a court can imply from the conduct of the parties and therefore can be created inadvertently. Because of the liability of one partner for the contracts and misdeeds other partners, the finding of such a relationship can have significant consequences for that person. This must be a consideration whenever someone is involved in any kind of business activity with another. Failure to appreciate this possibility can have disastrous financial consequences when one partner incurs liability to a third party.

Partnership can be created by conduct

Partnership Exists Where Business Is Carried on Together

Two brothers, Peter and Michael Boychuk, operated a series of businesses in St. Paul, including a taxi service, bowling alleys, billiard rooms, school buses, and the rental of buildings. Michael died without a will, and his wife brought an action for a declaration that the brothers were carrying on a business in partnership. The action was contested by Peter. Evidence showed that the brothers carried on their businesses together. There was also evidence that the taxis and buses were owned separately. The court looked at the licenses for the billiard rooms and the bowling alleys and saw that they were issued jointly to the Boychuk brothers. Also, income tax returns were filed as partners. The returns showed that they split the profits fifty-fifty. Since partnership is defined as parties carrying on business together with a view towards profit, this qualified as a partnership.

Boychuk et al. v. Boychuk (1975) 55 D.L.R. (3d) 751 (Alta. S.C.T.D.)

The partnership relationship is primarily one of contract, usually created by agreement, but this agreement often does not take a written form. The *Olson v. Gullo* case used to introduce this section is an instance where a court found that a partnership had been created by such an oral agreement.

In addition to setting out the responsibilities of partners to third parties, the *Partnership Act* also sets out the rights and obligations of the partners to each other. But like the *Sale of Goods Act,* the *Partnership Act* provisions, at least as far as the

Creation by Agreement

rights between the partners themselves are concerned, can be modified by the partnership agreement. It is important for the partners to enter into an agreement preferably in writing, setting out the exact nature of the relationship between them.

A partnership agreement should set out

- the duties of each partner
- what type of work or talent each is expected to contribute
- the amount of time to be committed to the business
- how the profits are to be shared and how the capital is to be distributed
- any limitations on the powers or authority of each partner
- methods of resolving any disputes between the partners, and
- the circumstances in which the partnership will be dissolved.

It must be remembered that the rights of outsiders dealing with the partnership are without notice, unaffected by any agreement between the partners. Outsiders' rights are determined by the provisions of the *Partnership Act* and partnership law generally.

It should also be noted that a partnership relationship can arise because of **estoppel**. If one of the parties represents to a third party, either by words or by conduct, that another person is a partner and that representation is relied on, the existence of a partnership cannot be denied, even if it can be clearly demonstrated that the two were not carrying on a business together. The principle of estoppel applies to partnership just as much as it does to agency because each partner acts as an agent for the partnership.

Holding out as Partner Creates Partnership

Mr. Lloyd owned and operated a truck purchased under a conditional sale agreement and used primarily to move mobile homes from one location to another, usually for dealers. Mr. Lloyd lived in British Columbia and was not able to deliver mobile homes from point to point in Alberta, just from Alberta to other locations. In an effort to remedy this problem he approached the principals of Caravelle Homes Ltd. with a scheme whereby they would purchase the truck. They declined this arrangement but agreed to a sham transaction in which they completed a bill of sale stating that they had purchased the truck for one dollar. They advanced money to pay Mr. Lloyd's arrears. They changed the insurance permits and other documents, which then showed the corporation's name as owner. Also, they added signs to the truck that indicated Caravelle was its owner. Whenever the truck stopped at weigh stations, Mr. Lloyd produced documents showing that the truck was owned by Caravelle. He continued his own independent trucking business separately from Caravelle. On one of these deliveries for Caravelle, to a business owned by Mrs. Poulos, he was careless in unhitching a mobile home, and it slipped and pinned Mr. Poulos' arm causing him serious injury. Mrs. Poulos sued Caravelle, claiming that Mr. Lloyd and Caravelle were partners. The courts decided that because the corporation allowed the truck to be held out as owned by them, they were a partner of Mr. Lloyd and were vicariously liable for the injury caused when he delivered the mobile home.

Poulos v. Caravelle Homes Ltd. (1995) 32 Alta. L.R. (3d) 76 (Q.B.); rev'd on other grounds (1997) 49 Alta. L.R. (3d) 385 (C.A.)

The Partner as an Agent

Every partner is the agent of the other partners and so has the power to bind them in contract as long as the contract involves the business of the partnership.[6] To properly understand the law of partnership, this chapter must be read in conjunction with Chapter 12 on agency. Even where the authority of a partner has been limited and the partner exceeds the power given, that contract will be binding if the third party is unaware of the limitation and the contract relates to the partnership business. For example, Akbari and Carlson operated a shoe store in partnership, and Akbari, while visiting his regular supplier in Toronto, purchased 500 pairs of yellow patent-leather oxfords he was unable to resist buying for only $5000. That contract would be binding on Carlson, even if the partnership agreement specifically set out that neither partner could make any purchase over $1000 without the other's approval. However, if Akbari bought a new boat during his trip to Toronto, this purchase would not be binding on his partner because the purchase could not be said to be made pursuant to the partnership business of selling shoes.

Laws of agency apply to partnership

Vicarious Liability

All partners are also vicariously liable in tort for both careless and intentional conduct of their partners in all business-related activities, including personal injury. Thus, if Agostino and Paradis were partners selling firewood, and Agostino negligently dropped a load of wood on a passing pedestrian, both Agostino and Paradis would be liable to pay compensation for the injury. Vicarious liability for intentional wrongs is illustrated by the case used to open this section. There, the partners of the lawyer who fraudulently acquired the $60 000 from his client were required to make good the loss, even though they were completely innocent.

Partners liable for each other's acts

Partners can also be held responsible for the breach of trust of their partners, such as the misuse of their clients' money. In such situations, all the partners are responsible for compensating the victim's loss. Note, however, that under the *Partnership Act,* the other partners are only liable if they have prior notice of the trust relationship.[7]

Partners liable for breach of trust

Since a partnership can employ individuals, the principles set out in Chapter 11 on employment law apply. Partners are vicariously liable for the misdeeds of their employees committed in the course of their employment. They must also adhere to government regulations on workers' compensation, employment insurance, and income tax.

Partners liable for wrongful acts of employees

For a businessperson, a serious risk associated with the law of partnership is the danger of becoming a partner inadvertently. This can come about by carrying on business together without realizing that a partnership has been created or by allowing oneself to be held out as a partner by someone else. The danger is the liability imposed by such a partnership both in tort on the basis of vicarious liability and in contract on the basis of each partner being an agent. This is unlimited liability, meaning a partner's entire fortune is at risk, and can lead to devastating results. Care should be taken to avoid the risk that an inadvertent partnership can create.

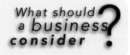

6. *Partnership Act,* s. 6, 7
7. *Ibid.* s. 14

Unlimited Liability

Partners share losses equally or proportionally by agreement

Like a sole proprietor, a partner's liability is unlimited, and their personal fortune is at risk to satisfy the claims of an injured party. With partners, however, they are liable not only for their own wrongful acts and those of their employees but are also responsible for the conduct of their partners. If the assets of a partnership are not sufficient to satisfy the claims of the creditors, the partners must make up the difference out of their own personal assets. This is done in the same proportion that they share the profits. Thus, if a partnership agreement provides that a senior partner gets 40 percent of the profits and each of the three junior partners gets 20 percent of the profits, the senior partners will bear 40 percent of the loss and the junior partners will bear 20 percent each of the loss.

Third party can collect from any partner regardless of agreement

Note that such a provision in the partnership agreement will only affect the relations between the partners. An outsider is not affected by any term in the partnership agreement that limits the liability of one of the partners and can collect all of what is owed from any partner. If one partner is particularly well off and the other partners have few personal assets, the injured party will look to the partner with significant assets for compensation once the assets of the partnership have been exhausted. That partner can seek contributions from the other partners on the basis of the partnership agreement if they have anything left to contribute.

In most provinces, partners are only **jointly liable** for the debts and obligations of the partnership as opposed to jointly and **severally liable**.[8] This means that for someone to seek a remedy against all the partners, they all must be included in the original action. Thus, if only two of the three partners are sued and it later turns out that they do not have enough assets to satisfy the judgment, it is then too late to sue the third. It must be emphasized, however, that when liability arises because of wrongful conduct (tort) or because of breach of trust, this liability is both joint and several. This means that it is possible for the injured party to sue one partner and still maintain the right to sue the other partners if the claim is not satisfied.[9] When an action is brought against the partnership in the partnership

All personal assets at risk

name, the plaintiff will be able to enforce the judgment against any of the partners. The result of this vicarious liability is that all the partners are personally responsible for the injuries incurred to the extent of their entire personal fortunes.

A retiring partner remains liable for any wrongs committed or liability incurred during the partnership period. This liability also continues for acts committed after the dissolution of the partnership or the retirement of the partner, unless the third party has been given notice that the retiring party has left the firm. The remaining partners or a new partner coming in can agree to take over these obligations in the partnership agreement but the new partner is not automatically liable. This is

Retiring partner remains responsible

why such care is taken to notify colleagues and customers when the membership of the partnership changes.

McDonic v. Hetherington (Litigation Guardian of)[10]

In 1985, two elderly sisters, Ms. McDonic and Ms. Cooper, on the advice of Ms. Cooper's son-in-law, retained Mr. Watt, a solicitor, to advise them on investments. Mr. Watt invested a considerable sum of money for them but failed to properly secure those investments. The result was that Ms. McDonic lost over $230 000 and Ms. Cooper lost over $10 000. Mr. Watt was sued and lost on the basis that he failed in

8. *Ibid.* s. 10
9. *Ibid.* s. 13
10. 142 D.L.R. (4th) 648 (Ont. C.A.)

his fiduciary duty to these clients. The problem here was for the court to determine whether his partners were also liable for these losses on the basis of vicarious liability. The partners denied liability, claiming that this was misconduct on the part of Mr. Watt outside the scope of the business, that Mr. Watt was acting as an investment advisor, not a lawyer, in these transactions, and on that basis they were not liable. The lower court agreed. However, the Ontario Court of Appeal decided that the partners were liable for the losses caused by their partner because Mr. Watt did what he did as a partner in the normal course of that partnership's business. The money went into a partnership trust account. It was dealt with like all other accounts, and the other partners actually dealt with those funds as well. In addition, he was liable as an agent acting within the apparent authority given by the other partners.

It is true that the transactions were not expressly authorized by the partners, but it is clear that he was acting within his apparent authority and, as such, made the other partners liable for his conduct. His office was part of the firm's offices, he used their letterhead, and in making the investments for the sisters, he used the facilities of the law office as well as the firm's accounts in the normal course of the firm's business.

All partners are liable to the extent of their personal fortune for the wrongful acts and mistakes of their partners. This example deals with the misuse of trust money in a law firm, but this is just one of the many examples that could be used where one partner's liability for the acts of another is present. We must use great care in choosing our partners and even then we face great risk of loss. This is one reason that incorporation had become much more popular as a method of doing business.

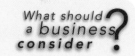
What should a business consider?

Registration

Most provinces require that a partnership be registered. Ontario, British Columbia, Alberta, and New Brunswick only require registration when the partnerships involve mining, trading, and manufacturing. Registration may also be required when all the partners are not listed or are in limited partnerships as discussed below.

Registration usually required

Failure to register properly can result in the imposition of a fine but typically will prevent the unregistered partnership from maintaining an action and cause joint liability to become joint and several liability. Note that an unregistered partnership can still be sued, and so, there are pressing reasons to register and no advantage in not doing so.

Rights and Obligations of the Parties

Fiduciary Duty

Each partner has a fiduciary duty to act in the best interests of the other partners. This duty imposes an obligation to account for any profits that have been made or for any partnership funds or property used. A partner who uses partnership property for personal benefit without consent must pay over any profit made and reimburse the partnership for any deterioration of the property. Property brought into a partnership for the purposes of the business becomes the property of the partnership, even though the title documents might not reflect this ownership. The partner with title is said to hold the property in trust for the partnership. This

Fiduciary duty exists between partners

Partners must account for any profits or use of property

was the situation in *Olson v. Gullo,* discussed earlier, and why Olson had the right to one-half of the profits from the sale of the property that Gullo had secretly purchased. It also underlines why the appeal court found it necessary to reverse the lower court's decision to award all the profits to Olson. This was inconsistent with the true nature of the partnership where they all shared the ownership of the property and thus the rights to the profits.

Partners cannot compete with partnership

If a partner operates a similar business without consent, he will be required to pay over any profits made to the partnership, which will then be distributed normally to all the partners. That partner, however, will not be reimbursed for losses. If a partner in a restaurant in Toronto were to open another in Hamilton without consent, any profits made from the Hamilton operation would have to be paid over to the partnership and then be distributed equally among them, but any losses would be borne by that partner.

Information must be disclosed

Any information obtained through a person's position as partner must be used to the benefit of the partnership, not for personal use. If Noorami came across a deal for some mining claims because of his position as a partner in a mining partnership, he would be required to inform his partners about the opportunity. If he bought the claims for himself without consent, he would have to turn over any profits earned to the partnership but suffer any losses himself. In effect, the information he used was the property of the partnership.

Hogar Estates Ltd. v. Shebron Holdings Ltd[11]

The defendant and plaintiff companies agreed to go into partnership to develop a certain parcel of land. Because the land was situated on a flood plain, it was difficult to get permission to build on it, and the land lay dormant for some time. Mr. Klaiman, the principal of Shebron Holdings Ltd., proposed to Hogar Estates Ltd. that Shebron purchase Hogar's interest in the property. Shebron was the active partner dealing with the planning authorities who had blocked the development of property, and Shebron was the partner who had informed Hogar of the problems with obtaining permission to build. After informing Hogar of this difficulty, Mr. Klaiman discovered that the planning authority was about to change its mind and that the prohibition on developing the property would be lifted. He failed to inform Hogar of the change and went through with the agreement to terminate the partnership. When Hogar learned that the property had been built on, it sued Shebron and asked the court to set aside the termination agreement.

It was clear that at no time did Mr. Klaiman lie or actively mislead Hogar. When Shebron stated that the land was tied up and could not be developed, that was accurate. They only learned subsequently that the conditions had changed and now they could develop the property. But they learned this before they had given notice to dissolve the partnership and the agreement for them to take it over was entered into. Their failure was to keep their partner apprised of the new developments. And the court found that because of the fiduciary duty between partners, they had a duty to let their partner know of the changes. Their failure to inform their partner of the changes made the agreement between them void, giving their partner a half interest in the property. Again, we see just how important fiduciary duty is. It is present when there is a relationship where one party places trust in another and is vulnerable if that trust is not honoured. Partnership is an important example of such a trusting relationship and of the imposition of the fiduciary obligations.

11. (1979) 101 D.L.R. (3rd) 509 (Ont. H.C.)

Provisions of the *Partnership Act*

The rights and obligations of partners to each other are set out in the *Partnership Act,* and these provisions apply, except where modified by the partnership agreement.[12] Some of the provisions of the act are as follows:

1. The partners will share profits equally between them. Similarly, any losses incurred are shared equally between the partners. This provision is often modified by a partnership agreement, but an outside third party will not be affected by any agreement, as they can recover losses from any partner who has the assets. That partner will then look to the other partners for reimbursement.

    Profits and losses shared equally or modified by agreement

2. The partners are entitled to reimbursement for any expenses they incur in the process of the partnership business. They are also entitled to be reimbursed for any money other than capital they have advanced to the partnership before the other partners can claim a share of the profits. In addition, the partner advancing such funds is entitled to the payment of interest on that money.

    Partners' expenses reimbursed

3. All partners have the right to take part in management and to have a vote in the firm's affairs. This provision is often modified by partnership agreements, which create different classes of partners, particularly in firms with a large number of partners.

    Partners participate in management

4. A partner is not an employee and is not entitled to wages or other remuneration for work done, only to a share of the profits. If one partner is to be paid a salary, this must be clearly stated in the partnership agreement. Such remuneration normally takes the form of a monthly draw against the yet-to-be-calculated profits of the partnership.

    No salaries paid to partners

5. No major changes can be made to the partnership business without the unanimous agreement of all the partners. No new partner can be brought into the partnership nor can a partner be excluded from the firm without the unanimous consent of all the partners. However, for the ordinary matters of the firm, a simple majority vote is sufficient, unless the partnership agreement states otherwise.

    Unanimous agreement needed for major changes

6. Partners do not have the right to assign their partnership status to some other party without the consent of the other partners. The benefits can be assigned, but the assignee will not have the right to participate in the operation of the business or in the decisions relating to it.

    Assignment requires consent of other partners

7. The business records of the partnership must be kept at the partnership office, and all the partners have the right to inspect them.

    Partners must have access to records

As can be seen from this summary, the general principle governing a partnership relationship is that the partners function as a unit and have a considerable responsibility to look after each other's interests.

Advantages of Partnership

Although the problems associated with a partnership may appear overwhelming, many of these difficulties can be overcome by proper insurance coverage. It should also be noted that a disadvantage to one person may be an advantage another. For

Insurance coverage important

12. *Partnership Act,* s. 24.

Unanimous consent protection

example, the unanimous consent required for important changes in a partnership may appear to interfere with effective management, but it does provide considerable protection to the individual partner. Such an individual partner cannot be outvoted by the majority, as is the case with a minority shareholder in a corporation. Similarly, the right of the individual partner to inspect all records of the business confers advantages not shared by minority shareholders in corporations to the same extent.

Partnership less costly to form

It is also normally less expensive to set up a partnership than a corporation and less costly to run because there are few formal requirements once the business has been established. For example, a corporation must keep certain types of accounting records and file reports with the appropriate government agency. A partnership, on the other hand, has only the needs of the partners to satisfy in this regard. But, as with sole proprietorships and corporations, there are other government regulatory bodies that require records, such as the taxation department, workers' compensation, and employment insurance.

It should not automatically be assumed that because of the unlimited liability and unwieldy management structure of partnerships, incorporation is a better way of carrying on business. Many of the apparent advantages of incorporation are illusory, and many of the disadvantages of partnership can be overcome. While it may be true that a corporation is the best vehicle for carrying on business in many situations, there are other situations in which a partnership is more appropriate. Some activities, such as the practice of law, accounting, medicine, and dentistry, are not allowed by statute to be engaged in by corporations. A partnership is the only alternative when more than one of these professionals wishes to join together to carry on business. Before a decision is made to incorporate, consideration should also be given to the pros and cons of using a partnership to carry on the business instead. Note that in some jurisdictions, it is possible for these professionals to carry on their practice as a professional corporation. But many of the advantages of incorporation have been removed, including limited liability. In Ontario, the *Partnership Act* has been amended to allow general partners to participate in limited liability partnerships. In these partnerships, partners are still liable for their own negligence but not vicariously liable for the torts of their partners. This important change only applies where the legislation governing the professional body allows such limited liability.[13] Note that the *Public Accountancy Act* of Ontario does permit such limited liability partnerships.[14]

Partnership may be only alternative for professionals

What should a business consider?

Business people should not be too quick to discard partnership as a valuable method of carrying on business with others. From an individual point of view, all partners have an equal say, and in all important matters, there must be unanimity. This eliminates the tyranny of the majority problem usually associated with corporations. The disadvantages, such as unlimited liability, can be overcome, to a large extent, by obtaining appropriate insurance, and the tax advantages are similar to corporations.

Dissolution of a Partnership

Dissolution—by notice, death, bankruptcy, or insolvency

Usually, a partnership is easy to end, requiring only notice to that effect by one of the partners. While this may seem to be an advantage to the leaving partner, to

---

13. R.S.O. 1990, c. P.5, s. 1 (1); 1998, c. 2, s. 1
14. R.S.O. 1990, c. P.37

the others, it can be a considerable disadvantage, requiring the sale of the assets for distribution to the partners. Usually, this is overcome by providing in the partnership agreement a mechanism whereby one partner can leave without causing the remainder of the partnership to dissolve.

The partnership is usually dissolved by the death, bankruptcy, or insolvency of any partner. This provision varies slightly from province to province. Dissolution can give rise to significant problems in ongoing, long-term partnerships of professional groups. Therefore, professionals will typically set out in partnership agreements that the death, insolvency, or bankruptcy of one partner will not dissolve the partnership and that, instead, the partner's share will be made available to the heir or creditor of the partner. Insurance coverage is often taken out to cover such a contingency.

Dissolution by death, bankruptcy, or insolvency

British Columbia's partnership legislation is unique because it establishes that when more than two partners are involved, the partnership will be dissolved only in relation to the partner who has died or become bankrupt. This provision can be modified by agreement, but its unique feature is that the death or bankruptcy of one partner will not bring to an end the whole partnership relationship in the absence of an agreement between the partners.[15]

A partnership that has been set up for a fixed term will end at the expiration of that term. Similarly, a partnership that is set up for a particular project or event will end when that project is completed or the event takes place. A partnership is automatically dissolved if the business engaged in by the partnership becomes illegal. In addition, a partner can apply to the court to dissolve the partnership if any one of the following factors are present.[16]

Partnership established for specified time will end at expiry

Partnership can be dissolved by request to the court

1. When it is clear that the partnership business will continually operate at a loss

2. When one of the partners has become mentally incompetent or otherwise unable or unwilling to perform partnership responsibilities

3. When the conduct of one partner is prejudicial to the partnership relationship or otherwise in breach of the partnership agreement

4. When there is a catch-all provision empowering the court to dissolve the partnership whenever it considers that there are "just and equitable reasons to do so"[17]

The effect of dissolution is to end the partnership relationship, oblige the partners to wind up the business, liquidate the assets to pay off any obligations to creditors, and then distribute any remaining assets and funds to the former partners. Individual partners should take care to give public notice of dissolution. The law may require that such notice be filed with the partnership registration office or registrar of companies, depending on the jurisdiction. For further protection, such notice should be sent to all regular customers of the business. Failure to do so may render each partner liable for the acts of the other partners even after dissolution. Note that although dissolution takes place, the partners still have the authority to act as partners and bind the other partners by their actions in doing whatever is necessary to wind up the business.

Public notice may avoid liability

15. *Partnership Act*, R.S.B.C. (1996) c. 348 s. 36

16. *Ibid.,* R.S.O. (1990) c. P.5 s. 35

17. *Ibid.* s. 35(f)

The Bank of Montreal v. Sprackman et al. (1977)[18]

The members of a partnership had a falling-out and agreed among them that one of the partners (Mr. Sprackman) would retire from the partnership. A handwritten letter was drawn up and signed, stating that Mr. Sprackman's interest in the partnership and responsibility for liability would be taken over by one of the other partners, Mr. Dinardo. Mr. Dinardo subsequently sold his interest in the partnership to a third partner, Mr. Gotzaminis, who subsequently became bankrupt. When the partnership was active, arrangements had been made for a $3000 loan and an overdraft arrangement with the Bank of Montreal. Mr. Sprackman verbally advised Mr. Martin, the bank manager, that he was retiring and that his obligation was being taken over by Mr. Dinardo. Mr. Martin agreed to release Mr. Sprackman from the loan if he paid $1500, which he did over some period of time. Unfortunately, neither side said anything about the overdraft, which amounted to $2899.66 at the time of Mr. Sprackman's retirement. This amount increased after Mr. Sprackman's retirement to $6029.82, including interest at 18 percent per annum. The bank then insisted on payment of this overdraft from Mr. Sprackman. One of the documents Mr. Sprackman had signed with the bank required that the overdraft arrangement would stay in force until "terminated by written notice."

The judge was not impressed by the conduct of the bank personnel in this situation. They had allowed Mr. Sprackman to believe that the $1500 settlement extinguished all debt. This was not the case, as it was clear that his obligation for the overdraft remained until ended with written notice. The judge reluctantly agreed that the bank was within it s rights to demand payment and gave judgment accordingly. The 18 percent interest also was upheld because this is the amount being paid on the overdraft when the firm was active and Mr. Sprackman was aware of this. The judge did show his displeasure by refusing to award the bank costs in the action.

This case shows how important it is for the terms of a partnership agreement to be clear and for each partner to know exactly to what they are agreeing. It also shows how important it can be for a retiring partner to make a clean break. It was fully appropriate for the partner who was leaving to enter into a separate agreement with the bank settling his liability, but the partner was not sufficiently careful in entering into that agreement and making all those terms clear. The devil is in the details, and in this case, the devil got Mr. Sprackman.

Distribution of Assets and Liabilities

Debts paid out of profits first, then capital, then personal assets of partners

When dissolving a partnership, the debts must be paid, first out of profits and, if they are insufficient, out of the capital the partners originally invested.[19] If there is still not enough money to pay the debts, the creditors can then turn to the partners themselves who are liable to the extent of their personal fortunes. On the other hand, once all creditors have been paid and the other obligations of the partnership satisfied, any assets still remaining are applied first to pay back the partners for expenses and then to pay back the original capital investment. Any remaining funds are divided among the partners on the established basis for sharing profits.[20]

18. (1977) 78 D.L.R. (3rd) 665 (Ont. H.C.)
19. *Partnership Act,* 44(1)
20. *Ibid.* s. 44(2)

The dissolution of the partnership and the distribution of assets may be a problem especially when some of the partners want to continue the business in a new partnership. To avoid this problem, the parties often agree to a different process in the partnership agreement. It should be noted that if one partner owes a debt to an outside creditor which has nothing to do with the partnership business, that creditor can claim against only the assets of that partner, including his or her share of the partnership assets left after all other claims against the partnership are settled.

Limited Partnerships

Additions to the legislation governing partnership in every province provide for the creation of limited partnerships. This measure gives some of the advantages of incorporation to partnerships. But partners can lose their status as limited partners if they fail to carefully adhere to all the requirements of the governing legislation, with the result that they are then deemed to be general partners with all the consequences inherent in that designation. The main advantage of a limited partnership is that it allows the partners so designated to invest money in a partnership but to avoid the unlimited liability that goes with being a general partner. The only loss a limited partner can incur is the original investment.[21]

Limited partners liable only to the extent of their investment

If Kimmel and Ingram were general partners with Pak, a limited partner, and Kimmel were to negligently injure a customer to the extent of $300 000 damages, Pak would only lose his $25 000 investment. Both Kimmel and Ingram would be liable for the entire $300 000, but Pak's liability would be limited to the $25 000 invested, even if the combined assets of Kimmel and Ingram were not enough to cover the loss.

The problem is that it is relatively easy for the limited partner to lose that status and become a general partner with unlimited liability. In the preceding example, if Pak had allowed himself to be represented as a partner in the business, allowed his name to be used in the name of the business, or actively participated in the partnership business or its management, he would have become a general partner and would have been required to pay along with Kimmel and Ingram with no limitation on liability.

To be a limited partner, the first thing one must do is register at the appropriate government registry by filing a certificate setting out such information as the terms of the agreement, the amount of cash contributed, and the way profits are to be shared. The name used by the partnership can contain the name of the general partners, but the name of a limited partner cannot be included in the firm name.

Registration required to become a limited partner

A limited partner can contribute money or property to the business but cannot participate in the management of the firm without becoming a general partner. The limited partner is not prohibited from giving the other partners advice, but since it is often difficult to determine where advice stops and participation in management starts, there is a considerable risk in doing so. When a business starts to fail, there is a great temptation for the limited partner to jump in to preserve the investment, but doing so raises the risk of becoming a general partner and should be avoided. It is not possible to form a partnership with only limited partners. The legislation requires that there be at least one general partner in the firm. A limited partner is not an agent of the firm and so does not have the power to bind the partnership in their dealings with outsiders.

Limited partners cannot participate in management

21. *Limited Partnership Act*, R.S.O. (1990) c. L.16 s. 9

Limited Partner Loses Status by Participating in Management

Zivot wanted to launch a magazine, but the corporate organization that he set up to do it was quite complex. He incorporated a company called Lifestyle Magazine Inc. with himself as an employee. He then had Lifestyle enter into a partnership, called Printcast, with himself and several other partners. Zivot and the other partners were limited partners, whereas Lifestyle Magazine was a general partner. Houghton supplied printing services to Printcast in order to produce the magazine and was not paid. He sued Zivot and another limited partner, claiming that because they participated in the general management of the business, they ceased to be limited partners and became general partners. The court agreed and declared Zivot and the other limited partner to be general partners and liable for the indebtedness of the partnership. Zivot had not only participated in management but also led people to believe he was an officer in Printcast; therefore, he was liable as a general partner.

Houghton Graphic Ltd. v. Zivot (1986) 33 B.L.R. 125 (Ont. H.C.); aff'd (1988) 38 B.L.R. xxxiii (Ont. C.A.); leave to appeal refused (1988) 38 B.L.R. xxxiii (S.C.C.).

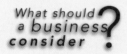

What should a business consider?

As was discussed above, the rights and duties between partners can be modified in a partnership agreement. This applies to the relationship between general and limited partnerships as well. Limited partnerships are attractive to people because of favourable tax implications. To obtain these tax benefits, one big advantage normally associated with limited partnership, limited liability, must be sacrificed to a considerable extent through modifications set out in the partnership agreement. Often, these changes are not brought to the attention of prospective investors. Great care should be taken before entering into such a limited partnership as an investment vehicle and to understand exactly what you are getting into.

Summary

Sole proprietors

- Carry on business by themselves and, with some government regulation, have unlimited liability for their debts and obligations

Partnership

- Involves two or more partners carrying on business together with a view to profits
- Controlled by the *Partnership Act* and by specific agreement of the partners
- Can be created by agreement but often comes into existence by inadvertence when people work together in concert in a business activity
- Each partner is an agent for the partnership, and all partners are liable for the contracts and torts of the other partners and employees. That liability is unlimited, and all the assets of the partners, including personal assets, are at risk to satisfy such debts and obligations

- Fiduciary duty
  - Partners must act in the best interests of the partnership
  - Partners must unanimously agree on major changes

- Dissolution
  - Partners to give notice to that effect
  - Upon death or bankruptcy of one of the partners, unless the partners have agreed otherwise in their partnership agreement
- Limited partner
  - Liable only to the extent of the investment made in the business, but to protect that limited liability status, partner must be registered as such and not participate in the partnership business or its management

QUESTIONS

1. Distinguish among a sole proprietorship, a partnership, and a corporation.

2. What risk does a businessperson face in a sole proprietorship or partnership that is avoided in a corporation?

3. What advantages and disadvantages are associated with carrying on business as a sole proprietorship?

4. What advantages and disadvantages are associated with carrying on business as a partnership?

5. What distinguishes a partnership from other types of joint activities?

6. Distinguish between sharing profits and sharing fees.

7. If two people enter into a business together with the object of making money but lose it instead, can the business still be a partnership?

8. Why must a person understand the law of agency in order to understand the law of partnership?

9. What danger exists when a third party is led to believe that two people are partners when, in fact, they are not? What legal principle is applied in this situation?

10. What is the significance of the existence of a partnership agreement for outsiders dealing with the partnership? What is the advantage of entering into a formal agreement?

11. Explain the different ways in which a person can become responsible for the acts of his or her partner and describe the limitations on this responsibility.

12. Describe the liability of retiring and new partners.

13. Partners have fiduciary obligations to each other. Explain what this means.

14. What will the consequences be if a partner operates a business similar to the partnership without the partners' consent or uses information acquired through the partnership to his or her own advantage?

15. What events may bring about the end of a partnership prematurely? Under what circumstances might it be necessary to get a court order to end a partnership?

16. What will the normal effect be on a partnership when a partner dies or becomes insolvent? How is the law of British Columbia significantly different?

17. When a partnership is being dissolved and does not have sufficient assets to pay its debts, how is the responsibility for these debts distributed? How are excess assets distributed?

18. Explain the significance of being a limited partner.

19. What must a person do in order to qualify as a limited partner? What happens when a limited partner fails to meet one of these qualifications?

CASES

1. Lambert Plumbing (Danforth) Ltd. v. Agathos

Magoulas was just starting up as the sole owner of Alpha Omega Construction Company when he signed a contract with Agathos, the owner of a Toronto radio station, for advertising over a period of time. Magoulas was unable to pay, but Agathos continued to give him advertising in hopes that the business would get going to the point that he would be able to pay. Agathos also helped Magoulas out in his business, signed many contracts, and performed other acts on behalf of Magoulas, including writing cheques on his personal account. In January 1971, Kreizman, president of the plaintiff corporation, entered into a contract to supply the Alpha Omega Construction Company with certain plumbing and heating equipment. This contract was entered into at the construction company, and the person Kreizman dealt with was Agathos. Kreizman thought he was dealing with the owner, and Agathos did nothing to dissuade him of this notion. In all the many subsequent dealings between these two parties, Kreizman continued to think that Agathos was the principal of the construction company, and Agathos did nothing to correct it. It is clear that there was no partnership agreement or arrangement between Agathos and Magoulas and that Agathos was helping Magoulas out gratuitously, hoping for eventual payment under the advertising contract. Magoulas only partially paid for the supply and installation of the plumbing equipment with $500 outstanding. Lambert Plumbing sued Agathos as a partner for the unpaid funds. Explain the arguments available to both sides and the likely outcome.

2. Klutz v. Klutz

The plaintiff and defendant had been married for 25 years when Mrs. Klutz left Mr. Klutz in 1958. During that period, two pieces of land had been obtained, both of which were in the husband's name. It was clear that Mrs. Klutz had done considerable work on the land, such as milking cows and feeding livestock, but she had made no financial contribution to the properties. She claimed that the property was held in partnership and demanded an accounting from the husband. Explain the likely outcome and arguments from both sides.

3. Barnes v. Consolidated Motors Co. Ltd.

Hall was negligently driving a motor vehicle when he struck and injured Mrs. Barnes. Hall was an employee of Distributors Used Car branch which was a business established by Consolidated Motor Co. Ltd., and Dan MacLean Co. Ltd., for the purpose of disposing of their used cars. J.M. Brown Motor Co. Ltd. later joined the business. The business had its own bank account, management, employees, and so on but the cars remained the property of the company that supplied them. Hall was driving one of the cars owned by Consolidated to the Distributors premises when the accident took place. Mrs. Barnes sued all three car companies, claiming that they were a partnership. Explain the arguments for each side. Discuss the likely outcome.

4. Castellan v. Horodyski and Lynkowski

Horodyski and Lynkowski were partners in the operation of a hotel, which they sold to Castellan in 1953. One of the assets sold in this transaction was a heater/boiler. Horodyski had made fraudulent misrepresentations about this boiler, which induced Castellan to enter into a contract for its purchase. Although Horodyski knew that what he said was false, Lynkowski was not aware of what was said or that there was any problem with the boiler. Shortly after Castellan's purchase, the boiler broke down and had to be rebuilt. Castellan sued both Horodyski and Lynkowski for the cost of rebuilding the boiler. Explain the legal position of the parties and the likelihood of success.

5. Dockrill v. Coopers & Lybrand Chartered Accountants

Coopers & Lybrand were a national partnership of chartered accountants, and they merged with a firm of chartered accountants carrying on business in Halifax. Subsequent to that, two managing partners in the Halifax office decided that as a result of the merger, there were too many partners in Halifax, and they terminated Mr. Dockrill. Before doing that, they had approached the partners in Toronto and obtained legal advice from an in-house counsel, which they relied on in asking for Mr. Dockrill's resignation. Mr. Dockrill brought this action for wrongful termination of his partnership and, in the process of the action, brought an application to the court for a copy of the information supplied by the Toronto lawyers to the Halifax partnership. Mr. Dockrill hoped that this information might contain disclosures that would help his case for wrongful termination.

Explain whether Mr. Dockrill is entitled to the information supplied by the Toronto lawyers. Would your answer be different if Mr. Dockrill had been asked to resign and then the Halifax partners had sought this legal advice? (See A. Akman & Son (Fla.) Inc. v. Chipman (1987) 45 D.L.R. (4th) 481 [Man. C.A.])

CHAPTER 14

Corporations

CHAPTER HIGHLIGHTS

- The process of incorporation
- Separate legal entity or corporation
- Funding a corporation
- Duties of corporate officers
- Advantages and disadvantages of incorporation

The previous chapter dealt with the simpler methods of carrying on business: sole proprietorship and partnership. This chapter will examine the third method, the incorporated company. Since incorporation is, by far, the most common means of setting up a large business organization, exposure to the concepts and forms that regulate this important aspect of the commercial world is a vital part of the study of business law. In this chapter, we will examine the process and effect of incorporation, some features of incorporated bodies, and the rights and responsibilities of the various parties involved.

Sinclair v. Dover Engineering Services Ltd. et al.[1]

Mr. Sinclair was a professional engineer who worked for Dover Engineering Services Ltd. for a number of years but was paid by Cyril Management Ltd. Mr. Goudal owned 50 percent of Dover, and he and his wife owned Cyril Management Ltd. Mr. Sinclair was discharged without notice and without cause. He initiated a wrongful dismissal action against Cyril Management Ltd., since Dover Engineering had no assets and was no longer in operation.

The question the court had to answer was which company had employed Sinclair: Dover Engineering or Cyril Management Ltd.? The judge decided that the close relationship between the two companies made them both Mr. Sinclair's employers. Sinclair was, therefore, successful in his action against Cyril Management Ltd.

This case illustrates the significance of the myth that each corporation is a legal entity, separate and apart from the people who make it up. It also demonstrates the court's willingness in some circumstances to ignore that separate existence by "lifting the corporate veil." This chapter will discuss the concept of the corporate entity and the legal benefits and responsibilities that result from the creation of a corporation.

1. (1987) 11 B.C.R. (2d) 176 (B.C.S.C.)

The Process of Incorporation

The concept of an incorporated company was developed in response to the need to finance large economic projects without the limitations associated with sole proprietorships and partnerships. What was needed was to have a large number of people participate in a venture without playing active roles in it. The incorporated company was the means to accomplish this end. The most significant feature of an incorporated company is that it has a separate legal personality from the people who own shares in it. The shares that represent an individual's interest in the incorporated company can be bought and sold; thus, the shareholders can be continually changing, while the company itself remains intact. This structure provides considerably more flexibility in meeting the needs of owners and directors and is a much more effective method of attracting capital.

Corporation is a separate legal entity

An early example of incorporation was when the monarch granted a royal charter to a town or university, thereby creating a separate legal personality. It was a natural step to extend that practice to commercial ventures. The Hudson's Bay Company is one of the earliest English commercial corporations created by royal charter. Parliament also got involved by creating "special act companies" when ventures were considered important enough to be incorporated by their own special legislation.

Royal charters created early corporations

Special act companies were corporations

At this stage, ordinary citizens could not incorporate, and so, they created their own unofficial companies through contracts called **deeds of settlement**. Parliament eventually permitted incorporation for private business activities, but in the process, they also had to accommodate the numerous voluntary contractual associations that were already in existence. The resulting legislation gave these companies formal status and the advantages of incorporation by allowing them to register at the appropriate government office and pay a fee.

Canada adopted many of the features of the British approach to incorporation. Both the federal and provincial governments have created many corporations through their power to pass special statutes. For example, the Canadian Broadcasting Corporation (CBC) and the Canadian Pacific Railroad (CPR) were created by special acts of parliament. Some Canadian jurisdictions adopted the British practice of incorporation through **registration**. Other jurisdictions developed their incorporation process from the royal charter approach and created incorporated bodies through the granting of **letters patent**. A third approach which has been borrowed from the United States is based on the filing of **articles of incorporation**. Although there are technical differences between these three methods of incorporation, it is important to understand that the practical effect of each system is the same. Each method is described in more detail below.

Three general methods of incorporation in Canada

A company may be incorporated at the provincial or federal level. If the activity is to be confined to a local area, it is likely that incorporation under the provincial legislation would be appropriate. Thus, a restaurant would be provincially incorporated. When the activity involves something that will be carried on in several provinces, such as a chain of restaurants, or generally across Canada, as with some service provided on the Internet, the federal option might be preferable. A provincially registered corporation can be registered to do business in other provinces, but a new fee will have to be paid in each province. If the company is incorporated federally, these separate provincial fees can be avoided.

Federal and provincial companies

Registration

Incorporation through registration recognizes the contractual relationship between its members and grants them corporate status. In British Columbia and Nova Scotia, the jurisdictions in which the registration system is currently used, registering a "memorandum of association" and "articles of association" with the appropriate government agency and paying the fee meet the requirements for incorporation.

The **memorandum of association** serves the same function as a constitution in that it sets out important matters, such as the name of the company, the authorized share capital (the total value of shares that can be sold), and, when appropriate, the objects of the incorporation.

The objects listed in the memorandum of association set out the purposes for which the corporation is created and also set out the limits of the capacity of the corporation to act. In British Columbia, "objects" are no longer permitted, but the law does permit the inclusion of "restrictions." The memorandum is difficult to alter once it has been registered, so care must be taken in its design. The selection of a name can be a difficult problem, whether a corporation, partnership, or sole proprietorship is involved, since several choices may not be available. A name search must be done to ensure that the name chosen is not already in use. This problem can be avoided by simply using the registration number as the name of the company. Some names are simply not appropriate or are prohibited, such as obscenities or words associated with royalty and used without permission.

The internal procedural regulations for governing the ordinary operation of the corporation are contained in the **articles of association** (not to be confused with the articles of incorporation used in other jurisdictions, discussed below). These articles deal with such matters as how shares are to be issued and transferred, requirements for meetings of the board of directors and shareholders, voting procedures at those meetings, regulations covering borrowing, powers of directors and other officers, requirements dealing with dividends, regulations concerning company records, and how notice will be given to shareholders. The articles also set out the procedures for altering the articles, so there is considerably less difficulty in changing them than in changing the memorandum. But because these articles are filed along with the other incorporating documents, subsequent changes are more difficult than in the jurisdictions where the corresponding bylaws are considered internal documents and need not be filed.

This method of incorporation is accomplished by registration only; the registrar has no discretionary right to refuse incorporation except when the requirements set out in the legislation are not complied with. Corporations created in a registration jurisdiction originally had their capacity to contract limited by their objects of incorporation. This has been modified by statute in both Nova Scotia and British Columbia. The *British Columbia Company Act* states that a corporation has "all the power and capacity of a natural person of full capacity."[2]

Letters Patent

The letters patent method of incorporation is based on the practice of the monarch granting a royal charter. The process involves an applicant petitioning the appropriate government body for the granting of the letters patent. The government representative, acting by statute, grants a charter of incorporation to applicants

2. R.S.B.C. 1996, c. 62 s. 21

who meet certain qualifications. Today, only Québec and Prince Edward Island use this method of incorporation.

Use of letters patent method declining

The letters patent sets out the constitution of the new company and contains such information as the purpose for which the corporation is formed, the name to be used, the share structure, any restrictions on the transferability of shares, and the rights and obligations of the parties. The rules governing the ordinary operation of the corporation are set out in separate bylaws. In letters patent jurisdictions, corporations have always had all the powers of a natural person to enter into contracts.

Articles of Incorporation

The other provinces and the federal government have adopted a system of incorporation, developed in the United States, based on the filing of articles of incorporation and the granting of a certificate of incorporation. The articles of incorporation method has features of both the letters patent and the registration methods. As with the letters patent, companies under this system are primarily the creations of government rather than based on contract. The articles that are filed are similar to a constitution or statute controlling the activities of the parties rather than a binding agreement between them. A company is granted a certificate of incorporation by filing the articles of incorporation and paying the appropriate fee. The articles of incorporation serve the same function and contain the same types of information as the memorandum of association and the letters patent in the other systems. The day-to-day operation is controlled through bylaws similar to those in a letters patent system, which need not be filed when applying for incorporation. It is also important to note that in this system, the government body assigned to grant certificates of incorporation has no general discretion to refuse the request.

Articles of incorporation method borrows features from each

Incorporation accomplished through granting certificate of incorporation

Other Incorporated Bodies

Cities, universities, and other public institutions are incorporated legal entities that can sue or be sued in their own right. Under both federal and provincial legislation, it is also possible to establish (incorporate) non-profit bodies, sometimes called "societies," or non-share capital corporations. These bodies are primarily cultural, social, charitable and religious organizations, such as the Society for the Prevention of Cruelty to Animals (SPCA), the Red Cross, and the Canadian National Institute for the Blind (CNIB). The one thing these bodies have in common is the non-profit nature of their activities. The legal obligations and technicalities associated with these bodies are much simpler and more straightforward than those associated with corporations generally. Business people often deal with such bodies and so should be aware of them and the statutes by which they are regulated. An examination of these non-business incorporations is beyond the scope of this text.

Societies also incorporated

Separate Legal Entity

Salomon v. Salomon & Co.[3]

In this case, Mr. Salomon ran a successful shoe manufacturing business that he decided to incorporate. He set up a company in which he owned almost all the shares. He then sold the business to that company. Since the company had no assets to pay

3. [1897] A.C. 22 (H.L.)

for the business, he loaned the company enough money to purchase the business from himself, securing the loan with a debenture similar to a mortgage on the company's assets. In short, Mr. Salomon loaned the company he "owned" enough money to purchase the business from him and had a mortgage on the assets of the business created to secure the loan.

When the business failed because of labour problems, the creditors turned to Mr. Salomon for payment. Not only did he refuse to pay but, as a secured creditor, had first claim on the assets of the company, leaving nothing for the unpaid creditors. In fact, the creditors had dealt only with Mr. Salomon and blamed him for their problems. They sued claiming that he should not only be prevented from claiming ahead of them but that he should also be responsible for paying them if the company's assets were not enough.

The court decided that since the company was a separate legal entity, it had a separate legal existence apart from Mr. Salomon and so he could indeed sell his assets to the company and could take security back. The end result was that Mr. Salomon was a secured creditor who stood in line ahead of the other unsecured creditors and thus had first claim on the remaining assets of the company. For the same reason, the court held that Mr. Salomon was a person separate from the company and was in no way responsible for its debts.

This case graphically illustrates not only what is meant by the corporation being a separate legal entity but also the consequences of limited liability on the part of the shareholder.

Corporation a separate legal entity

The most difficult concept to grasp in this area is that when the incorporation process is completed, there are two legal persons: the shareholder and an incorporated company. Although the corporation does not exist except on paper and is only a "legal fiction," all the forces of law assume that it does exist as a separate entity from the shareholder and that it can function in the commercial world. Shareholders often have difficulty understanding that they do not actually own the business or that the company they have incorporated does. Shares held in a company bestow the rights of control and only give the right to share in the liquidation of the assets (right to participate in capital) if the corporation is wound up.

The problem is the opposite when dealing with a large corporation. It is difficult to think of Sears Ltd. and Imperial Oil Ltd. as a fiction or myth. We make the mistake of thinking of the company's assets, its warehouses and stores, or its shareholders as the entity. But just as Vandenberg's car is not Vandenberg but an asset owned and used by her, so, too, is Sears Ltd. separate from its stores or shareholders. And at this level, the large corporation, just like the small one, is a legal fiction, often referred to as the "**corporate myth**."

What should a business consider?

Unfortunately, business people often act as if the corporation were a real person. Managers often make decisions they find repugnant and which they would not otherwise make because they think that the corporation they serve is real. They draw a distinction in their minds between the corporate entity and themselves as managers. While it is true that the legal duty of directors and managers is to the corporation, it must also be remembered that the corporation itself is merely a fiction. It has no mind or personality and cannot be an excuse for immoral conduct.

Courts will sometimes ignore separate legal entity

It is also important to recognize that the status of separate legal entity for a corporation is a flimsy one, and business people are often shocked to see the courts cast aside this aspect of the corporation to get at the shareholders. For example, the tax department will often deem several different corporations to be one person for tax purposes. Similarly, where the object of incorporation is to get around some government regulation or commit a fraud, the courts will ignore the legal entity aspect of the corporation, and "lift the corporate veil" to get at the shareholders or managers committing the fraud. The example used to introduce this chapter illustrates a situation where the courts were willing to lift the corporate veil.

Nevertheless, the separate legal entity aspect of a corporation is tremendously important for commercial activities. It allows for the acquisition of capital without involving the shareholders in the operation of the corporation. It also allows the purchase and sale of their shares without interfering with the ongoing operation of the business. Like sole proprietorships and partnerships, a corporation is responsible for contracts made on its behalf and for torts of their employees under the principle of vicarious liability. The corporation can even be convicted and fined for the commission of a crime. But it is the corporation itself that is liable, not the shareholders who have limited liability, since they can only lose their initial investment. It is this principle that protected Mr. Salomon in the case discussed above, where as a shareholder, he was not liable for the debts of the company and was also able to claim ahead of the others as a secured creditor.

Limited liability derived from separate legal entity

Today, creditors protect themselves by requiring shareholders to sign a personal guarantee and become a party to the debt along with the corporation, and thus, a significant advantage of incorporation, that of limited liability, is to a large extent lost. While there are examples, such as the *Sinclair v. Dover Engineering Services Ltd.* case used to introduce this chapter, where the courts are willing to lift the corporate veil, in most cases, the status of the corporation as a separate legal entity will be respected. This is an important institution in our commercial world, but it is important that business people do not take it completely for granted.

Court Will Lift Corporate Veil in Event of Fraud

Mr. Kehoe was the sole director, shareholder, and person in charge of Terra Nova Auctioneers Inc. and, in his auctioneering capacity, sold a number of vehicles on behalf of Newfoundland Telephone Company. He operated one bank account and put all the funds into that account and used the money to pay off bills. When came the time to pay Newfoundland Telephone, he was about $42 000 short. Newfoundland Telephone sued Mr. Kehoe in his personal capacity for that money, and the court was asked to hold the principal liable for the company's debts. The court said that it was the auctioneer's duty to hold the money in trust for the sale of the vehicles, and keep it separate from any of their own funds. This was not done. The money was commingled. The court found that Mr. Kehoe used the money for his own purposes in a fraudulent and improper manner. Therefore, it was appropriate to lift the corporate veil and hold him personally liable.

Newfoundland Telephone Co. v. Terra Nova Auctioneers Inc., (1992) 323 A.P.R. 121 (Nfld. T.D.)

Capacity

It was only in provinces using the registration system of incorporation where the capacity of the corporation to enter contracts was limited. That was more of a nuisance than anything else, and in the two provinces still using the registration system, the legislation was changed so that those corporations now have all the capacity of a natural person. The problem of capacity to contract still may arise when dealing with companies created by special acts of the legislature or parliament, where those

Registration jurisdictions limit capacity

acts limit their activities to specified areas. When dealing with such companies and the act, it seems that unusual care should be taken to check that there is no restriction on its capacity. In some jurisdictions, such as British Columbia, it is possible to set down restrictions on what the company can do, but outsiders dealing with that corporation would only be affected in the unlikely event that they had specific notice of the limitation.

The Role of Agents

Corporations must act through agents

Since the corporate entity is a legal fiction, all its activities must be carried out through the services of real people acting as agents. The principles of agency law set out in Chapter 12 are, therefore, extremely important when dealing with corporations. Employees, from directors and managers right down to the clerk, may have actual or apparent authority to bind the corporation, depending on the nature of their jobs. Historically, a company could be protected from unauthorized action from such employees simply by filing with the incorporation documents a specific limitation on the actual authority of an agent. Today, these limitations on authority, even though they are filed with the other incorporating documents, are no longer considered notice to the public.[4]

Filed documents no longer notice of limited capacity

Funding

Issued shares usually less than authorized share capital

Common practice to issue no-par-value shares

An important attraction of the corporation is the ability to acquire capital from a large number of sources through the sale of shares. While the **share** gives the holder an interest in the corporation, that interest falls short of ownership. The corporation remains an independent personality separate and apart from the shareholders or members who make it up. The share gives the shareholder control of the corporation and a right to the assets of the corporation upon dissolution.

Some jurisdictions still require that the authorized share capital be set out in the incorporation documents. This sets an upper limit on the shares that can be sold and is usually set quite high to avoid the problem of having to go back and amend those incorporating documents. It is difficult to justify this limitation, and some jurisdictions, including Ontario and the federal government, no longer require it.

Shares of public companies are traded on the stock exchange.
The Canadian Press/Toronto Star/
Richard Lautens

Par-Value versus No-Par-Value Shares

The practice of issuing par-value shares is declining. This involves each share being given a specific value, such as $1, at the time of issuance. This can be misleading, as the marketplace quickly sets a value on those shares that is not reflected in that stated par-value. The more common practice in Canada and the United States is to put no value on the share at all, making it a no-par-value share and allowing the marketplace to determine the value. Some jurisdictions, such as Ontario and the federal government, have abolished par-value shares altogether.[5]

4. *Ontario Business Corporations Act*, R.S.O. 1990, c. B.16 s. 18

5. *Canada Business Corporations Act*, R.S.C. 1985, c. C-44 s. 24(1)

Special Rights and Restrictions

The shares issued by a corporation are normally divided into different classes, usually called common shares and special or preferred shares. The rights and restrictions associated with special shares can be designed to accomplish many diverse objectives, but they usually give the shareholder preference when dividends are declared and are, therefore, called **preferred shares**. Usually, a preferred share will bear a promise to pay a specific dividend each year. This is not a debt, and the company is not obligated to declare a dividend, but once they do, the preferred shareholder has the right to collect first before the common shareholders. These rights are cumulative, and where there has been a failure to pay the promised dividend for a number of years, the preferred shareholder has a right to receive any back payments before the common shareholders get any dividends. If Bandura has 100 preferred non-voting shares in a corporation that committed to pay a dividend of $10 per share per year, she may receive $1000 in dividends from that corporation in any given year. She cannot force the payment of the dividend, but she does have the right to payment before any dividends are paid to the common shareholder. This includes any failed payments from prior years.

Usually, only common shareholders have the right to vote, but a preferred share contains a provision giving the right to vote when the company fails to pay the promised dividend. There can be a right to vote, even without such a provision, where major changes that would materially affect the position of the preferred shareholder are proposed. For example, a proposal to change the rights or nature of the preferred share or to sell the assets of the corporation could not be adopted without allowing the preferred shareholders to vote. Also, when a company is dissolved, preferred shareholders usually have the right to have those shares repaid before any funds are paid out to the holders of common shares.

Since a variety of rights and restrictions can be incorporated into these special shares, depending on the interests of the parties, it is important that these matters be negotiated before the shares are issued. When a closely held company is involved, it is common to include a restriction on the sale of the shares, such as requiring the approval of the directors before the sale can take place. (Closely held and broadly held corporations are discussed below.)

Special shares are used for other purposes, such as estate planning, where two classes of shares can be created: one with a right to vote and some control in the affairs of the company but no right to dividends or money upon dissolution, and the other with a right to dividends but no right to vote. Such a division allows the holder of the voting shares to maintain control of the operations of the company but to surrender the income and the beneficial interests of the corporation to any heirs.

It is relatively easy to incorporate a business, and today, the process is simplified to the extent that people can either do it themselves or purchase a simple off-the-shelf corporation, much like you would purchase a suit off the rack. But this misses some of the considerable flexibility that is available using this method of carrying on business. It is possible, by careful use of common shares, the creation of shares with special rights and restrictions, and shareholders agreements, to cater to a great variety of different relationships and needs giving different rights and obligations with unique advantages to the various players. In addition, through holding companies, companies working together, and even companies in partnership, there is no limit to the creative solutions that can be designed to deal with a variety of business problems and needs. Just as a personally tailored suit has advantages over an off-the-shelf one, business people should be aware that paying the extra to have

Different classes of shares can give some shareholders preference

Special shares used in estate planning

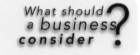

a lawyer custom design a company for their particular needs may well be worth the trouble and expense. Scrimping to save a few dollars at the outset may cause expensive problems later on.

Borrowing

The corporation can also borrow funds, thus accumulating debt. This can be done by borrowing large sums from a single creditor, such as a bank, and usually requires a mortgage on the property of the business. It can also be accomplished through the issuing of bonds or debentures, either secured or unsecured, to many different creditors. The result is the creation of a debtor-creditor relationship and an obligation that must be repaid. Where shares are involved, even preferred shares, there is no legal obligation to pay dividends, but failure to repay a debt constitutes a breach of the corporation's legal obligation. The creditor can bring an action, execute against security, and, once judgment is obtained, seize the assets of the business. If the company is unable to pay, bankruptcy will likely follow.

Corporation borrows funds by issuing bonds

Usually, the terms "'bond" and "debenture" are used interchangeably, but in Canada, a **bond** is normally secured by a mortgage, whereas a **debenture** is more likely to be unsecured. The corporation typically makes a debt commitment to a trustee who then issues shares in the indebtedness to individual bondholders. These bondholders are entitled to a portion of the repayment at a set rate of interest and are free to sell such claims to others, sometimes at a premium or discount, depending on the market.

Bondholder has right to payment

Shareholders are participants in the business, whereas bondholders are simply creditors. The company is in debt to the bondholder for the amount of the bond, but the company is not in debt to the shareholder. The bondholder can demand repayment and enforce that right in court, whereas a shareholder, even a preferred shareholder, has no similar right to demand payment of a dividend.

Bondholder has no right to vote

On the other hand, while shareholders can determine the operation of the corporation through the exercise of their voting power, a bondholder has no right to vote and cannot affect management decisions. In the event of a default, however, the bondholders usually have a right to take over the management of the corporation through the appointment of a receiver, similar to bankruptcy but without the requirement of court involvement. While the company remains solvent, however, the shareholders retain control through their voting power, and the bondholders only have the right to be paid on a regular basis. From the investor's point of view, the choice between shares at one end, bonds at the other, and preferred shares in the middle is likely to be simply a question of balancing risk and return. But in order to calculate the risks, a clear understanding of the legal differences between these vehicles is essential, not to mention an understanding of their different tax implications.

Most large corporations maintain a balance between common and preferred shares on the one hand and various types of debt instruments, such as large loans and secured and unsecured corporate bonds, on the other. To illustrate, suppose Bowman wanted to incorporate a small manufacturing business. There are several ways to transfer the assets of the business to the incorporated company. Bowman might incorporate a company that would acquire the manufacturing business and any property associated with it in return for all the shares of the company. But a better alternative might be to have the corporation purchase the manufacturing business as well as any property associated with it from Bowman, giving him a bond secured by a mortgage on the property as security for the repayment of the debt.

Bowman has all the shares in the company in either case. However, in the second case, instead of simply having shares in a company with significant assets, Bowman is a creditor of that corporation. Because the debt will be secured, he will be in a better position to get his money back if the corporation eventually runs into financial difficulties. This is similar to the situation in which Salomon found himself in the case described earlier. Before decisions are made with respect to these options, careful consideration must be given to the various tax implications of the choices.

Closely Held and Broadly Held Corporations

Traditionally, company law statutes in the various jurisdictions have recognized a distinction between broadly held and closely held corporations, which were usually called public and private corporations, respectively, and, in British Columbia, reporting and non-reporting corporations. In recent years, statutory provisions relating to these two classes of corporation have received considerable attention and have been significantly modified. In Ontario, corporations that offer shares to the public are called "**offering corporations**,"[6] and such corporations have more stringent auditing and reporting requirements.

A closely held corporation is one in which there are relatively few shareholders, and there are some restrictions on the sale of shares which cannot be sold to the general public openly or on the stock market. These are usually small corporations, such as a family business, that is managed by the shareholders. In those jurisdictions where the company law statute still distinguishes between closely held and broadly held corporations, the closely held company is much freer of government regulations and control. Some jurisdictions require the broadly held corporation to have more directors than the closely held company and to have more structured shareholders' meetings, more complete and audited financial statements, and more public access to company records and reports. Ontario requires three directors for an "offering corporation," but otherwise just one. The special requirements for broadly held corporations are found not only in the appropriate incorporation statutes but also in the securities legislation of that jurisdiction.

Broadly held corporations more closely regulated

Corporate Officers

Directors (Managers)

Within the Corporation

Deluce Holdings Inc. v. Air Canada[7]

Air Ontario was a small regional airline that had been owned and operated by the Deluce family for years out of London, Ontario. In 1986, a deal was struck with Air Canada, whereby they acquired a majority interest in the company. (Air Canada had a 75-percent share and the Deluce family a 25-percent share through separate

6. *Ontario Business Corporations Act*, R.S.O. 1990, c. B.16 s. 1

7. 98 D.L.R. (4th) 509 (Ont. Gen. Div.)

holding companies.) Air Canada had the right to appoint seven directors to the board of Air Ontario and the Deluce family was to appoint three. The deal also involved a separate shareholders' agreement, whereby Air Canada would have the right to buy out the Deluce interest when the employment of the last member of the family ended and that any disputes would be arbitrated. Stanley Deluce was chairman, and his two-year contract was not renewed when it expired. William Deluce, who was vice-chairman and CEO, was subsequently asked to resign. When he refused, he was fired. This was a complicated action, but basically, the Deluce family was claiming oppression on the basis that the seven directors appointed by Air Canada ganged up on the others, forcing William Deluce out so that Air Canada would then be able to buy out the Deluce interest as part of a general policy change, whereby Air Canada was now acquiring control of all its regional feeder airlines.

The question turns on the nature of the duty of the directors appointed by Air Canada. The court found that the directors had a duty of good faith to act in the best interests of the corporation that they were directing, Air Ontario. The court then examined the circumstances of the firing of William Deluce and found that the directors appointed by Air Canada, instead of acting in the best interests of Air Ontario, had acted on behalf of Air Canada so that they could buy out the shares of the Deluce family and take over the company. This was in violation of their duty and constituted oppression of the minority shareholders.

This case illustrates that directors owe a duty to the company that they are directors of, not to the interest group that appointed them. This can cause a serious dilemma to people acting as directors, especially where they owe their position to some other holding company whose interests they are expected to protect. This creates a classic conflict of interest. The case also shows the importance of shareholder agreements and the role they can play creating specialized relationships and obligations between the parties.

Shareholders choose directors

The shareholders normally exercise control over a corporation through the election of directors at the annual meeting. Once the directors are elected, the shareholders have little real say in the operation of the business until the next election, but the expectation is that if they want to be re-elected, the directors will follow the wishes of the shareholders. Sometimes, shareholders' votes will also be held when decisions involving a fundamental change in the business are to be made or where required by the incorporating documents. Smaller (closely held) corporations are more often run like an incorporated partnership. The shareholders are usually the managers as well as the directors and they participate in all important decisions.

For a person to serve as a director, he or she must be a mentally competent adult. The director cannot be an undischarged bankrupt or have been convicted of certain crimes, such as fraud. In most jurisdictions, the director no longer needs to be a shareholder[8] but because many corporations are foreign subsidiaries, usually a significant portion must be resident in Canada.

Director owes duty not to be negligent

A director owes a significant duty to the corporation to be careful. In common law, this duty was minimal, the director only being liable where there was some blatant or gross carelessness on his or her part. This standard has been significantly raised in most jurisdictions and now requires the director to exercise the care of a "reasonably prudent person" when carrying out the affairs of the business.[9]

8. *Ibid.* s. 118(2).

9. *British Columbia Company Act*, R.S.B.C. 1996, c. 62 s. 118; *Canada Business Corporations Act*, R.S.C. 1985; c. C-44 s. 122(1); and *Ontario Business Corporations Act*, R.S.O. 1990, c. B.16 s. 134(1.b)

Directors also have a **fiduciary duty** to the corporation. This requires the director to act in the best interests of the corporation, to be loyal, to avoid conflict, and to otherwise act honestly and in good faith towards the corporation. Directors are not permitted to take personal advantage of opportunities which arise because of their positions as directors, nor can they start a business in competition with the corporation. Any gains made by directors from such dealings must be paid over to the corporation, but any losses must be borne by that director alone. When a director is personally involved in some transaction that the company then becomes involved in, the director must disclose that interest by making a declaration to the board of directors, avoid any involvement in the discussion of the matter, and abstain from voting.

Director owes fiduciary duty

A major problem associated with director's **liability** is that they owe a duty to the company itself, not to the shareholders. This principle was clearly established in the case of *Foss v. Harbottle*[10] and has subsequently been incorporated into many statutes. Only the company can sue the director when this duty is violated. Since the directors decide what the company does, a decision to sue a director must be made by the directors, and they are not likely to decide to sue themselves.

Director owes duty to corporation, not to shareholders

To solve this problem, many jurisdictions give even minority shareholders the right to bring what is called a **derivative action** (or, in some provinces, a **representative action**) against the directors or others on behalf of the injured company.[11] This change, along with the change in the nature of the imposed duty to be careful, has significantly enhanced the peril associated with being a director. It has even been argued that the fiduciary duty of a director extends to the creditors of the corporation in some limited situations.

Representative action

Directors Owe a Fiduciary Duty to the Corporation They Direct

Canadian Airlines, a subsidiary of Pacific Western Airlines (PWA), entered into a limited partnership agreement with Canada's other major airline in creating a computer reservation system called Gemini. This agreement was to last for some time, but PWA and Canadian Airlines were having a difficult time and entered into negotiations with American Airlines to bail them out. Part of this arrangement required PWA/Canadian to get out of the Gemini computer reservation system. They tried to have the limited partnership dissolved in this action. The court found that the directors who were nominated by PWA/Canadian to sit on Gemini had a duty to disclose to Gemini the negotiations that were going on concerning their leaving the Gemini partnership. Even where a director is nominated from another corporation, he or she has a fiduciary duty to disclose all relevant information to the corporation or body of which he or she is a director. The directors failed to do this, breaching their fiduciary duty, and as a result, the application to have the limited partnership dissolved failed.

PWA Corp. v. Gemini Group Automated Distribution Systems Inc., (1993) 103 D.L.R. (4th) 609 (Ont. C.A.); leave to appeal refused (1993) 104 D.L.R. (4th) vii (S.C.C.).

10.(1843) 2 Hare 461 (H.C.C.)

11. *Ontario Business Corporations Act*, R.S.O. 1990, c. B.16 s. 246

Duty on insiders

Statutes in all jurisdictions also impose personal liability on directors if they allow dividends to be paid out to shareholders when the company is insolvent. Director's liability may also be imposed when they allow improper manipulation of shares, fail to give proper notice of shareholder meetings, fail to adhere to the restrictions on company power set out in the incorporating documents, or otherwise violate the specific responsibilities given in legislation. Securities legislation also prohibits directors from using "**insider knowledge**" to their own advantage or to the advantage of their friends or family, that is, directors who are aware of something about to happen that will materially affect the value of the shares, bonds, or other assets in the company are prohibited from using that knowledge to their own advantage, and they may be subject to fines and imprisonment if they do so.

External Obligations

Director's statutory duty for

• wages

Various federal and provincial statues impose personal liability on the director in primarily three areas. Directors can be held personally liable when a company fails while owing workers unpaid wages. Often, when a company is in trouble, directors will resign rather than face this risk. Sometimes, the company will agree to indemnify them, but if the company fails, such an agreement is useless. Insurance provides the best protection in these circumstances. Directors can also be held personally liable for breaches of the employment standards legislation as well as the workers' compensation and occupational health and safety legislation in place in the particular jurisdiction.

• taxes

A second area of personal liability for directors is for unpaid taxes. Under federal income tax legislation, the directors are personally responsible if back taxes are left unpaid. In many jurisdictions in Canada, if foreign firms wish to operate, they must have local resident directors. Local business people are often expected to act as token directors but are not actually expected to participate in the decision-making process of the corporation. Many take these positions not realizing their exposure, and if the company fails, leaving unpaid taxes and other obligations, the personal liability can be ruinous.

Directors May Be Liable for Unpaid Taxes

Stuart was a director of an incorporated company with employees. But he was a director in name only: he received no documents, reports, financial statements, and so on, invested no money, and was paid no dividends. When the company failed to properly deduct and remit taxes with respect to wages and salaries pursuant to the *Income Tax Act*, the court held Mr. Stuart vicariously liable, since a director can be held liable for such a failure. To avoid liability, he would have had to show that he had taken reasonable steps to ensure the deductions and payments were properly made, and, of course, because he played such a passive role, he could not show this.

Stuart v. M.N.R., [1995] 2 C.T.C. 2458 (T.C.C.)

• environment

The third area involves environmental regulation. Complicated statutes impose personal liability on directors for damages caused by the company to the environment. Contamination of property, pollution of the air, unexpected spills, and the cost of cleanup are examples of potential sources of a director's personal liability. In addition to potential fines and imprisonment, the directors face being personally responsible for the actual damages caused or the costs of cleanup in a civil action.

In a case involving Bata Industries, two directors were fined $12 000 each for failing to ensure that a waste storage site was cleaned up. This fine was reduced to $6000 on appeal.[12] Note that in this case, the directors were found liable not for what they did but for what they failed to do.

Usually, directors can only escape liability where they can show that they acted with "due diligence." What constitutes **due diligence** varies with the situation, but in general, they must show that they kept themselves informed of what was required of the company and what the company was doing to comply and that they did all that was reasonable to avoid the problem.

Individual liability has also been imposed on directors for offences under consumer protection legislation, such as the *Trade Practices Act*, the federal *Competition Act*, securities legislation, and provincial human rights codes. It is important to note that many of these statutes not only contemplate fines but also provide for imprisonment in extreme situations. Usually, both criminal and civil responsibilities may be imposed on the corporation itself, its directors, and officers.

• **other**

It should also be remembered that where the commission of a tort, such as misrepresentation or deceit, is involved, directors can be held personally liable if they were the one who committed the wrong. The corporate structure is no protection to the person who actually commits the tort.

Officers and Senior Executives

Roper v. Murdoch et al.[13]

Catalina Productions was involved in several high-profile programs, including "Let's Make a Deal," "The Tom Jones Show," and a game show called "Pitfall." They instituted negotiations with Richard Deacon, a well-known Hollywood personality, to produce a television news program called "Micro Magic,"' which involved microwave cooking and celebrity guests.

At the initial stage, the negotiations were handled by Catalina productions' owner Ian McLennan and then usually handed over to Bill Armstrong, the vice-president of programming. Unfortunately, in this case, because of financial problems and chaotic conditions at Catalina productions, the negotiations fell through, and on September 9, a letter was received from Richard Deacon's agent cancelling the deal.

On that same day, Northstar Productions Inc. was incorporated by Bill Armstrong and Bill Murdoch, formerly Catalina's vice-president of marketing, who had resigned from Catalina Productions in late August, and they concluded a deal with Deacon and his agent to produce the new "Micro Magic" show. That agreement contained virtually the same terms as the handshake agreement entered into with Ian McLennan and Catalina Productions. The project went ahead, and during the year 1981–1982, Northstar produced the show.

In this case, Murdoch and Armstrong had been executives and, as such, owed a fiduciary duty to Catalina Productions. Armstrong had been in the planning stages of "Micro Magic" while at Catalina Productions, and Murdoch in his position at Catalina was certainly aware of the project. The situation became even more complex because Catalina went into bankruptcy, and the trustee assigned any rights they had arising out of television production to Roper, who brought this action against Armstrong and Murdoch.

12. R. v. Bata Industries Limited (1992) 70 C.C.C. (3d) 394
13. (1987) 39 D.L.R. (4th) 684 (B.C.S.C.)

The court held that Armstrong and Murdoch, because of their position with Catalina Productions, owed a fiduciary duty to Catalina. It was clear from the evidence that on the day they resigned, Armstrong and Murdoch had it in mind to produce "Micro Magic." This opportunity came to them because of their corporate position, and they were prohibited from taking personal advantage of it. The court required them to pay over any profits they made from the deal to Roper, the successor of Catalina Productions.

This case shows clearly the fiduciary duty imposed on the officers and directors of a corporation and also how that duty continues after the officers' resignation. It is also interesting to note that the right to sue did not die with the bankrupt corporation but was subsequently exercised by a complete stranger to these dealings, the assignee Roper.

Although directors are legally responsible for management, in a large corporation, they usually appoint a managing director or CEO, who is given overall responsibility along with a managing committee of the directors to run the affairs of the corporation. The day-to-day operation of the corporation is assigned to others who report to the CEO. These officers may include a president, a treasurer, a secretary, and other senior executives, such as vice-presidents and managers, as deemed appropriate for the organization. In general, these officers and managers are in a fiduciary relationship to the corporation, similar to that of the directors. They owe the same types of general obligations and duty of care and competence to the company as the directors but may be held to an even higher standard. In the case of statutory obligations, they may have to pay any wages and taxes owing. They may be held personally liable for judgments against the company in human rights and consumer complaint actions as well as costs for cleaning up any environmental damage caused by the company. The legislation usually imposes the same obligations on officers as those imposed on directors. The Roper case shows the nature of fiduciary duty as well as how that duty can continue even after the employment relationship has ceased.

Similar duties owed by senior management

Promoters

Promoters also owe duties

A promoter is someone who participates in the initial setting up of the corporation or who assists the corporation in making a public share offering. Provincial securities statutes control the sale of shares to the public, whether through the stock exchange or other means. A **securities commission** is established to prevent fraud and to encourage a free and efficient market in corporate shares and other securities. This requires the complete disclosure of as much information as possible. To accomplish this, a proper prospectus must be issued when shares are to be sold to the public. The purpose of the **prospectus** is to disclose all pertinent information of interest to investors about the corporation and its business operations. The corporation and the promoters are responsible to ensure full disclosure and no misrepresentation in the prospectus. Significant fines and the possibility of jail sentences may be imposed when such misrepresentations take place.

Disclosure required

The securities commission is also charged with controlling other forms of abuse, including insider trading, where officers or people holding significant percentages of the shares of a corporation trade in those shares using their insider's knowledge to anticipate a rise or fall in prices. The securities commission also controls abuses by providing for the licensing and regulation of all those involved in the selling and marketing of shares and other securities, including brokers, sales personnel, and the issuers of the shares (the corporations) themselves.

Whether the promoters are officers of the corporation or not, just like directors and other officers, they have a fiduciary duty to that corporation. When property is acquired with the intention of incorporating a company and then selling that property to it, the promoter has a duty to act in the best interests of the corporation. The promoter cannot sell the property to the company at an excessive profit, must divulge the original price paid, and must not participate in the decision to purchase. The promoter has a fiduciary duty to the company and a duty to disclose any personal interest in deals in which the company is involved.

Fiduciary duty

Szecket v. Huang[14]

Dr. Szecket and Mr. Geddo developed a process for bonding different metals and entered into an agreement with Mr. Huang for funding further development. The deal involved Mr. Huang forming a company that was, among other things, to employ Dr. Szecket and Mr. Geddo for 3 years in Taiwan. Mr. Huang, "acting on behalf of a company to be formed," signed the agreement. The contract was not performed, and Dr. Szecket and Mr. Geddo brought this action for breach of contract against Mr. Huang in his personal capacity, since the company he claimed to be acting for was never incorporated. This is called a pre-incorporation contract, and the Ontario legislation permits such a contract to be adopted by a company once it comes into existence. But the statute also makes the agent acting on the yet-to-be incorporated company's behalf personally liable until the contract is adopted by the new corporation, unless it is made clear in the agreement that there is to be no such personal liability. Mr. Huang tried to argue that because a clause in the original offer making him personally liable was deleted, he had made his intention not to be personally liable clear to the plaintiffs. But the court found that this had to be made clear in the agreement itself. The agreement did make it clear that he was acting on behalf of a company yet to be formed, but the court found that there was no indication in that contract that he was not to be held personally liable. As a result, the action against Mr. Huang was successful.

Mr. Huang was acting as a promoter in these circumstances, anticipating that he would incorporate a company and that company would be liable under this contract. Here, the problems associated with pre-incorporation contracts and the separate nature of the corporation are dramatized. Normally, a company would not be bound by a contract entered into on its behalf before incorporation because it did not exist at that time and so could not ratify the agreement. This problem has been overcome by statute, but in this case, since the company never was incorporated, the non-existent company could not be liable. Therefore, under the statute, Mr. Huang who was purporting to act on its behalf was liable. Business people, especially promoters, have to be very careful to avoid personal liability when deals like this go sour. They have to make it absolutely clear in the agreement that they are not assuming any personal liability.

Promoters will often purchase property on behalf of a company before it has been incorporated and then have the company ratify the agreement after incorporation. Such ratification of pre-incorporation contracts is invalid in common law, since the company did not exist at the time the promoters were claiming to act on its behalf. Although this approach may be legally sound, it is not practical from a business point of view, and many jurisdictions (notably Ontario and the federal

Ratification of pre-incorporation contracts

14. (1998) 168 D.L.R. (4th) 402 (Ont. C.A.).

government) made changes permitting the later-incorporated company to ratify a pre-incorporation contract. The result is that the contract is valid and binding on the company once it is so ratified. Of course, if the company does not ratify or if a pre-incorporation contract is signed in a jurisdiction where the company cannot ratify, the promoter remains solely liable for any losses, since there was no authority to act.

Shareholders

Richardson Greenshields of Canada Ltd. v. Kalmacoff[15]

Two security companies were involved in this case, Security Home Mortgage Investment Inc., referred to as "Security Home," and Security Home Financing Ltd. referred to as the "advisor." Security Home was controlled by a small group of individuals holding 85 percent of the common shares. That same group largely owned the shares in the advisor company, which had a contract to manage and run the operation of Security Home. A large number of preferred shares in Security Home had been sold on the open market through the agent, Richardson Greenshields of Canada Ltd. These special shareholders only had the right to vote with respect to the management contract. Security Home ran into financial difficulty but renewed the management contract of the advisor anyway. Because renewal of the advisor's management contract also required the approval of the preferred shareholders, Richardson Greenshields obtained enough proxies from them to override that decision, and the contract was terminated.

It was at this point that the basis of the complaint arose. Instead of that being the end of the matter, the directors of Security Home, in order to thwart the spirit of the direction given them by the preferred shareholders, simply hired the people employed in the advisor company as managers for Security Home. In effect, they were doing exactly the same jobs they were doing before, but now they were employed directly by Security Home instead of the management company. In response to this, Richardson Greenshields bought 100 shares of Security Home on the open market and brought a derivative action against Security Home and its directors.

The question in this case was whether Richardson Greenshields had the right to bring such a derivative action, since they had acquired the shares after the conduct complained of. The appeal court decided that the issues involved were significant, that it did not matter when they obtained the shares, and that, as a shareholder, they had the right to ask the court for permission to commence a derivative action against the directors of the company, which permission was granted.

The court's decision here did not decide the merits of the dispute; it simply authorized the action to proceed. But it does illustrate some very important points. First of all, it shows how "preferred" shares can be set up with rights and obligations different from those of common shares and what the effects of those differences can be. It also illustrates how different corporate entities can be used and intermingled to accomplish different purposes, as was the case here with Security Home and the advisor company having essentially the same investors owning common shares in each. But for our purposes, the most important thing is the right of a disgruntled shareholder to overcome the tyranny of the majority and bring an action on behalf of the company against those who have, for their own ulterior purposes, made decisions not in the best interests of the company.

15. (1995) 123 D.L.R. (4th) 628 (Ont. C.A.); refused leave to appeal (1995) 126 D.L.R. (4th) vii (S.C.C.)

Shareholders have few obligations to the corporation or other shareholders other than not to use insider knowledge for their own purposes. The number of shares required to qualify as an insider varies from one jurisdiction to another, but shareholders who have been classified as insiders have the same obligation as directors not to use insider information to their own benefit or to the benefit of friends or relatives.

Rights

Shareholders do have significant rights and remedies. Certain records must be kept at a designated company office and made available to the shareholders. These records must include:

- the documents of incorporation;
- lists of all the shareholders;
- lists of transactions or changes in relationship to the shares;
- lists of officers, directors, and debenture holders, minutes of directors' and shareholders' meetings; and
- audited financial statements.

Some corporate records, including the actual financial records (the books), are not available to shareholders. Otherwise, such information could not be kept from competitors. Nonetheless, much important information is contained in documents that are accessible to anybody who holds a share in the company.

Shareholders are entitled to receive copies of any annual reports and the financial statements that accompany them, which must be audited when a broadly held corporation is involved. An **auditor** is an unbiased outside accountant, whose responsibility is to ensure that the financial statements use generally accepted accounting practices and are accurate. The auditor's duty is to the shareholders, not to the directors, and the auditors have access to the company's books to ensure the accuracy of their conclusions. In most jurisdictions, shareholders who have some doubts about the accuracy of these audited statements can have an inspector appointed to examine the auditing process.

The shareholders also have considerable power to affect the decisions made by the company. An **annual general meeting** of shareholders must be held, where the shareholders are given an opportunity to vote for the directors of the corporation, making the directors directly answerable to the shareholders for their actions. Advance notice of this meeting, including the appropriate financial statements, must be given to the shareholders. Any major changes that will affect the nature of the corporation must be placed before the shareholders to vote on before the decisions are implemented. If necessary, a special meeting can be called for this purpose. The incorporating documents or bylaws of the corporation may provide for the right of shareholders to vote in other situations as well. Shareholders at these meetings can put forward proposals concerning any matter for the decision of the other shareholders, but the management can refuse to submit them if the proposal is self-serving or is in some way an abuse of the process. Of course, it must be remembered that each vote is based on the number of shares held. Thus, someone holding a majority of the shares will always be able to outvote minority shareholders.

Shareholders can pass their right to vote on to someone else in the form of a **proxy**. These proxies can be very important when groups of shareholders band together to effect a particular result or to control which directors are elected at the annual general meeting. The rules for the creation and operation of proxies are

Shareholder has few responsibilities

Shareholder has right to see records and reports

Shareholders have the right to vote

Proxy can be passed to someone else

quite strict because of the potential for abuse. For example, in some jurisdictions, a management group soliciting proxies is required to state this fact in bold print on the face of the information circulated to the members.[16] The bylaws or articles set out how many votes each shareholder is entitled to, but this may vary with the type of shares held.

Holders of **common shares** are usually entitled to one vote per share, and **preferred shareholders** usually cannot vote, unless the promised dividend has not been paid.

A shareholder holding a significant portion of the shares can usually force the calling of an extra meeting, and someone with fewer shares, if they have good reason, can apply to the court for the same purpose. But such a right still only protects the majority shareholder, since a majority vote or greater is necessary to decide all matters once the meeting is held.

Preemptive rights entitle shareholder to be offered any new shares first

In many jurisdictions, shareholders have the right not to have their proportion of shares diluted by the sale of more shares to others. If there are 1000 shares outstanding and Pantaz has 500 of them, he owns 50 percent of the company. If the directors decide to issue 500 new shares and none are offered to Pantaz, his interest will be reduced to a one-third portion. In small companies, this is usually avoided by including in a separate shareholders' agreement, a provision requiring that a sufficient number of the new shares be offered to the existing shareholders first so that they may retain their proportionate share of the company. Such a right is called a preemptive right. In most jurisdictions in Canada, preemptive rights exist only where actually granted in the incorporating documents or shareholders' agreements.[17] British Columbia does provide such rights for a closely held corporation in the absence of a stated intention to the contrary set forth in the incorporation documents.[18]

Bell v. Source Data Control Ltd.[19]

Bell, Stewart, Williamson, and Wilmot were minority shareholders in Source Data Control Ltd. (SDC), each having a 10 percent interest. James Hood was the majority shareholder holding a 60 percent interest in the company. The company was successful for a number of years, but then, Hood became distracted because of personal problems. The business deteriorated. Relations between the shareholders became difficult, and finally, the minority shareholders wanted out. For several years, McLean-Hunter Ltd. had expressed an interest in purchasing SDC, and Williamson offered to sell his 10 percent interest to them for $200 000. McLean-Hunter refused, saying they were only interested if they could get majority control. Later, Hood offered to sell his shares to McLean-Hunter and demanded $2.1 million. (At that rate, each minority shareholder's 10 percent interest should have been worth $350 000). After considerable negotiation, it was agreed that they would pay this price for Hood's shares but a much lower percentage price for the minority shares (the $200 000 initially offered by Williamson). Hood met with the minority

---

16. *British Columbia Company Act*, R.S.B.C. 1996, c. 62 s. 157

17. *Ontario Business Corporations Act*, R.S.O. 1990, c. B.16 s. 2

18. *British Columbia Company Act*, R.S.B.C. 1996, c. 62 s. 41

19. (1988) 53 D.L.R. (4th) 580 (Ont. C.A.)

shareholders without telling them what he was getting for his shares or even that he was selling as well. He told them of the weak financial condition of the company and how poorly things were going. Without any suggestion from him, they told Hood they wanted $200 000 each for their 10 percent interests. At one stage, after the deal had been made, but before it was executed, Hood was specifically asked what he was getting, but he refused to divulge any information to the minority shareholders. The deal went through, and when the minority shareholders discovered that Hood was getting much more proportionally for his shares than they were, Bell and Stewart brought this action claiming that Hood had violated his duty to them.

At the trial, the judge found that there was no fraud, no breach of trust, and that the minority shareholders had not placed any reliance or trust in Hood. They suggested the $200 000 figure, and they wanted out of the company as quickly as possible. It was also found that it was not unreasonable for McLean-Hunter to be willing to pay a premium to the majority shareholder to get a controlling interest. And so the action was dismissed. On appeal, two of the three judges agreed, and so, the minority shareholders lost their action. The court found that there was no fiduciary duty between the majority shareholder and the minority shareholders (or a director and the minority shareholders) to disclose any of this information, and so, Hood was not in violation of any duty because none existed. Note, however, that there was a strong dissenting opinion.

This case nicely illustrates that while shareholders may have an obligation not to misrepresent or commit fraud, there is no general fiduciary duty that requires them to disclose information or otherwise act in the best interests of the corporation or other shareholders.

These shareholder rights may seem significant, but to a minority shareholder, that power may be an illusion. In large corporations with great numbers of shares distributed, any individual shareholder's rights may be very diluted, and the only practical recourse is to sell the shares. In small, closely held companies there is usually a restriction on the sale of shares. The "locked-in" shareholder may be unable to sell those shares and unable to influence the course of the company because of the overriding control exercised by the majority shareholder.

Weak position of minority shareholders

Shareholder Protections

To protect the shareholder from abuse in these circumstances, the statutes have provided several safeguards, the most important of which is the shareholder's right to sue the directors on behalf of the company when the directors have done something actionable. The right to **derivative** or **representative action** exists in British Columbia, Nova Scotia, and those jurisdictions that use the articles of incorporation method of incorporation.

Derivative or representative action

To succeed in these jurisdictions, a shareholder must show that the company was in some way injured by the directors' actions. In the Richardson Greenshields case used to introduce this section, the directors used a technicality to thwart the rights of the preferred shareholders to their detriment and that of the company. Richardson Greenshields as a shareholder was seeking permission of the court to bring an action on behalf of the company against those directors who were unwilling to bring an action against themselves.

Shareholders Have the Right to Bring a Derivative Action

Northwest Sports owned the Canucks hockey team and created a wholly owned subsidiary, Arena Corp., for the purpose of building a stadium in downtown Vancouver. Northwest also explored the possibility of getting an NBA franchise for Vancouver. Eventually, Mr. Griffiths, who was the president of Northwest Sports, pursued this opportunity on his own and made arrangements to obtain an NBA franchise for Vancouver with the cooperation of the McCaw Group. This required that Northwest sell out their interest to the new organization. The directors of Northwest, with Mr. Griffiths abstaining, agreed to this new arrangement. A few of the minority shareholders, however, did not like the deal. One of them brought

this action before the B.C. Supreme Court seeking permission to bring a derivative action against Mr. Griffiths and the other directors for violation of their fiduciary duty with respect to Northwest. The court granted leave for such a derivative action, noting that Mr. Griffiths had violated his fiduciary duty by taking advantage of a corporate opportunity. The other directors who were refusing to sue on behalf of Northwest were in no position to do so, since they would be suing themselves. This is an appropriate situation for a derivative action.

Primex Investments Ltd. v. Northwest Sports Enterprises Ltd. [1996] 4 W.W.R. 54 (B.C.S.C.); rev'd in part [1997] 2 W.W.R. 129 (B.C.C.A.)

Shareholders have rights to relief from oppression

In other circumstances, the shareholder might be able bring an **oppression action**. For example, the directors might arrange for the sale of shares just to weaken the voting position of a particular shareholder, or if the shareholder is an employee, the directors might fire the shareholder to force the sale of the shares. In some jurisdictions, both shareholders and creditors have the right to go to court and seek an order for relief from oppression if this type of abuse takes place. The court has the power to appoint a receiver to take control of the company or to provide for its dissolution if it feels that the complaint is justified.

Dissent provisions provide relief for shareholders

Sometimes, minority shareholders are adversely affected by a decision that is beneficial to the company as a whole. In the past, there was no recourse. In many jurisdictions, however, the injured minority shareholder can now file a **dissent**.[20] Such dissent procedures are implemented when major changes to the company adversely affect the shareholder and require that his or her shares be purchased at a fair price.

Re 85956 Holdings Ltd. and Fayerman Brothers Ltd. [21]

For several years, Sidney and Joseph Fayerman operated a wholesale/retail merchandising business through Fayerman Brothers Limited in Prince Albert. Because of their failing health and increased competition, it was decided by the directors and approved by the majority shareholders not to purchase any more inventory but simply sell off what they had. The minority shareholders opposed this. When the decision was made to continue the sell-off without replacing inventory, the minority

---

20. *Business Corporations Act*, R.S.O. 1990, c. B.16 s. 185. This is a very significant shareholder power, but it is only available in limited circumstances, such as when a decision is being made to amend the articles of incorporation in order to restrict the issue or transfer of shares, or to restrict the type of business the corporation can carry on. It is also available when amalgamation with another corporation is involved or when a significant portion of the assets of a corporation is going to be sold or leased. British Columbia, Nova Scotia, and the provinces that have adopted the articles of incorporation method of forming a company have similar dissent provisions.

21. (1986) 25 D.L.R. (4th) 119 (Sask. C.A.)

shareholders asked that their shares be purchased at a fair value. This was refused, and so this action was brought to force the share purchase at a fair price on the basis that the minority shareholders were dissenting. The *Saskatchewan Act,* like many incorporation statutes, has a provision that when "a sale, lease, or exchange of all or substantially all the property of a corporation other than in the ordinary course of business of the corporation" takes place and a shareholder does not approve such a sale, the dissenting shareholder can force the purchase of their shares at a fair price. The problem in this case was whether the choice not to replace the inventory changed this from being a sale done in the ordinary course of business triggering the dissent provision.

The court held that a sale in the ordinary course of business required the replenishing of the inventory. Not to do so amounted to a sale of all or substantially all the assets of the business, and the dissent provisions were triggered. The court found that the company was required to buy out the minority shareholders paying a fair market price for the shares.

This case illustrates how the dissent provision works and under what circumstances a minority shareholder is entitled to this protection. It is interesting to note that the company retained its considerable real estate holdings. Still, this was considered a liquidation of the assets of the business, and the minority shareholders were entitled to have their shares bought out.

Closely Held Corporations

Small, closely held corporations whose shareholders are also directors and managers of the company are often little more than incorporated partnerships. Often, they will also be full-time employees of the corporation, and when they have a falling out, the problems can go far beyond what can be remedied or even what has been anticipated in the legislation. The individual shareholder may lose not only the job as director and manager but also full-time employment and may still not be able to sell his or her shares. In such circumstances, the importance of a properly drawn up **shareholder agreement** cannot be overemphasized. Usually, the agreement will include a provision, whereby one shareholder must buy out the other if these types of events or other forms of dissatisfaction occur. Provisions relating to employment are often included in such agreements as well. Shareholder agreements are very important and can be used to set out many important obligations between the parties, much as a partnership agreement does in a partnership relationship.

Importance of shareholder agreements

Dividends

Shareholders have no legal right to force the payment of a dividend, although they can require payment if one has been declared by the directors. Their recourse is political, and if the directors fail to declare a dividend when the shareholders expect one, they are likely to be voted out at the next shareholders' meeting. But the shareholders cannot go to court and sue for a dividend even where preferred shares are involved, with the commitment to pay a specific dividend each year. Such preferred shareholders can force payment before any dividend is paid to the common shareholders and, where this right is cumulative, can also require the payment of any prior unpaid dividends on winding up or dissolution. The rights associated with the shareholders' position are rights of control, information, and protection, but there is no corresponding right to a specific return on the funds invested. Many provisions are in place to protect the position of shareholders, but it is important to balance these rights against some important drawbacks for shareholders.

Shareholders have no right to dividends

Pros and Cons of Incorporation

Advantages

There are several advantages associated with incorporation, most of which are derived from the concept of the separate legal personality of the corporation.

Limited Liability

Liability of shareholder limited to investment

As illustrated in the Salomon case, shareholders are not liable for the debts and other obligations of the corporation because the company, as a separate legal person, is responsible for its own wrongful conduct. Where the company assets are not enough to pay the unsatisfied creditors, they cannot turn to its shareholders for the difference. Shareholders can only lose what they have invested.

Even a Subsidiary Corporation Is a Separate Person

In 1981, two large oil companies, Sunmark Worldwide Services Inc. and Ocelot Industries, created two subsidiaries to explore for oil in the Sudan as a joint venture, Sun Sudan and Ocelot Sudan, respectively. When, after considerable exploration, the point came that Ocelot Sudan was to put more funds into the project according to the agreement, they were unable to do so. Sun Sudan sued the parent company Ocelot Industries, not the subsidiary. The court had to determine whether the parent company was responsible for the debts of its subsidiary. The court determined from the evidence that there was no fraud on the part of Ocelot Sudan or any of the parties and that a sub-

stantial effort had been made to provide funding. Also, there were good and valid reasons for creating the subsidiaries, not the least of which was to reduce risk and insulate the parent companies from liability. The judge found that because of the *Salomon v. Salomon* principle, each corporation had a separate legal personality and the parent Ocelot Industries was not responsible for the debts of Ocelot Sudan. He pointed out that these were sophisticated business people who knew they were dealing with limited liability companies and concluded there was no wrongdoing, and so, the separate legal liability element was in effect.

Sun Sudan Oil Co. v. Methanex Corp., (1992) 5 Alta. L.R. (3d) 292 (Q.B.)

Limited liability lost when personal guarantee given

This limited liability, although attractive and often the primary reason for choosing to incorporate, is often only an illusion. When dealing with a closely held company, banks and other major creditors will usually insist on a **personal guarantee** from the major shareholders or other principals, which effectively eliminates any advantage of limited liability for those asked to sign such a guarantee.

Still limited liability will protect shareholders from unexpected company obligations, such as vicarious liability for torts committed by employees or the failure to properly perform contractual obligations. Also, suppliers of materials usually do not obtain any personal commitment from shareholders, and so, they cannot seek compensation from them if the business becomes insolvent. For example, if a person operating a grocery business incorporates a company and borrows money from the bank for business purposes, that bank will probably insist on a personal guarantee from the shareholder, but a supplier of groceries would normally have no such personal commitment. If the business goes bad, the shareholder will have to pay the bank because of the personal guarantee but not the supplier, who must look to the corporation for payment. If an employee of the grocery business negligently injured a pedestrian while delivering groceries, the company would be vicariously liable for that injury, not the shareholder.

Even this amount of limited liability is not certain. As the case used to introduce this chapter illustrates, in rare cases, the courts are willing to look behind the corporate veil and hold the principals liable for the obligations of that corporation. This is especially true when there is any taint of wrongdoing or avoidance of obligations that ought to be honoured.

Taxes

Although tax reforms did away with many of the differences between the federal income taxes paid by sole proprietors, partners, and corporations, because the system is so complex, there still may be advantages available to the individual taxpayer through incorporation. At the least, the shareholder can leave the funds in the corporation and use it as a vehicle of investment, thus avoiding some taxes until a later date. In addition, as many provinces have not followed the federal lead, there may still be significant provincial tax advantages to be gained through incorporation.

However, federal and provincial income tax laws are extremely complicated. It is possible that incorporation will backfire and that the process will lead to more income tax rather than less. When losses are experienced, as is normally the case with a new business, the taxpayer is better off if the business is not incorporated so that these losses can be applied directly against personal income. Great care must be exercised in the process of tax planning for any business, and a prudent businessperson will seek expert advice in these circumstances.

Succession and Transferability

Because a corporation is a separate legal entity and a mythical person, it does not die unless some specific steps are taken to end its existence. When a partner dies, the partnership will usually come to an end. The death of even a 100 percent shareholder will not affect the existence of the corporation, although the loss may have practical implications, especially where the shareholder is involved in the ongoing operation of the business. The share is simply an asset in the hands of the shareholder, and, like any other asset, is simply distributed to the heirs.

Thus, where two people hold 50 percent each of the shares of a corporation and are both killed in an air crash, the company continues, and the shares go to the heirs, who become the new shareholders. If the two people were carrying on business as partners, however, the company would automatically be dissolved.

When a partner leaves a partnership, the process is complex, often requiring the dissolution of the partnership. Shares in a corporation, however, usually can be transferred at will without reference either to the other shareholders or to the corporate body. This free transferability of shares is one of the attractive features that led to the creation of the corporate entity in the first place, and it provides an effective method for the contributors of capital to restrict their relationship with the company. When closely held corporations, which often have the same kinds of relationships as partnerships, are involved, this free transferability of shares is significantly restricted.

It is often said that a corporation cannot die, but actually, there are several things that can cause an incorporated company to be dissolved. The ultimate end for a company going through the bankruptcy process is dissolution by operation of

But can be dissolved

law. Minority shareholders or creditors can bring application to the court to have a company dissolved because of oppression or some other inappropriate conduct by the other shareholders or directors, making it appropriate for the court to do so. The shareholders themselves can vote to bring the corporation to an end when they feel it is appropriate, filing a declaration to that effect at the appropriate government office. But the more common way is for the company simply to fail to file the required annual reports. Eventually, the company will be considered inactive and removed from the registry. Such companies can be restored by filing the missing reports.

Obligations of the Participants

No duty on shareholder in a corporation

Unlike partners, shareholders are generally free of any obligations or duties to the corporation or other shareholders. There is no fiduciary duty to act in the best interests of the corporation or even to refrain from carrying on business in competition with the corporation.

The extent of this freedom of action can be illustrated by the activities of several environmental groups. They acquire a few shares in the large corporations they consider a threat to the environment with the express purpose of using the special privileges available to shareholders (such as rights to information and to attend shareholders' meetings), which can be used in the battle against the polluting corporation. Even when the interests of the environmental group are diametrically opposed to, and interfere with, the profit-making ventures of the corporation and other shareholders, there is no obligation to act otherwise. Only when people acquire sufficient shares to be classed as insiders or become directors or officers, or when an individual has a majority of the shares, are certain restrictions placed on their activities. These restrictions usually take the form of rules, which prevent the shareholders from abusing their positions of power within the corporation and causing injury to other investors.

Management

Managers and shareholders separate

In a sole proprietorship, the business is controlled by the proprietor; in a partnership, each partner is entitled to participate in the business decisions of the partnership; in a corporation, however, it is common to separate the managers from the owners. The shareholders elect a board of directors who control the business. They, in turn, can hire professional managers who have the expertise to make sound business decisions on behalf of the corporation. The shareholders do not have to devote time or attention to managing, but they can change the management by electing different people to the board of directors if they are unhappy with the decisions being made.

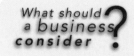

Businesspeople usually assume that the best way for them to carry on their business is through incorporation. While that may, in fact, be the case, consideration should also be given to the alternatives. Sole proprietorship and partnership are the only real alternatives discussed in this text, although if the enterprise is not for profit or does not involve an ongoing business, there are other possibilities. For example, societies are used for non-profit activities, such as charities, clubs, and religious organizations, and where property is shared, cooperatives and joint tenancy arrangements might be appropriate alternatives.

Even the choice between partnership and incorporation is not always clear. The unlimited liability of a sole proprietorship or partnership can be overcome by appropriate insurance. The tax advantages of incorporation have, to a large extent, been eliminated or extended to sole proprietorships and partnerships as well. The unique power of a single partner to veto the decisions of the others partners can be built into an incorporated company by a carefully drawn shareholder agreement. And many of the disadvantages that professionals experience because they are required to carry on their profession as partners can be overcome by creating a management company to manage the practice.

The point is that there are many different options and many different combinations available to a businessperson when structuring the tools used to carry on the business. Expert advice should be sought and careful consideration given to the options earlier rather than later in the process.

Disadvantages

A corporation is not always the best method of carrying on business. Many of the characteristics outlined above as advantages can just as easily be seen as drawbacks from another person's perspective.

It is helpful to compare incorporation with partnership to illustrate some of the disadvantages of incorporation. Partners who wish to change important aspects of their partnership arrangement need only reach an agreement to that effect. In the case of a corporation, however, the incorporating documents themselves may have to be altered, which is an involved and expensive procedure. A partner in a minority position still has considerable power. In a partnership, one partner can veto a proposal supported by 10 others. A minority shareholder in a corporation can do little to alter unsatisfactory decisions and may not even be able to sell his or her shares.

Weak position of minority shareholders in corporations

In closely held corporations, the free transferability of shares is restricted either through shareholder agreements or by limitations placed in the incorporating documents themselves. Often, the shareholders are required to get approval of the sale or offer the shares first to the other shareholders. As with partnerships, the reason people organize themselves into small, closely held corporations is often because of the individual skills each shareholder brings to the company. These shareholders are usually employees as well, and their contribution to the operation of the business is often vital to its success. Free transferability of shares in such circumstances might be a significant threat to the corporation, especially if the shareholder withdraws his or her services when the shares are sold.

A corporation is the most expensive way to operate a business; the initial incorporation process costs more in the first place and the ongoing operation involves more expense than either sole proprietorship or partnership. There are more formal record-keeping requirements and generally more government control exercised with a corporation.

Corporations more expensive than other forms of business

It is important to note as well that there are many variations on the corporate approach to business. Often, corporations are set up that merely hold shares in other corporations. Corporations may join others or individuals in joint ventures and partnerships usually for some major project or activity. Corporations may license others to use their products, software, or other forms of intellectual property, such as patents or copyrighted materials.

Corporation can be used to create a variety of business structures

It is also common to see small business enterprises that are part of a larger organization through **franchising**—business arrangements based on contracts of service and the supply of products between the larger and the smaller units. Fast food restaurants specializing in pizza and fried chicken, hamburgers, and so on are normally set up this way. Many difficulties can arise in such relationships, and the changing nature of contract law and corporate responsibility are softening the normally narrow approach to these businesses. For example, the good-faith requirements that are now being read into business contracts put franchisees in a much more favourable position than they have formerly been.

Termination of the Corporation

Corporations can be dissolved in several ways. The process can be voluntary by following the winding up procedure found in the company law statutes or in some jurisdictions in a separate winding-up act. If the corporation owns sufficient assets, it may be worthwhile to follow this process, but often, it is not worth the expense.

Dissolution can take place either voluntarily or involuntarily, and the procedure can be induced internally by the directors or shareholders or externally by a creditor. On occasion, a court will order a company to be dissolved when a minority shareholder has been unfairly treated. If there are more debts owing to the creditors than the company has assets to cover, the common procedure is bankruptcy, and the end result is usually the dissolution of the company. Under the current bankruptcy legislation, it is possible for the corporation to make a proposal to the creditors and, if accepted and followed, the company will continue.

Dissolution may be voluntary or involuntary

The process of distributing the assets upon winding up the company is set out in the various statutes and will not be dealt with here. It is important to note, however, that the directors have a considerable obligation not to allow any of the assets of the corporation to get into the hands of the shareholders until the creditors have been satisfied.

One of the commonest ways for companies, especially small, closely held companies, to come to an end is for the principals simply to neglect to file their annual report. In a registration jurisdiction, such as British Columbia, after a few years without annual reports, the corporation is simply taken off the registered list of companies, and that is the end of it. Some jurisdictions, notably Ontario and the federal government, have abolished the requirement that these annual reports be filed. In those jurisdictions, it is only necessary to report when changes are made in matters that were required to be filed in the original incorporating documents, and so automatic dissolution does not take place.

602533 Ontario Inc. v. Shell Canada Ltd.[22]

This action arose from a claim by the numbered company against Shell with respect to the installation of allegedly defective underground tanks. The plaintiff was seeking damages "for breach of contract, misrepresentation, deceit, breach of warranty, and negligent failure to warn and a declaration holding Shell responsible for any environmental damage caused by its conduct." Mr. John Pangos had been operating the service station in question through the numbered company for about five years, when it was discovered that the underground tanks were leaking. The company commenced the action against Shell in February 1990.

However, the numbered company used by Mr. Pangos to operate the gas station and bring this action had been dissolved by operation of law for non-compliance under the *Corporations Tax Act* in 1989. This was unknown to Mr. Pangos and was not remedied by reinstating the company until 1996. The point made by Shell in their application to dismiss this action was that at the time the statement of claim was

22. (1998) 155 D.L.R. (4th) 562 (Ont. C.A.)

issued, there was no 602533 Ontario Inc., and so, the non-existent company could not have commenced the action. To further complicate matters, the limitation period within which an action against Shell must have had to commence expired before the numbered company was reinstated.

The court dismissed the action against Shell, and that decision was upheld on appeal. The company could not bring an action against Shell when it was dissolved, and although the reinstatement of the company restored any rights that the company had when it was dissolved, that was subject to any rights that had been acquired by the other party during the dissolution period. The expiration of the limitation period was a right Shell had acquired after the plaintiff company was dissolved and could not be overcome by its reinstatement in 1996.

The case shows how careful business people must be to make sure they comply with government regulations. In this case, the consequence was dissolution of the company. Such a dissolved company no longer exists legally and loses the right to bring an action on its own behalf. The case also shows that such a dissolved company can be resurrected by following the appropriate procedure, but here, even that process could not overcome the consequences of allowing the company to become dissolved in the first place.

Often, when a company is to go out of business, a decision must be made whether to sell the shares of the company or sell the assets. If the shares are sold, the company continues as before. The debts and other obligations continue, but problems may arise if the purchaser decides to make changes in wages and contracts with suppliers. Because the corporation continues, the contracts stay in place and continue to bind the corporation even with new ownership. When the assets are sold, on the other hand, the purchaser is not affected by the contractual or other obligations of the company selling those assets, except if those assets are encumbered. If the asset in question has been used to secure a debt, that creditor has first claim against the asset, and any purchaser of the business would be well advised to search the title of the assets for such liens and charges before entering into the transaction.

Selling the shares or selling the assets

As explained in Chapter 10, some provinces have bulk sale statutes in place to protect creditors from the sale of all or substantially all the assets of the debtor. Any debts or other obligations that have been incurred by the selling company remain those of that company. After the assets are sold and the corporation no longer has a business, the company can be wound up.

Summary

Corporation
- A fiction or a myth that has a separate status as a legal person from the shareholders who make it up
- Methods of incorporation are registration, letters patent, and articles of incorporation
- Shareholders not liable for debts of company; they can only lose what they have invested (limited liability)
- Special statute corporations' capacity may be limited

- Funding may be derived from the selling of shares (which may be common shares or shares with special rights and restrictions); or through borrowing (which involves the sale of bonds and debentures, secured or unsecured)
- Broadly held corporations have more stringent government controls and greater reporting requirements than closely held corporations

Directors/officers

- Have a fiduciary duty
- Must act in the best interests of that corporation
- Must avoid conflicts of interest

Shareholders

- Very few duties to the corporation or other shareholders unless they have sufficient shares to be classed as insiders
- No right to sue the director when he or she acts carelessly or wrongfully in carrying out his or her duties
- In many jurisdictions, the shareholder can bring a derivative or representative action against the director on behalf of the corporation
- No right to dividends

Advantages of incorporation

- Limited liability
- Tax benefits
- Ease of transferring shares
- Separate management and ownership

Termination of corporation

- The corporation does not die with the death of shareholders

---

QUESTIONS

1. What is meant by a corporation having a separate legal identity?

2. Distinguish among companies that have been created by special acts of parliament, by royal charter, by registration, by letters patent, and by filing articles of incorporation.

3. Explain the significance of the memorandum of association in a registration jurisdiction. Contrast it with the articles of incorporation and the articles of association.

4. Explain how the liability of a shareholder is limited.

5. What is meant by a "preferred" share? Contrast this with the normal "common" share. Explain why the term "preferred shares" is misleading.

6. Explain why the concept of a par-value share is misleading and why such shares have declined in popularity.

7. Does a shareholder, whether preferred or common, have a right to a dividend? Explain.

8. What is the significant difference between a bondholder and a preferred shareholder, both of whom are entitled to a specified payment each year?

9. Distinguish between closely held and broadly held corporations and explain these differences in terms of the provisions in place in your jurisdiction.

10. Set out the nature of the duties owed by a director of a corporation. To whom are these duties owed? Who else in the corporate organization owes a similar duty?

11. Explain why it is becoming increasingly difficult to get prominent individuals to serve as directors of Canadian companies.

12. Explain any duties shareholders assume. Summarize the rights of the shareholders in relationship to other shareholders, the management, and directors of the corporation.

13. Explain what is meant by a proxy and why proxies can be so important at a corporation's annual general meeting.

14. Explain the advantages of free transferability of shares and how and why this right is often modified by shareholder agreement.

15. Set out and explain some of the disadvantages associated with the corporate method of carrying on business.

16. How can a corporation be terminated?

CASES

1. Re Graham and Technequip Limited

Graham was one of four shareholders in Technequip, and, according to the shareholders' agreement, he was a director and an employee as well. At one directors' meeting, the other three directors fired Graham from his position as director and from his employment. He retained only his status as a minority shareholder. What courses of action are available to Graham in these circumstances? Explain the likely outcome. How would your answer be affected by the knowledge that Graham was not adequately performing his duties as either employee or director and that the shareholders' agreement had a buyout provision Graham could have implemented but chose not to?

2. W. J. Christie & Co. Ltd. v. Greer

Greer was a longstanding employee of the plaintiff company W. J. Christie and had held the position of director and executive officer for 10 years. Greer left Christie and went on to establish his own company, Sussex Realty and Insurance Agency Limited. In the process, Greer approached several customers of Christie's and persuaded them to transfer their business to the new firm. In this action, W. J. Christie sued Greer for his conduct. Explain the arguments available to both parties and the nature of the compensation Christie would probably obtain, if successful.

3. Wedge v. McNeill

In this action, the appellants were directors and shareholders in the respondent company Hillcrest Housing Limited and, as such, had the right to vote at meetings of directors and shareholders. A bylaw of Hillcrest Housing Limited allowed the directors to vote in matters in which they had an interest after having made proper disclosure. The majority of the directors set up a company called Arcona Construction Limited which was fully owned by them. At various directors' meetings, after fully disclosing their various interests, they participated in the decision to direct considerable amounts of business to Arcona Construction Limited even though the directors representing minority shareholders, Richard and Mary Wedge, complained about this action and voted against it. Explain the nature of the complaint lodged by the Wedges, the arguments to be raised by both parties, and the probable outcome.

4. Re Keho Holdings Ltd. and Noble

Twenty investors came together and incorporated Keho Holdings Ltd., taking 100 shares each at one dollar a share. One member of that group, Oliver, voluntarily directed the company's affairs and did so very successfully, bringing the company's value up to $6 million. Oliver bought out some of the other shareholders and eventually acquired a 66 percent or greater controlling interest in the company. He then exercised control over those voting shares to his own personal advantage. The first complaint was that he used his position to structure the directors in such a way as to give him complete control over the company and its assets. He appointed himself, his two sons, and an ally, A. S. Cameron, as directors; the people representing the minority shareholders were completely frozen out. The second complaint was that Oliver had the shareholders grant him stock options for 12 500 shares of common stock priced at $1 per share. These shares were selling at $72 a share. This was supposedly done in recognition of his voluntary service to the company over the prior 25 years. The third complaint was that Oliver and the directors under his control voted to borrow $258 000 from the bank and then loaned that money to Gyron Petroleum Ltd. at 12-percent interest without any security. Gyron was Oliver's personal company.

Explain whether these complaints are valid and what course of action is available to the minority shareholders in these circumstances.

5. Mills-Hughes v. Raynor

Canadian Admiral Corporation Ltd. was a successful company until it was bought by York Lambdon Inc. from its previous parent company and brought under York's control. Admiral made significant loans against its assets to the point that when interest rates increased, they could not meet their obligations and went into receivership. They were forced into bankruptcy in 1981. Section 114 of the Canada *Business Corporations Act* governing this corporation holds the director of the corporation personally "liable to employees of the corporation for all debts not exceeding six months' wages ... for services performed for the corporation" while they were directors. The former employees of Admiral claimed against the directors personally for vacation pay, severance pay, and bonuses.

Discuss whether or not the directors are liable to pay these amounts. Would your answer be different if you understood that the bonus in question was a "guaranteed bonus of $3500 for the year 1981," and would it affect your answer to know that these parties appealing were all senior officers and managers of Admiral?

Property

Our legal system is often criticized for its historical preoccupation with property rights over other matters that might have been a greater concern of the law. Such property rights are normally a vital concern of business. Property is traditionally divided into personal property and real property. Chapter 15 examines personal property, including chattels (or movables) and intangibles or claims that one person may have against another. The rest of the chapter introduces real property, which concerns the rights of people in relation to land and things affixed to the land. Real property rights are examined generally, and the landlord and tenant relationship as well as mortgages are the concern of the rest of the chapter. Chapter 16 is devoted to a discussion of intellectual property, which, in modern times, has become a very important example of such intangible personal property. The final part of this chapter is an overview of insurance, which is often of vital importance where property considerations are involved.

PhotoDisc

CHAPTER 15

Personal and Real Property

CHAPTER HIGHLIGHTS

- Personal and real property: definitions and distinctions
- Bailment and its consequences
- Real property and ownership of land
- Landlord and tenant relationships
- Mortgages and their effect on real property

Property interests can be divided into real property and personal property. Intellectual property, which is separated for convenience, is in reality, a particular kind of personal property. The term "real property" means land and things affixed to it. Real property is immovable.

Mason v. Westside Cemeteries Ltd.[1]

Mr. Mason was a police officer in Ontario when his mother died in 1970. She was cremated, and Mr. Mason, being uncertain about his future plans, asked the funeral home to look after the ashes. They were placed in an urn and stored in their storeroom, pending further instructions. Several years later, his father died and was cremated, and the same funeral home was asked to look after both urns.

A few years later, he was informed that they could no longer keep the ashes, and arrangements were made to transfer them to the defendant Westminster Cemeteries Ltd. A fee was paid to the funeral home, which, in turn, paid Westminster Cemeteries for that purpose. Finally, in 1993, he decided on the final resting place for the remains and approached Westminster Cemeteries to make the transfer. The ashes could not be found. They had no record of them, and after an extensive search that included disinterring several crypts and examining the urns contained in them, it became clear that they would never be found. Mr. Mason sued, claiming that Westminster was a bailee, and the property had been lost due to their negligence. He was successful in the action, the court finding that Westminster Cemeteries Ltd. was indeed a bailee of these human remains, and, as such, they had a duty to show that the loss of the urns was not the result of any failure on their part to take reasonable care of them. Although they kept careful records, it was clear that someone had made a mistake, and so, they had failed in their duty as bailee and were liable for the loss. Mr. Mason had claimed $50 000 in damages, but the judge had difficulty placing a value on human remains. The court only awarded nominal damages for the loss of the urns, but the plaintiff was awarded $1000 damage for his mental suffering.

1. ? 135 D.L.R. (4th) 361 (Ont. Gen. Div.)

The defendants had been entrusted to care for items of property that were not theirs, making them a bailee with the special obligations that bailment imposes. This introduces the concept of property and the responsibilities imposed on those charged with looking after it. Both personal and real property and the obligations associated with it will be discussed below.

Introduction

While people usually think of property as a physical object, such as a boat, car, or land, "property," more correctly, refers to the relationship existing between the item and the individual who owns it. When a person says he owns a boat, it is descriptive of the nature of the interest he has in the boat rather than the boat itself, and this distinction must be kept in mind as we examine the nature of the different interests in property. Although ownership or title is the highest form of property right to a particular item, other lesser forms of interest are also possible. In our legal system, ownership or title can be separate from possession. Thus, one person might be in possession of something that belongs to someone else.

Ownership and possession separated

Personal property, on the other hand, is movable and can be divided into two categories.

Chattels are tangible personal property, consisting of movables that can be measured and weighed. An intangible right is a claim one person has against another, such as a claim for debt, and is called a **chose in action**, which is, in effect, a right to sue. Bonds, share certificates, and negotiable instruments are examples of choses in action.

Chattel—tangible property

Chose in action—intangible

A special category of intangible personal property is now called **intellectual property: copyright** gives an author control over the use and reproduction of his or her work; **patent** gives an inventor the right to profit from his or her inventions; **trademarks** protect the name or logo of a business; industrial designs, **confidential information,** and **trade secrets** are all examples of intellectual property.

Intellectual property deals with ideas and creative work

The first section of this chapter is devoted to tangible personal property, followed by an introduction to real property. Intellectual property is discussed in Chapter 16, with a concluding discussion of insurance.

A Taxi License Is Personal Property

Foster had a taxi license that he used as security in financial arrangements with several different people. These four creditors all claimed priority with respect to that license. The court held that although the license was subject to regulation, it still represented a valuable asset, and therefore it was a form of intangible personal property known as a chose in action. The security aspects of this case were discussed in some detail in Chapter 10.

Re Foster, (1992) 89 D.L.R. (4th) 555 (Ont. Gen. Div.)

Personal Property

Chattels

Chattels are movables, such as baggage, clothes, radios, animals, and boats. Even construction cranes and locomotives are chattels. **Real property**, on the other hand, is land and things fixed or attached to the land. A chattel can become part of the real property when it is attached to the land, and this can lead to a conflict with respect

Chattels are movable things

Things fixed to the land become real property

Chattels attached become part of the real property

to who has first claim to it. When a person buys and installs a furnace or a hot water heater in their home, the item that was a chattel becomes a **fixture**. Who has first claim will usually be determined by who installed the item, for what purpose, and to what degree it is affixed. If after buying a new hot water tank, Gauthier loses the house because he cannot make his mortgage payments, the mortgagee would only have a claim to the hot water tank if the default took place after it had been installed. It then has become part of the real property.

The owner of the land is free to remove a chattel that has become a fixture (severance) just as he or she was able to fix the chattel to the land in the first place. Difficulty arises when third parties, such as creditors or tenants, become involved and claim the property. Generally, when a chattel has been affixed to real property, it becomes part of that real property and cannot be removed. However, if a tenant of a commercial property attaches fixtures to enhance trade or carry on business, he or she has the right to remove those trade fixtures when leaving. In residential or commercial tenancies, non-trade fixtures attached for the comfort, convenience, or taste of the tenant, such as mirrors or paintings, can also be removed.

Trade fixtures can be removed by tenant

Of course, when those fixtures have been incorporated into the property in such a way that they clearly are intended to stay or where their removal will cause damage, they must stay.

In any case, these fixtures can only be removed during the term of the tenancy. When the tenant moves out at the end of the tenancy and takes the mirrors, light fixtures, rugs, and display cases that had been installed by the tenant, the landlord has no complaint. But if the tenant comes back for them after the landlord has retaken possession, it is too late. Those fixtures have become part of the property of the landowner. Of course, any provisions in the lease to the contrary override these general provisions.

Finders Keepers

A finder gets good title against all but original owner

When a person finds a watch or ring in a park, they have the right to that item against everyone except a prior owner. If that finder were to hand it to the police or the lost-and-found centre and the rightful owner could not be found, that finder would be entitled to it. Only the rightful owner or someone having a proprietary interest in it, such as a secured creditor, could demand it from the finder.

However, these rights may be different, depending on where the item was found. When found by someone on private property, the owner of the property is generally entitled to the item. But if found in an area frequented by the public, such as a store or mall, the finder has priority. If the finder is an employee of the property owner, the employer has the right to the chattel, no matter where on the property it was found. Whether the finder is the person entitled to the item or the owner of the property on which it was found, there is also an obligation, however slight, to return those goods in good condition to the proper owner. This obligation is based on the law of bailment.

Bailment

Amo Containers Ltd. v. Mobil Oil Canada, Ltd.[2]

In this case, Amo supplied containers to Mobil, which used them to transport goods to the oil rigs off the east coast of Canada. The particular containers in question were

2. (1989) 62 D.L.R. (4th) 104 (Nfld. C.A.)

being transported when the vessel sank with the loss of all on board. In this action, Amo, as bailor, was suing Mobil, as bailee, for the loss of its containers.

The court found, as a matter of law, that Mobil would be liable if it could be shown it was negligent. However, the court also found that, as a general rule, such negligence is presumed, and it is up to the bailee to show that there was no negligence. Since the goods were in the company's care and keeping, the onus was on it to show that there was no negligence. The one exception to this is when the bailee no longer exists and the goods are lost. The bailee, Mobil, still existed, and since an inquiry was going on, there was information available to establish whether the company was negligent or not. The onus, therefore, was still on Mobil to prove that it was not negligent.

This case is illustrative of bailment in several ways. First, it shows that bailment applies when personal property is used, even on a large scale, such as containers; and second, it shows that the principles can be quite significant in commercial relationships. Here, the bailment was one for value, and the obligation was on the bailee (the person or company holding the goods) to establish they were not negligent. It could not do so, and Mobil was liable for the loss.

A bailment exists when one person takes temporary possession of personal property owned by another. The owner giving up possession is called the **bailor** and the person acquiring possession the **bailee**. Although chattels are usually involved, intangibles, such as bonds, share certificates or negotiable instruments can also be the subject of a bailment. For a bailment to take place, the property must be delivered by the bailor to the bailee, making it clear that that the possession is only to be temporary, with the chattel to be returned at the end of the bailment period.

Bailment created by giving goods to bailee

Determining whether the goods have been delivered is not as easy as it may seem. When a car is left in a parking lot and the keys given to the attendant, a bailment has taken place because control and possession have been given to the car lot. But when a person drives onto a lot, parks the car, and takes the keys, there is no bailment. This is just a license to use the parking space, and the control and possession of the car stay with the driver. During the bailment, the title to the goods remains with the bailor, and only the possession goes to the bailee. Normally, a bailee cannot give the goods to someone else (a sub-bailment), unless there is permission to do so or where it is the custom of the industry, as might be the case if automobile repairs requiring the services of different specialists are involved.

When fungibles, such as timber, oil, and wheat, are placed in the care of a bailee, they can become indistinguishable from similar items being stored for others. In fact, the exact goods need not be returned, only goods of a similar quality and quantity. This situation is still a bailment and is treated under bailment law.

With fungibles, the same goods need not be returned

The primary concern of bailment law is the liability of bailees for damage done to goods in their care. Bailees are responsible for any wilful, negligent, or fraudulent acts of themselves or their employees' that cause injury or damage to the goods, although the standard of care used in establishing that negligence will vary with the type of bailment created.

Bailment For Value

Bailments are either gratuitous or for value. Bailment for value involves a mutual benefit or consideration flowing between the parties. Usually, the relationship is commercial, and the bailor pays the bailee to repair, store, or transport the goods. But

Bailee has a duty to care for the goods

Bailment for value—both parties receive benefit

Duty—reasonable person caring for own goods

a bailment for value can also arise where a friend stores something, such as a piano, for another in exchange for the right to use it. The standard of care required in such circumstances is simply the ordinary standard for negligence—that is, the amount of care that would be expected from a prudent person looking after his or her own goods in similar circumstances.

Thus, the amount of care that should be exercised will vary with both the value of the goods and their nature. More care would be expected where delicate or valuable items were involved, such as china or a rare violin, but where heavy-duty machines were being stored, the standard of care would be much lower.

Standard of Care

Duty may be determined by contract or common practice

If the bailment is based on a commercial relationship, the provisions of the contract and industry practice will be taken into consideration in determining the standard of care required. In the *Amo Containers* case, the standard of care imposed on Mobil would be based on the customs and traditions of the industry, but there was a complication in that instance. The containers were lost, and only Mobil was in a position to determine what had happened. The onus was, therefore, reversed, and Mobil had to prove that they were not negligent. Reversing the onus in this way is rarely done in our legal system, but with bailment, the bailee who has the care of the goods is often the only one who can establish what happened. This was also the situation in the *Mason* case used to open this chapter.

Exemption Clauses

Exculpatory clauses may limit liability

Contracts of bailment often contain exculpatory or exemption clauses which limit the liability of the bailee. An example of such a clause is, "Goods left on the premises are entirely at the risk of the owner. The proprietor assumes no responsibility for any loss, whether caused by damage, loss, or theft of those goods." The parties are free to include such clauses, but as was discussed in Chapter 7, courts interpret them narrowly, since they favour one side. To be enforceable, such clauses must be clear and brought to the attention of the customer at the time they enter into the contract.

Common Carriers

Common carrier has duty of insurer

A particularly heavy standard of care is imposed on innkeepers and "common carriers" (trucking and bus companies, railroads, airlines, and even pipelines). Common carriers must be distinguished from private companies or individuals that transport for a particular bailor. These private carriers are merely bailees for a reward and have the obligation of a reasonably prudent person in the circumstances. A common carrier offers transport services to the public generally and undertakes the standard of an insurer, which means that if the goods are damaged or destroyed while in its care, the carrier is liable even when the damage was not caused by its negligence. But even a common carrier will not be liable when the damage was beyond its control, as when the goods deteriorate because of some inherent problem or because the packaging provided by the shipper is inadequate. If an animal dies in transit because of a previously contracted disease or goods are destroyed by spontaneous combustion, there is no liability. A common carrier is also not liable where the damage is caused by an act of war or some condition of nature, such as flood or earthquake. Most common carriers limit their liability by contract and include a term such as "Not responsible for lost or stolen goods or damage over $500." Again, to be valid and binding on both parties, such a provision must be clearly brought to the attention of the shipper at the time the contract is entered into. Common carriers are usually controlled by statutory provisions regulating their industry.

Innkeeper's Liability

In common law, innkeepers are also treated like insurers and responsible for the lost or stolen goods of a guest, unless it can be shown that they were lost because of some act of God or negligence on the part of the guest. To succeed, the guest must show that the establishment qualifies as an inn offering both food and temporary lodging (transient-type accommodation).

Innkeeper has duty of an insurer

Most jurisdictions have significantly reduced the innkeepers liability by statute so that they are only liable when it can be proven that they or their servants have been negligent or acted wilfully. This protection is only available to the innkeeper when the act is properly complied with, which normally requires that copies of selected sections of the act be posted in every bedroom and public room and the office of the inn or hotel. When this is not done, the higher common law liability of the innkeeper (that of an insurer) prevails. In the case of Ontario, they have simply limited the innkeeper's common law liability to $40. Most statutes require the innkeeper to accept a guest's valuables and put them in a secure place assuming liability for them.

Liability may be reduced by statute

The law of bailment involves all those situations where one person's property is left in the care of another. From a business point of view, this affects not only service industries, such as restaurants and hotels, but also repairers, mechanics, and transporters of goods. Business people face a high standard of care towards these goods, and it is wise to both insure against loss and limit liability through use of an exculpatory clause included in the service contract or posted so that it is clearly visible on the premises.

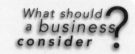

Gratuitous Bailment

A gratuitous bailment occurs when only one side receives a benefit. When the bailee receives the benefit, as when a friend borrows your car, the standard of care imposed is very high, and liability will be imposed even when the bailee has been only slightly careless. On the other hand, when it is the bailor who receives the benefit, as when you store furniture as a favour for a friend, the bailee is only liable if there has been gross negligence. Note, however, that courts today seem to be moving towards imposing the normal definitions and tests for negligence and standards of care, requiring a higher standard of care for the bailee, even when the benefit of the bailment is for the bailor.

Gratuitous bailment

• when bailee benefits, duty high

• when bailor benefits, duty less

It is also important to note that in a bailment action unlike a normal negligence action, the onus of proof shifts to the bailee. In these cases, once the bailment has been established and damage to the goods has been shown, the bailee is obligated to show that he or she was not negligent towards the goods belonging to the bailor.

Involuntary Bailment

McCarthy v. Matthews[3]

Mrs. McCarthy's mother owned the house in question and allowed Mrs. McCarthy and her husband to stay in it as long as they made the mortgage payments every month. Unfortunately, Mrs. McCarthy separated from her husband, and they left the house, making no further payments and leaving all her furniture and appliances in the house. When the mortgage was not paid, the mortgagee brought proceedings to foreclose, which eventually led to the house being sold. Mrs. McCarthy had, in the meantime, returned to the house to get her furniture and appliances, but the locks had been changed and she could not get in. The real estate agent

3. [1988] B.C.D.Civ. 2768-01 (B.C. Prov. Ct.)

involved in the sale had also informed the mortgagee about Mrs. McCarthy's belongings in the house and had offered to store them for her. That offer and advice were ignored, and when the cleaning crew came to prepare the house for sale, the mortgagee simply told them to discard the items. There were just a few things left, when Mrs. McCarthy requested the return of her belongings from the new owner. She refused to take the remnants and sued several people but was only successful against the mortgagee.

The court held that the mortgagee was an involuntary bailee "and was therefore under duty to exercise that degree of diligence which men of common prudence generally exercised about their own affairs." When the mortgagee treated the property as abandoned and told the purchaser the goods were abandoned, they had failed in this duty and were liable for Mrs. McCarthy's loss. Mrs. McCarthy was also held contributorily negligent because she had failed to take the few remaining goods when she had the chance. Her damages were, therefore, reduced by that value.

This decision was from a lower court but nicely illustrates the various levels of duty that different categories of bailees have. This case involved an involuntary bailee, and so, the duty was minimal and yet was still breached by the mortgagee.

Involuntary bailment—duty low

When someone leaves a coat in a restaurant or at a friend's home or you pick up a watch you have found on the sidewalk, an involuntary bailment has been created. The consent needed for a bailment relationship in these circumstances is established when you pick up the watch or in any way exercise some control over the goods. As soon as you exercise that control, the obligations of a gratuitous bailee for the benefit of the bailor arise, and you have a duty to take care of those goods. If someone were to walk by and in the course of a conversation with you and leave their coat on your fence, you would have no obligation until you move the coat. By picking it up, you exercise control over it and thereby assume the responsibility to look after the coat. Your responsibility as bailee is to keep the coat safe and return it to the bailor. Generally speaking, if the goods are returned to the wrong person, the bailee is responsible.

The Position of the Bailee

Contract terms prevail

The terms set out in the contract govern a bailment for value. Such provisions as the terms of payment, the requirement of insurance, and any exculpatory clauses are binding if they have been properly brought to the attention of the parties. An unpaid bailee has a common law right to a lien if he has repaired or otherwise worked on the goods, but there is no corresponding common law lien where the goods are just stored, as with a warehouse, or transported. Today, statutes have been passed, giving common carriers, repairpersons, storage facilities, and other bailees for value the right to retain the goods until payment is arranged. This statutory lien includes a right to resell, after giving the bailor appropriate notice, and an opportunity to reclaim the goods. When it is the bailor who has not been paid, as with rented tools or furniture, they can reclaim their goods and seek normal contractual remedies. Where no price has been agreed upon, the bailor is entitled to recover a reasonable payment on the basis of the principle of *quantum meruit*, as discussed in Chapter 7. Where consumers are involved, care must be taken to adhere to the consumer protection legislation, as discussed in Chapter 8.

Except where modified by statute

Real Property

Land Titles System Different from Registry System

Mr. Hill was a bad credit risk and had been turned down by Paramount Life Insurance Company when he tried to obtain a loan through a mortgage on the house that he and his wife owned. He then sold the property to his business partner and had his partner arrange for a loan with Paramount Life Insurance Company on the basis of a mortgage on the property. This mortgage was granted. The problem was that he had not obtained his wife's consent for the sale but had forged her signature on the documents. Neither the business partner nor the life insurance company knew this fact. Shortly after this transaction, Hill died. Because Paramount was not receiving mortgage payments, it foreclosed. It was then that Mrs. Hill found out what her husband had done. She fought the foreclosure action on the basis of her late husband's fraud, claiming she was entitled to the property. Because the court action took place in a land titles jurisdiction where the Torrens System (see later in this chapter) of land registry was in place and because the partner and Paramount were innocent of any wrongdoing, the court found that the business partner had obtained good title to the property and that the mortgage granted was good. The government, through the local Land Titles Office, had granted a certificate of title to the land to the partner. This certificate determines ownership against all other parties. Mrs. Hill was the victim of her husband's fraud and lost the property. This case illustrates the significance of the difference between the land titles system of registration used in some parts of Canada and the system of land registry used in the rest of the country. In the land titles system, a certificate of title which establishes ownership of the property is granted. Such a certificate had been issued to the business partner in this case. This chapter explores real property interests, which are created under these two systems as well as landlord/tenant and mortgage law.

Paramount Life Insurance Co., v. Hill (1986) 34 D.L.R. (4th) 150 (Alta. C.A.)

The need to understand the law of real property (land and buildings) extends beyond business relationships because accommodation is one of life's essentials. Whether shelter is obtained through ownership, rental, or even squatting, the relationships created are governed by real property law. Businesses also need accommodation, either rented or owned, and a significant industry has developed to serve the property needs of business, that is, the provision and management of space and the purchase and sale of property. There are several ways a businessperson can become involved with the use, possession, and ownership of real property, whether for investment or business purposes. The material in the rest of this chapter is necessarily abbreviated, but it will serve as an introduction to the most significant aspects of the law of real property: interests in land and their transfer, landlord and tenant relationships, and mortgages.

Legal Interests in Land

Real Property

The term "real property" includes land and anything affixed to it, such as buildings and chattels that are permanently attached. As far as the areas above and below the surface are concerned, only the portion that the owner can permanently use or

Real property is land or anything attached to land

occupy is now considered part of that property, and even this space will probably be restricted by local zoning regulations. A landowner has no complaint when an airplane flies over the property, but power lines or an overhanging building that permanently incur into this air space would give rise to a right to sue. As for the sub-surface rights, usually the Crown has retained the mineral rights, and the oil and gas rights. Property owners generally have no complaint when these rights are granted to others, and mine tunnels or oil wells are developed under their property. In these cases, the property owner is entitled to compensation for surface disturbance, in the form of access roads, shafts, and so on, but not to a share of the profits coming from the minerals, oil, or gas.

Interest in Land. The current law of real property is rooted in the ancient feudal system of England, in which people held rather than owned their land. The

All land owned by Crown

king actually owned the land, and the right to possession of it, called an **estate in land,** was granted on the basis of some obligation of service to the king. The original estates in land, which were numerous and based on the type of obligation owed to the king, have been reduced to a few significant types, known today as estates in fee simple, life estates, and leasehold estates.

Fee Simple. The greatest interest a person can have in land today and what we think of as ownership is an estate in fee simple. Although the Crown (the federal or provincial government) technically still owns the land, a fee simple estate gives

Fee simple comparable with ownership

the right to use or sell the land subject only to any local restrictions which have been imposed by agreement or legislation. This right to sell the land free from interference is why we consider fee simple equivalent to ownership in Canada today.

Still, the "owner" of land is subject to government and municipal regulations with respect to what the property can be used for, the nature and description of the buildings that can be erected on it, and the health, sanitary, and appearance standards to be maintained. The property may even be expropriated under certain circumstances.

Life Estate. Whereas a fee simple estate can be inherited, a life estate is more restrictive and cannot be willed to others. Both types of estate give exclusive possession of the property to the holder, but upon the death of the life tenant, the

Life estate divides fee simple

property reverts back to the original owner of the fee simple or that owner's heirs. This right to take back the property or **reversionary interest** may be transferred to a third party, who is then called the **remainderman** and has a right to the remainder of the fee simple after the death of the life tenant. Life estates are not particularly common in Canada and are usually used to ensure that some member of the family, such as a spouse, is cared for to the end of their life. The holder of a life estate has special responsibilities and must pay for normal upkeep, pay fees and taxes, and not commit "waste"—that is, not do anything to harm the value of the reversionary interest, such as cut down trees or damage the house.

In many provinces interests, such as life estates, are created through the operation of law. **Dower rights** were intended to protect women who lost any individual

Dower and homestead rights protect spouse

claim to property when they married. Dower provided the wife a one-third interest in the husband's land as a matter of right, but this also interfered with the free transferability of property. Dower rights were also lost when the couple divorced. Because of these and other problems, dower rights have been modified or, in most provinces, abolished altogether. Today, these rights are protected in most provinces by **homestead rights**[4] or in family law statutes that give the spouse a claim to a substantial portion of all family assets in the case of marriage breakdown.[5] These family law considerations are beyond the scope of this text but can have a significant impact on business people.

Leasehold Estates.   Fee simple estates and life estates are described as freehold estates because a person has exclusive possession of the property for an indeterminate time. Leasehold estates or leases are limited to a specific period of time, after which the property reverts back to the landowner. These leases may be short or long term (99 years) and may also be a periodic tenancy. This means that there is no definite termination date; rather, the term is an automatically renewable monthly or yearly tenancy, as when a person rents an apartment on a month-to-month basis without a lease. The tenancy arrangement continues until the landlord or tenant notifies the other that it is to end. This topic of leasehold interests is generally called landlord and tenant law and will be discussed in a separate section of this chapter.

Leasehold estates determined by time

• but may also be periodic

Lesser Interests in Land

Wells v. Wells[6]

The defendant and his brother, the plaintiff's father, obtained adjacent tracts of land under the *Veterans Land Act* in 1950 and 1957, respectively. The plaintiff inherited his property from his father in 1983. The defendant's only access to the property was across the plaintiff's land, which they had walked and driven across since 1950, seven years before the plaintiff's father had acquired it. This access had continued unabated for 40 years. Unfortunately, the plaintiff's property only had a 60-foot road frontage, and the access road of the defendant ran diagonally across that frontage area, making it useless for anything else.

The plaintiff now had an offer for the property conditional upon being able to relocate the defendant's access road so that it would go down the side of the narrow frontage section rather than diagonally, leaving room to construct a house. The defendant refused to give permission for the change, and this action was brought to ask the court to order such a change to be made. The court refused, finding that since the defendant had been using that access to property openly for 40 years and in a way adverse to the plaintiff, he had gained a right of way across that land by prescription. The court went so far as to agree with the defendant that the plaintiff's actions amounted to a trespass and awarded $2000 in damages. This case illustrates the nature of a right of way where one person has a right to cross another's property to get access to his own. This is a form of easement and is an important interest in land. This case also illustrates that it is possible to obtain such a right of way in many jurisdictions by prescription, which means by continuous use over a significant period of time.

4. *Homesteads Act*, 1989, S.S. 1989–90, c. H-5.1
5. *Family Relations Act*, R.S.B.C. 1996, c. 128, s. 56
6. (1994) 116 D.L.R. (4th) 524 (N.S.S.C.)

Easement gives right to use of land—not possession

Unlike freehold and leasehold, there are several lesser interests in land that do not convey the right to exclusive possession of the property. An **easement** gives a person the right to use a portion of another's land, usually for a particular purpose. The **right of way** is one of the most common forms of easement that allows a person to cross another's land, usually to get to their own property or to reach another point of interest, such as a lake or the sea. As illustrated by *Wells v. Wells* case discussed above, the owner of the property cannot interfere with the right of the holder of an easement to cross his property, but it should also be noted that the person with the right of way cannot stop, park his car, or build some permanent structure on the property. The property that has the advantage of the right of way is called the **dominant property,** and the property subject to it is called the **servient property**. Another form of easement involves a permanent incursion onto the property, where, for example, someone has been given permission to have part of a building hang over onto the neighbour's property. Interests like easements are created where power lines, sewer pipes, and other public utilities interfere with private property. These restrictions on the use of land are not easements in a true sense because there is no dominant tenement. They are created by statutes and impose similar rights and responsibilities and are sometimes called public easements.

Must be dominant and servient tenement

Property rights may be acquired by prescription

Other lesser interests in land include **licenses,** where a person is given permission to use another's land and which can be revoked at any time. Where such use continues unabated over a long period of time, in some provinces, this can become a permanent enforceable right as illustrated by the right of way obtained in the *Wells v. Wells* case discussed above. Acquiring such a right over property through use is called an **easement acquired by prescription** and to avoid this happening, the landowner must periodically exercise some control over the portion of land in question, such as blocking off public access from time to time.

—or by adverse possession

A right to actual possession of land can be acquired in the same way. This is called acquiring possession through **adverse possession** and occurs when someone has had possession of land for a number of years in an open and notorious fashion, tolerated by the actual owner. Several Canadian jurisdictions, specifically those using a land titles system, have abolished both the right to an easement by prescription and the right to acquire land by adverse possession.[7]

Mineral Claim Right in Property

Tener's predecessors in title obtained a right to the mineral claims on certain lands in British Columbia in 1937. These lands were later incorporated into a park—at first a class B park and then a class A park. The park's designation prohibited the development of lands within it, except where it would benefit the park. Tener, with others, applied for a permit to operate the mineral claims and was refused. They then applied for compensation for expropriation. This required the court to determine the nature of the mineral rights that were owned. The court found that they were a *profit à prendre*. The Supreme Court decided that this was an interest in land giving them rights to minerals below the land and a right to interfere with the surface of the land as much as needed to extract the minerals. When the permit was denied, this was a form of expropriation for which they were entitled to compensation.

The Queen in Right of British Columbia v. Tener et al., 17 D.L.R. (4th) 1 (S.C.C.)

7. *Land Title Act*, R.S.B.C. 1996, c. 250 s. 24

Another lesser interest in land involves contracts to take trees, gravel, soil, peat, sand, or some other valuable commodity from the land. These are referred to as a **profit à prendre.**

Another important right is a **restrictive covenant**. When someone sells land to another, they can place restrictions on the use of that land that will bind all subsequent holders. These restrictive covenants are typically restrictions as to the type of buildings that can be put on the property relating to their height, shape, and style, restrictions as to how the property may be used, such as for residential, commercial, or light industrial, and restrictions as to who can own the property, including prohibitions against children or specifying religious or racial qualifications. These latter discriminatory restrictions are often invalid, being prohibited under the provincial human rights law.

Restrictive covenant may bind future owners

Although these are lesser interests in land, they run with the land, meaning that they are tied to the property itself rather than to the owner of it and bind not only on the original purchasers but also any subsequent owners. They are better viewed as an interest in land rather than as a simple contractual relationship, and so, the rule of privity of contract does not apply.

For such restrictions to bind subsequent owners of the property, they must be negative rather than positive obligations. Thus, a requirement that no building over three stories be constructed on the property is a negative covenant and will bind future owners but requiring that a building be built within a certain time period imposes a positive obligation to do something and will only bind the initial purchaser. A **building scheme** involves the same restrictive covenants being placed on all the properties in a large development. Building schemes take on many of the attributes of zoning bylaws because the developers have imposed basic rules governing the construction and use of property in the development, just as a municipality would normally do through zoning bylaws.

Tenancy in Common and Joint Tenancy

When people own property together in a tenancy in common, they both have an undivided half interest in the land. The two share the property, and if one dies, that person's heirs inherit their interest. People can also share ownership of property in a joint tenancy relationship, but here, if one dies, the other will be left with the whole property. In effect, both individuals own the entire property outright, and when one dies the survivor continues to own the entire property. Where one joint owner of property dies, there is no inheritance, which avoids many of the problems encountered when property becomes part of the estate, such as probate fees and estate taxes. This is why joint tenancy is so attractive to couples holding property together.

Owning property together may be joint or in common

Only joint ownership creates right of survivorship

Where property is owned jointly and one of the parties does not want the other to get their interest, it is possible to "sever" the joint tenancy. Severance must take place before death and is accomplished by one of the parties acting towards the property in some way that is inconsistent with the joint tenancy continuing. Selling their interest in the property to a third party, for instance, would sever the joint tenancy, creating a tenancy in common between the other party and that purchaser. Creditors can also bring applications to the court to partition or sever a joint tenancy so that the debtor's half of the property can be sold to pay the debt.

Joint tenancy can be severed

To avoid the creation of a joint tenancy, terms such as "held jointly" or "joint ownership" should not be used in the title document. When such words do not appear, the creation of a tenancy in common is presumed.

Tompkins Estate v. Tompkins[8]

Mr. and Mrs. Tompkins owned their matrimonial home together as joint tenants. Unfortunately, their marriage broke down, and several times they discussed the sale of the home as they negotiated the settlement of their affairs. Their respective lawyers even wrote to each other "without prejudice," discussing the division of property, including the sale of the house. But before any of these matters could be finally settled, Mr. Tompkins died, and this action was brought to determine whether Mrs. Tompkins was still entitled to the house by right of survivorship.

The court held that the joint tenancy had not been severed and that Mrs. Tompkins was entitled to Mr. Tompkin's interest in the home. It is possible for a joint tenancy to be changed to a tenancy in common, but it requires that the property be transferred or that there be an agreement to that effect between the parties. In this case, there was no transfer of the property, even though a sale was contemplated, and although an agreement was being negotiated, it had not been completed when Mr. Tompkins died. An intention to sever had been demonstrated, but no severance had, in fact, taken place by the time of his death.

This case clearly shows the effect of a joint tenancy and how the surviving joint tenant acquires the other joint tenant's interest in the property upon the death. It also shows the danger of sharing interests in land in this way and how it can be changed if the parties wish. But the change from a joint tenancy to a tenancy in common requires some positive action on the part of the parties, and a demonstrated intention to do so is not good enough.

What should a business consider?

Shared property can be both a boon and a thorn in the side of the people who own it and those they deal with. Partners often find it efficient to own business property jointly so that if one dies the other acquires the whole property without having to deal with the estate or face government taxes. On the other hand, when a creditor is faced with property owned jointly or in common with someone else, it can be difficult to deal with the property, to realize on the security, or to enforce a judgment. The difficulty increases for creditors significantly when the property is shared by spouses, only one of whom owes the money. Great care should be taken to understand exactly what the rights of all the parties are when transactions involving such shared property interests are involved. For instance, it may be very attractive for partners to own assets jointly, but where this is the case and a person dies, that property does not go to his estate and is not available to his heirs. That may be an appropriate result if planned for and other arrangements are made to provide for the family, but it may be a tragedy if the implications of such a relationship were not fully understood.

Other Interests in Land

Option gives right to purchase

When an offer is made for the purchase of land, like other offers, it can be revoked at any point before acceptance. Such an offer can be made irrevocable when the offeree pays some additional consideration to keep the offer open for a specified period. This is called an **option agreement,** and when land is involved, it conveys with it significant rights, giving the offeree a right to purchase the land at a specified price, which can, in turn, be sold to someone else. When land is leased and

8. (1993) 99 D.L.R. (4th) 193 (B.C.C.A.)

improvements made, the lease agreement will often contain an option to purchase, but this option agreement must be registered to be effective against outsiders who may subsequently purchase the property.

When a person purchases land, paying for it by a series of installments, the transaction involved is often an **agreement for sale**. The agreement is secured by caveat, since the conveyance of the title is delayed until the last payment is made. This is much like a conditional sale of personal property, and in the event of a default, the seller can reclaim the land that he has title to. In the interim, the agreement for sale bestows a significant interest in the property on the purchaser, including the right of possession. Upon final payment, the purchaser can require transfer of the title, obtaining full ownership of the property.

Security given through mortgage or agreement for sale

A more common way of financing the purchase of property is through a **mortgage**. The creditor lends the borrower money to make the purchase, and the title of the property is conveyed (transferred) to the moneylender as security, to be reconveyed upon receipt of the last payment. Mortgages are not restricted to financing the purchase of property but are used to secure loans for any purpose. Because the use of mortgages is so common and important, special rules have been developed, and these will be examined in more detail in a separate section of this chapter.

Transfer and Registration of Interest in Land

Historically, land was transferred by grant. The document used to accomplish this transfer had to be under seal and was called a **deed of conveyance**, now shortened simply to deed. A problem with this system was that there was no way to keep track of the various deeds that would accumulate with respect to a particular property over the years. It was impossible to be certain that good title to the property had been transferred by the most current deed, without inspection of all the past documents. Two different solutions to this problem were developed, and either one or the other has been adopted in different jurisdictions in Canada.

Grants give title to property

Both systems require the registration of documents, but in most jurisdictions in Canada, the registration process does not affect the rights of the parties, which are determined by the registered documents. This is called the **registration system**, the registry being merely a repository of documents and providing assurance to the parties that they will not be affected by any unregistered documents. The purchaser must still "search the title" by examining the title documents and establishing a chain of valid deeds to determine whether the seller has good title. This usually means going back over the documents for a set period of time (40 years in Ontario) to make sure no mistakes have been made. Anything before that period is presumed to be correct.

Registration imposed to assist ascertaining title

The western provinces, New Brunswick, and some areas of Ontario, Nova Scotia, and Manitoba have taken the registry system one step further and adopted a **land titles system,** where the title to real property is guaranteed. In this system, once registration has taken place in a central registry, a certificate of title is created and registered that is binding on all parties. The government guarantees that the information on that certificate of title is correct. This information sets out the declared owner of the property as well as any mortgages, easements, or other interests that might be held by others. The key to understanding this system is that the certificate of title determines the interest of the parties listed on it to the land specified.

Some provinces guarantee title

9. R.S.B.C. 1996, c. 250 s. 23 (2)

For example, in British Columbia, the *Land Titles Act*[9] states that the **certificate of title** is conclusive evidence in any court that the person named on the certificate is the holder in fee simple of that property and that is the end to the matter. For this reason, in the example used to introduce real property, Mrs. Hill was not able to retain the property. Even though she was innocent and her signature had been forged, a certificate of title had been issued to Mr. Hill's partner, and this certificate extinguished any claim she had to the property. Both systems require registration, but in the registration system, it is up to the parties to sort out the legal relationships derived from those registered documents, whereas in the land titles system, the certificate of title determines the interests.

In both registry and land titles systems, great strides are being made to modernize the process using advanced data compilation technologies. This has already introduced significant changes in data storage, and more changes can be expected in the future. One very important change is in the process of filing the documents, which now can be done electronically.

Condominium Legislation

Condominium legislation allows vertical title

Condominium interest involves some shared property

Because traditional real property law did not recognize the difference between the land and the buildings affixed to it, it was incapable of handling the modern practice of creating ownership in suites stacked vertically in an apartment building or attached town houses. All the Canadian provinces have passed legislation allowing fee simple interest in individual units in a condominium structure. But because condominium ownership also involves a form of common ownership, many unique rights and responsibilities apply. Although individuals may own their separate units, all common areas, such as the halls, reception areas, and laundry facilities are owned in common.

The condominium association is a corporate body and functions in a way similar to a municipality, company, or society, holding regular meetings with each member (those owning apartments in the development) having a vote. Bylaws are passed that outline the rights and duties of members. These bylaws can often create hardship where rules are put in place that interfere with what would normally be considered a right of ownership, such as prohibitions on pets or children. The

Rules must be obeyed and fees paid

condominium association will also levy a fee on each member to pay for such things as repairs, the cost of management, and other services. If these fees are not paid, the condominium corporation has a right to place a lien on the title of the member and force a sale, if necessary, to recover the funds. When unexpected repairs occur, these fees or levies can be substantial. In British Columbia, there has been a particular problem with "leaky condos," the repair of which has required many condominium owners to pay levies sometimes in excess of $50 000, causing many to lose their homes. Each member of the condominium owns his or her own suite and the normal rules of real property apply; the suites can be sold, mortgaged, or rented, but the interest the member has in the common area goes with that conveyance and so do the responsibilities associated with it.

Apartments can be owned through cooperatives

A **cooperative** is a less common method of acquiring accommodation. Like with a condominium, all the members of a cooperative have shares in the apartment building. However, their rights to their individual suites are based on the terms of the contract and the bylaws of the cooperative, as opposed to a specific real property interest in the suite itself. In this case, the real property interest in all the suites and the common areas is held by the cooperative, which is a company composed of the members holding shares in it and the members do not have title to the specific suite that they occupy.

There are some disadvantages to condominium and cooperative ownership, such as submission to the bylaws and the monthly fee, but there are also significant advantages. This form of ownership is the only viable alternative to renting an apartment. Condominium or cooperative ownership provides greater assurance of a constant monthly cost, since the property is purchased rather than rented. Rents can change, whereas a purchase price is fixed. Monthly service fees, however, can increase over the years and be a significant cost in the ownership of the suite. In condominiums or cooperatives, residents can be required to leave if they violate the bylaws. For example, buildings can be designated as adults-only, and couples can be required to leave if they have children. (This particular provision may violate human rights legislation.)

The general requirements of contract law apply to leasehold estates.
Dick Hemingway

The Landlord-Tenant Relationship

Caldwell v. Valiant Property Management[10]

The Caldwells had leased two apartments in the building in question, and on two separate occasions, in 1995 and 1996, repairs had to be made to the building, causing noise and disturbance and interfering with their use of the property. They could not use their balcony or air conditioner, and also their use of the pool and parking lot were interfered with for a total period of about 12 months. Mrs. Caldwell had particular problems because she did shift work and the jackhammers and other noises interfered with her sleep, forcing her on several occasions to sleep in the homes of relatives. There was no doubt that the repairs were necessary and made in good faith, but the landlord had not given any notice to the tenants that the repairs were going to be made when they had renewed their lease.

After examining the authorities, the court found that there was a covenant implied into the lease of quiet enjoyment and that this covenant was breached. The judge adopted the words of the Ontario Law Reform Commission in their March 15, 1976, *Report on Landlord and Tenant Law,* stating, "...a breach of the covenant should arise from any acts which result in the tenant's reasonable peace, comfort, or privacy being interfered with, whether due to liquids, gases, vapours, solids, odours, vibration, noise, abusive language, threats, fire, the total or partial withholding of heat, electricity, water, gas, or other essential services, or the removal of windows, doors, walls, or other parts of the rented premises." A breach of the covenant of quiet enjoyment had occurred and this required a remedy of abatement (a reduction in the rent paid) to be awarded to the tenants. The rent was reduced by $200 per month for the 8-month period of greater disruption and $100 per month for the 3-month period of lesser disruption.

This case illustrates the principle of quiet enjoyment that is available in both commercial and residential tenancies. The specific covenants of the lease are important but may not be exhaustive of the rights of the parties. In residential tenancies, these requirements may be set out in statute, and modification may be prohibited.

10. (1997) 145 D.L.R. (4th) 559 (Ont. Gen. Div.)

Leasehold Estates

A leasehold estate lasts for a specific or determinable period of time, usually ending on a specified day. Like freehold estates, the tenant has exclusive possession of the premises, while the landlord retains a reversionary interest in the property. A **license** on the other hand is based on contract and gives the license holder a non-exclusive right, meaning that other people may also have a license to use the property. For example, if Jones rents a room in a hotel for a month, this is a license, and the hotelkeeper has the right to come in the room, make the beds, clean the room, do any repairs, and even move Jones to another location if it is deemed appropriate. On the other hand, if Jones were to lease an apartment for a month, Jones would have the exclusive right to use the premises and the landlord could not come in without Jones' permission. Because a lease is created by contract, Jones and the landlord could make a provision in the lease for the landlord to enter the premises under certain circumstances. However, in the absence of such agreement, Jones is entitled to exclusive possession of that apartment. Note that when occupancy is at some future time, this is an agreement for lease rather than a lease, which may give rise to different remedies in the event of a breach.

As with other business relationships, the general requirements of contract law apply to leasehold estates. Even though it is wise to do so, a lease for three years or less need not be in writing. Leases over three years, however, must be evidenced in writing to satisfy the *Statute of Frauds* or its equivalent in most jurisdictions.[11] The written evidence must specify the premises covered by the lease, the parties to it, the consideration or rent to be given by the tenant, the duration of the lease, and any other special provisions the parties may have agreed to. In the absence of written evidence, part performance, such as the occupation of the premises by the tenant, will satisfy this requirement. Provincial legislation may also require that the lease be registered to protect the tenant's interests against third parties.

Leases, like freehold estates, are interests that run with the land. Privity of contract does not apply, and so, when a landlord sells the property, the new owner is bound by the prior lease. Also, if the landlord mortgages the property after the lease is made and defaults, the creditor is subject to the lease arrangement, and if the property is seized or resold, the lease must still be honoured. Because of this, many jurisdictions require long-term leases to be registered along with other claims affecting the title of the property.

Like other contracts, a landlord who contracts with an infant, a drunk, or a mentally incompetent person runs into all the problems associated with incapacity, as discussed in Chapter 6, and the resulting contract may not be binding. Historically, frustration, as discussed in Chapter 8, did not apply to land.[12] Many jurisdictions have changed this with respect to residential tenancies so that if the property is destroyed or damaged rendering it unusable, the contract will be discharged by frustration, and the tenant's obligation to pay rent will cease. Most jurisdictions have introduced special legislative provisions determining the rights and obligations of landlords and tenants in residential relationships. Commercial tenancy law has also been modified by statute to a lesser extent. This legislation varies from province to province, so no attempt will be made to make a comprehensive summary of these statutory provisions, except to indicate some of the more interesting provisions in place.

11. R.S.O. 1990, c. S.19 s. 3

12. Paradine v. Jane (1647) Aleyn 26 (K.B.)

Types of Tenancies

Property may be leased for a specific period or time, such as for "one year" or "ending September 5," or it may be a periodic tenancy with no set duration. When such an agreement has a set duration, it is a term lease, entitling the tenant to exclusive possession of the property for the specified period. Where the lease allows assignment and the tenant does so, all rights and claims in relationship to the property are given up to the new tenant. However, if the property is sublet, the tenant retains a reversionary interest, giving the tenant the right to retake possession at the expiration of the sublease. Usually, leases contain provisions allowing for such assignment or subletting with the permission of the landlord, "which shall not be unreasonably withheld." This gives the landlord some say in who takes possession of the property but does not allow him or her to interfere unreasonably.

Property may be sublet

A **periodic tenancy** has no specific termination date; rather, it involves a specific lease period that is automatically renewed in the absence of notice to the contrary. The period involved can be weekly, monthly, or yearly, but the most common is the month-to-month tenancy. Without notice bringing the relationship to a close, a periodic tenancy will continue indefinitely. Any notice to end the periodic tenancy must give one clear period of notice. Thus, in a month-to-month tenancy, notice must be given before the end of one month to take effect at the end of the next. If Nilsson rents an apartment from Delgado in a month-to-month tenancy and pays his rent on the first of each month, the lease period ends at the end of the month. Notice to terminate must be given on or before the last day of the month to take effect at the end of the next month. If notice is given on the day the rent is paid to terminate at the end of that month it will not be effective because the lease period has already begun. This requirement has caused considerable problems and is an area that has been modified by statute with respect to residential tenancies in many jurisdictions.

Periodic tenancy usually month to month

Notice period is one clear rental period

Rights and Obligations of the Parties

Norbury Sudbury Ltd. v. Noront Steel (1981) Ltd.[13]

In this case, a landlord is claiming damages for the cleanup and repair costs they incurred at the end of a lease from their tenant, a steel manufacturing business. The case is complicated by the involved relationships between the parties. Mr. Segger and Mr. Nemis were in business together operating Noront Steel (1981) Ltd. In 1960, they set up another company, Norbury Sudbury Ltd. (the landlord) and sold the land and buildings to that company, but Noront remained as tenant with a 15-year lease. Although there was a legal difference between these two companies, they were, in fact, operated as one business. Over that 15-year period, many changes were made, expanding the plant and buildings. At the end of the lease, Mr. Segger and Mr. Nemis had a falling out, and as part of the resolution of the dispute, Mr. Segger bought out Mr. Nemis' shares in the landlord, Norbury Sudbury Ltd. Even though these companies and the shareholders were closely related and carried on business together, the judge decided that he should continue to treat them as separate legal entities and as separate landlord and tenant.

In 1977, the lease and an extension to it expired, and Noront Steel left. The landlord then had to prepare the premises for a new tenant and incurred considerable expense in cleaning up the property and getting it ready for the new tenant.

13. 11 D.L.R. (4th) 686 (Ont. H.C.)

The lease required the tenant to leave the premises clean and in good repair. The judge had to interpret these clauses, and after a careful examination of the terms, he concluded that this did not mean that the premises had to be left in good repair but only that they had to be left in the same condition they were in when the tenant took possession, except for normal wear and tear. The premises also had to be cleaned, but that term was relative, considering the nature of the business of the tenant, not with relation to the new tenant (which repaired heavy mobile equipment) moving in. It should be noted that this new company needed many changes to be made before it could operate its business. The judge, therefore, refused many of the expenses incurred by the landlord in cleaning and repairing to get the property ready for the new tenant, as this put a greater burden on the tenant than required in the lease. The landlord's claim was, therefore, reduced from over $69 000 to just over $33 000. The judge also allowed the tenant to set off against that claim certain improvements that had been made over the years, including a lunchroom and an extension to the other buildings, amounting to about $12 000. The result was that the entire award made against the tenant was reduced to $22 661.31 plus interest.

This case points out the nature of the relationship between commercial landlords and tenants, the importance of a carefully drawn lease, and how a tenant's normal obligation to clean and repair is determined by the condition of the premises when occupied and the nature of the business carried on in the premises. The case also shows that a tenant is not responsible for normal wear and tear but will be responsible for consequential damage. The example is used that the tenant will not be responsible for a tile that blows off a roof but will be responsible for any damage done to the premises when the hole caused by its loss is left open to the weather. It also shows how complicated these relationships can become when different companies with various shareholders are involved and the importance of each company being treated as a separate legal entity.

Obligations may be modified by statute

In common law, commercial and residential tenancies were treated the same way, but all provinces have passed statues modifying these rules. Some provinces use several statutes for their landlord and tenant law,[14] whereas others use only one,[15] but in all cases, the rules with respect to residential tenancies have been significantly modified. The following comments apply primarily to commercial tenancies. The unique rules associated with residential tenancies will be discussed under a separate heading. You should refer to the specific legislation in effect in your jurisdiction.

Lease sets out rights of the parties

Note that the lease is a form of contract that can be modified by the parties, and so, the following are the rights and responsibilities of the parties only if they have not agreed otherwise in their lease agreement. In addition to the rent to be paid and a description of the property, provisions often included in commercial leases relate to what use the property can be put to and who is responsible for the payment of utilities, taxes, repairs, and insurance. In special situations, such as services or retail stores in shopping malls, provisions may relate to the kind of businesses that can be located in the same mall. In the shopping mall situation, rent is sometimes fixed as a percentage of sales. Long-term commercial leases often include an option for the review of the rent at set periods or for its renewal.

14. *Commercial Tenancies Act*, R.S.O. 1990, c. L.7; *Tenant Protection Act*, 1997, S.O. 1997, c.24
15. *Rent Review Act*, R.S.N.S. 1989, c. 398; *Residential Tenancies Act*, R.S.N.S. 1989, c. 401

Vacant Possession. The landowner has an obligation to ensure that the premises are vacant and ready for occupancy at the time agreed for the lease period to start. A failure on the part of the landlord to deliver vacant possession to a new tenant may be caused by several factors, such as failure to eject an over-holding tenant, an error in calculating the prior tenant's rights to stay on the premises, or construction or renovation. The landlord's liability and the compensation due the tenant in these situations will be calculated on how much it costs the tenant to find other accommodation in the interim.

Landowner must provide vacant premises

Quiet Enjoyment. A landlord is obligated to give a tenant quiet enjoyment of the premises. This does not mean that the tenant has to be happy or like the premises, only that the landlord must ensure that nothing happens to interfere with the tenant's use of the property. Where Cho leases an office building from Rankin and then rents the office space to Coghlan and the deal between Cho and Rankin falls through, Coghlan will not be able to occupy the office space. This would be a breach of his right to quiet enjoyment of the lease, and Coghlan could take action against Cho. Also, if Coghlan rents office space in a building owned by Cho and cannot gain access to his office because the entrance is blocked by construction, this also would be a breach of his right to quiet enjoyment and be actionable.

Landlord must not interfere with the tenant's use of property

Repair of Premises. The landlord has no general obligation to deliver premises that are clean or in good repair. The tenant takes the property the way it comes, and if he or she wants it in better condition, the cost is the responsibility of the tenant. Only when the premises are in such disrepair that it amounts to a breach of quiet enjoyment can the landlord be held responsible. In the example above, Coghlan would have no complaint if the premises are not painted or the carpet is threadbare when he moves in, unless a provision to provide better facilities is in the lease. But if the structure of the building is in such poor repair that it is no longer capable of supporting a wall or a floor and a resulting cave-in would make the office unusable, that would be a breach of the covenant of quiet enjoyment, and Coghlan could sue. Usually, the parties specify changes to these obligations in the lease agreement but there are also many situations in which the courts will imply into the contract obligations on the parties because of the circumstances. For example, when a tenant rents only part of a building, the court will assume that the landlord has an obligation to provide heat, unless otherwise stated in the lease. But when the tenant leases the entire building, that obligation may be assumed to fall on the tenant.

No general obligation to repair

Termination. A lease that ends on a specific date, or is for a specified period of time, ends when specified, unless there is an agreement to extend it. But when a periodic tenancy is involved (for example, month-to-month) notice to terminate must be given. If the tenant fails to leave after the lease has expired or after being given the appropriate notice, a **tenancy at sufferance** relationship is established. When this happens, the landlord is entitled to compensation, but if the normal rent payment is made, there is a danger of creating a periodic tenancy requiring more notice before the tenant can be ejected. Periodic tenancies may be week-to-week, month-to-month, or year-to-year, but one clear rental period must be given for the notice to be effective. In most jurisdictions, the notice period has been extended when residential tenancies are involved.

Proper notice must be given

Frustration applies by statute

Frustration. Historically, the doctrine of frustration did not apply to real property, but many jurisdictions have modified this in their landlord and tenant statutes. In those jurisdictions, when the leased premises become unusable by some unforeseen event, the lease will be terminated by frustration. In Ontario, for example, the *Tenancy Protection Act* states that the " doctrine of frustration of contract and the *Frustrated Contracts Act* apply with respect to tenancy agreements." [16]

Tenants' Obligations

Tenant Responsible for Injury to Customer

Mr. Silad leased a laundromat where a customer was injured by a falling fluorescent light fixture. She sought damages from Mr. Silad, who paid $27 000, and in this action, he was seeking contribution from the landlord. The problem for the court to decide was whether the tenant or the landlord was responsible for keeping the premises in repair and also who was responsible for the injury to the customer. Under the *Occupiers' Liability Act*, it is clear the tenant occupier is responsible to the person using the premises, and because there was no provision in the lease making the landlord responsible for repairs, the occupier had no claim against the landlord for the condition of the premises, which were entirely within the control of Mr. Silad. This case shows how important it is to specify in a lease agreement which party will be responsible for repairs.

Barnett-Black v. Silad Investments Inc., (1990) 74 D.L.R. (4th) 734 (Ont. Gen. Div.)

Tenant must pay rent

The obligation of paying the rent at the appropriate time is independent of any special obligations that the landlord may have agreed to in the lease contract, such as a duty to make repairs. As a result, when the landlord fails in his obligation to make repairs, the tenant cannot withhold rent until the repairs are made. In these circumstances, the tenant can ask the court for an order of **abatement** that will reduce the rent to be paid to compensate for the landlord's breach of the lease obligation. The tenant has no obligation to repair normal wear and tear or even to make serious repairs when they occur, unless they are caused by waste (his or her own action). The landlord should be notified of any serious problems, but in common law, the landlord has no obligation to make these repairs unless failure to do so would interfere with the quiet enjoyment of the tenancy. If Coghlan rents an office from Cho and the rug on the floor wears out over the years, Coghlan would be under no obligation to replace it. But neither would Cho, since the landlord is not required to provide premises of any standard of fitness for the tenant. Of course, the landlord and tenant can agree otherwise, and in many lease agreements, the landlord assumes the responsibility for keeping the property in good repair.

Tenants not responsible for normal wear and tear

A tenant does have an obligation to make repairs when undue wear and tear takes place because the premises are used in a way not agreed to in the lease. The landlord can also evict the tenant. If Coghlan rents premises from Cho to be used as an office and instead it is used for manufacturing furniture, Cho could demand payment for any excessive wear and require Coghlan to vacate the premises, no matter how long the lease had to run.

16. *Tenant Protection Act 1997*, S.O. 1997, c. 24, s.10

When a tenant attaches something (a fixture) in such a way that it is clearly intended to become a permanent part of the building or will cause damage to remove it, they are not permitted to remove it when they leave. If Coghlan installed modern wiring and added a staircase to the second floor of his rented office, these fixtures would become permanent and he could not remove them when he left. Trade fixtures, on the other hand, such as shelving, display counters, machinery, decorative artwork, and signs can be taken away by the tenant who attached them, if no damage is caused. But they must be removed when the tenant leaves. If they are left by the tenant, they become part of the real property, and the tenant cannot come back later to recover them.

Tenants can remove his or her fixtures before termination of lease

Bowling Lanes Fixtures

Although this case does not deal with a landlord and tenant relationship, it does illustrate the nature of a fixture. The debtor in this case built a bowling alley in White Rock and acquired equipment from Florida, including 20 bowling alleys, complete with setters, lanes, gutters, ball returns, ball racks, score sheets, bowling seats, masking units, divisions, capping, and foundations. This equipment was installed in the building, and the dispute in this case is between the mortgagee and another creditor who has a chattel mortgage agreement in relation to the equipment. The court had to decide whether the equipment had become part of the realty, thus giving the mortgagee priority. The court decided that although it was possible to remove the equipment, including the lanes which had been securely attached by screws, their purpose was to remain attached. The mortgagee as a result had priority. Today, with the new *Personal Property Security Act*, the same challenge with respect to priorities would have a different result, but we can still appreciate the decision, which shows that affixed bowling alley equipment becomes part of the realty.

North West Trust Co. v. Rezyn Developments Inc., (1991) 81 D.L.R. (4th) 751 (B.C.C.A.)

Remedies

Breach of Lease. When the rent is not paid, the landlord can sue for the overdue rent. When some other breach occurs, the landlord may sue for damages and, in serious cases, may require the tenants to vacate the premises. This is called **forfeiture,** and when unpaid rent in a commercial lease is involved, no court order is needed, and forfeiture may be accomplished by the landlord simply changing the locks. When the tenant is in breach of some other term of the lease, such as the use of the premises or repair, the landlord must first give the tenant notice to end the breach and time to do so. When eviction is necessary, the services of a law enforcement officer, such as a sheriff, must be obtained, which can be a costly and time-consuming process. Residential tenancy statutes usually limit the availability of eviction as a remedy.

Landlord can sue for compensation when lease breached

When the landlord does retake the property for failure to pay rent prior to the end of the lease term, the tenant can apply to the court to have the lease reinstated. This relief against forfeiture is an equitable principle similar to a right to redeem an interest in real property after a mortgage has been foreclosed, which will be discussed below.

When the tenant abandons the premises, the landlord retains the right to payment of rent for the duration of the lease period. It should be noted that the landlord is normally not obligated to mitigate this loss, at least in commercial tenancies, by finding a new occupant for the premises until the expiration of the lease period.

Landlord can seize tenant's property when lease breached

The landlord also has the right to seize any property left by the tenant and hold it until the rent is paid or to sell the tenant's property to pay the rent owing. This is called **distress,** and when done, it often causes confusion because by so doing, the rent is paid and the lease continues. The landlord cannot treat the lease as ended and also distrain the tenant's property. This power to seize the tenant's property is usually significantly limited or eliminated in residential tenancy legislation.

Monetary compensation available for breach of lease

The landlord can also seek contractual remedies in the form of damages when the lease is breached. This usually amounts to the rent due but also may be compensation for the cost of repairs when damage is done to the premises.

The courts will also issue an injunction when either tenant or landlord carries on some activity inconsistent with the terms of the lease. Thus, when a tenant uses the premises for a purpose different from that contemplated in the lease, the landlord can get an injunction to prevent the misuse of the property.

Tenant has limited remedies

The remedies available to the tenant for the landlord's breach of the lease are more limited. The tenant is generally entitled either to sue the landlord for compensation for any injury suffered because of the breach or to seek an injunction. The tenant is not entitled to withhold rent to force the landlord's compliance with the lease obligations. But if the landlord's breach is significant enough to qualify as a breach of a major contractual term, the tenant may be entitled to treat the lease agreement as discharged and vacate the premises voluntarily, thus terminating the lease. For example, if the lease agreement requires the landlord to provide heat and water and those services are turned off, this would probably be a significant enough breach for the tenant to terminate the agreement. In any case, the tenant always retains the right to seek a court order that the lease be declared as ended or the tenant's obligation to pay rent be reduced because of the landlord's breach.

Occupier's liability on tenant

It is a principle of tort law that the occupier of property, including a tenant, is responsible for any injury caused to people using the property. The landlord may also be liable if the landlord is responsible for repairs under the lease and the tenant has notified the landlord but the repairs are not made. The landlord will be responsible for injuries to the tenant or the tenant's employees in these circumstances.

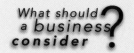

One of the most important transactions not directly associated with the focus of a business is the acquisition of physical space to carry on the activity. Whether it is office space, a manufacturing plant, or a warehouse, the space is usually leased rather than purchased outright. It is vitally important that the tenant understand the terms of the lease agreement; that appropriate modifications are made and that the lease provides for the possibility that the facility needs of the business might change in the future. Aside from not fully understanding what they are agreeing to, a common failing for tenants is to commit themselves for an extensive period without the flexibility to change as the business grows or declines. Great care should be taken when entering into these commercial leases to ensure that provisions are added or modified providing for as much flexibility as possible.

Residential Tenancies

Applewood Lane West Ltd. v. Scott et al.[17]

Thomas Scott and Dave Hinds were tenants, and Applewood Lane West Ltd. was
their landlord. They had a one-year lease running from the end of July 1985 to
end of July 1986. Their rent was almost $600 a month, and they had paid just under
$300 as a security deposit. In the fall of 1985, they decided they did not want to
live there any more and informed their neighbours and friends that they were
going to have a series of "lease-breaking parties," which they proceeded to do.
Several noisy parties lasting well into the morning were held. Neighbours complained, police attended, and finally the landlord was driven to give them notice to
vacate within five days. They did not leave until a month later and did not pay that
month's rent. The landlord retook possession of the premises, made necessary repairs, incurring expenses of $231 in the process, and was unable to rent it before
April 1. The landlord brought this action to recover the damages from the two
tenants. The tenants, on the other hand, applied to have their security deposit returned. The question was whether in evicting their tenants the landlord gave up any
claims to rights they had under the lease.

The Court of Appeal in this case made it clear that the conduct of the tenants
in deliberately provoking the landlord to terminate the lease constituted abandonment of the lease on their part. The tenants, not the landlord, had breached the
lease, therefore, the landlord was entitled to lost rent as well as the cost of repairs
and was successful in his action.

This case illustrates the nature of the landlord-tenant relationship and the obligations existing between them. It also shows how the interests of the parties in a
residential tenancy relationship can be quite different from those in a commercial tenancy; it also underscores the need for the introduction of special legislation to deal with those relationships.

Most jurisdictions have introduced special statutes to significantly modify common law where a tenant rents or leases premises for the purposes of acquiring living accommodation. In some provinces, these provisions are included in one
general landlord and tenant act, but most jurisdictions have special statutes dealing
with residential tenancies. Ontario, for example, has recently replaced their *Landlord
and Tenant Act* and the *Rent Control Act* with one statute, the *Tenant Protection Act.*[18]
These acts are like consumer protection statutes, altering the rights and obligations of the landlord and tenant. In some cases, they also introduce rent controls
and establish administrative tribunals in the form of a rentalsperson or rent review commission to handle disputes that normally would fall under the jurisdiction of the courts. Generally, the removal of landlord and tenant disputes from
the courts has been advantageous to both landlord and tenants. The rights of the
parties before such administrative tribunals were discussed in Chapter 3. In many
cases, the residential tenancy legislation restricts the number of rent increases that
can be imposed to one per year and, in some jurisdictions, restricts the amount
of increase to a certain percentage of the normal monthly rent or establishes guide-

**Residential tenancy rules
modified by statute**

**Some jurisdictions impose
rent controls**

17. 35 D.L.R. (4th) 287 (Man. C.A.)

18. *Tenant Protection Act,* 1997, S.O 1997, c. 24

lines to that effect.[19] This type of control is very controversial, and legislative changes occur regularly as one government is replaced by another. Readers are encouraged to study the current legislation in their own jurisdictions to determine what kinds of controls may be in effect.

Statutes often increase notice period

Only one clear month had to be given as notice of rent increases under common law. Most residential tenancy statutes increase this requirement to three months' notice.[20] Similarly, the notice to terminate required of the landlord has also been increased in some cases to three months.[21] Often, the landlord is also required to give reasons for the termination. Many provinces have extended the notice period still further when the landlord requires the premises for some specific purpose, such as for personal use or for conversion to condominiums.[22] Ontario requires the landlord to get permission for such conversions, and British Columbia requires the landlord to pay moving expenses as well. Often, these statutes require the landlord to give notice even when the lease is for a specific term. In most cases, the notice required of the tenant is only one month, and no reasons are necessary.

Qualities of facilities regulated by statute

Also, these statutes usually impose an obligation on the landlord to keep the property in good repair, to live up to the local health and safety bylaw standards, and to maintain the services that have been provided, such as laundry facilities and parking. The cost of such services is generally considered to be part of the rent and so is also governed by the controls placed on rent increases by statute. The landlord's right to enter the premises without notice is usually restricted to those situations where the tenant has abandoned the premises or in the case of an emergency. The landlord can enter for purposes of inspection or to do repair work but must give notice, and even this access is restricted to normal daylight hours. Most residential tenancy statutes require that a tenant be given a copy of a written lease before its provisions are binding.

Statute Overrules Lease

This case involves a lease entered into between a landlord and tenant for residential premises. The lease contained a provision indicating that in the event of termination, 30 days' notice would be given. The tenant stayed until the lease expired and then continued to stay from month to month. In 1993, the tenant served one month's notice on the landlord pursuant to the provisions of the lease for termination. This was rejected by the landlord, who insisted on two months' notice as set out in the *Landlord and Tenant Act* in force in the province. The court had to decide whether the provisions of the act would apply or whether they would be overridden by the terms of the lease. The act specifically states that its provisions applied despite any agreement or waiver to the contrary, and so, the court decided that the 60-day notice required by the act applied. The tenant was required to pay the landlord rent for one month more. Such legislation usually favours the tenant, but note that in this instance, it was the landlord that benefited.

Pinheiro v. Bowes, 109 D.L.R. (4th) 315 (Ont. Gen. Giv.)

Amount of security deposit restricted by statute

Where a security deposit is taken to cover damage or unpaid rent, as in the *Applewood* case discussed above, the legislation usually restricts the amount to one month's rent or less and often requires interest to be paid as well.[23]

19. *Ibid., part VI.*
20. *Residential Tenancy Act*, R.S.B.C. 1996, c. 406 s. 24(3)
21. *Residential Tenancies Act*, R.S.N.S. 1989, c. 401 s. 10(1)
22. Residential Tenancy Act, R.S.A. 1980, c. R-15.3. s. 10
23. *Residential Tenancies Act*, R.S.N.S. 1989, c. 401 s. 12(2)

In some provinces, including Ontario, the deposit is made to secure the payment of the last month's rent rather than provide security for damage. In those jurisdictions, the tenant obtains repayment simply by not paying the last month's rent after giving notice of leaving. When it is a damage deposit, however, the tenant must pay the last month's rent and apply for the return of the security deposit.

The statutes also usually impose a duty on the landlord to mitigate, and so, when the tenant abandons the premises, the landlord must try to re-rent rather than let the lease run out and retain the security deposit or seek out the tenant for further payment. Landlords of residential premises in many jurisdictions are not permitted to seize the personal property of tenants for unpaid rent but may be allowed to take goods that have been left after the tenant has abandoned the property.

Landlords must mitigate losses

The tenant is required to maintain reasonable health and cleanliness standards and repair any damage other than normal wear and tear. It may be possible for the tenant to assign or sublet the lease, but the landlord is usually given the right to veto this course of action as long as the consent to sublet or assign is not unreasonably withheld.

Although these changes to common law are significant, they should be viewed as a form of consumer protection legislation designed to prevent the serious abuses that have occurred in the past in landlord and tenant relationships.

Mortgages

A mortgage is a form of security usually involving large sums used to purchase the property in question. The borrower temporarily transfers the title in the property to the creditor as security for the funds advanced. Upon proper repayment, the creditor re-conveys the title, but if there is a default, the creditor has first claim on that property before other creditors.

The terminology used to designate the parties to such transactions can be confusing. The person who conveys the title (grants the mortgage) is the one borrowing the money and is called the mortgagor. The creditor is on the receiving end of the transfer of the title and is called the mortgagee.

Debtor is mortgager, creditor is mortgagee

Originally, the creditor actually took possession of the land, but this was inconvenient and not needed for the security, and the practice soon developed where the creditor was given title but the debtor kept possession of the property. In the event of default, the creditor had the right, because of title, to take possession of the property as well. Still, problems were associated with the process. Since the mortgagee had title, they could take the land upon default, but the debtor still had to pay back the loan, even though they had lost their land. Subsequent developments of the law of mortgages, especially in the Courts of Chancery, were intended to overcome these problems and have resulted in a unique body of law.

Mortgage involves transfer of title as security

Equity of Redemption

The law relating to mortgages is a significant example of how the Courts of Chancery stepped in to relieve the harshness or unfairness of common law. In common law, the mortgagor not only lost the property upon default but still had to pay the money owed. The Courts of Chancery recognized that the property was only intended to be security for debt and allowed the debtor to reclaim the property even after default by paying the money owed plus any expenses involved. This right to redeem became known as the **equity of redemption,** and it bestows on the mortgagor an interest in the land that goes beyond the basic contractual responsibility. If Nagai has property worth $100 000 and owes $60 000 on a mortgage owing to Dhillon, Dhillon can

Mortgager retains right to redeem after default

take that property in the event of a default. But the right to redeem gives Nagai the right to reclaim his property even after the default by making the $60 000 payment plus any expenses and interest. This right to redeem is an equitable interest in property, in this case worth $40 000. Today, we often use the shortened term "**equity**" to refer to the value left in any asset they own after they subtract what they owe. Thus, if I own a car worth $12 000 and I owe $5000, I will have $7000 equity in that vehicle.

Foreclosure

But this right to redeem causes problems for the creditor who is always in danger, even years later, of the mortgagor exercising his right to redeem and reclaiming the property.

Mortgagee can foreclose the right to redeem

The solution devised by the Courts of Chancery was to set a time limit within which the mortgagor's right to redeem must be exercised. If the mortgagor failed to pay within that time, an order would be made which forever foreclosed the mortgagor from redeeming the property. This combination—a right to redeem on the part of the mortgagor and a right to obtain foreclosure on the part of the mortgagee—has worked well and is the system in place in Canada today.

Foreclosure is a two-stage process

The process of obtaining foreclosure has two stages. Upon default, the mortgagee goes to the court and asks for an order establishing the time limit within which the mortgagor can redeem (called an **order nisi** in some provinces). This time limit will vary with the circumstances and from jurisdiction to jurisdiction, although it is usually not more than six months. If the property is not redeemed within the designated period, the mortgagee returns to court and asks for a final order of foreclosure (called an **order absolute**). This order, once obtained, prevents any further exercise of the equity of redemption on the part of the mortgagor. It should be mentioned that even then, in most jurisdictions, the court retains the discretionary right to reopen the redemption period if the circumstances warrant. (See the *Namu* case summarized below.) Once the property has been resold to a third party or once the order absolute is registered and a new certificate of title has been issued in a land titles system, the original owner no longer has a right to redeem the property.

355498 B.C. Ltd. v. Namu Properties Ltd.[24]

In 1995, Namu Properties Ltd. sold a townsite property on the British Columbia coast to EuroPacific Properties Ltd. with a mortgage back to the vendor. They also acquired a foreshore lease from the provincial government. They ran into financial difficulties at the outset and were unable to make proper payments on the mortgage. They also lost the foreshore lease because of their failure to make proper payments. The mortgagee made an application for an order nisi of foreclosure, which was granted by the court. The mortgagee then made an application for an order absolute of foreclosure. But this was adjourned several times as they tried to work things out. Finally, an order absolute was obtained from the court, but even then, the mortgagee agreed not to file it in the land registry if the appropriate payments were made. They were not, and the order absolute of foreclosure was filed at the appropriate land registry. Several months later, the mortgagor which had considerable equity in the property tried to redeem and was refused. In this application, the mortgagor was asking the court to reopen the order absolute and allow them to redeem the property. The mortgagee took the position that it was too late to do that. The court had to decide whether they would allow the redemption of the mort-

24. (1999) 171 D.L.R. (4th) 513 (B.C.C.A.)

gage even after an order absolute of foreclosure had been registered. The court held that they had a discretion to allow redemption even at this late stage and allowed the redemption of the mortgage by the mortgagor.

A mortgage is a transfer of the property interest to the creditor as security for the loan. The equitable right to redeem is a recognition of the security nature of that interest, giving the mortgagors a right even after default to reclaim their property upon payment of what is owed. The process of foreclosure (the order nisi and then the order absolute) puts an end to that right to redeem so that the security can be realized after allowing an appropriate time for the right to redeem to be exercised. This case shows how those various interests work and also the power, discretion, and willingness of the court to recognize the right to redeem even after an order absolute has been registered in the land registry, especially when the mortgagor has a substantial equitable interest in the property.

In a registration jurisdiction, the document filed actually transfers title to the mortgagee, but in a land titles system, the certificate of title remains in the name of the mortgagor. The interest of the mortgagee is merely noted as a charge against the property, much as an easement or a leasehold interest would be. But the rights bestowed are those of a mortgagee under common law and so the mortgagee (chargeholder) has the right in the event of default to start the foreclosure process. In the event of the property not being redeemed before the time limit specified, the mortgagee has the right to have a new certificate of title created in their name. Although the method of recording the relationship in land titles jurisdiction might be different, the effect is the same.

> **In land titles system jurisdictions, a mortgage is registered as charge on title**

Second Mortgage

The mortgagor's right to redeem is a valuable interest in land and can be used to secure further debt. When the debtor transfers this equity of redemption to another creditor to secure further debt, it is called a second mortgage. Since the title itself was transferred the first time the property was mortgaged and the right to redeem is an equitable remedy created by the Courts of Chancery, any subsequent mortgages after this first mortgage are called equitable mortgages. But even after a second mortgage is created, the mortgagor has a similar right to redeem by paying off the second and first mortgages. Thus, the mortgagor retains the right to redeem. In this way, third, fourth, and fifth mortgages can be created. The mortgagor always has a right to redeem any mortgage interest that has been created.

> **Mortgager can use right to redeem as security—second mortgage**

It should be obvious that the more mortgages involved, the weaker the security, so anything beyond first, second, and third mortgages is rare. To illustrate, if Redekop financed the purchase of a new home valued at $150 000 with a first mortgage with Johal for $90 000, he would retain an equity of redemption worth $60 000. If that were not enough to finance the purchase, he might borrow a further $35 000 from another creditor (Nelson) using that equity of redemption as security. This would be a second mortgage. But Redekop would still retain a right to redeem the property from the second mortgagee (Nelson). The value of that right to redeem would be $25 000 ($150 000 − $90 000 − $35 000 = $25 000). In other words, Redekop would have a $25 000 equitable interest in the property. There is no reason why Redekop could not grant a third or fourth or additional mortgage on the property if somebody was willing to take them.

Because the first mortgagee has the right to foreclose in the event of default, stripping the mortgagor or any subsequent mortgagee of any interest in the property the position of a second or third mortgagee involves considerably more risk.

> **Power to foreclose increases risk to second mortgagee**

They must be prepared to buy out the first or second mortgage above them to preserve their security. In the example above, if Redekop gave Johal a $90 000 first mortgage on the property and Nelson a $35 000 second mortgage, Nelson must be prepared to pay out the $90 000 owing on the first mortgage to protect his interest if Redekop defaults. This puts any subsequent mortgagees in a very vulnerable position. As a result, higher rates of interest are charged for second and third mortgages.

In land titles system, mortgages are listed as charges on certificate

In a land titles jurisdiction, the first, second, and subsequent mortgages are listed on the certificate of title as charges against the property, and the order of priority is established by the order in which they have been registered. This priority between mortgage holders is established by the date of registration rather than by the date of creation of the mortgage. In other registry jurisdictions, the rights of mortgagees will also be determined by the time of registration of their interest at the appropriate land registry office. The prompt registration of mortgages is vital in both systems. The whole purpose of a registration system is to notify people who are acquiring interest in the land of other claims against the property. Those other interests must be registered to be effective, and a person who fails to properly register an interest in a property will lose priority to any person who acquires an interest in that property afterwards and does register it. If Redekop grants Johal a first mortgage against his property and then grants Nelson another mortgage, Johal will have priority over Nelson if both have been registered. However, if Johal neglects to register his mortgage interest and Nelson is not otherwise informed about it, Nelson is said to be a *bona fide* third party and is not affected by Johal's unregistered first mortgage. Nelson would gain priority over Johal's interests in the event of Redekop's default. It is only if Nelson has notice of Johal's prior interest that she will not be able to claim priority.

Types of Mortgages

Mortgages which are used to finance some business activity usually in conjunction with a promissory note are called collateral mortgages. Also, in these circumstances, some third party often guarantees the debt secured by the mortgage. Although a mortgage may be amortized over a 30- or 40-year period which is the length calculated for repayment, the mortgage term is much less, usually one, two, or five years. The mortgage agreement expires at the end of that term and the entire amount left owing on the mortgage becomes due. The mortgagor must then pay it off or negotiate a renewal of the mortgage, usually at a different interest rate. This can work to the advantage of either party, depending on whether the interest rates have gone up or down. Some people use open-ended mortgages, wherein the mortgage continues, and a varying rate of interest fluctuating with changes in the banks' prime rate is charged.

Mortgages for shorter term thus amortized

Remedies upon Default

Regional Trust Co. v. Avco Financial Services Realty Ltd.[25]

Mr. and Mrs. Foster owned property on which they had a first and second mortgages. The first mortgage was to Regional Trust and the second was to Avco. They ran into financial difficulties and made arrangements with Avco to transfer their title to Avco in the form of a quitclaim deed. Avco made payments to Regional Trust for

25. (1984) 5 D.L.R. (4th) 670 (Ont. H.C.)

about a year and then defaulted. Regional Trust exercised their right to sell the property under the power of sale and then sought payment of the deficiency of $6500 from Avco.

This action was to determine whether the second mortgagee, Avco, was required to pay a deficiency in these circumstances. The court held that they were. When they had assumed title to the property, they had also assumed the obligations. They stepped into the shoes of the Fosters, and when the property was sold for less than what was owed, Avco was required to pay the difference.

This case illustrates the nature of first and second mortgages. When the Fosters transferred their title in the property to Regional as security for the loan they retained the right to redeem which they used to grant a second mortgage to Avco. But Avco's position as second mortgagee was precarious, and they had to be prepared in the event of default to pay out the first mortgage. Unfortunately for all parties, the market fell and the value of the property was not enough to cover the amounts owing. Likely this was not apparent to Avco when they obtained the quitclaim deed and attempted to continue making payments. Had the market rebounded and the value of the property increased, Avco would have taken advantage of any such increase, making a windfall profit, but as it continued to decline, it became apparent that it was not worth it for Avco to hold onto the property, and they allowed Regional Trust Company to exercise its power of sale. Because the Fosters had surrendered their interest rather than have Avco go through the foreclosure process, Avco was now responsible for any shortfall. Regional exercised its power of sale under the mortgage contract, retaining the right to demand any deficiency from the title holder, which was now Avco.

Had Avco remained as a second mortgagee, Avco would have no responsibility to Regional, and both Avco and Regional would have had a claim against the Fosters for any shortfall from the sale of the property. But by taking title from the Fosters, Avco also assumed its obligations.

This case not only illustrates the nature and distinctions between first and second mortgages and the rights associated with exercising a power of sale but also graphically illustrates the danger associated with the second or third mortgagee positions.

The process of foreclosure is just one of the remedies available to the mortgagee when the mortgagor fails to live up to the terms of the mortgage agreement. Mortgage contracts, in addition to the obligation to make payments, usually include an obligation on the mortgagor to insure the property. This ensures that the value of the assets remain high enough to secure the debt, even in the event of damage or destruction of the buildings. For the same reason, the mortgagor must pay property taxes, as failure to pay can result in seizure and sale of the property by the municipality.

Similar provisions require the mortgagor to keep any buildings on the property in good repair as well as refraining from committing waste (doing anything to the land or buildings to reduce their value). When second or third mortgages are involved, a provision making the failure to pay a prior mortgage a default will be included as well. Although the most common method of breaching a mortgage agreement is failure to make the appropriate payments, a breach of any of these terms will constitute default and entitle the mortgagee to seek a remedy.

Must keep property in good repair

The following is a summary of the types of remedies available to the mortgagee. Of course, the possibility of a negotiated settlement should always be explored.

There is no sense in incurring the legal expense of court action if the defaulting mortgagor can be persuaded to surrender the property, participate in a joint sale, or otherwise rehabilitate his or her position, for example, by accepting a different repayment schedule. It might be important for the creditors to protect their positions by obtaining a court order, even where there is a willingness to negotiate. The adversarial remedies discussed below are almost always time-consuming, especially with an uncooperative mortgagor, and when payments are not being made, the amount owing including interest can quickly grow. When this happens, most of the creditors will only partially recover what they are owed and the mortgagor will get nothing. Where a default does take place, an **acceleration clause** is usually included, provided that upon default, all that is owed becomes due and payable. Legislation normally requires the creditor to notify the mortgagor of the default and give a specified period of time to repay any arrears and costs and reinstate the mortgage. If such repayment is not made, the mortgagee can proceed to obtain the following remedies.

Suing on the Covenant.

As with other types of contracts involving security, the creditor has the right to sue on the promise to repay rather than seek other remedies, such as foreclosure. It should be noted that in most jurisdictions, the right to foreclosure is lost when the mortgagee follows this course of action because the two remedies are inconsistent. Once foreclosure has taken place and the mortgagee wants to sue on the covenant, he or she must be prepared to re-convey the property back to the mortgagor. If the property is sold after foreclosure and it is not enough to cover what is owed, it is too late for the mortgagee to sue for the deficit. They no longer have the property to re-convey to the mortgagor. Several provinces, including British Columbia, have incorporated into legislation this prohibition against suing after foreclosure. Note that where the power of sale is exercised or a judicial sale takes place, the mortgagee still has the right to sue for any shortfall.

Creditor can sue for breach of contract

Possession.

The mortgagee also has the right to ask the court for an order giving him or her possession of the property upon default of payment. The problem with this course of action is that any profits earned through the property must be accounted for and given to the mortgagor upon redemption. Nor is the mortgagee entitled to compensation for any expenses incurred in looking after the property, such as the cost of a caretaker. If any damage is done to the property while the mortgagee is in possession, the mortgagee is responsible to compensate the mortgagor upon redemption. The mortgagee will generally not seek an order of possession of the property if it appears that redemption is likely because of the responsibilities involved. Only when the property has been abandoned or is in danger of deterioration for some other reason will this course of action be used.

Right to take possession upon default

Foreclosure.

This remedy was discussed earlier, but it must be pointed out that its availability varies with the jurisdiction. For example, foreclosure is only available in Manitoba after attempts to sell the property by the court fail.[26] In other jurisdictions, the process of foreclosure is the usual course embarked on by the mortgagee in the event of default by the mortgagor. However, in the process, all interested parties, including the mortgagor and second and third mortgagees, must be notified of the foreclosure, giving them opportunity to seek other remedies, which usually results in the property being sold rather than foreclosure.

Foreclosure most common remedy used

26. *Real Property Act*, R.S.M. 1988, c. R-30 s. 138(2)

Second Mortgagee Retains Right to Sue

Macon owned a condominium and granted a first mortgage to Cooperative Trust Company and a second mortgage to Frank Laci. In both these cases, der Bach guaranteed or co-signed the mortgage debt. Macon defaulted on the mortgages and then sold the property to Mayr. The first mortgagee foreclosed, and the second mortgagee then paid off the first mortgagee and assumed the position of first mortgagee. The purchaser, Mayr, paid out sufficient funds to cover the amount of the first mortgage and the amount owing to Laci, and now Laci, the second mortgagee, wished to proceed by way of personal judgment against Macon and the guarantor der Bach. The question for the court was whether the second mortgagee, when he or she buys out the first mortgagee, retained the right to sue on the personal covenant. The answer was yes, and der Bach and Macon, the debtors, had to pay the shortfall. The foreclosure by the first mortgagee forced the second mortgagee to buy out that first mortgage, and the second mortgagee assumed those rights, but he did not lose the rights he had with respect to the second mortgage, that is, the right to sue on the covenant to repay.

der Bach v. Mueller, (1987) 46 D.L.R. (4th) 320 (B.C.C.A.)

Power of Sale and Judicial Sale. In almost all cases, the contract embodying the mortgage will contain a term called "a power of sale" giving the mortgagee the right to sell the property upon default without going to court first. This power to sell the property upon default is used in many jurisdictions, and in some, resort to this remedy is required by statute. In other jurisdictions the appropriate process is the judicial sale or a court-ordered and -supervised sale. This important but often misunderstood remedy involves an application to the court by the mortgagee, and sometimes the mortgagor, for an order that the property be sold under the court's supervision with the object of realizing as much money as possible from the sale for the parties.

Contract usually provides for right to sell property upon default

The actual procedure varies from province to province. In some jurisdictions, the property is sold at public auction in the case of both a judicial sale and a power of sale. The sale is advertised; tenders are invited; and sometimes, a reserve bid is included to make sure the interests of the parties are protected. In other jurisdictions, the responsibility to conduct the sale will be given to the party who has the incentive to obtain the highest reasonable price, usually the second or third mortgagee, depending on the value of the equity. The property is sold through a realtor in the normal way; when a purchaser is found, the parties, in the case of a judicial sale, return to the court, and the court gives its consent to the sale. It is important to understand the effects of this remedy. If the first mortgagee goes to court and asks for foreclosure, the judge will grant a specific redemption period, such as six months, during which time the mortgagor may redeem the property. The problem is that at the same time, an order to sell the property will be made, usually at the request of the second mortgagee, if there is sufficient value in the property. This order is designed to protect the financial position of the second mortgagee, by selling the property before the foreclosure can takes place. Thus, the person who acquires the order for the judicial sale obtains the right to have the property sold, not in six months, but immediately. The timing of the sale varies with the jurisdiction and the process involved, but it must take place before the end of the redemption period.

Court will authorize sale during redemption period

It is obvious that the effect of such a successful sale is to shorten the period available to the mortgagor to redeem the property.

In some provinces, an attempt must be made to sell the property before the foreclosure route can be taken. In every province, the mortgagor has the right to sell the property during the redemption period as long as the purchase price is high enough to cover the amount owed to the mortgagee. If the property has been sold by judicial sale or using the power of sale in the contract, and the total amount of money realized from the sale is less than the total amount owing on the mortgages, including accumulated interest and other costs, the original mortgagor will get nothing and will be still liable to pay any outstanding amounts.

Where judicial sale mortgagee can sue for deficit

This, of course, was the problem in the *Regional Trust Co. v. Avco* case discussed at the start of this section. Avco, by accepting the quitclaim, had put themselves in the position of the original owner of the property, and when not enough money was obtained from the sale of the property to cover the amount owing to Regional, they were responsible for the shortfall. One of the disadvantages of being a second or third mortgagee in the event of default is the necessity of taking over the property to protect your investment. The case illustrates that there may be even more dangers when that course of action is taken. In some provinces, a mortgagor does not have to pay a deficit where residential property is involved.

Bank of Montreal v. Allender Investments Ltd. et al.[27]

Allender Investments borrowed $46 000 from the Bank of Montreal, securing the loan with a mortgage against certain property. That mortgage was personally guaranteed by Mr. Neil. Allender then sold the property, which was again resold, with that purchaser then defaulting on the mortgage. With the mortgage in default, the bank exercised their power of sale as set out in the mortgage and offered the property for sale at auction. Unfortunately, the only bid was by the plaintiff bank, which purchased the property for a mere $100. The bank then sought to recover the shortfall or deficit from of $45 711 from the original mortgagor or the guarantor, Mr. Neil. The defendants argued that the bank had failed in a duty owed to get the best price possible for the property and certainly no less than its market value. The court found in favour of the plaintiff. The judge said that the plaintiff would only lose this right if they failed to proceed as required under the mortgage covenants or statutes or if they acted negligently in the sale itself. In this case, they acted properly, and the sale by auction was in no way negligent and so were still entitled to recover the deficit from the defendants. The judge also pointed out that the bank would not be making a windfall as the defendants still had the right to redeem the property upon payment of what was owed.

The power of sale gives the mortgagor the right to have the property sold in the event of default, and so long as they follow the provisions in the mortgage contract and statutory requirements and do not act negligently in the process of the sale, they will retain the right to recover any deficit. This is true even when the amount recovered is nowhere near the actual market value of the property.

On the other hand, in the case of *Bank of Nova Scotia v. Barnard*,[28] the court found that there was negligence in the sale and refused to allow the mortgagee to recover a deficit owing. In that case, the property involved had been appraised (for a quick sale) at a price below its true market value and sold at the price listed. The court held that there was a duty to take reasonable steps to obtain the market

27. 4 D.L.R. (4th) 340 (N.B.Q.B.)
28. 9 D.L.R. (4th) 575 (Ont. H.C.)

value of the property upon resale, and while that price may not be obtained, a reasonable process should be in place to accomplish that goal. Getting a below-market-value appraisal for a "quick sale" and listing it at that low price meant they could not get the actual market value, since no one would offer more than the listing price. This amounted to negligence and barred recovery for a deficit on the sale.

The message of these cases is that upon default, the power of sale allows the mortgagee to sell the property to recover on the security. Also, if there is a shortfall, the mortgagee retains the right to sue the debtor for any deficit. However, in exercising that power of sale, the mortgagee has an obligation to the debtor to try to get the market value of the property. That does not mean that he or she will lose the right to a deficit if the market value of the property is not obtained, only that the sale must be conducted in a reasonable way so as to get as much as possible towards that market price. In the first case, there was no negligence on the part of Bank of Montreal, even though only a nominal amount was obtained from the auction. In the second case, even though a much greater percentage price was obtained, there was negligence because the property was listed at a price below market value on the basis of a negligent appraisal.

Of course, any excess from the sale after costs must go to the mortgagor or subsequent mortgagees. The remedy of foreclosure, on the other hand, involves the seizure of the property and obtaining title rather than the payment of compensation. When this remedy is used and the property is sold later for more than is owed, the mortgagee is not required to pay over any excess to the mortgagor. For example, where Redecop financed the purchase of a home valued at $150 000 with a $90 000 first mortgage with Johal and a $35 000 second mortgage with Nelson, if Redecop were to default, Johal would start the foreclosure process. Nelson could either take over the payments and foreclose himself or ask for an order for judicial sale at the same time that Johal first goes to court to begin the foreclosure process. If the property is sold and the total amount of the sale is only $110 000, then Johal will get $90 000 plus any interest, charges, and costs, and Nelson will get the remainder. Since there will be a shortfall, Nelson will then turn to Redecop and sue for any outstanding balance. In addition to losing his house, Redecop will be required to pay Nelson, which may jeopardize any other assets he possesses. However, if Redecop mortgages his property valued at $150 000 with Nelson to secure the $35 000 loan and no other mortgage is involved, Nelson would likely initiate the foreclosure process if Redecop defaults. If the redemption period expires and a final order is obtained, and Nelson then sells the property for $125 000, he will not be required to pay any of this windfall profit to Redecop in most jurisdictions. To avoid this loss, Redecop will make great efforts to refinance and redeem his title in the property or sell during the redemption period. In most situations, therefore, the property is either redeemed by the mortgagor or sold under the supervision of the court.

Where judicial sale excess to mortgagor

Where all payments have been properly made and no default has taken place, the mortgagor is entitled to have that mortgage discharged. A discharge transferring the property to the mortgagor is filed at the appropriate land registry, providing notice that the legal title has been re-conveyed and the mortgagee no longer has any interest in the property. In a land titles system, a notice of discharge is filed at the land registry, and the mortgage charge is removed. Depending on the terms of the mortgage agreement, the mortgagor may have the right to pay off the mortgage or a portion of it prior to the expiration of the mortgage term. In many cases, under the terms of the agreement, the mortgagor will have to pay an additional amount to compensate the mortgagee for the interest that will not be earned because of the early

Discharge of mortgage

payment, especially if interest rates have gone down. This may be an important consideration when the property is to be sold and the purchaser will not be assuming the mortgage.

Business and personal leases and mortgages are some of the most intricate of legal relationships, and people are well advised to have the services of a lawyer when they enter such relationships. Unfortunately, because these are common transactions, the parties are often less vigilant and do not appreciate just what they are getting into. This becomes especially apparent when there is a default and the complex rights and obligations come into play, in particular, when second and third mortgages are involved. The court's power to sell the property, thus shortening the time given to the debtor to redeem, the speed at which the costs and interest eat up any equity, and the responsibility for any shortfall, all combine to create very involved and difficult problems for the parties.

Summary

Personal property

- Tangible, moveable property—chattels
- Intangible property—a chose in action
- Chattels can become fixed to real property, but where they are trade or tenant fixtures, they can be removed when the tenant leaves, if this can be done without damage
- Bailment—when property owned by one person is temporarily in the possession of another; imposes an obligation to look after that property; depends on contractual terms or on who benefits from the bailment when there is no contract

Real property

- Land and things attached to it
- Estate—right to exclusive use of the land
- Fee simple estate—complete ownership of the land
- Life estate—right to the land for life
- Leasehold estate—right to the land for a specific period
- Lesser interests—easements, restrictive covenants, and, in some cases, licenses
- Joint tenancy—when one of the parties dies, the other takes the whole property by right of survivorship
- Tenancy in common—separate interests remain apart even with death
- Land registry—depository of documents that affect the title. Government provides a certificate of title that is conclusive proof of the interests affecting the title of the land
- Leasehold estates involve landlord and tenant relationships
- Commercial tenancies are governed primarily by common law, with the rights of the parties set out in the lease
- Residential tenancies have been significantly modified by statute; notice must be given by the landlord to increase rent or terminate a lease; parties

have obligations to repair or pay security deposits; rent controls are in place in some jurisdictions

Mortgages

- Title to property transferred to a creditor/mortgagee as security for a loan
- Debtor/mortgagor retains a right to redeem the property
- Equity of redemption can also be mortgaged, creating an equitable second or third mortgage
- Upon default, the creditor seeks a foreclosure order, which ends the mortgagor's right to redeem; second mortgagee usually seeks an order for judicial sale of the property to ensure some payment before the operation of the foreclosure order takes effect

QUESTIONS

1. Indicate how personal property can become real property. Discuss why a determination of why and when this has happened may be significant.

2. What is a fixture, and under what circumstances can someone other than the owner of real property remove fixtures?

3. Explain what is meant by the saying "finders keepers" in terms of who is entitled to property that has been found.

4. Discuss the different ways in which a bailment may be created and the nature of the duty imposed on the bailee in each circumstance.

5. Distinguish between the obligation placed on a bailee for value and that imposed on a common carrier or innkeeper.

6. What does the purchaser get when he or she buys a house?

7. Distinguish between personal and real property.

8. What is meant by a fee simple estate in land?

9. Explain the rights and obligations of reversion and remainder when discussing a life estate.

10. Explain and contrast life estates and leasehold estates.

11. What is meant by an easement? Give examples and explain why an easement is called a lesser interest in land.

12. Explain the significance of dominant and servient tenements when dealing with easements.

13. What is meant by a restrictive covenant? Under what circumstances will such a covenant be binding on subsequent landowners? How does this relate to a building scheme?

14. Contrast a tenancy in common with a joint tenancy and indicate how one can be changed to another. Why is the distinction important?

15. How can failure to properly register a mortgage or deed affect the initial parties to an instrument in a registration jurisdiction? What happens when an innocent third party becomes involved?

16. How is a leasehold right different from the rights of a resident created under a license agreement?

17. Under what circumstances must a leasehold interest be evidenced in writing? Why?

18. What is a periodic tenancy? How does it compare with an ordinary lease arrangement? What special problems come into play with periodic tenancies which are not present with term leases?

19. Explain what is meant by a landlord's obligation to ensure a tenant's "quiet enjoyment."

20. What is meant by mortgage, equity of redemption, and foreclosure? Distinguish between the mortgagor and mortgagee.

21. Compare the terms "equity of redemption" and "equity in property."

22. What is mortgaged when a second or third mortgage is created? Explain how the risk of a second or third mortgagee is greater than that of the first mortgagee.

23. How is the registration of mortgages handled differently under a land titles system of land registry as opposed to the registration system in place in the rest of Canada?

24. Why is the time of registration of a mortgage significant in all jurisdictions in Canada?

CASES

1. Punch v. Savoys Jewellers Limited et al.

Mrs. Punch owned a very valuable antique ring, which was in need of repair. She took it to Savoys Jewellers who then sent it by registered mail to Walkers, a Toronto jeweller. By the time Walkers had repaired the ring, there was a postal strike in progress, so they used Rapidex, a branch of the Canadian National Railway, to transport the ring back to Savoys with their agreement. There was a provision on the bill of lading limiting Rapidex's liability for "negligence or otherwise" to $ 50. Walker put a $100 value on the bill of lading, when, in fact, the ring was worth about $11 000. The ring was never delivered, and Mrs. Punch sued Savoys, Walkers, and CN for the loss. CN had no record of what happened and was not able to show whether the ring had been lost or stolen.

Explain the nature of the duty owed by Walker, Savoys, and CN to Mrs. Punch and the likely outcome of her action against them for the recovery of the value of the ring.

2. National Trust Co. v. Chriskim Holdings Inc.

A bank and a restaurant were located on adjoining properties. The company operating the restaurant wanted to expand by extending the restaurant into a lane that it thought it owned but which, in fact, was owned by the bank. The restaurant only had a right of way across it. Unwittingly, the owners of the restaurant started the expansion but soon discovered their mistake. They sent a letter to the bank offering to pay an annual rental of $1 per foot. When the bank did not accept this offer, instead of stopping, they continued with the construction. The bank sued. The restaurant countersued; it seems a mistake had been made when the bank was built and it encroached slightly onto the property owned by the restaurant. The restaurant had been leasing the property since 1983 and had purchased it in 1987. Before this time, however, the former owner had used that right of way since 1952. The bank building had been at its location since 1967.

Explain the obligations and rights of the parties to each other in these circumstances and the arguments available to each in defending their positions. Would your answer be any different if this had taken place in a land registry jurisdiction rather than in a land titles jurisdiction?

3. Re Ramsay and Heselmann

The appellant was the owner of a property consisting of 12 furnished rooms, one of which was rented to the respondent. Rent was paid weekly. The respondent failed to make proper payments, and the appellant seized her clothing and personal effects as security for the non-payment of rent. (The *Innkeepers' Act* allows an innkeeper or boardinghouse-keeper to seize goods in this way. The *Landlord and Tenant Act* [R.S.O. (1980) Chapter 232] does not allow a landlord a similar right.)

The respondent brought this action, applying for a declaration that her goods and personal effects had been wrongfully seized. Explain the arguments on both sides and the likely outcome of the case.

4. North Bay TV & Audio Ltd. v. Nova Electronics Ltd. et al.

North Bay TV was the landlord, and Nova was the tenant operating a store selling audio and electronic equipment. They entered into a five-year lease agreement in 1981. In 1982, business started to go bad for Nova. They were late paying their rent in April and only paid partial rent in May and June. They failed to pay their rent in July altogether or make even partial payment for their share of the utility services supplied to the building. This caused North Bay's representative, Mr. Stanfall, to call Nova about these lapses. Mr. Smith and Mr. Becock were the principals involved in Nova. Mr. Becock informed Mr. Smith that he understood the landlord was intending to close the premises down, and he suggested to Mr. Smith that they remove as much inventory as possible that evening, which they proceeded to do. They removed three station wagon loads of electronic goods from the store. While they were doing this, Mr. Stanfall arrived, confronted them, and asked them what they were doing. The tenants told him they were moving out of the premises. When the tenants had left, Mr. Stanfall closed the shop door with a sign saying that the store had been closed by landlord, and anyone taking anything from the premises without permission of the landlord would be prosecuted. The next morning, they changed the locks.

Explain the rights and remedies available to each party. Who has terminated the lease? Who is entitled to any goods still on the premises? Would your answer be affected if you understood that several months later the landlord re-let the premises at a higher rent than they were receiving from Nova?

5. Sterne v. Victoria & Grey Trust Co.

Mr. Sterne owned a hobby farm, with a first mortgage held by Victoria & Grey Trust. Mr. Sterne was unable to make payments when they became due. The mortgagee commenced sale proceedings under their power of sale as set out in the mortgage. They obtained two appraisals, one for $190 000 and the other for $195 000. The mortgagee advertised the property, received an offer of $185 000, and sold it for that price. During this time, Mr. Sterne had listed the property and had received an offer for $210 000, but the offer had conditions, and the closing date was several months away, so the mortgagee went ahead with their deal for $185 000.

Explain the rights of the parties in these circumstances. Would your answer be any different if you learned that at the time of the sale, the mortgagee was aware of other appraisals which placed the value of the property as high as $240 000 and also that the property was listed only as "work" property not as a hobby farm and then only in the local newspapers?

CHAPTER
16

Intellectual Property and Insurance

CHAPTER HIGHLIGHTS

- Forms of intellectual property
- Legal protection of intellectual property
- Electronic technology and intellectual property
- Insurance

Intellectual property law attempts to balance the protection of the product of a person's mental effort on the one side and the free flow of new and innovative ideas, which stimulate the advancement of the commercial environment, on the other. Its primary focus is on the rights and responsibilities of individuals in relation to ideas, information, and other creative works, and how others use those products of the mind.

Imax Corp. v. Showmax Inc.[1]

Imax Corp. was the plaintiff in an application for an interlocutory injunction for trademark infringement against Showmax Inc., a company based in Montreal that opened a large-format motion picture theatre. Showmax promoted its grand opening on banners, in magazines, and on its Internet web site. The web site used a framing device to show multiple windows on its homepage. One of the windows linked browsers to the Old Port of Montreal web site, which, in turn, contained information and advertising regarding the Imax theatre at the Old Port of Montreal. The plaintiff argued that the arrangement of framing and linking would cause the viewer to think that Imax was responsible for or was connected with Showmax. The Federal Court of Canada agreed that there was evidence that the web site might lead consumers to believe that the Showmax theatre was operated and controlled by the same entity that controlled the Imax theatres. This evidence of confusion was sufficient to lead to the loss of "name, goodwill, and reputation." The judge concluded that there was a serious issue to be tried and the possibility of irreparable harm, and therefore granted the interlocutory injunction. This case illustrates that laws governing copyright and trademark infringement will be applied to internet communications, and web site managers must be careful that their links and frames do not mislead browsers as to the source of the information. It also illustrates how an injunction, and particularly an interlocutory injunction which is granted before the actual trial (as discussed in this chapter), can be an important remedy when such an infringement takes place.

1. Imax corp. v. Showmax Inc. 5 C.P.R. (4th) 81 (Fed. T.D.)

Intellectual Property

Intellectual property must be contrasted to other forms of personal property. When a chattel is stolen or destroyed, it is no longer available for the use of the original owner. When an idea is taken and used by somebody else, or confidential information is wrongfully communicated to another, the idea or information does not change. It is still available to the original holder, although its value might be considerably diminished.

As computer data storage and internet information transmission expand, intellectual property law has grown significantly in importance. The development of law has not kept pace with this information and technological explosion, but existing laws go a long way in establishing rights and obligations, and many recent changes have been made by both parliament and the courts.

Grad Student Finds Thesis Marketed for Profit On-line

A Canadian academic surfing the Internet was startled and angered to find her master's thesis marketed for US $ 69.50 on Contentville.com, an American web site. Graduate students submit copies of their work to the National Library of Canada when they complete their degrees, often without knowing their work could be sold for profit to others.

The academic, a doctoral student at the University of British Columbia, was shocked to see her thesis and others offered on the Contentville web site. "I never gave permission for them to use it. It was like it was stolen." The National Library of Canada argued that all graduate students give permission on a form they fill out when they submit a copy of their theses to the library. The form gives the library a limited license to reproduce and distribute them to make research available to other scholars. To cut costs, this service was contracted out to a private company, UMI Dissertations Publishing.

In early July, UMI decided to make part of its catalogue available to Contentville. Any sale made on Contentville is directly transmitted to UMI, which copies the thesis, sends it to the buyer, and collects the fee.

"We are simply attempting to broaden the access to dissertations," says Bill Savage of UMI. He notes the catalogue was already available to scholarly societies and libraries, as well as to UMI's own web site."[2]

Most legislation protecting intellectual property is federal, with copyright and patent legislation being exclusively granted to the federal government in the *Constitution Act (1867)*.[3] Such areas as confidential information, trade secrets, and passing-off are not considered property rights and are protected by common law principles. Some provincial statutes, such as privacy acts, can have an important impact in the intellectual property area.

2. Adapted from Chris Tenove, *National Post* Aug. 15, 2000 A4.

3. *Constitution Act (1867)*, Section 91, ss. 22, 23

Copyright

Boudreau v. Lin[4]

Paul Boudreau was a student taking part-time classes in an MBA program, when he wrote a paper for a directed readings course under the direction of the defendant, a professor at the university he attended. At the time, Boudreau was employed in a high-tech firm and based his paper on information gathered from his place of employment. He submitted his draft paper and, with suggestions from his professor, made changes and resubmitted the paper in its final form. In the meantime, his professor had been discussing the paper with a colleague at another university, and they jointly published the paper with only a few revisions, with themselves as authors and no mention of Boudreau.

When Boudreau discovered his paper with a different name and a few changes published in a casebook used by MBA students, he complained to the university. He also brought an action for the infringement of his copyright against the professor and the university. The court found that the student was the author and owner of the paper and, therefore, had the copyright in it. The professor claimed that he had made a minor error in leaving off the student's name and that they had previously discussed publication. The student denied this, and the court accepted that position. The university was deemed to have knowledge of the infringement, and thus shared liability with its employee. The professor claimed fair dealing, but the court found that his removal of the author's name, the change of the title, and his claim that the paper was his were inconsistent with fair dealing with the work. The university claimed that the work had been reproduced as a matter of private study, but the court disagreed, finding that reproducing the paper for the study of the whole class was no longer a matter of private study. Also, the author's moral rights were infringed because the integrity of the work had been interfered with (changed somewhat) and his right to have his name associated with it breached. Both the copyright and the moral rights of the students had been infringed. The court noted, "Plagiarism is a form of academic dishonesty which strikes at the heart of our educational system. It is not to be tolerated from the students, and the university has made this quite clear. It follows that it most certainly should not be tolerated from the professors, who should be sterling examples of intellectual rigour and honesty."

The case illustrates a problem that often arises in the university environment as to who owns the work that students produce. Here, the student was clearly entitled to the copyright in the paper he authored. In other situations, where university equipment and grants are involved, it might not be so clear. It should be noted that in the investigation process by the university, the interests of the student were given only cursory consideration, while the position of the professor was given considerable consideration and deference. This shows another regrettable situation where the students are often treated as second-class citizens in these situations. The case is interesting for our purposes in that it shows how copyright is established and also shows what is meant by the author's moral rights. It also indicates the narrow scope of the defences of fair dealing and private use.

The federal *Copyright Act* [5]gives the author or owner of the copyright a monopoly over the use of the created work prohibiting copying or reproduction of the

4. 150 D.L.R. (4th) 324 (Ont. Gen. Div.)
5. R.S.C. (1985)

work without permission. Only the actual work itself is protected, not the ideas or thought behind it. Thus, the actual expression of an idea in a book is protected, but someone else is free to express those same ideas in a different way.

The work is protected, not the idea

The federal government has the power to make law with respect to copyright. The *Copyright Act*, originally passed in 1928, has until recently remained surprisingly unchanged. But this legislation is now undergoing a major three-phase amendment process. The first changes were introduced in 1988[6] and the second in 1997.[7] The third and final phase should be submitted to parliament by September 2002. These changes are required because of significant technological advances, including the ease of reproducing written, musical, visual, and computer works, huge changes have taken place. Massive copying of books, records, tapes, CDs, videos, and computer programs is not only possible but is now common. This is especially true over the Internet, where compression software and CD burners have made the wholesale copying of recorded music so common that it has seriously affected the viability of the recorded music industry. The power to make copyright law has been given to the federal government exclusively, and the *Copyright Act* remained relatively stagnant for 50 years until significant amendments were made starting in 1988.

Matters Covered

Only original work that is the product of an artist's or author's own work or skill is entitled to copyright protection. The categories of copyrightable materials have recently been expanded and now include the following: literary works including tables, computer programs, and "literary compilations" such as poems, stories, and articles (books). Dramatic works include shows (movies, videos, television, and theatre) and mime performances, including choreography and scenery. Musical works include musical composition with or without words. Artistic works include paintings, drawings, charts, maps, plans, photos, engravings, sculptures, works of artistic craftsmanship, and architecture. Sound recordings include any kind of material record of sound, including tapes, CDs, and vinyl records. Performers' performances include those by actors, musicians, dancers, and singers, whether they are scripted or improvised. Communications signals include broadcasted (wireless) signals such as radio and television.

To be copyrightable, work must be original and the product of the author's skill

The problem of whether computer programs were protected by copyright was solved by the 1988 amendment to the *Copyright Act* that now specifically provides copyright protection for computer software and hardware. Prior to this, there was considerable debate and confusion as to whether unique computer software and hardware were protected under patent or copyright law and how extensive that protection was. A particular problem with computer programs is the difficulty in distinguishing between what constitutes the idea behind the software and its expression. The courts have concluded, however, that where one product has the same look and feel in its operation as the other, an infringement of copyright has taken place. Thus, even if the code is completely different, if what appears on the screen looks the same as another program, it is likely that there has been an infringement of copyright.

Computer programs protected

---

6. *Ibid.* c. 42, as amended by R.S.A. (1985) (4th Supp.) c. 10 and subsequent amendments

7. S.C. (1997), c.24, s.2

Creation

In Canada, the creation of the work generates copyright protection automatically. There is no need to register or even publish the work. Still, registration may be wise, since it establishes when the copyright was created and the presumption that the person named in the registration is the owner of the copyright. Although not specified in the Canadian legislation, there is a practice (following the provisions of the Universal Copyright Convention) of notification of copyright which generally takes the form of the symbol "©," sometimes with the word "copyright" beside it, followed by the year the copyright was first published and the name of the owner of the copyright. The United States and other countries that are parties to the copyright conventions discussed below recognize valid Canadian copyright, and so registration is not necessary, but notification as set out above is required; where the copyright is not registered, the remedies available for infringement may be significantly restricted.

For a person to obtain copyright protection in Canada, he or she must be a citizen or resident of Canada, or a citizen, subject, or resident of one of the countries that adhere to the *Berne Copyright Convention* or the *Universal Copyright Convention*—international agreements that set out common rules of conduct in matters concerning copyright. Berne Convention countries are also included when sound recordings, communication signals, or performances are involved. Residents of other countries may also be protected where the minister so designates and publishes notice in the *Canada Gazette*.

Many countries, for example, the People's Republic of China, do not have the same traditions of protection of artistic and literary works as in western countries, and the disregard for intellectual property protection in such countries has been a major stumbling block in the further development of trade relations.

Ownership

The copyright belongs to the person who created the work or to the employer where the work was created as part of employment, unless there is an agreement otherwise. Once the copyright has been created, its owner can assign or license it, all or in part, to someone else, although a court will presume the copyright is held by the creator unless there is evidence to show otherwise. The owner of the copyright can assign it to someone else, but even then, the author will continue to have **moral rights** in the work. These moral rights allow the author to demand that his name continue as author and that the new owner not change the work in such a way as to degrade it and bring harm to the reputation of the author. In 1982, an Ontario court granted an injunction to a respected sculptor when, to celebrate Christmas, Toronto's Eaton Centre put red ribbons around his sculptures of flying geese. Since the 1988 amendments, the moral rights of the authors and artists have been incorporated into the *Copyright Act* to protect such interests. Moral rights also require that the work not be associated with any product or activity that may harm the author's reputation without permission. The moral rights of an author are infringed when someone else claims authorship, or if the work is mutilated or modified in such a way that the reputation of the author is harmed. In such circumstances, the author can seek compensation even though someone else owns the copyright, providing the author has not waived their moral rights.

Copyright gives the owner control over the work, except for the moral rights, which remain with the author. No one else can perform, copy, publish, broadcast, translate, or otherwise reproduce the work without the permission of the owner of the copyright.

This protection extends for the life of the author plus 50 years, with some exceptions, such as photographs, where the protection is for only 50 years from the creation of the negative. Copyrights held by government are also only protected for 50 years.

Copyright holder has complete control over rights for author's life plus 50 years

Infringement takes place when anyone tries to obtain a benefit from the sale, distribution, performance, broadcast, or other commercial use of the work. The moral rights of an author are infringed when someone else claims authorship or if the work is mutilated or modified in such a way that the reputation of the author is harmed. In such circumstances, the author can seek compensation even though someone else owns the copyright, provided the author has not waived his or her moral rights.

The protection given under copyright and moral rights generally extends for 50 years after the end of the calendar year in which the author dies. There are several exceptions to this, such as government publications, where the protection granted is generally limited to only 50 years after the year of first publication. Photographs for which a corporation owns the copyright are also granted only 50 years protection, unless the creator was the major shareholder of the corporation. In that case, that major shareholder is considered to be the author and the general rule applies extending protection for 50 years after the end of the year in which the author dies.

Copyright Law Protects Artists

A young artist made two sketches of tall ships that he intended to have mechanically reproduced to sell to sightseers, when two tall ships visited a neighbouring community. The job of reproducing the prints was given to a print shop, where two employees ran off the requested 50 copies and then 60 more for themselves. The artist received his prints but decided not to sell them. The two print shop employees sold their copies of the prints and kept the profits. When the artist discovered this violation, he took the necessary steps to have them prosecuted.

The court decided that the artist owned the copyright in the two sketches and that the actions of the print shop employees went beyond mere copyright infringement and amounted to theft under the *Criminal Code*. They were convicted.[8] Although the artist retained the original sketches, reproduction of them without his permission not only was a violation of copyright but also amounted to theft. Art work, photographs, computer programs, compact discs, and videotapes are often improperly copied without authorization and without affecting the original.

Copyright gives the owner control over the work, except for the moral rights, which remain with the author. No one else can perform, copy, publish, broadcast, translate, or otherwise produce the work without the permission of the owner of the copyright. Infringement takes place when anyone tries to obtain a benefit from the sale, distribution, performance, broadcast, or other commercial use of the work. Plagiarism involving the copying of another's work and claiming authorship is also a violation of copyright.

Quotations from the work that are not extensive and are attributed to the author do not amount to an infringement of copyright. The *Copyright Act* specifically states that "any fair dealing with any work for the purposes of private study, research, criticism, review, or newspaper summary"[9] is not an infringement of copyright. There is considerable debate as to just what these words mean, and certainty will only be established where courts rule on specific practices. It is likely, however, that

8. R v. Wolfe and Campbell, 633-016. *The Lawyer's Weekly*, December 19, 1986.
9. *Copyright Act*, Section 27(2)(a)

where the reproduction, even for classroom or study purposes, is so extensive as to deprive the author of the market for the product, it would be an infringement of the copyright. Specific exceptions allowing copying for certain purposes are set out in the act. Non-profit educational institutions, such as schools, colleges and universities, have a very limited right to reproduce works used for study. Teachers can write materials on the board or include them in exams and not infringe the act. They can also record and keep for a limited period of time for study purposes radio, newspaper, and television material. Teachers can also project materials on a screen unless commercially available slides are available for that purpose. Libraries and similar institutions have similar rights. People who have reading or hearing disabilities can make copies to assist them, such as converting the work to braille. People can make one back up copy of their computer programs. And interestingly, anyone can make a recording of music tapes, records, and CDs for their own private use. Royalties are charged on blank tapes and other recording media to compensate artists and producers for this exception.

Copyright Protects Videotapes

The managers of Wall & Redekop were impressed with a set of videotapes titled "How to Master the Art of Listing and Selling Real Estate" that had been prepared by the plaintiff. In 1981, they obtained a used copy of the tapes, made 10 copies, and distributed them to their various offices. When the plaintiff was informed of this, they wrote to Wall & Redekop complaining about the infringement. Wall & Redekop immediately called in the 10 tapes and erased them. This action was successfully brought, claiming a violation of copyright and the tort of "conversion," wherein ownership in something is wrongfully taken over by another. Damages were awarded.

Tom Hopkins International, Inc. v. Wall & Redekop Realty Ltd., 20 D.L.R. (4th) 407 (B.C.C.A.)

Remedies

The normal remedies available in a civil action, including an injunction, are available when a copyright is violated. Sometimes, an **interlocutory injunction** is given before the actual trial to prevent further damage. This is an interim measure, and a permanent injunction may or may not be granted at trial. Often, the effect of the interim remedy may be so devastating to the offender that no further action need be taken. To obtain an interlocutory injunction, the plaintiff must establish a *prima facie* case that there has been an infringement of copyright and that if the injunction is not granted, irreparable harm will be suffered that could not properly be compensated for by an award of damages at the trial. The **balance of convenience** must also be in the plaintiff's favour. This refers to which side will suffer the greatest damage if the injunction is granted. Where a small business seeks an order to stop the production and sales of a much larger operation, it will not be granted if the order would cause that business more damage than the small one would suffer if the injunction were not granted. Courts are generally reluctant to grant interlocutory injunctions.

Sometimes, a court will issue an order even before trial that the offending material be seized. This is called an **Anton Piller order**. This is an *ex parte* procedure, in which the evidence must be seized by surprise before the goods or relevant documentation can be hidden or destroyed.

Schools have a limited right to reproduce works used for study.
PhotoDisc

The court will only issue such an order where there is clear and compelling evidence of the infringement of copyright, the danger of significant damage to the plaintiff, and some indication that surprise is needed to protect the evidence.

After the trial, one of the most important remedies is the **permanent injunction** prohibiting the production, sale, or distribution of any of the infringing products. If the copyright has not been registered and the defendant were unaware they were violating copyright, the only remedy under the act is an injunction, often with an order to surrender the offending documents. But where the infringement took place knowingly, damages or an accounting may be obtained. An award of **damages** is calculated to compensate the victim for the losses suffered, including the lost profits that would have been earned had the copyright not been infringed. An **accounting** is often given where it would be difficult to determine what actual damages have been suffered. This remedy requires that any profits made from the sale or rental of the offending product be paid over to the victim, even if this amount exceeds the damages suffered by the plaintiff. The court may also award **punitive damages** in cases of flagrant violation to punish the offender rather than simply to compensate the victim of the infringement. In any case, it must be noted that the limitation period in which an action should be commenced is three years, although this may be extended from the time the person learned of the infringement rather than from when it actually occurred.

One of the purposes of the recent revision of the act has been to make enforcement of its provisions more equitable. To that end, a simplified or summary procedure has been introduced, making enforcement much easier and less costly. In addition, the courts can now in their discretion award statutory damages in the range of $500 to $20 000 simply on the basis of affidavits. One of the serious problems of the old legislation, which is overcome by this provision, was the difficulty of proving actual losses.

In addition to these civil remedies, the *Copyright Act* provides for penalties of up to a million dollars in fines and five years in jail for the most serious cases. The provisions set out in the *Criminal Code*, such as those sections prohibiting theft and fraud, may also apply to the infringement of copyright cases.[10] The *Criminal Code* was used to impose the penalties in the example used to introduce this chapter.

Permanent injunction granted at trial

Damages can compensate for loss

Accounting requires handing over profits

Punitive damages may be available to punish wrongdoer

Statutory damages now available

Fine and imprisonment available for infringement

Criminal Code **may apply**

Untangling the WEB

Although the amendments to the *Copyright Act* have gone some way to alleviate the problem, the enforcement of copyright laws becomes increasingly difficult as the ease with which copies are made increases. Governments rely heavily on self-regulation, but studies have shown that this strategy, although acknowledged and respected by many professional and commercial users, will never be entirely dependable because the means of reproduction is readily available to private users. Hardware and software companies have devised methods to protect their products by using encryption coding and digital watermarks that do not prevent copying but help track how the copies are being used and who is responsible for misuse. While it is still possible to circumvent these protections, it is illegal to do so. Because the Internet has the potential to become a "vast copying machine for pirated software, CDs, and movies," laws are required that will protect intellectual property but still allow the kind of access to information that the Internet makes possible and the free flow of that information that the *Copyright Act* affords.[11]

10. *Criminal Code*, R.S.C. (1985) c. C-46

11. Turban, Efraim, Jae Lee, David King, H. Michael Chung. *Electronic Commerce: A Managerial Perspective*. Upper Saddle River, NJ.: Prentice Hall, 1999, p. 353

The Copyright Board

The *Copyright Act* establishes a board with broad powers to handle disputes between individuals and otherwise supervise and regulate the industry. The board's functions range from setting and reviewing fees and royalties for use of copyright materials to arbitrating disputes. Several associations have been created that represent the owners of copyright when they enter into licensing arrangements with others and to assist in the collection of royalties. SOCAN (Society of Composers, Authors, and Music Publishers of Canada) performs this service in the music industry, and CAN-COPY (Canadian Copyright Licensing Agency) serves a similar function in the literary field, entering into general licensing agreements. They collect royalties and fees for works to be photocopied or digitally reproduced, and pay the funds collected to the authors and publishers. These bodies can also launch a civil action on behalf of their members in the event of copyright infringement.

Patents

Patent creates monopoly

The idea is protected rather than the work

Must be original invention to be patentable

Theories, concepts, or obvious improvements are not patentable

A patent is a government-granted monopoly, giving only the inventor the right to produce, sell, or otherwise profit from a specific invention. Unlike copyright, the patent protection extends to the idea or concept expressed in the invention. To qualify, the invention must be new, in the sense that no one else has been given a patent for it. The patent will also be refused if the inventor or anyone else has disclosed the invention to the public over a year prior to application. This includes disclosure in an academic paper. The invention must also be the original work of the inventor. Thus, a person could not take an invention found in another country and patent it in Canada as his own. The invention must be unique and distinguishable from other products. It must have some utility or perform some useful function. It must also be possible to construct and use it on the basis of the information supplied to the patent office.

You cannot patent a scientific principle or abstract theory, such as Newton's discovery of gravity.[12] Nor can you patent obvious improvements to other products, inventions designed for illegal purposes, things that cannot work, and things generally covered by copyright law. Until recently, new varieties of plants, trees, crops, and animals were also not patentable, but this practice has recently been thrown in doubt by a federal court decision, stating that a genetically altered mouse

12. *Patent Act*, R.S.C. (1985) c. P-4 s. 27 ss. 8

with special value in cancer research could be the subject of a patent.[13] In Canada, as a general rule, computer programs cannot be patented and are now covered by copyright legislation, but such patents have been granted in the United States.

Creation

Unlike copyright, the patent must be registered before conferring rights on the inventor, and so, it is vital that a patent be applied for right away. If someone else beats you to it, you will not only lose the right to patent but also be prevented from producing or otherwise using or profiting from the invention. Employers are entitled to patent the inventions of their employees, and the holder of a patent can assign that patent to others. Joint patents can be obtained when two people have worked on the same invention.

Patent must be applied for and registered

The process of obtaining a patent is complex, requiring that patent records in the United States and Canada be searched to see if a patent already exists, and then submitting an application with supporting documentation and the proscribed fee at the appropriate patent office. These documents include a petition, specifications, claims statements, an abstract, and a drawing that set out not only what the invention is supposed to do but also enough information so that someone looking at them could build and use the item. The patent office then assigns an examiner, who may require further submissions from the applicant, and when all conditions have been met, the patent will be granted. If there are opposing applications, the patent will be granted to the person who first made an application. This process is usually handled by a registered patent agent with both legal and an engineering background and may take two or three years to complete.

Pursuant to international agreements, once a Canadian patent has been granted, application can be made for patents in other jurisdictions, but priority in those countries will be based on when the first application in Canada was made. The reverse is also true, and the Canadian patent office will grant a patent to a foreign applicant who applies in his or her own country before the Canadian applicant applies here. There is a limited period of time after obtaining the Canadian patent to make an application for a foreign patent, and so, this should be done without delay.

Date of application in own country determines priority

Once the patent has been issued, the patent number should be put on the manufactured item to which it applies. The use of "patent pending" has no legal effect but is put on goods to warn that a patent has been applied for. A patent gives its holder a monopoly for a maximum period of 20 years from the date of application, but it requires that the inventor publicly disclose how to make the item in documents that are open to public inspection. Secrecy is surrendered in exchange for the 20-year protection, the idea being that others will be stimulated to produce new inventions because of the disclosure of that information. The granting of the patent gives the patent holder exclusive rights to manufacture, sell, and profit from the invention for those 20 years, and it even protects someone who merely develops a variation of the product, providing that variation meets the general requirements of a patentable invention, as discussed above.

Patent grants monopoly for 20 years but requires disclosure

---

13. President and Fellows of Harvard College and Commisioner of Patents Federal Court of Appeals [2000 03 03] No. A334-98

Complete Disclosure Needed for Patent

Through a process of artificial cross-breeding, the appellant developed a new soybean having very significant advantages and applied for a patent. There were two problems the Supreme Court had to deal with: whether this was a patentable invention and whether there was sufficient disclosure. The court decided this case on the second question, not wanting to consider whether a new plant form created by genetic engineering was patentable. Because the particulars disclosed in the application failed to describe the genetic engineering process and even suggested that a certain amount of luck was involved, there was not sufficient disclosure and the patent application was refused. Disclosure must be sufficient for someone to be able duplicate the results. One of the main purposes of the patent process is to make the information associated with the invention available to others so they can duplicate it and resulting in the advancement of knowledge. This was not done in this case.

Pioneer Hybrid Ltd. v. Commissioner of Patents, 60 D.L.R. (4th) 223 (S.C.C.)

Remedies same as copyright

Because a patent protects the idea rather than its expression, another person would not be able to produce a simple variation of the product without breaching the patent. An infringement of patent may take place by an unauthorized person manufacturing, importing, selling, or otherwise dealing with or using the invention. The patent holder is entitled to the same remedies that would be available in any civil action, including injunction, damages, and accounting, as discussed above under the heading of copyright.

Often, the holder of the patent does not have the resources to manufacture or otherwise exploit the invention and will license its manufacture to another company. Where an important invention is involved, there is provision for compulsory licenses to be granted with the payment of royalties, even over the objections of the inventor.

It should be noted that by a 1987 amendment to the *Patent Act*, drug manufacturers were given more control over the production and sale of their products. This stopped the practice of competitors capitalizing on the research and development of those manufacturers and producing much cheaper "generic drugs." A Patent Medicine Prices Review Board was also established with broad powers, including the power to reduce the sale of patented medicines and pharmaceuticals.[14] This period of patent protection in this area has also been extended to 20 years.

Untangling the WEB

Information technology has created a new wave of patents, as hardware and software developers attempt to protect their rights. New methods of using the Internet are being patented, and this further blurs the distinction between what can be considered an invention and what is really just an idea that should be handled under copyright laws.

Trademarks

Symbols or designs of business protected as trademarks

Any term, symbol, design, or combination of these that identifies a business service or product is a trademark and protected by the federal *Trademarks Act*.[15] Examples of protected trademarks are such words as "Kodak" and "Xerox," symbols,

14. *Patent Act Amendments*, R.S.C. (1985) (3d Supp.) c. 33

15. R.S.C. (1985) c. T-13

such as the arm and hammer used on that company's baking soda box; combinations of words and symbols, such as the Apple logo on computers; and even the distinctive design of a product's container, such as the Coca-Cola bottle. Trademarks also include the special marks used by some organizations, such as Canadian Standards Association, to indicate quality or certification. The object is to protect the value of the good will and prevent people from misleading others by using the trademark words or symbols for their own purposes and to prevent the trademarks value from being diminished through association with inferior products.

Purpose to protect consumer deception

For a trademark to be protected under the act, it must be registered. As part of the registration process, it is published in the *Trademark Journal,* and if someone feels that it does not qualify, they can "oppose" the registration. Once registered, the trademark gives its owner an exclusive right to use it throughout Canada for 15 years (renewable). The registration also establishes a presumption of ownership so that in an action for infringement, a defendant claiming otherwise must produce strong evidence to that effect.

Registration protects trademark

A trademark can be any word, design, symbol, or packaging that distinctively identifies a business or product. It cannot be obscene or scandalous or just a sound or colour, although a distinctive colour may be part of the trademark. Nor can it be anything that resembles the insignia, crests, or other symbols of royalty, the government, or government agencies, such as the RCMP, service organizations, such as the Red Cross, or even names, portraits, or signatures of individuals, without their consent. There is also a prohibition against using any marks, symbols, or designs that resemble a well-known one, which would cause confusion with the products or services of that other body. Normally, simple surnames cannot be registered, and so, people can use their own surnames in their business without fear of violation. Only where the name has become associated with another product, such as McDonald's hamburgers or Campbell's soup, will the applicant run into problems.

Restrictions

Trademarks can lose their status through common use. Aspirin, trampoline, kleenex, and linoleum are examples of terms that have lost their unique status because people use them to describe the general type of product.

Trademark lost through common usage

Applying for trademark registration is a complicated process requiring the services of an expert, and once registered, there is an obligation to use the trademark. Failure to do so can result in the loss of the trademark through abandonment. Also, whenever the trademark appears, it should be marked with the symbol "®," indicating that the trademark has been registered. An unregistered trademark can be marked with "TM."

The object of trademark protection is to preserve the value of the good will associated with it by preventing others from using the mark to mislead others into thinking they are dealing with the owner of the trademark when they are not. To enforce that right, the owner must show not only that they own the copyright but also that the public would likely be confused by the wrongful use of the trademark causing damage to the owner.

If the action to protect a trademark is successful, the types of civil remedies available are the standard ones, discussed under copyrights and patents. A very effective remedy in the appropriate circumstances is an order giving the owner of the trademark custody of the offending goods. An action can be brought in the federal court when the infringed trademark has been properly registered under the act, but it may be more effective to bring the matter before the appropriate provincial court. Such courts are not limited to enforcing the statute (as is the federal court) but may rely on common law principles as well.

Remedies same as copyright infringement

Court Rules Lexus Can Be Both a Luxury Car and a Fruit Juice

Lexus Foods, a Québec company that produces canned fruit and vegetables, has won a legal battle against Toyota Motor Corp. The car manufacturer went to the Federal Court of Canada to stop the Québec company from using the name Lexus, arguing that most Canadians would associate the name with its luxury car.

The court decided that people were unlikely to confuse a can of fruit juice with a luxury car and reversed a ruling that would have prohibited Lexus Foods from using its name to market its products. "It is hard to see that anyone about to buy some of the canned fruit juice of the appellant would even entertain the thought that the Japanese automobile manufacturers of Lexus was the source of this product," Justice Allen Linden wrote in his reasons for the court's decision. The problem arose in February 1993, when Toyota unsuccessfully opposed the food company's application for registration of the trademark. Toyota pursued the matter, and the Federal Court of Canada overruled the Registrar of Trademarks.

In its unanimous decision, the three-member Court of Appeal panel dismissed that decision. Justice Linden wrote that trademark protection must be related to "certain wares or services" because confusion is less likely when the products in question are markedly different. Justice Linden noted that many other businesses unrelated to automobiles used the name, including Lexus Bath Mat, Lexus Cleaners, Lexus computer Training, and Lexus Realty.

From *The National Post*, November 29, 2000, p. A-4.

Common law passing-off action gives similar protection

In addition to the federal *Trademarks Act*, this area is also covered by common law in the form of a passing-off action. A **passing-off action** is founded in tort and prevents a person from misleading the public into thinking it is dealing with some other business or person when it is not. The court can order compensation be paid or that the offending conduct stop. This remedy is available even when an unregistered trademark is involved.

Public must be misled

For a passing-off action to succeed, it is necessary to establish that the public was likely to be misled. The plaintiff must show that its mark, name, or other feature associated with their business was used by the offending party in association with its own operation, causing confusion in the minds of the public, with at least the potential of causing damage to the owner of the copyright. It would be an actionable passing-off for an independent hamburger stand operator to put golden arches in front of his place of business so that people would assume they were part of the McDonalds' chain. But if a person were to use an attractive logo developed by someone else but not yet registered or used in association with any business, a passing-off action would not succeed because the logo had not become associated with any business and the public could not be misled.

Industrial Designs

Industrial Design Act— reproduced artistic designs must be registered

Registering a unique shape, pattern, or ornament under the federal *Industrial Design Act* can protect a unique design or pattern that distinguishes a manufactured article, such as the Coca-Cola bottle.[16] To be protected, the design must be registered within one year of being published, and every item (or label or packaging) should be marked with the letter "D" enclosed in a circle, and the name of the registered owner, or its normal abbreviation. Failure to mark the item in this way will limit remedies for infringement to an injunction if the defendant did not know of the registration. Most products with a distinctive shape or pattern can be regis-

16. *Industrial Design Act*, R.S.C. (1985) c. I-9

Untangling the WEB

Rights to names and trademarks present a complex problem for information providers and retailers on the Internet. The sheer volume of web sites and the significance of links between them has spawned the creation of private companies, such as Network Solutions Inc. (NSI), that have become registrars for domain names, administering TLDs (Top Level Domains) like ".com" and ".net." This function is now performed by ICANN, which has committed itself to create a number of new domain names to deal with disputes with respect to these domain names. Individuals and network service providers apply to use a specific name for their homepage and in its address. Names are issued and registered on a first-come-first-served basis—this is one of the first things a new business should do. If there is a dispute, the user must justify their right to use the name. Because domain names should be closely related to the product or service so that it can be easily found by browsers, there is always the danger that competitors will divert browsers to their own site, either by the use of hidden links or using a variation of their competitor's domain name. In Canada, people should further protect themselves by getting a trademark registration of their domain name, but it is easy to see how the official registration process would soon be swamped by such applications. Even without such registration, there still may be the option of bringing a passing-off action.

tered and will receive protection for a period of 10 years, provided all the requirements of the act are met.

The act is intended to protect attractive and distinctive patterns or shapes, as opposed to useful ones. As with copyrights, patents, and trademarks, the product involved must be original and not a copy of some product already on the market. In 1964, in a case before the Exchequer Court, a uniquely designed sofa was deemed to be protected by an industrial design registration.[17] As with copyrights, patents, and trademarks, the product involved must be original, and not a copy of some product already on the market, and the resulting interest can be assigned to others.

Intellectual property is fast becoming the most important asset of many businesses. Companies, not realizing their potential, often fail to properly protect or exploit those assets. Some large companies have discovered they have untapped resources in their trademarks and other intellectual property that they have not taken advantage of because they were not directly related to their primary business objectives. As businesses realize the importance and value of intellectual property, more resources will be devoted to protecting and exploiting it. The law to regulate such matters will continue to expand with the developing realization of the importance of intellectual property. The right to use such resources can also be abused. When an outsider recognizes the value of a name, logo, or concept to an established company and finds that the name or concept has not been registered, that individual may be able to register it and then attempt to sell the right to use the name or concept back to the company for exorbitant prices.

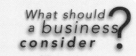

Confidential Information

Cadbury Schweppes Inc. v. FBI Foods Ltd.[18]

Duffy-Mott produced Clamato Juice in the United States. They entered into an agreement with Caesar Canning to produce the product in Canada. FBI Foods was further engaged by Caesar Canning to produce Clamato Juice for other parts of

---

17. Cimon Ltd. v. Benchmade Furniture Corp. (1964) 1 Ex. C.R. 811

18. 138 D.L.R. (4th) 708 (B.C.C.A.); S.C.C. decision 167 D.L.R. (4th) 577

Canada. One of the terms of the agreement with Caesar Canning was that as licensee it would agree not to produce a similar product for a period of five years after the agreement was terminated. Duffy-Mott provided a recipe to Caesar Canning and FBI Foods for the production of the juice; however, the special herbs and spices that were used to create its unique flavour were prepackaged and sent as a dry product to the licensees, and so, they did not have access to that part of the specific recipe.

Eventually, Duffy-Mott's shares were bought out by Cadbury Schweppes, and shortly after that, Duffy-Mott provided 12 months' notice to Caesar Canning that they were cancelling the agreement. In fact, Caesar Canning and FBI Foods had invested a fair amount in their plant and equipment to produce Clamato Juice, and with the cancellation of this license, they sought out another product. Lorne Nichlason, an employee of Caesar Canning, developed a new product called Caesar Cocktail to replace Clamato Juice.

The court found that Caesar Cocktail recipe copied the recipe of Clamato Juice. "It is beyond doubt that without the formula and process information about Clamato, Mr. Nichlason could not have developed Caesar Cocktail personally. He did not have the necessary skills." The trial judge found that even though they could have developed their own recipe within the 12-month time frame by hiring expert help, they chose instead to copy the Clamato recipe.

In determining whether a breach of confidence had taken place, the court looked for three elements that must be present. First, that the information in question was confidential; second, that it had been communicated in confidence; and third, that it had been misused by the party to whom it was communicated. In this case, all three of these requirements were clearly established.

Determining the appropriate remedy was a problem. The lower court awarded damages on the basis of what it would have cost the defendants to develop their own products, which was determined to be just short of $30 000. This was appealed to the British Columbia Court of Appeal, which issued a permanent injunction against the use of the information. On further appeal to the Supreme Court of Canada, it was held that this was an inappropriate case for an injunction because of an 11-year delay in bringing the matter to trial and the relative unimportance of the confidential information used. The Supreme Court of Canada awarded damages on the basis of the profits lost during the 12-month period of misuse.

For our purposes, this case is important because it shows what constitutes a breach of confidential information; it does not require a copyright, patent, or other form of government-provided protection. The information was given in a manner that indicated it was intended to remain confidential, so there is an obligation to keep it so. The case also provides an interesting insight into the way the court determines appropriate remedies.

Confidential information is given in circumstances where it is clear that the information is intended to remain confidential and not be disclosed. In business, it may be necessary that confidences be kept by insiders, such as managers, investors, and employees, as well as outsiders, such as contractors consultants and suppliers. The disclosure of confidential information can prove as devastating to the company as interference with other forms of intellectual property, and so, its protection is a vital concern of business. For information to be confidential it must not be generally known and not already disclosed to others. In fiduciary and other trust relationships, there is a common law duty not to disclose such information or to use it for personal benefit. Such a duty usually arises because of a special relationship, such as principal and agent, partnership, employer and employee, or between officers and their corporation. But the duty not to disclose or misuse confidential information is not restricted to fiduciary relationships. It can also arise in other situations, for example pursuant to express or implied contracts between the parties, as was the situation in the *Cadbury* case discussed above.

Duty to keep confidence

One of the most significant legal settlements in Canada arose out of such a duty not to use information obtained in confidence by LAC Minerals Ltd. from International Corona Resources Ltd. The case is very complicated but, in essence, Corona had obtained land claims in the Hemlo District of northwestern Ontario. Representatives of LAC entered into discussions with the representatives of Corona with the prospect of entering into a joint venture or partnership. In the process of these discussions, information was given to LAC in confidence to the effect that Corona did not own the surrounding gold claims but was in the process of negotiating for them. When negotiations broke down between LAC and Corona, LAC independently purchased the surrounding claims and made huge profits from the resulting mines. The court held that this was a violation of a duty imposed on LAC not to disclose or use the information for its own benefit, as a result of the special circumstances in which it was obtained. Although the court did not go so far as to find a fiduciary duty, a trust relationship had been established and the information gained because of it was intended to remain confidential. When the representatives of LAC used that information for LAC's gain at the expense of Corona, it was a violation of that duty of confidentiality.[19]

In both the *LAC Minerals* case and the *Cadbury* case, the courts found that the duty to keep information confidential arose when information was disclosed in circumstances that showed it was to remain confidential. The unauthorized use of that information was a breach of that duty of confidentiality.

Trade Secrets

A trade secret is a particular kind of confidential information that gives a businessperson a competitive advantage. Customer lists, formulas or processes, patterns, jigs, and other unique features unknown to competitors are trade secrets. Successful actions for the wrongful disclosure of trade secrets have been brought in such varied matters as recipes for fried chicken and soft drinks, formulas for rat poison, methods to flavour mouthwash, processes for making orchestral cymbals, and even the techniques prescribed in a seminar to help people quit smoking. A trade secret has the additional requirement that it be valuable to the business and not readily available to any other user or manufacturer. Customer lists available through government publication cannot be classed as trade secrets, nor can a process involved in the manufacturing of a product that is plainly discoverable simply by examining or disassembling the product.

Duty of confidentiality covers trade secrets as well

It should be noted that it is the conveying of the private information that is wrongful. There is no proprietary right in the idea or information itself. If Deng operated a company manufacturing tiddlywinks and had a secret process by which they could be produced more cost-effectively, which he failed to patent, and one of Deng's employees were to give that information to a competitor, it would be a wrongful disclosure of a trade secret. But if the competitor were to develop the same or a similar procedure independently, Deng would have no complaint, since he has no proprietary right in the idea or process.

19. LAC Minerals Ltd. v. International Corona Resources, as reported in *The Globe and Mail*, November 19, 1986.

Employees must not disclose trade secrets or confidential information

While an employee may be required either expressly or by implication in the employment contract not to disclose trade secrets and confidential information that he or she acquires in the process of employment, the employee can use the general skills and knowledge he or she gains on the job in another employment situation. An employee working in a guitar-manufacturing factory who acquires the skills of a luthier would not be expected to refrain from using any of those skills if he or she were to work for another manufacturer. However, specific processes or jigs used to make guitars might qualify as a trade secret. It is sometimes difficult to draw the line, and in such circumstances, it would be wise for the first manufacturer to include a **restrictive covenant** in the employment contract (a non-competition clause).

Although the courts are reluctant to enforce such covenants against employees, if the covenant is reasonable, and limited to an appropriate time and area, it may be enforceable. At the least, it will likely discourage the employee from seeking subsequent employment with a competitor. In any case, it is good policy to specifically include prohibitions and consequences in an employment contract dealing with the disclosure of confidential information and other forms of intellectual property of the employer.

Confidant should be advised of confidentiality

From a practical point of view, the owner of secret information can best maintain its confidentiality by informing the employee or other confidant that he or she is in a position of confidence and is expected to keep the information private. It is good policy to require them to sign a specific non-disclosure agreement with respect to that information. As mentioned above, with employees this agreement can be incorporated into the contract of employment. It is now common for businesses using co-op students on special projects in conjunction with their college to require such agreements.

Specify what is confidential

It is important to specify what information is confidential and what is not. Even the most honest employee can innocently disclose such information if he or she does not know it is confidential. No liability will be imposed for the disclosure of information if a person could not have been expected to know it was intended to be confidential. Steps should also be taken to minimize the number of people to whom the information is given or who have access to it, and to mark all distributed copies "Confidential."

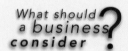

When a business has trade secrets and other forms of confidential information to protect they should take great care to impress upon their employees and those they do business with the importance of keeping it confidential. It is vital to make employees aware of their obligation of confidentiality in employment and service contracts as well as policy manuals and other forms of reminders. It is also important to identify just what is to be kept confidential. Even the most loyal employee cannot be expected to keep a confidence that he does not know is a secret. Employees should again be reminded of their obligations with respect to confidentiality when their employment comes to an end.

Care should be taken not to take this too far. If too much is marked confidential, the notification loses its effect. In addition, a person cannot be accused of wrongful disclosure of information if it has been widely distributed and is no longer confidential. It should also be noted that while in Canada, the law related to trade secrets is founded on common law and equity, in some parts of the United States, statutes have been passed to govern this area (*Trade Secrets Act*). Whenever those jurisdictions are involved, care should be taken to be aware of and comply with the appropriate statutes.

Remedies

Where someone wrongfully discloses information causing harm, the normal remedies of injunction, damages, and accounting discussed above may be available. The court, however, is reluctant to grant an injunction that will prevent an employee from earning a living, unless it is clear that the injunction is necessary to prevent the disclosure of confidential information. This usually happens when the employee goes to work for a competitor. Damages or an accounting are also available when confidences have been breached in this way. Even punitive damages have been awarded. Whether the confidant used the information personally or passed it on to someone else who used it to the detriment of the first party, either or both offending parties can be sued.

Disclosure must harm confider

Remedies similar to copyright infringement

Contract and tort law may be used to give increased protection to the various forms of intellectual property. There are often contractual provisions in service or employment contracts that prohibit the misuse of position or the misappropriation or disclosure of confidential information or trade secrets. Breach of the contract provisions will usually provide just cause for dismissal and may be grounds for obtaining an injunction. Employees often do not have sufficient assets to justify seeking damages from them, but the victim of the disclosure can often turn to the third party who profited from the disclosure or induced the breach of the contract for compensation. When the information holder has been enticed away and persuaded to breach the contract by a rival business, the victim can sue the competitor for the tort of inducing breach of contract. Although this tort was first developed to prevent one employer from luring away the employee of another, it has been expanded to many different kinds of contractual relationships and even to some relationships not based on contract. To succeed in such an action, the plaintiff is not required to establish malice on the part of the defendant, but it must be clear that the interference was intentional.

Other protection for intellectual property— contract

Tort
* *inducing breach of contract*

Ernst & Young v. Stuart et al.[20]

Mr. Stuart was a partner who had been working for Ernst & Young for a number of years, when he moved to a rival firm (Arthur Andersen & Co.) with only two weeks' notice. He found the working atmosphere at his new company much more attractive than the controlling and restrictive working environment at Ernst & Young. Unfortunately, there was a clause in his contract requiring him to give one-year notice upon leaving and not to work for a competing firm for a year after leaving. Ernst & Young sued both Mr. Stuart for breaching the partnership agreement and Arthur Andersen & Co. for inducing breach of contract.

The court found that the non-competition cause in the contract was unenforceable but that Mr. Stuart had breached the contract provision requiring him to give a one-year notice upon leaving. The court also had no hesitation in finding that Arthur Andersen & Co. had induced Mr. Stuart to breach his contract with Ernst & Young. The court found that Arthur Andersen & Co. knowing of the restrictive covenant provisions in the partnership agreement with Ernst and Young encouraged him to leave and had agreed to indemnify Mr. Stuart for any damages he had to pay for breaching that partnership agreement.

20. 144 D.L.R. (4th) 328 (B.C.C.A.)

The case illustrates not only how important the terms of a partnership agreement are and the difficulty of enforcing a non-competition clause but also the tort of inducing someone to breach a contract. In this case, the main difficulty for the court involving several different decisions at different levels was the determination of the appropriate damages to be paid. In fact, when Mr. Stuart went to Arthur Andersen & Co. in that first year, the section he supervised was extremely successful and earning more than anyone expected. Ernst & Young claimed that that was business they should have had and claimed the gross billings Arthur Andersen & Co. earned from those matters as damage. The court decided that only the profits (not the gross billings) could be claimed and then only what could have been expected if Mr. Stuart had stayed at Ernst & Young. Even that was not clear. The Court of Appeal did, however, award damages in the amount of $175 000 against Mr. Stuart and $75 000 against Arthur Andersen & Co.

Breach of Privacy

• breach of privacy

Some provinces, such as British Columbia, have passed privacy legislation that, among other things, makes it an actionable tort to use another's name or photograph without permission.[21] In other jurisdictions, the same effect may be accomplished indirectly by suing for breach of privacy. This happened in the United Kingdom when a manufacturer of a chocolate product promoted it by using a cartoon of a famous golfer with the package of the product in his pocket, and a British court held this action to be defamation because it communicated the idea that the golfer had lent his name to the promotion of the product, which would have been a serious violation of his amateur status.[22]

Injurious falsehood

Injurious falsehood, sometimes called trade slander, is a tort that can be pursued when someone misleads a customer about the nature or suitability of a company's product. For example, where a brewery spreads a false rumour that the employees of a rival brewery have contaminated the beer causing sales to fall, that competitor could bring a tort action demanding compensation for the damages done. The *Criminal Code* provisions relating to theft and fraud have also been used to deal with people who have wrongfully disclosed information or personally profited from its use. Even a civil action for **conversion** has been used to discourage such conduct.

Crime—fraud

Implications for Electronic Commerce

Securing information on Internet or email doubtful

Electronic mail and other Internet communications are subject to interception, and so, the security of matters discussed in e-mail and information provided when ordering products or services on the Internet is questionable. A company which gathers such information may make their data banks available to others for a fee, without the individuals being aware that their personal information is being disseminated. This information may be used by Internet service-providers to improve or customize their service, or it may be used to contact potential customers. It can also be used to track people's Internet browsing and buying habits. These lists may also get into the hands of scam artists or encourage the promotion of illegal activities. The information might also be used simply to generate unwanted junk mail (called "spam"). Protecting rights of privacy is an immense challenge, and the best advice is that the web users beware of giving out private or confidential

21. *Privacy Act,* R.S.B.C. (1996) c. 373, s. 3
22. Tolley v. Fry [1931] A.C. 333

information because there is no guarantee that this information will not be used inappropriately. This area is now regulated, to a limited extent, in Canada by the *Personal Information Protection and Electronic Documents Act.*[23]

The ease with which people can transfer material from another web site onto their own or link with a web site that contains information they wish to use while bypassing the home page of the originator of the site is also a cause for concern. A web site creator loses control of the site when someone deliberately bypasses a home page that may contain advertising and other controls that benefit the operator. These controls might include disclaimers, agreements for use, copyright limitations, and fee schedules. Trademarks and logos can be easily copied and used, and it may be difficult to track down the person responsible for the infringement. This was the problem acknowledged and remedied by the Federal Court in the case that begins this chapter.

Loss of control

Courts in the United States have demonstrated a willingness to hold offenders liable when they use information they have gleaned from a web site in a way that is detrimental to the originator. This may qualify as a case for a "passing-off" action, which may be remedied by an injunction. Voluntary compliance has not been an effective solution to these problems. Web users often impose sanctions on each other and report offenders to service providers or groups who patrol illegal activities on the net. This is known as "netiquette" and is a form of self-regulation provided by the services of Usenet. The Canadian Direct Marketing Association has a code of ethics and standards of practice that their members must comply with. The *Criminal Code* lists the interception of private telephone communications as a violation, and this can likely be extended to other forms of electronic communication. Again, the difficulty is in enforcement, as almost all businesses and most private homes now have the kind of equipment that makes all these offences possible.

***Criminal Code* provisions**

In addition to the problems related to the use of the Internet, we must contend with computer viruses that interfere with the operation of programs and corrupt or destroy data. Hackers can steal telephone services and access confidential or secret information through misuse of the phone system and the computers of other businesses. Outright piracy of computer programs, tapes, and videos is already a huge problem.

General *Criminal Code* provisions, such as theft, fraud, and mischief, and specialized provisions prohibiting the unauthorized use of computers are used to deal with these problems. Criminal prosecution can be effective, but the victim has no control and must rely on prosecutors who are usually under-funded and do not want to waste their resources on what they may consider to be a minor violation. Prosecutors also have to meet a much higher standard of proof in a criminal prosecution than in a civil action.

Where it becomes necessary to resort to the courts, often, the best route is civil rather than criminal, where the person bringing the action is in control of the process. Often, it is best to avoid legal proceedings altogether and seek an alternative method of resolving or avoiding disputes. The Internet is an example of how the rapid development of technology has outstripped the law. As a result, practical solutions, such as the development of data encryption codes to preserve privacy and security, may be much more effective than legal ones.

Civil action may be preferable

23. S.C. 2000, c.6

Insurance

Omega Inn Ltd. v. Continental Insurance Co.[24]

The Omega Inn Ltd. operated a restaurant in Nanaimo that burned down in December 1985. It carried both fire insurance and business interruption insurance with the defendant Continental Insurance Co. and applied for payment with respect to the loss. But Continental Insurance Co. suspecting arson, possibly at the hands of the plaintiff, refused to pay for some six months, while the cause of the fire was being investigated. After they did pay, it took a further four months to rebuild, causing a total of 10 months' interruption in the operation of the business. Continental Insurance Co. refused to pay the business interruption insurance for the 10-month delay. It claimed that the policy only required it to pay for the "length of time as would be required with the exercise of due diligence and dispatch to rebuild, repair, or replace such part of the described property as has been destroyed or damaged, commencing with the date of such destruction or damage." This was only the four months it took to rebuild, not the 10 months claimed. Omega, of course, claimed that the extra six months was caused by the failure of the insurance company to honour the policy and so should be included as part of the interruption in the business caused by the fire. At trial, the judge agreed with Omega, awarding payment based on a 10-month interruption period. This was appealed to the British Columbia Court of Appeal, where the judge overturned the lower court decision. The policy was clear and only required payment for the time the business would be interrupted while diligent effort was being made to rebuild. That obligation should not be affected by the fact that the insured did not have the funds to rebuild. "In my opinion, the impecuniosity of the plaintiff cannot be laid at the door of the insurer because it failed to pay more promptly. Its obligation and the full extent of its obligation, with respect to the business loss interruption coverage under the policy, was to pay for such length of time as would be required with the exercise of due diligence and dispatch to rebuild."[25]

Fire insurance and business interruption insurance usually go together, and this case shows their nature and how they work. It also forcefully points out the obligation on the insured to get back into business as soon as possible.

When property in any of its forms is the topic of discussion, insurance is an important consideration. Insurance was designed to provide compensation for damaged, lost, or stolen property but now also includes such areas as liability and life insurance, as well as business interruption insurance.

Insurance spreads risk

Spreading the risk reduces cost. Premiums paid cover the anticipated losses, the cost of administration, and a profit for the insurance company. The industry is regulated by the federal *Insurance Companies Act*.[26] This statute requires all non-provincial insurance companies to be registered and sets out other matters, such as the amount of reserves that must be retained to cover eventual claims. All provincial jurisdictions have similar insurance legislation. These provincial and federal statutes can be viewed as a type of consumer protection legislation in the field of insurance.

Industry regulated by statutes

24. 55 D.L.R. (4th) 766 (B.C.C.A.)

25. *Ibid.*, 768

26. S.C. (1991) c. I-11.8

Insurance companies use standard form contracts, the wording of which varies considerably between companies. Government controls help to ensure that the terms do not give unfair advantage to the insurance companies, but individuals should take care that the terms meet their needs. Each type of coverage has a different standard contract, and when modifications are made, they are attached as supplemental provisions called **riders**. Changes to already existing agreements are made by attaching an **endorsement**.

There is great danger that a business does not arrange for adequate coverage. Fire insurance, for example, will not normally cover damages caused by nuclear contamination, war, or insurrection, without a special rider to that effect. Similarly, burglary insurance would not cover shoplifting or theft by employees. Natural disasters, such as earthquakes or floods, are excluded from most standard form policies, at least in relation to some types of property loss. Most insurance contracts require insured parties to maintain certain safety and security standards to protect themselves against the risk of fire and theft.

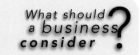

Property Insurance

The predominant form of property insurance covers losses to buildings and their contents due to fire. Co-insurance clauses are included in most fire insurance policies requiring that the insured maintain a certain percentage of coverage or bear some of he risk of loss themselves. Thus, in a policy with an 80 percent co-insurance clause, if the policy coverage was for less than that portion of the actual potential loss (say, only $60 000 coverage on property worth $100 000), the insured would have to assume a portion (20 percent in this example) of any loss that occurred. On the other hand, even if you overinsure a property, you cannot collect more than the loss. It becomes important, then, for the insured to have coverage that is at least close to the maximum potential loss and to obtain coverage for all types of loss, including fire, theft, natural disaster, and so on.

Business Interruption Insurance

Often, an ongoing business will find itself unable to function because of some unforeseen event that may or may not be covered by another form of insurance. For example, if Rampal operates a plant manufacturing widgets and the plant burns down, fire insurance and other forms of property insurance would normally cover the loss. Such insurance would not, however, cover the loss of profits suffered while the plant is not operational. Business interruption insurance will normally cover not only lost profits but also any added expenses incurred to bring the business back into production. Property insurance and business interruption insurance together are an attempt to put the insured in the same financial position they would have been in had the fire or other damage not occurred.

Life and Health Insurance

Life insurance provides security for a family or business against the death of the insured. Businesses take out life insurance against the death of key personnel to cover losses incurred from any disruption that may result from the death or illness of an executive or partner.

Death is inevitable, and so premiums are calculated on the basis of a prediction of how long a person of a certain age and health can be expected to live.

Chantiam v. Packall Packaging Inc. et al.[27]

In this case, Mr. Chantiam was working as the plant manager for Packall Packaging Inc., when he consented to a "keyman" insurance policy to be taken out on his life by the company. Under this type of policy, the employer is able to insure the life of important key employees so that if anything happens and their business is disrupted as a result, they will have the insurance coverage to compensate. About two years later, Mr. Chantiam terminated his employment and started up a business in competition with Packall. He had assumed that the insurance policy had ended as well, but several years later, he discovered that the company had maintained the policy and continued to pay the premiums. Mr. Chantiam brought this action, demanding that the policy be terminated or transferred to him.

Like other forms of insurance, there must be an insurable interest in the life being insured. In this case, there was such an insurable interest by the company in Mr. Chantiam's life at the time the policy was taken out, but Mr. Chantiam argued that since circumstances had changed, the policy should be cancelled. The trial court agreed with Mr. Chantiam, ordering that the policy be cancelled on the ground that it was not "in the public interest" that Packall be allowed "to continue insuring the life of its business competitor."[28]

But on appeal, that court held that the appropriate time to determine insurable interest was when the policy was made, and it did not matter that circumstances had changed since. The policy was valid and the company was within its rights to continue it. An insurable interest is determined by the company being in a position to suffer a loss if the insured-against event were to happen. In this case, because of his key position, there was no question that such an insurable interest was present at the time of the creation of the policy. Furthermore, the legislation involved stipulates that where the insured consents in writing to the creation of the policy, as happened here, that satisfies the insurable interest requirement. Since there was an insurable interest at the time the policy was created, there were no grounds to challenge the continuation of the policy by Packall.

A person taking out life insurance like other forms of insurance must be able to demonstrate an insurable interest in the life of the person insured. For businesses, it is a prudent and common practice to insure the life of key personnel. Any dispute as to whether there is an insurable interest in the life of such employees is overcome by having that employee sign consent in writing to the policy. This case illustrates that the question of insurable interest only relates to when the policy is taken out. Note that Manitoba has changed its legislation allowing a person to bring an application to the court to have the policy cancelled when that insurable interest is no longer present. But in this case, Ontario had no similar provision, nor does any other Canadian province.

There are various forms of life insurance to meet the needs of different individuals. Term insurance provides only a benefit upon death, and the premiums are lower than whole life insurance, which provides coverage in the event of death as well as investment potential and retirement income. These are just two of several variations of life insurance available.

Health and disability insurance usually part of group coverage

Health and disability insurance provides coverage during the life of the insured and is designed to pay health care expenses and provide an income for a person who is unable to earn a living because of illness or accident. Medical insurance can be

27. 159 D.L.R. (4th) 517 (Ont. C.A.)
28. *Ibid.*, 519

arranged individually or as part of group coverage. Health care services in Canada are funded through the government-sponsored medical system, which is often supplemented by plans providing extended coverage. In most Canadian jurisdictions, disability insurance can be obtained on an individual basis with an insurance company, but it is more often acquired by large organizations as part of an employee benefits package.

Liability Insurance

When injury or damage is caused by a person failing in their duty to others, the wrongdoer can be sued for the loss. Such carelessness can take place anywhere, and it can happen when the person acts in a business, professional, or personal capacity. In some occupations, professional liability insurance is mandatory. In all cases, it is important to maintain appropriate insurance coverage to avoid potentially disastrous consequences. Personal liability insurance and motor vehicle insurance go a long way towards protecting individuals from potentially devastating claims against them.

Liability insurance covers negligence by self or employees

Business people must also insure against vicarious liability, which may be imposed on them because of the wrongdoing of employees. Liability insurance does not excuse the insured from responsibility, and it is quite likely that the insured will have to go through a lawsuit, but in most liability insurance contracts, the insurance company arranges legal representation and covers the judgment up to the amount of coverage. The insured will be responsible for the amount of the judgment over the insured amount, and so, it is important to maintain adequate coverage in this area as well. If Jones has liability insurance for only $500 000 and causes a $750 000 loss, he will be required to pay the $250 000 shortfall. Liability insurance will not cover you for your own willful acts, such as assault, theft, or arson.

Only to extent of coverage

Many people assume that if there is insurance coverage any injury or damage will be compensated regardless of fault, but with liability insurance, the insurer will only pay where the insured was at fault. If there was no negligence or other wrongful conduct on the part of the insured, the insurance company will not pay. Many argue for no-fault coverage in these circumstances. No-fault insurance is similar to workers' compensation in that the injured party is entitled to compensation, no matter who is responsible. Liability coverage has become so important in the operation of automobiles that several provinces have instituted compulsory automobile coverage, and some have or are considering going to no-fault schemes.

Coverage only when insured is at fault

Insurable Interest

For insurance not to be considered a wager, the insured must be able to demonstrate an insurable interest in what is insured. That means that when the insured-against event happens, the insured must have suffered a loss for which the insurance payout provides compensation. Insurance is only intended to put the person who suffers a loss back in the original position he or she would have been in had the event not taken place. The contract for insurance is a contract of indemnity. Consequently, except in the case of life insurance, the insured can recover only what he or she has actually lost up to the limit set out in the policy. When the payout becomes a windfall, the insurance agreement is void as an illegal contract.

Must be insurable interest to avoid illegality

When a claim is made, the insured will only be able to collect up to the value of the insurable interest he has in the property insured. The insurable interest, then, is the amount he or she stands to lose if the insured-against event takes place. If Nahanee owned a half-interest in a house worth $150 000, Nahanee would have an insurable interest of $75 000. If Nahanee carried an insurance policy of $150 000 on the house and it was destroyed by fire, Nahanee would only be able to collect $75 000 for himself, even though he had insured it for the higher amount. Any other result would give Nahanee a windfall, which is prohibited. If this example were to actually happen, Nahanee would likely collect the entire $150 000 but be required to hold the other $75 000 in trust for the person who owned the other half interest in the house.

It should be noted that when life insurance is involved, the insurable interest is defined as the amount of insurance coverage contracted for, provided there is some sort of family or business relationship at the time the insurance is taken out. Where the lives of key business people are insured, the written consent of that person is also required.

Shareholders now have insurance interests in assets of corporation

In the past, it was thought that because a company was a separate legal entity, the shareholder had no insurable interest in the assets of the corporation. The Supreme Court of Canada, however, has decided that shareholders do have an insurable interest in those assets. The court held that it was not necessary for the person taking out insurance to actually have a legally enforceable interest in the property to insure it. It is enough that a relationship to the subject matter or a concern in it exists such that a loss would be suffered if the insured-against event took place.[29]

Other Features

Wellington Insurance Co. Ltd. v. Armac Diving Services Ltd.[30]

In 1978, a boat owned by Armac Diving Services Ltd. and insured by Wellington Insurance Co. Ltd. capsized. Armac made a claim against Wellington. The insurance company denied the claim, saying that the boat was not covered by the policy. Armac sued. Wellington settled the action and paid Armac half the claim, making it clear that they were doing so not pursuant to the policy, but rather to bring an early end to the legal proceedings and as a public relations gesture. Armac then successfully sued the third party that had caused the capsize of their vessel, obtaining judgment. In this action, Wellington takes the position that since they paid out on the policy, they were subrogated to the rights of the policyholder and had the right to collect the proceeds of any judgment taken against the person who caused the loss in the first place. But the Court of Appeal found that subrogation did not apply.

In marine insurance policies, as in most insurance policies, when an insurer pays out on a policy, it assumes the rights (subrogation) to any actions against anyone causing the loss. In this case, however, it disputed the claim, and when it settled the matter for half the amount claimed, it made it clear that it was settling a disputed action, not paying out on their policy. In fact, Wellington specifically stated that it was not admitting liability; therefore, the settlement with Armac was exhaustive of the rights between the two parties, and Armac was then free to carry on in its action against the third party.

This case illustrates the nature of subrogation and the right that the insurance company has once it pays out on a policy to step into the shoes of the insured in any actions that they may have against the party causing their loss. It also points to the limitations on that right.

29. Kosmopoulos et al. v. Construction Insurance Company of Canada Ltd. [1987] 1 S.C.R. 2 (S.C.C.)

30. 37 D.L.R. (4th) 462 (B.C.C.A.)

A relationship of trust exists between the insured and insurer creating an obligation to act in good faith. An important aspect of that obligation is the duty on the part of the insured to disclose pertinent information, especially where it affects the risk assumed by the insurer. Even after the contract is made, there is often a duty to notify the insurance company when circumstances change, as when an occupied building becomes unoccupied for a length of time.

Disclosure

When applying for property insurance, the insurer will want to know what the property will be used for, whether it is for a business, whether it will be vacant for extended periods, and what kind of security and safety equipment is in place. For life, disability, or medical insurance, any injury, disease, or other health problems that may affect that person's health must be disclosed. These factors affect eligibility or the rates charged for insurance, and since the insurer usually has no way of determining this information by itself, it must depend on the honesty of the insured to disclose it. Failure to disclose information material to the loss may be misrepresentation and may result in the loss being unrecoverable. Even where it is not relevant to the loss, if it is a material misrepresentation, it may cause the entire policy to be void. Legislation in some provinces upholds the insurance where the misrepresentation was innocent, but even in those jurisdictions, if the misrepresentation or failure to disclose was done knowingly, the insurance policy cannot be enforced.

Insured must disclose relevant information

Subrogation

The right of subrogation gives the insurance company, once it has paid out a claim, the right to take over the rights of the insured in relation to whoever caused the injury. The insurer steps into the shoes of the insured and can then sue whoever caused the loss as if it were the insured. Thus, where a neighbour carelessly allows a bonfire to get out of control causing Mrs. Kostachue's house to burn down, she would normally claim on her insurance and receive compensation. Her insurance company would then sue the neighbour for negligence and recoup what it can. In fact, if the neighbour had liability insurance, it would likely be their insurer that would ultimately pay. You should not assume when you are involved in an accident that just because the other person has insurance, you are protected. If it is your fault, that person's insurance company will seek to recover its loss from you.

The principle of subrogation is nicely illustrated in the *Wellington Insurance* case, but that case also graphically brings home how important it is for an insurance company to preserve that right. In that case, the right to subrogate was lost because in the settlement, it was made clear by the parties that that settlement was exhaustive of their rights. It was clearly stated that the money was paid as a matter of goodwill and not because they admitted any liability on the claim by the insurance company.

Another mistake people often make is thinking that when they have two insurance policies covering the same risk that they can collect on both. A basic principle of insurance law is that you can only recover what you have lost, and so no matter how many policies you have, the total you can collect from all of them is no more than what you have lost. If you take out two policies on a house for $100 000 each and you suffer $50 000 damage in a fire, you can collect only that $50 000 from either insurer, or each insurer will pay you $25 000. You will not, however, be able to collect $50 000 from each company, despite the fact that you have paid premiums to both.

Normally, insurance companies will also have the choice to rebuild, repair, or replace what is damaged so that it can minimize its cost. They also have the right of salvage. If stolen goods are recovered, for example, it can sell those goods to recover its costs. When personal property has been lost, the insurer usually only has to pay the depreciated value of the goods, not the replacement cost, unless it has agreed otherwise.

Right of salvage

Insurance companies will also normally have the choice to rebuild, repair, or replace what is damaged so that they can minimize their cost. They also have the right of salvage. If stolen goods are recovered, for example, they can sell those goods to recover their costs. When personal property has been lost, the insurer normally only has to pay the depreciated value of the goods, not the replacement cost unless they have agreed otherwise. Most personal household insurance policies today provide for the replacement of destroyed or stolen goods at their full retail value. When a loss does take place, there is a general requirement on the part of the insured to report that loss to the insurance company right away so that the insurance company can take steps to minimize the damage. There might also be an obligation to report the matter to the police if a crime is involved or if the loss resulted from an automobile accident.

Depreciated rather than replacement value

Insured can't profit from wilful misconduct

It should also be pointed out that the insured is not permitted to profit from his or her wilful misconduct. If the insured deliberately causes the loss, he or she will not be able to collect. Thus, if Fagan burns down his own house killing his wife in the process, he will not be able to collect on the fire insurance and he will not be able to collect on his wife's life insurance, even where he is named as beneficiary.

Insurance Agents

Most insurance is purchased through the services of an agent. An insurance agent acts on behalf of the insurance company, not the person purchasing the insurance coverage. A discussion of agency law and the responsibilities of such agents is set out in Chapter 12. Insurance agents owe an important obligation to their principals (the insurance companies), but they also owe an important duty to the customer and will be responsible if they fail to provide the insurance coverage asked for or otherwise fail to honour the instructions given. Customers are finding themselves increasingly successful in suing agents for negligence when mistakes such as these are made.

Agent normally acts for insurance company

Wrongdoing of Partner Does Not Affect Insurance

Higgins and Wood operated a sporting goods business as a partnership. They took out a fire insurance policy for their building and contents, naming themselves as the beneficiaries. Wood, without the knowledge of Higgins, conspired with a third party to intentionally burn down the store in order to defraud the insurers. He got caught. It was clear that Higgins was perfectly innocent and had no knowledge of the conspiracy or the attempt to defraud the insurance company. However, his claim under the policy was refused. The court had to decide whether as an innocent partner of a wrongdoer, he was entitled to collect on the policy. The court held that the wrongdoing of Wood, while forfeiting any claim he had under the policy, did not automatically deprive his innocent partner of the policy protection. He did have the right to claim and was successful.

Higgins v. Orion Insurance Co. Ltd. (1985), 17 D.L.R. (4th) 90 (Ont.C.A.)

People will also often find themselves dealing with insurance adjusters who are employees or representatives of the insurance company charged with investigating and settling insurance claims against the company after the insured-against event takes place. It is important to remember when dealing with adjusters that they are not normally looking after the interests of the person making the claim, but the insurance company instead.

There are also many independent people working in the industry available to assist both parties, to arbitrate disputes, to mediate, and to otherwise ensure that the interests of whoever they represent are protected.

Finally, when there is a situation of considerable risk to an insurance company, such as a large project that needs to be insured (for example, a new chemical plant), the company will often turn to other insurance companies so that the risk is spread among them all. This pooling of risk is called **re-insurance** and is an important aspect of the industry.

Insurance companies often re-insure

Bonding

While insurance coverage is not generally available for intentionally wrongful acts, such as assault, many business people insist on some protection against the people they deal with who act wrongfully in a more wilful sense. Bonding is available in these circumstances, and it takes two forms. Usually, an employer will pay a fee to have an employee bonded against that employee's own wrongful conduct (**fidelity bond**). If the employee steals from the employer or a customer, the bonding company will be required to compensate the employer for that loss. It must be emphasized, however, that this does not relieve the bonded employee of responsibility. The bonding company can turn to the employee and collect from that party, which is what distinguishes bonding from normal insurance arrangements.

Bonded parties still liable

The second form of bonding, a **surety bond,** occurs when the bonding is designed to provide assurance that a party to a contract will perform its side of the contract. For example, in a large construction project, the company doing the foundation may be required to put up a performance bond that it will finish the job at a specified level of quality and by a certain time. If it fails to complete or does not complete on time, the bonding company will be required to pay compensation. A standby letter of credit as discussed in Chapter 10 can also be used for the same purpose.

Summary

Intellectual property

- Protected by both federal legislation and common law
- Copyright protects literary, artistic, dramatic, and other works from being copied or used by unauthorized parties for the author's life to the end of the calendar year, plus 50 years. Producing the work creates the copyright
- Registration ensures international protection
- Remedies include injunctions, Anton Piller orders, damages, and accounting of profits

- Patent—registration gives international monopoly protection on the use of an invention for 20 years

- Trademark—registration protects certain terms, symbols, and designs associated with a business or product, prevents deception of consumer , and protects goodwill. Passing-off action may provide similar protection

- Industrial designs are protected by federal legislation

- Confidential information
  - In common law, an employee or associate under a fiduciary obligation is prohibited from disclosing confidential information including trade secrets
  - Damages or an injunction may be awarded when such confidences are breached.

Insurance

- Designed to spread the risk of loss

- Insured must have an insurable interest in the subject matter. Recovery limited to the extent of that insurable interest

- Property, business interruption, life and health, and liability are the primary forms of insurance available

- Liability insurance
  - Payment will only be made where the insured was at fault
  - When a claim is paid, the company is subrogated to the rights of the insured
  - Can salvage the property or take over the insured's right to sue a third party

QUESTIONS

1. What two principles does the law of intellectual property try to balance?

2. Explain how a copyright is obtained and the qualifications that must be met to obtain such protection.

3. Discuss the significance of the 1997 amendments to the *Copyright Act.*

4. Summarize the nature of the protection given to the holder of a copyright and indicate what remedies are available to enforce such rights.

5. Discuss under what circumstances an Anton Piller order would be given and indicate how this remedy might be more valuable than other remedies which might be available.

6. What is the purpose of patent law, and why is registration required for protection?

7. What kinds of things are protected by the trademark legislation, and how is that protection obtained or lost?

8. What kinds of material are intended to be protected by industrial design? How is this protection obtained?

9. How does the duty of confidentiality arise, and what protection or remedies are available to the confider?

10. What are some of the problems enforcing intellectual property regulations when the medium for transmitting information is the Internet?

11. Indicate how criminal law, tort law, and contract law can be used to protect intellectual property. How effective are such alternatives?

12. Explain conceptually the purpose of insurance and why it is not void as an illegal contract. (See also Chapter 7.)

13. Distinguish between business interruption insurance and fire insurance. Why might a business person want to have both forms of coverage?

14. What kinds of things cannot be covered under a liability insurance policy? Indicate any other methods a person or business might use to ensure that the people they are working with perform their jobs properly.

15. Discuss the similarities and differences between insurance and a wager.

16. What is meant by an insurable interest, and how does it apply to the various types of insurance discussed in the chapter?

17. Explain what is meant by the right of subrogation and how this may affect not only the insured but also the person who has caused the injury or damage. Also indicate what other means the insurance companies have to keep their damages as low as possible.

18. What is meant by bonding? In your answer, distinguish between bonding and insurance coverage.

CASES

1. Spiro-flex Industries v. Progressive Sealing Inc.

Mr. McLeod designed a new pump coupler (a device used in a circulating water pump), which he intended to produce and sell. But he could not produce a special spring used in the device and so had to turn to others. He produced freehand sketches of the product as well as directions and specifications and went to different manufacturers to have it made. He entered into an agreement to have the product marketed and provided a photograph of the device to illustrate a brochure. Once the device was on the market, several companies made copies of the coupler, including the people he originally asked to produce the device and some of those involved in the production of the brochure. Explain McLeod's rights against those parties.

2. Thurston Hayes Developments. v. Horn Abbott, Ltd.

The plaintiff was the developer of the board game "Trivial Pursuit," which had been on the market successfully for several years. The defendants brought out a new board game with the same approach but which involved a different subject matter and called it "Sexual Pursuit." The board used was essentially the same, the box the game came in was similar, and the games were even played the same way. Explain the nature of the complaint the plaintiff has, any legal action that can be taken to protect his rights, and the likely outcome.

3. Ciba-Geigy Canada Ltd. v. Apotex Inc.

Ciba-Geigy had the right to manufacture in Canada the product Metoprolol, a drug used for treating hypertension and angina. Under the *Patent Act* then in place, other manufacturers could acquire a license and manufacture and sell the product in Canada. These versions are known as generic drugs. Apotex and Novopharm both obtained licenses and, in the process, produced a drug with the same appearance as that produced by Ciba-Geigy. They used the same shape, size, and colour. Even the dosages were the same. In fact, these drugs were interchangeable with the original product. Given that these companies have the right to produce generic drugs that are similar and useable for the same purpose, is there any complaint Ciba-Geigy can use against these imitators? Would your answer be affected by the fact that only doctors and pharmacists are aware of the differences and the ultimate consumer would not notice the difference?

4. Allen v. Toronto Star Newspapers Ltd.

Jim Allen, a photographer, took a photograph of Sheila Copps, MP, wearing leather and sitting on a motorcycle. It was used on the cover of *Saturday Night* magazine, which had employed Allen to take the picture. Allen sold the picture on two other occasions. It became a matter of some controversy. *The Toronto Star*, without the photographer's permission, published the picture, including the cover, in their newspaper as part of a news story. No objections were raised by *Saturday Night Magazine*. What options are available to Jim Allen, and what defences are available to *The Toronto Star*?

5. Hammill v. Gerling Global Life Insurance Co.

Mrs. Hammill obtained a life insurance policy in which she stated that she had been a non-smoker for the past 12 months. In fact, this information was incorrect. It was clearly established that she had smoked considerably during this period. She had taken out the policy in 1985 and was killed in an auto accident on February 2, 1986. Although her smoking in no way contributed to the accident, the insurer refused to pay the beneficiary under the policy. Explain the legal obligations of the insurer in these circumstances.

The *British North America Act*

Sections 91 and 92*
VI.-Distribution of Legislative Powers

Powers of the Parliament

91. It shall be lawful for the Queen, by and with the Advice and Consent of the Senate and House of Commons, to make Laws for the Peace, Order, and Good Government of Canada, in relation to all Matters not coming within the Classes of Subjects by this Act assigned exclusively to the Legislatures of the Provinces; and for greater Certainty, but not so as to restrict the Generality of the foregoing Terms of this Section, it is hereby declared that (notwithstanding anything in this Act) the exclusive Legislative Authority of the Parliament of Canada extends to all Matters coming within the Classes of Subjects next herein-after enumerated; that is to say,

Legislative authority of Parliament of Canada

1. The amendment from time to time of the Constitution of Canada, except as regards matters coming within the classes of subjects by this Act assigned exclusively to the Legislatures of the provinces, or as regards rights or privileges by this or any other Constitutional Act granted or secured to the Legislature or the Government of a province, or to any class of persons with respect to schools or as regards the use of the English or the French language or as regards the requirements that there shall be a session of the Parliament of Canada at least once each year, and that no House of Commons shall continue for more than five years from the day of the return of the Writs for choosing the House: provided, however, that a House of Commons may in time of real or apprehended war, invasion or insurrection be continued by the Parliament of Canada if such continuation is not opposed by the votes of more than one-third of the members of such House. (39)

1A. The Public Debt and Property (40)

2. The Regulation of Trade and Commerce

2A. Unemployment insurance (41)

3. The raising of Money by any Mode or System of Taxation

4. The borrowing of Money on the Public Credit

5. Postal Service

6. The Census and Statistics

7. Militia, Military and Naval Service, and Defence

8. The fixing of and providing for the Salaries and Allowances of Civil and other Officers of the Government of Canada

9. Beacons, Buoys, Lighthouses, and Sable Island

10. Navigation and Shipping

11. Quarantine and the Establishment and Maintenance of Marine Hospitals

12. Sea Coast and Inland Fisheries

13. Ferries between a Province and any British or Foreign Country or between Two Provinces

14. Currency and Coinage

15. Banking, Incorporation of Banks, and the Issue of Paper Money

16. Savings Banks

17. Weights and Measures

18. Bills of Exchange and Promissory Notes

19. Interest

20. Legal Tender

21. Bankruptcy and Insolvency

22. Patents of Invention and Discovery

23. Copyrights

24. Indians, and Lands reserved for the Indians

25. Naturalization and Aliens

26. Marriage and Divorce

27. The Criminal Law, except the Constitution of Courts of Criminal Jurisdiction, but including the Procedure in Criminal Matters

28. The Establishment, Maintenance, and Management of Penitentiaries

29. Such Classes of Subjects as are expressly excepted in the Enumeration of the Classes of Subjects by this Act assigned exclusively to the Legislatures of the Provinces

And any Matter coming within any of the Classes of Subjects enumerated in this Section shall not be deemed to come within the Class of Matters of a local or private Nature comprised in the Enumeration of the Classes of Subjects by this Act assigned exclusively to the Legislatures of the Provinces.

Exclusive Powers of Provincial Legislatures

92. In each Province, the Legislature may exclusively make Laws in relation to Matters coming within the Classes of Subject next herein-after enumerated; that is to say,

1. The Amendment from Time to Time, notwithstanding anything in this Act, of the Constitution of the Province, except as regards the Office of Lieutenant Governor

Subjects of exclusive province legislation

2. Direct Taxation within the Province in order to the raising of a Revenue for Provincial Purposes

3. The borrowing of Money on the sole Credit of the Province

4. The Establishment and Tenure of Provincial Offices and the Appointment and Payment of Provincial Officers

5. The Management and Sale of the Public Lands belonging to the Province and of the Timber and Wood thereon

6. The Establishment, Maintenance, and Management of Public and Reformatory Prisons in and for the Province

7. The Establishment, Maintenance, and Management of Hospitals, Asylums, Charities, and Eleemosynary Institutions in and for the Province, other than Marine Hospitals

8. Municipal Institutions in the Province

9. Shop, Saloon, Tavern, Auctioneer, and other Licences in order to the raising of a Revenue for Provincial, Local, or Municipal Purposes

10. Local Works and Undertakings other than such as are of the following Classes:

    (a) Lines of Steam or other Ships, Railways, Canals, Telegraphs, and other Works and Undertakings connecting the Province with any other or others of the Provinces, or extending beyond the Limits of the Province;

    (b) Lines of Steam Ships between the Province and any British or Foreign Country;

    (c) Such Works as, although wholly situated within the Province, are before or after their Execution declared by the Parliament of Canada to be for the general Advantage of Canada or for the Advantage of Two or more of the Provinces.

11. The Incorporation of Companies with Provincial Objects

12. The Solemnization of Marriage in the Province

13. Property and Civil Rights in the Province

14. The Administration of Justice in the Province, including the Constitution, Maintenance, and Organization of Provincial Courts, both of Civil and of Criminal Jurisdiction, and including Procedure in Civil Matters in those Courts

15. The Imposition of Punishment by Fine, Penalty, or Imprisonment for enforcing any Law of the Province made in relation to any Matter coming within any of the Classes of Subjects enumerated in this Section

16. Generally all Matters of a merely local or private Nature in the Province

The Constitution Act (1982)

*Charter of Rights and Freedoms**
Schedule B
Constitution Act, 1982

Part 1: Canadian Charter of Rights and Freedoms

Whereas Canada is founded upon principles that recognize the supremacy of God and the rule of Law:

Guarantee of Rights and Freedoms

Rights and freedoms in Canada

1. The Canadian Charter of Rights and Freedoms guarantees the rights and freedoms set out in it subject only to such reasonable limits prescribed by law as can be demonstrably justified in a free and democratic society.

Fundamental Freedoms

Fundamental freedoms

2. Everyone has the following fundamental freedoms:
    (a) freedom of conscience and religion;
    (b) freedom of thought, belief, opinion and expression, including freedom of the press and other media of communications;
    (c) freedom of peaceful assembly; and
    (d) freedom of association.

Democratic Rights

Democratic rights of citizens

3. Every citizen of Canada has the right to vote in an election of members of the House of Commons or of a legislative assembly and to be qualified for membership therein.

Maximum duration of legislative bodies

4. (1) No House of Commons and no legislative assembly shall continue for longer than five years from the date fixed for the return of the writs at a general election of its members.

Continuation in special circumstances

    (2) In time of real or apprehended war, invasion or insurrection, a House of Commons may be continued by Parliament and a legislative assembly may be continued by the legislature beyond five years if such continuation is not opposed by the votes of more than one-third of the members of the House of Commons or the legislative assembly, as the case may be.

Annual sitting of legislative bodies

5. There shall be a sitting of Parliament and of each legislature at least once every 12 months.

Mobility Rights

Mobility of citizens

6. (1) Every citizen of Canada has the right to enter, remain in, and leave Canada.

(2) Every citizen of Canada and every person who has the status of a permanent resident of Canada has the right

    (a) to move to and take up residence in any province; and

    (b) to pursue the gaining of a livelihood in any province.

Rights to move and gain livelihood

(3) The rights specified in subsection (2) are subject to

    (a) any laws or practices of general application in force in a province other than those that discriminate among persons primarily on the basis of province of present or previous residence; and

    (b) any laws providing for reasonable residency requirements as a qualification for the receipt of publicly provided social services.

Limitation

(4) Subsections (2) and (3) do not preclude any law, program, or activity that has as its object the amelioration in a province of conditions of individuals in that province who are socially or economically disadvantaged if the rate of employment in that province is below the rate of employment in Canada.

Affirmative action programmes

Legal Rights

7. Everyone has the right to life, liberty, and security of the person and the right not to be deprived thereof except in accordance with the principles of fundamental justice.

Life, liberty, and security of person

8. Everyone has the right to be secure against unreasonable search or seizure.

Search and seizure

9. Everyone has the right not to be arbitrarily detained or imprisoned.

Detention or imprisonment

10. Everyone has the right on arrest or detention

Arrest or detention

    (a) to be informed promptly of the reasons therefor;

    (b) to retain and instruct counsel without delay and to be informed of that right; and

    (c) to have the validity of the detention determined by way of habeas corpus and to be released if the detention is not lawful.

11. Any person charged with an offence has the right

Proceedings in criminal and penal matters

    (a) to be informed without unreasonable delay of the specific offence;

    (b) to be tried within a reasonable time;

    (c) not to be compelled to be a witness in proceedings against that person in respect of the offence;

    (d) to be presumed innocent until proven guilty according to law in a fair and public hearing by an independent and impartial tribunal;

    (e) not to be denied reasonable bail without just cause;

    (f) except in the case of an offence under military law tried before a military tribunal, to the benefit of trial by jury where the maximum punishment for the offence is imprisonment for five years or a more severe punishment;

    (g) not to be found guilty on account of any act or omission unless, at the time of the act or omission, it constituted an offence under Canadian or international law or was criminal according to the general principles or law recognized by the community of nations;

(h) if finally acquitted of the offence, not to be tried for it again and, if finally found guilty and punished for the offence, not to be tried or punished for it again; and

(i) if found guilty of the offence and if the punishment for the offence has been varied between the time of commission and the time of sentencing, to the benefit of the lesser punishment.

Treatment or punishment

12. Everyone has the right not to be subjected to any cruel and unusual treatment or punishment.

Self-incrimination

13. A witness who testifies in any proceedings has the right not to have any incriminating evidence so given used to incriminate that witness in any other proceedings, except in a prosecution for perjury or for the giving of contradictory evidence.

Interpreter

14. A party or witness in any proceedings who does not understand or speak the language in which the proceedings are conducted or who is deaf has the right to the assistance of an interpreter.

Equality Rights

Equality before and under law and equal protection and benefit of law

15. (1) Every individual is equal before and under the law and has the right to the equal protection and equal benefit of the law without discrimination and, in particular, without discrimination based on race, national, or ethnic origin, colour, religion, sex, age or mental or physical disability.

Affirmative action programmes

(2) Subsection (1) does not preclude any law, program, or activity that has as its object the amelioration of conditions of disadvantaged individuals or groups including those that are disadvantaged because of race, national, or ethnic origin, colour, religion, sex, age or mental or physical disability.

Official Languages of Canada

Official languages of Canada

16. (1) English and French are the official languages of Canada and have equality of status and equal rights and privileges as to their use in all institutions of the Parliament and government of Canada.

Official languages of New Brunswick

(2) English and French are the official languages of New Brunswick and have equality of status and equal rights and privileges as to their use in all institutions of the legislature and government of New Brunswick.

Advancement of status and use

(3) Nothing in this Charter limits the authority of Parliament or a legislature to advance the equality of status or use of English and French.

English and French linguistic communities in New Brunswick

16.1 (1) The English linguistic community and the French linguistic community in New Brunswick have equality of status and equal rights and privilages, including the right to distinct educational institutions and such distinct cultural institutions as are necessary for the preservation and promotion of those communities.

Role of legislature and government in New Brunswick

(2) The role of the legislature and government of New Brunswick to preserve and promote the status, rights and privileges referred to in subsection (1) is affirmed.

17. (1) Everyone has the right to use English or French in any debates and other proceedings of Parliament.

Proceedings of Parliament

(2) Everyone has the right to use English and French in any debates and other proceedings of the legislature of New Brunswick.

Proceedings of New Brunswick legislature

18. (1) The statutes, records and journals of Parliament shall be printed and published in English and French and both language versions are equally authoritative.

Parliamentary statutes and records

(2) The statutes, records and journals of the legislature of New Brunswick shall be printed and published in English and French and both language versions are equally authoritative.

New Brunswick statutes and records

19. (1) Either English or French may be used by any person in, or in any pleading in or process issuing from, any court established by Parliament.

Proceedings in court established by Parliament

(2) Either English or French may be used by any person in, or in any pleading in or process issuing from, any court in New Brunswick.

Proceedings in New Brunswick courts

20. (1) Any member of the public in Canada has the right to communicate with, and to receive available services from, any head or central office of an institution of the Parliament or government of Canada in English or French, and has the same right with respect to any such institution where

Communications by public with federal institutions

  (a) there is a significant demand for communications with and services from that office in such language; or

  (b) due to the nature of the office, it is reasonable that communications with services from that office be available in both English and French.

(2) Any member of the public in New Brunswick has the right to communicate with, and to receive available services from, any office of an institution of the legislature or government of New Brunswick in English or French.

Communications by public with New Brunswick institutions

21. Nothing in sections 16 to 20 abrogates or derogates from any right, privilege or obligation with respect to the English and French languages, or either of them, that exists or is continued by virtue of any other provision of the Constitution of Canada.

Continuation of existing constitutional provisions

22. Nothing in sections 16 to 20 abrogates or derogates from any legal or customary right or privilege acquired or enjoyed either before or after the coming into force of this Charter with respect to any language that is not French or English.

Rights and privileges preserved

Minority Language Educational Rights

23. (1) Citizens of Canada

  (a) whose first language learned and still understood is that of the English and French linguistic minority population of the province in which they reside, or

Language of instruction

  (b) who have received their primary school instruction in Canada in English or French and reside in a province where the language in which they received that instruction is the language of the English or French linguistic minority population of the province, have the right to have their children receive primary and secondary school instruction in that language in that province.

Continuity of language instruction

(2) Citizens of Canada of whom any child has received or is receiving primary or secondary school instruction in English or French in Canada, have the right to have all their children receive primary and secondary school instruction in the same language.

Application where numbers warrant

(3) The right of citizens of Canada under subsections (1) and (2) to have their children receive primary and secondary school instruction in the language of the English or French linguistic minority population of a province

    (a) applies wherever in the province the number of children of citizens who have such a right is sufficient to warrant the provision to them out of public funds of minority language instruction; and

    (b) includes, where the number of those children so warrants, the right to have them receive that instruction in minority language educational facilities provided out of public funds.

Enforcement

Enforcement of guaranteed rights and freedoms

24. (1) Anyone whose right or freedoms, as guaranteed by this Charter, have been infringed or denied may apply to a court of competent jurisdiction to obtain such remedy as the court considers appropriate and just in the circumstances.

Exclusion of evidence bringing administration of justice into disrepute

    (2) Where, in proceedings under subsection (1), a court concludes that evidence was obtained in a manner that infringed or denied any rights or freedoms guaranteed by this Charter, the evidence shall be excluded if it is established that, having regard to all the circumstances, the admission of it in the proceedings would bring the administration of justice into disrepute.

General

Aboriginal rights and freedoms not affected by *Charter*

25. The guarantee in this Charter of certain rights and freedoms shall not be construed so as to abrogate or derogate from any aboriginal, treaty or other rights and freedoms that pertain to the aboriginal peoples of Canada including

    (a) any rights or freedoms that have been recognized by the Royal Proclamation of October 7, 1763; and

    (b) any rights or freedoms that may be acquired by the aboriginal peoples of Canada by way of land claims settlement.

Other rights and freedoms not affected by *Charter*

26. The guarantee in this Charter of certain rights and freedoms shall not be construed as denying the existence of any other rights or freedoms that exist in Canada.

Multicultural heritage

27. This Charter shall be interpreted in a manner consistent with the preservation and enhancement of the multicultural heritage of Canadians.

Rights guaranteed equally to both sexes

28. Notwithstanding anything in this Charter, the rights and freedoms referred to in it are guaranteed equally to male and female persons.

29. Nothing in this Charter abrogates or derogates from any rights or privileges guaranteed by or under the Constitution of Canada in respect of denominational, separate, or dissentient schools.

Rights respecting certain schools preserved

30. A reference in this Charter to a province or to the legislative assembly or legislature of a province shall be deemed to include a reference to the Yukon Territory and Northwest Territories, or to the appropriate legislative authority thereof, as the case may be.

Applications to territories and territorial authorities

31. Nothing in this Charter extends the legislative powers of any body or authority.

Legislative powers not extended

Application of *Charter*

32. (1) This Charter applies
    (a) to the Parliament and government of Canada in respect of all matters within the authority of Parliament including all matters relating to the Yukon Territory and Northwest Territories; and
    (b) to the legislature and government of each province in respect of all matters within the authority of the legislature of each province.

Application of *Charter*

   (2) Notwithstanding subsection (1), section 15 shall not have effect until three years after this section comes into force.

Exception

33. (1) Parliament or the legislature of a province may expressly declare in an Act of Parliament or of the legislature, as the case may be, that the Act or a provision thereof shall operate notwithstanding a provision included in section 2 or sections 7 to 15 of this Charter.

Exception where express declaration

   (2) An Act or a provision of an Act in respect of which a declaration made under this section is in effect shall have such operation as it would have but for the provision of this Charter referred to in the declaration.

Operation of exception

   (3) A declaration made under subsection (1) shall cease to have effect five years after it comes into force or on such earlier date as may be specified in the declaration.

Five-year limitation

   (4) Parliament or the legislature of a province may re-enact a declaration made under subsection (1).

Re-enactment

   (5) Subsection (3) applies in respect of a re-enactment made under subsection (4).

Five-year limitation

Citation

34. This Part may be cited as the Canadian Charter of Rights and Freedoms.

Citation

Part II: Rights of the Aboriginal Peoples of Canada

35. (1) The existing aboriginal and treaty rights of the aboriginal peoples of Canada are hereby recognized and affirmed.

Recognition of existing aboriginal and treaty rights

   (2) In this Act, "aboriginal peoples of Canada" includes the Indian, Inuit and Métis peoples of Canada.

Definition of "aboriginal people of Canada"

   (3) For greater certainty, in subsection (1) "treaty rights" includes rights that now exist by way of land claims agreements or may be so acquired.

Land claims agreements

Weblinks

General

The following sites on the World Wide Web (WWW) provide links to information in the area of business law and are relevant to all chapters. Sites listed subsequently have been chosen for specific chapter topics.

Access to Justice Network
www.acjnet.org/
Provides access to legislation, court reports, people and organizations, publications, databases, and discussion forums on justice and legal issues.

Canadian Legal Information Centre
www.wwlia.org/ca-home.htm
A Canadian non-profit corporation based in Victoria, British Columbia, making legal information available to everyone 24 hours a day.

Canadian Legal Resources on the WWW
www.mbnet.mb.ca/~psim/can_law.html
A list of resources on Canadian law and government maintained by Peter Sim, Barrister and Solicitor, Winnipeg.

Virtual Canadian Law Library
www.lexum.umontreal.ca/index_en.html
Canadian legal documents on-line.

Osgoode Hall Law Journal
www.osgoode.yorku.ca

Hieros Gamos-Law and Government
www.hg.org/
Comprehensive international law and government site with over 20 000 original pages, more than 70 000 links, and information on over 6000 legal organizations.

Canada: Ministry of Justice
www.canada.justice.gc.ca/

Canadian Bar Association
www.cba.org

Chapter 1

Canadian Law: A History
www.wwlia.org/cahist.htm
Significant events in legal history, indexed and annotated.

Canadian Constitution
www.canada.justice.gc.ca/ Charter of Rights and Freedoms
www.solon.org/Constitutions/Canada/English/ca_1982.html

Canada: Supreme Court of Canada
www.scc-csc.gc.ca/

Chapter 2

ADR Centre—links to Canadian sites
www.acjnet.org

Canadian Foundation for Dispute Resolution
www.cfdr.org

Alternative Dispute Resolution - An Introduction
www.wwlia.org/adr1.html

Dispute Resolution Project, Department of Justice Canada
www.canadajustice.gc.ca/en/ps/drs/object.html

Dispute Resolution and Avoidance in Electronic Commerce
www.law.ualberta.ca/alri

Alberta Arbitration and Mediation Society
www.aams.ab.ca

Ontario Mediation Centre
www.interlog.com

B.C. International Commercial Arbitration Centre
http://www.bcicac.com/cfm/index.cfm

Common Ground – An Alternative Dispute Resolution Company
www.outofcourt.com/

Canadian Motor Vehicle Arbitration Plan
www.canvap.ca/index.html

U.S. site with links to International ADR sites
www.netlegal.com/adr.html

Chapter 3

Canadian Institute for the Administration of Justice
www.ciaj-icaj.ca/

Industry Canada Regulatory Affairs Information
www.strategis.ic.gc.ca/sc

Canadian Competition Bureau
www.strategis.ic.gc.ca/sc

Environment Canada
www.canada.justice.gc.ca

Canadian Environmental Assessment Agency
www.ceaa.gc.ca/

Canadian Environmental Law Association
www.cela.ca

International Institute for Sustainable Development
www.iisd1.iisd.ca/

West Coast Environmental Law
www.wcel.org

World Resources Institute (WRI)
www.wri.org/wri/

Canadian Institute for Environmental Law and Policy
www.cielap.org

Chapter 4

Provincial acts can be found on provincial government web sites, which can be accessed through **www.acjnet.org** under legislative materials.

Supreme Court of Canada decisions can also be accessed at **www.acjnet.org** under legislative materials.

Chapter 5

Canadian Contract Law Centre
www.wwlia.org/ca-con1.htm

Roger Bachelor's Contract Law Page
www.qsilver.queensu.ca/~law120/index.htm

Duhaime's Contract Law Centre
www.duhaime.org/ca-con1.htm

Industry Canada Consumer Information
strategis.c.gc.casc_consu/Consaffairs/engdoc/oca.html

Chapter 6

The *Uniform Electronic Commerce Act*
http://www.law.ualberta.ca/alri/

Queen's University on Contract
http://qsilver.queensu.ca/~law120/index.htm

B.C. Infants Act
www.qp.gov.bc.ca/stat_reg/statutes/22300.htm

B.C. Law and Equity Act
www.qp.gov.bc.ca/stat_reg/statutes/25300.htm

Chapter 7

High Court of Australia: *McRae v. Commonwealth Disposals Commission* (1951) 84 CLR 377
www.austlii.edu.au/do2/disp.pl/au/cases/cth/high_ct/84clr377.html

Supreme Court of Canada: Rulings: *BG Checo International Ltd. v. British Columbia Hydro and Power Authority*
www.droit.umontreal.ca/doc/csc-scc/en/pub/1993/vol1/html/1993scr1_0012.html
Supreme Court of Canada: Rulings: *London Drugs Ltd. v. Kuehne & Nagel International Ltd.*
www.droit.umontreal.ca/doc/csc-scc/en/pub/1992/vol3/html/1992scr3_0299.html

Chapter 8

Alberta Frustrated Contracts Act
www.gov.ab.ca/qp/ascii/acts/F20.txt

Chapter 9

Canadian Consumer Information Gateway
www.consumerinformation.ca

United Nations Office of Legal Affairs, International Trade Law Branch
www.un.or.at/uncitral/

World Trade Organization
www.wto.org

The Better Business Bureau Central Web Server for U.S. and Canada
www.bbb.org/

Market Place on CBC TV
www.tv.cbc.ca/market/

Chapter 10

TD Business Banking Centre
www.tdbank.ca/tdbank/bizexch/index.html

Canadian Imperial Bank of Commerce: Small Business Information Exchange
www.cibc.com/SmallBusiness/

Business Development Bank of Canada
www.bdc.ca/

Office of the Superintendent of Bankruptcy
strategis.ic.gc.ca/sc_mrksv/bankrupt/engdoc/superint.html

Canada: *Bills of Exchange Act*
canada.justice.gc.ca/FTP/EN/Laws/Chap/B/B-4

Canada: *Bank of Canada Act*
canada.justice.gc.ca/FTP/EN/Laws/Chap/B/B-2

Canadian Consumer Information Gateway
www.consumerinformation.ca

Chapter 11

Charter of Rights and Freedoms
www.solon.org/Constitutions/Canada/English/ca_1982.html

An Annotated Bibliography for *Canadian Charter of Rights and Freedoms* Research
www.law.utoronto.ca/conlit/bibliog2.htm

Canadian Human Rights Commission
www.chrc.ca/

Worksafebc.com
www.wcb.bc.ca/

B.C. Workers' Compensation Act
www.qp.gov.bc.ca/stat_reg/statutes/49200.htm

Human Resources Development Canada: Employment Insurance
www.hrdc-drhc.gc.ca/ei/common/home.shtml

WWW Virtual Library: Labour and Business History
www.iisg.nl/~w3vl/

Canadian Labour Congress
www.clc-ctc.ca/

Public Service Alliance of Canada
www.psac.com/1993scr1_0087.html

Chapter 12

Canadian Institute of Chartered Accountants
www.cica.ca/

Alberta Powers of Attorney Act
www.gov.ab.ca/qp/ascii/acts/P13P5.txt

Chapter 13

Government of Alberta: Small Business Guide Series
www.edt.gov.ab.ca/guides/
Six "booklets" designed to help with various aspects of planning, setting up, and running a small business: (1) *Starting a Small Business*, (2) *Starting a Home-Based Business*, (3) *Marketing a Small Business*, (4) *Managing a Small Business*, (5) *Record Keeping for Small Business*, and (6) *Financial Planning for Small Business*.

New Brunswick Partnership Act
www.gov.nb.ca/acts/acts/p-04.htm

Chapter 14

Canada Business Service Centres
www.cbsc.org

TSE-The Toronto Stock Exchange
www.tse.com/

Montreal Exchange
www.me.org/

Canadian Venture Exchange
www.cdnx.ca

Chapter 15

Real Estate Institute of Canada
www.reic.ca/

Canada Mortgage and Housing Corporation
www.cmhc-schl.gc.ca/

Chapter 16

World Intellectual Property Organization
www.wipo.org/

SOCAN-Society of Composers, Authors and Music Publishers of Canada
www.socan.ca/

CANCOPY's Home Page
cancopy.com/

Canada: Patent Act
canada.justice.gc.ca/FTP/EN/Laws/Chap/P/P-4

Canadian Patents Database
www.cbsc.org/english/fedbis/bis/2030.html

Electronic Frontier Foundation "Intellectual Property Online: Patent, Trademark, Copyright" Archive
www.eff.org/pub/Intellectual_property/

Industry Canada, Task Force on Electronic Commerce, The Protection of Personal Information: Building Canada's Information Economy and Society
http://strategis.ic.gc.ca/privacy

Personal Information Protection and Electronic Documents Act
http://info.ic.gc.ca/cmb

Insurance Canada
www.insurance-canada.ca/

Insurance Bureau of Canada
www.ibc.ca/

Electronic Privacy Information Center
www.epic.org

Risk and Insurance Management Society, Inc.
www.rims.org/

Intellectual Property Magazine
www.ipmag.com

The Uniform Electronic Commerce Act
http://www.law.ualberta.ca/alri/ulc

Uniform Rules on Electronic Signatures
http://www.un.or.at/uncitral/english/sesions/

References

Part I

Anisman P, Reid RF. *Administrative Law: Issues and Practice.* Scarborough, Ont.: Carswell, 1995.

Banfield J, Moore D, eds. *Readings in Law and Society,* 8th ed. Toronto, Ont.: Captus Press, 1999.

Blake S. *Administrative Law in Canada.* 2nd ed. Markham, Ont.: Butterworths, 1997.

Carleton Department of Law Casebook Group, eds. *Introduction to Legal Studies,* 2nd ed. Toronto, Ont.: Captus Press, 1995.

Elliott DW. *Administrative Law and Process,* 3rd ed. Toronto, Ont.: Captus Press, 1999.

Funston B, Meehan E. *Canada's Constitutional Law in a Nutshell,* 2nd ed. Toronto, Ont.: Carswell, 1998.

Greenbaum A, Wellington A, Baar E, eds. *Social Conflict and Environmental Law* (2 vols.) Toronto, Ont.: Captus Press, 1995.

Jones DP, de Villars AS. *Principles of Administrative Law,* 2nd ed. Scarborough, Ont.: Carswell, 1994.

Olivo LM, ed. Introduction to Law in Canada. Toronto,Ont.: Captus Press, 2000.

Ponte LM, PonteTD. Cavenagh. *Alternative Dispute Resolution in Business.* Cincinnati, OH: West Educational Publishing Company, 1999.

Sanderson JP, Q.C., McLaren RH. *Innovative Dispute Resolution: the Alternative HC.* Toronto, Ont.: Carswell, 1995.

Smyth JE, Soberman DA, Easson AJ. *The Law and Business Administration in Canada,* 9th ed. Toronto, Ont.: Prentice Hall Canada, 2001.

Yates R, Yates R, Bain P. *Introduction to Law in Canada,* 2nd ed. Toronto, Ont.: Prentice Hall Canada, 2000.

Part II

Fridman GHL. *The Law of Contract in Canada,* 2nd ed. Toronto, Ont.: Carswell, 1986.

Linden AM. *Canadian Tort Law,* 4th ed. Toronto, Ont.: Butterworths, 1988.

Owen DG. *Philosophical Foundations of Tort Law.* Oxford, UK: Clarendon Press, 1995.

Smyth JE, Soberman DA, Easson AJ. *The Law and Business Administration in Canada,* 9th ed. Toronto, Ont.: Prentice Hall Canada, 2000.

Turban ELJ, King D, Chung MH. *Electronic Commerce: A Managerial Perspective.* Upper Saddle River, NJ: Prentice Hall, 2000

Wright CA, Allen ML, Lewis NK. (ed. Priscilla Darrel). *Canadian Tort Law,* 8th ed. Toronto, Ont.: Butterworths, 1985.

Part III

Bennett F. *Bennett on Bankruptcy,* 5th ed. North York, Ont: CCH Canadian Ltd., 1998.

Falconbridge JD, Crawford B. *Banking and Bills of Exchange,* 8th ed. Toronto, Ont: Canada Law Book, 1986.

Fridman GHL. *The Sale of Goods in Canada,* 4th ed. Toronto, Ont: Carswell, 1995.

McLaren RH. *Secured Transactions in Personal Property in Canada,* 2nd ed. Toronto, Ont: Carswell, 1997.

Ogilvie MN, ed. *Consumer Law: Cases and Materials.* Toronto, Ont: Captus Press, 1993.

Sarna L. *The Law of Bankrupcty and Insolvency of Canada.* Montreal, Que: Jewel Publications, 1997.

Part IV

Arthurs HW, et al. *Labour Law and Industrial Relations in Canada,* 4th Ed. Markham, Ont.: Butterworths, 1997.

Bell SR. *Canadian Employment Law.* Aurora, Ont.: Canada Law Book. [Updated annually.]

Canadian Labour and Employment Law Journal. Toronto, Ont.: Carswell. [Volumes bound annually.]

Corry DJ. *Collective Bargaining and Agreement.* Aurora, Ont.: Canada Law Book. [Updated annually.]

England G, Innis C. *Employment Law in Canada,* 3rd Ed. Toronto, Ont.: Carswell. [Updated annually.]

Harvey C. *Agency Law Primer,* 2nd Ed. Toronto, Ont.: Carswell, 1999.

Smyth JE, Soberman DA, Easson AJ. *The Law and Business Administration in Canada,* 9th Ed. Toronto, Ont.: Prentice Hall Canada, 2000.

Part V

Goode P, ed. *The Future of Corpoate Law.* Queen's Annual Business Law Symposium Scarborough, Ont.: Carswell, 1999.

Manzer AR. *A Practical Guide to Canadian Partnership Law.* Aurora, Ont.: Canada Law Book, 1994.

McGuinnes KP. *The Law and Practice of Canadian Business Corporations.* Markham, Ont.: Butterworth's, 1999.

Peterson, D. *Shareholder Remedies in Canada.* Markham, Ont.: Butterworth's. [Updated annually.]

Smyth JE, Soberman DA, Easson AJ. *The Law and Business Administration in Canada,* 9th Ed. Toronto, Ont.: Prentice Hall Canada, 2000.

Part VI

Kratz MPJ. *Canada's Intellectual Property Law in a Nutshell.* Toronto, Ont.: Carswell, 1998.

Mackaay E, Gendreau Y. *Canadian Legislation on Intellectual Property.* Toronto, Ont.: Carswell, 2000.

Mann JF. *Information and Technology Law.* Toronto, Ont.: Carswell, 2000.

McKeown JS. *Fox: Canadian Law of Copyright and Design.* Toronto, Ont.: Carswell, 2000.

McGill University Faculty of Law. *Making Business Sense of Intellectual Property.* Montreal, Que.: Faculty of Law, McGill University, 1996.

McNaim CHH, Scott AH. A *Guide to the Personal Information Protection and Electronic Documents Act.* Toronto, Ont.: Butterworths, 2000.

Table of Statutes

Note: The page numbers given in parentheses at the end of each entry refer to pages in this book.

Table of Cases

Note: The page numbers given in parentheses at the end of each entry refer to pages in this book.

Index

Note: Boldface page numbers indicate definitions.